Slow Train to Paradise

How Dutch Investment Helped Build
American Railroads

Slow Train

to *Paradise*

How Dutch Investment
Helped Build American
Railroads

Augustus J. Veenendaal, Jr.

STANFORD UNIVERSITY PRESS
Stanford, California

Stanford University Press, Stanford, California
© 1996 by the Board of Trustees of the Leland Stanford Junior
University
Printed in the United States of America

CIP data appear at the end of the book

Stanford University Press publications are distributed exclusively
by Stanford University Press within the United States, Canada,
Mexico, and Central America; they are distributed exclusively by
Cambridge University Press throughout the rest of the world.

Preface

At first glance *Slow Train to Paradise* may seem to be a fanciful title, without any bearing on the subject of Dutch investment in the American railroad network, but it is, in fact, an apt metaphor. Though Dutch investors initially believed they had discovered a shortcut to El Dorado by buying American railroad securities, it turned out that only long-term investment brought financial paradise within reach of the average Dutch investor. As always, of course, a few lucky speculators and gamblers struck it rich and made a fortune in a very short time, thereby reinforcing the existing craze. However, for the average Dutch investor only holding on to securities for a very long time brought pecuniary gain. In the end, however, such patience was well rewarded.

The purpose of this study is to follow the complex history of American railroad securities on the Amsterdam Stock Exchange from 1855 until 1914. English investment in the United States, both in railroads and in other fields, has been amply studied in recent years, while the Dutch contribution has remained much less well documented. Yet the Dutch have been large investors in the United States for more than a century and a half; only recently have they been passed and pushed back into third place by the Japanese.

The year 1914 has been chosen as the end of the period covered by this study. After an era of almost uninterrupted growth of foreign investment in the United States, the outbreak of war caused a complete and sudden change. The belligerents withdrew their capital invested in American securities on an unprecedented scale to finance their own war efforts, and even the Netherlands, although neutral in the conflict, were affected. Government control, lack of independent means of communication across the Atlantic, and shortages of every kind caused by the war badly depressed the Amsterdam stock market for a time. Moreover, the available statistics on Dutch investment in American securities are particularly unreliable for this era because of large sales of German-held American paper through neutral Amsterdam after 1917, when America entered the conflict and sequestrated all German assets in the United States. Only after 1919 did the Dutch market return to some semblance of normality.

The first eleven chapters of the book discuss in broad terms the process and consequences of channeling Dutch capital into American railroads. Chapters 12 through 14 cover a few outstanding railroads in some detail. These railroads have been selected because of the size of the Dutch investment, their importance in forming the Dutch attitude toward investment in American rails in general, or other special qualities that distinguish them from the run-of-the-mill Dutch investment in American railroads. Chapter 15 reviews the various Dutch funds that invested in American rails.

To avoid overloading a work on financial history such as this with figures, I have moved most of these data to Appendixes A and B. The interested reader will find there the hard facts on Dutch investment in American railroads, grouped conveniently together, chronologically in Appendix A and alphabetically in Appendix B. Details of the Dutch protective committees are given in Appendix C. A list of abbreviations of railroad names used is given in Appendix D.

This book is definitely not a railroad history. Others have done that before, and better, and their work has been gratefully used in the following pages. However, a financial history such as this one cannot stand on its own without giving some kind of framework of the corporate history of the companies involved, and readers will also find at least a few facts about the way the Dutch money was spent—and sometimes wasted—on tracks, bridges, depots, and locomotives.

I will not try to find an excuse for my life-long love for trains. From early childhood I have been impressed by the sight of a working steam locomotive—unfortunately already a nearly extinct species even then. My first memories are of the few Dutch steam engines still left after World War II, and later those of other countries. Most impressive in my eyes have always been the American steam locomotives, but only in pictures, as I have never been able to see them in regular revenue service, apart from museum or tourist operations. And although a diesel horn may be a poor substitute for the steam whistle wailing in the night, the sound of American trains is still something special and never fails to impress me. When I lived in Baton Rouge, Louisiana, for a few months, Illinois Central and Kansas City Southern trains passed close by, and later, when I was in Riverside, California, the Union Pacific and Santa Fe again rolled visibly and audibly through the night with headlights blazing and horns blaring. They recalled the days when railroads were young and when the Dutch investor, although thousands of miles away, played a crucial role in the drama of the building of the American railroad network.

Acknowledgments

Of all the people who have helped me in collecting the material for this book, one stands out: Mr. Herbert W. Günst, documentalist of the Vereniging voor de Effectenhandel (Association for the Trade in Securities) in Amsterdam, now retired. We met by chance at a meeting of the Dutch Business Historians club, now many years ago when I was researching Gerrit Middelberg and the Oklahoma Central Railway, and discussed—among other things—American "rails." Almost casually he then remarked, "I think we have something on that road at the Stock Exchange." The next day found me in Amsterdam on the first of a long series of visits to Beursplein 5, where a veritable treasure trove lay waiting for me. Without Herbert Günst's help this book could not have been written, as the archives were essentially closed to the general public. I also have to thank the chairman of the Vereniging voor de Effectenhandel, Baron B. F. van Ittersum, for allowing me in and extending his hospitality to a historian with no money to invest.

Two other friends have contributed materially to this book. Professor Johan de Vries, historian of De Nederlandsche Bank at Amsterdam, has witnessed the slow growth of the work almost from the start, and he never failed to encourage me and help me with his advice. The other is Professor Mira Wilkins, of Florida International University, Miami, who first contacted me soon after my opening article on the subject came out. Since then we have been in regular correspondence, and we finally met in person in Pasadena in March 1992. She always urged me on, saying, "We don't know anything about Dutch investment, and you are in a position to tell us something." She commented extensively on earlier versions of this book, and I have used her remarks gratefully. I hope I have not disappointed her.

Other friends and colleagues never tired of listening to my stories and offering advice on subjects with which I was unfamiliar. Of all these I want to thank Wantje Fritschy, Joost Jonker, and Keetie Sluyterman in particular. They helped me over difficult spots now and then, and opened new and profitable views on the subject.

Without the generosity of the Huntington Library, San Marino, California, in awarding me a grant to research their vast holdings in business history, I could never have found the opportunity to be in that beautiful place, so fertile in scholarly ideas. I am particularly grateful to the board of my Institute of Netherlands History in The Hague for giving me a six-months' sabbatical to do more research and finish the writing of the book. That half year (and some more months) were spent at the University of California, Riverside. I want to thank the chairman and the colleagues of the History Department for their hospitality in accepting me in their midst and including me in their social life as well. My thanks also go out to the staff of the Rivera Library at Riverside for their unfailing help and attention to my needs. They have probably never seen so many Dutch books pass through their hands in such a short time.

Finding the illustrations for this book proved to be a challenging task from across the Atlantic. My friends H. Roger Grant and Don L. Hofsommer were most helpful in this endeavor, and directed my search in several libraries and museum collections. I owe them much.

From the start, Norris Pope, director of the Stanford University Press, was enthusiastic about this project and never failed to encourage me. George W. Hilton, Professor Emeritus at the University of California, Los Angeles, read and commented on the first version of the manuscript. His ideas regarding reorganization of the material in this book proved to be most refreshing, and I am glad to have been able to use them here. Ellen Smith of the Stanford University Press editorial staff undertook the somewhat thankless task of converting my work into an orderly manuscript. I owe each of them a great deal for the final result.

Last, and most important by far, has been my wife, Jannie. She never tired of listening to my stories, and she accompanied me gladly on almost every trip to the United States. In the midst of summer she traveled with me, without ever complaining, into the backwoods of Arkansas or Oklahoma to see some forgotten railroad line or depot, taking excellent pictures on the way and generally enjoying herself mightily. She is the only one who has seen this work grow from the very first faint stirrings, in Baton Rouge in 1981, to what it is now. Without her encouragement and her almost unlimited confidence I could never have finished it.

Contents

x ■ Contents

Photo sections follow pp. 68 and 154.

Tables

Slow Train to Paradise

How Dutch Investment Helped Build
American Railroads

One

Dutch Investment at Home and Abroad

The Kingdom of the Netherlands, to give its full name, was and is a small European country on the shores of the North Sea, bordered on the east by Germany and on the south by Belgium. In 1815 it measured only some 32,500 square kilometers[1] and had a population of around 2 million; this had grown to 3.2 million in 1855 and to just over 6 million in 1914.

But this minute country has had a disproportionately large influence on European and even world affairs. Originally part of the Spanish Empire, it liberated itself through a fierce war that began in 1568 and did not end until the Peace of Westphalia of 1648. The country that emerged from this struggle, the Republic of the Seven United Provinces (or Dutch Republic for short), became the foremost economic power in western Europe for at least a century, until surpassed by Great Britain in the eighteenth century. Constitutionally, the country was a republic, something unusual for the period, and it remained so for most of its independent existence. The *stadholder* was the highest elected official and commander in chief of its armed forces. The office of stadholder had developed during the time of the Spanish kings, who generally resided in far-away Spain. The stadholder functioned as their trusted lieutenant in the Netherlands. After the virtual independence of the Seven Provinces, the office of stadholder was retained, although strictly speaking it was no longer needed after the king was officially deposed in 1581. William I (the Silent) of Nassau-Orange, leader of the struggle against Spain, was the first new stadholder, and during the next two centuries his descendants rose to an almost semimonarchical position in an otherwise republican society. The province of Holland became the nerve center of the Dutch Republic and the nucleus of its economic and financial power, thereby giving the colloquial name of Holland to the whole country.[2]

During this blossoming of the Republic, its East and West India Companies acquired a colonial empire larger than any other except Spain's. The Indonesian archipelago, with Batavia on the island of Java as government center, became the most important part of the Dutch East India Company (the first joint-stock corporation in the world), but Ceylon (now Sri Lanka), Malaya, a number of settlements on the Indian coast, the Cape of Good Hope in South Africa, and the small but important island of Deshima in the Bay of Nagasaki (Japan), all contributed to the company's wealth. The West India Company was less important, but did acquire New Netherland in North America (lost to England in 1666), a number of islands in the Caribbean, Surinam in South America, a couple of forts on the African Gold Coast, and even Brazil for a number of years.[3]

In the eighteenth century, constitutional deadlock and internal strife between democrats, who called themselves Patriots, and the established regents of the Stadholder party contributed to economic decline, causing the Republic to lose some of its luster, but it remained a highly important financial center. The country was overrun by French revolutionary troops in 1795; it was transformed into the short-lived Batavian Republic, with the Patriots in power, and finally ended up as part of Napoleon's French Empire. All colonies, except Deshima and the Gold Coast, were lost to Great Britain in 1795.

The Congress of Vienna of 1815 wanted to set up a strong barrier against new French aggression, and so the Kingdom of the Netherlands was incorporated, now enlarged with the former Austrian Netherlands (modern-day Belgium), a union which lasted only until 1830. The son of the last stadholder became William I, the first king of this new country. Great Britain returned most colonies, but the Cape of Good Hope, Ceylon, and some territories adjoining Surinam stayed in English hands. The remaining Dutch possessions in India and Malaya were voluntarily transferred to Great Britain in 1824, while the fort of Elmina on the African Gold Coast, which had lost its importance since the abolition of the slave trade, was sold to Great Britain in 1872. Thereafter the Dutch East Indies (Indonesia) formed the most important part of the Dutch colonial empire, with the Caribbean islands and Surinam playing a less conspicuous role.[4]

In the early years of the nineteenth century, after the newly won independence of the Netherlands, the general stagnation of the economy of the Napoleonic period did not end as had been hoped. In the northern part of the new country, the old Dutch Republic, economic problems were especially severe. The southern part of the Netherlands, modern-day Belgium, was already more industrialized and had been able to profit from the Continental System imposed by Napoleon, which effectively closed off his European dominions from the products of British industry. The more mercantile north, with its staple market and the closely connected shipping industry, which was already in decline before 1795, had been much harder hit by the wars. The traditional role of the Dutch as the middlemen of Europe had been lost, never to return.

Ownership of securities had been widespread during the eighteenth century. Not only had the old mercantile classes invested part of their surplus capital in securities, but small shopkeepers, domestic personnel, military officers, and widows and spinsters had done so too. But Dutch capital losses during the Napoleonic period had been enormous, estimated at between 90 and 120 million guilders, and many investors had been forced to sell their securities.[5] Of course, the small saver was forced to sell first. Nevertheless, the Amsterdam money market still flourished to a certain extent under the French regime. Continental loans continued to be floated there, but London had taken over the role as the primary European money market.

And yet, despite widespread poverty and the grass growing between the cobblestones in the streets of Amsterdam, there were still large quantities of capital available, enough to make Amsterdam a financial center once again, albeit on a smaller scale. The many Dutch merchants and industrialists who had already been withdrawing from active business during the eighteenth century had managed to keep much of their accumulated savings intact. The surviving great mercantile houses of Amsterdam, which had seen their traditional trade dwindle to almost nothing, had much capital now unused and were waiting for an opportunity to invest it somewhere.[6]

Fortunately the Dutch government could absorb most of this money. Its public debt, already at an astronomical level before 1795, had again—out of sheer necessity—been allowed to grow during the Batavian-French period. Despite forced reduction and deferment of interest payments on part of it, the servicing of this debt remained a heavy burden on the young state, which was already wrestling with unemployment, loss of export markets, and other economic ills. The secession of Belgium in 1830 and the state of war existing between the two countries until 1839 meant a further growth of the debt, which mushroomed to an almost unbelievable 1.3 billion guilders by 1840. About 53 percent of the government's income was needed for redemption of and interest payments on this monstrous debt.[7] New loans had been necessary over the years to finance the annual deficits and most Dutch surplus capital had been absorbed in this way by the domestic market.

The year 1850 signals the turning point. Successive Dutch governments now tried hard to reduce the public debt, helped in no small measure by the growing revenues flowing in from the Dutch East Indies. The growth of such cash crops as coffee, tea, sugar, and other tropical products was being forcibly expanded, and the revenues from the colonies were mounting accordingly. Except for a very small number of municipal loans, no new government loans were floated after 1840 and older, high-interest ones were forcibly converted or redeemed. It was not until 1870 that new public loans would be issued again.

Over the first half of the nineteenth century the total of Dutch-held domestic (including colonial) securities—mostly public but a few private—had grown until it had reached a total of more than 1 billion guilders by 1850. During the same period the amount of Dutch-held foreign securities had remained fairly constant at about 600 million guilders. Only after midcentury did the foreign share start growing rapidly, and a mere ten years later it was equal to the domestic stocks held in Holland.[8] The stockbroking business in Amsterdam naturally profited from this development and flourished as never before.

Until the mid-nineteenth century surplus capital had been chiefly "old" money, derived from the enormous capital accumulated during the golden years of the Dutch Republic. In the somewhat stagnant phase of the Dutch economy until 1850 it was not possible to set aside much "new" surplus capital for purposes of investment elsewhere.

After 1850, agriculture did rather well in a market of steadily rising prices, and farmers could possibly have saved enough to invest some money in securities. Especially in the north, where the large farms of the Groningen region were thriving, much surplus capital was generated in the 1870's, capital that was at least partly invested in foreign securities.[9] This may explain the relatively large number of stockbrokers operating in that small northern center, as well as the several financial weeklies published there. (See Chapter 4 for details about the Dutch financial press.) In 1878, a general agricultural crisis ended the prosperity of this segment of the economy.

Industry was slow in developing, although some branches, such as the gin distilleries of Schiedam, did very well with their massive export to the United States. It remains doubtful, however, that the distillers could accumulate enough savings for investment outside their own businesses.

One branch of industry that may have influenced the reception of the sudden flood of American railroad stocks on the Amsterdam Exchange in the early 1870's has yet to be mentioned. Amsterdam had already been the center of the diamond trade for centuries, with most of the raw material coming from India and Brazil. Now this industry suddenly blossomed into something previously unknown. The newly discovered diamond fields of the Cape Colony in South Africa—a Dutch possession until 1795— started producing on an unprecedented scale in 1870, and as most of this production eventually found its way to Amsterdam to be cut and polished, it caused a boom of massive proportions there. Wages in the diamond industry, already higher than in other trades, shot up to new heights. Weekly wages of 200 guilders (also known as Dutch florins and abbreviated hereafter as Dfl) and more became common, and raises of between 100 and 200 percent are reported in 1872. Comparable wages in other trades, such as the printing business, were 7 or 8 guilders a week, while foremen in these industries could go home on Saturdays with maybe 11 or 12 guilders. A resulting torrent of money swept through the city. Young boys and girls were drafted into the diamond industry without much education, and with the high wages then current they—and their elders as well—were prone to spending their "surplus" money on luxuries, alcohol, and gambling.

A common form of gambling was speculation in securities on the Bourse (exchange). It is not unreasonable to assume that the boom in American "rails," with their promise of quick gains, was at least in part fueled by the money being made so easily in the diamond industry. Most diamond merchants and workers were Jewish, and a number of Jewish stockbroking houses in Amsterdam, such as Teixeira de Mattos Brothers and Lippmann, Rosenthal and Company, were doing a brisk business in these years. The growth and decline of another Jewish stockbroker, Lion Hertz, is nearly concurrent with the Cape diamond boom. Hertz was noted in Amsterdam for the somewhat shady nature of many of the American rails he brought to market, and he may well have catered to the most daring among the gamblers. The diamond boom came to an end in the worldwide economic crisis of 1873, as did the American investing craze at the Amsterdam Exchange, but the South African fields continued to produce on a high level well into 1876. The Amsterdam diamond business was still doing relatively well at the time that the first new American railroad loans were introduced in Amsterdam after the 1873 crisis.[10]

What were the options open to Dutch investors in the 1850's and 1860's? We have seen that the domestic debt, mostly carrying an interest rate of between 4 and 5 percent before 1850, and even lower thereafter, was largely held at home and gave a safe but not very spectacular yield. Large-scale domestic industrial enterprises were still very few in that period and did not require large amounts of capital. Shipping did absorb some capital. The system of regular, government-sponsored chartering in rotation in the trade between the homeland and the Asian colonies for Dutch ships of a certain size made the building of new ships attractive. Shipyards were busy again, and ancillary industries profited accordingly. Marine insurance was another branch of commerce that could absorb large amounts of capital. After 1857 the abolishing of the regular East Indies chartering and the world-wide slump in international shipping meant a severe decline in the navigation business in general, only alleviated by the advent of a few new, capital-intensive steamship lines. The successful Koninklijke Nederlandsche Stoomboot-Maatschappij (Royal Netherlands Steamship Company) was incorporated in 1856, and it did need—and easily found—large amounts of capital. Dutch shipbuilding took a long time to switch over from the traditional wooden ships to modern iron steamers, however, and only a few shipyards were equipped to deal with the latter.[11]

The only really large-scale, capital-intensive businesses after 1835 were the railways. The first Dutch line was opened in 1839 as a private enterprise, while the second line was helped by personal intervention of the king and was later transferred to a limited company. These domestic railways offered relatively safe but low-interest bonds—between 4 and 4.5 percent—while the shares of the two companies involved, the Holland Railway and the Dutch Rhenish Railway, generally yielded no more than 3 percent, reason enough for Dutch investors to dispose of them after their initial high hopes of 8 percent or more had proved unfounded. A few mortgage banks offered a 4-percent return on investment, and an Amsterdam city loan offered 5 percent, but these were the highest rates available in domestic finance.[12]

The private company established to operate the government-built railway system after 1863 needed large amounts of capital, but Dutch investors were slow to support this enterprise. Only after the government had helped it did it attract private capital on some scale. Much the same happened to the Amsterdamsche Kanaal Maatschappij, which in the 1860's built a shipping canal connecting the port of Amsterdam with the North Sea at IJmuiden.

With this relative lack of opportunities for investment in domestic securities, and with the freeing of large sums as a result of the redemption of the domestic public debt it is only natural that Dutch investors looked elsewhere to place their surplus capital. In itself, this was nothing new, of course. The Amsterdam Stock Exchange was the first exchange in the world where foreign securities were traded on a large scale, and this trend, which dated back to the eighteenth century, continued (after the interruption between 1795 and 1815) even stronger in the next.[13]

Investment in foreign securities was officially forbidden at the beginning of the nineteenth century by a measure that dated to the time of the French-dominated Batavian government and which was continued under the kingdom. But it could never really be enforced and was abolished in 1824. Income from interest and dividends—

domestic or foreign—was not taxed and securities were not included in property taxes. On the other hand, all securities were included in estate taxes, and from 1824 until 1859 foreign paper was taxed at twice its current market value. A stamp duty was levied on all securities, and only stamped paper could be officially traded. Under this stamp duty foreign stocks were taxed at 30 cents for every Dfl 100 of par value, reduced in 1856 to only 5 cents, the domestic rate. In short, in the first half of the nineteenth century, investment in foreign securities was penalized.[14] (See the section "A Note About Currency" in Chapter 3.)

■ Foreign Investment Opportunities in the Nineteenth Century

English consolidated bonds (consols) were popular in Holland, but they paid 3 percent or less. Although the Dutch owned a large part of the British public debt before 1795, most of it had been returned to London by the second half of the nineteenth century. French "rentes," or government bonds, were not held in Holland to a large extent. In 1816 foreign credit had helped the new French regime on its feet, when Francis Baring and Company (London) and Hope and Company (Amsterdam) together had sold French government bonds worth Fr 6 million in England and Holland. Later French domestic savings were largely invested in the domestic debt, and foreign influence had diminished. Yet these bonds, and French railway shares, were held in Holland, especially after the English sold off large blocks in the 1840's to make room for their own railway shares during the British railroad building boom known as the "Mania."[15]

Italy offered a rather dismal picture, with a government deficit growing from year to year and with little promise for the future. Spain was seen as even worse. Initially Dutch investors assumed large amounts of the Spanish public debt, and in 1851 they ranked a close second to the English as Spanish bondholders. But the reactionary regime of Isabella II was essentially in default for most of the period and could count on little support from foreign lenders. After the forced conversion of these bonds in 1851, the London and Amsterdam stock markets were virtually closed to any new Spanish government borrowing, and although the revolution of 1868 held out some promise for improvement of the public credit, the situation in Spain remained not very favorable to foreign investment. Spanish railway debentures were held in France, Belgium, and Germany in the 1860's, but never on a very large scale in Holland.[16]

Russia was a country where Dutch investors had traditionally looked for safe opportunities coupled with high returns on their money. In the eighteenth century the Dutch had invested heavily in Catherine II's government, and the pattern continued after the establishment of the Kingdom of the Netherlands. Russian government loans in the first half of the nineteenth century were relatively few, but the Russian railways did absorb an enormous amount of Dutch money. The first railway in Russia, from St. Petersburg to Moscow, built by Americans in the 1830's, was largely financed by Germany and Holland. The Grand Société des Chemins de Fer Russes, although engineered and run by the French, was built with money supplied by Amsterdam.

English investment in Russia was small. The British seemed to abhor the autocratic czarist regime, and the Crimean War, of course, meant a complete stop to British investments in the enemy country. Holland, neutral in the conflict, took over as the chief supplier of capital to Russia until well into the late 1860's. Then the Russian demands became so large that Amsterdam alone could not fill them, and Germany and France stepped in. This did not mean that Dutch investment in Russia ceased altogether, only that it diminished in comparison with other European countries. Russian railway bonds continued to be bought in Holland, especially when they were guaranteed for interest and principal by the Russian government. Loans to the Russian government itself remained popular as well.[17]

Austria was another great user of Dutch capital to finance its government, its enormous military establishment, and its railways. Apparently the Dutch had fewer problems with financing an authoritarian regime than the British did, and they kept propping up the imperial government, which was already staggering under an enormous debt. New military expenditure resulting from the war with Prussia at last required drastic measures. In 1868 the Austrian government forcibly converted its debt into two new loans that paid lower rates of interest. Of an estimated £300 million in debt outstanding before this action, about one-third was held abroad. Of this £100 million, the Netherlands held some £33.5 million, more than any other country. Of course an outcry was raised in the creditor countries involved, but the measure was executed, with the predictable result of totally destroying the Austrian government's credit abroad for a number of years.[18] And as this conversion coincided with the flood of American railroad loans in Amsterdam, Dutch brokers were quick to point out the advantages of exchanging Austrian securities for American bonds.

Other European countries such as Portugal and Turkey now and then applied for loans in Amsterdam and elsewhere, but they were never very popular. The Ottoman Empire was considered a most risky customer, always on the brink of financial disaster, and able to survive only because of the mutual distrust of the great powers. Egyptian and Tunisian loans were offered in Amsterdam in 1868–69, as was a Romanian railway loan paying 7.5-percent interest, but even at that high rate Dutch investors were advised to keep out.[19]

Outside Europe the Dutch East Indies offered some possibilities in railways, and a few of the early private agricultural companies operating there attracted some capital. Their real growth came later in the century, when rubber, tobacco, and other agricultural products from the Indies brought in enormous profits. But even in the early years of the twentieth century complaints were still heard about the lack of enthusiasm on the part of the Dutch capitalists for investing in their own colony, when they were pouring large amounts of money in speculative ventures elsewhere.[20] In the Dutch West Indies and Surinam, opportunities for investment were even smaller, and the African Gold Coast (a Dutch colony until 1872) did not figure at all in the minds of Dutch investors. During the nineteenth century Dutch colonial securities generally ranked as domestic paper and were classified as such.

In the Americas, the young independent states in the south had attracted some Dutch capital. New Granada, later divided into Colombia and Ecuador, had a loan held in Amsterdam for a time, but generally these states had a most dismal record of financial performance. Only Brazil—where the Dutch had long had interests in the sugar industry—could command higher confidence, and some of its public debt was held in Holland.[21]

The general Dutch lack of knowledge of the young South American republics, however, was made abundantly clear in 1825 when a certain enterprising American gentleman, posing as the English representative of the Republic of Poyais, turned up in Amsterdam. There he managed to sell a loan of this "state" on most attractive conditions, and it was even officially listed on the exchange for a short time. When the imposter suddenly disappeared with the cash thus raised, Dutch investors discovered that even the best and most recent map of South America did not show a Republic of Poyais.[22]

■ Dutch Nonrailroad Investment in the United States to 1850

The United States of America from its inception as a nation commanded some degree of sympathy among Dutch financiers, especially among the so-called Patriot or anti-Orangist circles. Dutch merchants had made enormous profits by running supplies to the revolutionary army from the Caribbean island of St. Eustatius. The Dutch Republic's war with England that resulted from this large-scale smuggling had been disastrous for Holland's trade, and it never really recovered. Yet the sympathy for the young American republic remained, and in 1782 the first loan explicitly meant for the United States was floated in Amsterdam. The credit of the young nation was not yet established, and it took French intervention and a guarantee by the Dutch States-General to interest the Amsterdam bankers in this loan of Dfl 5 million.[23]

When the credit of the United States proved better than expected, it was easier to float new American loans on the Amsterdam market. Interest was paid regularly and a policy of regular redemption was practiced by the American Treasury to bolster its credit even more. But unknown to the Dutch investors the money the United States needed to service and redeem its debt was found only by floating new loans, as the tax income of the young state was still insufficient for these purposes. Before 1794 the Americans borrowed a total of Dfl 30,450,000 in Amsterdam, but what remained of the proceeds, after the payments of interest, had been largely spent in redemption of loans previously advanced by France and Spain.

The French conquest of the Dutch Republic in 1795 and the ensuing French domination meant a temporary stop to the floating of new American loans in Amsterdam, but after the Peace of Amiens in 1802 contacts between America and the Netherlands were resumed. Napoleon was willing to sell the French North American colonies, taken over from Spain only a few years before, to the United States government for a most reasonable price—$15 million—to be paid chiefly in 6-percent U.S. Government bonds maturing between 1819 and 1821.[24] The French government reserved the right to market these bonds when possible, and as Napoleon greatly preferred cash instead of bonds, Francis Baring and Company of London and its traditional partner in Amsterdam, Hope and Company, offered to take over the U.S. bonds, but at a discount, of course. It is possible that the original idea of the sale of the U.S. "sixes" in England and

Holland was first circulated by Theophile Cazenove, who had been agent of the Holland Land Company in America until 1799 and who was at the time employed by the French minister Talleyrand. In any event, together the two firms acquired the $11,250,000 in bonds at a price of 78.5 percent of par just before the hostilities between Napoleon and Great Britain were resumed. Hope, joined by the Amsterdam firms of W. and J. Willink and R. and Th. de Smeth, offered $5 million of these bonds in Amsterdam at par and the success was enormous. Six-percent interest was high for the time, and because of the wars few possibilities existed for Dutch capitalists. These American sixes were quoted in Amsterdam at around par long after 1804. Baring marketed the rest in London with equal success, and together the firms must have made a substantial profit on the deal. Part of the English share in the business later turned up on the Amsterdam market, where these "English" American sixes were separately administered by the firms of N. and J. and R. van Staphorst, Ketwich and Voombergh, and Willem Borksi.[25]

After the establishment of the Kingdom of the Netherlands (1815) part of the United States public debt continued to be held in Amsterdam, but the American policy of redemption resulted in an almost total absence of federal securities in Dutch portfolios by 1835. The Mexican-American war and other federal commitments resulted in a slight growth of the U.S. public debt to $68.3 million in 1851, of which two-thirds were said to be held in Europe.[26] And indeed Dinger's first investors' guide lists a 6-percent U.S. loan of 1848, held in Holland and marketed by Hope and Company in certificates of $400 (Dfl 1,000).[27] New issuances of American bonds held in Amsterdam, largely U.S. government paper but probably also the first Illinois Central Railroad bonds, suddenly grew from about $500,000 in 1856 to a high of $11 million in the next year, only to fall again to some $4 million in 1858.[28]

U.S. government securities did not represent the total Dutch commitment in the young republic. One of the greatest assets of the United States was its wealth in land, uncharted and undeveloped but with great possibilities. Small wonder that this land had early drawn the attention of Dutch capitalists in Amsterdam. The result was the Holland Land Company, established in 1792 by six Amsterdam trading and banking houses (Stadnitski and Sons, Van Staphorst, P. and C. van Eeghen, Ten Cate and Van Vollenhoven, W. and J. Willink, and R. J. Schimmelpenninck). These firms were all involved in the international financial business on a large scale; Schimmelpenninck would eventually gain fame as grand-pensionary or first minister of the Batavian Republic. After many legal and political problems were successfully overcome, the Holland Land Company held title to some 5 million acres in western New York and Pennsylvania, with headquarters in Batavia, New York, and with (the second) New Amsterdam, later called Buffalo, as its principal settlement. The later history of the Holland Land Company need not be recounted here, and it must suffice to say that not much ever came of its grand projects for settling the land with Dutch and German farmers. The European revolutionary wars intervened and after 1815 the Dutch interest in American land waned. Yet it was not until 1858 that the partnership behind the Holland Land Company was finally dissolved.[29]

Not only the Holland Land Company was active in the purchase of American lands.

Other, smaller Dutch enterprises operated in the same promising market. New York and Pennsylvania were the states where the Dutch were chiefly interested in land, but even Georgia attracted some Dutch money in an abortive agriculture company. Another scheme in which the Amsterdammers invested some money was Alexander Hamilton's Society for Establishing Usefull Manufactures of 1790. His project proposed the building of large industrial enterprises on the Passaic River in New Jersey, utilizing the waterfalls there to power the necessary machinery. The success was only slight, but Paterson did grow into an important industrial town. Dutch investors sold their small $6,500 interest between 1808 and 1810.[30]

Besides the federal loan mentioned above, other American securities were held in the Netherlands after 1815. Holland had funded in part the defunct first Bank of the United States and had helped the Second Bank of the United States, which had encountered much opposition at home, to be established in 1816. The new bank's 20-year federal charter lapsed in 1836 and was not renewed; after that it operated under a Pennsylvania charter only and on a more limited scale. Burdened by excessive capital (most of it in the form of loans) and reckless investment, it suffered greatly from the difficulties resulting from the panic of 1837. But before it finally closed its doors in 1843, the bank had attracted large amounts of Dutch capital. Its shares had been marketed in Holland as certificates issued by Hope and Company, Ketwich and Voombergh, and Wed. W. Borski, but no dividend had been paid since 1839. In addition, two loans, both bearing 5-percent interest, of the same Second Bank of the United States were floated by Hope in Amsterdam in 1840. The first (per 1845)[31] was for Dfl 5.5 million and was offered at a first price of 90 percent of par. The second loan, of Dfl 4.5 million, also per 1845, was offered at 95.5 percent of par. As collateral for these two loans a large amount of American state government bonds had been deposited with Hope and Company. These loans, on which payment of interest would cease in 1842 and which spurred the creation of the first investment fund in the Netherlands, are discussed in greater detail in Chapter 15.[32]

In 1839, even before these Dutch loans, the Second Bank of the United States had floated a 6-percent loan with Rothschild's of Paris and London, totaling £900,000 or Fr 22,770,000. Servicing of the debt was postponed in 1842, as it was with the Dutch loans, never to be resumed. Apparently quite a few of these bonds were held in Holland, but to what extent is unclear; the fact that they were officially quoted in Amsterdam would indicate a sizable Dutch interest. Rothschild's had an agent in Holland, who marketed securities handled by the London and Paris houses.[33]

The spending spree on internal improvement of the 1820's and 1830's in most American states had financial consequences for Dutch investors. But even in an earlier period, Dutch monies had been sunk—literally—in canal or river improvement schemes. The James River improvement company in Virginia (1775–98) had operated with some Dutch money, but the single largest such enterprise to attract capital from Amsterdam was the Connecticut River scheme of 1792. Only in 1810 did the Dutch manage to sell the last of their interest, after suffering continuing losses.[34]

Of the United States's great internal improvement works of the early nineteenth century, the Erie Canal was undoubtedly the largest. A project of this magnitude needed an unprecedented amount of capital, and naturally the promoters looked to

Europe for at least part of the money they needed. A first tentative offer to the parties behind the Holland Land Company to participate in the financing of the canal in 1817 did not result in any Dutch capital being made available, but the company itself gave away some 100,000 acres of land for the construction of the canal.[35] The state of New York eventually financed the Erie Canal through the sale of bonds abroad, but no trace of New York State bonds has been found in Holland. Other American canals did attract some Dutch monies. In 1829 Daniel Crommelin and Sons offered Dfl 3,750,000 in 5-percent bonds of the "Drie Steden," the three cities of Washington, Georgetown, and Alexandria. This loan covered the share of the three towns in the building of the Chesapeake and Ohio Canal. When the canal company went bankrupt in 1834, payment of the interest ceased, but one of the provisions of the company's original charter held that in case of default the president of the United States was authorized to sell sections of the three cities involved to pay off the creditors. The thought that a part of the capital city of the United States was thus about to fall into the hands of Dutch brokers and stockjobbers must have been so abhorrent that Congress decided to take over the loan. Payment of interest was resumed in 1836 and the bonds were redeemed over a 25-year period ending in 1865.[36]

Less fortunate were the owners of Dfl 1,875,000 of bonds of the Morris Canal and Banking Company. Willem Willink, Jr., had offered these bonds in Amsterdam in 1830, and interest was paid until 1841, when the canal company defaulted. As no federal guarantee was available in this case, most of the Dutch investment had to be written off.

In 1837 the same Willink offered bonds of the Batavia-Buffalo Railroad and of the Tonawanda Railroad, both operating in western New York, where the Holland Land Company had been active, and both under the presidency of David E. Evans, who was also the company's agent there. The success of these issues (Dfl 1 million each) was very limited.[37] Both railroads were included in the 1853 merger which created the New York Central system.

Daniel Crommelin and Sons had better luck in 1839, when they offered $200,000 of 3-percent State of Maryland bonds, issued in support of the Baltimore & Susquehanna Railroad, later part of the great Pennsylvania Railroad. This issue was eagerly taken up in Amsterdam. It is probable that they are the same as the 3-percent Maryland bonds mentioned in 1873, against which Tutein Nolthenius and De Haan had issued certificates. Maryland went into default in 1842 but resumed the interest payments in 1847.[38]

An example of a more shady internal improvement scheme was presented by the Bank of Pensacola, chartered in 1831, and the Union Bank of Florida, chartered in 1833, with initial capital to be raised by the sale of territorial bonds. Although there were some doubts about the legality of issuing securities in a territory, the bonds were duly issued and marketed chiefly in Europe. A certain Colonel Gamble—auspicious name—set out for Europe in 1834 and managed to sell one hundred bonds ($1,000 each) to Hope and Company at 97 percent of par.[39] Doubts about the solidity of the territorial bonds lingered, however, and Francis Baring and Company warned their Dutch associates to be careful. And indeed, Hope refused to market more of these bonds some years later. Gamble managed to sell the rest of the bonds in England, but not to Barings, who refused to have anything to do with them.

The results of both banks were predictable. Operating under a large debt in a poor territory with a very small population, they soon went bankrupt. The Florida territorial legislature in 1842 refused to honor its earlier pledge and declared itself not responsible for the debts of the banks. Thus in effect Florida repudiated a debt of $3.9 million mostly held in England, in one stroke. When Florida applied for statehood in 1844, the frustrated European bondholders petitioned the U.S. Congress not to allow the new state into the union without some agreement about the territorial debts, but to no avail. At the Anglo-American Claims Convention of 1853, the British representative tried to make the federal government liable for Florida's debt, but the mediator, while acknowledging the legality of the claim against Florida, denied any federal responsibility.[40]

In the end the British managed to unload some £1 million of their holdings on Florida planters in 1869 at a 50-percent discount. In 1870 the state of Florida, then desperately in need of new European loans, which could not be obtained while the problems of the earlier bonds remained unresolved, offered £10 for each £100 bond plus some claim on land. The British bondholders agreed, and in 1870 the state paid £2 per bond to indicate its good faith (but nothing further was done). In that same year the new 8-percent Florida State bonds were successfully marketed in Holland, so it is apparent that the Dutch had got rid of their earlier holdings somehow. It is also possible that they were led into believing that a new era had dawned and were willing to let bygones be bygones. In any case Florida was able to sell the new bonds in Holland.

Other state loans also circulated in Holland before 1851, but it is not quite clear who originally introduced them. Ohio sixes, Pennsylvania fives, and Illinois sixes (the latter to a total Dfl 1 million) were held in the shape of certificates issued by Hope and Company, Ketwich and Voombergh, and the Wed. W. Borski. Ohio had never ceased the payment of interest on its bonds; Pennsylvania had defaulted in 1842 but had resumed payment in 1845; Illinois had also defaulted in 1842 but had partly resumed payments by 1847, and Hope and Company had paid out whatever became available. A 5-percent loan of the city of Mobile, Alabama, was also sold by the same Dutch combination against their certificates. The certificates of all of these bonds were in denominations of $200 or $400, or Dfl 500 and 1,000.

A 5-percent sterling loan of the state of Massachusetts was also marketed in Amsterdam by Hope and Company, but it is not known when or to what extent. It is not mentioned in Dutch stockbrokers' guides in 1851, but appears in Dinger's 1873 guide. Massachusetts was safe and never defaulted.

An early American bank that became known in the Netherlands was the Farmers Loan and Trust Company of New York. Between 1833 and 1836 this mortgage bank had purchased large tracts of land from the Holland Land Company, which was then selling out.[41] The bank's 5-percent bonds (per 1856) were already offered in Holland in 1838 to a total of $1 million, but must have been available even earlier. Hope and Company included them in their investment fund in 1838 at a first price of 91.50 percent of par. At the same time Hope probably also offered 5-percent bonds of the closely connected Farmers Fire Insurance and Loan Company of New York.[42] These bonds were later exchanged for other American securities within Hope and Company's investment fund.

One other American security with a long history in Amsterdam remains to be mentioned. In 1833 the Citizens Bank of Louisiana was established in New Orleans. The promoters of the bank applied at once for a loan with Van Eeghen and Company of Amsterdam, but without success. The Dutch had no confidence in this bank in which the shareholders did not supply any actual money but only signed mortgages to the amount of their participation. In 1835 W. Willink, Jr., tried again to raise some money on behalf of the bank, but again without results. The state of Louisiana then decided to support the bank by issuing $12 million in 5-percent bonds in denominations of £100 (Dfl 1,200) each. Of this total, $7 million was then sold in Amsterdam by Hope and Company at 101 percent of par in 1837.[43]

The Citizens Bank was soon in trouble, and in 1842 the payment of interest ceased. Unpaid coupons were converted into new 5-percent bonds, on which interest payments were suspended until 1848, when they were resumed. However, the redemption of the first bonds in 1849 had to be postponed, and they were extended.[44] Legal troubles then emerged, but were solved when Louisiana passed a law in 1852 that gave a new charter to the bank. For a time, the business seemed to prosper. N. G. Pierson, a young Dutch cotton broker who would later become one of the leading Dutch financial experts, visited New Orleans in 1859 and expressed great confidence in the bank, despite its somewhat tarnished reputation with Dutch bondholders.[45] During the Civil War years payment of interest on the bonds still outstanding was surprisingly regular, but in 1865 bondholders learned that during these years interest had been paid out of capital and not out of earnings. The bank's depleted capital had to be augmented again, and the Dutch bondholders once more agreed to a deferral of interest payments for several years. Even this did not help, and in 1873 they had to accept a new postponement. After a reorganization in 1882, in which Hope and Company played an important role, new Louisiana 5-percent certificates were issued, which remained listed in Amsterdam until 1903.[46]

This survey of American securities circulating in Holland before 1850 is by no means complete, but only includes those that were actually listed in the official Amsterdam price lists, published by the Stock Exchange. There are indications that large numbers of other American bonds were widely held in Holland without any formal listing or official introduction on the Amsterdam Exchange. Dutch investors (through Dutch brokers) probably acquired these in London or purchased them on other European exchanges; some could even have been purchased in the United States. Some Amsterdam notaries public specialized in forwarding the coupons of these bonds to London or America to cash the interest for their Dutch customers. Amsterdam brokers also had the necessary contacts to expedite such transactions. It is impossible to say with certainty how much of this unlisted paper—of course, not only American in origin—was actually held in Holland, but it may have been considerable.[47]

▪ *Dutch Nonrailroad Investment in the United States after 1850*

With the Louisiana Citizens Bank we have already taken the story of Dutch investment in American securities other than railroads into the twentieth century, but in this chapter some attention should be paid to the new loans introduced in Amsterdam in the 1860's. The U.S. Civil War, of course, meant an enormous expansion of public debt, both of the Union and of the new Confederacy. Part of the costs of the war were funded by printing paper money, but the rest had to be borrowed on the capital market, both at home and abroad.[48]

The debt of the federal government, which stood at about only $68 million in 1851, had swollen to a staggering $2.67 billion in 1865. Most of this was raised in America through the efforts of the financier Jay Cooke, but now and then access to foreign markets was sought. England was hostile to the Union to some extent and was reported to be more in favor of the Confederacy. On the European continent Union loans were readily accepted.[49] Apart from a pre–Civil War 5-percent loan of 1858 (per 1874), the following Union loans were held in Holland and listed officially as of 1873: 5-percent 10-40s (maturing between 1874 and 1904) of 1864; 6-percent of 1861, per 1881; 6-percent 5-20s (maturing between 1867 and 1882) of 1862; 6-percent 5-20s (maturing between 1869 and 1884) of 1864; 6-percent 5-20s (maturing between 1870 and 1880) of 1865. How much of these loans were actually held by Dutchmen and exactly when they were purchased is not known; estimates vary widely. An estimate of $250 million in Union loans held in Holland and Germany in March 1865 seems reasonable.[50]

After the end of the war rumors about the redemption of all outstanding loans in paper instead of gold, and even of the total repudiation of the government debt, flew about and were only ended by the election of General Ulysses S. Grant as president in 1868. As a presidential candidate Grant had made nonrepudiation of the U.S. debt a special plank in his election platform, and foreign creditors had high hopes on his election. In 1871 a new consolidated gold loan at 5 percent was created to convert the earlier loans and restore confidence in the U.S. government. A large number of bonds from the 6-percent loan of 1862 was redeemed by these new fives. The scarcity of capital in Europe as a result of the Franco-Prussian war, however, made a conversion of all 6-percent loans impossible. New U.S. loans, apart from the 1871 consols, came on the Amsterdam market in 1873 (6-percent loan), in 1877 (6-, 5-, and 4.5-percent loans), and also in 1879 (4-percent loan). The latter was listed in Amsterdam until 1906 and generally quoted over par.[51]

Whereas by war's end Union securities were reasonably attractive to Dutch investors, the Confederate issues were of far less interest. The Southern cause was definitely unpopular in Holland, and the Confederate loans were not taken up to any extent. Trade in the 7-percent cotton loan of 1863 was very sluggish, although the newly issued bonds were offered in Amsterdam by B. H. Schroeder and Company, the Dutch connection of the house of J. Henry Schroeder and Company of London, who together with Emile Erlanger of Paris had underwritten the loan. Another Confederate loan of 1863, paying 8 percent, was also offered in Holland, and there are rumors that Rotterdam interests bought a large number of these bonds from England in 1864, when their price had fallen dramatically. Apparently they had some hopes of a recovery, which would result in a handsome profit, but they were disappointed when the Confederate securities became completely worthless after Appomatox. In 1865 these bonds were quoted in Amsterdam at around 1 percent of par![52]

After 1865 several new state loans were offered in Amsterdam. An old acquaintance,

Louisiana, issued several loans for the construction of levees along the Mississippi River. The first one, of 1867, carried 6 percent, while the second (1867) and third (1870) carried 8 percent. All three were marketed in Amsterdam, and all three were in trouble in 1873, when payment of interest stopped. Louisiana tried to reorganize its debt in 1874, but loud protests from the English and Dutch bondholders resulted in a kind of stalemate that was not resolved until 1884.[53]

Florida, just after having settled earlier claims of European bondholders, managed to sell new state bonds in Amsterdam and Rotterdam, issued in support of the Jacksonville, Pensacola & Mobile Railroad. These bonds will be covered in more detail in Chapter 8. The city of Mobile, Alabama, also an old customer in Amsterdam, issued a new 8-percent loan in 1870 in support of the Mobile & Alabama Grand Trunk Railroad. Payment of interest on the loan ceased in 1873; how much of this issue was held in Holland is not known. The 8-percent bonds were converted into new 6-percent bonds in 1875, and two years later the city defaulted again.[54] The railroad was reorganized in 1886 as the Mobile & Birmingham and was later taken into the fold of the Southern Railway.

The Dutch had better luck with a 6-percent loan of the city and county of New York of 1871. This $15 million loan was marketed in all leading European stock exchanges, including Amsterdam, where D. L. Goldschmidt offered the $500 or $1,000 bonds at a first price of 98.25 percent of par. How much Goldschmidt sold is not known because the bonds were never officially included in the Amsterdam price lists.[55]

Although these Dutch investments in the American public sector were impressive, they were tiny compared to the flood of American railroad securities that swept through the Amsterdam Stock Exchange after 1865. By 1890, when many of the more shady railroad bonds had already disappeared from the Amsterdam market, 123 of the 141 American securities officially listed were railroads; the remaining 18 included principally federal, state, and occasional local American government securities, often residues of issues made decades earlier. There were some land companies, but in the post–Civil War era, railroads dominated Dutch investments in America.

Two

The Stock Market
in the Netherlands

During the second half of the eighteenth century throughout Europe the line between the trade in goods and capital was not strictly drawn. This was especially true in the Netherlands. Most of the great Amsterdam brokerage houses with American connections, such as Willink, Van Eeghen, Stadnitski, Ketwich and Voombergh, Hope, and Crommelin, were active in traditional commission trade and at the same time in the stockbroking business. Some had traded with the English colonies in America and, after the independence of the United States in 1776, had provided the newly independent nation both with loans and with goods. The same houses were also involved in the land business, such as the Holland Land Company and other schemes of the same nature.

After 1815 the bottom dropped out of the commission trade because American merchants had by then established direct links with European houses, thus obviating the need for middlemen. What little remained of this kind of business had been taken over by other, mostly British firms. For the Dutch the role of suppliers of capital remained, but gradually the established Amsterdam houses divested themselves of this side of their activities in the United States as well. One by one they curtailed their operations or closed their doors completely until only very few remained. Of these survivors Stadnitski was one of the few that entered the field of American railroad securities on a limited scale, and only two or three other names from the earlier era will be heard as the story of America's railroads unfolds. Of all the eighteenth-century firms only Hope and Company made the trade in American railroad stocks one of its main spheres of business in addition to the Russian, Austrian, and other European loans with which it was involved. Except for Hope and Company, the great upsurge in the trade in foreign securities which took place after 1850 largely bypassed the old houses. Most of them were simply out of business or had been taken over by newcomers in the 1850's. A whole new set of bankers and brokers took their place. The tremendous growth of the trade in foreign securities was reflected in the number of stockbrokers in Amsterdam: between 1850 and 1870 their number doubled, from 113 to 232.[1]

16

This study will not give a complete survey of all the new brokers who became active in the 1850's and 1860's in the business of American railroad securities. Some of the more prominent, however, appear and reappear in our text and so do qualify for a closer description. These were the intermediaries who made the transmission of Dutch capital to America possible on an unprecedented scale.

One of the most outstanding was the firm of Wertheim and Gompertz, which was already active in the affairs of the Galveston, Houston & Henderson line beginning in 1860–61. Abraham Carel Wertheim (1832–97) was an Amsterdam Jew whose uncle Abraham Wertheim had operated a small bank with his partner Leon Gompertz since 1834. Through their wives Abraham Wertheim and Gompertz were both related to the Königswärter family, renowned in continental banking circles, and young Abraham Carel learned the trade in the Amsterdam office of Julius Königswärter. He became a partner in the firm in 1858, and with the son of his uncle's partner, Leon B. Gompertz, he became the leading force of the family firm in Amsterdam. In 1868 Wertheim and Gompertz, with Westendorp and Company and F. W. Oewel as partners, established the Administratie Kantoor voor Amerikaansche Spoorwegwaarden (Administrative Bureau for American Railroad Securities).[2] An *Administratie Kantoor*, literally translated an administrative bureau or office, acted as a specialized intermediary between investors and firms—or governments—in need of capital to facilitate foreign investment by taking care of all paperwork. (These Kantoren are discussed in greater detail later in this chapter.) Wertheim and Gompertz was to play a leading role in the Amsterdam stockbroking business. Wertheim was the chief partner in Amsterdam while Oewel often went to America as the firm's representative when the need arose.

Other Jewish firms were numerous. Gebr. (*Gebroeders*, or brothers) Teixeira de Mattos, an Amsterdam banking firm since 1822, became involved in the American rail craze early when they started selling, in the late 1850's, Illinois Central bonds and shares.[3] They often teamed up with the Christian firm of Gebr. Boissevain when the business was exceptionally large. Lippmann, Rosenthal and Company, established in 1859, became under the vigorous leadership of Leo Lippmann one of the prominent houses in Amsterdam, closely cooperating with Wertheim and others and deeply involved not only in American securities but also in Russian finance and Dutch domestic banking. Lippmann was one of the founders of the Amsterdamsche Bank in 1871.

Alsberg, Goldberg and Company was active in several American railroads and generally acted as the Dutch partner or representative of the New York firm J. and W. Seligman and Company and its associated house of Seligman & Stettheimer of Frankfurt.

The house of Becker and Fuld, operating in Amsterdam from 1858 till 1898, also had close ties with Frankfurt colleagues (probably all relatives) and was among the founders of the Amsterdamsche Bank. This house also served as the Rothschild representative in Amsterdam.[4] Just as Lippmann, Rosenthal often did, Becker and Fuld regularly collaborated with Wertheim and partners when business was too large to handle alone.

Lion Hertz is one of the more obscure figures in the Dutch stockbroking world; he disappeared from sight in 1876, when his firm was dissolved, after having brought to market numerous of the more dubious American railroad securities.[5]

Of the Gentile firms, one of the oldest was the famous house of Hope and Company. It was established by merchants of Scottish ancestry in Amsterdam early in the eighteenth century and operated under the name of Hope Brothers until 1762. The firm naturally had strong links with Scotland and England, but was also active early in America. Relations with the London house of Baring Brothers were also established, and were cemented when Pierre César Labouchère (1772–1839), one of the trusted servants of Hope and Company, married Dorothea Baring, daughter of Sir Francis, in London during the firm's exile in England while Holland was overrun by French revolutionary troops. After 1802 Labouchère became chief of the firm's Amsterdam branch and a partner as well. On the death of senior partner John Hope in 1813, the old firm was dissolved and largely taken over by Baring Brothers, although the Amsterdam office continued to operate with Labouchère as partner (although he resided in England most of the time). His younger brother Samuel Pierre Labouchère (1778–1867), a Rotterdam merchant, later became partner as well, and Samuel's son Henri Matthieu (1807–69) carried on the family tradition. Later Labouchères were Charles Henri (1863–1906), also partner of Hope and Company, and Ernest Samuel (1856–1932), who established the firm of Labouchère, Oyens and Company, which was also active in American business. Labouchère, Oyens was taken over by the Rotterdamsche Bank in 1913 but continued to operate under its old name.

A house closely linked with Hope and Company and often acting as its broker was the ancient house of the Weduwe W. Borski (the widow of Willem Borski), which was taken over by Van Loon and Company in 1885. Under the new name it continued to act as broker for Hope and Company. Hope took over Van Loon in 1937.[6]

Another established house was Daniel Crommelin and Sons, with its manifold American relations, operating since 1859 as Tutein Nolthenius and De Haan. Under the latter name, this firm played the leading role in one of the key Dutch-American railroads, the Kansas City, Pittsburg & Gulf. New firms in the 1850's and 1860's included Elix and Broekman (later Broekman and Honders, and even now active on the Amsterdam Exchange, under the Broekman name) and Broes, Gosman and Company. The latter firm, together with Ten Have and Van Essen and Jarman and Sons, operated one of the other leading Administratie Kantoren dealing with American rails. J. L. ten Have also served as a director of the Chicago & North Western Railroad for many years.

Hendrik Oijens (1778–1851) was the founder of the firm H. Oijens & Sons, bankers and stockbrokers, in 1836. His son Hendrik Gerard Oijens (1804–86) continued the business with his younger brother Gerrit Hendrik (1811–83), who called himself De Marez Oyens. Gerrit Hendrik's son Hendrik Jan de Marez Oyens (1843–1911) became a partner in the family firm, and was instrumental in the reorganization of several American railroads and served for many years as a director of the Missouri, Kansas & Texas Railroad. Later Oijens and Company merged with Labouchère to form the present-day Labouchère, Oyens and Company (the "ij" has recently been changed to "y").[7]

Another famous name in Amsterdam banking and American railroad finance was Boissevain. The Boissevain family had been long established in the capital of the Netherlands, chiefly involved in the shipping and insurance businesses. The brothers Daniel (1804–78) and Edouard Constantin (1810–85) founded their own stockbroking–banking firm, at first operating under the name Holjé and Boissevain and then (sometime around 1876, when silent partner Holjé left) as Gebr. Boissevain. The firm soon made a name for itself in American business, especially under the leadership of Gideon Maria Boissevain (1837–1925), Daniel's son and an economist of note. Gebr. Boissevain also branched out to London, where a cousin, Athanase Adolphe Henri Boissevain (1843–1921), set up an office (until 1901) in partnership (with two brothers from Boston named Blake) under the name Blake, Boissevain and Company. In 1875 this same A. A. H. Boissevain set up his own business in Amsterdam under the name Adolphe Boissevain and Company, often cooperating with Gebr. Boissevain. Adolphe Boissevain and Company was deeply involved in the Union Pacific reorganization of 1893–94. A New York office of Gebr. Boissevain was added later, when Daniel Gideon Boissevain (1867–1940), the son of Gideon Maria, set up business there toward the end of the century. Daniel Gideon himself became a director of several American railroads, among them the Kansas City Southern.[8] Not only did the Boissevains operate under their own names, they also became involved in many other banks and stockbroking firms, and their sons and daughters intermarried with the other leading Amsterdam banking families, thus forming an intricate network of family relations important at that time when business was still very much a personal affair.

Kerkhoven and Company was an Amsterdam firm founded in 1812 by Johannes Kerkhoven (1785–1859) and active in many projects, among them the ill-fated St. Paul & Pacific Railroad. Johannes's son Willem Octavius (1825–97) and grandson Johannes (1859–1927) were in time partners of the firm. A brother of the first Johannes Kerkhoven, Theodorus Johannes (1789–1817), and his two sons Pieter Jacobus (1826–94) and Jan Willem (1828–1913) were also stockbrokers in Amsterdam and connected with Kerkhoven and Company. Jacob van Oosterwijk Bruyn (1794–1876) and his sons Willem (1829–1903) and Pieter Adolf (1837–1900) were also partners in the same Kerkhoven firm, and played a role as members of several American railroad reorganization and bondholders' protective committees.[9] The name Kerkhoven lives on in the American town of Kerkhoven, Minnesota.

Willem Frederik Piek (1838–1916) was a relative newcomer. He was born in a family of prosperous lumber merchants in Holland and set up a stockbroking firm of his own in Amsterdam in the early seventies. The Van Ogtrop family also played a role in American business: Hendericus Joannis van Ogtrop (1803–65) founded a stockbroking firm in partnership with his son Petrus Antonius Ludovicus (1835–1903), operating under the name H. J. van Ogtrop and Son.[10]

A late arrival among the Amsterdam stockbrokers was the firm of Hubrecht, Van Harencarspel and Vas Visser, founded in 1880 under the leadership of Dr. Henri François Rudolph Hubrecht (1844–1926), a cousin of the cofounder of the Rotterdamsche Bank Paul François Hubrecht. H. F. R. Hubrecht had a degree in chemistry from Heidelberg University but apparently found more opportunities in stockbroking. His younger relative Pieter Glaudius (1871–1929) was later cofounder of the firm Van der Werff and Hubrecht.[11]

This short survey is by no means comprehensive. Many more names of Amsterdam brokers will appear as the story unfolds, but the ones recorded above were among the most prominent in the American railroad business. Unfortunately the records of many firms have been lost; a complete history of the Amsterdam stockbrokers remains to be written.

There was little in the way of a dividing line between Jewish and Christian firms in Amsterdam. Jewish houses, especially those of Portuguese or Sephardic denominations, had been established in the seventeenth century and had risen to preeminence in the financial world. Jews were freer in the Dutch Republic than anywhere else in the world to engage in business, and although collaboration between Christian and Jewish firms may have been rare before 1795, a number of Jewish firms acquired solid respectability by that time. After the Napoleonic period, when all existing limitations for Jews in certain trades were abolished, cooperation between Christian and Jewish stockbroking houses became commonplace, as the following pages will show. Internationally, however, foreign Jewish firms—American, German, or otherwise—tended to do business with Jewish counterparts in Amsterdam when they needed Dutch cooperation or support.

Outside Amsterdam, only a few houses were important. In Rotterdam the firms of A. J. and M. Milders and H. C. Voorhoeve and Company merit attention. Milders usually cooperated with the Boissevains, and Voorhoeve teamed with Kerkhoven to do business in the St. Paul & Pacific Railroad. In The Hague it was not until the first years of the twentieth century that some brokers came to the fore: Salomon Frederik van Oss set up his own firm there in 1903, and Oppenheim and Van Till was operating in that city at the same time. These firms did not do much more than pick up the crumbs left by the older Amsterdam firms. But Van Oss shares with Kerkhoven the distinction of living on in the name of an American town: Vanoss, Oklahoma, population 75!

Most of the Amsterdam firms mentioned earlier handled both banking and stockbroking businesses indiscriminately, although gradually a certain specialization became evident. Modern specialized commercial banks came to Holland only in the 1860's, though several of the large Jewish European houses had established branches in Amsterdam by the 1820's. The previously mentioned German banker Julius Königswärter had an office in the city from 1817 to 1856. The Bischoffsheims had started what would become their worldwide business in Amsterdam in 1820, when Louis Raphaël Bischoffsheim (born in Mainz in 1800, died in Paris in 1873) founded his own banking firm there. He soon branched out to Antwerp, Belgium, London, and Paris. His son Raphaël Louis (1823–1906) was born in Amsterdam—he was naturalized as a French citizen only in 1880, but probably held Belgian nationality in between—and operated the Amsterdam family firm until 1848; when he moved to Belgium the importance of the Amsterdam house was considerably reduced; only a representative was left there.[12] We will encounter the British Bischoffsheims later.

Other international Jewish banking firms such as S. Raphael and Company and Joseph Cahen established branch offices in Amsterdam, Raphael in 1818 and Cahen in 1845. Only Cahen became involved in American railroad securities, and then only on a limited scale.[13] Disappointment with the lack of Dutch support for crédit mobilier–like operations is the most probable cause for the early disappearance of these particular international firms.

One of the first modern banks in the Netherlands was the Twentsche Bankvereeniging, which developed from the operations of a notary public in the town of Enschede, one B. W. Blijdenstein, Jr. Blijdenstein specialized in banking and had felt the need for a simple way of financing the growing exports of the cotton textile industry in his area, Twente. Toward this end he opened an office of his own in London, and in 1861 he established in Amsterdam the Twentsche Bankvereeniging B. W. Blijdenstein and Company as a limited partnership.[14] The Twentsche Bank, as it was known, would soon enter the American railroad business. The London office operated under the name B. W. Blijdenstein and Company, but always worked in close cooperation with the Twentsche Bank.[15]

Rotterdam, as the center of Dutch shipping and commerce, also needed modern methods of providing credit for commercial operations. In the same year, 1861, the brothers C. J. J. M. C. and V. C. G. M. van Geetruyen established the Commandietkas, again as a limited partnership. Bad management—it was sometimes called the Banditkas—soon led to its downfall, but in its short years of operation it did some business in American rails. The Van Geetruyens also operated branches in Amsterdam and other cities.[16] More important for the present study is the Rotterdamsche Bank (a limited company), founded in 1863, initially to finance commercial operations in the Dutch East Indies. It soon entered the American railroad business.[17]

The Rotterdamsche Bank was clearly inspired by the ideas of the French protagonists of crédit mobilier, and this movement was even stronger in Amsterdam. After the initial refusal of the Dutch central bank, the Nederlandsche Bank, to facilitate the founding of banks along these lines in the 1850's, new and now more successful attempts were made in the 1860's to provide Holland with modern banking systems and credit facilities.[18] The first in Amsterdam was the Algemeene Maatschappij voor Handel en Nijverheid, founded as a limited company in 1863. (By 1868 this firm had dissolved in a strong smell of fraud and mismanagement.) The same year, 1863, also saw the founding of the Nederlandsche Crediet- en Deposito-Bank of Amsterdam, a venture of the noted doctor-philanthropist and friend of A. C. Wertheim, Dr. Samuel Sarphati. It branched out with an Antwerp office, formerly the Bischoffsheim office there, and a Paris office, which soon became more important than the original Amsterdam establishment. Already by 1866 its affairs in Holland had started to decline, and the bank was converted to the (French) Banque de Paris et des Pays-Bas in 1872. The Amsterdam *Succursale* (branch office) of this bank rarely entered the field of American bonds.[19] For a couple of years, Mijnhard Johannes Boissevain (1845–1917) was chief of the Amsterdam branch.

Much more important and successful was the Amsterdamsche Bank of 1871, founded by the Bank für Handel und Industrie of Darmstadt, Germany, together with several other German, Austrian, and Dutch houses. Among the Dutch participants were Wertheim and Gompertz, Lippmann, Rosenthal and Company, Becker and Fuld (all of Amsterdam) and the Rotterdamsche Bank. Of the bank's initial capital of Dfl 10 million only about Dfl 2 million came from the Dutch side, the rest from Germany. The bank was run by a well-connected Dutchman, F. S. van Nierop, and A. C. Wertheim was a member of the Board.[20] Almost from its inception the Amsterdamsche Bank was active in American securities; it was reported to have participated in an underwriting syndicate for a 7-percent loan of the New Orleans, Jackson & Great Northern in 1872.[21]

With the Banque de Paris et des Pays-Bas and the Bank für Handel und Industrie we have already touched on the subject of foreign banks operating in the Netherlands. Most large American banking dynasties of this period, such as the Morgans, the Speyers, and the Seligmans (many of them of German origin) established branches, often staffed by family members, in many European capitals, but they did not do so in Holland until almost the end of the century. German influence was strong in the Amsterdamsche Bank, as we have seen. Despite an apparent absence of direct foreign influence, there was a closely knit network of international financial relations, of course, in which Dutch houses were as involved as other European countries. Earlier we noted that the Barings had virtually taken over Hope and Company by 1813; the Speyer firms in New York, London, and Frankfurt usually did business with Gebr. Teixeira de Mattos; Becker and Fuld acted as Dutch agents of the Rothschilds; Seligman acted often, but not always, through Alsberg, Goldberg and Company. Jacob Schiff, of Kuhn, Loeb and Company of New York, made it his policy to establish links with more than one house in each country, and so he did business in Holland with Hope, the Amsterdamsche Bank, Wertheim and Gompertz, Adolphe Boissevain, and Alsberg, Goldberg and Company, as circumstances demanded.[22] There was, in short, a well-established network of international financial dealings. However, more often than not, a regular pattern of financing did not exist, and most business was done on an ad hoc basis. When a new firm entered the market, it went for all business it could get; it dealt directly with the railroads and was often prepared to take more risks or be content with lower commission fees.

Most Dutch brokers did form alliances with others in Holland. Gebr. Boissevain often worked with Gebr. Teixeira de Mattos; Kerkhoven (Amsterdam) and Voorhoeve (Rotterdam) cooperated in several cases. Holjé and Boissevain, forerunners of Gebr. Boissevain, formed an alliance with the Milders's firm of Rotterdam. S. F. van Oss of The Hague went hand in hand with Van der Werff and Hubrecht of Amsterdam. From time to time the bigger Dutch firms also formed part of international underwriting syndicates, usually teaming up with their customary domestic and international partners.

A typical Dutch institution was the so-called Administratie Kantoor or administrative bureau. The chief aim of these Administratie Kantoren was to facilitate the payments of dividends and the transfer of original shares to new owners. Transfers of American railroad shares generally had to be executed in the railroad company's offices in the United States, which was an expensive nuisance for foreign owners. Further, dividends were only paid to owners registered in the company's books. To facilitate investment, the Administratie Kantoor bought the shares with money advanced by Dutch investors, had them transferred en bloc to the name of the Administratie Kantoor, and then issued certificates to each individual Dutch investor according to the amount of his or her contribution. The Kantoor then cashed the dividends and paid them to shareholders, charging a small commission. The Kantoren made it even easier for investors by issuing certificates for one, five, or ten original shares, and even for fractions of the original shares to accommodate the small investor. For issuing a certificate of $500 or more they generally charged a commission of 1 percent, with 1.5 percent for smaller fractions.[23]

An added advantage of the Administratie Kantoor, with all Dutch holdings united in one hand, was the possibility of immediate intervention if the need arose. When an American railroad went bankrupt or seemed in trouble, the officers of the Kantoor could act promptly and expertly in the interests of all parties concerned, including their own.

Administrative bureaus were not set up specifically to deal in American railroad securities. They had been used to buy Russian securities since the eighteenth century, and Hope and Company had something along the same lines for its dealings in American securities early in the nineteenth century, although this bureau soon expanded into an investment fund. The first Administratie Kantoor intended explicitly to cash American railroad dividends seems to be the one organized informally by Holjé and Boissevain and Gebr. Teixeira de Mattos in 1864 for Illinois Central shares. In that year these companies asked Dutch shareholders to exchange their shares (then already circulating in Holland) for the certificates of the Administratie Kantoor to make the payment of dividends easier.[24]

Railroad shares were most often exchanged for certificates of some kind issued by an Administratie Kantoor, but bonds were occasionally converted to such certificates as well. At the time interest on bonds was generally payable to bearer, and therefore relatively easy to cash. In some instances, however, bonds were also handled by a Kantoor, as in the case of the Atlantic & Great Western in 1867, when Lippmann, Rosenthal and Company, Wertheim and Gompertz, and Alstorphius and Van Hemert opened an Administratie Kantoor for these bonds.[25] The road was in financial problems, which was the most apparent reason for this rather unusual move on the part of the Dutch brokers.

Most of the larger stockbrokers in Amsterdam opened their own Administratie Kantoren in due course, not for one specific security, as in the case of the Atlantic & Great Western, but for American railroad securities in general. The Kantoor operated by Wertheim and Gompertz, Westendorp and Company, and F. W. Oewel, the Administratiekantoor voor Amerikaanse Spoorwegen, was created in 1868 and over the years introduced a large number of American railroad shares, such as Erie commons, Baltimore & Ohio commons, and many others, in the shape of its certificates. In 1883 this Kantoor was reincorporated as a limited company. Oewel was dead by then.[26]

Broes, Gosman and its partners were the next firms to establish their Administratie Kantoor voor Amerikaansche Fondsen, which was also very active in the American railroad business. This Kantoor was converted to a limited company in 1881 with A. A. H. Boissevain as one of its directors.[27]

The early very informal Boissevain–Teixeira de Mattos operation was gradually formalized and incorporated as the Administratie Kantoor van Amerikaansche Spoorweg-Aandeelen. Gebr. Boissevain had already earlier, in cooperation with Kerkhoven and the Rotterdamsche Bank, opened a Kantoor for Milwaukee common and preferred shares only, but transferred those certificates to Broes, Gosman in 1879.

A fourth general Kantoor was the Algemeen Kantoor van Administratie onder directie van Stadnitski and Van Heukelom, Wurfbain and Son, H. Oijens and Sons, Jolles and Company, and Tutein Nolthenius and De Haan, which did not specialize in American rails only but did business with other countries as well. In 1880 the new firm of Hubrecht, Van Harencarspel and Vas Visser opened an Administratie Kantoor (instead of the already more common limited company) for several American railroad stocks under the name of Vereeniging tot Administratie onder directie van Hubrecht etc. In 1884 they changed over to the format of a limited company as well.[28] As will be noted, almost all of the leading brokers were involved in one of these five administrative bureaus. All these Kantoren operated for reasons of profit. They made the marketing of American railroad shares much easier, the actual work involved did not amount to much (unless a railroad went bankrupt), and the commission they charged could mean a tidy extra profit. Investors could trade the certificates easily because they were included in the Amsterdam price lists. Quite often the original railroad shares continued to circulate as well and both shares and certificates were included in the Amsterdam stock market price lists and were regularly quoted. Generally quotations in Amsterdam were in guilders; only when little trading had been done in the more obscure American securities in Amsterdam would the New York quotations in dollars be given instead.

In cases where the Dutch interest in a company in trouble was particularly large, the holdings were transferred from the Administratie Kantoor to a *Vereniging* (association; during the period of this study the word was commonly spelled *vereeniging*) incorporated especially for the purpose, as in the case of the Missouri, Kansas & Texas in 1888 and the Atchison, Topeka & Santa Fe in 1895. This was chiefly done to ensure impartiality; brokers could easily be suspected of acting in their own interest above all, while a neutral association of all certificate holders would cater equally to each investor, large or small. After the reorganization of the troubled railroad company, the new shares were made out in the name of the asssociation, which in turn issued new certificates. These Verenigingen were a kind of half-way measure between the Kantoren and the more typical and more extreme protective committees, which were set up by brokers, the Stock Exchange Association, and the Administratie Kantoor. These protective committees will be covered more fully in Chapter 9.

A special case resulted from the accumulation of a large amount of Central Pacific common stock in Dutch hands. Most shares circulating in Europe in the 1880's were in the names of Leland Stanford and C. P. Huntington and their associates or in the name of clerks in the Central Pacific's New York office. To ensure inclusion in the price lists of the Amsterdam Exchange it was necessary to transfer title of these shares to new Dutch owners, but complications arose over a clause in the corporate laws of California which stated that every stockholder in an enterprise incorporated in the state was fully liable for the total debt of that corporation. This caused many European shareholders to delay the transfer of their shares to their own names.[29] It also meant that Huntington and Stanford, despite their minority holdings in their own names, continued to exercise almost complete control through the proxies of these European shares, which were still officially in the names of their New York clerks. In 1893, out of a total of 385,348 shares, Stanford owned only 4,983 and Huntington a meager 500. But C. E. Bretherton of London, representing the English shareholders, had proxies for 73,786 shares, and A. K.

van Deventer and S. A. van der Veer, both of New York (despite their Dutch names), held proxies for 44,330 and 61,729 shares respectively. Could they have been the representatives of the Dutch shareholders?[30]

This continued influence of Huntington and Stanford was frowned upon in England, where most Central Pacific shares outside America were held. The English Association of American Bond and Share Holders opened a lively correspondence with the Amsterdam Stock Exchange Committee with the intention of cooperating more closely to exercise the influence of more than $23 million in common stock held in both countries.[31]

These problems led to the incorporation in 1897 of the N. V. Maatschappij tot beheer van aandeelen in de Central Pacific Railroad Company (Company to Control Central Pacific Shares, Ltd.) in Amsterdam. At the first shareholders' meeting on 2 July 1897 in Amsterdam, 23,500 shares (of $100 each) were represented, 17,100 by Gebr. Teixeira de Mattos alone. All Dutch-owned shares were transferred to the name of the Maatschappij, thus obviating the danger of total liability of individual shareholders. As a limited company, the Maatschappij could never be held liable for more than the shares made out in its name. A London company organized along the same lines, the Central Pacific Railroad Shareholding Company, was established on 8 February 1898. Out of $68 million in outstanding common stock, $52 million was held in Europe at that time, mostly in England and the rest in Holland and Germany.[32] The Dutch shares were converted to certificates of the Maatschappij, but because Dutch limited companies were by law restricted in their actions, a protective association of those owning certificates was also founded on 11 January 1898, called the Nederlandsche Vereeniging ter behartiging van de belangen van houders van bewijzen van aandeel in de Central Pacific Company (Association for the Protection of the Interests of Central Pacific certificate owners). California law was thus circumvented to limit the liability of the individual foreign shareholders to the extent of their own holdings only.

Three

The Amsterdam
Stock Exchange

*T*he early history of the Amsterdam Stock Exchange is not remarkable as much for its organization as for its lack of it. Trading in stocks in the late seventeenth and most of the eighteenth centuries took place in a corner of the Bourse, a marketplace primarily for commodities and goods. Anyone could call himself a stockbroker and buy and sell stocks. Some semblance of order was created toward the end of the eighteenth century when the Collegie tot Nut des Obligatiehandels (College for the Benefit of the Trade in Bonds) was set up to formulate some rules and to weed out dubious or insolvent traders.[1] One of the most important actions of this body was to issue the first official price list, the *Prijscourant* of 1795. A drawback of this weekly price list was its use of very wide margins, sometimes 30 points or more, which prohibited an exact survey of prices. To give more precise and dependable quotations, a number of stockbrokers in 1833 founded the Nieuwe Handel-Societeit (New Society for Trade), which started to publish its own price list according to new, stricter standards.[2] Almost from the start this authoritative list became the most widely used.

The fast-growing trade in securities in the 1850's necessitated a stronger organization, and in 1856 the old Collegie and the Nieuwe Handel-Societeit together set up the Algemeen Beurs-Comité voor Publieke Fondsen (General Exchange Committee for Public Securities) with the explicit intention to watch over the interests of both stockholders and owners of securities. The next year the Beurscomité issued a set of rules, the "Reglement voor de Handel in Publieke Fondsen," which were generally accepted by the trade. In the same year the two old stockbrokers' organizations merged into one new Effecten-Societeit (Securities Society).

The new organization meant a distinct improvement, although not all dubious stocks could be repressed, and unreliable or insolvent traders could not be completely kept out. Moreover, complaints were heard about the autocratic way the Beurscomité tried to impose its will, which came more and more into conflict with the more liberal and democratic feelings of the time. After several years of wrangling, a new organization was at last founded, the Vereeniging voor den Effectenhandel (Association for the Trade in Securities), incorporated in May 1876 and still the only organization regulating the trade in securities in Amsterdam. A. L. Wurfbain became the first chairman, and board members were (among others) A. C. Wertheim, P. A. L. van Ogtrop, J. L. ten Have, P. A. van Oosterwijk Bruyn, and F. S. van Nierop.

Membership in the first year stood at 465, and grew to almost 1,300 in 1914. Only individual bankers (not banks), stockbrokers, and their staffs whose businesses were located in Amsterdam could be members, and apart from a few dissenters all bankers and brokers joined the new association. Members were expressly forbidden to do business with nonmembers outside the official Exchange. The association developed and published a new set of rules governing the trade in securities and began to put out an official daily price list. With few alterations, these rules were maintained throughout the period covered by this study.

The Vereeniging affected only the Amsterdam market because only brokers with their main sphere of activity in Amsterdam could be members. Rotterdam had a Bourse of its own, but this was of small importance for the trade in securities. Consequently the Vereeniging van Effektenhandelaren te Rotterdam was not very influential. The domination of the Amsterdam Vereeniging was broken with the incorporation of the Bond voor den Geld- en Effectenhandel in de Provincie (Union for the Trade in Money and Securities in the Provinces) in 1903, in which brokers and bankers outside Amsterdam and Rotterdam united to break the stranglehold of the Amsterdam Vereeniging. The Bond grew quickly to some 650 members in 1905 (818 in 1914), and soon the Amsterdam brokers, the Rotterdam Vereeniging, and the new Bond came to terms, making it possible for all parties to trade under the same conditions.[3]

Despite the generally accepted respectability of the Amsterdam Vereeniging, not all members were of the same quality. Complaints about some brokers were heard, and quite a few were certainly less than respectable and involved in many shady deals. In 1914 the total number of stockbrokers in Holland was said to be about 1,500, which would mean one for every 4,000 Dutchmen.[4] Small wonder that there was some chaff among the wheat.

The decision to include a given security in the Amsterdam price lists was made by a committee appointed by the board of the Vereeniging. A few conditions had to be observed, among them that the broker or banker involved had to deposit Dfl 500 for every newly listed bond or stock. Moreover, the broker had to publish a prospectus in one of the daily newspapers and present a copy of the articles of incorporation of the company, a copy of the latest annual report and balance sheet, a certified copy of the official mortgage document when a bond issue was secured by such a mortgage, and other documents proving that the company in question was bona fide and in business. Over the years more conditions were imposed and the cost per listing was not fixed but made relative to the sum traded. In order to obtain a daily quotation at least Dfl 2,000 of a security had to be traded that particular day.

The exceptional circumstances of World War I necessitated closer supervision of the trading of stocks by the Dutch government. After the assassination in Serajevo on 28 June 1914, a financial panic broke out all over Europe. Most bourses closed their doors, and the one in Amsterdam followed suit at the urgent recommendation of the Netherlands government. On 29 July 1914 the Stock Exchange was closed, and reopened only on 9 February 1915. The Beurswet (Exchange Law) of September 1914, although meant to be only temporary, gave the Minister of Agriculture, Fisheries, and Industry (later more appropriately the Minister of Finance) permanent general supervision over all Dutch bourses. Among other powers, the minister decided which securities were to be added to the price lists. Moreover, every bond or share issue from this point was required to have a par value of Dfl 500,000 or more to qualify for a listing.[5]

The actual building in Amsterdam where the trade in securities took place was the famous old Merchants' Exchange on the Rokin, built by Hendrick de Keyser in the early 1600's. In a corner of this building the stockbrokers gathered and did their business. By the 1840's this old Beurs had become so dilapidated that a new building was necessary. Designed by Zocher, the new Merchants' Exchange opened in 1845 on the Dam in Amsterdam. Again, the actual stock exchange was only a corner in the new edifice, while the rest was used as a bourse for commodities. Despite many attempts to acquire a separate stock exchange building, the Vereeniging was not successful. In 1903 a new Merchants' Exchange, designed by H. P. Berlage, was opened, but a separate room for the trade in stocks was the best that could be obtained. When this room soon became too small for the growing number of members of the Vereeniging, the urge for a real stock exchange became stronger, and at long last the present Stock Exchange building, designed by Jos. Th. J. Cuypers, was opened in 1913, next door to the Merchants' Exchange.[6]

■ *Government Intervention*

After the establishment of the Kingdom of the Netherlands in 1815, William I, "the merchant-king," pursued an active policy of mercantile and industrial development. In his view the drain on capital resources resulting from investment in foreign countries was a hindrance to development at home, and as we have already noted, foreign investment was for a time—until 1824—officially forbidden, except with special royal permission.

All securities traded in the Netherlands were subject to a stamp duty levied by the government, and foreign paper was taxed at a rate of 30 cents for every 100 guilders of par value. In 1856, as noted, this relatively high duty was reduced to only 5 cents, the same as for domestic paper.

Other than this, the Netherlands government generally abstained from interference with the stock market or the trade in foreign securities. This may have made the trade relatively easy and free from bothersome regulations, but on the other hand it also meant that Dutch investors in foreign securities, when in trouble, could not count on much support from their government. In 1817 Dutch diplomatic representatives all over the world were ordered to act on requests for help by private parties only after careful examination of the case by the Dutch authorities and after formal authorization by the Foreign Office in The Hague. This, of course, could mean long delays in the days before the telegraph.[7]

When differences arose between Dutch merchants or investors and foreign private parties, generally no official steps were taken by the government in The Hague. When a foreign government became involved, the Netherlands Foreign Office sometimes did act, but usually in an unofficial and unobtrusive way, as befitted a small country. Arbitration was generally favored to solve differences between governments peacefully, and this form of bilateral transaction became very popular, especially when the United States was the other party involved. Only rarely was the Netherlands' envoy in Washington instructed to act in his official capacity, as in the case of goods belonging to Dutch merchants seized by the Union Army in New Orleans in 1862.[8]

In disputes over financial matters between Dutch investors and American banks, railroad companies, or stockbrokers, the government in The Hague only gave unofficial support when requested by Dutch citizens. Dutch consuls in American cities such as Galveston did act now and then in the interests of Dutch nationals, but never through pressure, and always by way of mediation and advice. A succinct statement of 1867 by the Minister of Foreign Affairs, count J. P. J. A. van Zuylen van Nijevelt, explains the official Dutch policy nicely: "It is not the duty of the Netherlands Government to favor foreign, and sometimes risky, investments, and to expose itself thereby to international problems."[9]

Among the authorities, American (and Russian) railroad securities were not seen as a very safe medium of investment, even if some of them, such as the stocks and bonds of the Illinois Central and other companies considered sound, were deemed suitable for orphans and spinsters. The Nederlandsche Bank, the nominally independent but actually government-sponsored national bank of the Netherlands, categorically refused to accept American railroad paper as collateral for loans to other banks or private persons. Only during the monetary crisis caused by the Franco-Prussian War in 1870 did the bank for a time accept certain selected classes of American and Russian railway paper, but only the best, and even then only with some restrictions.[10]

Dutch consuls, usually an unpaid honorary appointment, acted as representatives of the government especially in commercial and personal matters all over the world. The stationing of these consuls in the United States came in for some criticism. The consulate general was in New York, with a handful of consuls in port cities such as Boston, Philadelphia, Baltimore, Norfolk, Charleston, and Savannah. On the Gulf coast Mobile, New Orleans, and Galveston were fairly obvious choices for a consulate, but surprisingly Key West also supported a Dutch consul, until he was transferred to Pensacola in 1880. Port Arthur, Texas, was added in 1906, reflecting the Dutch interest in the area, but Shieldsboro, Mississippi, established in 1889, is a surprising choice; the vice consul there was transferred to Gulfport in 1907. Dutch consulates in inland cities, apart from obvious candidates such as St. Louis and Cincinnati, were even more strangely placed; Keokuk, Iowa, held a Dutch consul for a number of years, until abolished in 1866. Portage City, Wisconsin, north of Madison, had a consulate until it was transferred to Winona, Minnesota, in 1869. One writer in 1870 wondered why Chicago had no Dutch consul while Winona, where probably no Dutch were living, did. The same was said of St. Louis, where not more than a handful of Hollanders could be found. Chicago held a sizable Dutch contingent, with two Dutch churches, among its 300,000 inhabitants, and consulates of all countries, "even of Belgium, Hesse, and Italy," were already in place there.[11] Fortunately for our writer the Dutch consulate at

Winona was transferred to Chicago in the next year. St. Paul, Minnesota, got a vice consulate in 1873, but Grand Rapids, Michigan, an established center for Hollanders, had to wait until 1885. On the West coast San Francisco had had a consulate since the end of the Mexican War, and Los Angeles and Seattle were added to the list early in the twentieth century.

The consular reports were closely followed by the Dutch brokers, as is clearly seen in the 1878 annual report of the Administratie Kantoor van Amerikaansche Spoorweg-waarden (Administrative Bureau for American Railroad Securities) set up by Wertheim and Gompertz and partners. The Kantoor's actions came in for a lot of criticism after having exchanged in 1873 6-percent Central Pacific bonds for the same of the Paducah & Memphis, which soon ceased to pay any interest. Wertheim defended his policy by quoting from the reports of the Dutch consul in San Francisco, James de Fremery, who in 1872 had written that the Central Pacific was in a very bad financial shape and likely to collapse any time.[12] Unfortunately for Wertheim, De Fremery was wrong, and the Central Pacific continued to pay interest regularly, while the Paducah & Memphis soon folded. De Fremery, himself a merchant of note in San Francisco and founder of the Chamber of Commerce there, recognized the need for more factual information about California, and he privately published abridged versions of his annual consular reports over the years 1861–90. In his 1871 report he paid much attention to the railroads of California and their financial situation. He lamented the lack of information on the part of the railroad managers, who had regularly referred him to the brokers who were handling the sale of the securities of that particular road regarding a railroad's solvency. Only the directors knew for sure how solid a company actually was, and they made sure that De Fremery did not find out.

Even when several American states repudiated their debts in the 1830's and 1840's, which caused widespread displeasure among the Dutch holders of these state bonds, the Dutch government abstained from interfering officially. Successive American envoys in The Hague were bombarded with protests by Dutch individuals or bankers, but the Dutch Foreign Office took no official steps. The American diplomats did recognize the justice of the Dutch claims, but could do little because the U.S. federal government was singularly uncooperative. Harmanus Bleecker, an American envoy of Dutch descent who valued American society much more than Dutch, in 1842 acknowledged one severe fault of his American countrymen, their "indifference to pecuniary obligations."[13]

Upon entering the country in 1842, his successor in The Hague, Christopher Hughes, was welcomed with a report drawn up by A. van der Hoop, of the influential Amsterdam firm of Hope and Company, titled, "Holland held up as an example to the United States of North America in respect to the payment of their debts." Hughes could not avoid forwarding this manifesto to the U.S. State Department, and when that did not bring payment on U.S. debt, a deputation of bankers again pressed him for action and presented him with a petition signed by 165 bondholders of American loans. Only then did the acting Secretary of State, Hugh S. Legare, inform Hughes that the federal government did not feel responsible for the debts engaged by the several states, and thus declined to act. Economic growth would soon solve all problems, according to Legare.[14]

Unlike other European powers, the Netherlands government did not pursue an active policy of establishing or extending spheres of influence. The British financial and commercial influence in Mexico, Argentina, and the Middle East, largely through financing, building, and operating railways, or the German drive for Baghdad with the Baghdad railway, was not imitated by the Dutch. This did not mean that no Dutch capital was invested in those areas at all, but it was never used to obtain special commercial favors from the local governments. The domestic heavy industry in the Netherlands was slow in developing, and exports of rails and other iron products were negligible. An industry to build tramway and railway cars had been established and operated on a scale of some consequence since the 1870's. Exports of streetcars and railway rolling stock to foreign countries became common enough, but never through the efforts of the home government. No railroad equipment was ever exported to the United States. Mexican railways had attracted Dutch capital, but again little or no rolling stock was sold to that country. Turkish (or Ottoman) government bonds were also held in Holland, but without any visible Dutch influence on the Ottoman railways.

The Kingdom of the Netherlands was already in possession of a vast colonial empire in the East and West Indies that was almost too large for a small nation to handle, and the scramble for colonies in Africa and Asia involving England, France, and Germany was closely watched but not imitated. Only in one instance did an official interest in a railway in a foreign country become slightly visible. In Transvaal, which had regained its independence from Britain after the first Boer War, the building of a railway toward Portuguese Mozambique was undertaken by a Dutch company, the Netherlands South African Railway Company, incorporated in 1889. The line was largely financed from Holland and Germany, engineered by the Dutch, built by Dutch contractors, with most iron and steelwork supplied by Dutch firms, equipped with German and Dutch locomotives and rolling stock, and staffed by a motley international crew headed by Dutchmen. To overcome strong political resistance on the part of Britain and the British Cape Colony against this enterprise, which was bound to loosen the stranglehold of the British colonies on landlocked Transvaal, the Dutch government pursued a rather active policy in support of the railway company. Apart from financial and commercial considerations, other arguments in favor of helping the Boer republics were also heard. Transvaal—and the Orange Free State—were peopled by brothers, Dutch-speaking and Calvinist, and both republics were seen as a field where the surplus Dutch population could go to help build a new nation. Emigration of Dutch citizens was actively promoted in the Netherlands, and thousands served not only on the African railway but also in industry, education, and even in the Transvaal government offices.[15] South Africa, however, remained the one and only example of an active Dutch foreign policy in support of Dutch-owned and Dutch-built railways in other, politically independent countries.

■ A Note About Currency

The unit of currency in the Netherlands was and is the *gulden* or guilder, abbreviated in international trade as Dfl (Dutch florin). In 1847, after many years of bimetallism, the Netherlands government adopted the silver standard and the existing gold pieces were slowly withdrawn, until in 1850 gold was officially demonetized. In the following years a general decline of silver prices led to slow inflationary pressure. To obviate this, gold was again introduced for coinage in 1875. The old silver coins remained in circulation, but for all intents the Netherlands were among the many countries that adhered to the gold standard since that year.[16] During the years of this study the American gold dollar was worth Dfl 2.50 with only slight fluctuations, while the English pound was worth Dfl 12, again with little or no fluctuation. The value of the paper dollar, of course, changed almost daily during its existence and was generally well below that of the gold dollar.

The difference between the gold and paper dollar could cause complications, as becomes clear from an episode with the Illinois Central in the years 1864–68. That company wanted to redeem its 7-percent construction bonds by converting them into 6-percent redemption bonds, but the directors met much opposition to this reduction of interest. Few bondholders volunteered to exchange their securities on these conditions, whereupon the company simply announced that the first 3,000 of the construction bonds were to be redeemed at 120 percent of par in cash. However, the redemption was made not in gold but in currency; when the bonds were originally issued no specification had been made about paper or gold, paper dollars not existing at that time. In 1864 the gold dollar was valued at slightly more than Dfl 2.40, while the greenback was only Dfl 1.00. When the Illinois Central executed this plan, bondholders realized only about 48 percent on every $1,000 bond.

Small wonder that an outcry was raised in England and Holland against such an arbitrary action, although it was acknowledged that the measure was legal and that the company had the right to take it. The forced conversion did nothing to enhance the credit of the road, of course, and a sharp drop in the price of its securities was the result. President William Osborn did his best to defend the measure against the Dutch opposition, but to little avail.[17]

Yet, apparently pleased with the result of this first redemption, the company announced a second conversion of $3 million worth of sevens into new sixes, again under threat of redemption in currency. This time the protests of the bondholders were such that the redemption was annulled and only those bonds offered voluntarily were converted. Then in 1868, with the paper dollar at Dfl 1.65, the next sevens (numbered 3001 to 4000) were redeemed at 120 percent in currency, despite new protests of the bondholders, who again had to accept a loss.[18] Loans issued after 1862 always carried an explicit statement about being in gold or in currency, and foreign investors could not be fooled anymore in this way. Currency loans were seen as less attractive and were therefore generally quoted a few points lower than contemporary gold loans.

■ *The Character of the Dutch Investor*

Much effort has been spent trying to explain the high risks Dutch investors took in the finance of projects in America, Russia, and other countries. Did they favor the risky American rails over their own country's consolidated debt, and if so, why? This study is not meant to dissect the psychology of the Dutch investor, but will attempt some explanation of his behavior.

As we have noted in the previous chapter, around the middle of the nineteenth century the wealth of the Dutch was still large and probably spread over a larger segment of the population than elsewhere in the world. On the average the wealth of the individual investor may have been smaller than in England, but the number of small capitalists in the total population was larger.[19] In 1860 it was estimated that around 100,000 Dutch possessed securities of some kind or other, and their number grew during the rest of that century.[20] This trend was not a phenomenon of the nineteenth century only. It had already been seen in the eighteenth, when the number of small rentiers who had retired from active business with capital large enough to support them comfortably was substantial. This group had always looked at investment of its capital with an eye toward high returns combined with a reasonable measure of safety.

The degree of national feeling among them was negligible when it came to a choice between high-paying foreign securities and low-paying domestic paper. The revenues were all important, and investors were willing to take a certain amount of risk. Only when domestic enterprise promised a high yield, such as the first railways in the country did, was the Dutch rentier willing and even eager to place his money there. The old theory that he was out of principle averse to all domestic enterprises has been sufficiently demolished by now. He was perfectly willing to put his savings in the home railways, but only when the return was as high as he could obtain with Russian, Austrian, or other "safe" securities. Dutch industry simply did not yet require much capital.[21]

The Dutch investor's instinct for safety led him to spread the risk over a large number of securities. A common Dutch proverb was (and is) "don't put all your eggs in one basket," and acting on that principle the cautious Dutchmen hardly ever invested all their surplus capital in one enterprise, domestic or foreign. The later investment funds, of course, found favor with Dutch investors by spreading their capital in the same way over large numbers of different enterprises in many countries.[22]

Another characteristic of Dutch investors was their preference for relatively high-paying bonds with which they were willing to take a certain amount of calculated risk. Not only the speculative element among them, but also the cautious investor, was apt to choose the foreign bonds that promised a yield of 1 or 2 percent more over the solid but low-paying domestic government loans. The high return was generally sought first, and the safety of an issue came in second place.[23]

A very important aspect of the trade in securities in Holland was what was called the system of the *prolongatie* loan. A private person could buy securities with borrowed money, generally for two or three months, in the hope of realizing some gain during that time. Money was available in large quantities. Large mercantile companies, industries with extra cash on hand, and rich private persons were willing to lend money on easy terms for this purpose. Until 1853 banks did not pay any interest on deposits, and even after such payment became customary with most banks, many businessmen and private persons preferred to lend their surplus capital themselves in prolongatie loans. Moreover, the short-term interest rate in the Netherlands during the period covered in this study was generally very close to the long-term rate, so there was little incentive to put surplus capital away for long terms in savings banks and similar institutions. Large amounts of capital were thus on hand, and the closely knit network of stockbrokers and agents all over the country, combined with excellent communications with the Amsterdam Stock Exchange by means of telegraph, railway, and postal service, made it possible for persons with little or no capital of their own, anywhere in Holland, to buy securities with money borrowed on easy terms. The only condition was that the securities had to be popular and frequently traded, so as to be easily disposable at the end of the loan period. American and Russian railroad securities fitted the bill admirably: much trade, great popularity, and a good chance of rising prices. This kind of paper was seen as almost the same as cash.[24]

Banks themselves did lend money in this way, with the stocks thus bought by the borrower serving as security. The few figures available indicate that some banks, such as the Savings Bank of Rotterdam during the period 1868–88, had between 68 and 46 percent of their total capital put out in this way.[25] The system of buying on prolongation came to grief in 1914. The general and widespread fall in price of all securities caused by events in Serajevo meant that people, at the end of the loan period, would have to supply the difference between the principal of their loan and the current market price of their securities. This could have led to a large-scale liquidation of portfolios, followed by a further fall in prices and great losses for all parties involved. This was one, but certainly not the only, reason for the closure of the Amsterdam Exchange on 29 July 1914. The consequent problems of liquidity for many firms, which saw their surplus capital placed in short-term loans suddenly transformed into loans with indefinite terms because of the impossibility of sales on the Exchange, were solved with the help of the Nederlandsche Bank.[26]

Many foreign writers have seen Dutch capitalists as most accomplished speculators and reckless gamblers, as "le joueur le plus déterminé du monde."[27] Sweeping statements like these are always hard to prove, and may be partly true, but certainly not completely so. Of course, quite a number of the investors in American railroad securities were speculators, buying at low prices in the hope of a rise, and selling again when the price had climbed enough for realizing a nice profit. But another trend is visible also, quite opposed to the speculative one: buy when prices are low but then hang on to your securities regardless of market prices. A relatively large number of the Dutch-owned American issues covered in this study clearly show these latter characteristics. Through defaults and reorganizations the Dutch owners tenaciously clung to their bonds, apparently in the hope that ultimately they would come out ahead. Moreover, by hanging on to one's original securities, the stamp duty and the brokers' commissions could be kept to a minimum. The "short-term–high-return" kind of investment mentioned by many as a national preference of the Dutch (and Scottish) capitalists clearly was not the favorite (at least in the case of the Dutch).[28]

A clear distinction should be made between the large group of Dutch investors, who were looking for high-paying but reasonably safe securities, and the much smaller group of speculators, going all-out for quick profits only. The first group, generally requiring a long-term investment, did indeed favor American railroad stocks and bonds for their high yield. In the 1860's and 1870's 6, 7, or even 8 percent could be had in American railroad bonds, and not only in the more fancy or fraudulent schemes. In combination with the price of these bonds—generally well below par—an actual return of some 10 percent could thus be obtained. For the time this was extremely high, and the attraction of this kind of bond or stock is not difficult to explain. Furthermore, among these American railroads there were quite a few most respectable companies that did indeed honor their obligations. Many securities of such companies as Illinois Central or Chicago & North Western were among the earliest shares offered and bought in Amsterdam, and quite a few are still included in the price lists today. Illinois Central common stock, first introduced in 1856, was still listed in 1992, 136 years later.

The more speculative group of Dutch capitalists was chiefly attracted by the prospect of quick gains. The element of lottery in the riskier of the many schemes offered in the years after the Civil War strongly appealed to their gambling instincts. When introduced on the European markets, some of these railroads were nothing more than schemes, able to show only a charter, a prospectus containing the most glowing terms, and sometimes a few miles of jerry-built road from nowhere to nowhere in particular, without any real earning capacity. These roads were selling their bonds at a great discount, and as long as they paid the first few semi-annual coupons the market price of their bonds generally rose. A shrewd speculator could buy this kind of paper at a very low price and unload it on an uninformed public with a nice clean profit before the inevitable crash came. But if he waited too long, the speculator himself was of course caught with the worthless bonds or stocks still on his hands. Apparently in almost every group of Dutch investors were some affected with the gambling spirit. Bakers and grocers, farmers and artisans were all reported to indulge in a gamble of this kind now and then, sometimes with borrowed money, as noted above. And when the crash came, as happened several times, they were the losers.

After every crash the moralists lectured loudly in public on the depravity of mankind and assumed righteously that these sinners only got what they deserved. A case in point is the unholy glee of the public when in 1884 the local Barneveld (province of Gelderland) press noted with some satisfaction that one of the most vehement opponents of a proposed local railway line, which promised to be important for regional development, had been rewarded for his troubles by losing his private fortune in the American "swindle" of the Oregon & California.[29]

Around the turn of the century this speculative element became less important. American railroad loans were no longer carrying 7 or 8 percent, but 4 or 5 at the most, and their price at introduction was generally not much below par, making them no longer suitable for speculative purposes. American industrial shares and also the domestic oil, rubber, and agricultural companies in the Dutch East Indies had opened new fields which now offered rich rewards for shrewd and daring financiers, making the American railroad securities pale in comparison. Yet, in 1903 it was noted that Dutch losses resulting from the American crisis of that year were still considerable, especially in the smaller towns. Army officers in Amersfoort (province of Utrecht) had indulged in too much speculation and were now caught short.[30]

It should be noted that not only individuals invested their capital in American railroad paper. Small industrial companies, with modest capital needs, sometimes put their surplus capital in securities of all kinds, including American rails. The most important condition for choosing what kind of paper these companies would buy was that it had to be readily marketable. At short notice the company could need the money again, and then the securities in question had to be sold or pawned quickly. Russian securities and American railroad bonds were considered almost as liquid as cash and were widely held as such. This kind of paper could easily be sold, and also pawned, if the shortage of liquid funds was expected to be of short duration.[31] The gambling element was probably completely absent in this kind of transaction. Toward the end of our period the large industrial companies then emerging in the Netherlands also held some foreign securities. The same has been noted for England, where banks and other firms owned substantial blocks of American railroad securities. There is no reason to assume that Dutch companies did not do the same.[32]

Some American railroad presidents now and then complained that the foreign stockholders in their companies were interested in regular high dividends and nothing else. Apparently these foreign investors were supposed to have had no idea that some of the earnings of a railroad had to be used for improvement of the property; when all improvements would be charged to the capital account, the capital stock would increase to such an extent that in the future dividends would be rendered almost impossible.[33] This may have been true of the average Dutch stockholder, but the Amsterdam brokers and their representatives were well aware of those facts and tried to explain the financial situation of the American railroads as well as they could through their Administratie Kantoren. Of course, in the end, investing in American railroads was strictly a business proposition, not a charity. All investors, foreign and domestic, expected—and still expect—to make money and the Dutch were—and still are—no exception to that simple fact.

Four

American Railroad Loans in the Netherlands: Information and Opinions

One wonders what, if anything, the Dutch investing public knew about the United States during the second half of the nineteenth century. How did the available information about possible investment there reach them? Dutch brokers and bankers with well-established contacts on the other side of the Atlantic (such as the firms mentioned in the preceding chapters), of course, had some knowledge of the American need for capital to develop the young country. The links between Amsterdam and New York trading firms, dating back to the eighteenth century, ensured a regular flow of information about the financial situation of the United States, but the export of capital to America had remained a rather specialized branch of trade activities until the 1850's. The general public had little or no access to this information. With the growing interest in investment in foreign stocks and bonds in the 1840's and early 1850's, however, the need for more information made itself felt. Thus the first investors' guides in the Netherlands came to be published.

Even when the possibilities for investing in American securities were still limited, several of the new investors' guides started to pay attention to the American situation. J. Dinger, a stockbroker himself, published his first survey in 1851, and some fifteen pages of this brochure are dedicated to America.[1] In successive editions the American section would be greatly expanded, reaching more than 200 pages in the fifth and last edition of 1873.

Willem van Oosterwijk Bruyn, a partner in the firm of Kerkhoven and Company, followed up an earlier specialized guide for American securities with two annual surveys for 1868 and 1869, in which he highly recommended American securities. Compared to Austrian or other European paper, he considered American rails and state loans much more secure.[2] Austria was seen as a particularly bad opportunity because the Empire had repudiated part and forcibly converted the rest of its outstanding debt in 1868. Inasmuch as the Dutch were easily the largest foreign creditors of that country, holding an estimated 426 million Austrian florins out of a total foreign-owned debt of just over one billion florins, this conversion made a great impression. Dutch investors were understandably starting to look elsewhere.[3]

The first specialized investors' guide for American railroads only, by J. J. Weeveringh, came out in 1870 and totaled a meager 32 pages. This brochure was published just before the great flood of new loans, and consequently the last edition of the same work of 1887 had grown to 157 pages, a clear indication of the growth in popularity of these securities in Holland.[4] Another guide for investors willing to risk their money in American rails came out in 1873, just before the general economic crisis of that year, written by N. J. den Tex, another stockbroker and leading Amsterdam businessman.[5]

Complaints were heard that most of these guides were written by stockbrokers, whose own financial interests were at stake, and who therefore were believed to be inclined to paint a rosier picture of the situation in America than warranted by actual facts. J. Pik, editor of the independent financial paper *De Financier* (published in Groningen, far from the Amsterdam financial crowd), set out to rectify this situation. His 1879 book is much more critical than the others, and he sometimes even attacks Amsterdam stockbrokers directly for lack of sound judgment, if not for actually misleading their customers, the public.[6] While most other guides were strictly factual, mentioning only figures from annual reports and such, Pik explains the situation of every railroad in question, with remarks about the management in America and the actions of the Dutch protective committees. Pik's book differs in one more respect from the other guides then available: it includes an excellent map, based on Appleton's railroad map, with the lines with Dutch financial input highlighted in many different colors. (Even so, Pik's spelling of American place-names is full of errors. Still, if he errs now and then, how would the average Dutch investor know? Would he have known Paducah from Cairo, or Rockford from Rock Island?)

Later guides, like the one by Santilhano, grew into complete books, and gave not only the latest figures on every American railroad whose securities were known in Amsterdam, but also a kind of financial history, including some information about corporate mergers, defaults, and reorganizations. The most complete was, of course, S. F. van Oss's *American Railroads as Investments*, published in New York, London, and Amsterdam in 1893, and widely known in the Netherlands. Van Oss also published in 1903 a smaller guide for Dutch capitalists, in which he warned of the pitfalls of investing in U.S. rails. He would soon become entangled himself in the Oklahoma Central Railway.[7]

In 1903 this same Van Oss started his annual *Effectenboek* (Securities Book), meant as a guide for brokers and investors alike, and giving details of the corporate structure of all companies with securities on the Amsterdam Exchange, together with the usual information about financial performance, capital and funded debt, and the current market price of the stocks and bonds. As his coverage was worldwide, the series soon expanded into two annual volumes, one for domestic and one for foreign paper, and each running to more than 1,200 pages of minute print. For contemporary financiers, and for later historians, the *Van Oss' Effectenboek* has been invaluable.

The independent Dutch financial press also provided information about possibilities and dangers of investing in domestic and foreign securities. The *Amsterdamsch*

Effectenblad (since 1843 the successor to the venerable *Prijscourant der Effecten*) and, after 1870, the *Nieuw Algemeen Effectenblad* (also published in Amsterdam), gave information but little comment. Other weeklies (or biweeklies), such as *De Nederlandsche Financier* (which first came out in Amsterdam in 1864), *Kapitalist* (published in Groningen since 1874), and the *Nieuwe Financier* (published by stockbroker T. A. Huizenga in Groningen since 1875), gave editorial commentary in addition to statistical information. The latter two journals were merged in 1880 into the *Nieuwe Financier en Kapitalist*, which then came out twice a week and quickly became an influential source of information. From 1903 the editor was S. F. van Oss, the noted financial journalist and stockbroker. J. Pik, author of the critical guide on North American railroads, started his own weekly *De Financier* in Groningen in 1877. He did not confine himself to American securities only, but also wrote extensively on more general topics such as taxation, free trade, and banking.

The daily press, especially the papers published in the two trading centers of Holland, also provided much information for the Dutch investors. The Amsterdam *Algemeen Handelsblad* and the Rotterdam *Nieuwe Rotterdamsche Courant* both catered to a public that included capitalists interested in financial matters. Groningen, although without a stock exchange of its own, had become a kind of secondary center for international money matters, as we have noted from the several weeklies published in that northern town. Interest in financial matters must have been sufficient for the regional daily *Provinciale Groninger Courant* to include in its pages from 1877 an elaborate price list of all current stocks on the Amsterdam Exchange.[8]

Even the specialized brokers in Holland recognized the need for more regular information about the American railroad business. In 1873 the well-respected Amsterdam firm of Wertheim and Gompertz, Westendorp and Company, and F. W. Oewel convened a meeting of interested parties to discuss establishing an information bureau as a kind of central point where brokers and bankers could obtain the necessary information to better judge the solidity of the schemes offered to them. Although this happened just before the crash of 1873, and the idea would seem to have been most reasonable, support was sadly lacking, and Wertheim had to abandon the idea completely.[9]

■ Travel Accounts

An important source of information about America and American railroads was the many travel books published in Holland and elsewhere from the late 1850's onward. Dutch travelers to the United States in the second half of the nineteenth century felt the same urge as the average Englishman to write about their experiences in that strange country, and many of them knew enough and saw enough to be able to say something useful for prospective Dutch investors in American railroads. One of the first to publish his impressions, the influential member of Parliament W. T. Gevers Deynoot, rode many American railroad trains in the eastern states in 1859, but he did not say much about the Dutch investments, which were still few at the time. He did, however, travel over the recently finished Illinois Central and he concluded that its shares and bonds were a safe investment.[10] He was to be proved right. Coming down on the IC (for a complete list of all the abbreviations for railroads used in this study, see Appendix D) from the north, he changed trains for St. Louis at Sandoval, Illinois, where the broad-gauge Ohio & Mississippi crossed the standard-gauge Illinois Central on the level. Why he did not use the more convenient connection with the Terre Haute route at Vandalia is hard to say, but he may have wanted to inspect the O&M in view of possible investment in that road. There was some talk at the time in Amsterdam about the Ohio & Mississippi being a suitable vehicle for investment.

Dutch interest in the United States after the Civil War grew enormously, and books about the history, the manners of the people, and the experiences of travelers in that country became popular in Holland. Bancroft's history of the United States was translated into Dutch and published in Holland. English and French travel books were reviewed in Dutch periodicals.[11] Among the books reviewed by R. P. A. Dozy, noted professor of history at Leiden University, in *De Gids* of 1871 were Rae's *Westward by Rail* and William Blackmore's *Colorado*. Rae described the alternative route to the Far East by way of the new transcontinental railroad, while Blackmore wrote in depth about the resources of Colorado and the Trenchera and Costilla Estates, soon to attract millions of Dutch guilders.[12] In 1870 Dozy had also reviewed—and completely demolished—Chester's *Transatlantic Sketches* as being written by a most narrow-minded and conceited John Bull, who condemned everything that was even slightly different from his own English customs and practices, without having any regard at all for local circumstances and history. Dozy's views were much more lenient. Without closing his eyes to the evils of reconstruction in the South, he thought that at least some allowance should be made for the American republic, still a relatively young state, regarding abuses in the judicial system and elsewhere.[13]

A later Dutch writer on America was G. Verschuur, an experienced traveler, who had already crossed every continent. He wrote after the general crisis of 1873, which for Dutch investors had been so catastrophic, and exhorted his readers, who were supposedly shuddering when hearing the words "American railroads," to forget about those brightly colored pieces of paper and think only of the advantages of railway travel in the United States. He then continued with a most enthusiastic description of the American railroad passenger car and its luxuries and comforts.[14]

At the same time a Dutch protestant minister who had traveled for six months through the United States wrote in the same vein. Martinus Cohen Stuart was Dutch delegate at the convention of the Evangelical Alliance, held in New York in 1873, and he wanted to see as much of the country as possible. He was skeptical about American railroads because of the bad reputation (not without reason) of American railroad stocks in Holland, but concluded that some distinction should be made between being a railroad shareholder and a railroad traveler. In the latter capacity he found little to complain about.[15] All convention delegates were presented with a free pass on the Erie Railroad, a wise move on the part of a company with a very bad reputation in Europe. Cohen Stuart was most optimistic about the profitability of the Erie because of its heavy traffic and the wealth of the coal and oil regions it traversed.[16] He failed to mention the detrimental influence of the bad management and the malversations of Jay Gould, Jim Fisk, and their cronies, who had only just been thrown out and who had left the company in terrible shape. It is hard to believe that he simply did not know about all this, because every newspaper in the Netherlands and in America had been full of the Erie scandals.

Riding the Des Moines Valley Railroad to Pella, Iowa, Cohen Stuart noted that he was seeing names familiar from the Amsterdam Stock Exchange list, with all their unfortunate connotations. He clearly saw that if the Dutch capitalists had had a more profound knowledge of the geographical circumstances, they would never have been led to expect a return of between 10 and 15 percent on their money right from the start. The land, however fertile they had been promised it would be, could attain its real value only after the railroads had been built, and even then a yield of more than 10 percent was probably much too optimistic. A slight consolation might be that future generations would profit from the original investments. In this latter respect Cohen Stuart curiously enough echoed Ralph Waldo Emerson who, already in 1844, had written, "We build railroads, we know not for what or for whom, but one thing is certain, that we who build will receive the very smallest share of benefit."[17] Cohen Stuart may well have known Emerson's works, but certainly not the American poet's private diaries, which were only published at a much later date, and it is noteworthy to see how Stuart elaborates on the great importance of the railroads for Americans as the only means of linking the vast West with civilization and with the world, and binding the country together, much as Emerson had written in his diary: "We could not else have held the vast North America together which we now engage to do." The pious Dutch minister concluded, "The steamcar is the ramrod which will open the west to civilization, will people and farm the wilderness, and convert the empty prairies into farmland as God intended."[18] But where David Henry Thoreau poetically had called the locomotive whistle "the scream of a hawk" and the steam "a banner streaming behind in golden and silver wreaths," the Dutchman more prosaically claimed to have heard the sighs of the Dutch bondholders in the hissing of the steam engines of the unfortunate St. Paul & Pacific![19]

Later Dutch travelers were commonly as impressed by the splendors and comforts of the American railroad cars as Cohen Stuart had been. J. van 't Lindenhout, a fellow minister and director of a large orphanage near Nijmegen, made the usual grand tour of the Dutch colonies in Michigan and Iowa in 1886. He correctly attributed the excellent service on most lines to the great competition between the several railroads, something that the owners of railroad shares certainly would not like to hear about, because this kind of competition was apt to reduce the annual dividends.[20]

In 1892 J. C. Wijnaendts Francken rode the trains all over the American continent. Although he stated that his book would not give any financial information, he was aware of the fact that his readers, on seeing the words "railroads in America," would think of the many millions lost by the ordinarily cautious and prudent Dutchmen driven by the quest for high returns and their love of gambling. A description of the United States without paying any attention to the railroads would not be complete, however, given their enormously important role in the opening and developing of the country. Again, he too was impressed by the Pullman cars and by the enormous distances covered in them in relative comfort. His travels even brought him to Georgetown, Colorado, where he had a pleasant discussion—in French—of the latest philosophical topics with Louis Dupuy, the famous owner of the Hotel de Paris there.[21]

A special case is the beautiful book *Nieuwe Wereld* (New World), written by R. P. J. Tutein Nolthenius and originally published in 1900. It was so successful that a second edition was necessary two years later. Tutein was a civil engineer, a pioneer in building with that promising new material, concrete, and was also interested in the history of engineering as well as that of his own family. Moreover he was connected with, and for a number of years even a partner in, the Amsterdam firm of Tutein Nolthenius and De Haan, which was the broker behind the formidable Dutch participation in Arthur Stilwell's Kansas City, Pittsburg & Gulf Railroad. His description of his travels along that road, in the splendor of Stilwell's private business car, complete with a pipe organ among other comforts, through Arkansas and Louisiana vividly conveys the majesty of the virgin forests along the right of way and the fertility of the still empty land. Naturally, he was a vociferous advocate of Dutch investment in the United States, a country with a tremendous future.[22]

The decline in importance of the Dutch investment in American rails when compared to investment in other industries is clearly reflected in the account of another Dutch civil engineer, J. C. van Reigersberg Versluys, in 1917. On his way to take up his post in the Dutch East Indies he traveled by way of America because of the German submarine danger and crossed the continent from New York to San Francisco by train. His book is full of technical descriptions of great engineering works in the States, but he did not fail to note that the average interest on capital invested in American railroads had declined to 3.5 percent generally, with a high of 4.4 percent only in exceptionally good years such as 1914. His statement is a concise explanation of the decline of investment from Holland in this particular field.[23]

One more Dutch traveler in the United States remains to be mentioned, for two reasons: first, his book was extremely well-written; second, he carried a famous name, which gave him access to all American financial establishments. He was Charles Boissevain, related to all the Boissevains of banking and stockbroking circles, a young journalist who was from 1885 to 1908 editor in chief of the leading Amsterdam newspaper *Algemeen Handelsblad*. He traveled extensively in the United States, by train of course, and because he must have known the price lists of the Amsterdam Exchange by heart, his remarks about railroads with Dutch capital are to the point. His description of the Wall Street Stock Exchange, where he was received with open arms, is most accurate and funny at the same time, and he explained all the jargon in use there to his Dutch readers.[24]

Boissevain also provided the European investors with some ideological background for investing in American railroads. Only through the capital they put up for railroad building had it been possible to develop the vast unbroken prairies into the bread basket of the world, thereby forever banning the spectre of famine from their own European continent. Moreover, the United States was not burdened by a large standing army, and every man could do useful work and contribute to the national economy, while in Europe the enormous armies drew millions of young men away from more profitable pursuits while saddling the governments with heavy debts.[25] The latter argument had already been put forward more poignantly by W. van Oosterwijk Bruyn, when he wrote in 1868 that capital invested in a democratic America was not going to be used for the production of arms, which in time could be used "against our own children." Compared to autocratic Prussia or Austria, he certainly had a point.[26] These arguments in favor of American investment can be seen as a kind of follow-up to the arguments heard in Holland back in the eighteenth century for supporting the sister republic across the ocean in her struggle against a tyrannical monarch.

But Boissevain was not blind to the dangers which threatened American democracy. Poverty and socialism posed the greatest threat to the old world, and America should take care that something similar would not happen there as well. At the same time, the new class of "money-aristocracy" that had risen, the monopolists, could also easily trample the little plant of democracy underfoot. Still, the great democratic republic had succeeded in paying off most of its debts without any repudiation or forced conversion, and according to Boissevain this success was to be attributed more to her capitalists, railroad directors, and farmers, than to her politicians.

■ Emigration and Investment

Solid information about most areas of the United States was difficult for interested Dutchmen to get, but this was certainly not the case with such states as Michigan and Iowa. Since 1848 thousands of Dutch emigrants, staunch Calvinists fleeing from oppression at home, had settled in and around Holland, Michigan, and Pella, Iowa. These transplanted Dutch men and women initially were most active in the building of harbors and canals to facilitate the transport of their products to markets. Although several of them were soon doing well, there is no evidence at all that they participated in investment in the railroads in their area, apart from working for the roads as laborers or station staff.[27] But despite this notable lack of financial interest in these railroads, the presence of a large body of transplanted Dutch meant that a lot was known about these parts of the United States through letters to relatives home and oral travel accounts from the many visitors. Dutchmen worked for the railroads in these states and this must have contributed to the general knowledge of American railroads back home. In 1881 a Michigan railroad company, the Grand Rapids & Indiana, hired Dutchmen to act as its land agents with the specific purpose of attracting more Dutch settlers. These efforts had some success, as the development of the settlements of Cadillac, Vogel Center, and Moddersville in Michigan proved.[28]

Of the numerous travel accounts and descriptions of Michigan and Iowa, one of the more precise and influential accounts was by A. E. Croockewit, published in *De Gids* in 1870. He was no stranger to this Jerusalem for he was related to the G. A. Croockewit who would soon be involved in the American railroad business as representative of the Dutch in the Missouri, Kansas & Texas Railroad. Croockewit described the railroads in Iowa and Michigan, the transportation business in general, and the future of the area and the Dutch there in great detail.[29]

An example of the continuing relations between the Dutch settlers in Michigan and the homeland from a much later period was the popular series by Theo De Veer in the weekly *Eigen Haard*, published in 1907 and 1908.[30] Although he did not mention any financial details, he gave a very concise description of the Dutch communities there and of their great prosperity.

The links between Holland and the expatriate Dutchmen in Michigan and Iowa contributed to the flow of information across the Atlantic. It is hard to believe that it was just a coincidence that almost all of the railroads in Michigan had Dutch money in their capital structure. The Michigan Central was the first in the late 1850's, and the Lake Shore, the Port Huron & Lake Michigan, and even the obscure Traverse City companies all had attracted some Dutch capital. The same holds true for many Iowa railroads, including the troublesome Des Moines & Fort Dodge, which connected Pella with Keokuk and Des Moines. Yet it is striking that Dutch brokers did not often use this proximity of an American railroad to a center of Dutch settlement as an added sales incentive. When in 1905 Van der Werff and Hubrecht of Amsterdam and Van Oss and Company of The Hague advertised a 4-percent bond loan of the Pere Marquette Railroad, they failed to mention in their prospectus that this road traversed the "Dutch" area of Michigan and that it had depots in Holland and Zeeland.[31]

Another part of the United States that generated much Dutch interest was Minnesota. In connection with the unfortunate St. Paul & Pacific Railroad (in which millions of guilders had been sunk between 1865 and 1871), the "Maatschappij van Grondbezit in Minnesota," commonly known as the Minnesota Land Company, was set up in Amsterdam in 1866. Directors were H. Kloos and L. August Bruijn; Kloos's brother Johan H. Kloos was engineer in charge of construction of one of the St. Paul's lines in Minnesota. Land could be bought for cash or for bonds of the railroad—one $1,000 7-percent bond for 200 acres—and emigration to Minnesota was to be actively promoted.[32] Another Dutch land agent operating in Minnesota for the Land Company was M. E. d'Engelbronner, civil engineer and member of the prestigious Royal Institute of Engineers in the Netherlands.

In 1867 Johan Kloos himself wrote a book about Minnesota which was explicitly meant for both emigrants and investors, and he was considered an impartial expert on all matters concerning that state.[33] In 1872 another Dutch writer, S. R. J. van Schevichaven, wrote in glowing terms along the same lines, stating in his foreword that "it must be of some concern to the owner of American railroad securities to know the look of the land, that has been developed with his money."[34] J. Knuppe, a former Dutch army officer employed by the St. Paul railroad as treasurer of the land department of the St. Vincent Extension, who later took up farming in Crookston in the Red River valley, also wrote a kind of guide for prospective settlers, aptly named *Land and Dollars.*[35] Knuppe was the brother-in-law of Johan Carp, who was to play a conspicuous role in the negotiations with James J. Hill over the sale of the St. Paul & Pacific in 1877–78.[36] Because of the short life of the St. Paul & Pacific, nothing much came of the emigration schemes, but at Kerkhoven, west of Minneapolis, there was a successful settlement of farmers from Holland.

Other instances of a combination of Dutch investment and emigration are found in Colorado and New Mexico. In Colorado the Costilla Estate attracted investors from Holland who were interested in opening up the empty land by means of General William J. Palmer's Denver & Rio Grande Railroad. The Maxwell Estate, or more accurately the Maxwell Land Grant Company, was taken over by Dutch interests from an English investors' group in 1874, and actively promoted emigration to its more than

2 million acres of land in New Mexico. Again the area was to be opened up by the Dutch-financed Denver & Rio Grande railroad, but when that company was barred access to New Mexico by the aggressive policy of the competing Atchison, Topeka & Santa Fe, the emigration schemes fell flat. Much slimmed down, the Maxwell Company survived and is still listed in Amsterdam as the Maxwell Investment Fund, a blue chip company investing in Royal Dutch Shell oil shares.[37]

Dutch emigration to the United States was not always associated with Dutch financial interest in the railroads of the region in question. The Northern Pacific was active in promoting European emigration to its lands, jokingly known as "Jay Cooke's Banana Belt." G. P. Itmann, Jr., was the NP's chief agent for the Netherlands with an office in Rotterdam, but although he had some success in attracting Dutch settlers, Dutch investment in the railroad itself never amounted to much.[38] Itmann was also behind the incorporation in 1873 of the Vereeniging tot ondersteuning der emigratie van minvermogenden naar den Noordamerikaansche Staat Minnesota (Association for supporting the emigration of the indigent to Minnesota). The association was reported as also being willing to help the more affluent prospective emigrants.[39]

Another author on Minnesota, N. J. den Tex, the same who had earlier published an investors' guide of his own, wrote his article as a kind of addition to the Dutch translation of Fr. Gerstäcker's *Naar Amerika*, which came out in 1874.[40] Den Tex's concept is clear: without railroads America would not amount to much, and "many an American railroad would not have been built or extended if Holland had not advanced the necessary capital." Railroads were of the greatest importance for agriculture, although he acknowledged the tensions about freight rates existing between railroads and grangers.

One other combined emigration and settlement scheme remains to be mentioned, although here the railroad element came first and emigration was only added as an afterthought. The Boissevains of Amsterdam were very active in the floating of Norfolk & Western securities in Holland. After they set up a branch office in New York, they started buying land along the N&W for development. Although these ventures were generally quite successful from a purely financial point of view, the number of Dutch actually settling in those places remained neglible. Only the small Virginia towns of Boissevain and Holland keep this venture alive.[41]

In conclusion it can be said that Dutch emigration to the United States did not materially influence the amount of Dutch investment in American railroads. Generally the two elements were kept apart, and in the few cases that both emigration and railroad financing were the combined goal of the Dutch backers of a scheme, the emigration came to little or nothing. That there was some link, however, between the two is proved by the concentration of Dutch-financed railroads in the only areas where Dutch settled in large numbers, Michigan and Iowa.

■ Doubts in Holland About the American "Craze"

In Holland the craze for American rails was seen well before the flood of new loans in the late 1860's and early 1870's. Already in 1864, at the opening of the "Paleis voor Volksvlijt," a sort of Crystal Palace in Amsterdam, tickets for the opening gala were selling like hot cakes and were even traded at the Stock Exchange, where they were said to be "as popular as Americans."[42]

Not all information available to prospective Dutch investors was positive, however. Several observers were vociferous in denouncing the wisdom of investing in American railroads. The craze for American loans in Amsterdam drew many adverse comments from different quarters. It was generally believed that the flow of Dutch capital across the Atlantic was actually causing a shortage of money for building the domestic railway system, and many scathing remarks were made about the Dutch money-grubbers who were only interested in lining their own pockets at the expense of stagnation of commerce and industry at home. And although it has been clearly proved that the slow construction of a railway network in the Netherlands cannot be attributed to a lack of available capital, this belief was widely held at the time. Dutch investors were always interested in a high return on their money, and when the first Dutch railways in the 1830's and early 1840's promised dividends of 8 percent or more, their shares were eagerly taken at home. As soon as it turned out that these expectations had been much too optimistic, however, and that dividends did not exceed 3 or 4 percent, the Dutch sold their holdings to foreign parties, mostly Germans in the case of the Holland Railway and English interests in the case of the Rhenish Railway.[43]

Of course, this was not unique to the Netherlands. The same remarks were heard in England, where investment and speculation in American railroads and mining ventures was even more widespread than in the rest of Europe. Where sinking money in American railroads was seen as a calculated risk, investing in gold and silver mines was almost asking for trouble. Curiously enough, however, while the Dutch invested and speculated heavily in American rails, they hardly touched the American mining businesses at all. English, French, German, and other European capitalists were risking their money on a very large scale in gold and silver mines in California and Nevada, but in the Netherlands there was only one early mining venture officially listed in Amsterdam, the Winnamucca Silver Mines in Utah. There may have been some unofficial trading of American mining shares on the side, but that kind of activity has left little trace. The California gold rush was, of course, commented on in Holland, and adventurous Dutch souls were no doubt attracted by the easy riches. However, the cautious capitalists abstained from any participation. In 1849 Jacob van Lennep, a popular writer of the time, produced A *California Dream*, a musical comedy in which he mocked the whole idea of getting rich quickly in America.[44]

Of course, there were warnings, both in England and in Holland, against reckless speculation in a country where business ethics seemed to differ greatly from those at home. Anthony Trollope, who was widely read in Holland, speaking out of his own experiences in America, fulminated in 1862 against the American way of doing business: "It seems to be the recognized rule of commerce in the Far West that men shall go out into the world's markets prepared to cheat and to be cheated. It may be said that as long as this is acknowledged and understood on all sides, no harm will be done. It is equally fair for all."[45] This may have been true when both parties in a transaction were American, but when one of them happened to be from Europe, the cheating was chiefly done on one side only, as European investors were soon to find out. Trollope also accurately recognized that land played an important role in the financing of

American railroads. Land grants became valuable when the railroad in question was completed, and prices of land could increase fivefold or more. "It may easily be understood that a railway, which could not be in itself remunerative, might in this way become a lucrative speculation."[46]

In his 1876 novel, *The Way We Live Now*, Trollope gives even better proof of his clear understanding of the way American railroads were being built and financed. His colorful but shady financier Augustus Melmotte seems to have been modeled after the real life Baron Albert Grant, né Gottheimer, an international financier of doubtful reputation. The great project of Melmotte and his American partner Hamilton K. Fisher, a line from Salt Lake City to Mexico, sounded somewhat like a "castle in Spain," but "a fortune was to be made, not by the construction of the railway, but by the floating of the railway shares."[47] This is a most accurate description of many American railroad schemes.

The 1875 publication in Holland of a sensational book did not augment the confidence of the Dutch in railroads in the Carolinas. In that year James S. Pike, former American envoy in The Hague, had seen his book about South Carolina under Negro rule published in a Dutch translation.[48] One chapter was full of horror stories about enormous frauds perpetrated in the construction of railroads in that state. Dutch investors should have abstained from sinking money in railroads in states of this caliber, but in 1870 they had already invested in the Port Royal Railroad in South Carolina, with rather disastrous results, not so much as a consequence of government by former slaves as of lack of traffic and revenues.[49]

An anonymous Dutch author, writing under the initial H., is much more outspoken than any of the others in his opinions. In 1868 this man vehemently denounced the speculation going on in Amsterdam and condemned the sharp financial practices as a cancer eating away at society and preventing any serious investing business from being done. His chief culprit is the French crédit mobilier banking system with its ramifications in other countries, but all speculation in domestic and foreign securities is denounced as dangerous.[50]

In 1870 another anonymous writer who claimed to be a stockbroker wrote a pamphlet chiefly directed against the Belgian financier J. Langrand Dumonceau, the "Great Bank Juggler," and his creations. At the end of his vehement monologue, the writer adds a caution to the Dutch investors who speculated heavily and unwisely in American railroads, which he claimed were just as rotten as Langrand's financial castles in the air.[51]

Directed straight at the American railroad business was the series of brochures written by T. A. Huizenga, the stockbroker and financial journalist from Groningen, and published between 1873 and 1875. He was not opposed to investment in American rails as such, but he urged Dutch investors to be more careful in selecting their securities. American railroad promoters should never be taken at their word, but everything should be checked by impartial experts. He scolded the Dutch brokers for having shamelessly recommended the most risky and worthless securities, without any critical examination of the profitability of the railroad in question.[52] But at the time of his writing it was already too late and the crisis of 1873 had caused enormous losses to the Dutch.

Apart from the numerous articles in newspapers and journals warning against the dangers of reckless speculation in American rails, which need not be specified here, one 1886 booklet stands out because of its thorough and personal character. A. W. de Klerck, a former teacher at the gymnasium of Deventer, who traveled extensively in America (where he met a variety of people, including President Grant and the great financiers of the day), wrote a short but venomous study of the investing habits of the Dutch public.[53] Although the title of his brochure, *The Impoverishment of the Netherlands in Relation to the Import of American Railroad Shares*, is misleading because he does not really explain why the Netherlands were actually becoming poorer by investing in American rails, he seems to have a clear understanding of how the Dutch stock market was organized.

After making the rounds of European countries where the Dutch had traditionally invested, De Klerck concluded that not a single one of these countries really deserved any Dutch money: they were either autocratic, militaristic states such as Austria and Russia; or oppressed segments of their population, such as Great Britain did in Ireland; or were simply so unstable, as were Turkey or Portugal, that investing in them would be a waste of money. Only the United States remained as a democratic, nonmilitaristic country where investment could be fruitful, but dangers were lurking there as well: the newly rich and the monopolists were taking over the government with scant regard for democratic principles. Directors of railroads were without distinction called swindlers and frauds, out for the money of the innocent Dutchmen.

The Amsterdam stockbrokers had to bear the brunt of his poisonous attacks. Dr. Hubrecht, of Hubrecht, Van Harencarspel and Vas Visser, was accused of voting the Santa Fe shares held by his Administratie Kantoor against the interests of the certificate holders. F. W. Oewel, the former grocer turned stockbroker, who was dead by then, was accused of having given his brother-in-law Schaap a well-paid job as director of the Costilla Estate in Colorado at the expense of the Dutch owners. Teixeira de Mattos was said to have spread rumors about the bad situation of the Illinois Central, then sent H. J. de Marez Oyens as its representative to America to inspect the property and report negatively. When the price of shares had dropped enough after all this bad news, they quietly bought them for themselves at very low prices and sold soon after at much higher prices when the road's situation turned out to have been less unstable than originally thought.[54] Most of De Klerck's accusations seem to have been founded on half-truths, but some of his mud slinging must have been effective.

De Klerck's writings were not the last. With every investment in American railroads that went wrong for some unforeseen reason, there were writers who stood up to warn their countrymen against the sharp practices of American railroad directors, and of the Dutch bankers and brokers as well.

Five

The Capitalization of American Railroads

*B*efore embarking on the history of Dutch investment in the railroad network of the United States, it is necessary to provide some overall information about how American railroads were financed. The methods of railroad capitalization will only be described in general and as far as they affected the flow of Dutch capital across the Atlantic. Exhaustive studies have already been written, to which the reader is referred.[1]

In the young United States just one thing was plentiful: land and the natural resources provided by that land. Labor was scarce, hence the early introduction of all kinds of labor-saving machinery. Large-scale immigration from Europe and high birth rates eventually solved the labor problem, but shortages of both skilled and unskilled labor continued to plague the railroads throughout the best part of the nineteenth century.

▪ *Capital in America*

If labor was scarce, capital was even scarcer. First France, then the Dutch republic, and then Great Britain supplied the United States with most of the capital needed for the construction of its early infrastructure. This regular flow of money from Europe to America was temporarily halted now and then by recurring crises in America. The financial panic of 1837 was the first to curb the development of the newfangled steam railroads, almost drying up the source of capital for construction. Then in the 1840's the defaulting of many states on their internal improvement loans made foreign investors shy away from America for a period. The economic crisis of 1857 caused a slowdown once more. The Civil War meant an almost complete stop to foreign investment in the railroads of the United States, both North and South, but the building boom after peace returned swelled the flow of capital to unprecedented levels. The decade between 1865 and 1874 saw more than 38,000 miles of new railroad constructed, compared to only 20,000 miles in the preceding decade. The 1873 general economic crisis ended this building spree for a time, but in the early 1880's a new construction boom resulted in a renewed flow of European capital across the Atlantic on an even larger scale. Railroads became the largest single sector where European capital was invested, and without this massive infusion of money the development of the American railroad network would have been notably slower.

Later economic crises in America, especially the severe one of 1893, had the same effect of temporarily slowing down the influx of European capital, but eventually European investors always resumed buying bonds and shares of American railroads. After the turn of the century, other investments in America gradually became more attractive and put the railroads in second place. Large industrial firms such as United States Steel promised higher yields, while the emergent oil industry seemed even more promising, syphoning off a large amount of the European capital available for investment in America.

The very first railroads in America were financed largely by England, more often than not in the form of an exchange of railroad securities for iron rails, machinery, and locomotives. British-built engines operated on some of the first roads, but quickly the American industry—firms such as Norris and Baldwin—took over and supplied virtually all the needs of the domestic railroads. Iron, however, especially rails, continued to be purchased in large quantities in Britain well into the 1860's. Germany and Belgium also supplied some railway iron for American railroads, but on a much smaller scale. The Netherlands had no blast furnaces and rolling mills until well into the twentieth century, so exports of railway iron to America were practically nonexistent.

■ *Shares versus Bonds*

Most early American railroad companies started with the issue of capital stock, to be fully paid in several installments, to provide the actual capital to pay for construction of the line. Subscriptions were opened locally at first, but when the results of the canvassing of communities along the line were disappointing, the promoters of the road started looking elsewhere. In relatively prosperous and densely populated regions such as New England, local capital was generally sufficient for building most of the early roads. Even outside New England, the first construction costs of roads such as the Illinois Central could actually be defrayed by the first installments on the stock. The Pennsylvania Railroad was also planned to be built with capital raised by the issue of stock only.[2] Most companies, however, soon found out that, in addition to the capital stock, bonded loans were necessary as well.

The idea of raising construction capital through stock issues was quite common at the time all over the world. In England much of the railway building was financed that way, and on the Continent the picture was much the same. America in these early days was no exception to this general rule and in 1855 the capital stock of all American railroads was still 42 percent larger than their total bonded debt.[3] By 1914, at the very end of our period, the situation had changed dramatically. Of the total long-term capitalization of the American railroads, 70 percent was then in the form of bonded debt, and the rest in the form of capital stock.[4]

As long as railroad building was confined to the prosperous East, local capital was generally adequate, but as soon as the first roads were extended into the unpopulated West, other methods had to be found. Shrewd investors, both in America and Europe, saw all too well that such roads would take years before being able to earn a reasonable return on the invested capital; stocks, especially those of young companies of still unknown financial strength, were therefore generally considered to be too speculative. On the other hand, bonds carried interest obligations irrespective of earnings and might be more suitable to attract possible investors. Construction loans, more often than not secured by a mortgage on part of the property, became for the railroads a suitable means to procure the money needed, presumably without exposing the investors to unnecessary risks.

From the mid-1850's, but especially after the Civil War, most foreign capital was attracted to American railroads in the form of mortgage loans, although shares of many railroads continued to be held widely in Europe. Shares of newer companies were hardly ever fully paid up, and were often offered to subscribers of loans as a bonus, without any real current value but with a (more often than not remote) possibility for profits when the railroad in question proved to be a money maker. Numerous bond issues were floated, generally secured by some form of mortgage on the railroad or on parts of the land grant, if available. The healthier companies could easily raise enough capital through the sale of first mortgage bonds, which constituted the first and only lien on the property. These companies could also sell these bonds straight to the public without having to resort to bankers to underwrite the issue. The risk of having to sell at a lower price than intended was small in the case of these roads with a good financial reputation.

Railroads with less respectable financial histories, of which there were all too many, often resorted to financing through second, third, fourth, or even fifth mortgage loans, where the security of the bonds in question was down to almost nil, resulting in a price far below par. They could dispose of these unsecured bonds only through bankers, who, of course, exacted a stiff price for their services, resulting in an even lower actual yield for the company. Some roads resorted to the issue of consolidated mortgage loans, which often came after an already existing first lien on the property and made these consols generally less secure. Bankers could charge a fee of up to 2.5 percent for selling railroad bonds to the public in America and Europe. In instances where a bank or a combination of banks and brokers underwrote a new issue, thereby guaranteeing the railroad company that they would sell the bonds not below a certain price, their commission could climb to 10 percent or even more, depending on the anticipated risk in disposing of the bonds at the price agreed upon.[5]

All mortgages, whatever their names, were mostly dependent on the operation and the earning power of the railroad itself. When traffic was too low, or when competition forced the road to ruinously low rates, the best mortgage was worthless. Even a mortgage on a company's land grant was of little value until the road had been actually built. Western land without transportation available was next to worthless. All mortgage loans, whatever their actual yields, constituted a fixed debt of the company, which had to be serviced regularly and redeemed at the dates stipulated in the mortgage instruments. All too often the debt contracted in this way turned out to be too heavy at the slightest downturn of the economy. Then the assumption of investors that there was little risk often proved false. Crises such as the ones in 1873 and 1893 brought down many railroads which were staggering under a debt load they could hardly carry when times were good.

■ *Government Support for the Railroads*

Financial help by the federal or state governments for construction of railroads took any of several forms. Some states, such as Michigan, Pennsylvania, and Virginia, built their first railroads in the 1830's as state enterprises, financed and constructed by the state. Most of these state-owned roads were subsequently sold to private enterprise, more often than not at a great loss to the public.

Other state governments encouraged railroads within their borders by buying the capital stock of such roads that were considered vital for the local economy, and thus became part owners of the roads. Still other states lent money to a railroad against the security of state bonds, which were sold both at home and in Europe. Towns and counties often made land for depots and roadbed available through donation or sale on easy terms, and could also participate in the capital stock or even issue bonds of their own in support of the railroad. Provision of federal funds for internal improvement schemes was considered unconstitutional, but donation of land from the public domain was allowed and was first practiced in 1850 with the land grants to the Illinois Central and the Mobile & Ohio railroads. In later years federal land grants became quite common to western railroads, which operated, of course, where the public domain was the largest.[6] The Union Pacific–Central Pacific transcontinental line was the first to be supported through its early, difficult years not only by land grants but also directly by the issue of U.S. bonds. A few of the later transcontinental railroads, such as the Kansas Pacific, also claimed some federal support in the form of U.S. bonds issued to the railroad company.

■ *Other Forms of Bonded Debt*

A later development in the way the railroads tried to procure necessary capital was the issue of income bonds, which received interest only when the company earned an income, making them a kind of halfway house between mortgage bonds and stocks. The holders of these bonds did have a claim on the assets of the company, but participated in the revenues only when there actually were some. This type of bond became a popular means of scaling down the fixed-interest indebtedness of many railroads during the reorganizations of the 1870's and 1890's, but because of their unpredictable yield they were never popular with investors and could only be sold well under par.

Collateral trust bonds were first used as a means to circumvent the limitations in the charter of the Union Pacific. By its original charter, that company was not allowed to build any branches. When it proved necessary to provide the mainline with feeders, separate companies were set up to build them. These companies then issued bonds, which were taken up by the UP in return for construction capital, and the Union Pacific itself issued bonds of its own, with the branchline bonds as collateral, a kind of mortgage on stocks and bonds of other railroads. Later this practice became common-place during the era of the great mergers and the holding companies in the early years of the twentieth century. In 1903 an estimated one-tenth of all American railroad bonds was in the form of collateral bonds.[7]

During the early 1900's convertible bonds also became very popular as an extra incentive in attracting new capital. These bonds could be converted into common shares at the will of the owner during a certain stipulated period of time. The convert-ible bond itself was not a new invention and had already been used during the regime of Jay Gould on the infamous Erie Railroad in the 1860's, but it acquired a new popularity after 1900.

One last kind of loan should be mentioned, although it remained rather rare in American railroad finance. The debenture was common in England, where it was considered a kind of stock without voting power but with preference as to dividends. In the United States the debenture was a bond, in some cases with interest only payable when earned, but without any specific mortgage or foreclosure power, which ordinary bonds did have. It is no wonder that this rather unattractive form of loan remained a rare occurrence in America. It was generally resorted to only when the company was reorga-nized and its debt scaled down, and had mortgaged everything to the hilt.[8]

All this was long-term borrowing, for periods running from 25 to 100 years, on the part of railroad companies. When part of their debt was falling due, most companies generally resorted to refunding of the old debt with new bonds, if possible at a lower rate of interest. With the general rate of interest on railroad loans continuously falling from between 6 and 8 percent in the 1860's to between 3.5 and 5 percent in the early 1900's, most companies did indeed manage to reduce their fixed charges. Moreover, most roads were able to finance a lot of necessary extensions and improvements by using their own internal revenues. While in the 1880's an estimated 98 percent of all new financing still came from outside the railroad companies through the domestic and foreign sale of bonds and stocks, by 1910 this percentage had dropped to 60, with the rest being generated by the railroads themselves internally.[9]

Although of little importance for this study, mention must be made of several kinds of short-term borrowing. Whenever a company was in serious trouble, with a large floating debt, it often resorted to issuing notes, running for a couple of years only, and generally at a ruinous rate of interest. Equipment trusts were used when the railroad itself, the depots and shops, the land, and everything else had already been mortgaged as far as possible. Notes were issued to buy a specific number of cars or locomotives, which remained the property of the owners of the notes, and were let to the company for a sum large enough to pay the interest on the notes. Although some of these classes of se-curities were held in Holland from time to time, they never played a significant role in the Dutch investment in general.

■ American and European Sources of Capital

Not all capital needed for the construction of the American railroads came from Europe, of course. New England financed most of its own roads, and later invested heavily in railroads in other areas in America as well. Boston merchants and bankers, their fortune often built on the Asiatic trade, financed the construction of the Boston & Albany and other lines radiating from their hometown. In the 1840's they transferred their interests into the West, where the Michigan Central was taken over from the state by a group of Bostonians headed by John M. Forbes and James F. Joy.[10] Later this same group of Boston financiers moved even farther west into the Chicago, Burlington & Quincy and its predecessors such as the Hannibal & St. Joseph.

Another group of Boston capitalists, headed by David A. Neal, was behind the Illinois Central from the start, bringing much needed capital and introducing a conservative and cautious way of railway financing, which made the "Boston" railroads a favorite place for foreign investment. Still later both the Union Pacific and the Atchison, Topeka & Santa Fe attracted much capital from New England, and early leadership was provided by directors from the Northeast. Boston banks, such as Kidder, Peabody and Company and Lee, Higginson and Company, with their worldwide contacts played a significant role in American railroad finance.

Most of the China merchants of Boston already had contacts all over the world. In the 1830's and 1840's Forbes regularly did business with the Amsterdam firm of Daniel Crommelin and Sons, and other Boston firms had the same advantages. Later, when confronted with the enormous sums of money needed for the new railroads, it was only natural that they looked for additional capital to their European contacts. Forbes, in 1849, wrote prophetically, "The time will come within ten years when European capital will find its way to this country freely and all these things [American railroad securities] will be sought and I should not be surprised if it should be soon! Who that knew any thing would hold English, French or German funds when they can get Boston 6% stock at under par, and various sure 8% stocks—railway shares and bonds—at par and under?"[11]

And indeed, within a decade after these words were written, the Illinois Central, Michigan Central, and other "Boston" railroads were eagerly sought by English and Dutch investors. Forbes himself went to England, using his established business contacts there, and David Neal did the same thing in 1855 and managed to interest Amsterdam investors in both the Illinois Central and the Michigan Central, thus starting the long history of Dutch investment in American railroads. Neal's efforts are discussed in greater detail in Chapter 6.

An even earlier source of American railway capital was the merchants and bankers of Philadelphia, although the contacts existing between them and the Amsterdam commercial and financial circles seem to have been less developed than in the case of Boston. In the early 1830's, before the financial crisis of 1837, Philadelphia seems to have dominated the field of American railroad finance, and English investors were attracted from the start. Only in the 1840's did Boston grow into the most important market for railroad securities, until it in its turn was surpassed by the New York Exchange in the late 1850's, a position which Wall Street never relinquished, although both Philadelphia and Boston continued to play a secondary role.[12]

Figures on the foreign share in the capitalization of the American railroads vary widely, but most sources do agree that the railroads attracted a sizable amount of the total foreign investment, especially during the great building booms after 1865 and again after 1876, when the effects of the severe crisis of 1873 had worn off. In 1853 a U.S. Treasury report gave the following figures: of 244 American railroads, 3 percent of the stock and 26 percent of the bonded debt were held in foreign countries.[13] By 1873 the foreign-held portion of the total American railroad securities outstanding (at nominal value) still stood at only 20 percent, climbed to 33 percent in 1890, and declined to 30 percent in 1914.[14] All such estimates should, however, be used with the greatest caution; exact figures are impossible to come by and consequently estimates may vary widely.[15]

■ Influence of Bond- and Shareholders on Railroad Management

Shareholders, being owners of a company, had a vote in its management through the annual election of the board of directors. They were also liable for the full par value of their shares, paid up or not, in cases of bankruptcy, but as most shares were not even partially paid up, shareholders did not lose much in the case of a bankruptcy. Most reorganizations did indeed include provisions in favor of the bondholders, who had put up most of the capital for construction. Foreign shareholders, of course, had difficulty in exercising their rights. The system of collecting proxies by unscrupulous American directors was open to fraud and abuse. After the 1873 crisis the Dutch made sure that their interests in railroads with large-scale Dutch investment were represented either by Dutch members on the board—as in the case of the Chicago & North Western, the Milwaukee, the Missouri, Kansas & Texas, and others—or by a trusted American acting for them. In 1881 Anthony G. Dulman of New York was director and representative of the Dutch on roads such as the Rock Island, the Canada Southern, the New York, Pennsylvania & Ohio (the former Atlantic & Great Western), the Cleveland, Columbus, Cincinnati & Indianapolis, the Chicago & North Western, and the Missouri, Kansas & Texas, all railroads with a large amount of Dutch capital.

Bondholders, who had generally put up the money for the actual construction of a railroad, had no direct influence in the management of the road. And as long as the interest on the debt was paid regularly, they had no reason to complain. Whenever a company was unable to service its debts, it defaulted and some agreement with the bondholders was commonly sought first. When the default was deemed temporary, as a result of bad harvests or other nonfundamental causes, the directors often tried to bring the bondholders to agree to a postponing of the interest payments wholly or in part, or the funding of the unpaid coupons by the issue of new bonds (which, of course, only served to increase a debt that was probably already too large). If no agreement could be reached, or when the railroad was in such a bad shape financially that no hope for speedy recovery existed, the company was placed under the care of a receiver, who was to manage the property until some reorganization could be executed.

In such cases the bondholders usually organized themselves to be able to act in a body and thus make their financial influence felt and their interests as safe as circumstances would permit. These so-called protective committees are discussed in greater detail in Chapter 8.

The often-heard remark that foreign bond- and shareholders had no influence at all on the management of the railroads they owned is certainly not true. This does not mean that actual control was in the hands of these foreign owners; day-to-day operation was left in the hands of Americans. Dutch and also English financiers generally abstained from active participation in the running of their railroads in America, but they did protect themselves against the manipulations of American directors and made sure that their interests were well taken care of. There are numerous examples of railroad company boards wholly or partly appointed by foreign bondholders, and Dutchmen and Englishmen actually served on the boards of some companies.[16]

■ Railroad Receiverships

As outlined above, when a railroad could no longer carry out its financial obligations toward its bondholders, a receivership was necessary.[17] A receiver was appointed by federal or state court depending on whether the railroad crossed state lines. In theory a receiver was expected to guard the property in the interest of all parties, including the traveling public, against abuse by any of the parties involved until either a reorganization could be effected or a suit brought against the company by a party of creditors. A receiver was ideally a completely disinterested person, capable of running as highly complex an organization as a railroad for the benefit of all parties involved. Such a person was sometimes hard to find, and in practice one of the directors of the company was often appointed as receiver. In this way a person who was at least partly responsible for the failure of the railroad was also made responsible for its recovery. Abuses from this practice were many and varied, making bondholders' committees even more necessary.

A perfect example of how "friendly" receivers could be appointed is given by the Wabash, St. Louis & Pacific in 1884. When it became clear that the June 1884 coupon of its outstanding loan could not be paid, the notorious Jay Gould, director of the road, took steps to avoid the appointment of a receiver on behalf of the bondholders. He and his henchman Russell Sage personally held some notes of the railroad, which also fell due in June of that same year. They found a friendly judge willing to appoint the receiver of their choice. The bondholders were not even notified of this decision, and thus found their efforts to take action forestalled. The bondholders were by far the largest creditors, but found themselves excluded by a relatively small creditor. Technically this may have been legal, but ethically it was a most dubious trick.[18]

The position of receiver gradually developed from that of trustee of a mortgage after the latter were found to have not enough legal powers to protect well the bondholders for whom they were supposed to hold the mortgage in trust. Trustees continued to be appointed for every mortgage, however, and they often acted in concert with the receiver. In the early years private individuals generally acted as trustees, and names of certain railroad experts, such as Louis H. Meyer, are found again and again among the trustees of railroad mortgages where a large Dutch interest was at stake. Meyer was one of the directors of the Pittsburgh, Fort Wayne & Chicago, and he often acted for the Dutch interests. Toward the end of the nineteenth century big trust companies began to act as trustees for mortgages, and the individuals gradually disappeared. The trust companies could lend more force to the protection of the bondholders, although abuse in another form could be practiced now. More often than not these trust companies were in the same monopolistic hands as the banks and the railroads involved, making the individual bondholder more vulnerable than ever.

When a receiver was appointed to run a railroad, he was often in dire need of funds to be able to continue safe operation of the road. Urgent repair of bridges or track might be necessary, while new rolling stock could be immediately required. Payment of the wages of the road's workforce was another drain on the cash position. In such cases the receiver could be authorized by the court to issue receivers' certificates to raise the necessary money. Such certificates generally carried a higher rate of interest than the railroad's bonds, sometimes as high as 10 percent, and they were considered superior to all existing bonds, including the first lien bonds. For that reason bondholders often objected to the issue of receivers' certificates in large amounts, as this tended to diminish the value of their bonds when the road was sold.

When no amiable agreement with all creditors could be reached, the court could, on behalf of the creditors, order the railroad to be sold at foreclosure to the highest bidder. When only one class of bonds was outstanding, the road was sold to the bondholders who thus recovered their property. In this way quite a few American railroads ended up in the hands of Dutch bondholders' committees. (Again, these committees will be discussed in more detail in Chapter 8.)

In cases of reorganization of railroads, the stockholders generally bore the brunt of the cost. This was considered right, as these stockholders had not paid much—if anything at all—toward the actual cost of construction, while the bondholders had indeed invested their money in the road. Stockholders who wanted to retain their interest in the company were required to pay an assessment on their shares, while the senior bondholders generally exchanged their old bonds for new ones at par. Quite often the bonds of the old company were not disturbed at all and were continued until their stipulated date of redemption, with the interest paid by the newly incorporated successor road.

The junior bondholders, however, did not escape so easily. Their second mortgage bonds could be converted into stock or income bonds, without any obligation on the side of the company to pay interest or dividends until prosperity returned. Of course, this resulted from the policy to reduce materially the fixed charges of the new railroad, which could be done by reducing the rate of interest paid out, in conformity with the falling rate of interest on railroad loans toward the end of the nineteenth century. The principal of the debt could also be reduced by converting old bonds into new ones below par, sometimes as low as 50 percent. A third way of reducing the fixed charges was the replacement of the fixed-interest-bearing debt with charges contingent upon earnings, such as income bonds or preferred stock. Quite often a combination of all three measures was sought, to spread the burden over all classes of creditors. One thing was certain, however: when a reorganization failed to reduce the fixed charges of the railroad materially, the company was bound to be in trouble again at the very first downturn of the American economy.

Sometimes a railroad failed through fraudulent dealings of its directors or promoters. American railroads acquired a bad name in this respect in Europe. Chapter 10 will cover frauds and swindles in more detail.

Six

American Railroad Promoters in the Netherlands

Having seen the reluctance of Dutch bankers and stockbrokers to enter the American market after the many disappointments caused by defaulting American state governments, it will come as no surprise that in the 1850's the initiative to interest Dutch financiers in the potential of railroad investment lay chiefly with American railroad promoters. Moreover, the Dutch were preoccupied with Austrian and Russian finance at the time and as yet had little incentive to turn to the American market. So the Americans had to go and find them.

A very early instance of Americans sailing for Europe with the express purpose of seeking capital for railroad construction was the attempt of John Buchanan and Thomas L. Emory in 1837. They were commissioned to market Maryland state bonds issued in support of the Baltimore & Ohio Railroad in London, Paris, Antwerp, and Amsterdam, but they had no success in any of these places.[1] Two years later the Dutch house of Daniel Crommelin and Sons managed to market a small amount of Maryland State bonds issued in support of that other Baltimore railroad, the Baltimore & Susquehanna.[2]

■ David A. Neal: Illinois Central

After this early and unsuccessful marketing attempt, nothing much happened for a number of years, until in 1851 another American crossed the Atlantic and the North Sea in search of Dutch financial assistance for a railroad: David A. Neal, of Salem, Massachusetts. Neal was a merchant in India and the Dutch East Indies and one of the prosperous and energetic New England businessmen behind the fledgling Illinois Central Railroad, chartered in 1851. He had one more asset: through his trading in the Dutch colonies he had acquired Dutch contacts, which now became useful. Another promoter of the Illinois Central, Thomas W. Ludlow, had the same advantage: he was American agent of the old established Amsterdam mercantile and banking house of Daniel Crommelin and Sons.[3] To Neal and Ludlow Amsterdam must have seemed a most natural source of capital.

The capital stock of the Illinois Central was initially set at $1 million, and some $17 million in construction bonds (per 1875) was deemed necessary to finance the actual construction of the road. Robert J. Walker, Mississippi lawyer, financial expert, and former U.S. Secretary of the Treasury (and as such well known in European financial circles), was hired to sail for Europe to market the Illinois Central bonds there. Walker was a free-trader and well respected by English liberals such as Richard Cobden, who was to become a large stockholder of the Illinois Central.

Accompanied by David Neal, Walker sailed for Europe in 1851, but the two met with little success. Walker commenced his operations in London, but banks there hesitated because the state of Illinois still had a bad name since it had declared itself unable to pay any interest on its bonds between 1841 and 1846. In Paris Walker had no chance at all, due to the coup d'état by Louis Napoleon, later to become Emperor Napoleon III. In Amsterdam, which had been taken on by Neal, Hope and Company and Mr. Labouchère did not dare to decide without first referring to London.[4]

In the end only London proved willing to take up some of the construction bonds, which carried 7-percent interest. Early in 1852 $5 million worth of these was sold through Charles Devaux and Company and $4 million worth more was disposed of in America.[5] British ironmasters were also willing to accept the bonds at par as payment for the necessary 80,000 tons of English iron rail, not a bad start for a young undertaking. The few Dutch factories manufacturing railway iron on a modest scale were not in position to do the same.

A setback was the Schuyler scandal of 1854. Robert Schuyler, former president of the Illinois Central, was found to have fraudulently issued New Haven Railroad stock for his own benefit and had to flee the country in disgrace.[6] And although he had stepped down as president of the Illinois Central one year before and that company was not involved in the fraud, its securities depreciated considerably. The last portion of the 7-percent bonds could only be marketed at a large discount. It is not known how much the Schuyler fraud influenced the Dutch. Schuyler, of course, was a scion of an old Dutch-American family, and his name must have been known in Holland.

The immediate results of Neal's visit to Amsterdam may have been disappointing, but the seed had been sown and Dutch financial circles had become aware of the new opportunities offered. Illinois Central securities soon found a ready market in Amsterdam, although it is not clear through whom they were offered. The first quotations of IC 7-percent construction bonds have been found in early 1856.[7] Shares of the company were first mentioned in the Dutch financial press one year later, when they were already quoted at 137–38 percent of par. Over the next months a brisk trade developed, and when the bonded debt of the company was enlarged from $17 million to $25.5 million in 1857, two Amsterdam stockbrokers announced that they were taking care of the preferential rights of Dutch shareholders. The two Dutch houses involved were Alstorphius and Van Hemert and Gebr. Teixeira de Mattos, and it is probable that they had handled the earlier sales in Amsterdam as well. Because shares were freely transferable by simple endorsement, the stockholders' lists of the company were generally not quite up to date. This was a problem because the dividends were only payable to shareholders listed in the company's books. To deal with this situation Gebr. Teixeira de Mattos opened an Administratie Kantoor for these shares in 1863, issuing certificates in return. These certificates were for $100, $500, or $1,000, and they were officially included in the price lists in Amsterdam along with the original shares, which continued to be traded as well.[8]

When the Illinois Central encountered difficulties in 1857, its president William H. Osborn sailed for Europe to quiet the unrest of the English and Dutch investors. In July of that year he arrived in Amsterdam from London and managed to establish an excellent understanding with the Dutch houses involved.[9] The company soon became one of the pet investments of both English and Dutch, and by 1877 it was reported by William Osborn that nine-tenths of all its common stock was held by 1,650 shareholders in England and Holland. Other contemporary sources credit England with 54 percent of the stock and Holland with 26 percent. Not surprisingly the Dutch had a representative on the Illinois Central board in the person of Anthony G. Dulman, a New York Dutch-American banker.[10]

With this early large Dutch interest in the Illinois Central, it is not surprising that the railroad soon drew the attention of Dutch travelers in America. W. T. Gevers Deynoot, a member of the Second Chamber of Parliament, was one of the first to write about his experiences in the New World, and while he was generally critical of America and the Americans, he gave much praise to the Illinois Central. He was impressed by the wealth of the company, in his opinion chiefly the result of the extensive land grant, and he was sure that its bonds would be a safe investment. With wise and honest management, the future of the railroad seemed assured. Gevers Deynoot's favorable impression was enhanced by his knowledge of the activities of Abraham Lincoln as lawyer for the IC. When Gevers's book was published, Lincoln had already been elected president of the United States.[11]

After these endorsements Illinois Central securities always found a ready market in Amsterdam, of which particulars will be found in Appendix B. One early bond issue of a later subsidiary of the IC, the New Orleans, Jackson & Great Northern, should be mentioned here, however. The first mortgage bond issue of this company, part of the IC connection to the South, is a perfect example of the indirect way in which many securities came to Amsterdam. The London house of J. Henry Schroeder and Company had marketed $2 million worth of these 8-percent bonds in 1857 and had apparently placed part of this issue in Amsterdam through its partner in the Dutch capital, B. H. Schroeder and Company. The latter firm advertised twice in the Dutch press that coupons of this loan were payable in London.[12] They were never listed in Amsterdam.

■ David A. Neal: Michigan Central

When David Neal was in Amsterdam in 1851, he acted not only on behalf of the Illinois Central. He was also interested in another young railroad, the Michigan Central, and tried to peddle the stock of that company as well. This railroad, later part of the Vanderbilt empire, had been incorporated in 1846 as successor to the state-owned Central Railroad of Michigan. A Boston consortium, headed by John Murray Forbes and Thomas H. Perkins, bought the line in 1847 and finished its Chicago–Detroit main line. In the latter city it connected, by ferries to Windsor, with the broad-gauge Great

Western of Canada. A third rail was soon laid, and standard-gauge through trains could then run from Windsor to New York by way of the suspension bridge over Niagara Falls. This route soon became popular with Dutch emigrants on their way to Michigan. But despite Neal's useful contacts, and just as with the Illinois Central, the Dutch bankers could not yet be persuaded to take the plunge, and it took several years more before American railroad securities were regularly marketed in Amsterdam. Did the Michigan Central's new Rogers locomotive, delivered in 1855, get the name "Foreigner" to attract more capital from Europe, or was it actually paid for with foreign money?[13]

Just as with the Illinois Central, however, Dutch investors soon started to buy the Michigan Central's securities. On 27 October 1857 the anonymous Dutch agents of the company announced in the *Amsterdamsch Effectenblad* the issue of $2 million in 8-percent first mortgage convertible 25-year bonds. Shortly after, on 9 February 1858, Hope and Company made known that they had invested $94,000 in these bonds as replacement for other securities, which they held as collateral on their investment fund, the Gemeenschappelijk Bezit van Amerikaansche Effecten, Series B. At the same time they invested $107,000 in Michigan Central common shares (of which more later) and $24,000 in 7-percent Central Railroad of New Jersey bonds, plus other nonrailroad stock.[14] What happened to the MC bonds is not clear; they were never listed in Amsterdam, but some must have been held there because later announcements about their redemption or exchange were regularly made in the Dutch press.

With the Michigan Central common shares we are on firmer ground. After Hope and Company acquired the first block in 1857, Wertheim and Gompertz and partners issued certificates for one, five, or ten shares (of $100 each) in 1869. These shares were attractive enough, as dividends of 10 percent had been paid from 1869 to 1872; the 1873 dividend, however, was paid mostly in scrip because of the crisis of that year.[15] The news of the takeover by the Vanderbilt interests in 1877 was favorably received in Holland, as it was thought that the Michigan Central as part of the large New York Central system would be able to pay regular dividends more easily than before.[16] The Vanderbilts continued buying up the MC stock, and by 1898 most ($16,814,300 out of a total of $18,738,000) shares were in their hands. In that year an offer was made to the few remaining outside shareholders of $115 in 3.5-percent New York Central bonds for every $100 worth of MC commons. The railroad had been paying dividends of 4 percent in the years before this offer, and some stubborn Dutchmen must have had their doubts about the benefit of such an exchange, for in 1919 some of the MC certificates—by then 50 years old—were still in Dutch hands. In 1922 a new offer was made to buy up the remaining commons at 345 percent, at least 10 points higher than the current market price, but even as late as 1933 a single certificate of 1869 was still outstanding. The MC shares were only dropped from the Amsterdam price lists in 1937![17]

■ *Edward Miller and J. Edgar Thomson: Pennsylvania Railroad*

One year after David Neal another American railroad man came to Amsterdam to solicit funds for his company, the Pennsylvania Railroad. Edward Miller, chief engineer of that line, was sent to London, Paris, and Amsterdam in 1852 to find the capital necessary for further construction. He seems to have had little success in London and none at all in Amsterdam. It is not known to which bankers or brokers he turned when in Holland, but the results of his visit were completely negative. The Dutch market was not yet ready to buy American railroad securities, although large amounts of Pennsylvania State improvement bonds were held in Holland. One year later J. Edgar Thomson, the Pennsylvania's president (whose father, John Thomson, had been employed as a surveyor by the Holland Land Company back in 1795), went over to Europe himself, but with no better results. It has not been recorded if he went to Amsterdam at all.[18]

■ *Charles Moran: Erie Railway*

Another unsuccessful bid for Amsterdam capital was made by Charles Moran in 1856 for the Erie Railway, which was by then already floundering in a morass of debts. Moran, a Belgian by birth and chief partner of Moran Brothers Bankers (earlier Moran and Iselin) of New York, went over to Europe to raise a loan there. It is not certain if he turned up in person in Amsterdam, but he must have made use of the existing close contacts between Antwerp and the Dutch capital. It is not known if he did raise any money in Amsterdam, but as a reward for finding some capital in London he was made president of the Erie at the outrageously high annual salary of $25,000.[19] Two years later he crossed the Atlantic again and managed to float a *fifth* mortgage loan, unsecured by anything of real value, in Europe.[20] Again, Dutch investors were conspicuously absent. In 1859 the Erie went bankrupt, and it took years to reorganize the road. Only in 1868 were the reorganized line's first securities sold in Amsterdam.

■ *James McHenry: Atlantic & Great Western*

In the late 1850's another colorful character showed up in Amsterdam to raise money for his railroad: James McHenry, an American of Irish descent, who had gone to England to set up as a grain merchant and who then became European agent of the young Atlantic & Great Western Railway. Later he was described as "contractor, foster father and finally . . . near [to] being the funeral undertaker of the Atlantic & Great Western." As European agent of this largely British-financed road, he is reported to have persuaded Henri Gompertz of Amsterdam to take up some bonds of the New York and Pennsylvania sections of the A&GW in 1856, but other investors failed to follow suit. McHenry was a master of advertising. He brought in personalities such as the Spanish Marquis of Salamanca, noted as a railway entrepreneur in Europe, and Sir Morton Peto, the great British contractor who was then building the Grand Trunk Railroad of Canada. In 1864 Peto organized a tour of the A&GW for prospective investors; no Dutchmen participated, but James Staats Forbes, director of the London, Chatham & Dover and the Dutch Rhenish railways, was a member of the party. Only in 1864 were the first A&GW securities traded in Amsterdam, again by way of Antwerp, where G. H. Levita handled a 7-percent loan of the Ohio section, later taken over and monopolized by F. W. Oewel of Amsterdam.[21] These "Ohio sevens" were to become notorious in the international financial world as the "Oewel certificates," and are discussed in greater detail in Chapter 7.

■ *Jay Cooke: Northern Pacific Railroad and Pennsylvania Railroad*

Jay Cooke, the Philadelphia financier who had successfully set up a complex European network for marketing Union bonds during the Civil War, had remarkably little luck in selling railroad bonds in Holland. He had his agents there, but apparently they were not in the right position to approach the Amsterdam money market adequately. Early in 1870 he undertook to sell $30 million worth of 7.3-percent Northern Pacific bonds, but his Amsterdam office managed to market at best only a few, and probably none at all. His timing was said to have been completely wrong, for at the time the Dutch market was saturated with St. Paul & Pacific bonds. A disgusted Cooke wrote, "Europe is now flooded with bonds offered by every little Dutch house with whom we should have to compete, unless backed by a great house whose recommendation would give them preference."[22]

In 1870 another syndicate set up by Jay Cooke—the first modern underwriting syndicate—to sell Pennsylvania railroad bonds in Europe, had no success on the Dutch market either.[23] Only much later did Dutch brokers begin to handle the Pennsylvania securities.

Not all American railroad tycoons who came to Holland for capital returned empty handed; Neal, Miller, and Thomson just happened to be too early in the field, when the Dutch were not yet ready to enter the American market on any scale. After the end of the Civil War the trickle of railroad paper offered in Amsterdam grew into a veritable torrent, and Dutch investors became willing participants in the "American railroad craze" and more receptive to the lures of American rails.

■ *William J. Palmer: Denver & Rio Grande*

One of the first to profit by this change of attitude was General William Jackson Palmer, the man behind the Denver & Rio Grande railroad. This famous road has always played a conspicuous role in American railroad history; its narrow gauge, its mountainous terrain, and its colorful past have made it appear almost larger than life in American railroad lore.

The railroad was the brainchild of Palmer, a Civil War hero and, like so many of his fellow officers, active in the railroad business after the war. He had been in charge of the construction crews of the Kansas Pacific, building westward through Kansas, and had become a director of that company. Even before the KP reached Denver in 1870, Palmer was already working on schemes for connecting lines south and west.

In October 1870 he chartered the Denver & Rio Grande Railway Company to build a network with Denver as its nucleus. One line was to run south to Colorado Springs and Pueblo, then west to Alamosa, and from there south following the Rio Grande to Santa Fe, New Mexico, and El Paso, Texas, where a Mexican connection was projected. Another line was to run west from Denver across the Rockies to Salt Lake City by way of Grand Junction, with a couple of branches penetrating the booming mining districts of Colorado.[24]

Because of the mountainous terrain, the narrow gauge of three feet was chosen. The slim gauge was just coming into vogue, inspired by the Festiniog Railway in Wales, which operated successfully with steam locomotives on an even narrower gauge of two feet. Colorado Springs, soon to develop into the fashionable resort jokingly called "Little London" because of its popularity with wealthy Britons, was reached from Denver in 1871. One of Palmer's close friends, William Bell, an English medical doctor who had accompanied him on his explorations into the mountains and who had come under the spell of the Colorado wilderness, became the Rio Grande's best advocate in Europe. He promoted Colorado Springs and praised it as a retreat for his tired, affluent countrymen.[25] Pueblo, 115 miles from Denver, was reached in the next year. A change of plans had been made by then, and it was proposed to build from Pueblo south instead of southwest, across Raton Pass, the only mountain pass suitable for railroad traffic, straight into New Mexico Territory. But the Rio Grande construction crews came too late and found the pass securely in the hands of the engineers of the Atchison, Topeka & Santa Fe and thus saw the path to El Paso blocked. Palmer had to content himself with building west into the mountains of Colorado.

Not unexpectedly, money for the construction of these lines was initially sought in England. As has been noted, English interest in Colorado ran high at the time, and William Bell never tired of promoting the wonders of Colorado in books, articles, and speeches. He became the link between his friend Palmer and the European capitalists who might be interested. Later, he had to confess that his career as a stockbroker had been unfortunate, and he was indeed quite unsuccessful in marketing the Denver & Rio Grande's bonds in London. Money there was tight, and, because of the Franco-Prussian War, France and Germany were for the time not interested in foreign investment at all.[26]

Because money from London was forthcoming only in a trickle, it was Amsterdam that supplied most of the initial construction funds. Palmer had become a great admirer of the Dutch and their heroic revolt against Spain in the sixteenth century through his readings of John Lothrop Motley's account of the birth of the Dutch Republic. The idea of enlisting Dutch financial help for his railroad must have appealed to him.[27] Through Bell's friend William Blackmore, the English financier, the Amsterdam house of Wertheim and Gompertz was contacted late in 1870. Palmer's original idea had been to incorporate several companies, each to build a part of the proposed network, but F. W. Oewel, partner of Wertheim and Gompertz, insisted that only a single company be incorporated and that the line must pass through the Costilla Estate, which was being financed jointly by Wertheim and Gompertz and Oewel. A meeting in Amsterdam in January 1871 of all parties concerned—Blackmore, Palmer, James C. Parrish (American friend and partner of Blackmore), Oewel, and A. C. Wertheim—brought about an agreement. The Dutch bankers took up $480,000 worth of 7-percent bonds, with an option on the same amount again after three months. The price to be paid by Wertheim was 64.50 percent of par for the first portion, and 66 percent of par for the optional sum;

both prices were on the low side and indicative of the risks expected to be incurred in financing such an undertaking. Wertheim also stipulated that Louis H. Meyer of New York, director of the Pittsburgh, Fort Wayne & Chicago Railroad who often acted for Dutch interests, be added as a trustee of the mortgage.

Thus the Rio Grande's first mortgage gold loan of 1870 was introduced in Amsterdam by Van Vloten and De Gijselaar, who acted for Wertheim and Gompertz. First price for the public was set at 70 percent of par, and the bankers and brokers made a nice profit on the deal. Oewel himself got the usual 1 percent commission plus 7 percent in stock of the railroad.[28] Interest was payable in New York and London, and in guilders in Amsterdam as well, indicating that Dutch interest was expected to be high. And apparently with good reason, as Wertheim and Gompertz offered another $750,000 of the same loan nine months later.[29] This meant that almost all of this first loan was sold in Holland. The sale of bonds of $2,225,000 par value had netted the company $633,062.65 from Wertheim and Gompertz, $456,000 from American subscribers, and only $147,000 from England, altogether only 58.65 percent of par.[30]

Contemporaries were amazed at the ease with which the Rio Grande's bonds were taken up in Amsterdam. Writing about the Santo Domingo Land Company, which need not concern us here, a certain Edward M. McCook notified the well-known railroad financier and lawyer Samuel Barlow in 1871 of the favorable prospects of floating his company's bonds in Europe: "Certainly when the bonds of a road like the D. & Rio Grande, with nothing earthly for a basis except the right of way, are eagerly sought after, the bonds of a corporation with millions of acres of good land as a foundation, should find no obstacle in the way of their speedy negotiation."[31]

A number of land and townsite companies were already operating in Colorado and New Mexico, and one of these, the Costilla Estate, had attracted large amounts of Dutch money. This Costilla Estate formed part of the million-acre Sangre de Cristo Grant in southern Colorado and northern New Mexico. The northern part had been taken over by the English Trinchera Estate company, while the southern half was set up as a separate company, the Costilla Estate. The promoter of this land company was the same William Blackmore, lawyer and capitalist, who was behind the Rio Grande as well. This Dutch-owned land company will be covered in more detail in Chapter 7.

Another famous land company, the Maxwell Land Grant and Railway Company, was taken over by Dutch capitalists from the English incorporators in these same years. Already in 1870 a Maxwell Land Grant & Railway loan of £700,000 (Dfl 8,400,000), with coupons payable in sterling or guilders, had been floated in Amsterdam by Holjé and Boissevain and in Rotterdam by A. J. and M. Milders. Two years later Lion Hertz sold another Dfl 3.3 million of Maxwell bonds when Dutch interest in Colorado and New Mexico was at its peak. Palmer had been deeply involved in the Maxwell Company as well, and it was hoped that his Rio Grande Railway would help materially in developing the estate.[32] When the Rio Grande lost the struggle for Raton Pass, Palmer's interest waned and he soon sold out to the Dutch. The Maxwell Company never became a pot of gold for them, but was later converted into an investment company, its shares still listed in Amsterdam and doing well.

For a time interest on the Rio Grande bonds was paid regularly, and the little road even weathered the crisis of 1873, although new construction came to a halt. Wertheim and Gompertz were unwilling to sink more money in the scheme because of the generally unsettled state of the money market, and they were disappointed that Palmer had not yet built through their Costilla Estate as promised. Later other Rio Grande securities were successfully marketed in Amsterdam, but this would be after Palmer's ouster as director of the road.

A trip to Paris undertaken by Palmer in 1875 to promote Colorado and to raise new capital proved to be fruitless. An office was opened and a French prospectus printed, and Parrish was active in briefing the French press, but all to little avail.[33] The French were too busy paying off their war indemnity to Germany and were more interested in Russian government and railroad bonds. Palmer got into trouble over interest payments in 1877. Earnings from traffic were not enough to cover the fixed charges, although the Rio Grande's rates were higher than anywhere else in America. While on most eastern and midwestern roads 2–3 cents per mile was the usual passenger fare, the "Narrow Gouge," as it was called by its critics, charged no less than 10 cents a mile. Complaints over the high rates were many, and ten years later the adventurous anthropologist Herman ten Kate still mentioned the outrageously high 8 cents per mile charged for traveling in its diminutive cars between Antonito and Silverton. The scenery, however, he found superb, better than along the Schwarzwaldbahn in the south of Germany and comparable to the mountains traversed by the Austrian Brenner railway.[34]

■ *Levi Parsons: Missouri, Kansas & Texas*

Judge Levi Parsons, president of the Missouri, Kansas & Texas Railroad, the erstwhile Union Pacific Southern Branch, was in Europe for most of the year 1873, commuting between London, Paris, and Amsterdam. The Dutch had invested heavily in his road, and it is therefore small wonder that he visited Amsterdam when he was in need of more capital. He also had to explain away some little difficulty over the mortgage of one of the MKT loans listed in Amsterdam.[35] His visits were in vain, however, and the economic crisis of 1873 proved to be too much for the tottering company; the "Katy" was one of the first of the bigger railroads to collapse.

■ *General Warner and William Mahone: Excuses*

Not all American railroad directors came to solicit new monies; some found it wise to appear in person to explain to the Amsterdam bankers why their rosy visions of great profits for investors had come to naught. Nasty questions were asked about how the money Dutch and other Europeans had pumped into American railroads had been spent or misspent, and the feelings of the investing public had somehow to be placated to induce them to advance more capital. In April 1874 General Warner, president of the Marietta & Pittsburg and the St. Louis & Southeastern, came to Amsterdam for this purpose. He was particularly unlucky, as both his railroads had defaulted after the 1873 crisis, and he would have needed great rhetorical talent to persuade a hard-headed businessman such as Abraham Wertheim to put up more Dutch money. His plan for the Marietta & Pittsburg, to raise capital through a second mortgage loan, was refused by the Dutch, who then joined forces with their British counterparts.[36]

Warner's proposal for the refunding of the floating debt of the St. Louis & Southeastern met with no more success, although the Germans in this case tended to go along with him, but Wertheim refused and managed to obtain better results through a separate sale of the several divisions of the road to interested American parties.[37]

Another who found out, to his own disadvantage, that he had better not ignore the concerns of Amsterdam investors was William Mahone, president of the Atlantic, Mississippi & Ohio, forerunner of the Norfolk & Western. Mahone, nicknamed the "Railroad Bismarck" for his arbitrary ways of governing his road, did not think it worthwhile to explain his problems to the Dutch, although they held more than $2 million worth of the AM&O's securities. In October 1875 he was in London trying to settle his problems with the English but did not take the trouble to come over to Amsterdam in person, an omission strongly resented there.[38] After his failure to smooth the ruffled feathers of the Dutch, his credit with them sank to a low ebb, which materially contributed to his downfall in 1881.

▪ *Arthur E. Stilwell: Kansas City, Pittsburg & Gulf*

Not only in the 1870's did American railroad directors sail for Holland to seek capital for their companies. Early in 1894 Arthur E. Stilwell, a real estate tycoon from Kansas City, came to the Netherlands to find the money needed for his projected Kansas City, Pittsburg & Gulf Railroad.[39] Stilwell's case is exceptional: he hated the established American banks and brokers, the "Cannibals of Wall Street" as he used to call them, and tried to circumvent them whenever possible. He was in a position to do without Wall Street because he had made some most useful acquaintances on an earlier pleasure trip to Holland. One of these was Jan de Goeijen, Jr., a rich coffee broker of Amsterdam, who had become a close friend. Moreover, Stilwell had a Dutch partner in his Kansas City real estate business, Jacques (Johannes Jacobus) Tutein Nolthenius. Tutein's relatives operated a stockbroking firm in Amsterdam, Tutein Nolthenius and De Haan, specializing in American railroad securities, so Stilwell was able to go straight to the source of Dutch capital without having to navigate the existing contacts between American and Dutch stockbrokers. Altogether, in just a few years, Stilwell and his Dutch associates managed to sell stocks and bonds worth some $26 million (par value) in his several companies to the Dutch public, making this the largest single target of Dutch investment, with the possible exception of the Chicago & North Western. The Kansas City, Pittsburg & Gulf is discussed in more detail in Chapter 14.

▪ *Dorset Carter: Oklahoma Central*

An American promoter who imitated Stilwell ten years later, although on a very small scale, was Dorset Carter from the town of Purcell in what was then still the Indian

Territory. Carter came to Holland for capital for his Oklahoma Central Railway, a 132-mile short line in rural Oklahoma. He went, not to Amsterdam as was usual, but straight to The Hague to contact S. F. van Oss, the broker-journalist who had just set up in business there for himself. It is most likely that Carter and Van Oss had met earlier, because the Dutchman had visited the Indian Territory a short time before. Carter was successful in obtaining almost a million dollars through Van Oss to build his road. The venture ended in disaster for the Dutch investors, however, and Van Oss soon regretted his involvement.[40]

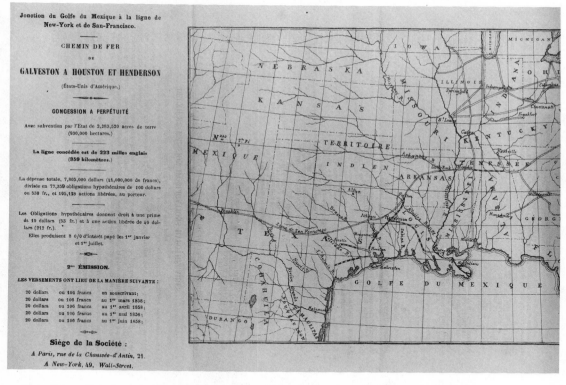

Part of the original prospectus for the 8-percent loan of 1857 for the Galveston, Houston &
Henderson, the third American railroad to be offered on the Amsterdam Stock Exchange (after
the Illinois Central and the Michigan Central); $1 million of this loan was sold in Amsterdam.
(Veenendaal)

Construction to extend the St. Paul, Minneapolis & Manitoba across the prairies of North Dakota in the 1880's. Some of the capital for this road, later part of the Great Northern, came from Amsterdam. (James J. Hill Papers, James J. Hill Reference Library, St. Paul)

Facing page:

Top: An 1873 view of the first Minneapolis railroad station of the St. Paul & Pacific; the railroad was financed from Amsterdam and already in receivership by this date. One of the engines shown may be the StP&P no. 16, "Kerkhoven," named after the Amsterdam brokers who invested millions in this predecessor of the Great Northern. (Great Northern Railway photo, Don L. Hofsommer Collection)

Bottom: A group of officials of the St. Paul & Pacific at Breckenridge, Minnesota, in October 1871. The man in the light suit and white hat in the middle is Leon Willmar, the representative of Dutch bondholders. (Great Northern Railway photo, Don L. Hofsommer Collection)

Top: Chicago, Rock Island & Pacific engine no. 109, "America." Built by the Grant Locomotive Works of Paterson, New Jersey, it was exhibited at the 1867 World Exposition in Paris and was used to open the Rock Island's line to Leavenworth, Kansas, in September 1870. Because the Dutch-financed bridge over the Missouri at Leavenworth was not finished by that time, the official train got no farther than Stillings Junction. (State Historical Society of Iowa)

Bottom: A Rock Island train in the station at Horton, Kansas, north of Topeka, in 1914. By that year the once-solid CRI&P was on the verge of bankruptcy. (DeGolyer Library, Southern Methodist University, Dallas)

Top: The Michigan Central's engine no. 74, "Quickstep," in Chicago in the 1870's. The MC, part of the New York Central system after 1877, was, in 1857, the second American railroad company to enter the Dutch market. (Smithsonian Institution)

Bottom: In a photo dating from 1905–9 the famous Lake Shore & Michigan Southern "Twentieth Century Limited" speeds through LaPorte, Indiana, behind a Prairie 2-6-2 engine, no. 4685. The LS&MS was also part of the New York Central system. (LaPorte County, Indiana, Historical Society)

The Boston, Hartford & Erie engine no. 10, "Onward," on a siding in the 1870's. Although the BH&E was bankrupt by 1870, common shares were sold in Amsterdam in 1872, one of the first instances of fraud on record. (Collection of Dr. S. R. Wood, DeGolyer Library, Southern Methodist University, Dallas)

Engine no. 6 of the Milwaukee & St. Paul, forerunner of the Chicago, Milwaukee & St. Paul, leaves an unidentified station in 1910. The road was first traded on the Amsterdam Stock Exchange in 1872 and had a Dutch director on its board from 1872 to 1876. (Library of Congress)

Top: The Eau Claire, Wisconsin, roundhouse of the West Wisconsin Railway in 1871. Dutch investment in the West Wisconsin began in 1868. Later the road was held by the Chicago & North Western, which probably received more Dutch capital than any other American railroad. (Collection of Dr. S. R. Wood, DeGolyer Library, Southern Methodist University, Dallas)

Bottom: Two ten-wheelers, dating from the turn of the century, haul freight on the Chicago & North Western line between Rapid City and Pierre, South Dakota, in 1933. The line was opened in the early years of the twentieth century, when Dutch interest in the C&NW was still strong. (Otto Perry photograph, Denver Public Library)

Top: A Missouri, Kansas & Texas train in Parsons, Kansas, in 1880. The town was named for Judge Levi Parsons, director of the MKT, who was well known in Amsterdam. (Collection of Dr. S. R. Wood, DeGolyer Library, Southern Methodist University, Dallas)

Bottom: The Pensacola, Florida, depot of the Louisville & Nashville in 1908. Among southern railroads the L&N probably made the greatest use of Dutch capital. (DeGolyer Library, Southern Methodist University, Dallas)

A freight train of the Atlantic & Pacific crossing Canyon Diablo, Arizona, in the 1880's. The Dutch had a large stake in the loan for the Western Division of the A&P; this part of the line was later sold to the Atchison, Topeka & Sante Fe. (William H. Jackson photograph, Colorado Historial Society)

A double-headed "California Limited" of the Atchison, Topeka & Santa Fe on the former Atlantic & Pacific lines in the Mojave desert in the 1890's. The AT&SF has been traded on the Amsterdam Stock Exchange from 1872 to the present day. (William H. Jackson photograph, Colorado Historical Society)

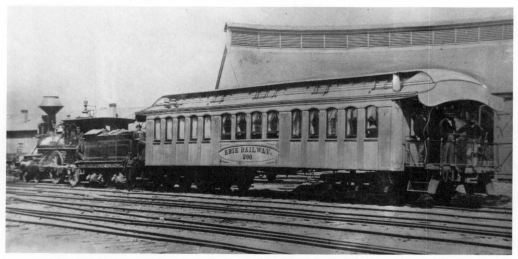

Top: The St. Louis & San Francisco ten-wheeler no. 411 south of Cordell, Oklahoma, in 1904. The Dutch were early investors in the StL&SF and many of its predecessors, and investment remained high during the many reorganizations and receiverships. (Collection of Dr. S. R. Wood, DeGolyer Library, Southern Methodist University, Dallas)

Bottom: Jay Gould's Erie Railway presidential car, ca. 1867–72; Gould is one of the men on the car's platform. Although the Erie's shares were traded in Amsterdam from 1868, it never attracted much Dutch investment. (Smithsonian Institution)

Seven

Dutch Brokers and Bankers in America

As discussed in the previous chapter, American railroad promoters first had to go to Holland in search of capital, and after some years a regular flow of money across the Atlantic ensued. Dutch brokers, now alerted to the new possibilities, then crossed the Atlantic in the other direction in search of opportunities for investment. Of course, quite a few American railroad securities, especially in the early years, also came to Amsterdam by way of foreign, mostly English and German, bourses, but when the market clamored for more American "rails," Amsterdam brokers went out themselves in search of more of this attractive paper.

For a few years in the 1830's Dutch bankers had already been active in this field, but with little or no lasting results. The little Tonawanda Railroad in upstate New York must be given the honor of being the first American railroad to receive Dutch money in its early years, although it was never listed in Amsterdam. This road, incorporated in 1832, ran from Rochester to Attica by way of Batavia, altogether some 43 miles, and was modestly capitalized at $500,000.[1] It is not surprising that Dutchmen would be interested in the little line. Batavia had been the headquarters of the Holland Land Company since its inception. The railroad reached the town from Rochester in 1837. In that same year Dfl 1 million ($400,000) in bonds of the road was offered in Amsterdam by W. Willink. Despite the "Dutch" background of the road, interest in Holland was small, and little money was forthcoming.[2] To tide the road over the difficult time, the state of New York advanced $100,000 in 1840 to finish the line to Attica, which was reached two years later. Its corporate existence ended in 1850 when it was merged into the Buffalo & Rochester.[3] The only Dutch name on the board was that of Abraham M. Schermerhorn, of the well-known New Amsterdam family, but it is not known if he was in any way connected with the Holland Land Company.[4] The Tonawanda was one of the more successful of the early lines. In 1844 it started paying regular dividends and consequently had no trouble selling its stock, but little or none of it turned up in Amsterdam.[5] In its turn the Buffalo & Rochester was consolidated with many other smaller lines into the New York Central Railroad Company in 1853.

Another pioneer railroad that had been looking to Holland for construction capital was the Baltimore & Susquehanna. This early road was chartered in 1828 and completed to the Maryland-Pennsylvania border ten years later. The state of Maryland issued improvement bonds to help finance the line, just as the city of Baltimore did on a smaller scale. The Maryland State bonds were widely held in Europe, especially in England but also in Holland, and in this roundabout way Dutch investors helped finance this early road.[6] In 1854 the Baltimore & Susquehanna was merged with others into the Northern Central Railroad, which in turn ended up in the Pennsylvania system in 1863.[7]

▪ F. W. Oewel

The Dutchman who was probably most active in America in the 1870's was F. W. Oewel of Amsterdam. Little or nothing is known about the man himself, apart from the fact that he started his career as a grocer and entered the stockbroking fraternity only later. In 1868 he joined forces with A. C. Wertheim and others in the Administratie Kantoor van Amerikaansche Spoorwegwaarden Wertheim and Gompertz, Westendorp and Company and F. W. Oewel, with the express purpose of marketing American railroad bonds and shares in Holland.[8] But although a partner in this successful venture, he continued to import under his own name bonds of American railroads such as the Traverse City in Michigan and the Elizabethtown & Paducah in Kentucky in 1871.[9] One year earlier he appears to have underwritten a part of a loan of the North Missouri, which operated between Kansas City and St. Louis. Oewel had these bonds marketed by Elix and Broekman in Amsterdam with much success. The North Missouri was one of the few American roads on the Amsterdam Exchange that was really in operation, and its bonds soon rose appreciably in price. In the partnership with Wertheim and Westendorp, Oewel was clearly the traveling partner, with A. C. Wertheim managing the affairs in Amsterdam.

Oewel became deeply involved in the affairs of the Atlantic & Great Western, although he appears not to have imported bonds of this company himself. Several kinds of A&GW securities, including debentures, had been introduced on the Amsterdam Exchange in 1864 and 1865. This paper, guaranteed by the Consolidated Bank of London, was generally considered safe as houses.[10] In England the A&GW was seen as a first-class road, "one of the best, if not the very best railway in the U.S."[11]

A meeting in 1865 of parties interested in the A&GW in London, where Sir Morton Peto (the great English railway contractor and friend of James McHenry, the A&GW's boss) reported on his inspection of the road, was commented upon favorably in the Dutch press. Shortly afterward the new consolidated mortgage of 1865, totaling £2,771,600 ($13,858,000), was also offered in Amsterdam.[12]

How much of these loans was actually held in Holland is, as always, hard to establish, although it was said that the Dutch interest was considerable. Regular quotations of the A&GW's Ohio Division first and second mortgages and the consols and debentures have been found since 1863. In 1866 Dutch holdings were given as $430,000 in Ohio Division bonds (out of a total of $3,740,900); $743,000 in consols (out of a total of at least $18,961,500); and £220,000 in debentures (out of a total of £2,800,000). After 1866 most of the consols and debentures must have been sold, because Pik wrote in 1879 that the Ohio Division firsts were held in Holland, but only small sums of the others. Oewel later stated that at least $3 million of the Ohio firsts were in Dutch hands.[13]

The financial crisis in England of 1866, which started with the failure of Overend, Gurney and Company, put an end to all high hopes of success for the A&GW. It was said that Overend had extended itself too much in this and other railroads, and many other banks, including the Consolidated Bank, also failed. The great contracting firm of Peto and Betts also went under, with debts estimated at £4 million. McHenry was exposed as a financial juggler, and although he continued to declare that all was well, his credibility was seriously impaired.[14] The payment of interest on most if not all of the A&GW securities ceased. In London a protective committee was organized, rumored to hold $40 million in securities.

F. W. Oewel was appointed Dutch representative in that committee, and some members, Oewel among them, went in person to America early in 1867 and were joined there by the young English engineer Francis E. Trevithick, then in charge of construction of the Grand Trunk of Canada. Dutch bondholders deposited their securities and coughed up one guilder for every £100 to pay for Oewel's travel expenses. To make a stronger stand, Lippmann, Rosenthal and Company, Wertheim and Gompertz, and Alstorphius and Van Hemert announced the opening of an Administratie Kantoor for A&GW securities.[15]

Oewel was back in July of 1867 and reported that the A&GW was not yet really finished, despite some $60 million spent. He was confident that under good and honest management the road would have an excellent future. Trevithick was less optimistic, stating that at least $2 million was needed for the most urgent repairs.[16] Oewel next sought the support of the Netherlands government. The Minister of Foreign Affairs was willing to lend a hand where possible, but not in any official capacity, "as it is not the duty of the Netherlands Government to favor foreign, and sometimes risky investments, or to expose itself thereby to international problems."[17]

There is no need to follow the several reorganization schemes closely. McHenry was replaced as president by General George B. McClellan to give some lustre to the tarnished image of the road.[18] The London committee was dissolved in July 1868, but Oewel continued his activities and in May 1870 came up with a new plan for reorganization that, not surprisingly, benefited the holders of the 7-percent Ohio Division bonds, chiefly Dutchmen. The English security holders, united in a new committee, did not favor the Oewel plan and came forward with one of their own, which was endorsed by McHenry, who was again riding high as the leader of the opposition against Jay Gould of the Erie, which had leased the A&GW. (See Chapter 10 for more discussion on the Erie's troubles.) McHenry wrote triumphantly to Samuel Barlow that his plan for reorganization of the A&GW was supported by bankers in Frankfurt and Amsterdam, and he even foresaw a merger with the Ohio & Mississippi.[19] The English plan did not differ materially from Oewel's plan, but it gave voting rights to second and third (consolidated) mortgage holders.

Oewel tried to reach an agreement with Bischoffsheim and Goldschmidt, the European agents of the A&GW, who had been in charge of the reorganization, but in vain, as

McHenry, despite being called an untrustworthy fellow by Oewel, seemed to have his way. Lion Hertz, acting as agent for Bischoffsheim, handled the conversion, which was duly announced in the Dutch financial press.[20] The old Ohio Division firsts (per 1876) that had been deposited with Oewel were not converted, however. Even better, Oewel managed to get some payment for overdue coupons, probably through the good offices of the Dutch-German-American banking and trading firm of Bunge, Burlage and Company of New York, which often acted as intermediary between Dutch and Americans. Rudolph C. Burlage was Dutch consul general in New York between 1855 and 1893. In July 1869 this firm wrote to Barlow, who was then in Europe,

We have received from Mr. F. W. Oewel, Amsterdam, a large parcel ($110,000) of overdue coupons of the Atl. & Gr. W. RR. Cy. Mr. Oewel is an old and highly esteemed correspondent of my firm who represents the interests of the Dutch creditors of the AGW Cy. Some years ago when Mr. Oewel was in New York [1867], he gave the business to Mr. Clarkson N. Potter and the coupons are deposited with us for safekeeping and collection. I know from Mr. McFarland [Barlow's partner] that your firm represents a large interest against the Atl. & G. W. and we would like that all interest should be one, that is, in your hands. We wrote to Mr. F. W. Oewel that your firm is working at a consolidation of the A & G W debts and if you should receive a letter from him, you would greatly oblige my firm by giving him your opinion of the matter.[21]

Somehow Oewel managed to keep the Dutch Ohio Division bonds outside the consolidation of the debt. It took much time and a great deal of correspondence between Bischoffsheim and Goldschmidt on one side and McClellan, Thurman and Butler, trustees of the new A&GW mortgages, on the other, before everything was straightened out. Only in March 1873 was a final agreement signed and forwarded to Van Nierop, of the Amsterdamsche Bank, who was now acting as agent of Bischoffsheim and Goldschmidt after Lion Hertz had left the business.[22] Not all Dutchmen agreed with Oewel's stubbornness, and advocated the new first mortgage bonds instead, because the latter were in gold, while the Ohio Division bonds were in currency.[23]

When a new Atlantic & Great Western was incorporated in 1871, it was agreed that the Oewel certificates, as the old Dutch-held Ohio Division bonds were now generally known, would be redeemed according to plan in 1876. But despite a new and more advantageous lease of the A&GW to the Erie, the company was in receivership again by the end of 1874. A. C. Wertheim and Oewel then threatened foreclosure if interest on the Dutch bonds was not paid, and finally they agreed to a three-year extension of the redemption date, with payment of interest in gold instead of paper. But even this arrangement could not be fulfilled, and after new threats of foreclosure, a new and final agreement was reached in December 1879. Each old $1,000 Ohio Division bond was redeemed for Dfl 2,800 ($1,120), including the coupons unpaid since 1874. After the accounts of the Dutch committee had been closed, an additional sum of Dfl 80.03 ($32) was left for every bond. This was not a bad deal, as the original bonds had been in currency and not in gold. Oewel's stubbornness had brought some results after all.[24]

Apart from these Atlantic & Great Western bonds, Oewel, again in his own name only, imported currency bonds of the Elizabethtown & Paducah, a 175-mile line in western Kentucky. In the summer of 1872 he went there in person to inspect the property. While there, he also paid attention to the Paducah & Memphis and the Cairo & St. Louis roads, whose securities he had also sold in Holland.[25] Despite this personal care, the E&P, described as "merely two streaks of rust in the grass," defaulted in 1874 and was sold at foreclosure to the bondholders, in the person of H. W. Smithers, who acted for Oewel.[26] The road was reorganized as the Paducah & Elizabethtown in 1877. Wertheim and Gompertz and partners exchanged some 3,000 bonds ($1,000 each), so the Dutch holdings had indeed been substantial.

Another railroad in which Oewel had interested himself was almost as unfortunate as its neighbor, the Elizabethtown & Paducah. The Paducah & Memphis, operating in the same Kentucky area, defaulted one month before the connecting E&P, in August 1874. A new company was then incorporated, the Memphis, Paducah & Northern, with H. W. Smithers and Eckstein Norton as directors. Norton was partner in the New York commission house of Norton, Slaughter and Company and was to remain a representative of Dutch interests in other railroads, such as the Louisville & Nashville in the 1880's.[27] To have a firmer hand on the new company, Oewel managed to get his brother-in-law, Caspar W. Schaap, in the position of secretary of both the MP&N and the P&E. Through several reorganizations these railroads ended up in the possession of Collis P. Huntington's Chesapeake, Ohio & Southwestern, and the Dutch did not lose too much in the process. Oewel, in this case aided by the partnership with Wertheim, managed to save a substantial amount of the original investment.

Before this rather favorable outcome was reached, Oewel and Wertheim had come in for a lot of criticism. In 1873, just before the general crisis of that year, they had exchanged the Central Pacific bonds held in their investment fund for Paducah & Memphis securities. The P&M bonds had not paid any interest, while the CP had not defaulted and was not likely to do so. Wertheim defended himself by saying that they had acted on the negative reports about the Central Pacific for the year 1872, reports that had been confirmed by James de Fremery, Dutch consul in San Francisco, in his consular report for that year. Moreover, Eckstein Norton, president of the Paducah & Memphis, had a very sound reputation, and he had personally recommended the P&M bonds.[28]

A third railroad in the same area that Oewel had fancied was the Cairo & St. Louis, across the Ohio River in Illinois. This road too defaulted in 1874, but Oewel, again ably assisted by H. W. Smithers, managed to save the investment. The Cairo & St. Louis ended up in complete Dutch ownership and will be described in more detail in Chapter 9.

A last center of Oewel's activities in America was Denver, Colorado. As has been noted earlier, General William J. Palmer had been in Holland to solicit construction capital for his Denver & Rio Grande Railroad. Wertheim and Gompertz had obliged by advancing a lot of money on the railroad's bonds, and as usual Oewel was sent to Colorado to inspect the property.

Dutch interest in Colorado and New Mexico was at a high point in these years. Oewel, J. S. Smithers (one of the two Smitherses who often acted for Wertheim in American railroad business), and R. M. Krapp, also of Wertheim's office, visited Colorado Springs in July 1872 and were much pleased by what they saw.[29] A popular book of the time by Albert van Motz, *Colorado uit een geographisch en huishoudkundig oogpunt beschouwd* (Colorado from an Agrarian and Economic Point of View), published in 1874, boosted Dutch interest even more. Van Motz was a Dutch civil engineer who had assisted in early surveys for the railroad in the area of Pike's Peak and who then lived in Manitou, near Colorado Springs.[30]

Opposing Palmer's original plan to split the building of his Rio Grande railroad into several small corporate entities, Oewel persuaded him to incorporate only one company, and also insisted on the construction of the line through the Costilla Estate, a land company then being developed by Wertheim and Gompertz and partners on part of the old Spanish-Mexican Sangre de Cristo land grant in southern Colorado and northern New Mexico.[31] Oewel became a director of this Costilla Company, and of the affiliated United States Freehold Land and Emigration Company, set up by William Blackmore, English financier and friend of Palmer, and financed by Wertheim and Gompertz.[32] Directors of this company were, besides Oewel: Louis H. Meyer, who was also trustee for the Denver & Rio Grande railroad loans; Rudolph C. Burlage of the Amsterdam-New York banking firm Bunge, Burlage and Company and Dutch consul general in New York; Gustav Bunge of Cologne and partner of Burlage; and William Gilpin, former territorial governor of Colorado.[33] Wertheim and Gompertz took up $1 million of the Land & Emigration Company bonds at a discount of 50 percent. Of the total capital stock of $2 million, they held $1 million, with Oewel owning $100,000 and P. W. Scholten, employee of Wertheim and Gompertz, another $10,000. Gilpin became resident manager while another employee of Wertheim, Caspar W. Schaap (Oewel's brother-in-law, whom we have met in Paducah, Kentucky), became county recorder.[34] M. de Gempt, another Dutchman, was the representative of the company on the eastern seaboard to meet the expected emigrants and conduct them to the estate.[35] Despite this splendid array of names, the number of emigrants was disappointing, and many problems were encountered with squatters on the estate, although Wertheim had paid much attention to the validity of the company's title to the grant. In the end the Costilla Estate never lived up to expectations and became a serious loss to the Dutch investors involved.

Wertheim and Oewel personally had done well: the railroad's bonds were bought by them at prices of between 64.50 and 66 percent of par, and sold at 70. Moreover, Oewel got the usual 1-percent broker's commission, plus 7 percent in stock of the railroad.[36]

Besides being a director of the Costilla Estate and the Freehold and Land companies, Oewel was also involved in the other land company in the area, the Maxwell Land Grant and Railway Company of Amsterdam, taken over from English interests in the early 1870's, which has been described in the previous chapter.

Oewel's early travels to the United States had been chiefly in search of opportunities for investment, drumming up business, but gradually the character of his activities there changed out of necessity. The investments were threatened, especially as a result of the 1873 crisis, and his presence was now chiefly needed to salvage as much as possible from the wrecks. In the latter capacity he was quite successful, and he managed to keep the Dutch interests in "his" railroads together as much as was possible.

■ *Nicolaas Jacob den Tex*

Another Dutchman who came to America in the early years to see if business could be profitably done was Nicolaas Jacob den Tex, an influential Amsterdam businessman and from 1863 to 1877 the secretary of the Amsterdam Chamber of Commerce.[37] Whereas Oewel came of his own accord, Den Tex came by invitation. Early in 1871 he was the only Dutch member of a party of American and European (mostly German) investors, bankers, and prospective land buyers who toured the Red River of the North country and the new Northern Pacific Railway then being built.[38] Jay Cooke, the Philadelphia financier behind the NP, was looking for European capital, and promotional tours such as these were becoming a common attraction to lure possible investors. The party was taken as far as the railhead in the Dakotas, wined and dined, and sent back to Europe to report positively, it was hoped. All participants took copious notes and were presented with much promotional literature, but unhappily lost everything in a railroad wreck on the return trip.[39] Yet Den Tex managed to write an account of his journey, apparently from memory.[40] His story was positive enough, but no Dutch capital was forthcoming for the building of the Northern Pacific, and when Jay Cooke's banking house crashed in the panic of 1873, the railroad collapsed too.

Initially Den Tex and Oewel had come to the United States to boost sales of railroad securities at home, and only later had Oewel's purposes changed. As discussed below, other Dutch brokers came to America for the express purpose of safeguarding existing Dutch interests, or for visual inspection of problematic or threatened properties in which the Dutch already had a stake.

▪ Hendrik J. de Marez Oyens

Hendrik Jan de Marez Oyens started his long career as a representative of the Dutch financial interests in the United States in 1866, when he was a young man of 23. In that year he inspected the ill-starred St. Paul & Pacific in Minnesota, in which so much Dutch money had been sunk.[41]

His next American assignment came in 1875, when he was sent to inspect the troubled Missouri, Kansas & Texas. He was a member of the protective committee in Amsterdam, which had worked out a deal with the MKT board for conversion of the outstanding debt. In New York Oyens signed the necessary documents on the part of the Dutch and returned home.[42] Another Dutchman had already been in Kansas before him. Late in 1874, G. A. Croockewit had been sent out by Wertheim and Gompertz to inspect the MKT and report. Other inspections had already been made on behalf of Louis H. Meyer, who acted for Wertheim as well.[43] Early in May 1876, Oyens was back in Amsterdam to report on his findings and to explain the solution reached.[44] It was not his fault that the Katy was soon in trouble again. Oyens was to serve on a Dutch MKT protective committee again in 1887 and in 1889–90 was the Dutch member of the so-called Olcott Committee, which reorganized the Katy for the second time. Frederick P. Olcott, president of the Central Trust Company, took the lead in the restructuring of the debt-ridden Missouri, Kansas & Texas; Oyens then took care of the large Dutch, German, and French interests.[45]

After Oyens's visit to Kansas he was given little respite before being sent out again. In the same year, 1876, he was the Dutch member of the international committee set up to rebuild the Gilman, Clinton & Springfield in Illinois, which had defaulted in 1874. (See Chapter 8 for more details about his activities there.) Soon after the successful outcome of this assignment he had to go to Illinois again. The Illinois Central was seen in London and Amsterdam as one of the gilt-edged investments, and when in 1876 a sharp drop in the company's revenues occurred, this naturally caused concern among the many European shareholders. Although this decline was thought to be a belated result of the crisis of 1873 and likely to be soon overcome, the Dutch shareholders were convened in Amsterdam in January 1877. Banker August Philips chaired the meeting, where only one-tenth of the total of 70,000 Dutch-held shares was present.[46] It was decided to send a representative to America, together with an English expert, and despite his protests that he had already been in America hardly a year before in the business of the Missouri, Kansas & Texas and the Gilman, Clinton & Springfield, Oyens was persuaded to go again. His English colleague was Captain Sir Douglas Galton, Royal Engineers, an expert on American railroads.[47] Their joint report on the IC was generally favorable, and revenues did indeed increase soon. As a result the dividend for 1878 was raised to 6 percent, and unrest among the shareholders subsided.[48] While in Chicago Oyens had made a very favorable impression on the IC directors, and afterwards they regularly informed him of the problems of railroad operation among a host of competing lines.[49] Their policy, approved by Amsterdam, was conservative, paying more attention to improvement of the road than to increasing the dividends. While other roads watered their stock extensively, the IC never did so, and it was in much better physical shape too.[50]

This did not end the American career of Oyens, for he continued to be active in the brokerage business, and he served on countless Dutch protective committees and on the board of the MKT almost until his death in 1911.

▪ *Pieter van Weel*

Pieter van Weel, a director of the Rotterdamsche Bank, was sent out in 1885 as representative of Dutch bondholders of the ailing former Florida Central & Western Railroad, then already merged into the new Florida Railway & Navigation Company. The Dutch held at least $500,000 worth of still older Florida Transit bonds (now also merged into the Florida Railway & Navigation Company), and Van Weel was sent to check the books of the new Railway & Navigation Company to see if interest payments could be expected or not. His report has not been found, but it cannot have been very positive; in 1886 the Railway & Navigation Company went into receivership.[51] This Florida business was not Van Weel's only American assignment; his other activities there are discussed in Chapter 9.

▪ *Jacobus Wertheim*

Jacobus Wertheim, an Amsterdam lawyer and cousin of A. C. Wertheim,[52] was active on the part of Dutch investors in the Florida frauds (see Chapter 10 for more on that side of his activities in America). In the summer of 1879 this same Wertheim was also acting for Dutch bondholders in the affairs of the Marietta & Pittsburg, then in default. Its president, General Warner, had already been in Amsterdam in 1874 to explain matters, and the Dutch had then joined forces with the Railway Share Trust Company of London. Francis Pavy, the representative of the Trust, corresponded with the Amsterdam Stock Exchange and with Berlin and Hymans, the Dutch brokers involved. Through his activities a reorganization had taken place, and a new company, the Marietta, Pittsburg & Cleveland, had been incorporated in 1877.[53]

Apparently the Dutch were not content with the marginal financial performance of the new road, and in June 1879 Wertheim was dispatched to Marietta, Pennsylvania, to investigate. In his very thorough report to the Dutch bondholders of 6 September 1879, he stated that the railroad was too long and too crooked, with trestles in bad shape and depots and shops hardly in existence. The ties were rotting and needed renewal, and only the rolling stock was in good repair. He strongly recommended cooperation with other roads to gain access to Cleveland, for which no less than $500,000 would be needed; for improvements another $300,000 were necessary.[54] Apparently these sums horrified the Dutch bondholders so much that they sold off their holdings to English parties soon after.[55] The Marietta, Pittsburg & Cleveland itself ended up in the Pennsylvania Railroad.

▪ Johan Carp

Johan Carp, prosperous manufacturer and broker of Utrecht about whom little is known, turned out to be a stubborn and successful negotiator. In the complicated affairs of the St. Paul & Pacific he proved to be a match for the Canadian-American mastermind, James J. Hill, and it was largely through his activities that the enormous Dutch interest in that road was not completely lost. Carp's activities are discussed in greater detail in Chapter 12.

▪ A. A. H. Boissevain

Athanase Adolphe Henri Boissevain (1843–1921) was one of the leading personalities of the Amsterdam stockbroking fraternity. After serving his apprenticeship with other brokers, in 1875 he set up his own stockbroking business in Amsterdam under the name of Ad. Boissevain and Company. His office was active in the Union Pacific affairs and had introduced several of that company's securities in Holland since 1880. A. A. H. Boissevain was more personally involved than Dutch brokers generally were in such cases. Along with many other European investors, he was not happy with the leadership of that controversial railroad tycoon Jay Gould, who had been in control of the UP from 1874 to 1883, and who had returned again as its leader in 1890, a position which he retained until his death late in 1892. Boissevain took the lead in a coup of European bondholders, early in 1892, to oust Gould from the board. He was almost successful, but the defection of one London banking house meant that Gould remained in control by a very small margin.[56] It was a pyrrhic victory, however, for Sidney Dillon, Gould's appointee for president of the road, died soon after, while Gould himself passed away in

December 1892. Without a strong leader and with the general financial crisis of 1893 making matters worse, a receivership could no longer be avoided. In October of that year receivers were appointed for the whole system.

A Union Pacific Reorganization Committee was formed in November 1893, in which Boissevain represented all foreign bondholders. He played a conspicuous role and came forward with a first scheme to set the company on firm footing again, while at the same time solving the problem of the company's debt to the U.S. government, which resulted from the subsidies advanced by the federal government during the early construction of the road. Owing to the indecisiveness of the government, nothing came of his plan nor of several others that followed over the next few years.[57] When it appeared that Congress would accept only a cash payment for the full debt plus interest accrued, the committee stepped down in March 1895. Only in the fall of that year was a new committee set up, but leadership was uncertain. Boissevain was still seen as the man best suited for this difficult task, but he was away in Holland, and it was Jacob H. Schiff, of Kuhn, Loeb and Company, who was at last persuaded to take the lead.[58]

At long last a solution was reached and the Union Pacific Rail*way* was sold at foreclosure on 1 November 1897, and a new Union Pacific Rail*road* was incorporated. Through these years, Boissevain had remained a member of the International Reorganization Committee as representative of the European bondholders, most of whom were German and Dutch. At the same time he was also active as a board member of the Dutch Association of Those Interested in the Union Pacific, set up in 1894 to protect the substantial Dutch investment in the transcontinental road.[59]

While in America for the affairs of the Union Pacific, Boissevain also served on an international committee to reorganize the bankrupt Norfolk & Western in 1895, again as sole representative of the European bondholders.

Later, in 1908, he served in a similar capacity when he was the only European representative in the reorganization committee of the Wabash Pittsburgh Terminal. This company, incorporated in 1904, was envisaged to fill the last gap in the truly transcontinental system pieced together by George Gould, son of the notorious Jay Gould. Construction proved to be ruinously expensive, and only fresh capital injected by Gould's Wabash Railroad made progress possible. The Terminal defaulted in 1908, and it turned out that some $1.5 million of its second mortgage loan had been sold in Holland; the rest of the $20 million had been taken up in America.[60] The reorganization committee consisted of Boissevain and John W. Castles, of New York, representing the Americans. Its success was slight, and with the 1917 reorganization of the Terminal into the Pittsburgh & West Virginia, the seconds were virtually wiped out.

■ *Johan Luden*

A role similar to that played by A. A. H. Boissevain for the Union Pacific fell in 1893–95 to Dr. Johan Luden (born in 1857), chief partner of Hope and Company of Amsterdam, during the reorganization of the Atchison, Topeka & Santa Fe. The Atchison's[61] securities were widely held in Holland, although Hope had not touched them until 1892. But Barings, Hope's English partners, had been acting as financiers of the Atchison for a long time already, and when they got into trouble in 1892 over their Argentine business, Hope took over some of their ATSF securities. First the Amsterdam house undertook to convert the Atchison's existing income bonds into second mortgage bonds, no doubt at the request of Barings.[62] Next the road's "Guarantee fund notes" of 1888, renewed in 1891 for two more years, were introduced by Hope in Amsterdam toward the end of 1893.[63] All this financial juggling proved to be in vain, however, as the Santa Fe went bankrupt in December of the same year. A Dutch protective committeee was formed, and Luden was elected to represent the Dutch and the Germans in America. Robert Fleming, a Scotsman with a large experience of American finance, represented the British bond- and shareholders, and Edward King, of the Union Trust Company of New York, did the same for the Americans. Together the three formed the General Reorganization Committee, and they hired the noted financial analyst Stephen Little to get some insight in the condition of the road.[64] Because this condition turned out to be much worse than originally thought, it took some time before the so-called King plan, hammered out between King, Fleming, and Luden, could be published, but in March 1895 it was ready.[65] Hope and Company organized the conversion of old into new securities for the Dutch holders, and most owners agreed with the terms set in the King plan, which were not unfavorable. Altogether they converted just under $40 million worth of three different classes of bonds and some 50,000 common shares for the Dutch owners.[66] On 10 December 1895 the old Atchison, Topeka & Santa Fe Rail*road* was sold to Edward King, acting for the Reorganization Committee, for $60 million and a new AT&SF Rail*way* was incorporated. The American-British-Dutch triumvirate had done its work well.

Luden had to act again for Dutch bondholders in 1912, when the Wabash Railroad defaulted on the payment of interest. It had overextended itself in support of the Wabash Pittsburgh Terminal, which went down in 1908, and now the parent company itself was in trouble. The final result of the reorganization was a new Wabash Rail*way*, incorporated in 1915, in which the Dutch still had a sizable stake.

▪ S. F. van Oss

Salomon Frederik van Oss (1868–1949) is the last of the Dutchmen in this gallery.[67] Born in the Netherlands, he moved to London as a young man and started a career as a journalist, specializing in such financial subjects as South African mining investment, Russian government finance, and American railroads. Traveling extensively, he acquired a deep knowledge of these subjects and wrote authoritative articles and books, which were widely read in the financial world. He boasted that he rode every main line in the United States at least once, and it is only natural that investors sought his advice in these matters. When the De Goeijen–Tutein Nolthenius group of Amsterdam was contemplating investment on a large scale in Arthur Stilwell's Kansas City, Pittsburg & Gulf, it asked Fred van Oss to inspect the road as far as it was finished by then and to report on its viability, on the terrain left to be traversed, on the traffic potential, and so on. Although his report has not been found, it must have been positive enough, for the Dutch took the plunge. (See Chapter 14 for the story of the Kansas City, Pittsburg & Gulf.)

In 1902 Van Oss decided to move back to the Netherlands, where he became editor of one of the leading financial journals, the *Nieuwe Financier en Kapitalist*. At the same time he started his famous annual series of *Van Oss' Effectenboek*, first published in 1903, which established itself as an invaluable manual for investors and brokers (and for business historians as well). Writing was apparently not enough for Fred van Oss, however; he wanted to take part in the actual business of brokerage and investing as well. In 1903 he founded, with his brother A. M. van Oss and J. D. Santilhano (also a financial writer of note), the firm of S. F. van Oss and Company of The Hague, specializing in American railroad and oil business. It must have been clear to them that most of the railroad network in the United States was finished and in place by that time, and that only in relatively undeveloped areas such as Oklahoma and Alaska was new construction of any importance possible. He therefore started with marketing securities of roads such as the Eastern Oklahoma (a Santa Fe subsidiary), the Texas & Oklahoma, and the Missouri, Kansas & Oklahoma (both MKT subsidiaries).[68]

In view of Van Oss's activities in the Indian Territory and Oklahoma, it is not surprising that Dorset Carter, the promoter of the Oklahoma Central, turned to the Dutchman for construction funds for his railroad. Van Oss knew the ground, had met Carter in the Indian Territory before, but apparently did not trust him too much, and therefore sent out an independent representative of his own first. This was Gerrit A. A. Middelberg (1846–1916), a well-known Dutch railroad engineer in retirement. Middelberg had been chief mechanical engineer of the Holland Railway, one of the leading railways in the Netherlands, and from 1889 to 1899 had been director of the Netherlands South African Railway Company, the Dutch company that built the railroads in President Paul Kruger's South African Republic (Transvaal).[69] Van Oss had met Middelberg in Pretoria, Transvaal, when he had been there to investigate the South African mining industry in 1897–98.

Gerrit Middelberg sailed for America in September 1905, had talks with the directors of the Western Trust & Savings Bank, business relations of Van Oss in Chicago, and arrived in Chickasha, Indian Territory, in December of that year to inspect the future Oklahoma Central Railway.[70] But he had made one other stop before that. Van Oss was also interested in Alaska and so, undaunted by the harsh winter, Middelberg traveled by train to Seattle and sailed for Seward, Alaska, to investigate the Alaska Central, then under construction.[71] Eventually Van Oss declined to act in the Alaska business, but he did underwrite the Oklahoma Central's bond issue to the tune of $1 million.

While in Chicago, Middelberg had also discussed the affairs of the Chicago & Milwaukee Electric Railroad, one of the newfangled interurbans, in which Van Oss was also interested. The C&ME's securities had been offered in Amsterdam, and Middelberg was asked to report on this property as well. His opinion was favorable, but the financial crisis of 1907 meant a fatal downturn of the company's fortunes with the road not yet finished and it defaulted. Reorganization took a long time, and it proved necessary for Van Oss to travel to Chicago in person in 1908. Another Dutch representative, Louis den Beer Poortugael, partner of Oppenheim and Van Till of The Hague, one of the brokers involved, was sent out in 1909, and only two years later could the Dutch bonds ($1,642,000 par value) be redeemed at 62 percent of par, a sizable loss.[72] The interurban itself was reorganized as the Chicago, North Shore & Milwaukee and became one of the best run and longest-lived of the American interurbans.

Despite the personal attention of Fred van Oss and Gerrit Middelberg, the construction of the Oklahoma Central went slowly and was accompanied by a smell of fraud. Therefore Van Oss judged it better to have a representative on the spot, in the person of Martin Middelberg (1872–1925), Gerrit's son, also a railway engineer with considerable experience in the Transvaal and the Dutch East Indies. But even Martin's presence in the town of Purcell during most of 1907 could not prevent the fraudulent dealings of some of the Americans involved in the construction company behind the railroad. It is surprising that an old hand such as Fred van Oss could be fooled by their tricks.

Although Van Oss may have lost on the Oklahoma Central deal, he made good again in the oil business in Oklahoma, acting on the advice of Martin Middelberg, who knew something about oil too. With the proceeds Van Oss could withdraw from the brokerage business and follow an old dream, the founding of a weekly paper of his own, *De Haagsche Post*, which is still flourishing. In 1913 the firm of S. F. van Oss and Company was converted into a private investment company. His name lives on in Oklahoma in the town of Vanoss. The town of Middleberg, a bit farther down the line of the old Oklahoma Central, was named for Gerrit, and it is even smaller than Vanoss.

Eight

Dutch Protective Committees

*I*n cases of impending bankruptcy or receivership of an American rail- road, Dutch bondholders usually organized themselves in order to act as one body, thus making their financial influence felt and keeping their interests as safe as circumstances would permit. The initiative was generally taken by the Dutch banking house or brokerage firm that had originally marketed the bonds in question. When more than one bond issue was outstanding, as was the case with most of the larger railroads, several bondholders' protective committees (whether exclusively Dutch or including members of other nationalities) could exist at the same time. This occasion- ally led to conflicts of interest.

When a railroad with a large Dutch share in its capital structure defaulted, the Dutch brokers and bankers involved usually called the owners of the shares and/or bonds together to discuss joint action. In many cases the actual shares were held by an Administratie Kantoor set up by the brokers, as explained in Chapter 2, which made it easier to act speedily and effectively. Bonds were generally owned by private individuals all over the country, and it often took a long time before a sufficient number of these investors could be reached. In some cases where the Dutch interest was particularly large, as in the Missouri, Kansas & Texas and others noted below, a formal association, a *vereniging* in Dutch, of stock- and/or bondholders might be incorporated, which held the shares or bonds in its name, and thus protected the interests of the individual investors even better.

Whether or not the bondholders' protective committee was a Dutch invention is not certain, but by actively employing these emergency measures the Dutch did acquire a good name in international financial circles. The London *Times* complained before 1878 that some protection was needed for English security owners against the manip- ulations of unscrupulous American managers. The unsigned article continued, "I be- lieve such arrangements are well understood and in operation in Holland and other parts of the Continent. The very knowledge of such means of defense being at hand would have a deterring effect and often nip in the bud attempts by some 'ring' of unscrupulous men to plunder the foreign holders unprotected by any prevailing interest held in America."[1]

It is doubtful if the protective committee was indeed a Dutch invention. A London committee for the Marietta & Cincinnati is mentioned in 1860, and a more or less permanent British Illinois Central committee was in existence in the 1850's.[2] But apart from these, and a few others such as those connected with the Erie and the Atlantic & Great Western in the 1860's, it is true that British protective committees for defaulting American railroads are fairly rare until the mid-1880's. In those same years, especially during the 1870's, the Dutch protective committees indeed proliferated.[3]

An added means of protection, and one which may explain the relative absence of British committees, was the establishment in 1884 of the English Association of American Bond and Share Holders Ltd., which soon became a power to be reckoned with under its forceful first director Joseph Price.[4] A similar organization was mooted in Holland by Wertheim and Gompertz, but never materialized. Interest shown by the stockbroking fraternity in Amsterdam was only lukewarm at best, and Wertheim had to drop the idea. Separate protective committees remained necessary whenever a sizable Dutch investment in an American railroad was threatened.

There appears to have been no established level of ownership before forming such a committee, although the general rule seems to have been that a minimum of around $1 million (par value) of a given security in Dutch hands was the first condition for forming a bondholders' committee. Yet, in some cases when more than that sum was outstanding in Holland, it was not deemed advisable to set up a separate Dutch committee because Dutch ownership, though large in itself, was just a drop in the ocean of securities of the company in question. In 1908, for instance, when the Wabash Pittsburgh Terminal defaulted, A. A. H. Boissevain was appointed as a member of the American committee to represent the Dutch, who held at least $1.5 million of the road's bonds. Of the total outstanding of $20 million this was apparently not deemed enough to act independently. On the other hand, even when Dutch participation in a railroad was known to be larger than the generally accepted minimum, the bondholders themselves sometimes were hard to prod into some kind of concerted action. When in 1874 the Amsterdam notary public J. C. G. Pollones[5] wrote 152 firms and individuals about the threatened investment in the Missouri, Kansas & Texas, only 37 took the trouble to answer at all.[6]

Further, when a Dutch committee was formed or proposed and not enough bondholders came forward to vote and authorize the committee to act for them the whole proposal would come to naught. A three-quarters majority was generally deemed necessary for a clear and undisputed mandate to the members of the board of a committee.

As noted, the stockbroker who had imported the defaulted bonds usually took the initiative in forming a committee, and the Stock Exchange Board then added one or two members, including the chairman, and appointed a secretary, who probably did most of the work. The next step was then to call the individual bondholders to deposit their bonds in exchange for certificates issued by the committee. Only then could an accurate count be made of how many bonds were actually in Dutch hands. The certificates usually replaced the original bonds in the price lists of the Amsterdam Exchange.

It is not necessary to follow the actions of all Dutch bondholders' committees known to have existed before 1914. A few of them will be described in other chapters: the Galveston, Houston & Henderson committee of 1860, the first on record, is found in Chapter 11; the St. Paul & Pacific committee of 1873 in Chapter 12; the Missouri, Kansas & Texas of 1875 in Chapter 13; the Denver Pacific of 1877 in Chapter 9; and finally the Union Pacific and Atchison, Topeka & Santa Fe committees of 1893 in Chapter 7.

▪ *International Protective Committees*

Joint English-Dutch or German-Dutch protective committees were also known. The Atlantic & Great Western committee of 1866, with F. W. Oewel as Dutch member, has already been noted in Chapter 7. A Dutch Kansas Pacific committee was mooted in 1873 by Kerkhoven and Wertheim and Gompertz, but interest was only lukewarm, and in the end it sufficed to collaborate closely with the German committee chaired by Henry Villard.[7] The same year saw the incorporation of a German committee for the bondholders of the Oregon & California, with F. S. van Nierop, director of the Amsterdamsche Bank, as sole Dutch member to take care of the interests of his fellow countrymen.[8]

No fewer than two international committees were set up in 1876: one for the Atlantic, Mississippi & Ohio, and one for the Gilman, Clinton & Springfield. An English committee had already been set up for the AM&O, chaired by Henry W. Tyler, and the Dutch sought cooperation with him. W. F. Piek and H. J. de Marez Oyens were added as members of the English committee, but in 1877 the Dutch felt left in the dark by their English counterparts and withdrew, leaving the field to Tyler and John Collinson, the London broker who had handled the securities originally. Piek and Oyens strongly warned against the English plans, but in the end their own plan for reorganization did not differ materially from Collinson's.[9] Differences were apparently smoothed over, because Oyens was again mentioned as a member of the English committee in 1880, and the final reorganization and foreclosure sale of the AM&O had the same results for all bondholders: they could choose between a cash settlement of Dfl 3,230.62 per $1,000 bond, including accrued interest since 1876, or new bonds at par after paying an assessment of £10 per $1,000. Not a bad result after all. Altogether 2,190 bonds of $1,000 each were paid off or exchanged by the Dutch committee.[10]

In the same year an international committee was called for to reorganize the 111-mile Gilman, Clinton & Springfield Railroad in Illinois. A strong smell of fraud hung around this road, and to clear things up a committee was formed by the banks most involved: Morton, Bliss and Company, of New York, in the person of George Bliss; Charles S. Seyton for Borthwick and Company of London; and H. J. de Marez Oyens for the Dutch interests.[11] The line was leased to the Illinois Central and later sold, and old GC&S bonds could be exchanged for IC bonds at 80 percent, which, of course, meant a sizable loss.

■ *The 1870's*

Des Moines Valley

A truly Dutch committee was formed in 1871 to watch over a Des Moines Valley Railroad loan. This road ran through Pella, Iowa, the center of *Dominee* (Reverend) Hendrik P. Scholte's Dutch colony, and as such was well-known in Amsterdam.[12] Of this loan of 1868, bonds worth $400,000 had been sold in Amsterdam by H. Franco Mendes and J. A. Matthes and Company, partly secured by a mortgage on the line and on 100,000 acres of the land grant. This security turned out to be of little value, however, when the company defaulted in October 1871. The committee was formed by the brokers involved, reinforced by the firms of H. Oijens and Sons and Burdet and Druijvesteyn. It took some time before a deal was worked out with Morton, Bliss and Company of New York, the representatives of the American bondholders. A total of 774 $1,000 bonds were exchanged by the Dutch committee, indicating a sizable Dutch interest.[13] The road was reorganized as the Des Moines & Fort Dodge Railroad in 1873, still with strong Dutch backing. So strong in fact, that in 1886 Broes, Gosman and Company asked for authorization of the Dutch bondholders to lease the road to a large neighboring line, the Rock Island, for 18 years.[14] That they were able to do this without consultation of other parties indicates a clear Dutch majority in the road's bonded debt.

Toledo, Peoria & Warsaw

In 1877 a committee was established for the Toledo, Peoria & Warsaw, a small road that tried with little success to build a line from Warsaw, Illinois, on the Mississippi River opposite Keokuk, to Toledo, Ohio, by way of Peoria. The tracks never went farther east than the Illinois–Indiana state line. At least $500,000 of the road's consolidated mortgage bonds had been marketed in Amsterdam by Elix and Broekman in 1871.[15] In 1873 the TP&Wa defaulted, and it turned out that not all earlier loans had been converted into this consolidated loan, as had been the intention. Wrangling between the old first and second mortgage holders and the consols took years, and only in 1877 was a Dutch committee finally incorporated to help speed matters along. H. J. de Marez Oyens was a member, together with representatives of Kerkhoven and Company and Elix and Broekman. It is not apparent that the Dutchmen influenced matters much, but a solution was finally found in cooperation with the American parties involved. A new Toledo, Peoria & Western was incorporated, and this road was leased to the Wabash, St. Louis & Pacific, which guaranteed 4 percent on the old consols, which were to be converted into new second mortgage income bonds. These new seconds could in their turn be converted into Wabash preferred shares, if the holder so desired, and the old coupons, unpaid since 1873, were to be paid in new TP&We common shares, which could also be exchanged for Wabash commons at 30 percent.[16] In 1880 this conversion was successfully executed by Stadnitski and Van Heukelom, which issued certificates against the new TP&We seconds and commons. A fair result for all, especially as the Wabash was considered a strong and well-managed road and its securities were commanding high prices. The Dutch committee was honorably discharged.

This was not to be the end of the Peoria story. For a few years the Wabash did indeed pay the 4 percent, but when that road was plunged into receivership in 1884 by the machinations of Jay Gould, the lease of the Peoria was canceled and interest payments stopped. Stadnitski called the bondholders together to discuss the situation. Harsh words were exchanged during this meeting: Oyens was furious at those bondholders who had not exchanged their TP&We bonds for Wabash preferred shares. At the then ridiculously high prices of Wabash stock they could have made a handsome profit instead of hanging on to the doubtful Peoria paper. Of the total of $2.9 million in TP&We income bonds in Dutch hands in 1880, almost $1.8 million had indeed been exchanged for Wabash preferred stock, but at least $450,000 was still held by Stadnitski against their certificates; the rest had probably been sold off over the years.[17] Stadnitski refused to act, but something had to be done and a new TP&We committee was set up in 1885. It was all to no avail, however, as the holders of the second mortgage income bonds had little power against the owners of the first mortgage. At the reorganization of the road in 1885, nothing remained for the seconds, and the Dutch holdings were simply wiped out: 464 certificates of $1,000 became wastepaper.[18] Of course, Oyens was right when he told the Dutch that they had been stupid not to convert in time, but one wonders if Stadnitski should not have warned them too.

■ *The 1880's*

New York, Ontario & Western

Not surprisingly the economic crisis of 1884 plunged other American railroads into receivership too, which resulted in the incorporation of a couple of Dutch protective committees. Shares of the New York, Ontario & Western Railway, the former New York & Oswego Midland, had been traded in Amsterdam from 1880, both as original $100 shares and $1,000 certificates issued by Gebr. Boissevain and Gebr. Teixeira de Mattos. But things were not going smoothly, and the representative of the British shareholders, Joseph Price, took the initiative and sought the cooperation of the Dutch in early 1884.[19] A letter from General E. F. Winslow, president of the NYO&W, to Price, which was forwarded to Amsterdam, explained the situation.[20] A new loan was needed to fund the floating debt, but such an issue had to be authorized by a majority of all shareholders, common and preferred. The latter were Americans and they managed the railroad, while the former, mostly British and Dutch, had no say in the running of the road at all.

A London shareholders' meeting had already been held, and a similar meeting was convened in Amsterdam on 2 February 1884, where $1,982,000 of commons was represented. Out of a total of $58 million this amount seems insignificant, but quite a number of shareholders could not be reached in time.[21] Two days later a protective committee was formed, chaired by P. A. L. van Ogtrop, with R. van Rees as secretary. That the trouble was taken to form a committee meant that the Dutch holdings were considerably greater than the dollar amount represented at the first meeting; apparently the Dutch were sluggish in their reaction. To stay in close touch with the English committee, the ubiquitous H. W. Smithers was named as associate member of the Dutch committee, and Van Rees was sent to America by way of London. In August of 1884 he was back and reported to the committee.[22]

He had found the problem twofold. First, the Ontario & Western management was in the hands of the preferred shareholders, all Americans and also the men behind the West Shore Railroad, which provided the NYO&W with its vital connection with the Weehawken, New Jersey, terminus. This combination of interests resulted in unfavorable contracts for the Ontario for the use of that terminal.

The second problem was the floating debt of more than $1.5 million. It was proposed to issue $2 million in bonds to pay off that debt and to convert the preferred shares at the same time. The English committee had already assented and their Dutch colleagues strongly advised their countrymen to do the same, as sufficient guarantees had been obtained that the European common shareholders would become the real power in the company and that the contracts with the West Shore would be revised. In a last paragraph of their report Van Rees and Van Ogtrop complained about the incredible lack of support from the Dutch shareholders. Only when united, they stated, could something be saved of their large interest, but if their support was not forthcoming, others would take matters into their own hands.

Although the future of the Ontario & Western certainly looked brighter after these measures, not everything was yet in order. The new contracts with the West Shore were not quite to the liking of Van Ogtrop, and only in 1886, after the New York Central had leased the West Shore, was a better arrangement finally obtained. The majority of the preferred shareholders agreed to exchange their shares for first mortgage bonds, and control of the company passed into the hands of the common shareholders. According to Van Ogtrop, this was by far the best that could now be obtained, although in 1885 better terms could have been had if only the Dutch shareholders had supported the committee more strongly.[23]

With the 1886 reorganization a new chapter in Ontario & Western history began. Work was started on a branch from Cadosia, New York, to Scranton, Pennsylvania, to take advantage of commerce with the coalfields. This "pet project" of the Dutch and English shareholders proved to be a godsend for the company. The coal traffic became its mainstay, and careful management did much to put the road on a secure footing. Because of the close cooperation of the British and Dutch committees good results had been obtained, but it is apparent that the initiative in this case came from London, not Amsterdam.

Denver & Rio Grande

In the same year another American railroad in trouble called for not one but two Dutch protective committees. The Denver & Rio Grande, which had been helped to firm financial footing with Dutch money, had overextended itself in support of the Denver & Rio Grande Western, its link with Salt Lake City. Its bonds had been popular with Dutch investors, and Hubrecht had even introduced the Rio Grande's common shares. General Palmer, who was held responsible for the downturn in the company's fortunes, had been forced out early in 1884, and Louis H. Meyer had taken a seat on the board for the Dutch. The new management came too late, however, and the Rio Grande had to default in July of that same year. The Dutch were quick in the field with a protective committee for the 7- and 5-percent bonds, chaired by De Marez Oyens and with P. C. A. M. van Weel and T. H. A. Tromp as members.[24] Van Weel and Tromp were sent to Colorado forthwith to inspect the property, with representatives of the Scottish and English bondholders. Tromp was in Colorado again in the spring of 1885, where he prepared a most thorough report on the condition of the road. He laid the blame for its misfortunes mostly at Palmer's door, although he criticized the new management as well. He also noticed that a road like the Rio Grande, which followed the fortunes of the mining camps so closely, was bound to be hit hard when the mines were worked out, as was the case in Colorado.[25]

A reorganization plan was hammered out by George Coppell (erstwhile English consul in New Orleans) for the English, Robert Fleming for the Scots, and Tromp for the Dutch. In the spring of 1886 everything was ready. The old railway was sold at friendly foreclosure to the bondholders, and a new Denver & Rio Grande Railroad was incorporated. The results of the conversion of the old securities were not too bad, although some losses had to be accepted. The Dutch committee reported that no less than $6,382,500 of the first mortgage bonds had been deposited in Amsterdam, with only $2,800,000 in Frankfurt.[26]

With the owners of the firsts and consols reasonably well taken care of, the owners of junior securities felt left out in the cold. Willem F. Piek therefore objected to an assessment of $6 per share, and he also called the Dutch 5-percent general mortgage holders together. At their meeting on 22 December 1885, 656 commons certificates (of $1,000 each) were represented, and a separate committee was formed to defend their rights and those of the 5-percent bondholders as well. Piek and J. L. ten Have were elected to the protective committee, but the result of their attempts to get a better deal were negligible.[27] Apparently their combined strength was not enough to oppose the other groups of security owners successfully.

Chicago & Atlantic

This problem of opposing groups of bond- and shareholders fighting each other instead of cooperating often caused delays in the reorganization of a bankrupt company and sometimes even prevented a solution acceptable to all parties. Interests of bond- and shareholders were almost always conflicting, and the latter, having put up little or no real money, had to bear the brunt of the losses. But even among the bondholders, junior and senior security owners could have different views, as sketched above in the case of the Rio Grande. In one specific case the Dutch found a novel way of removing such opposition of other bondholders by buying them out.

The Chicago & Atlantic was a railroad with a main line from Marion, Ohio, to

Hammond, Indiana, giving the Erie access to Chicago. It was controlled from the start by the Erie, which guaranteed the interest on its bonds. A first mortgage loan of $6.5 million had been issued in 1880, and Broes and Gosman had sold these bonds in Amsterdam. When the Erie got in trouble in 1884, the guarantee of the C&A interest was canceled and the November coupon of that year could not be paid. A Dutch protective committee was quickly formed, with Ten Have, Piek, De Marez Oyens, and Van Rees as members, all old hands at this game. One of their first actions was sueing the Erie for nonpayment of interest; it was stated that the majority of the firsts had been sold in Holland.[28] The committee's suit was thrown out by the courts, however, and a settlement was then worked out by J. P. Morgan.

A new company was to be incorporated after the foreclosure sale of the old Chicago & Atlantic. The required foreclosure sale, however, was opposed by owners of older second mortgage bonds, which had never been sold in Holland. Oyens, who was already in America, was then authorized by the Dutch to buy a majority of the old seconds to move their opposition out of the way. He managed to obtain bonds worth $773,000 (par value), for which he had to pay $580,000. Earlier, in the spring of 1890, a fund of Dfl 1.7 million ($680,000) and carrying 10-percent interest had been set up by the Dutch committee for just such a contingency. With the opposition thus removed, the road was sold under foreclosure in August 1890 and was reorganized as the Chicago & Erie.[29]

A total of 5,961 of the 6,500 old $1,000 Chicago & Atlantic firsts had been deposited with the Dutch committee, and it now proceeded with the conversion. Total expenses, including the purchase price of the old seconds, were estimated at Dfl 2.6 million.[30] Not a mean sum, but the money had served a good purpose. At least 7,000 $1,000 bonds of the new first mortgage loan of the Chicago & Erie ended up in Dutch hands after the unpaid coupons, and the old seconds bought up by Oyens, were converted into new firsts.

Florida Railway & Navigation Company

Among the many victims of the 1884 crisis in America were two Florida railroads, both with unsavory reputations, in which the Dutch had a large stake. In 1884 the old Florida Railroad, then already part of the Florida Transit, and the Florida Central & Western had been merged by the British Reed consortium into the Florida Railway & Navigation Company. Both the old roads had sold bonds on the Dutch market, and these loans had been continued after the 1884 merger. Problems soon arose, and in 1885 the September coupon of the old Florida Transit loan could not be paid. Dutch bondholders, representing $500,000, decided to send Van Weel to America to check the books of the parent Railway & Navigation.[31] The next year the Railway & Navigation itself went under and was in receivership. Two Dutch committees were formed early in 1886: one for the Florida Transit bonds, and one for the Central & Western bonds, a clear indication that Dutch interest in both companies was still extensive.[32]

Receivership lasted until 1889, when the New York financier, W. Bayard Cutting, bought the Railway & Navigation at foreclosure and incorporated the Florida Central & Peninsular Railway Company. A new loan was issued in 1888 and the old bonds of the predecessor companies were exchanged for the new ones at par. Except for the unpaid coupons, bondholders did not lose much this time when compared to earlier reorganizations.

Missouri, Kansas & Texas

The second default of the Missouri, Kansas & Texas necessitated a new Dutch protective committee in 1887. For better protection of the interests of the Dutch bond- and shareholders, an association, the Nederlandsche Vereeniging, was formed to safeguard the rights of those interested in the MKT system. One year later a separate committee was set up for the old Union Pacific Southern Branch bonds and the earlier MKT sevens. (See Chapter 13 for more details on the MKT.) Heavyweights such as Wertheim, Van Nierop, and De Marez Oyens again figured conspicuously in both committees, but history repeated itself. This second reorganization of the Katy was not the last, and another default took place in 1915. Again, two Dutch protective committees were necessary to help clear up the mess.

Chicago & Grand Trunk

The Chicago & Grand Trunk had been set up in 1880 as a successor to the old, largely Dutch-owned Peninsular railroad. (See Chapter 9 for details on the Chicago & Grand Trunk.) Wertheim and Gompertz had been instrumental in this incorporation, and they also recommended a later reduction of the interest on the road's income bonds from 7 to 5 percent. Even this reduction, however, could not save the Chicago & Grand Trunk from receivership in 1890, as the bonded debt was still much too large for the relatively small road. A reorganization was necessary, which took time. Only in 1899 were plans formulated for a conversion: a new first mortgage loan and new second mortgage income bonds were to be created. The existing seconds were to be converted into the new seconds at only 25 percent of par, thus wiping out three-quarters of the original investment.

Naturally, the Dutch bondholders balked at the idea and, as usual, a protective committee was formed, with some financial experts among the members: Van Ogtrop, De Gijselaar, Luden, and Piek, all experienced in American railroad finance. At the first meeting of the committee 830 bonds were represented, while many others could not be reached in time.[33] Despite strong opposition on the home front, the plan was approved, because the committee saw all too clearly that only a substantial reduction of the debt could bring some semblance of prosperity to the old Chicago & Grand Trunk. A new company, the Grand Trunk Western, was incorporated in 1900, and the proposed new loans were duly issued and introduced in Amsterdam. The Dutch bondholders had to swallow severe losses. It was evident that even a strong protective committee could not turn a company burdened by too heavy a debt into a prosperous enterprise overnight.

■ *The 1890's*

Chicago Great Western

In 1890 another Midwestern railroad, the Chicago Great Western, a road with strong British influence, ran into difficulties. Hope and Company had introduced its bonds in 1887, when it was still called the Chicago, St. Paul & Kansas City.[34] A scheme was worked out whereby unpaid coupons were converted into a priority (sterling) loan, and the Dutch holders assented.[35] Success was still elusive, however, and the railroad sank deeper and deeper into debt. A. B. Stickney, the road's president, was closely acquainted with Charles W. Benson, a St. Paul financier, and through Benson a reorganization scheme was drawn up in cooperation with his family firm, Robert Benson and Company of London. A London committee took care of the details; J. G. Sillem, of Hope and Company, was the Dutch member.[36]

A typical British solution was found in which no new bonds were to be issued but only stock, both common and preferred, and debentures carrying 4-percent interest. In England, debentures were a common way of raising capital for railways, but they were practically unknown elsewhere. They represented a general lien on the railroad, sometimes paying a fixed interest, but in this case they more closely resembled income bonds: when revenues were not enough to pay the 4-percent interest, the debenture holders were not entitled to anything. A new Chicago Great Western Railway was incorporated in January 1893, and took over all properties of the old CStP&KC. Owners of the old bonds did suffer a considerable loss on this deal, because a dividend was paid on the preferreds only between 1899 and 1907, and reached the promised 5 percent in only five of those years. Yet the bondholders had little choice, and most accepted. Times were bad after 1893, with numerous railroads in the hands of receivers; it was a miracle that the Chicago Great Western survived at all.

East Tennessee, Virginia & Georgia

The general economic crisis of 1893 caused many railroad bankruptcies, but even before that year one company was already plunged into receivership through overexpansion, internal struggles, and mismanagement. The East Tennessee, Virginia & Georgia had been reorganized in 1885 after an earlier receivership. The Scot Robert Fleming had played a conspicuous role in helping the company regain its viability then; one year later the Richmond Terminal Railroad had acquired a controlling interest in the ETV&G.[37] Although the problems besetting the East Tennessee must have been common knowledge and should have made investors wary, its extension bonds were introduced in Amsterdam by Hijmans and Sons in 1888. Two years later, when the road was already in serious trouble, Jos. Thors offered another part of the same loan.[38] They should have known better. An independent report by the New York banker F. J. Lisman had brought to light many irregularities in the financial management and bookkeeping. Dividends had been paid not out of earnings but out of capital; an already enormous floating debt had been allowed to mushroom, and the financial structure of the system was so complicated that no real insight could ever be obtained. This report was published in the *New York Herald* of 8 August 1891 and struck the American financial community like a bolt of lightning. It must have been known in Holland very soon.

Attempts at reorganization were of no avail. In 1892 the whole system was in the hands of receivers and payment of interest stopped. A Dutch bondholders' protective committee was formed, again with Wertheim and De Marez Oyens as members. Bondholders were invited to deposit their bonds in exchange for certificates, and at the first meeting on 26 January 1893, a total of $616,000 of the ETV&G bonds was represented. A. Palache had $96,000 in proxies, Ad. Boissevain $87,000, and H. J. Huffers $105,000.[39]

As part of the impending reorganization, the extension bonds of the East Tennessee could be exchanged dollar for dollar for general mortgage bonds of the same company. By the middle of 1893 $996,000 worth of Dutch-held bonds had thus been converted into general mortgage bonds.[40] So far so good, but the plan finally presented by Drexel, Morgan and Company caused some alarm. Under this plan every old $1,000 bond was to be converted into $250 worth of new 5-percent bonds, plus $800 in preferred stock.[41] Yields would thus be reduced to one-fourth, as the preferred stock was at best only a source of revenue in the remote future. The Dutch committee requested a mandate to protest against the Morgan plans, but when it became known that the New York bondholders' committee had been dissolved because of internal strife, Wertheim gave the Dutch a very slim chance to protest the plan effectively on their own. When news came through that the majority of the American bondholders had assented to the Drexel plan, Wertheim strongly advised the Dutch bondholders to do likewise.[42] His advice was followed because the Dutch interest was relatively small. Of course, a million dollars was a sizable sum at that time, but of the $140 million worth of new bonds of the newly created Southern Railway the Dutch contribution was only a tiny drop in a vast ocean of new securities.

Not surprisingly, the year of crisis, 1893, saw the formation of several Dutch protective committees: one for the Western New York & Pennsylvania; one for the Atlantic & Pacific; one for the St. Louis & San Francisco; one for the Union Pacific; and two for the Atchison, Topeka & Santa Fe. One year later, as a kind of afterthought, a committee for the Oregon Short Line & Utah Northern was organized as well. In view of the very large Dutch investment in Union Pacific (par value of at least $14 million plus shares) and Atchison (par value of at least $39 million plus shares), formal Dutch associations were set up to keep the Dutch interest in one hand. For the Oregon Short Line securities ($1.2 million) a separate Dutch association was set up for legal reasons, which was almost a replica of the UP association. Van Ogtrop was chairman of all three. Dutchmen were members of the international reorganization committees for the three roads as well: A. A. H. Boissevain for the UP and OSL, J. Luden for the Atchison.

Western New York & Pennsylvania

The Western New York & Pennsylvania was one of those American roads, of which there have been all too many, with a dismal financial record. In an earlier incarnation as the Buffalo, New York & Philadelphia it had already caused substantial losses to its security holders, mostly German and Dutch. In Holland both common and preferred shares and bonds had been circulating, marketed by Hubrecht and Alsberg, Goldberg. On the incorporation of the WNY&P in 1887 the old bonds had been converted into second mortgage bonds at a considerable loss to the owners. Yet a new issue of firsts was sold by Oyens and Sons in Amsterdam in 1887. The crisis of 1893 caused earnings of the WNY&P to drop so low that even the 3-percent interest on the seconds could not be paid, although the firsts were not yet affected. A Dutch committee was formed, with Piek, Van Nierop (Amsterdamsche Bank) and Van Oosterwijk Bruyn (Kerkhoven and Company) among the members. At its first meeting 433 bonds ($433,000 par value) were represented.[43] This cannot have been all, however, for a protective committee would never have been needed for such a small holding. The committee, in a letter to the owners, explained that Germans had a large share in the seconds too, but only together with the Dutch could the Germans ever be able to establish a majority. A plan for reorganization had been proposed by C. E. Bretherton (London) and Carl Jaeger (Frankfurt), but the board of the Dutch WNY&P Association (incorporated on 15 September 1893), which had taken over from the committee, did not agree. The bondholders in his case, however, did not support their board and the association was dissolved early in 1894. Most Dutch owners then deposited their bonds with the Amsterdamsche Bank in exchange for trust receipts.

According to the English-German reorganization plan of 1 December 1893, the firsts would remain undisturbed. The $20 million in seconds was to be converted into $10 million of new fixed interest bonds, at 2 percent until 1897, 3 percent for the following four years, and 4 percent after 1901. Moreover, they got 25 percent of their old holdings in income bonds, plus 25 percent in negotiable trust certificates. The latter two types of securities would probably never bring in any revenue, so the holders of the second mortgage had to be content with a reduction by half of their holdings, but with a somewhat better prospect of regular payment of interest. Shareholders could exchange their commons for new commons plus new income bonds, after paying an assessment of $7 per $200 par value; refusal to pay the assessment would mean loss of rights.[44] The Amsterdamsche Bank executed the conversion in June 1895, after the new Western New York & Pennsylvania Railway had been incorporated. The 2- to 4-percent general mortgage, the income bonds, and the common certificates were all included in the price lists in Amsterdam, while the undisturbed firsts of 1887 were continued. In 1905 the Pennsylvania bought up all outstanding shares and income bonds, thus relieving the Dutch of their unwanted holdings, which had never given much revenue.[45]

Atlantic & Pacific

While the Dutch investment in the WNY&P was relatively unimportant, participation in the Atlantic & Pacific was much greater. The Western Division of that road (Albuquerque, New Mexico, to Needles, California) was constructed with the help of the Santa Fe, which guaranteed the A&P loans until its own receivership in 1893; all payment of interest then ended. A Dutch bondholders' protective committee was formed; at a first meeting in January 1894, 1,291 bonds were represented. By the end of that year a total of $4,364,000 had been deposited with the committee. In Germany

$5,140,000 had been turned in, and this, combined with some $1,000,000 in New York, made up a large majority of the loan. Still, some Dutch-owned bonds were not yet accounted for.[46]

Closely cooperating, the German, Dutch, and American committees now set about to save the investment. It was clear that the Atlantic & Pacific formed a vital western connection to the Santa Fe, and they consequently first tried to sell out to that road. The Santa Fe offered to buy the $16 million worth of bonds for 35 percent in new ATSF bonds plus 50 percent in preferred shares, but this was refused indignantly. The bid was next raised to 45 percent in bonds and 55 in preferred stock, but this too was considered too low. For a time the committee even toyed with the idea of remaining independent and continuing the Atlantic & Pacific as a separate company, cooperating with the Santa Fe if possible or, if necessary, building a connecting line across Kansas and Missouri. Because of the expense involved, the latter idea was soon dropped, and one more attempt was made to get better terms from the ATSF. That road, now again on its feet after emerging from receivership, did indeed raise its bid somewhat to 52.5 percent ($8,400,000) in 4-percent bonds and 57.5 percent ($9,200,000) in preferred shares. Reluctantly the three committees accepted. The Santa Fe, moreover, agreed to pay off the floating debt of the A&P plus the expenses of the committees. Each $1,000 A&P bond was exchanged for $446.95 in ATSF bonds and $489.51 in preferreds.[47]

A smaller number of the A&P Central Division (Seneca-Sapulpa, Indian Territory) bonds (worth $2,794,000) was also held in Holland, but these were kept out of the deal with the Santa Fe. Obviously the newly reorganized St. Louis & San Francisco would be more interested in this property, and the Dutch committee managed to sell the bonds to the StL&SF for $300,000 in cash and $1,500,000 in StL&SF bonds; the bondholders reluctantly accepted. Each old bond was paid off with $70 in gold plus the new bonds.[48]

Thus ended the troubled story of the Atlantic & Pacific, a railroad of great expectations and great hopes but disappointing in both traffic and financial rewards. Dutch capitalists had sunk large sums in the road and in the end the protective committee, by closely collaborating with the Germans, managed to recover most of it, although at much reduced rates of interest.

St. Louis & San Francisco

The St. Louis & San Francisco, already mentioned above, had been taken over by the Santa Fe in 1890. With the default of that company in 1893, the "Frisco" was dragged down too; in December of that year receivers were appointed. What had become the expected Dutch bondholders' protective committee was organized, with Sigmund Alsberg, of Alsberg, Goldberg, among the members.[49] An inventory was made of the Dutch holdings in the several StL&SF securities outstanding: of the original bonds only some $100,000 was represented at the first meeting. The 1890 StL&SF consols, guaranteed by the Santa Fe, formed a clear majority: 510 bonds (of $500 or $1,000) were represented, giving a total of between $225,000 and $510,000.[50]

As junior securities, these consols were usually the most threatened in any reorganization. The Santa Fe guarantee had lost its value after that road entered receivership, and because it was reported that the Germans were already organizing themselves for other Frisco bonds, quick action on the part of the Dutch was urgent. In March 1894 an association, the Nederlandsche Vereeniging ter behartiging van de belangen van houders der 4% StL&SF geconsolideerde hypotheek obligatiën (Netherlands association to protect the interests of holders of 4-percent consols) was formed and certificates were issued.[51]

Pending its own reorganization, the Santa Fe had always kept open the option of acquiring the Frisco again, but at the end of 1895 it was finally decided not to include that road in the new ATSF system.[52] The several committees and the Netherlands Association, represented in New York by Sigmund Alsberg, who went over to America as member of the official reorganization scheme early in 1896, now hammered out a compromise. A new St. Louis & San Francisco Railroad was chartered in June 1896, which took over the property of the old railway.[53]

All old Frisco securities were initially to be left undisturbed, but as this would not reduce the new railroad's fixed charges enough, it was finally decided to exclude the 1890 consols, of which some $11,490,000 were outstanding, and convert them into new second preferred and common stock. The new securities were temporarily marketed in "blocks" (which held one of each of the following: common, first and second preferreds, and 4-percent consols), and Dutch interest in these blocks was great; they were at once included in the price lists in Amsterdam. A new Dutch association now replaced the old: the Nederlandsche Vereeniging van Aandeelhouders in de StL&SF RR Cy. (Netherlands StL&SF Shareholders Association), and the new shares were made out in the name of this association.[54] Out of 2,968 certificates for old Frisco consols, 2,131 were exchanged and the rest were unaccounted for, while a total of 2,901 blocks of the new securities were issued to Dutch owners, which meant a sizable Dutch share in the new company's capital structure.[55] The outcome of this reorganization was rather favorable, again thanks to an active protective committee. Yet, as a result of becoming an object of speculation after a takeover by the Rock Island, the Frisco was to crash again in 1913.

Chesapeake, Ohio & Southwestern

At the same time as the collapse of the Frisco, Collis P. Huntington's Chesapeake, Ohio & Southwestern, successor to the two unfortunate "Dutch" roads (the Paducah, Memphis & Northern and the Paducah & Elizabethtown), fell on hard times. Wertheim and Gompertz called a bondholders' meeting in February 1894. It turned out that first mortgage bonds worth between $3.5 and $4 million were in Dutch hands; the second mortgage bonds and the stock had meanwhile been bought up by the Illinois Central.[56] Wertheim smelled a rat, however, and he thought that it would not be wise to give up a first mortgage that had 17 more years before it was to be paid off on a property that seemed eminently suitable to pay the 6-percent interest. He thought that the nonpayment of the February 1894 coupon was a trick to force the road into receivership and consequently bring foreclosure on the mortgage in an attempt to make the Dutch sell out at a rockbottom price to the Illinois Central. A protective committee was set up, with

Wertheim and Luden among the members. Although the defaulted February coupon was indeed paid after all, it was not cashed by the committee, but reserved for future expenses.[57] The outcome is not clear, but the Illinois Central did buy the road in 1896, after three years of lawsuits and other entanglements, and the Dutch fared not too badly.

Norfolk & Western

The Norfolk & Western, successor to the old Atlantic, Mississippi & Ohio, had developed into a well-run and financially stable company, but the general crisis of 1893, combined with miners' strikes and other reverses, brought the road to the hands of receivers in 1895. An international committee was appointed to reorganize the property, with A. A. H. Boissevain as the Dutch member. A separate Dutch protective committee was also set up, chaired by Van Nierop, and with G. Vissering, who had just been appointed as secretary of the Stock Exchange Association, as secretary.[58] In close cooperation with similar committees in London and New York, the committee worked out a deal: old bonds were converted into new consolidated mortgage bonds at 62.5 percent of par, plus 75 percent in new preferred shares. This was not a bad arrangement at all, although the revenue went down considerably for a time, until the preferreds started paying a dividend in 1898. A large number of common and preferred shares came into Dutch hands as a result of the conversion, and a Dutch association was set up to keep the shares in one hand; the association issued certificates in return for the shares, as usual. In 1933 the association still held almost $200,000 of N&W prefs.[59]

■ After 1900

The several protective committees set up after the default of the Kansas City, Pittsburg & Gulf and its associated railroads in 1899 need little attention here, as they will be covered in more detail in Chapter 14. The same applies to the Oklahoma Central, which defaulted in 1908 and for which a Dutch committee was set up as well; this committee will be covered in Chapter 10.

Chicago & Milwaukee Electric

The only Dutch protective committee for an American electric interurban railroad was organized in 1908. Bonds of the Chicago & Milwaukee Electric Railroad worth about $1.6 million had been sold by several Dutch brokers, including S. F. van Oss and Oppenheim and Van Till, both of The Hague. Despite personal attention of some Dutch bankers and brokers, only about two-thirds of the original investment could be saved when the railroad defaulted, and it took three years to do so.[60]

Chicago, Rock Island & Pacific

At the very end of our period several big American railroads collapsed, causing much alarm to stock- and bondholders, including the Dutch. In the nineteenth century the

Chicago, Rock Island & Pacific had been a solid, profitable company, and its stock and bonds commanded high prices in Amsterdam. In 1902 the road was taken over by the Reid-Moore syndicate. From that year on expansion took place at a breakneck speed, and financial mismanagement and outright fraud became the order of the day, until the whole structure came crashing down in March 1914. The Dutch were caught with at least $8.5 million in collateral bonds (12 percent of the total outstanding) on their hands, plus some other securities including stock; a protective committee was set up.[61] At the railroad's reorganization, which took many years, bondholders had to swallow several losses, while shareholders were virtually wiped out.

Missouri Pacific

The Missouri Pacific, part of the Gould system, went under in 1915 as a result of the severe drain on the company's coffers when it tried to keep the ailing Western Pacific and the equally fragile Denver & Rio Grande afloat. Two Dutch protective committees were set up, one for the 5-percent bonds and another for the fours. At least $6,376,000 of the latter had been sold in Holland, with some $1 million of the fives, and possibly much more.[62]

The Western Pacific itself had already defaulted in March 1914, and as the Dutch held at least $3.2 million worth (6.5 percent of the total) of its bonds, a committee was formed immediately. An international reorganization committee was also set up in 1915, in which a Dutchman had a seat together with American interests.[63] Despite this representation, bondholders had to accept a large loss at the reorganization of 1916.

Chesapeake & Ohio

The railroad reorganizations described until now have made clear that in cases where Amsterdam had a large investment at stake, a Dutch protective committee or an association was usually set up. But now and then it happened that even when a great deal of Dutch capital was involved no separate committee was formed. An example of the absence of a Dutch committee, despite important holdings, is presented by the Chesapeake & Ohio in 1887. This road was one of Collis P. Huntington's eastern railroads, united under his holding company, the Newport News & Mississippi Valley Railroad. This holding company crashed in 1887 and with it the Chesapeake & Ohio, which then entered receivership. It was proposed to reduce the interest of all outstanding C&O loans from 6 to 4 percent; in Amsterdam a meeting was called to unite the Dutch bondholders. At least $746,000 in bonds was represented there on 29 September 1887, but no common stand on the proposal could be reached.[64] In the end the holders of Dutch bonds worth $1.2 million (par value) assented to the reduction of interest, and $600,000 did not. Both parties deposited their bonds with Broekman and Honders, who took care of the transfer to America.[65]

J. P. Morgan, meanwhile, carried out the reorganization. Huntington was bought out and the C&O emerged again in 1888. The old first mortgage holders came out best: every old bond of $1,000 was converted into $666 worth of new bonds, plus $333 in new preferred shares. Broekman and Honders and Gebr. Teixeira de Mattos were authorized by Drexel, Morgan and Company to execute the conversion for Dutch owners.[66] So, despite the absence of a Dutch committee, the bondholders in Holland came out well.

Another example of a railroad in default for which a separate committee was not deemed necessary will be mentioned in passing only. After the Erie (then operating under the name of New York, Lake Erie & Western) went bankrupt for the third time in 1893, final reorganization of the road was undertaken by the houses of Drexel, Morgan and Company of New York and J. S. Morgan and Company of London. Although Dutch interests were involved to a certain extent, Morgan explicitly dissuaded them from establishing a protective committee of their own, because he felt not enough European, non-British capital was involved.[67]

Wisconsin, Minnesota & Pacific

In 1912 there was some talk in Amsterdam of setting up a committee for the Wisconsin, Minnesota & Pacific, a railroad bought by the Chicago Great Western in 1901, but which had issued a loan under its original charter just before the purchase in 1900. Some bonds had been sold in 1905 in Amsterdam by Van der Werff and Hubrecht, but most had been marketed in London, where the CGW had always found a willing market.[68] The parent road stopped payment of interest on the WM&P bonds in 1912, and a London committee was constituted. After some consideration, it was not thought worthwhile to do the same in Amsterdam. Gebr. Boissevain then offered to deposit Dutch-held bonds with the London committee in exchange for certificates. In the end the CGW agreed to buy out the bondholders for $500 in CGW bonds plus the same in preferred shares for every old WM&P $1,000 bond, plus $123.74 in cash for unpaid coupons.[69] This was a most reasonable result, but was reached without much pressure from Amsterdam. Dutch holdings were too small to exert influence.

In retrospect the activities of Dutch protective committees were generally beneficial to the bondholders, although in some cases the railroad in question was so rotten that little or nothing could be saved. In almost every case the personal presence of a member of the protective committee was necessary, and such men as De Marez Oyens, Piek, and Van Weel, to name but three, sailed the Atlantic many times to inspect railroads and to confer with other interested parties, generally with some measure of success. Back in Amsterdam such bankers as Wertheim and Van Nierop did their best to unite the Dutch bondholders in order to make a strong stand against American parties and other European victims at the same time. Now and then the results of their exertions were disappointing, as has been noted above. In most cases, however, their attempts to solidify the bondholders were successful, and the financial results were often the best that could be obtained, and were sometimes even better than had been hoped for.

Nine

The Dutch in Control

Unlike the English, the Dutch never intentionally tried to gain complete control of an American railroad in which they invested. Whenever the financial participation from Amsterdam warranted it, Dutch investors wanted to be represented on the board to protect their interests, but they never concerned themselves with the actual operation of the railroad. Though cases such as the Alabama Great Southern, which was owned by British interests and operated by British managers, may have been more the exception than the rule, English and Scottish engineers and managers were numerous on those roads where the British financial interest was great. In contrast, Dutchmen in leading positions on U.S. railroads were few, even in cases where considerable Dutch financial interests were at stake.

Control usually was exercised through stock ownership, when a majority of the shares was owned by one person or at least represented by a single party. But possession of a majority of a company's stock did not always bring control. In the case of the New York, Ontario & Western, the majority of the common shares was held in London and Amsterdam, but actual control was only exercised through the preferred shares, held solely by Americans. As a condition for pumping more money into the road by means of a new bond loan, the British and Dutch shareholders in 1886 gained full voting power and could then appoint their directors to the board. Only then could they execute their pet project, the Scranton branch, which soon became the main source of revenue for the chronically ailing NYO&W.[1]

One other way of gaining control was possible, which was when a railroad in receivership was given over to the bondholders by court order. The bondholders generally were the only ones who had invested some real money, because stock was hardly ever paid in full. A judge could allot such a road, after it defaulted on the payment of interest, to the bondholders. This happened several times to railroads where the Dutch held the majority of the bonds outstanding, and in this way they gained full ownership.

When the Dutch held a substantial number of shares, they were generally content to have one or more seats on the board of the railroad in question. In this they did not differ materially from other European parties. They sometimes teamed up with British or German interests, and more often than not they appointed Americans or Englishmen to represent their interests. This made sense given the geographical distances and modes of transportation involved. H. W. Smithers, an English native living in Louisville, Kentucky, is one of the foreign names that is found again and again as a director, receiver, or member of a protective committeee, always representing the interests of the Dutch. Another was Louis H. Meyer, of German extraction but living in America, who was a director of the Pittsburgh, Fort Wayne & Chicago and who often acted for the Dutch as well. W. F. Whitehouse, a New York banker, represented the Dutch in the Louisville & Nashville in the 1880's, and Eckstein Norton, a New York cotton merchant, was even made president of that road in 1886 at the explicit behest of the Dutch shareholders.[2]

Anthony G. Dulman was a banker, merchant, and partner in the house of Dulman and Scharff of New York. He was of Dutch extraction and, as his business ties seem to have been mostly with the Netherlands, he was seen as an eminently suitable person to represent Dutch interests. So we find him on the board of the Illinois Central as representative of the 26-percent Dutch ownership in the 1880's, on the Chicago & North Western board from 1869 to 1890, on the boards of the Rock Island, the Missouri, Kansas & Texas, the Canada Southern, the New York, Pennsylvania & Ohio (formerly the Atlantic & Great Western), the Cleveland, Columbus, Cincinnati & Indianapolis, and others.

Besides these pseudo-Dutchmen, Dutch natives also figured as directors of several American railroads. J. L. ten Have, of the Amsterdam brokers Ten Have and Van Essen, had a seat beside Dulman on the Chicago & North Western board (1869–1879), reflecting the great Dutch interest in that road. F. A. Müller, a director of the Rotterdamsche Bank, was a director of the Chicago, Milwaukee & St. Paul from 1872 to 1879. H. J. de Marez Oyens, of the Amsterdam brokers H. Oijens and Sons, was not only active in many Dutch protective committees, but was also a director of the Missouri, Kansas & Texas, again with Dulman, at least until 1908.

In a few isolated cases Dutch control went further than just having one or more members on the board. Now and then, generally unintentionally and through circumstances beyond their control, the Dutch bankers ended up in complete control of a road. Although they sometimes seem to have toyed with the idea of running the road themselves, practical problems of operating a railroad in a distant foreign country soon caused them to look for a suitable buyer or lessee instead. A few of these cases will now be described, to better judge the different ways the Dutch bankers set about to get the best deal for their customers, the investors.

■ Denver Pacific

One of the roads that came under Dutch control accidentally was the Denver Pacific Railway and Telegraph Company, which in 1870 opened a line from Denver to Cheyenne, which was on the Union Pacific's main line. Closely cooperating with the Kansas Pacific, finished into Denver some months later, the 108-mile Denver Pacific was at once an important feeder to the Union Pacific and, together with the Kansas Pacific, a possible dangerous competitor.[3]

A first mortgage bond issue of $2.5 million had been authorized in 1869, with coupons payable in dollars and sterling, of which $1 million had already been sold in America, while the rest was offered in 1870 in London by Huggins and Rowsall, in Amsterdam by Holjé and Boissevain, and in Rotterdam by A. J. and M. Milders. A first price was not specified, but in 1870 these bonds were quoted in Amsterdam between 61 and 80 percent of par.[4]

A related issue, sold in Amsterdam in the next year, was the first mortgage loan of the Denver & Boulder Valley Railway, a branch of the Denver Pacific, which later guaranteed the interest. Coupons were payable in dollars, sterling, or German reichsmark. Wertheim and Gompertz sold 300 bonds of $1,000 in Amsterdam at a first price of 75 percent of par. In 1871 they offered 250 more of the same at the same price.[5] As the total issue had meanwhile been reduced in America to $550,000, we see that this whole loan was sold exclusively in Holland.

In 1877 a competing line, under strong Union Pacific influence, was opened between Denver and Hazard, just west of Cheyenne. Traffic on the Denver Pacific fell off immediately; the May 1878 coupon could not be paid. In March of 1877, however, even before that ominous news, the Dutch interests had been called together. At this meeting it was rumored that the Kansas Pacific, which had acquired the common stock of the Denver Pacific and more or less guaranteed the interest on its bonds, would be unable to pay the next coupons due. It was stated that of the total $2,310,000 worth of DP bonds, more than $2,000,000 had been sold in Holland. A protective committee was formed, with A. C. Wertheim and J. L. ten Have among the original members and W. F. Piek joining later. One of the original trustees of the loan had died in the meantime, and the committee named Anthony G. Dulman as his successor. It also decided to take care of the interests of the owners of Boulder Valley bonds at the same time.[6]

It took some time before the Dutch bondholders deposited their bonds, but by mid-April 1877 more than half of both Denver and Boulder Valley bonds were in the hands of the committee.[7] The same receivers had been appointed for both the Denver Pacific and Kansas Pacific, but early in 1878, at the request of trustees Dulman and John Evans, former governor of Colorado Territory, separate receivers were appointed for the Denver road. The receivers took care that its revenues would not leak away to the Kansas Pacific, which had by then fallen into the hands of Jay Gould.[8]

Dulman and Evans next requested the court to place the road in their hands as trustees for the bondholders, but their authority was disputed in the Denver courts by the stockholders, mostly Kansas Pacific men, for whom Carlos S. Greeley, closely connected with Jay Gould, was acting. Piek hurried off to New York in 1878 to confer with Dulman and then took the train to Denver with a suitcase full of Dutch bonds to prove that he indeed represented the majority. He was well aware of the fact that even if the court granted the trustees' demand, the Dutch bondholders would be saddled with a railroad in sorry shape, requiring much additional capital to bring it back to some form of prosperity, capital that they were probably unwilling to contribute.

The court postponed a decision and during this delay Piek returned to Holland to explain the situation. He argued that it would be better to sell out to American parties when a satisfactory price could be obtained, because "they [the bonds] could be of some value when in the hands of rich and influential Americans, a value which they could never have for Europeans without any inclination for cooperation and without willingness to put up the required monies."[9] He must have been thinking of Jay Gould of the Union Pacific, but mentioned no names.

Apparently Piek managed to make these thoughts agreeable to his backers, and toward the end of that year the committee was authorized to sell the Denver Pacific and Boulder Valley bonds if a good price could be obtained.[10] Piek returned to the United States to press the lawsuit, and with success, for on 10 July 1879 the U.S. Circuit Court in Denver decided to place the railroad in the hands of the bondholders as of 1 August of that year. Greeley immediately appealed the decision to the U.S. Supreme Court and threatened to build a road parallel to the Denver Pacific, depriving the "Dutch" road of all traffic.

In the middle of this stalemate, a mediation offer made by a certain Mr. Vis, a Dutchman acting as secretary for Jay Gould, came as a godsend. Gould, who was in Paris in the summer of 1879, sent Vis to Amsterdam to soften up the Dutch and make a first offer. He was told that the Denver Pacific and Boulder Valley bonds could only be sold together, and that the asking price was par. This was a stiff price, as Denvers were being quoted as low as 40 percent of par, with the Boulder Valleys even lower; of course, when news of the negotiations leaked out, prices rallied to over 70 percent of par. But Gould was in a hurry, and he wanted the Denver road badly to avoid costly new construction and endless litigation. He came over to Amsterdam in person with an offer for 50 percent of par on the Denver bonds and 40 for the Boulder Valleys. The Dutch, headed by A. C. Wertheim, refused. Gould next raised his bid to 60 and 50 percent respectively, but still Wertheim held out. New negotiations brought a compromise: 74 percent for the Denver Pacific and 57 for the Boulder Valley, more than the Dutch committee had ever hoped for or expected. All lawsuits pending were dropped immediately.[11]

Gould's later retelling of his dealings in Amsterdam sounds a little bit too simple: "I supposed they [the Dutch] would take a day or two smoking before they would make up their minds . . . and it would take more time than I had. Finally I went over there and saw them. I got in there in the morning at 10 o'clock and washed and got my breakfast, and let them know that I was there, and they met me at 11 o'clock, and at 12 o'clock I bought them out and paid them."[12] He forgets to mention that he had sent his secretary first to sound out the Dutch bankers, and that he had to raise his offer twice!

Gould paid $1,045,620 for 1,413 Denver Pacific bonds and $204,060 for 358 Boulder Valley bonds. This converts to Dfl 1,675 for every DP $1,000 and Dfl 1,250 for each BV bond. At the final closing of the accounts in 1880 an extra Dfl 107.20 was paid for every old bond.[13] Complaints were heard about the high expense account of the committee, but these differences were smoothed over.[14] After all, Piek had traveled to America twice and Ten Have at least once, and the costs of the legal procedures must have been high as well. The favorable outcome of the sale silenced most of the opposition.

▪ *Cairo & St. Louis*

A second case of accidental Dutch ownership is presented by a narrow-gauge line in rural southern Illinois, the Cairo & St. Louis. This line, one of the most successful of the narrow-gauge roads, was 146 miles long and passed through mostly easy terrain, with some difficult stretches on the southern half. It had been chartered in 1865 as a standard-gauge line, but when finance proved to be a stumbling block, its backers changed to the 3-foot gauge to reduce construction costs. Only in 1871 was actual work begun. By then the narrow-gauge movement had gained momentum and the Cairo & St. Louis was envisaged as part of the Grand Narrow Gauge Trunk, which was projected to run from Toledo, Ohio, all the way down through Arkansas to the Gulf of Mexico.[15] Although this Grand Trunk never operated as such, the Cairo & St. Louis indeed operated for a number of years.

The capital necessary for construction came from Amsterdam. A first mortgage loan of $2.5 million was issued in 1871 and marketed by Wertheim and Gompertz and F. W. Oewel early in 1872 at 81 percent of par. Interest was payable in New York, London, Amsterdam, and Cologne, but there is no indication that this loan was ever sold in England.[16] Apparently the portions of the loan that had been intended for other countries could not be marketed, and in September 1872 the remainder, another $1,180,000, was again offered by Wertheim and Gompertz.[17] The 1873 crisis caused the road to default on the April 1874 coupon; revenue had fallen disastrously, and although the floating debt was small, there was no money in the till for payment of interest.[18]

Construction of the line meanwhile had come to a standstill, and it was not until 1875 that a through service of sorts between East St. Louis and Cairo was at long last opened. The Dutch bondholders were represented on behalf of Oewel by the ubiquitous H. W. Smithers, who kept a close watch on revenues. These revenues turned out to be disappointing as a result of a multitude of causes: sloppy construction, strikes, and other mishaps. To make matters worse, part of the road's only tunnel, at Kaolin, collapsed in 1877, which effectively cut the line in two. J. Pik, the Dutch financial expert, then saw little hope for the unfortunate Dutch investors, who meanwhile had given a blank power of attorney to Oewel to represent their interests.[19] Prices of the bonds hit bottom at 10 percent of par in 1878.

Ferdinand Canda, a Chicago car builder and the road's largest shareholder, forced the Cairo & St. Louis into receivership in December 1877, and H. W. Smithers was appointed receiver. Smithers, still acting for the Dutch, now set about to make the Cairo & St. Louis a paying road again, and with some success. The tunnel was reopened late in 1877, and through service resumed. The entry into Cairo was also much improved, but for technical reasons it was impossible to lay a third rail (making the road compatible for narrow-gauge lines) on the Eads Bridge across the Mississippi at St. Louis. By 1881 the road was in the black again, and reorganization could be undertaken.

Wertheim and Gompertz and F. W. Oewel now set about to do their best for the Dutch bondholders. As usual, a protective committee was formed (in May of 1878) and bondholders were requested to deposit their bonds in exchange for certificates.[20] But not only bonds were in Dutch hands by that time; somehow stock had also been bought up. In 1880, out of a total of almost 50,000 shares, more than 15,000 were held in Holland. The largest Dutch owner, or representative of owners, was C. W. Schaap (Oewel's brother-in-law) with 9,567 shares, followed by Gebr. Boissevain with 2,360 and Gebr. Teixeira de Mattos with 1,650. Curiously enough, Wertheim and Gompertz and Oewel owned or represented only 125 shares each.[21] Early in 1881 the protective committee requested the deposition of all the bonds (by now exchanged for certificates) with the Associatie Cassa of Amsterdam, because a representative of the Illinois court was to arrive in Amsterdam to check the number of Dutch-held bonds to make sure that the Dutch indeed held the majority.[22]

A new company, the St. Louis & Cairo Railroad, was incorporated in June 1881. At the foreclosure sale of the old Cairo & St. Louis, W. F. Whitehouse of New York, who also represented Dutch bondholders in other roads such as the Louisville & Nashville, bought the property on behalf of the bondholders. Smithers, as receiver, could not legally bring out a bid, so Whitehouse had to be brought in. The new company was under strong Dutch influence from the start; Wertheim and Gompertz were authorized by the bondholders to continue their supervision over the road. The old 7-percent Cairo & St. Louis bonds were converted into 5-percent first mortgage income bonds, with the right to appoint a majority of the board if three-quarters of the old bondholders assented. In May 1882, 2,495 of the Dutch certificate owners had done so, while 1,163 were unaccounted for, and one owner dissented.[23] It is clear from these figures that the old loan of the Cairo & St. Louis had been held almost exclusively in Holland.

Almost all new income bonds ended up in Holland. The unpaid coupons since 1874 were converted into new common stock: $500 worth for every old $1,000 bond. Total share capital was set at $6.5 million, of which $3.8 million was held by Wertheim and Gompertz and issued to their customers in the form of certificates.[24] Not all of these Dutch holdings were acquired by way of compensation for the unpaid coupons. Only $1.25 million had to be used for these, while the rest of the Dutch shares were already in Dutch hands or were bought by Wertheim and Gompertz and later sold at prices of between 5 and 7 percent of par; no dividend was ever paid.

The St. Louis & Cairo now started on the second stage of its career in almost complete Dutch ownership: more than half of the stock was held in Holland, while nearly all the bonds outstanding were in Dutch hands. Wertheim and Gompertz, by now old hands at the American railroad game, clearly saw that a short line such as this could never be profitably run on its own, and certainly not under management from Amsterdam. They started looking around for a partner, and found the Mobile & Ohio interested in acquiring the St. Louis road as an extension of its own line, which would make it independent of the Illinois Central, which until now had provided the connections for the M&O north of Cairo. In 1885 an agreement was reached: the Mobile & Ohio would lease the St. Louis & Cairo for 45 years, for $165,000 annually, effective from 1 February 1886.

A new first mortgage loan was to be issued by the StL&C to the tune of $4 million. For every $1,000 in old income bonds plus $400 cash, $1,500 in new bonds would be issued. Wertheim strongly recommended the conversion, for the 5 percent on the old income bonds had been paid only once, in 1882, while prospects for a more regular payment of interest were certainly not bright. The new arrangement, although requiring a cash outlay, promised to be more profitable, because interest would be guaranteed by the Mobile & Ohio. Most owners went along with Wertheim and by mid-June of 1886 2,527 out of a total of 2,600 income bonds had been converted. The cash thus raised was used for the widening of the road to standard gauge and to make the connection with the M&O (which itself had been narrowed from its original 5-foot gauge to standard gauge the year before). At Cairo the Illinois Central bridge, then being built, was to give running rights.[25] By 1904 most of the original shares still in Dutch hands had been converted into new Mobile & Ohio bonds, $3,000 in stock for $1,000 in bonds; not a bad deal, as no dividend had ever been paid on the stock.

By prudent management and stubborn tenacity Oewel and Wertheim and Gompertz had managed to save a sizable Dutch investment from being completely wiped out. Their solution, a lease of their road to a stronger neighbor, worked out very well for all parties concerned.

■ *Peninsular Railway*

At about the same time, Wertheim and Gompertz also had to act for a third victim of overoptimism, the Peninsular Railway of Michigan. This road was the result of an 1869 merger of several earlier lines, and had issued two loans in 1870 and 1871. A $700,000 first mortgage loan for the Indiana section was sold in Amsterdam only, while the majority of a first mortgage loan for the Michigan section of $1.8 million was marketed there.[26]

As so often happened, high hopes were soon dashed when the Peninsular, even before the crisis of 1873, proved to be unable to pay the June 1872 coupon of both loans. Already in March of that year alarming rumors had spread that the road was in trouble.[27] Wertheim and Gompertz, who had not been responsible for the original marketing in Amsterdam, created a committee then to exchange the bonds for certificates, but could do little more.[28]

After June the Dutch bondholders responded quickly and deposited their bonds with the committee. Of the Michigan section loan of $1.8 million, $1,414,000 worth was in the hands of Wertheim and Gompertz by the end of 1878, indicating the overwhelming preponderance of the Dutch in this loan. Of the 700 bonds of the Indiana section loan, 594 bonds had been exchanged by the end of 1878. Wertheim forwarded the bonds to America to be exchanged for new securities.[29]

The Peninsular Railway was sold at foreclosure to H. W. Smithers, again acting for the Dutch, for a sum of $500,000. After payment of the preferred creditors, nothing was left for the small number of bondholders who had not taken part in the reorganization. Smithers next charged the Grand Trunk with the operation of the line, and an arrangement with the old bondholders, now owners of the line, had to be worked out.[30] The results turned out to be fairly satisfactory after all. Every $1,000 bond of the old Michigan section was converted into $1,000 worth of second mortgage income bonds of the Chicago & Grand Trunk Railway Company, while each $1,000 bond of the old Indiana section was good for $500 worth of the same. The difference was caused by the debt per mile of the old Peninsular: the Michigan section was burdened with only $16,500 per mile, while the Indiana section struggled under more than twice that sum. Bondholders had to pay Dfl 58 or 29 per bond toward the cost of conversion. The Chicago & Grand Trunk issued $4 million of these second mortgage income bonds, and Smithers was one of the trustees of the loan. He and his colleagues also had full authority over all expenditure of the company. A first mortgage loan of $6 million was created at the same time to finish and upgrade the road and to buy much-needed rolling stock. Dutch interest in this loan was only slight, as far as can be ascertained. Taken all together, the arrangement as worked out by Smithers and Wertheim was judged by all parties to be the best that could be obtained for the bondholders.[31] The new income bonds were included in the Amsterdam price lists in November 1881, replacing the old securities.[32]

Again Wertheim and Gompertz had managed to save a substantial part of the original Dutch investment, but they could hardly have foreseen that the Chicago & Grand Trunk would run into grave trouble right from the start. A conversion to lower-interest-bearing securities was necessary, but even this was not enough to save the road from receivership in 1890. A second reorganization had to be carried out, and this took some time. After a severe reduction of the debt, in which the Dutch bondholders lost 75 percent (nominal value) of their original investment, a new Grand Trunk Western finally steamed to some prosperity, which lasted until the end of World War II.

■ Kansas & Missouri Bridge

A fourth example of Dutch ownership ended with less success than any of the others. Closely connected with the Chicago & South Western (which was itself under control of the Rock Island), the Kansas & Missouri Bridge Company was incorporated in 1869 to build a bridge across the Missouri at Leavenworth, Kansas. Leavenworth was slowly losing its race for preeminence with Kansas City, which already had a railroad bridge over the river.[33] The bridge company was locally sponsored and only unofficially aided by the Rock Island, but the bridge itself was not completed until the end of 1870, too late in fact for the ceremonial "opening" of the Rock Island's line from Chicago to Leavenworth in September of that year. The special excursion train, carrying among other guests President Ulysses S. Grant and his wife, could not go further than Stillings Junction, just across the river from Leavenworth.

A first mortgage loan was floated on the Dutch market in July 1871 by the Rotterdamsche Bank and the Associatie Cassa of Amsterdam. The loan of $600,000 was offered only in Holland, at 82.75 percent of par, and interest was guaranteed by the Chicago & South Western but not by the Rock Island.[34] Of course, this guarantee by the C&SW did not offer much extra security after that road defaulted in November 1872. When the revenues of the bridge itself turned out to be insufficient for the 8-percent interest, the Rotterdamsche Bank offered to buy the unpaid coupons to restore some confidence in the venture.[35]

The Bank next called upon the bondholders to deposit their securities, and by 6 November 1874, 441 of the 600 bonds had been turned in.[36] A foreclosure sale on behalf of the first mortgage holders was then requested, and on 15 June 1876 the bridge was sold to Pieter C. A. M. van Weel, the Dutch representative, for $155,000.[37]

A new company was now set up, the Leavenworth Bridge Company, with capital of $600,000, of which one-tenth was paid in; existing bondholders got one $100 share plus one $1,000 bond of the new company for every old $1,000 bond. Pieter van Weel became president, with M. B. Haas of Leavenworth vice president and H. M. Aller director in Leavenworth. It took some time before the new securities arrived, but in 1881 the Rotterdamsche Bank announced that the exchange was about to be made.[38] What happened next is not clear; the Rock Island bought the bridge—probably including all Dutch shares and bonds—some years later. In 1879, *Poor's Manual* reported that the bridge at Leavenworth was owned by a company controlled by the Rock Island through stock ownership, and was operated by the Iowa Southern & Missouri Northern, the Chicago & South Western's successor.[39] It is not known how much the Rock Island paid for the securities, as nothing has been found in the Dutch financial press of the day. It is safe to assume that the Dutch lost substantially on the deal.

■ Cleveland, Akron & Columbus

One more Dutch-owned American railroad deserves our attention. The Cleveland, Mount Vernon & Delaware Railroad was created in 1869 with a line from Hudson, Ohio, to Millersburg, Ohio, 65 miles in all.[40] The new company was under strong influence of the mighty Pennsylvania, then busily expanding in Ohio and Indiana. The CMV&D had already issued a loan of $1.5 million and in 1872 issued another for $1 million to extend the line from Millersburg to Columbus, Ohio. The Pennsylvania did not guarantee the CMV&D bonds, but it controlled the line through stock ownership by the Fort Wayne, which in its turn was leased to the PRR.

The first loan, at 7 percent, was introduced in Amsterdam by Oewel and Wertheim and Gompertz in 1870 at 80 percent of par, and yielded a rewarding 8.75 percent. The 1872 Columbus Extension loan was also easily sold by the same brokers, but now at a price of 90 percent of par. Of this $1 million, a sum of $200,000 was used to redeem the same amount of the first loan, leaving the company with a total funded debt of $2.3 million in 1872. Oewel confidently predicted that the bonds would be much sought after.[41]

But the market was uneasy, even before rumors of financial troubles of the CMV&D reached Amsterdam. Oewel had to announce that the July 1874 coupon could not be paid, and he had to confess that the PRR, although the major stockholder, felt no obligation to advance the interest due.[42] An agreement between railroad and bondholders was reached early in 1875: the July 1874 coupon would be paid in full, and the coupons from January 1875 through July 1877 would be paid half in gold and half in 7-percent certificates of deferred debt. Of course, deferring the debt was only done in the fairly optimistic hope of an early return of prosperity. More than 70 percent of the bondholders agreed with the plan.[43]

For the next few years this arrangement indeed seemed to hold, but in 1877 payment of the interest fell behind and soon stopped altogether. Pik neatly figured out that the revenue of the road would never be sufficient to resume payment of interest even at the 3.5-percent level. He considered the Columbus Extension loan the weaker of the two, because it was secured only by a first mortgage on 33 miles and by a second mortgage on the other 111 miles, while the first loan had a first mortgage on those same 111 miles.[44]

Clearly, reorganization was needed, and the Dutch bondholders were invited to deposit their bonds with J. C. G. Pollones, notary public in Amsterdam.[45] By the end of 1880, $741,000 worth of the first loan (of a total $1.35 million still outstanding) had been deposited with Pollones, and $368,000 worth of the Columbus Extension loan (out of a total of $950,000).[46] The road was sold at foreclosure on 20 August 1881 and reorganized as the Cleveland, Akron & Columbus Railroad. In March of 1882 the court, for reasons unknown, annulled the earlier sale and ordered a new sale. That sale took place on 9 June 1882 to a committee representing the Dutch bondholders, among whom was—as usual—H. W. Smithers of Louisville. He had been in Amsterdam in April to explain the situation, and after these consultations a plan for reorganization, which contained some unusual points, was developed by Wertheim and Gompertz.[47] The bondholders, representing the only real capital in the road, were to choose between new income bonds or new shares of the company to be created. Both had the same rights to the earnings of the road, but income bonds would have no voting power while, according to existing law, the shares would have that power. Wertheim and Gompertz strongly recommended the shares. Of course, the existing major shareholder, the Pennsylvania, objected, because its holdings in the old CMV&D would be wiped out. After some legal wrangling, however, the Dutch had their way.

Thus, in 1886, the Cleveland, Akron & Columbus Railway was born, with a stock capital of $4 million and a funded debt of $1 million. The old $1,000 bonds were converted into ten new common shares of the CA&C of $100 each. Shareholders had preferential rights in subscribing to $600,000 worth of the new first mortgage bonds. Moreover, each share obtained a right to 1/4,000 of the results of the lawsuit pending against the shareholders of the old Cleveland, Mount Vernon & Delaware (i.e., the Pennsylvania).[48] Wertheim and Gompertz notified the Stock Exchange that it held a total of 39,993 shares against the certificates; what happened to the other seven shares remains a mystery.[49] Caspar Willem Schaap, Oewel's brother-in-law, was one of the directors of the new company and acted as treasurer at the same time. A certain E. L. Smithers was clerk at the company's offices.[50] Was he a relative of H. W. Smithers?

Despite a 1.5-percent dividend in 1886, it soon became known that the company was not doing well. To reduce the fixed charge of the annual interest payments, the 6-percent bonds were replaced with a new 5-percent loan in 1887 (per 1927). The conversion was readily accepted by the Dutch bondholders.[51]

For some unknown reason Wertheim and Gompertz closed its department for Cleveland, Akron & Columbus securities in 1895 and the certificates were transferred to the Nederlandsche Vereeniging van Houders van Amerikaansche Spoorwegaandeelen (Netherland Association of Shareholders of American Railroads).[52]

After the 1886 reorganization, Dutch-held shares had been regularly sold to buyers in the United States, until only a large minority interest remained in the hands of the Dutch Association. In 1899 the Pennsylvania, apparently still smarting from the loss of the CA&C in 1886, bought $2,237,000 worth of commons from the estate of the American financier Calvin S. Brice and thus with one stroke acquired a majority in the road. The position of the Nederlandsche Vereeniging became more difficult as a consequence, and its board voiced the opinion that it might be better to sell out to the PRR completely. The PRR also wanted to issue a new loan, for which the shareholders would have preferential rights. To exercise these rights, the remaining owners of Dutch certificates were asked to deposit their stock and give their opinion about selling out to the Pennsylvania at the same time. By May 1900, $1,594,800 in stock had been deposited out of a total of $1,763,000 still in Dutch hands.[53] The unexpected outcome of the query was that most owners refused to part with their stock, and they showed enough interest in the new loan to warrant its introduction in Amsterdam. The board of the Vereeniging, apparently more inclined to make a deal with the PRR, did not want to be involved in the new issue, stepped down, and a new Cleveland, Akron & Columbus Vereeniging was constituted, with W. F. Piek on the board. The new association subscribed to the new loan and issued certificates in exchange for the bonds.[54]

The large minority of shares in Dutch hands remained a thorn in the flesh of the Pennsylvania, and in 1911 the company again attempted to buy them out. The last quotation in Amsterdam (in 1909) had been at 85 percent of par, and the PRR now offered to buy at that price, not bad in view of the dividends of only 4 percent or less over the last years. But Ad. Boissevain and Company advised against accepting the bid, and a shareholders' meeting hastily convened on 20 March 1911 shared its views.[55] The Pennsylvania then raised its offer to 92, much above the current market price, and only then did the Dutch accept. Each certificate ($1,000) was paid off with Dfl 2,210.30, after deduction of expenses.[56] This was not a bad ending for a long, drawn-out affair. After its acquisition of the Dutch stock, the PRR reorganized the road as the Cleveland, Akron & Cincinnati, a wholly owned paper company.

These five cases represent the only instances of American railroads whose destinies were decided in Holland. In certain other cases, such as Arthur Stilwell's Kansas City, Pittsburg & Gulf, a sizable Dutch investment was combined with a large personal involvement, but actual control of the railroad remained in America and was never completely in Dutch hands. (The Kansas City, Pittsburg & Gulf is discussed in greater detail in Chapter 14.)

Ten

Frauds, Swindles, and Malversations

*I*nto every commercial transaction, large and small, some form of fraud can creep, despite the most stringent checks applied. Man is reported to incline toward all evils, and even the most righteous attitudes and business ethics of those involved in a deal of any kind can never completely keep out malversations. In a business of a magnitude previously unknown, such as the building and financing of the American railroad network, where millions and millions of dollars were changing hands, it seems only natural that fraud and malfeasance became commonplace occurrences. The enormous distances in space and time (which diminished only somewhat with the opening of the first Atlantic telegraph cable in 1866),[1] the lack of knowledge in Europe of American business practices, and the initial absence of control on the side of European bankers and brokers, all contributed to the ease with which fraud could be perpetrated. Given the casual way in which European money was transferred to and spent in America, it must have been tempting for people with weak consciences to embezzle some of this wealth for their own private use. It is not the purpose of this book to study fraud in depth, but some of the clearest cases in which the Dutch became involved will be described here.

There were many ways in which railroad investors, American as well as foreign, could be cheated out of their capital. A mild form of fooling outsiders was stock speculation on the part of the American promoters or directors, which temporarily drove up the price of the securities, only to let them crash down again later. Because of the lack of timely information, these tricks could catch foreign bond- and stockholders unawares, causing great losses and much ill will. Gentlemen like Jay Gould, Daniel Drew, and Jim Fisk had acquired thoroughly bad names over the years with their manipulation of the Erie securities. Later Gould may have mended his ways, but his name never had a good ring again in Europe, and investors eyed him warily. Commodore Vanderbilt was another tycoon who was not averse to manipulation of the stock market to reach his goals, and his name was also well-known in European financial markets.

The most common kind of swindle in the early days was, of course, the selling of securities of companies that existed only on paper. A beautifully printed prospectus, describing in glowing words the rich agricultural or industrial area to be traversed, was easy to produce, and the gullible investing public might easily swallow it all. Not only the Dutch public was eager to buy such American stocks; in Germany the craze for everything American was just as great, while in England the situation was not much different. Sometimes such a paper company did indeed manage to lay a couple of miles of track and provide some kind of train service, which strengthened public confidence, making it possible to sell still more securities. During the boom years of the late 1860's and early 1870's, scores of railroad securities were thus floated in the European markets. The 1873 crisis separated the good from the bad, and it turned out that the latter category was all too large.

Of course, the bankers and brokers who had marketed these securities should have made sure that the railroads involved were bona fide enterprises, but in practice most of them had been too lax in this respect. Only after the enormous losses caused by the economic crisis of 1873, when many roads defaulted, did the Dutch investing public become more cautious and the brokers more adept at importing only the better classes of securities. The bad name acquired in Europe by American rails became a cause of concern in American money circles too, as it tended to harm or even destroy American credit there. As one American banker, Henry Clews (himself involved in many doubtful schemes), put it, "The law has permitted these undertakings [the railroads] with so much concealment, misrepresentation and actual fraud, and has so disregarded the rights of the bondholders, that American credit has become a scandal and a byword on the European bourses."[2]

Another voice from the American banking world was that of Joseph Seligman, of the New York house of J. and W. Seligman and responsible for the marketing of the Atlantic & Pacific bonds in Europe through his many connections there. By 1872 Seligman wanted to get out of all western railroad business. In July of that year he wrote to his London connection, "Experience has taught me that American railroads . . . extend and expand too fast, taking every dollar of earnings and proceeds of loans to branch out into new lines and new schemes, and while ultimately the great majority of railroads will pay dividends . . . the banker issuing a loan is morally drawn in by degrees to lend large sums, ostensibly to protect the coupons, but actually to extend the line."[3]

During the 1873–74 crisis, the famous Commodore Vanderbilt is reported to have said:

There are a great many worthless railroads started in this country, without any means to carry them through. Respectable banking houses in New York, so called, make themselves agents for the sale of the bonds of these railroads and give a kind of moral guarantee of their secureness. The bonds soon reach Europe, and the markets of the commercial centers, from the character of the endorsers, are soon flooded with them. The roads get into difficulties, and bad language is heard all around. These worthless roads prejudice the commercial credit of our country abroad. Building railroads from nowhere to nowhere at public expense is not a legitimate undertaking.[4]

Clews, Seligman, and Vanderbilt were not the only ones to express themselves in this way, but there is every indication that their wise words were falling on deaf ears. Dutch investors and brokers should have heeded these remarks more than they did.

Despite the honest words of the financial wizards just mentioned, practices such as stock watering, especially favored during the 1860's and early 1870's, were never completely stamped out, and foreign investors had to remain alert and careful. Speculation in American railroad stock in America itself was also a common phenomenon, and it continued well into the twentieth century when, for example, the Rock Island, formerly a pillar of strength, was suddenly transformed into a speculative venture by the actions of an aggressively expanding syndicate of Wall Street speculators.

A case of fraudulent sale of shares is presented by the only New England railroad company whose securities were ever handled in Amsterdam. The Boston, Hartford & Erie, incorporated in 1864, intended to build a line from Boston to New York City by way of Hartford, Connecticut, and to link up with the Erie Railway by way of a ferry service across the Hudson River. The board of the Hartford turned out to be corrupt to the core, even more so than that of the "friendly" Erie itself. The state of Massachusetts had supported the road, but when it was learned that most of this public money had disappeared into the pockets of the directors and their cronies, the state refused to come to the rescue again, and the line went bankrupt in 1870. After several years of turmoil, it emerged in 1875 as the New York & New England.[5]

In 1872 common shares of the Boston, Hartford & Erie, then already in receivership, suddenly turned up in Amsterdam. Someone must have tried to unload his practically worthless stock on an uninformed Dutch public. The unscrupulous Daniel Drew was one of the original Hartford stockholders, as was Commodore Vanderbilt—whose righteous words have been quoted above—and both were fully capable of every trick in the trade to save their skins, but there is no evidence that they were the crooks behind this shady scheme.

The records of the Amsterdam Stock Exchange show that the respectable houses of Wertheim and Gompertz and Gebr. Teixeira de Mattos had been active in the Hartford business. They had issued certificates for these shares until the time when the company's books were reopened and transfers were made possible again, so it is probable that they knew that the company was at the time unable to register new stockholders. Did they also know that it was in receivership? If so, they should never have marketed the shares without a warning. Other stockbrokers such as Lion Hertz apparently also sold some of the shares; on 22 May 1872 it was stated that Wertheim and Teixeira de Mattos between them had sold 5,630 shares, while other brokers had disposed of some 4,700 more. There was a public outcry when it became known that the stock was practically worthless, and Lion Hertz was even sued in 1872 by an irate customer who felt cheated.[6]

By then it must have been obvious that something was definitely wrong. The rumors of the bankruptcy had been confirmed, and the Beurscomité called the unlucky owners of the shares together to discuss what action should be taken.[7] Nothing has been found about the results, if any, of this meeting, and it is not clear what happened to the some 10,000 Dutch-held shares. Possibly the loss was quietly written off, but even at their lowest price of 7 percent of par, the total was still close to $70,000, a significant sum in those days. In 1873 the Hartford's shares were quietly dropped from the price lists.

■ *The Construction Company*

By far the most common kind of swindle in the American railroad business was through the medium of the construction company.[8] As long as a newly incorporated railroad company existed only on paper, without any revenue from traffic of its own, its securities were often hard to sell to the investing public. To advance the necessary capital for construction, a so-called construction company was commonly set up. The actual building of the railroad was generally farmed out to smaller contractors, who were paid by the construction company. The construction company in its turn was paid by the railroad, not in cash but in bonds, stocks, and land (if a land grant had been given or if counties and towns had donated land). Almost invariably, the actual cost of construction of the road was much lower—often by as much as half—than the sum in bonds given to the construction company, because these bonds could only be sold to the public at a great discount. This meant that the fledgling railroad was saddled with a heavy debt right from the start. Experts estimated that 60 percent or more of all railroads constructed were heavily overcapitalized and overburdened with debt, leading to bankruptcy at the very first crisis.[9]

The construction company itself was not fraudulent per se. It became so because the promoters of a railroad were generally also the men behind the construction company. The latter company could be nominally independent and the railroad promoters might not even appear on the construction company's list of directors, but more often than not the real owners were the same as the original shareholders of the railroad. They contracted with themselves and paid themselves a handsome sum in bonds, which could then be disposed of to the investing public as long as the railroad still paid interest regularly. When the railroad company eventually defaulted, the promoters had usually already sold their bonds and had only stock in their portfolios, worthless by then, but for which they had never paid a cent. If the railroad turned out to be a paying proposition after all, they were still in control through their stock ownership and could pay themselves fat dividends.

The Credit Mobilier of America, which acted as the finance and construction company of the Union Pacific, is one of the more glaring examples of the abuses connected with such companies, but many more instances of swindling by way of construction companies can be found.[10] Many times all the bondholders of a railroad company, certainly not only Dutchmen, were caught by fraudulent practices of this kind.

An early instance of construction funds disappearing mysteriously is given by the Arkansas Central Railway, chartered in 1871 to build from Helena, Arkansas, 100 miles westward toward Little Rock. The gauge was to be 3 feet, but for some reason it was changed to the "English" 3.5-foot gauge during construction. A portion of the main line from Helena to Duncan and Clarendon, totaling 48 miles, was opened in 1872, but Little Rock was never reached.[11]

The state of Arkansas came forward with a subsidy of $2,225,000 in state bonds, but because Arkansas had converted and refunded its debt in 1869, with consequent losses to bondholders, the new bonds could be sold only at a large discount; in 1876 the state defaulted again.[12] The railroad itself had issued an 8-percent loan of $1.2 million, which was introduced in Amsterdam by Lion Hertz in 1872.[13] When price and interest were combined, these bonds promised an almost unbelievable yield of 10.50 percent. With the seemingly unlimited confidence in American railroads in general, they found a ready market in Holland. Most of a first offering of $575,000 was sold there, while a next series of $420,000 was chiefly marketed in London.

With the general economic crisis of 1873, the little narrow-gauge road was soon in trouble. The last quotation found in Amsterdam was in 1874; soon after interest payment must have come to an end. In 1877 the road was sold. What happened to the Dutch interests is not known; the Arkansas Central simply disappears from view in 1876. The last time the bonds were mentioned was in September of that year, when it was announced that 400 of the total of 750 bonds had been sold in Amsterdam and the rest in London. The firm of F. W. Ziegelaar, Gerlings and Binger of Amsterdam took charge of depositing the Dutch bonds with the Union Trust Company and received the assessments of 10 shillings per bond needed for the reorganization.[14] From that moment on a profound silence descended over the railroad and the fate of the $400,000 (par value) of Dutch money remains shrouded in mystery. It is possible that the bonds were converted into new shares; if so, the Dutch most likely disposed of this worthless paper as soon as possible.

It is hard to avoid the thought that some considerable fraud must have been perpetrated in the construction of the line. In 1875 it was described as a road with bad financial management, made worse by the anomalous condition of affairs in the state of Arkansas.[15] To build 48 miles of narrow-gauge line through relatively easy country a sum of over $2 million had been available.[16] This would have meant almost $42,000 per mile, which was outrageously high at a time when narrow-gauge lines generally did not cost more than some $15,000 per mile, including rolling stock. After all, the chief advantage claimed for the 3-foot gauge was its cheapness of construction. A considerable amount of money must have disappeared.

Another early instance of the all too common trick of fraud by means of a construction company was the Gilman, Clinton & Springfield in Illinois. This road was incorporated in 1867 by local businessmen who intended to build a line from Clinton, on the Illinois Central's Chicago–Centralia line, southwest by way of Clinton to Springfield, 111 miles in all. By September 1871 the goal had been reached. To finance construction the company had issued a 7-percent loan of $2 million, and many of the bonds were sold in Amsterdam by Elix and Broekman early in 1872. Morton, Rose and Company handled the loan in London.[17] For a time interest was paid regularly, until at the end of 1873 the first rumors about financial problems filtered through. It was stated that the line had cost $4 million or more, and that at least $2.5 million had disappeared into the pockets of the enterprising gentlemen of the railroad and the Morgan Improvement Company, the construction company which had "built" the road. Through the flat Illinois terrain the actual cost of construction cannot have been much more than $15,000 per mile; the actual cost had been $40,000 per mile, certainly much too high.[18]

However this may have been, the March 1874 coupon was not paid and the road was placed in receivership. An international committee was formed, consisting of Charles S. Seyton of Borthwick and Company of London, H. J. de Marez Oyens of Amsterdam, and George Bliss, of Morton, Bliss and Company of New York.[19] The road was sold at foreclosure to this bondholders' committee in 1876, and leased (and later sold) to the Illinois Central.

That the Dutch had at last seen through the trick with the construction company was illustrated by the Kansas City, Pittsburg & Gulf affair in 1894. When Arthur Stilwell, the flamboyant promoter of this road, came to Amsterdam looking for capital, Dutch brokers were willing to oblige, but only on the condition that he would turn over to them both construction companies involved. As expected, they lost on the investment in the railroad itself, but the profits made with the construction companies, especially in acquiring land, easily offset the losses. In fact, the Dutch found themselves with virtual ownership of Port Arthur, Texas, and parts of the famed East Texas Spindletop oil field.[20]

After the successful outcome of the KCP&G affair, it is hard to believe that the trick of the construction company was used once more. What's more, this time the victim was the thoroughly experienced S. F. van Oss. He had set up in business as a stockbroker in The Hague after a distinguished career as financial journalist in London, and he claimed to know the thorny field of American railroad finance as no other. Yet he advanced money to the Oklahoma Central Railway, money which was indeed spent on the construction of the railroad. The gentlemen behind the construction company, however, who had carefully kept Van Oss out of that organization, promised to advance the same sum as the Dutchman, but kept their money in their pockets and cheerfully let the railroad go bankrupt instead, with Van Oss bearing the losses.[21]

■ Townsite Companies

Another favorite of swindlers was the townsite company, meant to develop new towns along the railroad on company land. Just as with the construction company, a townsite company could be set up by the promoters of a railroad, more often than not through dummy companies. Towns and counties were persuaded to donate land for the railroad and its depots, or to float a bond issue in support of the road. The proceeds of such an issue or of the sale of the land not needed for the road itself could mean a significant sum for the townsite company. Unscrupulous promoters could easily pocket the money with nobody being the wiser.

A clear example of such a townsite company was the one connected with the South Pacific Railroad of Missouri, a forerunner of the St. Louis & San Francisco Railroad. This road, originally the southwest branch of the Pacific Railroad of Missouri, came into the hands of John C. Frémont in 1866. Frémont was known as an intrepid explorer and a capable officer, but proved to be less so as a businessman; his Memphis, El Paso & Pacific Railroad proved to be rotten to the core. But he was the son-in-law of the powerful senator from Missouri, Thomas Hart Benton, and was therefore a figure in the state. He incorporated the South West Pacific Railroad, which was seized by the state in 1867 for nonpayment of interest and sold next year to the South Pacific Railroad Company.[22]

As usual, the finances of the railroad were shaky in the extreme, but it had a valuable asset in a land grant of about one million acres. To sell the land, a deal was concluded with the American Emigrant Aid and Homestead Company. Agents of the Homestead Company swarmed out over Scandinavia and brought over hundreds of Danish and Swedish farmers who settled in Rolla, Missouri, and other places along the line. The early days of Rolla have been well documented by the noted English novelist Anthony Trollope, who visited there in 1862 and left a vivid, but not very favorable, description of the place in his *North America*.[23]

The townsite activities of the railroad company came in for much criticism, and the South Pacific was probably the model for the railroad in Mark Twain's *Gilded Age*. Twain's Salt Lick Branch of the Pacific Railroad laid its tracks from Slouchburg via Poodleville and Hallelujah to Corruptionville, creating new towns on the way while bypassing the established towns.[24] Travelers were not impressed by the quality of the towns along the road either: "The few towns were indescribable—no streets, no regularity, no paint, no style." And west of Rolla the country was even worse.[25] The agents of the Emigrant Company managed to sell some bonds in Germany, but it is not clear how the Dutch market was worked: in 1869 Joseph Cahen offered $1 million worth of bonds of the railroad in Amsterdam, but it has not been recorded if the Emigrant Company was involved too.[26]

■ Carpetbagger Swindles

One of the most conspicuous examples of outright embezzlement by corrupt politicians and railroaders after the Civil War is that of the Jacksonville, Pensacola & Mobile Railroad in Florida, chartered in 1869. Although this road itself did not sell its bonds in Amsterdam, the state of Florida in 1870 floated a loan of $4 million on its behalf. The corrupt carpetbagger government had issued this loan at the request of two notorious railroad promoters, George W. Swepson and Milton S. Littlefield, who had already embezzled millions with fraudulent railroad deals in North Carolina. The precious pair had obtained the JP&M in 1869 with the money stolen from North Carolina, and they now proceeded to milk the Florida treasury for a couple of million more.[27]

The Florida State bonds were sold in Europe, but little if anything of the proceeds reached the railroad, most being pocketed by Swepson and Littlefield and their corrupt henchmen in Tallahassee. In Holland the respectable firms of Holjé and Boissevain of Amsterdam and A. J. and M. Milders of Rotterdam offered the bonds in 1870. They should have used more discretion, for Florida had once before repudiated its debt to European bondholders. In 1873 it did so again and the July coupon went unpaid; the security of the railroad as collateral of the loan was of most doubtful value.[28] At least $1,384,000 worth of these bonds had been sold in Holland, and probably even more; 1,384 certificates had been issued by Boissevain against bonds, but another 421 bonds could not be traced. It was even rumored that the whole issue had been sold in Holland, but it is more probable that a number remained unsold.[29]

Unrest in Holland ran high. The Amsterdam lawyer Jacobus Wertheim[30] was dispatched to Florida at once, but only in 1882 could a settlement be reached, when the state bonds were converted into an equal amount of railroad bonds, plus some stock of doubtful value thrown in, a very meagre result.[31] Meanwhile, Wertheim continued his efforts to claim the whole amount of the original bonds from the state of Florida. The Florida Supreme Court declared in 1876 that the 1870 issue of bonds had been unconstitutional, and thus had relieved the state of its responsibility to the bondholders. But Wertheim fought on, and in 1879 the U.S. Supreme Court issued a judgment in his suit *Holland* v. *State of Florida*: the issue of bonds by a state legislature may have been subsequently declared unconstitutional, but Dutch bondholders, who had bought these bonds in good faith strictly as a business venture, could not possibly be expected to have known the motives and machinations behind this measure and could not be made to suffer for the misdeeds of former legislators and state officials. A lien was granted against the railroad company amounting to the market value at the time of purchase of the original state bonds sold in Holland—some $3 million—thus further swelling the Dutch holdings in the Jacksonville, Pensacola & Mobile and its successors.[32]

Another railroad in Florida that strongly smelled of fraud was the Florida Railroad, incorporated in 1855 to run from Fernandina on the Atlantic coast to Cedar Keys on the Gulf, 156 miles long.[33] In 1869 it had floated a loan of $2.5 million to finance the reconstruction of the road after the war, and Lion Hertz introduced the bonds in 1871 in Amsterdam.[34] Soon it turned out that the little road was in serious trouble; the July 1873 coupon could not be paid.

This was not all; there were also rumors about frauds with bonds traded elsewhere. Hertz announced that he had sold $520,000 (par value) in bonds and that other bonds circulating were irregular; he advised legal action.[35] This was to be his last communication regarding the Florida Railroad, and he subsequently received much criticism. J. Pik, generally reticent on the matter of the honesty of Dutch bankers and brokers, could not restrain himself. He commented scathingly on the prospectus issued by Hertz and the glowing terms in which the decrepit railroad was described. A couple of swindlers had gotten hold of the bankrupt road for $320,000, and they had managed to lead the gullible public, including Mr. Hertz, to believe that it was a veritable gold mine. A stock capital of $3 million had been "furnished" with which the line had been constructed and equipped. As if an American railroad was ever built out of capital, Pik sarcastically commented, and asked his readers why, if true, would the railroad then need a bond issue at all? And Hertz appeared to have believed everything instead of having been critical, as would have been his duty to his customers, the prospective investors. In an article in the *Nederlandsche Financier* of 30 September 1871, Hertz had recommended "his" bond issue, giving incorrect figures and too optimistic an outlook.[36]

As so often, Pik was right. The bondholders, after having been milked, were considered to be a nuisance, and the directors in Florida simply refused to provide them with any information about the earnings of the company. In Amsterdam in 1875 the price of the bonds—more than twice secured by the revenue of the road, according to Hertz—had dropped to the lowest possible level, 1 percent of par. There was some talk about the formation of a Dutch committee, but both L. H. Weetjen, chairman of the Stock Exchange Committee, and A. C. Wertheim refused to act. In 1879 a committee consisting of C. D. Willard, an American, and Jac. Wertheim was at last formed; the latter sailed for America to try to save something from the wreck, not only for the Florida

Railroad bondholders, but also for the owners of the Florida State bonds, as has been noted above.[37]

It took some years before the Florida Railroad was sold at foreclosure on behalf of the bondholders, who lost about two-thirds of their original investment. An English consortium, headed by Sir Edward J. Reed, bought the road, reorganized it several times, and finally sold it to the Seaboard Air Line System.

Another case of carpetbagger politics in which the Dutch became entangled brings us to Alabama and the Alabama & Chattanooga Railroad. Two unscrupulous carpetbaggers, the brothers John C. and Daniel N. Stanton (originally from New England), had arrived penniless in Alabama and had soon established a secure position among the politicians in Montgomery. Backed by the New York banking houses of Henry Clews and Company and Soutter and Company, they incorporated the Alabama & Chattanooga Railroad in 1868. Alabama then initiated a system of state support for its railroads by guaranteeing their bonds to a maximum of $12,000 per mile. Governor William H. Smith stretched this favorable law to the utmost, endorsing, and thus guaranteeing, the A&C's bonds to the tune of $5.3 million for the 295-mile line, or almost $18,000 per mile; only 225 miles were in actual operation in 1870. Even more fraudulent was the direct support of the road by the state through the issue of $2 million in state bonds in 1870, before Smith was thrown out of office. The state bonds thus obtained by the railroad were quickly unloaded on European markets.[38]

Under Smith's successor the state aid was no longer available and the Stantons got into financial trouble. In 1871 the road was in receivership and in such terrible shape that it was often impossible to operate any trains at all. When trains did run, it was chiefly for the private benefit of conductors and trainmen.

Both the bonds of the A&C and the Alabama State bonds were marketed in England, but only the railroad bonds reached Amsterdam.[39] In London the house of J. Henry Schroeder, agents of Alabama, sold the bonds easily, because the state had had until then an excellent credit rating. In Holland the $3 million A&C loan, guaranteed by the state, was offered in 1869 by the Commandietkas of Amsterdam, Rotterdam, and The Hague. Other portions of this same loan were sold in Frankfurt and Paris by the Erlanger firms.[40]

For a short while interest was indeed paid, but early in 1871 trouble came; the January 1871 coupon could not be paid and the governor of Alabama was reported to have declared that the guarantee by the state would not be honored and, later, that interest would be paid in currency, not in gold.[41] A further problem arose when Alabama announced that it intended to pay interest only on bonds numbered from 1 to 4,720, because the higher numbers were said to have been issued illegally. This news soon became known in Amsterdam, where it was rumored that the higher numbered bonds being traded there had come from a foreign bourse. Apparently someone must have thought the Dutch too dumb to notice. These controversial bonds had been sold in Amsterdam by respectable firms in good faith, and they were not thought to be fraudulent. The Stock Exchange Committee was requested to publish a warning against them to make sure that no more flooded the Dutch market.[42]

In the end the number printed on the bond was of no consequence, as the state stopped payment of interest on all bonds irrespective of numbers in July 1872. Years of struggle followed, in which the Stantons, the state of Alabama, the bondholders, and other interested parties tried in vain to get the upper hand.[43] Dutch interest in the A&C declined, although the *Nieuw Algemeen Effectenblad* in 1877 continued to report the news about it. No Dutch protective committee was formed and most of the Dutch-held bonds were deposited with a Frankfurt committee.[44] The road was taken over in 1877 by a British consortium headed by Emile Erlanger and Company, and it incorporated a new company, the British-owned and -managed Alabama Great Southern. Later the Southern Railway leased the AGS and since then the "Queen and Crescent Route" has formed an integral part of that system while still operating under its old corporate name.

What happened to the Dutch holdings—probably never very large—in the Alabama & Chattanooga is not clear. The last quotation found was in 1874. Neither the Alabama Great Southern securities nor the state bonds created at the sale of 1877 were ever listed. It may be assumed that the Dutch had sold most of their bonds to Germany.

▪ Simple Swindles

A case of outright fooling of prospective investors by unscrupulous promoters is presented by one of the more unfortunate railroads to be known in Amsterdam, the Rockford, Rock Island & St. Louis of Illinois. Chartered in 1869 to build a line between the cities in its name, in the end it managed to reach only Rock Island over its own rails.

In 1869 its $9 million loan was introduced in Germany, and by S. de Vita in Amsterdam.[45] People looking for a solid investment must have shied away from these bonds, but for speculative purposes they were attractive. In any case, the issue was eagerly taken up, mostly in Germany. The RRI&StL even had a transfer agent of its own, William H. Truesdale, in Frankfurt am Main in 1872–73, and business must have been brisk.[46] The buyers of the bonds, however, soon regretted their lack of caution. The prospectus issued proved to be full of lies: the land grant mentioned never materialized and the coal mines owned by the company were "salted." A few holes in the ground filled with coal dust were considered enough to fool prospective buyers. It was a simple trick, but apparently effective enough.[47] The company was soon in trouble and was unable to weather the 1873 crisis. Over the next few years the financial press in the Netherlands was silent on the RRI&StL, indicating the small Dutch interest in the road. Only in 1876 was news about the reorganization given. The German bondholders' committee had succeeded in buying the road at the foreclosure sale for $1,320,000, and they reorganized and then sold it to the Burlington. Bondholders had to be content with a pittance of 13.5 percent of their holdings. Moreover, they had to pay 765 reichsmarks per each $1,000 bond for expenses in return for new bonds. Most Dutch bondholders had sold their RRI&StL bonds before that, at prices of about five cents on the dollar.[48]

▪ The Scarlet Woman of Wall Street

Of all American railroads there is probably none with a financial history more infamous than the Erie Railway. All frauds, swindles, manipulations, watering of stock, common theft, and other crimes that have been known to investors seem to have been practiced on the Erie. The very name Erie Railway stood for everything that was wrong in American railroad finance, which led to its eventual designation as the "Scarlet Woman of Wall Street." And as the securities of the Erie had found a ready market overseas, its bad reputation eventually became common knowledge in the financial capitals of Europe.

The New York & Erie Railroad was incorporated in 1832, and in 1851 the 447-mile-long line—the longest in the world—was declared open.[49] Despite technical success, the financial position of the road went from bad to worse. After a first receivership, a new Erie Railway started in 1860 with a clean slate and great expectations. The company's securities were described as "among the steadiest of the railway shares."[50] This unfounded optimism was soon shattered. The conflict over control of the company, the so-called "Erie Wars" between Vanderbilt, Drew, Jay Gould, and Jim Fisk have been described elsewhere and need not be recounted here. By 1868 Jay Gould was firmly in control, however, ably assisted by Fisk and some other notorious rascals.[51] The enormous amounts of convertible bonds and new stock issued during the fight are of some consequence for this story, because some of it ended up in Amsterdam.

The capital stock of the Erie in 1868 stood at more than $46 million and grew by another $10 million in the next year. None of the old stock was held in Holland, but the Dutch became interested in the new issues. The low price was the attraction, although the brokers involved must have known the character of Jay Gould and his henchmen and the way they "managed" the road. In 1868 Wertheim and Gompertz first introduced certificates of Erie commons. Dinger, otherwise always very factual in his investor's guides, denounced the Gould administration most vehemently and was pessimistic about the prospects for the shareholders. Pik, writing some years later, is even more scathing about the possibility of a dividend and saw no chance at all in the near future for a better yield.[52] And indeed, apart from a small dividend for purposes of publicity in 1873, it was only in 1942 that the first regular dividend on Erie common stock was announced. Jay Gould himself is reputed to have said, "There will be icicles in Hell when Erie common pays a dividend," and another popular saying on Wall Street was, "Three things are certain: death, taxes, and no dividends for Erie common."[53]

The English shareholders were naturally unhappy with the way their interests were represented on the Erie board, and they set out to oust Gould, who was seen as the chief villain. Bischoffsheim and Goldschmidt, the London banking house with large interests in the matter, sought contact with other English firms and with Wertheim and Gompertz.[54] James McHenry, who was already in control of the Atlantic & Great Western, also solicited support for his plan to get rid of Gould and his cronies.[55] Samuel L. M. Barlow, the American railroad lawyer, cooperated, and this international coalition managed to throw Gould out in March 1872. General John A. Dix, of Union Pacific fame, became the new Erie president and Barlow one of the directors. Although most investors were happy with Gould's ouster, others had little faith in McHenry. While congratulating Barlow with his success in removing Gould, one of his correspondents remarked, "I am sorry that you were compelled to use a greater scamp than Gould to oust him," meaning McHenry.[56]

Although prosperity did not return immediately, some Dutchmen had enough faith in Dix and Barlow to recommend an exchange of the once popular Austro-Hungarian railway shares for Erie stock.[57] The pleasant surprise in the shape of a 2.75-percent dividend on Erie common in 1873, already mentioned above, of course did help in restoring the hopes of the stockholders, but it soon became known that the dividend had not really been earned but paid out of capital to improve the position of the company in Europe.

Captain Henry W. Tyler, Royal Engineers, inspected the Erie property on behalf of the English stockholders in 1874 and his report was mostly negative; quotations of Erie stock in London fell from 36 to 27 percent of par, and in Amsterdam it went down from 44 to 22. Much opposition continued to exist in England against the way the road was managed: "While the anomaly must exist by the law of the United States that a railway owned almost entirely by Englishmen is managed exclusively by a board of Americans, the English proprietors must, in our opinion, insist on a machinery which will afford them an efficient control over their property."[58] The same could have been said of the smaller number of Dutch stockholders.

Burdened by a heavy funded debt and hit by the recession of 1873, the Erie struggled on until May 1875 before defaulting once again on the payment of interest. Sir Edward Watkin, M.P., director of several English railways, went to America and drew up a plan for reorganization. A new company was incorporated in 1878; the New York, Lake Erie & Western Railroad took over the property of the old Erie. Dutch names are absent in the reorganization committees; their interest must have been too small to warrant members of their own.[59] The Dutch stockholders exchanged their shares for certificates of NYLE&W shares issued by Wertheim and Gompertz.

In the case of the Erie it is clear that the Dutch were well aware of the possible risks when they started buying into the road. Gould's name was known, although the extent of his financial manipulations was probably underestimated in Amsterdam. The low price of Erie common was tempting enough to persuade a well-respected firm such as Wertheim and Gompertz to issue certificates. In the end the market must have been limited, as indicated by the absence of Dutch names in the protective committees.

■ Ben Holladay, Swindler

An example of fraudulent dealings of a railroad promoter is given by the Oregon & California Railroad, organized in 1869 by Ben Holladay, a colorful operator of stagecoach and steamboat lines in Oregon. His line was meant to be built southward from Portland to meet its counterpart, the California & Oregon, creeping slowly northward from Sacramento.[60]

A loan had been issued in 1870 and the German and Swiss markets were flooded with bonds; they were offered not only in financial strongholds such as Frankfurt and Berlin, but also in small places like Fürth and Heidelberg. The house of Bischoffsheim of Frankfurt was active in the matter, and also tried to unload some of this issue through its London branch, with little success.

In Holland the bonds were marketed by the Amsterdam firm of Ter Meulen and Boeken, and two years later another portion was sold by Lion Hertz.[61] Despite this influx of capital, construction was slow. Holladay may have been a colorful figure, but he was no railroad operator and certainly not an honest businessman. Rumors of his having appropriated funds raised through the sale of bonds for political purposes soon were flying about, and in the end the affairs of the railroad turned out to be in terrible condition. The land grant was said to have been sold at ruinously low prices, and even land not yet turned over to the road by the government had already been squandered.[62] The German investors grew restless, so a bondholders' protective committee was formed. The sole non-German on this committee was F. S. van Nierop, director of the Amsterdamsche Bank, the Dutch bank with a strong German interest behind it.

In the Dutch financial press Holladay was depicted, not without reason, as the villain of the episode, and investors were urged to take strong measures and remove him as soon as possible.[63] The Frankfurt committee managed to reach an understanding with him, but the arrangement lasted only for a short time. Three Germans obtained seats on the board of the O&C, one of them the well-known Henry Villard, who was already active in the Kansas Pacific. In a meeting in October 1874, the Dutch bondholders decided to join forces with the Germans and place their affairs in the hands of Villard. At that meeting only 138 Dutch bonds (worth $113,500) were represented, hardly the total of Dutch holdings, although Germans made up a clear majority.[64]

For several years affairs were at a kind of stalemate: officially Villard was at the head of the company, but for all practical purposes Holladay was still in charge. Villard was in no position to act strongly, because he was in faraway New York; Pik thought that he might as well have stayed in Frankfurt. In Portland the German engineer Richard Köhler was Villard's representative, but he did not exert much influence either. After many years of wrangling, Villard at last succeeded in removing Holladay from the board, but the slippery fellow then threatened to duplicate the already unprofitable Oregon & California line with a new line of his own, the Oregon Central. To remove his sting, the O&C proposed to take over that line as well. The idea was accepted by the Frankfurt committee and the Amsterdamsche Bank agreed to cooperate.[65]

Pik had little praise for the arrangement: buying up an unprofitable road to shore up the already insolvent Oregon & California was to him throwing good money after bad. He failed to see that it was imperative to get rid of Holladay at any price.[66] The Oregon Central was duly taken over; Holladay was ousted and ended his career in poverty. The Oregon & California struggled on to a new receivership in 1885 and eventual takeover by the Southern Pacific.

▪ Bad Bookkeeping

Besides the examples given above of clear-cut cases of fraud and malfeasance, there are also many instances of irregular transactions, shady dealings hidden behind shoddy bookkeeping, often bordering upon fraud but without clear proof of real malversation.

An early example is the trouble over the shaky Peninsular Railway, running from Lansing, Michigan, to Chicago. In June 1872, even before the 1873 economic crisis, the road was thrown into receivership because of nonpayment of interest on its loan, which was largely held in Holland. W. L. Bancroft was appointed receiver for three separate sections of the road, one of which (Flint to Lansing) was in Vanderbilt hands. Bancroft was accused of not keeping the receipts of the several sections separate and of favoring the "Vanderbilt" section too much. His administration was a complete mess, and the debts he contracted saddled the successor road, the Chicago & Grand Trunk, with an uncontrollable debt load, under which it was to sink again soon.[67]

The cesspool uncovered by the report of Stephen Little after his examination of the books of the Atchison, Topeka & Santa Fe upon its 1893 default is another good example.[68] While there is no hint of any personal enrichment by the Santa Fe directors, the company's books had been found full of irregularities, resulting in incorrect figures for almost everything and, even more important, much lower figures for revenues than the public had been led to believe. Of course, the directors responsible were fired.

■ Frauds by the Dutch

Until now only swindles and frauds perpetrated by Americans have been discussed. The question arises, of course, whether there were any frauds on the part of Dutch brokers and bankers involved. To their credit, it must be stressed that no cases of outright fraud have been found. The only reproach that can be made against them is a gross negligence on their part in checking the soundness of the securities they imported. Not only firms with a somewhat unsavory reputation such as Lion Hertz, but also well-run and well-respected firms such as Wertheim and Gompertz or Gebr. Boissevain, were culpable of this same lack of caution, especially during the years before the great crisis of 1873.

The Amsterdam firm of Lippmann and Rosenthal was accused of having manipulated the prices of the St. Paul & Pacific securities to its own advantage (see Chapter 12). Gebr. Boissevain was the target of an attack as a result of its handling of an 1872 loan of the Maxwell Land Grant Company. It was said to have made excessive profits on the deal and to have fooled ignorant investors with tales of future riches. In a letter to the Stock Exchange, G. M. Boissevain defended himself honorably and maintained that Cimarron, New Mexico (headquarters of the Maxwell), was bound to surpass Denver some day in wealth and population.[69]

Wertheim and Gompertz was said to have sold bonds of the Paducah & Memphis, which it had imported but found hard to market, to its own mutual fund for a price higher than the current market value and thus to shift its own loss to the shoulders of the owners of the mutual fund shares. Nothing was ever proved, but if true it would have been a nasty trick played on unsuspecting investors.[70]

The Boissevain and Wertheim firms were certainly among the best in Amsterdam, but there were others with less positive reputations. The Commandietkas of Rotterdam and Lion Hertz of Amsterdam had poor names, and it is hardly accidental that quite a few of the securities they imported fell flat after 1873. We have noted Hertz's operations in the Florida Railroad and Oregon & California affairs above. In Chapter 4, accusations, probably partly true, by Dr. de Klerck have been noted. Hertz's firm had already been dissolved by the time of De Klerck's 1886 brochure; otherwise he would most certainly have borne the brunt of the attack. In general, however, it may be concluded that most Dutch brokers were honest and did their best to protect the interests of their customers along with their own.

Eleven

The First Large-Scale Fraud: Galveston, Houston & Henderson

One example of a swindle with American railroad securities requires more attention, because it is illustrative of all-too-common practices in the early days. The second American railroad company ever to enter the Amsterdam Stock Exchange with its securities proved to be one of the most fraudulent. In the process of issuing fraudulent mortgage loans it acquired notoriety as few others have done.

After the Illinois Central shares and construction bonds began to be traded in Amsterdam in 1855–56, Dutch brokers became aware of the business opportunities offered by this new interest. As a result of the IC's favorable reception, the securities of a second American railroad were introduced in Holland in 1857. This one, however, turned out to be a costly lesson for the Dutch.

The Galveston, Houston & Henderson Railroad was a Texas short line that, despite its name, never reached any further than the 50 miles between Galveston and Houston. The road was incorporated in 1853 to promote trade by building a line between Galveston, with its fine natural harbor, and eastern Texas as far as the Sabine and Red Rivers. Henderson, a small town southwest of Marshall, was the goal, although never reached.[1] Both Galveston and Houston supported the project financially and the state of Texas awarded a land grant totaling 611,840 acres to the fledgling enterprise.[2] Despite this support, construction was slow and Houston was reached only in 1859, while the bridge connecting Galveston with the mainland was not finished until 1860. In Houston the road reached other railroads but did not actually connect with them because of differences in gauge.[3] Time-consuming and costly transshipments were necessary.

The financial history of the Galveston reveals the utmost shabbiness. Even before being finished in 1860, it had already been sold to its creditors, and the new owner, B. F. Terry, reorganized it under the same name and the same charter in March 1860. Before this, though, foreign money was already involved in the GH&H.

It was French, not English, capital that played a role in the development of the

Galveston. The French had not been great investors in the United States in the nineteenth century; they started to invest on a large scale in American railroads only in the twentieth. But Texas had long been a point of special interest for the French. During the existence of the independent Republic of Texas (1836–45), the French king Louis Philippe had a representative in Austin, and the French had absorbed a large Texas loan.[4] The incorporation of Texas into the United States had changed that special position, but French interest remained strong. A French colony, La Réunion, had been established in 1855 on the Trinity River in the vicinity of what is now Dallas, founded by Victor-Prosper Considérant, an early follower of Charles Fourier, the French utopian socialist. Considérant had left France in 1849 for America, but his Texas brainchild met with little success. His book, *Au Texas* (1855), however, found a large readership in France, Belgium, and Switzerland, and emigrants from these countries had arrived in numbers.[5]

Political interest in the Texas area was also strong in France. During Emperor Napoleon III's Mexican adventure (the attempt to set up a French puppet regime in Mexico by installing an emperor from the Hapsburg line), the idea was fostered of France somehow aligning itself with Texas. The American Civil War even encouraged French ideas of taking Texas over outright, although the Confederate government strongly dissuaded Napoleon III from pursuing these fantasies.[6] Connected with these political ambitions were the plans for a southern transcontinental railroad under the name of Memphis, El Paso & Pacific Railroad. John C. Frémont was brought in as a director because of his useful contacts in France, and he had some success, because Henri Probst, who was also supplier of the French armies in Mexico, undertook to sell its bonds in Europe. It is unnecessary to follow the history of this road, which ended in complete disaster. Large-scale frauds, in which Frémont was also implicated, brought about its downfall in 1871. By then the French emperor, who had strongly supported the project, had other problems on his hands with the Franco-Prussian War. In Paris in 1873 Frémont was sentenced in absentia to a 5-year prison term for his part in the fraud, but he had fled in time and managed to avoid extradition to France. An outcome of this most unfortunate affair was the Franco-Texan Land Company, set up in 1877 in Weatherford, Texas, on parts of the original land grant of the Memphis, El Paso & Pacific.[7]

In view of this strong French interest in Texas, it is not surprising that the Galveston, Houston & Henderson Railroad had an early entry on the Paris bourse. But the French brokers involved also sought outside support in Germany and Holland. In 1857, 9,000 bonds (out of a total of 26,250) of $100 (or Fr 530) each, paying 8-percent interest, were offered in Amsterdam by G. A. van der Voort at a price of 95 percent of par. Every bond, when fully paid up, gave right to one share of $40. The rest of the issue had already been sold in Galveston, Paris, and on several German bourses.[8] A year after the first Illinois Central securities had been introduced in Amsterdam, this second issue was well received. The European agent of the company, a certain Mr. Vasbenter, was quoted as having said that the Galveston had already paid out 58 percent on its shares, largely out of the revenues generated by the sale of lands.[9] It is hard to believe that the Dutch investors really thought that this bold assertion could ever have been true. Even the prosperous Illinois Central could not show a similar favorable result.

For a short time things went well. The Comité Européen in Paris, chaired by Count d'Alton Shée, a French nobleman and railroad promoter of Irish ancestry,[10] announced the payment at the Amsterdam Associatie Cassa of the July 1859 coupon with Dfl 10 ($4) per bond. Shortly after, however, he had to deny rumors about financial problems of the company. He stated in the Dutch press that William J. Valentine of London, general European agent of the company (successor to Vasbenter?), had just arrived in Galveston with money, and other agents were on their way to the United States with more money and iron rails for finishing the line. The January 1860 coupon was to be paid as usual.[11]

This was to be the last positive news ever about the Galveston road. In 1860 it became known that, apart from the French-Dutch loan, other loans were outstanding, all secured by a purported "first mortgage" on the property. Which loan was really first was not clear. In Frankfurt a committee of holders of 10-percent bonds requested preference over the later 8-percent bonds, although this 10-percent loan of 1855 ($750,000 par value) was supposed to have been redeemed by the 8-percent loan of 1857. In its turn the 10-percent loan was said to have been used for redemption of a still earlier 6-percent loan of 1853, also of $750,000.[12] More disturbing news followed, when the *Galveston Union* newspaper reported that the railroad had been sold on 9 March 1860 to Messrs. Kyle & Terry, acting for the American bondholders of the $750,000 6-percent loan of 1853! Meanwhile d'Alton Shée had organized a bondholders' protective committee to rescue the French-Dutch loan.[13] Not surprisingly, prices of the Galveston bonds in Amsterdam were falling fast, from a high of 93 percent of par in 1858 to a low of 57 percent early in 1860.

Action was clearly needed, so on 18 May 1860 a meeting was held in Amsterdam, where d'Alton Shée, E. C. Nicholls, and Alfred Joly, all members of the Comité Européen, were present. To head off the pretentions of the holders of the 10-percent bonds, it was proposed to sell more 8-percent bonds: every owner of three 8-percent bonds was requested to buy a fourth nonissued bond at 70 percent of par, to be paid for with the three coupons per July 1860 ($12), plus $58 in cash. Every new 8-percent bond issued in this way would be used to redeem one 10-percent bond. After much discussion this proposal was grudgingly accepted, but the price of $70 for a $100 bond was considered too high when the market value of the same bonds had fallen to 57 at the time. On the other hand, if nothing was done, it was clear that the owners of the 8 percents were in danger of losing their security altogether. A committee was elected to execute this proposal, to which L. H. Weetjen, president of the Stock Exchange Committee, G. A. van der Voort, and M. S. Boon Hartsinck were appointed.[14] The sets of four 8-percent bonds, called *stellen* in Dutch, were separately listed in Amsterdam, and during 1860 were generally quoted a little higher than the original single bonds. The new bonds, which made up the fourth of the *stellen*, were called the "whites," and only these were considered secured by the mortgage.[15]

Altogether 1,500 new 8-percent bonds were created, and Wertheim and Gompertz, who had been charged with the actual execution of the scheme by the Dutch committee, announced early in 1861 that 1,000 of these had already been taken up. The other 500 could be bought for the July 1860 and January 1861 coupons ($24 altogether) plus

$52 in cash. It was rumored, but never substantiated, that an English consortium had taken up these 500.[16] Payment of interest on the 8-percent bonds had been discontinued by July 1860, and prices of the sets and the single bonds had fallen to 17 and 16 percent of par respectively.

The Paris protective committee then asked for an assessment of 1 percent per bond for the expense of sending a representative to Texas. By August 1860, holders of 987 Dutch bonds had paid the Dfl 2.50 ($1) requested, and 33 more came through the next year.[17] The Paris banking house of Van den Broek and Company, clearly of Dutch ancestry or with Dutch connections, organized the transfer of the assessments. The existing Dutch committee was expanded to a full protective committee with the addition of three more members in June 1861, and a lively correspondence with d'Alton Shée and his committee developed. Of the French-held bonds, 5,306 joined in the assessment of the 1 percent with the 1,020 Dutch bonds.[18]

A profound silence then descended over the affairs of the Galveston road. During the American Civil War most connections with Europe were severed and little or nothing was heard. Galveston was in Confederate hands, except for a short time when the Union Army controlled the port. After the end of hostilities, attempts to obtain exact information were resumed and the sorry state of the bondholders' affairs was soon fully revealed.

A number of interested parties were cooperating, or sometimes fighting each other, regarding the affairs of the road. The New York firm of Dulman and Scharff offered their help in the matter in a letter (in Dutch!) to Weetjen, and a certain Mr. Kimball came to Amsterdam in September 1867 with a plan for reorganization of the company. As has been noted earlier, Anthony G. Dulman later was director of many American railroad companies where he represented the Dutch stock- and bondholders, but this was his first appearance in the railroad business. Kimball did bring a plan, in which the 8-percent bondholders were not very favorably treated and which therefore found little acceptance.

At the same time a suit was filed against the company in Galveston by N. A. Cowdray, supported by the New York firm of Boonen, Graves and Company, another of the New York "Dutch" mercantile houses. Cowdray requested the transfer of the railroad to the bondholders and the appointment of a receiver in the person of Tipton Walker. Cowdray was a relative of the first partner of Boonen, Graves and Company, and he had requested their help in obtaining the support of the Dutch bondholders.[19]

Meanwhile, a retired Amsterdam notary public, J. J. A. Biesman Simons, had initiated another way of protecting the interests of the Dutch. He had written to the Dutch Minister of Foreign Affairs, Count van Zuylen van Nijevelt, in December 1866 with a request for help. Van Zuylen in turn asked the acting Dutch consul in Galveston, Adolph Heydecker (probably of German nationality), partner in the trading firm J. Kaufmann and Company, for information. Heydecker replied (in English) on 29 June 1867 and offered his help if the Dutch were willing to place their business in his hands.[20] He held out little hope, however: "I repeat it is important that prompt and combined action should be taken, as some of the 1st mortgage bondholders might try to carry their point to the exclusion of those who have not presented their claims in proper time. The whole history of the GH&H RRd has been a very dark one from the beginning, and if ever bondholders get any of their money back, they may consider themselves fortunate." In his letter he enclosed a statement of his attorneys, Messrs. Tucker and Leane of Galveston, with a survey of all outstanding loans, from which it was clear that the 6-percent loan of 1853, of which nothing was known in Europe when the 8-percent French-Dutch loan was issued, had never been redeemed and was considered to constitute the real first mortgage on the property. The 10-percent loan of 1855 was also still outstanding as a second mortgage, and the 8-percent loan could at best only be seen as a third mortgage.[21] Before asking Heydecker to take care of the Dutch interests, the Dutch committee wanted to await the arrival of Clarkson Potter, attorney from New York, who was on his way to Europe chiefly for the business of the Atlantic & Great Western but who was also reported to have new information concerning the Galveston as well.[22]

From all this sometimes conflicting information one thing was evident: immediate and joint action was needed. The Dutch protective committee requested the bondholders most urgently to deposit their bonds before 1 May 1868, but with little success, and a meeting convened for 27 April of that year met with even less support. On 15 May 1868, disappointed by so much lethargy, the committee decided to step down.[23]

Things were now moving fast, but without any action on the part of the Dutch. Tipton Walker, who had been receiver of the road since 1867, was replaced by Cowdray himself, but apparently the Dutch had little confidence in him. At least this was the opinion of a merchant from Rotterdam, Kuyper van Harpen, who again urged his fellow bondholders to join forces if any result was to be obtained. The firm of Boonen and Graves was the only means to gain some influence over Cowdray, and the Rotterdammer thought that at least Boonen himself could be trusted.[24]

Late in 1869, when it was rumored that most of the land grant of the company was to be sold at foreclosure in March 1870, Wertheim and Gompertz made a last attempt to get the Dutch together to try to postpone—or prevent if possible—such a sale. But, again, the support forthcoming was disappointing, and by February of that year only $300,000 worth of Dutch bonds had been deposited, not enough to act on, and nothing was done. Fortunately for all parties concerned, the sale of the land was postponed.[25]

It was Heydecker who warned the Foreign Office in The Hague of the last act of the drama, the impending sale of the property, and Van Zuylen in turn informed the Stock Exchange. *All* foreign bondholders were to deposit their bonds with the U.S. Circuit Court in Galveston before 1 December 1870 if they wanted to be recognized officially as parties to the sale and reorganization of the company. This idea had originated with Tucker, who had also managed to postpone the sale of the land grant earlier in the same year.[26] Only with this news of impending disaster did the Dutch bondholders wake up at last. Kleeblad and Sons and H. Franco Mendes, stockbrokers in Amsterdam, convened a meeting of interested parties on 20 October 1870, and it was decided to deposit the bonds with Heydecker in Galveston. Wertheim and Gompertz, despite their earlier disappointments, offered to dispatch the bonds, and a sufficient number arrived in Galveston in time. It turned out, however, that this belated action had been to no avail. In December 1871 the road was sold at foreclosure to a certain F. P. Jones for only $675,000, not enough to pay the holders of the 8-percent bonds any compensation.[27]

The entire French-Dutch investment had to be written off, but it took some time before the bondholders got used to that idea. In 1877 Wertheim and Gompertz announced that the original bonds, worthless by now, had been received back from Galveston and could be claimed by the owners if they wanted them. The capital sum of Dfl 2.75 per $100 bond was available, left over from the earlier assessments for expenses.[28] The bonds were last quoted at 9 percent of par in 1870, for both the sets and the singles. Years later they were still circulating in the portfolios of investors, in the hope that some day they might be worth something. As late as 1884 the heirs of the Amsterdam liquor distiller Theodorus Luns found among his securities $2,100 (par value) in worthless Galveston, Houston & Henderson bonds.[29]

It is difficult to assess how many of the 8-percent bonds were actually held by Dutchmen. An indication may be the $300,000 deposited with Wertheim and Gompertz in February 1870, which fell far short of the necessary majority. About three-quarters of the total of any security sold in Holland was usually considered a sufficient majority to act in cases of default or bankruptcy. In the GH&H case, of the total of 26,250 bonds, 9,000 had been offered for sale in Amsterdam, with 6,000 more in Paris in 1858. Just over 8,000 had been held back in the coffers of the company. The rest must have been sold in America and Germany. It is probable that the 9,000 offered in 1857 by Van der Voort had indeed been sold, and with the formation of the sets in 1860, 1,000 more had been issued, bringing the Dutch total to 10,000 bonds, or $1 million nominal value.[30]

The railroad itself never amounted to much. In the early 1870's speeds on the line were terribly slow. As one traveler wrote in 1873, "The 'mixed train' for Galveston left [Houston] at half-past 2, and consumed four hours in going the fifty miles."[31] Later, while still operating under its original name, the line was leased jointly to Jay Gould's International & Great Northern (Missouri Pacific) and the Missouri, Kansas & Texas. Today it still provides the Union Pacific, now owner of the Missouri Pacific and the MKT, with an access to the port of Galveston.

The Dutch broker G. A. van der Voort was clearly at fault here. Acting on a request from his business relations in Paris, he introduced the Galveston bonds in Amsterdam without checking the nature and the validity of the mortgage that secured the bonds, as he should have done. Lack of experience probably caused this grave mistake; after all, the Galveston was only the second American railroad on the Amsterdam Exchange, and most brokers did not yet know what to expect or how to avoid problems such as these. Van der Voort never again touched American railroad securities. Later brokers learned to avoid this particular mistake, but this did not imply that they introduced only the very best of American securities. As has been noted in the previous chapter, again and again new frauds were practiced, not only on Dutch brokers and bankers, but on others, European and American, as well.

Twelve

The St. Paul & Pacific

The St. Paul & Pacific Railroad of Minnesota stands out as a road of great significance for Dutch investors. A large amount of Dutch money was invested in the line, with a great deal of personal involvement on the part of Dutch brokers. The experience eventually meant substantial losses for the Dutch bond-holders, although there was never any clear indication of large-scale fraud.

When the Minnesota Territory was organized in 1849, there was no special demand for improved transportation, but in the next decade the clamor for railroads got stronger. In 1857, one year before statehood, the first company, the Minnesota & Pacific Railroad, was chartered to build west from St. Paul. Construction was slow because local capital was barely forthcoming, small wonder in a state with a total population of only 150,000. The Civil War only made conditions worse, and in 1862 the Minnesota & Pacific surrendered its charter and passed out of existence.[1]

Not all was lost, however, because the same promoters incorporated a new company in the same year and named it the St. Paul & Pacific Railroad Company, which again planned to build a main line from St. Paul west to Breckenridge with a branch to St. Vincent on the Canadian border. The land grant of its predecessor was also taken over.[2] Construction remained slow until a contract was signed with Electus B. Litchfield and Company of Brooklyn, New York, for construction of part of the line in exchange for shares of the railroad plus some cash.[3] By that time the first ten miles, between St. Paul and what is now Minneapolis, were in operation.

A first loan of $120,000 had already been issued, secured by a first mortgage on those ten miles, and in 1862 a new 7-percent issue of $700,000 (per 1892) was floated, secured by a second mortgage on the same ten miles, plus a first mortgage on 70 miles of the branch line. As this was not yet enough to cover construction costs, a third issue was floated the same year, again at 7 percent, but this time for $1.2 million and secured by a third mortgage on the first 10 miles, a second mortgage on the 70 miles of the branch, plus a first lien on 307,200 acres of the land grant.

Because of legal complications in the original charter, a new company, the St.

Paul & Pacific Railroad, First Division, was incorporated in 1864, comprising both the branch to Sauk Rapids, then under construction, and the main line, which was slowly creeping westward from Minneapolis. Litchfield held all the common stock of this new First Division company. It was supposed that foreign investors would be more willing to put money into a smaller undertaking, with definite goals, than in a company pretending to build as far as the Pacific Ocean.[4] The Northern Pacific, then also under construction, saw the St. Paul as a useful connection with St. Paul and Chicago, and contracted with Litchfield to buy his shares. For a time the NP thus controlled the destiny of the St. Paul.[5]

The 1862 issue of $1.2 million was marketed chiefly in Europe through E. Darwin Litchfield, brother of Electus, a banker in London. Robert Benson and Company of London also sold some of these bonds, but the bulk was taken up in 1864 in Holland by Kerkhoven and Company at a first price of 66 percent of par. An added incentive was that bonds could be used to buy land in Minnesota.[6] How much Benson sold is not known, but it cannot have amounted to much, as it turned out later that almost all had been marketed through Kerkhoven.

The next issue came in 1865, this time a 7-percent consolidated mortgage to clear up the financial structure. The total of this issue was $2.8 million, which was chiefly used to withdraw the two earlier loans. The remainder, some 780 bonds (of $1,000 each) was to be sold through Benson, but again turned out to be marketed primarily in Amsterdam by Kerkhoven, and also in Rotterdam by H. C. Voorhoeve, at 70 percent of par. Later statements claim that the Amsterdam firm of Lippmann, Rosenthal and Company also sold these bonds, but the facts do not corroborate this. Lippmann was to come in only in 1871.[7] The loan was secured by a mortgage on 80 miles of the branch line from St. Paul to Watab, plus 512,000 acres of the land grant (which totaled some 5 million acres according to some sources, but only 2,748,450 acres to others).[8] An added incentive for buyers of the new bonds was that 10 percent of the total was to be invested in United States 6-percent bonds to guarantee the payment of interest on the consols for some years. Despite all this, repeated calls resulted in no more than about half of the two 1862 loans being deposited for conversion into the new consols.[9]

The need for money was still pressing, and in 1866 the St. Paul issued a new loan (called the second section loan in Holland) of $3 million (per 1896), also at 7 percent, and secured by a second mortgage on the main line from Minneapolis to Big Stone Lake (part of the line to Breckenridge) plus a first mortgage on 576,000 more acres of the land grant. Again Kerkhoven and Voorhoeve marketed most of this loan, although a part seems to have been sold in England as well.[10] Because Kerkhoven wanted to have someone on the spot to guard the now large Dutch interests, Johan H. Kloos, a Dutchman with a degree in engineering from Delft Polytechnic, was sent out, ostensibly as a construction engineer, but more probably to keep an eye on the railroad and the way the Dutch guilders were being spent. Other Dutchmen traveled to St. Paul as well, to see the sights and to give their opinions on the future of Minnesota. C. A. Crommelin, of a famous Amsterdam banking family, and H. J. de Marez Oyens, later deeply involved in the Illinois Central and the Missouri, Kansas & Texas railroads, were a few of those who went to Minnesota in 1866.[11]

The $3 million of 1866 was apparently not enough to cover construction to Brecken-ridge, and in 1869 a new loan was floated, this time for $6 million and again with 7-percent coupons. Security was provided by a first mortgage on the whole main line from Minneapolis to Big Stone Lake (210 miles) and a first lien on 768,000 acres of the land grant. The same combine of Kerkhoven and Voorhoeve marketed the bonds at 70 percent of par. Sales were slow, however, and it must have been apparent that the Dutch market was becoming saturated with St. Paul bonds. To overcome the hesitation, 20 percent of the total issue was retained by the brokers and again invested in U.S. Government bonds to guarantee the regular payment of interest for three years. The total net yield of this loan for the railroad thus was very small, of course, the more so because early subscribers got an even lower price of 65.50 as an added incentive.[12]

Although at the end of 1869 some $13 million (par value) in St. Paul & Pacific securities had thus been sold in Holland, not enough of this enormous sum was left for actual construction of the road. Of course, the bonds had been sold at a considerable discount, but that was nothing unusual in those days. More unusual was how between 10 and 20 percent of some issues was held back by the brokers as added security, which diminished the net yield for the railroad still further, to less than half the nominal value. There were rumors of fraud (again, as usual), but such accusations are always hard to prove. The $8 million that one writer claims was embezzled by certain parties seems excessively large.[13]

More money was urgently needed to finish construction, because the land grant would have to be forfeited if the deadlines stipulated in the contracts were not met. An enormous loan of $15 million was now issued for the St. Vincent and Brainerd branches. These 7-percent bonds were secured by a first mortgage on the lines from St. Cloud to St. Vincent, 293 miles, and from Watab to Brainerd, 55 miles. The floating of an issue of this size needed more backing than the earlier loans. Benson and Company now teamed up as underwriters with Lippmann, Rosenthal and Company, and the actual marketing was executed for them by C. van Rinsum, Jr., Kerkhoven and Company, Leembruggen, Guépin and Muysken, all of Amsterdam, and Voorhoeve of Rotterdam. Almost all of this issue was sold in Holland, and only a small number of bonds remained in England. The price was 70 percent of par, and again 20 percent of the issue was set apart to guarantee the payment of interest for the first three years. The net yield for the company, after deduction of the brokers' commission, was thus only some $7 million, and the real rate of interest to be paid after the guarantee expired was just over 14 percent.[14] Harsh as these terms may seem, no one was prepared to advance money to the financially shaky road for less.

Construction did proceed for a time, but rumors about impending troubles flew about. Iron rail was almost unavailable, and the engineers in charge bought whatever they could lay their hands on, which resulted in no fewer than 13 different types of rail being used. Hermann Trott, a colorful German engineer and treasurer of the company, came to Holland in 1872 to defend his tactic of halting all building during the harsh Minnesota winter and starting again in the next spring.[15]

As many had predicted, the general crisis of 1873 was too much for the hard-pressed St. Paul. To make matters worse, 1873 was the year of the first of several consecutive grasshopper invasions in Minnesota, which destroyed all crops.[16] In May 1873 the StP&P had to stop payment of interest, except for the last loan of 1871, which was guaranteed until July 1874. A bondholders' protective committee was formed in Amsterdam, in which the firms of Lippmann and Rosenthal, Kerkhoven, Tutein Nolthenius and De Haan, Wurfbain and Sons, and Chemet and Weetjen (all of Amsterdam), Voorhoeve (of Rotterdam), and Johan Carp (of Utrecht) were represented. The latter was dispatched to America immediately. Meanwhile, the public was invited to exchange its original StP&P bonds for certificates issued by the committee, and the certificates then replaced the bonds in the price lists.[17]

Upon the news of the default of the St. Paul, prices of all bonds fell dramatically. The first section bonds went from 77 percent of par in 1872 to a low of 27 in 1874; the consols dropped from 74 to 10; the second section bonds from 77 to 12; the 1869 bonds from 76 to 11; and the St. Vincent Extension bonds were down from 76 to an abysmal 5 percent of par.

In that fateful year 1873 the Reverend Martinus Cohen Stuart was traveling in the United States. He came as the Dutch delegate to the conference of the Evangelical Alliance in New York, and when delegates were given free passes for a number of railroads, he decided to see as much of the New World as he could. He was a shrewd observer, with sympathy for the young country. Although a minister, he seems to have had a most thorough sense of business. In his opinion railroads through empty country such as the St. Paul could only be profitable in the long run, and the high prices commanded by its securities had no ground at all. He was severely critical of the St. Paul's management: it may not have been a case of outright fraud, but there had been great carelessness on the part of the directors, while the commission charged by the bankers had been much too high. In short, Cohen Stuart stated that the capital put up by the Dutch was lost. He even got access to the company's books and concluded that the last part of the $6 million loan was already used up at the end of August 1869, while the main line was still far from being finished and without any chance of receiving more funds soon. He ended his story on a poetical note: it seemed to him as if the sighs of the Dutch bondholders could be heard in the hissing of the St. Paul & Pacific's locomotives![18]

One other result of the 1873 crisis was the collapse of the Northern Pacific after the house of Jay Cooke had to close its doors. The NP could not live up to the terms of the contract signed with Litchfield, and as a result the St. Paul & Pacific shares were returned to him; Litchfield did indeed reclaim his property. To protect their interests against him, the Dutch committee appointed the New York banker John S. Kennedy as its representative, with Leon Willmar, a native of Liechtenstein, as their director in St. Paul. As representative of the bondholders, Kennedy requested the appointment of a receiver for the original StP&P; Jesse P. Farley was named for the post by the courts. The same Farley, a slow, old man, but one with railroad experience, was also appointed manager of the First Division—not yet in receivership because of the interest guarantee—by Kennedy, acting as trustee for the bondholders.[19]

To make sure that the valuable land grant would not be forfeited, it was necessary to finish the line to St. Vincent before the end of 1873. The money needed for this extension was found by issuing $5 million in 5-year receiver certificates at 10-percent interest. They were secured by a first mortgage on the St. Vincent line, coming before the existing St. Vincent loan. Coupons of this latter loan, which were guaranteed until mid-1874, were to be taken in partial payment, but the success of the new receiver's certificates in Holland was less than expected, even at the price of 85 percent of par, which gave a net yield of 11.76 percent. Therefore a new proposal was formulated, to convert the last two guaranteed coupons (3.5 percent each) of the extension bonds, of which 10,635 had been sold, into 10-percent receiver certificates, which would mean some $700,000 in cash. The bondholders would not lose anything but would only capitalize their interest. Carp, back from the United States, strongly advocated this proposal.[20]

Meanwhile, Kennedy, ably assisted by Kloos (who had gone to Washington for the purpose), lobbied for an extension of the deadline for receiving the land grant, as the line could not possibly be finished before the end of 1873. They were successful, and the term was extended.[21]

Carp, together with Kennedy and the Litchfields, now designed a plan of reorganization. Old bonds were to be exchanged for new ones, but at a considerable loss to the bondholders. Several meetings were held in Amsterdam during 1875 and 1876, and some adjustments were made, but the necessary majority of 90 percent was not forthcoming and the plans had to be shelved.[22] Lippmann and Rosenthal came in for a lot of criticism; they were accused of having taken a special, higher-than-usual commission for marketing the St. Vincent Extension bonds, but they vigorously denied these charges. Pik, always very critical, made no mention of any unfair dealings on the part of Lippmann, and the matter fizzled out.[23]

St. Paul affairs now were at a kind of stalemate. Feelings in Minnesota ran high against the "stupid and greedy Dutch"; the people wanted railroads at any price, and the Dutch were accused of hindering development by their refusal to give up their investment. Kennedy did his best to depict them not as grasping capitalists but as small artisans, farmers, and widows, who had invested their little savings in the railroad in the hope of making a small but honorable profit.[24] He was probably not exaggerating, as the St. Paul securities had been recommended as suitable for just this kind of people. The bonds were mostly in denominations of $250, $500, or $1,000, making them easier to sell. Governor Austin of Minnesota also voiced a more reasonable opinion. He urged considerable attention to the claims of the Dutch creditors and asked the state legislature to bear this in mind. His pleas may have fallen on deaf ears, however, as the "Granger" movement, with its strong pressure to regulate railroads, was gaining momentum in those years.[25]

However this may be, it was clear that something had to be done. The effects of the 1873 crisis were gradually wearing off, the grasshoppers had gone, and Minnesota agriculture was booming, with positive effects on the railroad. Carp was in St. Paul again in 1876, and on his return to Holland he reported favorably. A new plan was slowly maturing, and, to be well prepared for every contingency, all Dutch holders of certificates were again urgently requested to deposit their holdings with the committee.[26]

The new plan came from an American-Canadian combination consisting of James Jerome Hill, Donald A. Smith, George Stephen, and Norman W. Kittson. The latter was a St. Paul businessman and partner of Hill in a transportation company. Smith was a Canadian, an official of the Hudson Bay Company and later elevated to the British peerage as Baron Strathcona and Mount Royal. Stephen was also a Canadian, governor of the Bank of Montreal and later knighted as Baron Mount Stephen. Hill himself was born in Canada in 1838 and had come to St. Paul in the 1850's, where he had set up several enterprises in the transportation and coal businesses, operating between St. Paul and the Canadian frontier and beyond in the valley of the Red River of the North. He had been the freight agent of the St. Paul & Pacific almost from the beginning, and he knew the company inside and out. Moreover, he had useful connections; his partner in one business was Egbert S. Litchfield, half brother of Darwin and Electus, the shareholders of the railroad. Maybe more important, his neighbor in St. Paul was a certain C. Klein, a Dutchman who was related to L. H. Weetjen, the chairman of the Dutch bondholders' committee and president of the Amsterdam Stock Exchange.[27]

It was Hill who originally came up with the idea of taking over the St. Paul & Pacific, but lacking financial backing, he brought in his two Canadian partners. They had useful connections in the English financial world and through them it might be possible to buy out the Dutch bondholders and the Litchfields.[28] Hill had already met Johan Carp during the Dutchman's earlier visits and had formed a favorable opinion of the honesty of the Dutch representative. In the winter of 1877 he came forward with a proposal to buy part of the property, but without real hope that the Dutch would accept. Carp refused, as expected, but at least direct negotiations had been opened. Hill made a second proposition in May 1877, this time for buying the whole railroad for cash. Where the cash was to be found was not explained, but bargaining over the price could now begin in earnest. Hill started by offering from 80 to 11 percent of par value for the various bond issues, with the lowest bid reserved for the St. Vincent Extension bonds.[29]

Carp came with the expected counterproposal in October 1877, in which he set the value of the railroad at $6,866,759; this sum also included the money needed to finish construction of the lines as chartered. Hill's own valuation had come out much higher, at almost $20 million, but he was careful to keep his figure secret.[30] Hill's American-Canadian consortium now made a firm offer to the Dutch committee in the form of a lump sum to be divided over the several classes of bonds by the committee itself. Apparently the shrewd Hill foresaw much bickering over the price and rank of the bonds and he gladly left that disagreeable task to the Dutch themselves. The committee refused to fall into the trap, however, and demanded a separate bid for every class of bonds. Hill could do little else but comply. He offered 70 percent of par for the first section, 26 percent for the consols, 27.75 percent for the second section, 32 percent for the 1869 bonds, and 13.25 percent for the St. Vincent Extension, all to be paid in gold.[31] The total cost to Hill did not differ materially from his first ideas, but he did have to raise the 11 percent for the extension bonds somewhat, while he could lower the first section bonds to 70. The Dutch committee did not recommend or advise against the bid at first, but after some careful massaging by Kennedy, who considered this opportunity too good to be missed, it decided to back Hill's offer. Future problems with other railroads and with the Litchfields were foreseen, and it seemed best to close the deal and sell out. A large majority of the bondholders assented, and now it was up to Hill to find the cash.

Stephen was sent to London to try to raise a loan with Morton, Rose and Company, but after much hesitation and bargaining, and after an inspection of the road by General Edward Winslow, the London house flatly refused to advance the requested $5 million to Stephen and his associates. Hill then considered the deal with the Dutch off, because he had worded his offer as an *option* to buy, on condition that the cash became available. In their turn the Dutch were angry because they had thought that the contract was firm and that it was Hill's problem to find the cash needed.[32] Hill was desperate, because the railroad that he coveted so much seemed again out of reach. The Dutch committee was in the same mood, because all its hopes had been dashed. Both parties were willing to renew the negotiations.

Hill then prepared a new offer: all bonds were to be exchanged for new 6-percent bonds of a new railroad to be incorporated, and until the new bonds could actually be issued he would pay 7-percent interest on the old. As a bonus, each new $1,000 bond would include $250 in new preferred shares. The Dutch were well aware of the great risk they were taking in accepting this new offer. After all, Hill still had to prove that he was able to make the St. Paul & Pacific a paying proposition again, and he had no experience at all in running a railroad. On the other hand, they also saw clearly that by refusing they would be mired in a morass of litigation with Litchfield, and it was not at all certain that they would ever get any of their money back. The committee, strongly urged on by Kennedy, decided to go ahead, but requested a higher price: 75 percent of par for the first section, 28 percent for the consols, 30 percent for the second section, 35 percent for the 1869s, and 13.75 percent for the extension bonds. Moreover, the new bonds were to bear 7 instead of 6 percent, and for those who did not want the $250 in preferred shares, a 10-percent discount on the new bonds was requested. Two Dutch-appointed directors were to have seats on the board of the new road, and $280,000 in cash instead of the $125,000 offered was required toward the expenses of the Dutch committee.[33]

Hill could do little but consent, and the final agreement was signed in Kennedy's office in New York by all parties on 13 March 1878. Hill and his partners agreed to buy from the Dutch committee:

> $625,000 of the $1.2 million first section loan of 1862 at 75 percent of par
> $760,000 of the $2.8 million consolidated loan of 1865 at 28 percent of par
> $907,000 of the $3 million second section loan of 1866 at 30 percent of par
> $3.52 million of the $6 million 1869 loan at 35 percent of par
> $11.4 million of the $15 million St. Vincent Extension of 1871 at 13.75 percent of par

Because most of the Dutch bondholders who participated were not interested in the new preferred shares and requested payment in new bonds only, the 10-percent discount stipulated in the contract made the total price even higher, from over 83 percent of par for the first section bonds to about 14 percent for the extension bonds.[34]

The great majority of the Dutch assented, and wisely so. Hill's price was far above the current market price in Amsterdam, where the extension bonds had been quoted as low as 3 percent of par in 1877, while the best first section bonds were never higher than 61 in the same year. The committee strongly advised nonassenting owners to come forward, and even after the stipulated time limit had lapsed owners were still called up. The Hill consortium was willing to extend the deadline for conversion, but only if the extension bonds were now bought in at 11 percent instead of the earlier 13.75.[35]

Not all Dutch bondholders participated in the sale, and there were even rumors that Lippmann and Rosenthal was behind this opposition for reasons of its own, although it too had signed the contract. It is true that at least $600,000 of the extension loan marketed by Lippmann was still missing, but there are no reasons to suspect the brokers of foul play. Kennedy advised Hill to buy up as many of the dissenting bonds as possible to avoid later problems, and John S. Barnes, Kennedy's partner, was sent to Amsterdam to straighten matters out, with a little "friendly blackmail" to get George Rosenthal in line.[36] What this "friendly blackmail" was has never been satisfactorily explained.

As soon as the Hill associates owned most of the outstanding bonds, the railroad was sold at foreclosure. Out of the proceeds the nonassenting bondholders were paid off in 1879. Each bond ($1,000 nominal value) of the first section brought $901.40; the consols of 1865, $163.69; the second section, $171.53; the 1869s, $343.27; and the St. Vincent Extensions, $52.20. These figures make it clear that nonassenting owners generally got less for their old bonds than the many owners who did participate. Only the St. Vincent Extension bonds and the few outstanding first section bonds brought more at the foreclosure sale than Hill had offered to the participating bondholders. It should be remembered, however, that in the meantime the assenting owners were paid 7 percent on their certificates since December 1877, while the nonassenting owners had received nothing.[37]

As part of the deal with the Dutch, Hill had promised to build a connecting line between Breckenridge, the end of the main line, and Barnesville, north of Fergus Falls on the branch line to St. Vincent. The Dutch committee undertook to help Kennedy to advance the money needed for this construction. In July 1877 subscriptions were invited by the Dutch committee for 7,200 shares of this line, soon to be named the Red River & Manitoba Railroad. Shares of $40 each could be bought for Dfl 94.50, a discount of some 20 percent. Interest was lukewarm at first, and after one week only 1,620 shares had been taken, but some weeks later a total of $200,000 had been raised and construction could be started. After the sale of the St. Paul these Red River & Manitoba shares could be returned to the Associatie Cassa of Amsterdam for Dfl 95.38.[38]

The receiver's certificates created in 1874 were offered at 85 percent of par, but few had been taken. The most pressing needs had been met by converting the guaranteed January and July 1874 coupons of the St. Vincent Extension bonds. For every coupon of $35, one $40 receiver's certificate had been issued. As some 12,000 bonds were circulating in Holland, the $70 per bond must have meant a significant sum. In the end only $100,000 worth of coupons had been used, and on every certificate $29 was refunded. The new certificates were included in the price lists and were generally quoted at prices far above the other St. Paul securities, as the 10 percent was paid regularly; they were redeemed at par in 1879. For those who had been willing to take the risk, they had been an excellent investment.[39]

Even after the 1878 sale of the railroad, some people continued to object to the low price Hill had paid for the property. Traffic receipts had been growing over the last years and the future, now that the lines were finished, looked brighter than ever. Some felt that they had been cheated. The Dutch committee announced that the sale was final and that no appeal was possible, but the dissenting group continued its efforts to get better terms.[40] Nonassenting owners who had not yet sold their bonds were requested to contact Hagbarth Sahlgaard, Swedish vice consul in St. Paul, or his representative, W. 't Hooft, notary public in Rotterdam. Owners of St. Vincent Extension bonds were said to predominate among the dissenters—small wonder, of course, when the low price of 13.75 cents on the dollar is remembered. Their action was in a way supported by a lawsuit of receiver Farley against the Hill associates. He claimed a share of the spoils, because he stated that he had undertaken, in collusion with Jim Hill, to mismanage the railroad so as to drive down the price. His recourse to the law brought him no success, however, and in 1893 the U.S. Supreme Court finally dismissed his claims.

His actions did strengthen the hand of Sahlgaard to some extent, and 't Hooft called upon his adherents to deposit their bonds with the German American Bank of St. Paul. If Sahlgaard managed to obtain better terms, 50 percent of the proceeds was to go to the owner of the bond, the rest to the bank. Some people must have had high hopes of Sahlgaard's chances, for they were trying to buy up bonds, especially the first and second section and the 1869 bonds.[41] In the end they had little luck, for Sahlgaard's request to declare the sale of the railroad void was dismissed twice, and as a compromise he obtained little more than the prices paid by Hill after the foreclosure sale. From the figures given by Sahlgaard in a printed circular of 28 August 1879 it transpires that he represented only small sums of the several classes of bonds.[42]

In a final move in May 1879 the Hill associates incorporated the St. Paul, Minneapolis & Manitoba Railway, and all property of the old St. Paul was transferred to the new company.

Over the years few large business transactions have acquired as unsavory a name as this one, and it is time now to explode a few myths. That the Dutch had been greedy, as stated repeatedly by Holbrook and others, is not corroborated by the facts. Investing in a railroad under construction in almost virgin country was considered a risky but regular matter of business. While the risks may have been taken too lightly by some of the Amsterdam houses, these brokers apparently knew very well what they were doing, because they built in some extra safety by holding back a percentage of the loans as guarantees for the payment of interest. They even sent out engineers of their own to keep an eye on the way their money was being spent, and while some small-scale frauds may have taken place, there is no proof at all that large sums disappeared. Hill tried to drive a hard bargain, and of course he expected the Dutch to do the same. Clearly he did not consider them philanthropists or fools, but hard-headed businessmen, and he knew that he needed them as much as they needed him. That the Dutchmen lacked faith, as Holbrook states, is pure nonsense.[43] They had been willing to buy the receiver's certificates, they advanced the money for Hill's connecting line, the Red River &

Manitoba, and as supreme proof of their faith they invested millions in Hill's St. Paul, Minneapolis & Manitoba instead of insisting on payment in cash (where shortly before a leading London bank had flatly refused to risk any money on this road). Later developments proved the Dutch right, and Hill turned out to be an expert railroader, but at the time he still had to prove his worth.

On the other hand, the rumors that Hill enriched himself in the deal are exaggerated as well. He may have got hold of the St. Paul on the cheap, and he and his associates did extremely well later, when the railroad had been turned into a profitable undertaking, but at that point the other shareholders, many of them Dutch, were doing well also. The statement that the land grant of the St. Paul was sold immediately after Hill took over cannot be proven. The land was sold slowly in small parcels, not in a single multi-million-dollar deal.[44] As for the banker John Kennedy, this was his first plunge in railroad finance, and he came out very well. He took great risks in advancing money to Hill, but, just as the Dutch, he was later amply rewarded.[45]

The name Kerkhoven lives on in Minnesota. Just west of Litchfield the small town of Kerkhoven lies along the main line of the former St. Paul & Pacific. A contemporary Dutch writer, when passing through, said of the town, "The St. Paul & Pacific road owes so much to the Amsterdam firm that we cannot but think of the name of this town as a tribute." A tribute, certainly, but a poor one, to the role Kerkhoven played in promoting the first railroad in Minnesota. The firm had one other rare honor bestowed upon it: St. Paul & Pacific locomotive no. 16, built in 1870, was named Kerkhoven, and it was retired only in 1916 (as Great Northern no. 240, having long lost its name by then). No other Dutch banker or broker was ever honored in a similar way anytime or anywhere in the United States.[46]

After the incorporation of the St. Paul, Minneapolis & Manitoba, the Dutch interest in the road and its successor, the Great Northern Railway and its subsidiaries, continued to be very large, and this situation changed little over the years. Even today securities of the ultimate successor to the ill-starred St. Paul, the giant Burlington Northern system, are listed at the Amsterdam Stock Exchange. Kerkhoven is still a small but prosperous town in Minnesota, keeping the history of the Dutch connection alive.

Thirteen

The Missouri, Kansas & Texas

The Missouri, Kansas & Texas Railway was originally chartered in 1865 as the Union Pacific Railway, Southern Branch. It should be stressed, however, that the transcontinental Union Pacific had no legal connection with the Southern Branch, a fact which confused many outsiders, including Dutch investors. The railway was to start in Fort Riley, Kansas, on the projected Kansas Pacific line, and proceed southward through the former Osage Indian nation toward Fort Gibson or Fort Smith and ultimately to New Orleans.[1]

Congress accorded the company a land grant in the region just vacated by the Osages and gave it the right to build through the Indian Territory—but only with the consent of the Cherokee Indian Nation—to Fort Smith, Arkansas. Little actual construction was done until late in 1866, when a new board, led by Judge Levi Parsons (a wealthy New York lawyer), and including such eastern financiers as Levi P. Morton (of Morton Bliss and Company), Joseph Seligman (of J. and W. Seligman), young August Belmont (whose father had been American minister in The Hague), George C. Clark (of the New York firm Clark, Dodge Investment Company), and George Denison (also of New York), took matters firmly in hand. Denison was said to provide badly needed respectability to the young railroad, but it is doubtful if his name meant more to eastern and European financiers than the names of Belmont, Morton, and Seligman.[2] However this may have been, construction was now pushed forward, and 61 miles of track, from Junction City (near Fort Riley) to Emporia, Kansas, had been completed at the end of 1869.

Parsons, however, had greater things in mind. He was well aware of the fact that the treaties between the U.S. government and the Cherokee Indians would allow only one railroad through the Indian Territory, and he wanted to make sure that his road would be the one. Other railroads were already building southward from Kansas City and Leavenworth, and Parsons went all out to obtain this prize, which was thought—erroneously—to include a 3 million acre land grant. Until this point the line really ran from nowhere to nowhere in particular, and Parsons decided to switch the general direction of the road to the northeast, to Kansas City and St. Louis. To better illustrate the new policy, the road was rechartered as the Missouri, Kansas and Texas Railway Company in March 1870.

As usual, the capital stock of the railroad was not meant to be used for actual construction, and for that purpose a first mortgage totaling 4.25 million was created in 1869 on the first 170 miles of railroad. Right from the start the eastern financiers had these 6-percent bonds marketed in Europe, not in England, but in Holland, Germany, and France. In Amsterdam, Becker and Fuld teamed up with Wertheim and Gompertz and offered the UP Southern Branch bonds, as they were then still known, at 70.50 percent of par, thus giving an actual yield of 8.50 percent.[3] These Southern Branch bonds were widely held in Holland and were considered a good investment, even better than 6-percent U.S. government bonds; because of the lower price of the railroad bonds, the investor's annual interest could be an extra Dfl 300. And if the reduction of the interest on the government bonds from 6 to 4 percent was really carried out, as was rumored, then the yield of the railroad bonds would stand out even more favorably. Despite their early popularity it was not until 1871 that the Southern Branch sixes were officially included in the Amsterdam price lists, although daily quotations have been found from 1869.[4]

Meanwhile, building of the railroad continued, and to finance the expansion the MKT, or "Katy" as the company was popularly known, issued a new loan of $3,855,000 in 1871 (per 1904), with 7-percent coupons payable in New York or Amsterdam. Becker and Fuld and Wertheim and Gompertz underwrote the loan, and their agents Leembruggen, Guépin and Muysken, and C. van Rinsum, Jr., invited subscriptions in May 1871 at 80.60 percent of par. Louis Cohen and Sons of London were also mentioned as underwriters, but there is no evidence that the bonds were actually sold in England. Gradually more of these same bonds were issued, keeping pace with the expansion of the network, until a total debt of $16.5 million was reached by the end of 1872. To make matters more complicated, the old Southern Branch bonds could be exchanged for the new MKT bonds, and at the end of 1872 only $3,250,000 worth of the sixes was still outstanding.[5] There were some problems with bonds numbered 14,001 to 16,000: they were secured by a mortgage on the Tebo to Neosho line but not, as the lower numbers were, on a part of the land grant as well, and for that reason were not considered equal to the earlier issues, as Parsons himself explained in Amsterdam in July 1873.[6]

St. Louis was reached on the rails of the Missouri Pacific and the North Missouri (Wabash). From Parsons, Kansas, the line continued south to Indian Territory, and when the Katy won the race to the Cherokee border, permission was granted to build through the Indian lands. At the end of 1873 the Red River was crossed into Texas, where the town of Denison was founded. The system was then 787 miles long.

Denison town had a very mixed reputation. On the one hand it was described by Edward King in his widely read book *The Southern States of North America* as a den of iniquity, consisting chiefly of saloons, gambling halls, and bordellos, full of depraved, profane, and hideous ruffians and lewd women. Life was short and violent, and many died with their boots on, especially after Captain Lee "Red" Hall was brought in as peace officer to clean up the town. Yet the great traveler J. H. Beadle stated after his visit to Denison that the place was "the quietest railroad town I ever saw. In two days there I did not see a drunken man, notice a knife or pistol in anyone's belt, or witness a brawl. . . . There is rather more security for life than in Eastern places of the same size."[7] The explanation may well be that the Denison townsite company, set up by the MKT, enforced a strict separation of the lawful and the lawless elements. Main Street was most respectable, while the streets behind it were indeed full of filth and vice. It is too bad that the thoughts of the virtuous Dutch have not been recorded. King's book was well known in Holland, and the Dutch investors may have been aware of what was being done with their money.

The investors soon had other, more serious problems. The rapid growth of the funded debt as a result of the expansion made the road most vulnerable for any decline in revenues, and the general economic crisis of 1873 hit hard. President Parsons had been in Europe for most of 1873, but when he returned to Kansas in August of that year he could show few results from his talks with financiers in London, Paris, or Amsterdam. A proposed new issue of $10 million in second mortgage bonds to pay off the floating debt could not be marketed; European houses refused to underwrite it.

One of the first financial institutions to close its doors in the fall of 1873 was the New York Warehouse and Securities Corporation, which had financed part of the construction of the MKT. The Union Trust Company of New York, trustee for the mortgage, also was in trouble, and early in 1874 Parsons had to announce that the January and February coupons of the Southern Branch sixes and the MKT sevens would not be paid.[8]

Parsons went to Europe again with hat in hand to propose a funding of the unpaid coupons: the first two coupons would be good for one preferred share, while the next three were to be paid half in cash and half in preferreds. For the Southern Branch sixes this would mean two coupons ($60) for $84.75 in preferreds, while for the MKT sevens ($70) $98.87 in prefs would be given.[9] This was not bad on paper, but in practice was not desirable because it was not expected that the road would be able to pay any dividends in the foreseeable future. Several inspections of the property were made, the first one by G. D. l'Huilier, an engineer sent out by Louis H. Meyer as representative of Wertheim and Gompertz, early in 1874, and later in the same year by G. A. Croockewit, a Dutch stockbroker. Both reports were not unfavorable, and the prospects of the company seemed to be good.[10]

Meanwhile, establishing a bondholders' protective committee proved to be more difficult than expected. J. C. G. Pollones, the notary public in Amsterdam, had written to 152 persons and firms interested in the MKT about organizing a committee, but only 37 answered. He was so disappointed with the results that he wanted to lay down this self-imposed burden. In the meantime, William Bond, a henchman of Jay Gould, had been appointed receiver for the road, whereupon the Dutch renewed their attempts at organizing. They had success this time; in February 1875 a protective committee was at last formed. F. S. van Nierop, of the Amsterdamsche Bank, became chairman, with members A. C. Wertheim, E. Fuld, G. A. Croockewit, and H. J. de Marez Oyens among others. It was stated during the first meeting on 10 February 1875 that the majority of the MKT sevens was in Dutch hands, but no actual figures were given, except for the fact that 5,942 bonds were represented at this meeting.[11]

An agreement was worked out with the Katy management. The unpaid 1874 and 1875 coupons of the sevens were to be funded by new 6-percent second mortgage income bonds; the coupons for 1876–78 were to receive 4 percent in gold and 3 percent in income bonds. For 1879–81 the rate would be 5 percent in gold and 2 in income bonds. After 1881 the full 7 percent was to be paid in gold again. All coupons which had earlier been converted into preferred shares were to get the same amounts of income bonds as the unconverted bonds. In a meeting in Amsterdam of 26 July 1875, $2,276,000 in MKT sevens, $747,000 in Southern Branch sixes, and $5,591,819 in shares and scrip for income bonds and preferred shares was represented. H. J. de Marez Oyens sailed for New York to finalize the deal. After his return he presented the details of the scheme in a meeting early in May 1876, which followed along the lines given above. The chief difference was that the preferred shares were to be withdrawn and exchanged for income bonds. The French bondholders were said to be content, while the Americans would probably not object.[12]

For a short time interest was paid as agreed, but in 1878, when already more than $6 million in income bonds had been issued, the 4 percent in gold could not be found. A new inspection by T. Haskins Du Puy resulted in a new report, very unfavorable this time because of the terrible physical shape of the road.[13] But despite all pessimistic expectations, interest payments were resumed in October 1879, and even all arrears were settled. Jay Gould, by then firmly in control of the Katy, wanted to get rid of the claims of the Dutch bondholders, who threatened to foreclose, and he had his Missouri Pacific raise enough cash to pay all claims. There was some urgency in the matter: the Burlington had actually put out feelers to buy all Dutch MKT bonds. Fortunately for Gould, John Murray Forbes, president of the Burlington, thought the 5-percent interest guarantee asked by the Dutch too high, and he backed off, leaving the field to Gould.[14] After appointing one director, the trustworthy A. G. Dulman of New York, the Dutch committee dissolved.

Quotations of Katy securities in Amsterdam fluctuated wildly with the fortunes of the company. From a high of around 80 percent of par the Southern Branch sixes had been down to a low of 31 in 1875, but rallied again to par in 1880. The sevens gave much the same picture, from a low of 29 in 1875 to a high of 116 in 1880. Only the 6-percent income bonds, included in the price lists from 1880, did poorly: starting at 18, they had dropped to 8 in 1878 but advanced again to a high of 90 in 1881.

The new Gould management set to work to consolidate its new southwestern system. The International & Great Northern, the southern connection of the Katy, then being extended from San Antonio to Laredo, Texas, was taken over in 1881. The Katy was then leased to the Missouri Pacific, on terms favorable to the latter. To finance the transactions the Katy issued a $45 million general consolidated mortgage loan in 1880, underwritten by the Mercantile Trust Company of New York.

These 5-percent consols of 1880 were not immediately introduced on a wide basis in Holland, although a few may have been sold there from the start. Only in 1884 did W. F. Piek request their inclusion in the price lists, stating that they were meant in part to withdraw the 6-percent income bonds. Unpaid coupons of the income bonds were also converted into the new consols: $1,000 new fives for $600 in coupons. Two years later Van Vloten and De Gijselaar introduced a second portion of this same loan but now at 6-percent interest. All quotations found are of the fives, however, and the sixes were apparently never widely held.[15]

The prospects of the MKT must have been sufficiently high for the introduction in Holland of its common shares in 1880. A number of stockbrokers—Wertheim and Gompertz among them—applied for a listing, and the first price found reflects this optimism. A high of 54 was recorded in 1881, although no dividend was ever paid on them; in 1884 they were quoted at a more realistic 9 to 23 percent of par.[16]

New rumors of impending disaster were heard in 1885, when Wertheim and Gompertz announced that it was willing to act for the Dutch shareholders: because the shares were circulating in many different names, action could only be taken if a sufficient number was deposited in a single place. After one month only some 20,000 shares had been handed in, not enough to act on, and Wertheim and Gompertz withdrew. Piek, who had supplied the Stock Exchange regularly with traffic figures of the Katy, announced in 1887 that he had obtained more detailed information and that there was no floating debt and no reason for panic. But the railroad had lost $1.3 million that year, and the outlook was bleak because the Santa Fe had just finished a line parallel to the Katy all the way down to Houston and Galveston.[17]

In December of 1887 several brokers asked the Stock Exchange Committee for a protective committee, which was incorporated with F. S. van Nierop as chairman and many well-known names from the stockbrokers' fraternity, such as H. J. de Marez Oyens, as members. An inquiry was started to establish the number of shares held in Holland, but results were slow in coming. Early in January 1888 only 57,500 Dutch-held shares had been located, out of a total of some 470,000. It was said that English holdings were also extensive, but no London committee was ever established. For legal reasons the committee was reorganized as an association, the Nederlandsche Vereeniging ter behartiging van de rechten van belanghebbenden bij de Missouri, Kansas & Texas Railway Company (Netherlands Association to Protect the Rights of Those Interested in the MKT), which received royal recognition on 1 March 1888. R. V. Martinsen of New York was appointed representative of the Association in America.[18]

By 25 April 1888 Martinsen had received a majority of the stock, including the English and Dutch proxies. The Gould board was ousted in June and replaced by a new board made up chiefly of representatives of the major security owners. The lease to the Missouri Pacific was annulled, and two receivers were appointed to guide the Katy until reorganization; George Eddy and Harrison C. Cross took over in June 1888.[19]

The new board at once ordered a full and thorough report to be made on the state of the property. The results were published in August 1888 and turned out to be disappointing. The road was generally in a bad shape, with light and worn rail, rotting ties, and no ballast; some bridges needed to be replaced immediately; all depots needed a coat of paint at least. Rolling stock was generally found in fair condition, although the large number of locomotives from many different builders required a much-too-large stock of spare parts. The accusation that the Missouri Pacific had laid its hands surreptitiously on the Katy's newest rolling stock in exchange for older stock of its own was found unsubstantiated. A result of the lease to the MP was, however, that traffic had been siphoned off in favor of the larger road, starving the Katy line to Hannibal,

Missouri, and the Wabash connection there, of traffic. On the other hand, part of the cash necessary to pay the MKT coupons had been advanced by the MP.[20]

When the Dutch stockholders organized their defense, their association also took care of the 5- and 6-percent consolidated mortgage bonds. Certificates were issued and included in the price lists. At least $550,000 in fives was held in Holland, and some $260,000 in sixes, although the latter had never been included in the price lists.[21]

Only the holders of old Southern Branch and 7-percent MKT firsts decided to act for themselves. A separate committee was incorporated in October 1888, under the chairmanship of M. C. van Hall of the Banque de Paris et des Pays-Bas, with A. C. Wertheim among the members. At a meeting of 17 October a total of $469,000 of sixes and $648,000 of sevens was present.[22]

Several reorganization schemes were proposed, differing in details, but all agreeing on the most important point, the scaling down of the fixed charges. In the end the so-called Olcott plan was adopted, as proposed by a committee chaired by Frederick P. Olcott, president of the Central Trust Company, with H. J. de Marez Oyens among the members. The new Katy issued $40 million in 4-percent first mortgage bonds; $20 million in 4-percent second mortgage bonds; $13 million in 4-percent preferred shares; and $47 million in common shares. The old 6-percent consols were good for $640 in new firsts, plus $550 in new seconds, plus $275 in preferreds. The old 5-percent consols got $550 in firsts, plus $500 in seconds, plus $200 in preferreds. Common shares were to be exchanged at par upon a cash payment of $10, and in return for this the same sum in new seconds was given. A cash fund of $18 million was to be created by selling $22.5 million of the new firsts and $5.4 million of the new preferred shares on the market, with very favorable subscription rights for existing bond- and shareholders. For a cash payment of $400 bondholders got $500 of new 4-percent firsts plus $120 in preferreds; for $1,600 in cash shareholders could have $2,000 in 4-percent firsts plus $480 in preferreds. With the money thus raised the old MKT sevens and Southern Branch sixes were to be paid off at par, including all unpaid coupons.

The holders of the old 6- and 7-percent Southern Branch–MKT first mortgages were not satisfied. In theory they could have insisted on the execution of the mortgages on their portion of the system, but this would have meant a dismemberment of the network, with a loss of revenue enough to jeopardize all future earnings. After some wrangling to get better terms, the Van Hall committee accepted the terms of the Olcott plan, and sent all Dutch bonds to New York to be canceled and paid off.[23]

It is of course interesting to try to establish how much of the several MKT securities was actually held in Holland at the time of reorganization. A press cutting of 5 March 1890 gives the following totals for Dutch-held securities that had agreed to the Olcott plan: $4,416,000 in 5-percent consols; $3,346,000 in 6-percent consols; and $9,020,000 in common shares. In the cash fund of $18 million, a sum of $9 million had been subscribed to in New York, while Amsterdam had signed up for $4 million. Old MKT sevens and Southern Branch sixes were also taken in lieu of cash when subscribing to new securities, as outlined above, and it is possible that some Dutch owners of these old securities did not opt for cash redemption, but had their old paper converted into new in this way. A later report, of 16 January 1892, gives a total of $9,617,000 in old common shares held by the Dutch association, but does not mention other securities.[24] Later figures indicate a continued Dutch interest in the MKT stock. In 1900 the association was reported to hold 102,210 of commons, plus 4,705 of preferreds, while a number of Dutch stockbrokers still had some 4,000 commons on their hands. At the same time the English Association of American Bond- and Shareholders held 125,940 of commons, out of a grand total of 549,500 in circulation.[25]

Receivers Eddy and Cross operated the railroad until July 1890, when it was returned, in much better condition, to the directors. Henry C. Rouse was the new president and among the directors were well-known names such as John D. Rockefeller, certainly no friend of Jay Gould. H. J. de Marez Oyens, that veteran of many reorganizations, also got a place on the board as the representative of the Dutch interest; in 1908 he was still mentioned as a director.

All new securities were immediately listed in Amsterdam. The shares, both commons and preferreds, in the shape of certificates of five or ten, were issued by the Dutch MKT Association, which thus controlled the destiny of the road to a certain extent. Holdings of commons slowly grew: from the 102,210 reported in 1900, ownership grew to 155,580 in 1905. Four years later the association held only 127,517 commons, with several Dutch brokers accounting for another 500. Germans held only 390 shares in that year. After 1910 total Dutch holdings remained around the 100,000 mark.[26] No dividend was ever paid, and quotations were never higher than 50 percent of par, with lows of 10 percent in the years before 1900 and again in 1914.

The number of preferred shares in Dutch hands was always much smaller than the number of commons, usually around 2,000 but increasing to 5,136 in 1912. In 1906 the first 4-percent dividend was paid, causing an upsurge in the price of preferreds in that year to 74. The last dividend was paid in 1913, and quotations dropped to a low of 26 in 1914. Other MKT bond issues, among them of the Dallas & Waco subsidiary, were also taken up in Amsterdam; details are to be found in Appendixes A and B.

For a time the Missouri, Kansas & Texas seemed to be in good shape. An honest management did its best to improve the road, and access over its own rails to the terminals of St. Louis, Kansas City, Houston, and Galveston made it independent of competitors. In the eyes of Dutch investors, the MKT was seen as a reasonably safe investment, and new securities continued to be marketed in Holland after the turn of the century. But the expansion of the system had been too much for the financially fragile company. Much of the new trackage was in relatively unremunerative branch lines, which contributed little to revenues but formed a heavy burden in the funded debt. When a large amount of short-term notes fell due in 1915, the company was unable to refund them because of the war in Europe, which had cut off most of the capital markets. Default was the result, and in June 1915 a receiver was appointed.

The reorganization took a long time, partly owing to the federal control of all railroads between 1917 and 1920. In 1922 a new Missouri-Kansas-Texas Railroad finally emerged, with a restructured debt. It is not necessary to follow this third reorganization closely, but it may give some insight into the extent of Dutch holdings. Dutch protective committees were formed for both the 4-percent first and second mortgage loans of 1890, indicating a large interest in Holland. In 1918 Dutch holdings were stated as

$15,711,000 in commons, $882,000 in preferreds, $14,720,000 in 4-percent firsts, and $7,071,500 in 4-percent seconds. Dutch holdings in the Dallas & Waco were given as $454,000 in 1919.[27]

Although beyond our period, it is worthwhile to follow the later fortunes of the Dutch association. After the reorganization, the Dutch MKT Association issued new certificates for common shares, of which $3,141,000 was still in Dutch hands in 1934. New 7-percent preferred shares, created in 1922, were also held in Holland, and they were quoted in 1939 between $3.00 and $7.50. New prior lien bonds, series A (5 percent), were quoted between 12 and 15.25 percent of par and series B (4 percent) between 10 and 13. The old second mortgage fours of 1890 had been converted into 5-percent cumulative adjustment mortgage bonds in 1922, and these were quoted in 1939 between 5.75 and 13 percent of par, with the payment of interest again in arrears. Only the old 4-percent firsts of 1890 were undisturbed by the 1922 reorganization, and they commanded their best price in 1939: between 19 and 39 percent of par. The Dallas & Waco bonds were converted into new MKT prior lien bonds, series A, but in 1939 $114,000 worth of old Dutch-held bonds was still unconverted. Their last price was given in 1937, when they were quoted between 64 and 70.25 percent of par.

Fourteen

The Kansas City Southern

One of the last main lines built in the United States was the Kansas City, Pittsburg & Gulf. The idea of a railroad from Kansas City south to the Gulf had already been mooted as soon as that city started its strong growth into a commerial center. Midwestern farmers complained about the long and expensive haul their crops had to make to the eastern seaboard and from there to the markets of Europe. A line to the Gulf of Mexico seemed an attractive proposition and one sure to make transportation cheaper.[1] The stranglehold in which the eastern railroads held the Midwest could only be broken by building an independent line south to the tidewater.

Although many plans were proposed over the years, it took decades before anything really happened. It was Arthur E. Stilwell, a Kansas City real estate tycoon and railroad promoter who was already involved in terminal and belt railways around that city, who would at last realize the dream. In 1893 he incorporated the Kansas City, Pittsburg & Gulf Railroad to build a line to the South. He bought up several existing lines, and the KCP&G, or "PeeGee," as it was locally known, reached Pittsburg, Kansas, and its coal mines in June 1893. Siloam Springs, Arkansas, was reached early in 1894, but construction halted there for a time, while Stilwell went in search of additional capital.[2]

With so many American railroads already in receivership, it was a most importunate moment to ask investors to sink more capital in a railroad like the PeeGee, which had been shaky from the start. Moreover, Stilwell had no confidence in Wall Street and its bankers and brokers, whom he termed the "Cannibals of Wall Street," and he had always tried to avoid them whenever possible. He knew, of course, that the Dutch had invested heavily in the United States, but at that point even they were in no mood to help his ailing road without more incentives than the customary promises of high rates of interest.

But Stilwell was in the unusual position to reach the Dutch capital market without the use of middlemen. He had met and befriended a rich Dutch coffee broker, Jan de Goeijen, Jr., on one of his earlier trips to Europe, and he had as an associate in his Kansas City real estate business Johannes Jacobus (Jacques) Tutein Nolthenius, scion of an old Dutch family with a flourishing Amsterdam brokerage business. The firm of Tutein Nolthenius and De Haan, successor to D. Crommelin and Company, was a conservative establishment specializing in American railroad securities and exactly what Stilwell needed. When he arrived in Amsterdam in 1894 he persuaded the firm to participate, jointly with Jan de Goeijen, in his railroad, but at a price.

These firms undertook to market the bonds of the PeeGee, but as extra security they wanted control of the two construction companies set up by Stilwell as well. Dutch brokers must have known about fraudulent practices with construction companies, but never before had they participated in any of them. Tutein Nolthenius and De Haan and De Goeijen now took over the Arkansas Construction Company, which was to build the road from Siloam Springs to Shreveport, Louisiana, and the Kansas City Terminal Construction Company, which was to continue the line south from Shreveport to the Gulf. In return these brokers undertook to float the KCP&G loan on the Dutch market.

A 5-percent first mortgage gold loan totaling $23 million was authorized. Despite De Goeijen's buy recommendation and despite the low first price of around 60 percent of par, sales were slow, even when shares of the railroad were thrown in free as a bonus. To boost sales De Goeijen incorporated the "Vereeniging van belangen bij obligatiën en aandeelen van de Kansas City, Pittsburg & Gulf, N.V." (Association of Those Interested in Securities of the KCP&G Ltd.) in the form of a limited company, which had its charter approved by royal decree on 5 July 1895.[3] Capital stock was set at Dfl 1,250,000 (Dfl 500,000 paid in), and De Goeijen himself was the largest shareholder. The purpose of the new company was stated as the purchase of KCP&G securities and the keeping of the enormous Dutch interest in the road in one hand. A total of Dfl 5 million in 4-percent bonds of the association was issued between September 1895 and May 1896 with which at least $3.1 million worth of KCP&G securities were acquired and possibly as much as $3,472,500.[4]

Other brokers were active in the same field. The firm of Rutgers and De Beaufort of Amsterdam also sold KCP&G bonds, but how many is not known. Tutein Nolthenius and De Haan, through their Amsterdamsch Trustee Kantoor, issued trust certificates of PeeGee shares. These were for $1,000 each, and they were quoted at a low 15 percent of par in 1897, after 885 of them had been issued.[5] Needless to say, interest was never paid on them. In that same year the bonds were quoted at 70 below par.

With the Dutch millions Stilwell managed to finish his road to the gulf in September 1897, some 800 miles in all. As a terminus a site on Lake Sabine was chosen, which Stilwell modestly named Port Arthur after himself. Although its traffic was booming soon after the completion of the line, the company's financial structure remained shaky. Lack of rolling stock, sloppy construction, and cutthroat competition from other railroads made things worse, and by 1899 the railroad was in receivership.

Personal involvement of the Dutch in the Kansas City, Pittsburg & Gulf was exceptionally large. Usually investors were not interested in the actual running of "their" railroad, but in this case the opposite is true. Jan de Goeijen was appointed the European representative of the Missouri, Kansas & Texas Trust Company, Stilwell's vehicle to finance his earlier undertakings, while Jacques Tutein became manager of the foreign department of the same company in Kansas City. Gerard M. Titsingh, a former

Dutch naval officer and partner in the brokerage of Rutgers and De Beaufort, became vice president of the KCP&G, while Hendrik Visscher was treasurer. S. F. van Oss, the well-known financial journalist who was then living in London, was hired to inspect the line in 1896. A Dutch civil engineer of note, Rudolph P. J. Tutein Nolthenius, cousin *and* brother-in-law of Jacques and partner in the family business, also inspected the railroad, traveling in style in Stilwell's ornate private car in 1899. He has left us a vivid description of the railroad and the country it traversed in his popular travel book.[6] After the demise of the PeeGee and the incorporation of the Kansas City Southern, Daniel G. Boissevain, of the famous Amsterdam banking house, was director of the railroad while Visscher continued as treasurer.[7]

Before the story of the KCP&G is continued, it is necessary to look at some of the other railroads in Stilwell's empire that also attracted Dutch capital. The Kansas City Suburban Belt Railway had been set up in 1886. Three years later Stilwell got involved in the project, which comprised a line from the confluence of the Missouri and Kaw rivers that circled Kansas City, Missouri, and linked up with the Atchison in the west. Drexel and Company of Philadelphia invested some capital in the project, but the line was not finished and continued to operate in the red. Tutein Nolthenius and De Haan sold some of the Suburban Belt bonds in Amsterdam but with little success. Surprisingly, a better trade developed in Belt Railway stock, of which 5,000 shares at $100 each were introduced at the request of De Goeijen in 1895.[8] They were apparently easily sold at the low price of 25 percent of par and were included in the price lists; Hubrecht even issued certificates against them. Besides these certificates, shares in a shareholders' association set up by Tutein Nolthenius were also included in the price lists. This was the Nederlandsche Maatschap van aandeelhouders in de Kansas City Suburban Belt Railroad [sic] Comp. (Netherlands partnership of shareholders of the KCSB), founded in May 1896.

Even earlier than the Suburban Belt, however, another of Stilwell's creations, the Union Terminal, had been introduced in Amsterdam. This Union Terminal was meant as an extension of the Suburban Belt to connect both ends of the Belt in Kansas City, Kansas, including two bridges over the Kaw River. Total length was some 7 miles only, but the two expensive bridges necessitated much extra capital. A first mortgage loan of $2 million was authorized in 1893, with 5-percent coupons. Only half of this loan was issued at first, and $375,000 of the first half was offered by Tutein Nolthenius and Jan de Goeijen jointly in October 1893 at 87.50 percent of par. Interest was guaranteed by the Suburban Belt itself. Rutgers and De Beaufort also offered these bonds, and in the end bonds worth a total of $1.55 million appear to have been sold in Amsterdam.[9]

Despite the apparent ease with which the securities of the Stilwell companies were sold to an unsuspecting Dutch public, there were warning voices. Without openly accusing De Goeijen of actual dishonesty, one writer, Dr. I. A. Lamping, was severely critical of his actions. The highly complex building of companies on top of each other, associations for the acquisition of securities of other companies, and syndicates acting as holding companies, all hid the real state of affairs for the simple investor. Lamping correctly saw the Kansas City, Pittsburg & Gulf as the only item in the complex structure of companies that really mattered and the only one that would in time actually be able to make money. All other components depended on this road in some measure. He was also critical of De Goeijen's reports about the earnings of the PeeGee. All his figures for receipts and expenses were much too optimistic, and every year there was some plausible reason why the road had been prevented from actually making a profit. S. F. van Oss, writing in 1903—after the crash—characterized all KCP&G and related securities as highly speculative, but it was easy for him to be wise after the fact.[10]

The crash came in 1899: between April and August of that year, all of Stilwell's railroads were placed in the hands of receivers and, as usual, the Dutch participants were called on to deposit their securities and form bondholders' committees to protect their interests. First in the field were the Belt Railway shareholders in September 1899, and they organized an association, the Kansas City Suburban Belt Vereeniging, in October. At a meeting of interested parties in Amsterdam on 5 October of that same year, $1,792,000 in shares was represented, of which Jan de Goeijen himself owned (or represented) no less than $1,428,000. Jules L. N. de Gijselaar, R. Bloembergen Ezn., Jan de Goeijen, and E. van Essen, all brokers involved in the scheme, were members of the committee.[11]

A Nederlandsche Vereeniging ter behartiging van de belangen van houders van 5% obligatiën der Kansas City, Pittsburg & Gulf (Dutch Association for 5-percent KCP&G Bondholders) was incorporated next on 25 September 1899. Veteran stockbroker H. J. de Marez Oyens acted as chairman, while R. Bloembergen and Jan de Goeijen were among the members.[12]

Meanwhile, a fight had developed in America over the control of the railroad between John W. Gates, the noted Wall Street speculator, and Edward H. Harriman, who was then already in control of the Union Pacific and well on his way in his meteoric career. In his desperation, Stilwell had sought help from Gates to keep his companies afloat, but soon Gates joined forces with Harriman to oust Stilwell. De Goeijen was caught between his personal loyalty to his friend Stilwell, his own financial involvement, and his responsibility to the Dutch security owners who had trusted him. After some hesitation he joined forces with the Gates-Harriman group, and, with De Goeijen's Dutch holdings, the new consortium easily acquired a majority of both stock and bonds of the old Kansas City, Pittsburg & Gulf. By mid-1900, $12,660,000 in KCP&G shares plus $7,277,100 in bonds had been deposited by the Dutch committee.[13] The Harriman-Gates group soon incorporated the Kansas City Southern Railway, which took over the PeeGee and all its subsidiaries.

The conversion agreed upon was not too disadvantageous for the old bondholders. Every old $1,000, 5-percent bond of the KCP&G was exchanged for $750 in new KCS 3-percent bonds plus $500 in new preferred shares. The old common shares could be exchanged for new ones on payment of $10 per share, but most KCP&G shareholders had not paid anything for their original stock anyway, as the shares had been given away as a bonus.

The Suburban Belt $1,000 bonds were exchanged for $1,330 in new 3-percent bonds plus $250 in new preferred shares. The Union Terminal bonds were exchanged for $1,000 in new 3-percent bonds, again plus $250 in new preferreds. What happened to the Suburban Belt stock, which was widely held in Holland, is not clear. Probably it was also exchanged for new commons and preferreds, but at what rate has not been determined.[14] In the long run this conversion was not too bad: at first the yield dropped from $50 to $22.50 per $1,000, but after the preferred shares started paying the promised 4 percent in 1907, the yield rose to $42.50. De Goeijen himself did come out much better: the reorganization committee paid him a commission of $37,500 over the first $10 million deposited with it, plus 0.25 percent over the rest, which must have brought him another $20,000 or so.[15]

In the copybook of the Dutch KCP&G committee a list has been found of all old fives that were offered for conversion. This list, which covers the period from July 1900 until 19 March 1901, is not complete, but it indicates that at least 5,815 of old KCP&G bonds were offered for exchange during that period. This would mean, of course, that a minimum of $5,815,000 (par value) of old bonds had been owned in Holland. A letter from the Dutch KCP&G committee to the reorganization committee, 5 October 1900, mentions a total of $26 million (par value) in KCP&G securities (common stock and bonds) held in Holland.[16]

After the conversion, large amounts of the new Kansas City Southern securities were held in Holland. Certificates for commons were issued by the Amsterdamsch Trustee's Kantoor (i.e., Tutein Nolthenius and De Haan). Original shares were also held, and they too were regularly quoted. Because no dividend was ever paid, prices remained low, with a high of 49 in 1910. The 4-percent noncumulative preferred shares were also held, both in certificates and originals. Original preferreds came in blocks of five or ten, but the certificates were issued for one, two and one-half, five, or ten shares. They too started rather low, around 30 percent of par, but rose to a high of 72 in 1908 after the first dividend in 1907. Dividends were regular until the end of our period, and prices remained constant around 60 percent of par.[17]

The 3-percent first mortgage loan of the new KCS (per 1950) was very popular, although its price never climbed higher than 75 percent of par because of the low rate of interest. As a result of the conversion, at least some $5 million worth of these bonds must have ended up in Dutch hands.

To tide the company over a sudden shortage of cash in 1906, a total of $5 million worth of 5-percent, 6-year collateral trust notes was issued and sold at a price of 95 percent of par. They soon rose to almost par before being withdrawn in 1909; other KCS securities were introduced in 1909.[18]

The Kansas City Southern securities continued to be a popular paper on the Amsterdam Exchange. In 1934 the Administratie Kantoor reported that it still held 2,705 common shares, plus 44,286 of preferreds, against the certificates in circulation, exclusive of the many original shares also in Dutch hands. Quotations of the commons in 1939 were from $4.50 to $7.90 per share, while the preferreds were higher at between $10.25 to $17.65. The 3-percent bonds of 1900 were quoted from 46.50 to 55.50 percent of par, while the fives were doing between 44.75 and 56.

One more related loan was introduced in Holland after 1914, although strictly speaking not part of the Kansas City Southern itself. In 1910 all railroads entering Kansas City had decided to construct a new Union Terminal, to be used jointly. The Kansas City Terminal Railway was incorporated for the purpose, and it issued a first mortgage loan (per 1960) of $50 million. In 1925 Stuecker and Vié offered these bonds at 94; in 1939 they were still regularly quoted between 72 and 80. The resulting beautiful, neoclassical Kansas City Union Station is still standing, although hardly used by passenger trains anymore.

Although the story of the Kansas City, Pittsburg & Gulf has now been told, something must be said about the fate of the two construction companies. In 1894 De Goeijen had incorporated the Arkansas Construction Company Syndicaat, with a capital of Dfl 5 million, later raised to 6.5 million. Certificates of Dfl 1,000 ($400) were issued at 92.50 percent of par and easily taken up. Stilwell transferred $2,340,000 worth of commons and $520,000 of preferreds of his Arkansas Construction Company to the Dutch syndicate, giving De Goeijen a majority. Much the same happened with the Kansas City Terminal Construction Company (KCTCC) in 1895, for which a second Dutch syndicate was incorporated, capitalized at Dfl 6.5 million, which in its turn held $2,340,000 in KCTCC shares and a same amount of bonds, again a majority.[19]

The two construction companies did indeed construct the railroad and were mostly paid in KCP&G securities and in land, which was given away by the counties (parishes in Louisiana) and towns through which the railroad passed. In the 1900 reorganization both syndicates remained independent, and they continued their existence, albeit more as investment companies. Already in 1897 and 1898 the full purchase price of the certificates had been refunded to the Dutch owners, while dividends or interest continued to be paid to the tune of some 5 percent annually. In 1901 the Internationaal Land Syndicaat (ILS) was incorporated by De Goeijen with the purpose of taking over all landed properties of both syndicates, which were soon dissolved. Owners of syndicate certificates could exchange them at par for new ILS securities. This new company succeeded to the ownership of the Port Arthur Townsite Company and a rich variety of oil-, rice-, and timber-producing land in Texas, Louisiana, and Arkansas. Great profits were made for a number of years, and dividends of 30 percent were not uncommon. Slowly the land was disposed of, and in 1911 the ILS was converted into the Holland-Texas Mortgage Bank of Amsterdam, with the ownership of the Port Arthur Townsite Company as its most valuable asset. In 1938 the bank still owned 128 town lots in Port Arthur plus almost $1 million in mortgages outstanding.

One other offshoot of the construction companies remains to be mentioned. As part of the spoils after the line had been built, the owners of the two Dutch syndicates had acquired some $100,000 in first mortgage bonds (per 1927) of the Kansas City, Shreveport & Gulf Terminal Railway, a company set up to build and operate the terminal facilities in Shreveport. During the process of dissolving the two syndicates, these bonds were sold out of hand in Amsterdam in 1905 at a price between 56 and 65 percent of par. No stockbroker was involved in this operation, and the bonds were never included in the price lists, but they were held in Holland until redemption.[20]

The Dutch investment in the Kansas City, Pittsburg & Gulf and its affiliated companies was the last large-scale financial operation organized from Amsterdam to funnel capital into a particular group of railroads. Of course, Dutch investment in American railroads did not cease after De Goeijen withdrew from the business, but never again were so many millions pumped into one road. In addition, this investment differed in many respects from earlier and later financial operations from Amsterdam. Never before was there such a large personal involvement of the Dutch capitalists in their American companies, and, with the possible small-scale exception of the Oklahoma Central, there would never be another like it. Never before had the Dutch capitalists taken over a construction company, that vehicle eminently suitable for making quick profits, as De Goeijen was to prove once again. And never before or after would there be such a string of Dutch place-names along a railroad built with Dutch money: Amsterdam, Missouri; Mena (named after Queen Wilhelmina of the Netherlands), De Queen (named after De Goeijen, a name no American could pronounce correctly), and Bloomburg (named after R. Bloembergen), all in Arkansas; Zwolle and De Ridder in Louisiana; and Nederland, Texas, just north of the terminus of Port Arthur (and later to become the famous birthplace of cowboy singer and film star Tex Ritter). Not even the Oklahoma Central could boast such a proud array of Dutch names.

Top: The Union Pacific bridge across the Missouri River at Omaha, which opened in 1872. Construction capital raised in Amsterdam helped construct this bridge. (Union Pacific Railroad Museum Collection)

Bottom: Construction of the Kansas Pacific across the Kansas plains into Colorado in the 1860's. Bonds of the KP were held chiefly in Germany and the Netherlands; the road was later a subsidiary of the Union Pacific. (Union Pacific Railroad Museum Collection)

The first train of the Denver Pacific in Greeley, Colorado, in 1870. The DP, closely connected with the Kansas Pacific and chiefly financed from Amsterdam, was taken over by the Dutch bondholders when it defaulted in 1878; it was subsequently sold to Jay Gould. (Denver Public Library, Western History Department)

Two helper engines, Utah & Northern no. 85 and the leased Denver, South Park & Pacific no. 158, in Beaver Canyon near the Idaho-Montana state line in 1885. A narrow-gauge road financed in part from Amsterdam, the U&N later became part of Union Pacific's Oregon Short Line. (Montana Historical Society, Helena)

An Oregon Short Line passenger train crossing the Snake River between Idaho and Oregon in the 1880's. A Union Pacific subsidiary, the OSL was well known on the Amsterdam Stock Exchange. (M. Hazeltine photograph, Oregon Historical Society)

Top: The Union Pacific "Overland," westbound in Fish Cut, Utah, in 1904, along a recently double-tracked stretch of the line. Such construction was part of E. H. Harriman's rehabilitation of the UP's physical plant, which was partly financed by Dutch investment. (Wyoming State Museum)

Bottom: The Denver & Rio Grande depot at Colorado Springs (soon to be known as "Little London") in the 1890's. The first stretch of the line from Denver to Colorado Springs was financed exclusively by the Amsterdam firm of Wertheim and Gompertz in the early 1870's. (Colorado Springs Pioneer Museum)

Construction on the Central Pacific–Southern Pacific Lucin Cut-off, a line crossing part of the Great Salt Lake by trestle. Almost a quarter of the loan to finance the work was subscribed in Amsterdam in 1904. (Southern Pacific photograph, Don L. Hofsommer Collection)

Facing page:
Top: A 4-4-0 engine of the narrow-gauge Cairo & St. Louis (after 1881, the St. Louis & Cairo), the "W. F. Whitehouse," in front of engine-yard workshops, probably in East St. Louis. The StL&C was one of the few American railroads in complete Dutch ownership and control. (Smithsonian Institution)
Bottom: A Southern Pacific engine crossing the Colorado River toward Fort Yuma, Arizona, in October 1877. For its expansion southeastward out of California, the SP had some of its bonds and shares sold in the Netherlands. (Southern Pacific photograph, Don L. Hofsommer Collection)

A New Orleans City Railroad car at the corner of Carondelet and Canal streets around the turn of the century. The successor line, the New Orleans Railways, was one of the few streetcar and interurban companies to seek capital in Amsterdam. (Library of Congress)

Facing page:
Top: Kansas City, Pittsburg & Gulf engine no. 140 at the Rich Mountain, Arkansas, depot in 1900. The last American railroad built almost entirely with Dutch capital, the KCP&G was already in receivership at the time of this photo. (Collection of Dr. S. R. Wood, DeGolyer Library, Southern Methodist University, Dallas)
Bottom: To boost the enthusiasm of Dutch investors in the Kansas City, Pittsburg & Gulf, Arthur Stilwell built a fashionable resort on top of Rich Mountain, near Mena, Arkansas. Although Queen Wilhelmina never came to the room reserved for her, the building continues today as a hotel and restaurant in Queen Wilhelmina State Park. (Veenendaal)

Nederlandsche Vereeniging ter behartiging van de rechten van belanghebbenden bij de MISSOURI KANSAS & TEXAS RAILWAY COMPANY.

(DUTCH ASSOCIATION TO PROTECT THE RIGHTS OF PARTIES INTERESTED IN THE MISSOURI KANSAS & TEXAS RAILWAY COMPANY.)

CERTIFICATE

Serie B. № _____

This is to certify that the undersigned has received the **6 pCt. General Consolidated Mortgage Bond of the Missouri Kansas & Texas Railway Company** of

ONE THOUSAND DOLLARS

№ _____

with coupons from June 1st 1888, (inclusive) on the conditions mentioned in a deed executed the 30th of June 1888 before J. C. G. POLLONES, Notary public at Amsterdam.

Amsterdam, _____ 188 .

Nederlandsche Vereeniging
ter behartiging van de rechten van belanghebbenden bij de
Missouri Kansas & Texas Railway Company.

Countersigned,

Notary Public.

Example of a certificate of a Dutch Protective Committee. Such certificates were given out in exchange for original bonds deposited with the committee. This unissued certificate was for the 1888 default of the Missouri, Kansas & Texas Railway; the reverse has the same text in Dutch. (Veenendaal)

Fifteen

Investment Funds

*I*nvestment funds dealing with American securities exclusively were already set up in the Netherlands in the first half of the nineteenth century. Because several of them held very large blocks of American railroad paper, some attention must be paid to this typically Dutch phenomenon of the investment fund.

The modern investment fund, now so popular with savers, seems to have been a Dutch invention. A first *negotiatie*, as it was called in Holland, was opened back in 1774 by the Amsterdam stockbroker Abraham van Ketwich. It contained most elements of modern mutual funds except that it was limited to a period of 25 years. Every share cost Dfl 500 and gave the owner a right to a portion of a portfolio which consisted of ten different (in this case, all foreign) bonds. American securities were not yet included in this and other negotiaties set up along the same lines. Most of these early funds ended in losses for the investors, chiefly as a result of the French revolutionary wars, which could hardly have been foreseen by the initiators.[1]

For a time Dutch interest in these investment funds seemed to disappear, and the first one of the nineteenth century was only born accidentally. The Second Bank of the United States in Philadelphia had attracted Dutch capital with two loans in 1840 totaling Dfl 10 million negotiated through Hope and Company. As collateral for the first loan of Dfl 5.5 million a total of Dfl 6,875,000 par value ($2.75 million) in state bonds of Pennsylvania, Maryland, Mississippi, Illinois, and Michigan, all paying 5 or 6 percent, had been deposited. For the second loan of Dfl 4.5 million, 5- and 6-percent bonds of Pennsylvania, Maryland, Louisiana, Mississippi, Illinois, Michigan, and Indiana, plus bonds of the Farmers Loan and Trust Company of New York, had been deposited with Hope and Company. Together these had a par value of $2.25 million, or Dfl 5,625,000.[2]

Most of the states involved sooner or later defaulted, and the yield of the collateral was insufficient to pay out the promised 5 percent, but what little interest came in was channeled by Hope to the Dutch bondholders of the bank. At the same time, sale of the collateral at a good price was almost impossible, because most of these defaulted loans were quoted much below par. By 1847 the situation had slowly improved, and some of the states resumed interest payments.

With the final liquidation of the Second Bank of the United States in 1853, Hope and Company acquired more securities as partial payment of outstanding debts. Among these was some paper of early American railroads, chiefly in the Philadelphia area, such as the Philadelphia, Germantown & Norristown, of which Hope got 341 shares, valued at $18,755, plus $19,800 in bonds. Other railroad securities thus acquired were $11,000 in bonds of the Beaver Meadow Railroad; 15 shares, valued at $600, of the Mount Carbon Railroad; 35 shares of the Petersburg (Virginia) Railroad, valued at $2,275; plus some canal company shares and bonds. The total was estimated at just below $100,000. At the next distribution, Hope got an additional $222,000 worth of securities formerly held by the bank, including bonds of the Alleghany Portage Railroad and the Philadelphia & Columbia Railroad.[3]

Most sensibly, Hope and Company decided not to keep these small fractions but sold them as soon as a good price could be obtained. In 1855 the larger holdings of the former collateral—the state bonds and the Farmers Trust and Loan bonds—were officially transferred to Hope and Company, which decided not to sell but to set up a kind of investment fund called Gemeenschappelijk Bezit van Amerikaansche Effecten bij Hope & Co. (Mutual fund of American securities with Hope & Co.), split into two series parallel to the two original loans to the Bank of the United States.[4] Series A held only American state bonds, while series B also held state bonds, Wabash Canal Company stock, and $300,000 of Farmers Loan and Trust Company bonds (per 1857). In 1858 these latter bonds, then in default, were exchanged for $77,000 worth of Michigan Central Railroad shares, later augmented to $129,700; $68,000 worth of Michigan Central 8-percent bonds, later raised to $94,000; $17,000 worth of Central of New Jersey 7-percent bonds, later raised to $24,000; plus state bonds of Missouri, Virginia, and Tennessee, and City of St. Louis bonds.[5] Later changes saw the sale of the Central of New Jersey bonds and the inclusion of North Missouri Railroad 6-percent bonds ($50,000 par), plus city bonds of Chicago, Boston, and New York. Only in 1890 were both series finally liquidated. The disaster that had threatened the Dutch bondholders of the Second Bank of the United States in the 1840's had been most successfully averted, and the operation had even ended in a small profit for the participants.

■ *Vereenigde Amerikaansche Fondsen*

While the investment fund set up by Hope and Company may be seen as improvisational and organized for the purpose of rescuing anything from failing investments, the next fund was set up with the explicit purpose of reducing risk and facilitating investment for small capitalists, while at the same time guaranteeing a reasonable yield. In 1869 Kerkhoven and Company and Gebr. Boissevain opened their Vereenigde Amerikaansche Fondsen (United American Funds). Their first series consisted of Dfl 1 million in shares, called certificates of participation, worth Dfl 50, 100, or 1,000 each and carrying 5-percent interest. The surplus income from the investment, if any, was to be used for redemption of the shares through drawings. The portfolio was assembled from the following American securities:

6-percent United States federal bonds
7-percent first mortgage St. Paul & Pacific bonds
6-percent first mortgage Central Pacific bonds
6-percent first mortgage Union Pacific Southern Branch bonds
Illinois Central stock
7-percent guaranteed Pittsburgh, Fort Wayne & Chicago stock
7-percent preferred Chicago & North Western stock
Chicago, Rock Island & Pacific stock

For every Dfl 1 million in shares of the investment fund, the fund bought $50,000 worth of each type of security listed, making a total (par value) of $400,000 (Dfl 1 million). The first series was designed for a maximum investment of Dfl 5 million, but only some 2 million were actually received, which meant that about $800,000 worth of the American securities listed must have been bought, of which $700,000 was in railroad securities.

A second series was opened in 1870, which amounted to Dfl 4 million and held $200,000 of each of the following American securities:

7-percent Chicago & Southwestern first mortgage bonds
8-percent Alabama & Chattanooga first mortgage bonds
6-percent South Missouri first mortgage bonds
6-percent Central Pacific first mortgage bonds
6-percent Louisiana Levee bonds
7-percent guaranteed Pittsburgh, Fort Wayne & Chicago stock
7-percent preferred Chicago & North Western stock
Cleveland, Columbus, Cincinnati & Indianapolis stock

In this way another $1.4 million (par value) worth of American railroad securities were held in Amsterdam.

The success of this second series caused Kerkhoven and Boissevain to open a third, starting in 1872. A total of a little under Dfl 4 million was subscribed to in one year, and the portfolio this time held the following securities:

7-percent Atlantic, Mississippi & Ohio first mortgage
7-percent St. Paul & Pacific, St. Vincent Extension first mortgage
7-percent Toledo, Peoria & Warsaw first mortgage
6-percent Union Pacific main line first mortgage
6-percent Chesapeake & Ohio first mortgage
6-percent California & Oregon or Central Pacific San Joaquin Valley first mortgage
7-percent preferred Chicago, Milwaukee & St. Paul stock
Cleveland, Columbus, Cincinnati & Indianapolis stock

This third series held another $1.6 million in American railroad securities.[6]

Of course, the slump of 1873 meant great losses for the three series; many of the railroads involved defaulted, dividends were cut or reduced, and the yield of the fund's shares diminished considerably. One of the articles of incorporation of the Vereenigde Amerikaansche Fondsen held that shareholders could withdraw their original invest- ment at will, but only in return for one $1,000 bond or share of each of the securities involved in that series, meaning that withdrawals could only take place in blocks of $8,000, or Dfl 20,000. Despite this impediment, 28.6 percent of the second series and 30 percent of the third series were withdrawn between 1875 and 1879. The first series clearly had given the best results, as most of the roads involved did not default, and nothing was withdrawn from this first series.[7] Because all securities included in the fund were also traded regularly in Amsterdam, the bonds or shares withdrawn from the second and third series could easily be sold on the open market.

Despite the fact that by 1879 payment of the regular dividend on the fund's shares had not yet quite reached the original 5-percent level, Kerkhoven and Boissevain tried to start a fourth series at the end of that year. This time they decided on a solid and safe portfolio paying 6 percent, but this series never advanced beyond the planning stage. Apparently the Dutch investors thought the price at introduction—103.50 percent of par, the result of the quest for solidity—was too high. The first series had been issued at 77.375 percent of par, the second at 77 flat, and the third at 80.25. The annual redemp- tion drawing at par could thus mean a sweet profit, but not so with the projected fourth series.

It is not necessary to follow the history of the three series of the Vereenigde Ameri- kaansche Fondsen in detail, but some attention must be paid to its holdings of Ameri- can railroad securities. In 1886 the first series, after redemption drawings and voluntary withdrawals, still consisted of some Dfl 1.3 million in certificates of participation. In that year it was enlarged to Dfl 3,925,000, with an equal expansion of the portfolio, again mostly in American railroad securities.

The old second and third series were joined in 1890 and then totaled Dfl 3.2 million still outstanding; the rest (out of an original total of almost Dfl 8 million) had been withdrawn or redeemed over the years. Only in 1921, profiting from the favorable rate of exchange, were both series liquidated and the rest of the portfolio sold. It is almost impossible to follow the portfolios of both series closely. Bonds and shares were sold and bought, and with every reorganization in America old securities were exchanged for new ones, making for a most complicated picture. Some figures for 1914 are available. In that year the first series consisted of:

$125,000 in preferred stock of the Chicago & North Western
$125,000 in guaranteed stock of the Pittsburgh, Fort Wayne & Chicago
$125,000 in Illinois Central stock
$125,000 in the 4-percent first refunding mortgage of the Central Pacific
$125,000 in the 4-percent general mortgage of the Norfolk & Western
$125,000 in 4-percent convertible bonds of the Southern Pacific
$125,000 in 3.5-percent convertible bonds of the Pennsylvania Railroad
$125,000 in 4.5-percent convertible bonds of the Chicago, Milwaukee & St. Paul

It will be noted that the first three securities were old faithfuls, which had been in- cluded in the portfolio right from the start and which had always given good results.

Other old stocks, such as the Rock Island shares, were still held in 1903, but had been disposed of by 1909, when that road got into serious trouble.

In 1914 the second series contained the following securities:

$105,000 in preferred stock of the Chicago & North Western
$105,000 in preferred stock of the Chicago, Milwaukee & St. Paul
$105,000 in the 4-percent first mortgage of the Union Pacific
$105,000 in 4-percent convertible bonds of the Atchison, Topeka & Santa Fe
$105,000 in the 5-percent first mortgage of the Oregon & California
$105,000 in the 5-percent consolidated first mortgage of the Utah & Northern
$105,000 in the 4-percent first mortgage of the Chicago Great Western
$90,000 in Illinois Central stock
$95,000 in the 4-percent collateral mortgage of the Atlantic Coast Line[8]

Again many old standbys will be noted, but there are also some new names. All these railroads were known on the Amsterdam Stock Exchange, although not all of these securities were included in the price lists there in 1914.

Taken together, the results of the Vereenigde Amerikaansche Fondsen were positive, apart from the years between 1873 and 1879 when the promised 5-percent yield could not be attained. Of course, there were always critics who attacked the selection of the securities, but generally the managers of Kerkhoven and Gebr. Boissevain did a good job. The results of the first series have been computed at 9 percent and those of the second and third series at 7 and 3 percent, respectively. The new first and second series both reached 4.5 percent during their life span, again not bad, although certainly not outstanding.[9]

■ *Vereenigd Bezit van Amerikaansche Hypothecaire Spoorweg-Obligatiën*

With the apparent success of Kerkhoven and Boissevain in their investment fund, it was only natural that others would try to imitate them. Six months after the pioneers issued their first series, the Maatschappij tot Beheer van het Administratie Kantoor van Amerikaansche Spoorwegwaarden, opgericht door Wertheim & Gompertz, Westendorp & Co., en F. W. Oewel (Company for the Administration of the Administrative Bureau for American Railroad Securities, Founded by . . .) started its Vereenigd Bezit van Amerikaansche Hypothecaire Spoorweg-Obligatiën (United Property of American Railroad Mortgage Bonds). Wertheim and partners set up an almost perfect copy of the Vereenigde Amerikaansche Fondsen of Kerkhoven and Boissevain and in 1870 issued their first series of Dfl 1 million in certificates of participation (Dfl 1,000 each) at a first price of 77.25 percent of par. This first series, paying 5 percent, was heavily oversubscribed, and Wertheim immediately issued a second one with the same success, and continued until a ninth series was issued in January of 1873. All series were of Dfl 1 million, and all were fully sold, except for the last one, of which only some Dfl 100,000 was sold before the general economic crisis hit. Price at introduction had risen from the first 77.25 to about 86 of par for the eighth. Nevertheless, the redemption drawings at par, which were stipulated in the charter, could mean a significant profit.

Each series was secured by a portfolio consisting of $40,000 worth of the following bonds held in equal amounts:

7-percent California Pacific
7-percent California Pacific Extension
7-percent Oregon & California
7-percent St. Louis & South Eastern
7-percent Chicago & Southwestern
7-percent Kansas Pacific
7-percent Denver Pacific
7-percent North Missouri
7-percent Union Pacific Southern Branch
7-percent Central Pacific

Even when the last and incomplete (ninth) series is left out, this means that $320,000 worth of each of these bonds was held by Wertheim and partners before 1873, making this a sizable investment in the roads in question.[10] But unfortunately many of the railroad companies involved were among the first to default during the slump of 1873. As a result it was jokingly said that Mr. Wertheim's railroad arsenal looked more like a hospital.[11] And there were other critical voices: one of the few solid investments, the bonds of the Central Pacific, had been exchanged in 1873 for securities of the Paducah & Memphis, which was closer and therefore easier to supervise. At least those were the reasons Wertheim gave for the exchange. It was said, however, that Wertheim's Administratie Kantoor, caught with a large number of unsold Paducah & Memphis bonds on its hands, had been trying to unload them on the Dutch public. The success had been minimal, but instead of taking the loss itself, the firm had sold them, for a "reasonable" price, to its own investment fund.[12]

Because of the defaults of most of the railroads in Wertheim's "hospital," the regular payment of the 5 percent could not be resumed until 1881. By then the portfolio had been reduced through redemption drawings (510 before the end of 1873) and voluntary withdrawals, which together amounted to almost 40 percent of the total before 1880. In March 1880 the collateral was reported as consisting of $227,000 of each of the following bonds:

7-percent Cairo & St. Louis
7-percent North Missouri
6-percent Kansas Pacific
8-percent Elizabethtown & Paducah
7-percent Paducah & Memphis
7-percent St. Louis & South Eastern
7-percent Cleveland & Mount Vernon
6-percent Union Pacific Southern Branch (MKT)
6-percent prior lien New York, Pennsylvania & Ohio

The portfolio also contained £45,400 (sterling) in 6-percent Chicago & Grand Trunk bonds and $13,000 in 8-percent Paducah & Elizabethtown bonds.[13] Again, this portfolio was certainly not a show of strength, holding as it did a number of financially weak issues and few truly strong companies. With some lucky sales, however, the 5 percent could again be paid out after 1882, and the redemption drawings were resumed in the same year.

A complete reorganization was undertaken in 1892, when Dfl 3,713,000 of the original Dfl 8,100,000 was still outstanding. The exclusively American character was abolished, and railroad bonds from elsewhere were included. New subscriptions came in after the change, and early in 1915 the total outstanding was Dfl 4,525,000. The collateral then consisted of $181,000 of each of the following American railroad bonds:

5-percent Florida Central & Peninsular
4-percent Grand Trunk Western
4-percent Mason City & Fort Dodge
3-percent Kansas City Southern
5-percent Buffalo & Southwestern, guaranteed by Erie
4.5-percent Missouri, Kansas & Texas

Additional holdings included two Mexican, one Brazilian, and one Philippine railway loan.[14] After 1914 the yield of the fund declined steadily, until in 1938 a low of 0.99 percent of par was all that could be obtained. Final liquidation followed in 1939.[15]

■ *Vereenigd Bezit van Amerikaansche Fondsen*

Operating on a much smaller scale than the two earlier funds was the Vereenigd Bezit van Amerikaansche Fondsen (United Property of American Securities), established in 1887 by the N. V. Maatschappij tot Beheer van het Administratie Kantoor van Amerikaansche Fondsen opgerigt door Broes & Gosman, Ten Have & Van Essen, en Jarman & Zoonen. The Kantoor followed largely the examples set earlier by Kerkhoven and Wertheim and started with an issue of Dfl 2.5 million in certificates of participation of Dfl 1,000 or 500 each, introduced at a first price of 80.25 percent of par. This was relatively inexpensive, because the certificates of the other two funds were being quoted around par. The dividend was fixed at 3.5 percent and the portfolio was assembled from 21 different American securities, mostly railroad paper. The Dutch investing public received the new offering less than enthusiastically. The portfolio was seen as a hodgepodge of too many dubious bonds, with little security, and only about Dfl 1 million in certificates could be sold. Yet the 3.5 percent was regularly paid.[16]

In 1915, with only Dfl 873,500 in certificates still outstanding, the portfolio consisted of $17,000 worth of each of the following securities:

6-percent first mortgage of the Northern Pacific Terminal
6-percent improvement bonds of the Norfolk & Western
5-percent first mortgage of the Chicago & Erie
4-percent first mortgage of the Union Pacific
4-percent consolidated mortgage of the Denver & Rio Grande
4-percent first mortgage of the Missouri, Kansas & Texas

4-percent first mortgage of the Rio Grande Western
4-percent first mortgage of the Peoria & Eastern
4-percent first mortgage of the St. Louis South Western
4-percent consolidated mortgage of the St. Louis & San Francisco
preferred stock of the Chicago, St. Paul, Minneapolis & Omaha
4.5-percent first mortgage of the National Railways of Mexico
5-percent first mortgage of the Manitoba & South Western
Canadian Pacific stock
two nonrailroad loans[17]

All American railroads included were known and listed on the Amsterdam Stock Exchange, with the exception of the Peoria & Eastern, which later became part of the Cleveland, Cincinnati, Chicago & St. Louis.

In 1920 the Vereenigd Bezit van Amerikaansche Fondsen was finally liquidated. Of the original Dfl 1.25 million in certificates, only Dfl 761,000 was still outstanding; the rest had been redeemed by drawings over the years.[18]

■ *Other Dutch Investment Funds*

Apart from the relatively large investment funds described above, which specialized in American railroad securities, there were others which included a few such securities but which were organized along different lines. Still others were hardly to be called investment funds, but did operate along somewhat the same principles. The Administratie Kantoor of Broes and Gosman and partners had done well marketing several Chicago & North Western issues since 1870, and it decided to cash in on the success by issuing certificates of its own, held against a collateral of suitable North Western securities, somewhat along the lines of an investment fund. In 1878 they opened a department for first mortgage railway bonds in certificates of Dfl 1,000 ($400), paying 7 percent and issued at 92 percent of par. They were secured by $400,000 worth of 7-percent Menominee River Railroad bonds (per 1906); $200,000 worth of Minnesota Valley 7-percent bonds (per 1908); $200,000 of Rochester & Northern Minnesota 7-percent bonds (per 1908); and $100,000 of 7-percent bonds of the Plainview Railway (per 1908). It will be noted that none of these securities as such was listed in Amsterdam, although all were guaranteed by the Chicago & North Western. Pik was doubtful about the collateral. He was not sure that the total of only 91 miles covered by these lines would be sufficient to guarantee a 7-percent interest, but he was proved wrong, and payment was never suspended. The certificates became very popular and prices rose to well over par, reaching a high of 135 in 1895. They were redeemed in 1908 at par, paying Dfl 987.21 after deduction of costs. They had been an excellent and carefree investment, and one wonders why the same consortium did not buy more of the same.[19]

The Groningen firm of Messrs. Van Viersen, Trip and Feith had a different experience. Prompted by the many losses suffered by small Dutch investors as a result of the 1873 crisis, this firm set up an investment fund of its own in 1876. It remained, however, relatively small. Besides a few American railroad securities, it mostly held Austrian and Russian government bonds. In 1890 about 900 certificates of participation of Dfl 100 each had been sold, and this number grew to a maximum of almost 14,000 in 1920. Despite its relatively small size it had a long life and was finally liquidated only in 1955.[20]

A short-lived latecomer was the Hollandsche Beleggings Compagnie established in 1904 jointly by Hope and Company, the Nederlandsche Handel-Maatschappij, and J. D. Santilhano. This fund invested in American railroad stocks and bonds among many other securities, but it is not known to what extent railroads formed part of the total portfolio. American securities—government bonds, industrial stocks, and railroad and other transportation company securities—predominated in the fund; Kuhn, Loeb and Company of New York acted as American representative. In 1911 the Beleggings Compagnie was dissolved and the proceeds of the sale of the securities were distributed among the owners.[21]

The Hollandsche Beleggings Compagnie was the last of the pre–World War I Dutch investment funds with American railroad securities in their portfolios. Their importance as part of the total Dutch investment in the American railroad network was never very great, except for the years just prior to the 1873 crisis. In that year the total amount invested in American railroad securities by the two investment funds of Kerkhoven–Boissevain and Wertheim and partners was at least $6.9 million (par value), plus some $273,000 in the old fund set up by Hope and Company, bringing the grand total to well over $7 million in 1873. In 1914 the total was down to $1,893,000 for the three funds of which the portfolios are known, plus some more for the unknown ones, making it safe to assume that between $2 and $2.5 million in American railroad securities was still held in the various Dutch investment funds just prior to World War I.

Conclusion

Dutch investment in the American railroad network did not coincide with the beginnings of railroad construction in America, but when it finally came it soon grew into a flood. In the 1830's Dutch investors seemed not to be interested in American railroad securities, and American promoters visiting Amsterdam in the hope of obtaining capital returned empty-handed. This lack of interest persisted in the 1840's and early 1850's, when Dutch–American financial relations were at a low ebb. Many states had gone into default on loans held in Europe in the 1840's, and the losses suffered had been sufficient to turn the participants in the Amsterdam money market away from America toward brighter prospects in Russia and Austria. The few railroad loans that were floated in Holland before the Civil War were introduced at the initiative of foreign promoters or bankers: the Illinois Central securities after David Neal's visit to Amsterdam; the New Orleans, Jackson & Great Northern through the Dutch branch of the London house of J. Henry Schroeder and Company; the Galveston bonds through French bankers and their Dutch affiliates. The arteries through which Dutch money had been flowing across the Atlantic in the late eighteenth and early nineteenth centuries seemed to have become clogged. By the 1840's the land business—principally the Holland Land Company—was being wound up, the old Dutch trading houses with connections in America had for the most part closed down, and of the few Dutch bankers that were still in business, Hope and Company was in serious trouble with its American portfolio and was turning its attention more toward Russia. Small wonder that Dutch investors were not much interested in the new American adventures.

Moreover, the Dutch did not acquire American railroad securities as partial payment for iron rails and rolling stock, as English ironmasters habitually did, because industrial production of these items in Holland was very limited. In 1856, roughly $500,000 (par value) in American railroad securities were sold in Amsterdam; the annual amounts, however, grew in the late 1850's.

With the outbreak of the American Civil War, Dutch interest in American railroad securities evaporated, but not that in American bonds in general, as some federal government bonds were successfully marketed in Holland. For years a profound silence must have reigned in the American rails corner in the Amsterdam Stock Exchange. Only in 1864 were new securities introduced, at first again by a Belgian broker offering Atlantic & Great Western securities. This was to be the last offering by a non-Dutch house, however, for from that year on Dutch brokers were sufficiently interested to act for themselves. Houses such as Gebr. Boissevain, Gebr. Teixeira de Mattos, Kerkhoven, Wertheim and Gompertz, Broes and Gosman, and many others entered the American railroad market and soon the "craze" was well underway. The popularity of American rails was chiefly caused by their high interest rates combined with offering prices well below par, thus giving the buyer actual returns of around 10 percent or even higher. Most were new issues, some even aimed specifically at the Dutch market, in which cases coupons were payable in guilders as well as dollars. Older issues, often remnants of issues meant for other markets, were also imported occasionally. When political circumstances in Europe made the successful floating of new issues on other bourses impossible, underwriters sought an alternative market in Amsterdam. The popularity of American rails was helped in no small measure by the Austrian forced conversion of 1866, which threw a great deal of capital on the market for which few outlets existed outside Russian securities. The great rush to American rails, however, really started in 1869 with eight new offerings; Table 1 gives a comparison of these new issues to the number of new issues in London from 1869 until 1873.[1] The Dutch apparently dropped out of the race much earlier than the British did. The year 1874 seems to corroborate this: only two new securities were introduced in Amsterdam, of which one was in part a refunding of an earlier loan, compared to seventeen in London.

The reason for this sudden caution on the part of the Dutch was the large number of railroads in default as a result of the 1873 crash. Of the 55 American railroad companies known in Amsterdam in 1873 (many with several issues of bonds or stock), no fewer than 30 defaulted in or shortly after 1873. Of course, the British were also hard hit by the many defaults, but it might be argued that Continental investors were for a time less inclined to buy new American railroad securities than their British counterparts.[2] In some cases the Dutch investment had to be completely written off, but in many other cases at least part could be salvaged during the ensuing reorganization of the bankrupt road. Some companies proved to be fraudulent to the core, with the Galveston, Houston & Henderson as the first and most glaring example. Others were only overly optimistic, and despite warnings in the Dutch financial press, investors had eagerly taken up securities that should never have been offered at all. Brokers, tempted by the high commissions, all too often did not check the figures offered and statements made in the prospectus and simply recommended the paper to their clients, with disastrous results. As noted in Chapter 2, the Stock Exchange Committee did not yet supervise the brokers to any extent, so the wisdom of investing in a specific issue depended on the honesty and acumen of the individual broker involved. Not only small brokers such as Lion Hertz failed to show the necessary caution; the bigger firms also made the same mistake. After the 1873 crash brokers became more cautious and regularly sent repre-

TABLE 1
*New Issues of Railroad Stock in London
and Amsterdam, 1869–73*

	London	Amsterdam
1869	4	3
1870	10	10
1871	9	8
1872	20	24
1873	23	3

SOURCE: London figures from D. R. Adler, *British Invest-ment*, Appendix I; Amsterdam figures from AASE.

sentatives of their own to America to check on the railroads whose securities they were handling.

Dutch investors were not interested in active participation in the management of the railroads whose securities they owned. Theirs was the perfect example of passive portfolio investment, and only when their investment seemed to be threatened did they send an agent to America to act for them. The names of W. F. Piek, F. W. Oewel, P. C. A. M. van Weel, H. J. de Marez Oyens, and others come up again and again, defending the Dutch interest against supposedly grasping American financiers, hostile federal and state courts, and, in some cases, other foreign investors as well. When a railroad ended up in Dutch ownership and control after a foreclosure sale, as was the case with the Denver Pacific in 1878, the Dutch were happy to sell the road when an acceptable offer from an American buyer could be obtained. There are no instances of American railroads run by the Dutch for more than a few years, as was the case with the British and their Alabama Great Southern (an unusual situation for the British as well). Only the Cairo & St. Louis; the Paducah & Elizabethtown; the Memphis, Paducah & Northern; and the Cleveland, Akron & Columbus—all in the hands of Wertheim and Gompertz—came close, with a number of Dutch and Dutch-appointed officers in leading positions. However, these too were emergency measures. As soon as the roads could be sold or leased on reasonable conditions, Wertheim was only too willing to let go of the actual management, even if his control of the Cairo & St. Louis lasted for decades. In the 1890's only the Kansas City, Pittsburg & Gulf adventure was comparable, with many Dutch engineers and financiers actively participating in the actual running of the railroad for some four years. Again, this was a short-lived and isolated case, with no consequences except for the land and mortgage activities that grew out of the investment in the railroad itself and in its affiliated construction companies.

All this does not mean that the Dutch were not interested in how "their" railroads were run. Yet as long as interest was being paid, no one complained or had reason to take action. To make sure that the local management would do its best for the foreign bond- and shareholders, the Dutch regularly appointed directors or board members to represent their interests, just as the British did in comparable cases. More often than not these men were Americans, such as the New York banker-merchant of Dutch extraction

Anthony G. Dulman, who acted as "Dutch" director of numerous American railroads in the 1870's and 1880's. Another common name is H. W. Smithers of Louisville, Kentucky, probably of English descent. He was the regular correspondent of Wertheim and Gompertz in most of its ventures and acted as receiver or director of many of the roads that firm came to control. A third was Louis H. Meyer, the senior partner of the German-oriented investment bankers Meyer and Stucken of New York. His name was familiar as a trustee of many railroad mortgages or as "Dutch" director of railroads with large amounts of Dutch money in their capital structure.

In a few cases in which the Dutch interest was particularly large but without a clear majority of the equity outstanding, Dutch bankers were appointed to the board of the railroads in question, such as the Chicago & North Western, the Milwaukee, the Illinois Central, and the Missouri, Kansas & Texas, to name but the most important cases. It is doubtful, however, if these men could have done more than attend the annual stockholders' meetings, if that. Their commitments both at home and abroad were so extensive that they did not take part in the day-to-day business of the railroads on which they served.

■ *Geography and the Dutch Investor*

It has been supposed that the Dutch, coming rather late in the field, had to be content with the securities of railroads left over by the British, and for that reason Dutch investment in eastern railroads was negligible and was instead concentrated in the Midwest and the West. It is true that large New England companies attracted little Dutch investment; on the other hand, such eastern roads as the Morris & Essex and the Baltimore & Ohio were well-known and popular among Dutch investors. However, the railroads in the Old Northwest—Ohio, Michigan, Indiana, and Illinois—were most dependent on Dutch capital. Those of the Mississippi Valley also received special attention by the Dutch. In the South, the Louisville & Nashville, the Norfolk & Western, and the Chesapeake & Ohio all used Dutch money on a large scale. The Southeast was almost completely absent from the Dutch portfolios, apart from a few minor Florida roads acquired in the early 1870's. Political preferences seem to have had little weight with Dutch investors. Although the former Confederacy had never been popular in the Netherlands, the Dutch invested happily in the Atlantic, Mississippi & Ohio of Confederate war hero William Mahone.

The most important regions for Dutch capital involvement were by far the Midwest, Northwest, and Southwest. Almost all the roads running from Chicago to the Northwest and West were supported by Dutch capital. Consequently, their names became household words in Amsterdam and in the Dutch press. Southwestern roads such as the Atchison, Topeka & Santa Fe, the St. Louis & San Francisco, and especially the Missouri, Kansas & Texas all worked with very large amounts of Dutch money. All transcontinentals, with the sole exception of the Northern Pacific, were at least partly dependent on the Amsterdam Exchange for their financial needs. It was, however, the sprawling system of the Southern Pacific, including all of its predecessors and subsidiaries, that had the largest number of issues regularly traded in Amsterdam, a total of 29. Runner-up was the Union Pacific with 26; behind that road came the Great Northern with 23. The Chicago & North Western, although one of the American railroads with the largest amount of Dutch capital, had only 10.

Some roads would probably have failed during their start-up phases but for the infusion of Dutch capital: General Palmer's Denver & Rio Grande would not have laid a single mile of rail in the early 1870's without the money advanced by the descendants of Palmer's heroes, the Dutch freedom fighters of the sixteenth century. In the same years, the St. Paul & Pacific would have been stuck in the Minnesota prairies without the millions from Amsterdam, and Stilwell's projected line "straight as the crow flies" from Kansas City to the Gulf could only be realized with the guilders advanced by De Goeijen and his fellows in Amsterdam in the 1890's.

The preference of the Dutch for Midwestern and Western roads probably has less to do with timing than has been suggested. These roads, generally built in virgin territory, were not expected to be profitable for many years, and consequently their securities commanded lower prices. With the Dutch love of a bargain, these cheap securities found a ready market in Holland, sometimes with disastrous results, but often also with profits in the long run. When comparing the list given by Adler with the one given here for the years 1869–73 (Table 1), it is striking to note that the first prices of London-bought securities were generally much higher than the Amsterdam ones. While among the latter low 70's were quite common, in the English list prices in the 80's and low 90's seemed to be the rule. Erie commons became a rage in Amsterdam only when their price dropped to below 50 percent of par in 1868, while on the other hand Baltimore & Ohio commons, introduced in 1870 at 110, never did sell as well as the cheap Eries. Common stock of the already bankrupt Boston, Hartford & Erie worth $1 million (par value) found a ready market in Amsterdam in 1872 at bargain prices between 8 and 13 percent of par, apparently in the hope of selling soon at rising prices, again proof of the love of cheap paper on the part of at least a segment of the Dutch investing public. The more conservative group of investors opted for safer paper, such as the Fort Wayne 7-percent guaranteed shares, introduced in 1869 at 107 over par.

■ *Types of Dutch Investment*

Initially Dutch investors had a clear preference for bonds instead of shares. Of the 83 issues of American railroad paper circulating at the end of 1873 (refundings excluded), 71 were bonds and only 12 stocks, commons as well as preferreds. Indeed, Pik, who has often been quoted before, warned against all stock, even that of respectable companies such as the Chicago & North Western or Illinois Central, which were paying regular dividends and were widely held in Holland already. He was right as far as Eries and some others go, but many other shares did pay handsome dividends over the years and proved to be an excellent investment, commanding high prices in Amsterdam.

After the general crisis of 1873 American rails were, for a time, definitely unpopular in Amsterdam, and most new offerings there were refundings of earlier loans in default or securities of reorganized companies. Apparently, the hardship suffered by Dutch investors after the crisis was soon forgotten, for in 1879 new issues were picking up again, reaching a total of 22 in 1880 and 17 in the next year, again not counting refundings. When refundings and reorganizations are included, it is noticeable that a much larger proportion of stock to bonds was now offered: over the three years 1879–81 no fewer than 24 different shares were introduced, against 32 bonds. Among the shares were those of financially weak lines such as the Toledo, Peoria & Western and the New York, Lake Erie & Western, but also of solid companies like the Pennsylvania or the Milwaukee. In later years stock was often included as an extra bonus when buying bonds, indicating the small value of this watered stock. Such shares were held in Holland, although their prices remained generally very low. On the other hand, shares of the better railroads continued to be highly valued and every new addition to the capital stock of such companies was taken up eagerly in Amsterdam. The American railroad securities listed today in Amsterdam are the stocks, not bonds, of such companies as the Illinois Central, the Union Pacific, and the Santa Fe.

■ *Protecting the Dutch Investment*

When an American railroad encountered serious financial trouble despite the caution used by the brokers, the customary Dutch reaction was to organize a protective committee. This device was probably not a Dutch invention, but it was used by them very early and with some success. The brokers involved, assisted by members appointed by the stock exchange, called bondowners and/or shareholders together, asked them to deposit their securities with the committee, and requested authorization to act for all. In this way it was usually possible to rescue some part of an original investment from a wrecked road. Quite often cooperation with English or German protective committees was sought to make an even stronger stand. In other cases the Dutch interests were entrusted to a British or German representative, and Dutch bankers and committees also acted for foreign security owners from time to time. The setting up of a nationwide organization of American security owners was attempted once or twice, but without success. A Dutch equivalent of the English Association of American Bond and Share Holders Ltd. of 1884 remained a dream.

To obviate legal and financial problems with American railroad shares, Amsterdam brokers early set up the so-called Administratie Kantoren, or administrative offices, as described in Chapter 2. Investors were saved the bother of cashing dividends or transferring shares in return for a small fee. In cases of trouble the managers of such a Kantoor could take prompt and efficient action without first having to call together all individual owners. They also catered to all kinds of investors, large and small. One of the attractions of American rails—apart from their high rate of interest—was their small nominal value, sometimes as low as $50 (Dfl 125). Certificates were issued in small denominations of $100 or less, which was attractive to the small saver. At the other end, certificates for blocks of 10 or more shares, to accommodate the rich men, were also known.

To make investing in American rails even easier for lazy or timid capitalists, early forms of investment funds were organized by several Amsterdam brokerage firms. In this way millions more were channeled to American railroad companies, generally with a profit to investor and broker alike.

■ *The Amount of Dutch Investment*

Firm figures of how much the Dutch actually invested in American railroads over the years are hard to come by, and estimates vary wildly. The sums offered for sale in Amsterdam are known sometimes, but that hardly means that all that was offered was actually sold. Loans were generally offered in many European bourses at the same time, and how much each country absorbed remains unknown. Moreover, there was a continuous buying and selling between countries, depending on market prices and general state of the economy and money market, and what was originally held in Holland could be sold again almost overnight without leaving any trace at all. Only when a road defaulted and its bondholders were called together by a Dutch protective committee can a close estimate be made of the Dutch holdings of that particular moment. Yet in Table 2 I have attempted to establish some sound figures, at least for the early years.

Table 2 gives a survey of securities of American railroads (mostly new issues) sold in Amsterdam until the end of 1873, based on my own computations and without the figures for the investment funds as given in Chapter 15. After 1873 the picture becomes blurred by refundings, redemptions, and reorganizations of roads under different names, with some old loans being continued while others were refunded with new paper. For

TABLE 2
*Totals of Dutch Investment in New Issues
of American Railroads, 1856–73*
(in U.S. $ par value)

	Known Dutch purchases	Probable Dutch purchases[a]	Total
1856	—	500,000	500,000
1857	8,000,000	3,000,000	11,000,000
1858	—	4,000,000	4,000,000
1859	—	—	—
1860	—	1,500,000	1,500,000
1861	—	—	—
1862	—	—	—
1863	—	—	—
1864	3,625,000	1,000,000	4,625,000
1865	760,000	1,000,000	1,760,000
1866	907,000	—	970,000
1867	—	500,000	500,000
1868	300,000	4,000,000	4,300,000
1869	3,520,000	6,000,000	9,520,000
1870	14,801,500	12,300,000	27,101,500
1871	30,452,500	10,100,000	40,552,500
1872	17,651,000	11,500,000	29,151,000
1873	5,000,000	1,000,000	6,000,000

SOURCE: All figures are based on my own computations as given in Appendixes A and B. It should be stressed that these figures do not reflect divestments by Dutch investors in the same years, for which no figures are known.

[a]These issues were offered in Amsterdam but not necessarily sold there.

TABLE 3
*Securities Listed on the Amsterdam
Stock Exchange, 1855–1914*

	No. of securities listed	No. of foreign securities listed	No. of American railroad securities listed	
1855	?	76	—	
1860	?	78	(5)	
1865	116	89	8	(14)
1870	159	129	18	(28)
1875	238	184	63	
1880	299	222	65	
1885	432	281	98	
1890	611	368	123	
1893	(829)	—	(154)	
1895	782	458	150	
1900	1,010	531	147	
1905	1,253	596	168	
1910	1,471	727	185	
1914	1,796 (1,512)	840	194	(179)

SOURCE: Based on my own computations as given in Appendix A. Figures in parentheses are from other sources, as mentioned in the text, or from my Table 2 for the years until 1873.

that reason it is dangerous to give even crude estimates of Dutch holdings after 1873. A complete list of all new issues of securities, stocks, bonds, refundings, and so on is given in Appendix A.

Table 3 illustrates the importance of American railroad securities on the Amsterdam Exchange over the chosen period 1855–1914. These figures are based on Berghuis,[3] but should be used with caution. Figures from *Van Oss' Effectenboek* 1914 give different, lower figures for most categories, while a copy of the *Gids bij de Prijs-Courant* (Guide for the official price list) for 1893 gives higher figures than Berghuis does for 1890 or 1895. Establishing totals is hazardous; some sources list three portions of the same loan issued at different moments as three different securities, while others list them as one; some give original shares and certificates for those same shares as one, while others treat them as two different entries, which partly explains the differences in numbers.

Table 4 takes the figures given in Table 3 for 1893 and 1914 and breaks them into more categories, based on the 1893 *Gids*, mentioned above, and *Van Oss' Effectenboek* for 1914. These figures show clearly the many new options open to Dutch investors toward the end of the century in the field of industry, both at home and abroad, and in agricultural companies chiefly operating in the Dutch East Indies. This helps explain the gradual shift away from American railroad loans, where only between 3 and 5 percent could be had, to more profitable securities elsewhere. Moreover, the speculative element of American rails had been lost by then. Their issuing price was generally not far below par, and they held little chance for a lucky gamble.

Although estimates of total Dutch investment in American railroads made over the years have tended to vary wildly, they nevertheless show some common patterns. Again,

TABLE 4
Securities Listed on the Amsterdam Stock Exchange in 1893 and 1914

Type of security	Domestic[a]		Foreign (excluding American)		American	
	1893	1914	1893	1914	1893	1914
Government	36	111	155	211	2	4
Banks	101	173	34	48	5	—
Industry	28	116	3	23	3	58
Agriculture	62	155	—	3	—	1
Mining	2	25	2	7	1	7
Oil	13	27	—	14	—	2
Shipping	17	37	—	1	—	4
Various	33	78	12	22	8	20
Railways	71	106	87	80	154[b]	179[c]
TOTAL	363	828	293	409	173	275

SOURCE: 1893: *Gids bij de Prijs-Courant.* 1914: *Van Oss' Effectenboek.*

[a]Domestic includes Dutch colonial securities.

[b]The 154 American railroad securities equaled 18.57 percent of the 1893 total of all securities (829).

[c]The 179 American railroad securities equaled 11.83 percent of the 1914 total of all securities (1,512).

all figures should be used with greater caution, and it should be remembered that they are estimates and nothing more. Table 5 lists the several estimates.

The first two estimates seem sensible enough, with the slight drop between 1873 and 1876 explained by the losses after the crisis. My own total from Table 2 of slightly over $131 million worth of new issues sold in Amsterdam is based on very conservative estimates, which may easily explain the divergence of less than $30 million with the figure of Von Reibnitz. Moreover, my Table 2 does not include purchases of traded securities (not new issues), for which no figures are available. The figures in Table 5 do include these, as they are "stock" rather than "flow" figures.

To give a better idea of the enormous sums involved during these early years, some comparison may be helpful. In 1860 the Netherlands government decided to build a railway network of 800 kilometers (520 miles) to supplement the lines already constructed by private companies. This network proved to be quite an achievement, involving some ten great river bridges, including the mile-long Moerdijk bridge, then the longest in Europe and a stupendous work for the time. For this network a total outlay of Dfl 100 million ($40 million) was deemed sufficient, in annual installments of Dfl 10 million. Compared to this, the $131 million (nominal value, possibly $75 million market value) of Dutch investment in American railroads in the same period seems enormous.

The 1899 figures in Table 5 are possibly a bit low, although it might be expected that Boissevain, as one of the foremost Dutch brokers involved in the American business, knew what he was talking about. The sudden rise to the 1906 figure seems too high, although during the early years of the twentieth century a great deal of railroad paper was acquired in Holland. Inflation also pushed up the twentieth-century figures. Moreover, Van Pellecom in his unpublished manuscript seems to have been very careful in

TABLE 5
*Level of Dutch Portfolio Investment
in the United States, 1873–1914*
(in millions of U.S. $ [par value])

	Total	Railroads		Total	Railroads
1873	260	160	1908	750	140–150
1876	236	136	1910	700	—
1899	223	214	1913	400	400
1906	—	600	1914a	700	—
1907	700	—	1914b	600–800	—
			1914c	500	300

SOURCE: 1873, 1876 data from Von Reibnitz, *Amerika's internationale Kapitalwanderungen*, p. 41; 1899 data based on Von Reibnitz, p. 50 (figures by A. A. H. Boissevain), quoted in Bosch, *Nederlandse beleggingen*, p. 470; 1906 data from Van Pellecom, *Nederlandse kapitaalexport*, pp. 47–48; 1907 data from Von Reibnitz, p. 54; 1908 "Total" from Lewis, *America's Stake*, p. 530, based on computations by George Paish; 1908 "Railroads" from Vissering, *Giroverkeer*, p. 78 (includes only shares held by Administrative Offices in Holland); 1910 data from Von Reibnitz, p. 57; 1913 "Total" from Bosch, *Nederlandse beleggingen*, p. 470, which quotes *The Economist* February–March 1913; 1913 "Railroads" from Kiliani, *Grossbanken-Entwicklung*, p. 11, also quoted in Brandes de Roos, *Industrie*, p. 74; 1914a data from Von Reibnitz, pp. 60–61; 1914b data from Bosch, *Nederlandse beleggingen*, p. 470, which quotes the Federal Reserve Board (the 800 figure may also include direct investments in land, mortgages, and oil companies); 1914c data from Lewis, *America's Stake*, p. 546.

his estimates. His figures do not diverge much from those of Von Reibnitz of one year later, nor indeed from Paish's 1908 totals, which are considered too high by Cleona Lewis and Mira Wilkins. Vissering's 1908 figures cover shares held by Administratie Kantoren only, and so most of the railroad bonds held in Holland are not taken into account and should be added to his totals. The 1913 figures from the *Economist* are almost certainly too low, the more so when the continuing growth of Dutch investment in U.S. industry other than railroads during those years is taken into consideration.

Two totals of 1914, by Von Reibnitz and the Federal Reserve Board, are similar, and probably not far from the truth. Lewis's figure for the railroads alone seems low, while her total, to which should be added her $135 million in direct investments, comes close to the other totals from the same year. It is fair to assume that Dutch investment in the American railroad network at the outbreak of World War I still stood at more than $300 million, possibly even some $400 million. Of a key railroad such as the Missouri, Kansas & Texas, the Dutch still held more than $38 million in stock and bonds even after 1914. Of the dubious Rock Island collateral trust bonds per 2002, the Dutch held over 12 percent, or $8.5 million worth, and it is safe to assume that it was no different in the case of other early popular roads. A total of just below $400 million at the end of our period seems therefore not preposterous. Kiliani even gives a figure of Dfl 1,250 million ($500 million) for 1917, after many sales of Dutch-held American securities back to U.S. investors because of rising prices.[4] His high figure may be correct after all, when it is taken into account that many German-owned securities were sold by way of neutral Amsterdam, thus inflating the Dutch figures during the war years.

With the total foreign investment in U.S. railroads in 1914 estimated at the staggering sum of $4,170 million, of which the British alone held $2,800 million, the Dutch share—whether $300 or $400 million—seems insignificant. Yet it was as high, and possibly higher, than the German participation, and was certainly more than that of France and other countries.[5] This was not a bad showing for a country of about 6 million people in 1914. Great as the Dutch investment in the United States may seem, the interest that Dutch investors had in czarist Russia was almost as great. According to a report by the Nederlandsche Bank, drawn up in 1918 after the Russian Revolution, the total Dutch interest in Russia stood at Dfl 1,500 million ($600 million), of which about two-thirds was in securities with the rest in outstanding bills, deposits, and direct investment in oil and related industries.[6]

The total of all foreign securities (excluding direct investments and Dutch colonial paper) held in Holland in 1914 has been estimated by Meijers, based on the legacy duties, at between Dfl 1,800 million and Dfl 3,700 million (or between $725 million and $1,500 million).[7] With $500 million in American and $400 million in Russian securities alone, Meijers's lowest figure is simply impossible, and his highest is probably still too low. Recurrent evasion of the legacy duties may be one of the reasons for his low estimates. Other estimates, as recorded by Wilkins, based on Staley and others, give $2 billion for the Dutch total of foreign investment, which seems more reasonable in view of the American and Russian figures.[8] Large amounts of Dutch money had been sunk into European government loans other than Russian, while industry and banking all over the world had attracted Dutch monies as well. It is safe to say, however, that in 1914 American securities, both railroad and nonrailroad, were still the single most important category on the Amsterdam Stock Exchange and in the portfolios of Dutch investors, large and small.

After reading this book, one may wonder why the Dutch took the trouble to invest in American railroads at all. The long story of defaults, reorganizations, frauds, and other pitfalls and mishaps may give the impression that it was at best a question of avoiding losses instead of making profits. Yet it should be remembered that many railroads never defaulted and always honored their obligations to their stock- and bondholders during the period of this study. Roads such as the Illinois Central and the Chicago & North Western, to name but two, became blue-chip investments in Amsterdam because of their excellent credit rating. But there is little to be said about these railroads; they floated their loans in Amsterdam, redeemed them on time, floated new ones, and so on; details of their financial performance will be found in the Appendixes. Of course, more can be said about the other category of railroads, those that did go bankrupt, several times in some cases, with consequent losses to stock- and bondholders. These railroads predominate in this book, but the reader should not be deceived by the horror stories: investment in American railroads was a profitable business in the long run.

When the first American railroad securities came on the market in Amsterdam, many Dutch investors assumed that this kind of risky investment was certain to bring quick gains and lead straight to a financial paradise. Appearances were deceptive, however, and quite a few investors and speculators lost heavily as a result of the recurrent crises in America. Yet it turned out that in the long run careful investment in the better roads meant a slow but sure way to financial gain, a true "slow train to paradise."

Appendixes

Chronological Survey of American Railroad Securities Introduced and/or Listed in Amsterdam, 1856-1914

The following list of American railroad securities introduced or listed on the Amsterdam Stock Exchange between 1856 and 1914 has been compiled directly from materials in the exchange's archives.

Each entry consists of two lines. The first line gives the abbreviated name of the railroad involved, the year (in curly brackets) of the first issue of the loan in question, and the broker(s) who sold the issue. In the second line, the first column gives the type of security issued. The second column gives the par value of the security in general or the amount offered, but not necessarily sold, in Amsterdam; figures in square brackets are amounts known to have been sold and/or held in Holland. The third column gives the issue price as a percentage of par value. An asterisk indicates a refunding of loans previously listed in Amsterdam. A hash mark (#) indicates that securities were introduced and sold in Holland, but an official Stock Exchange listing was refused.

The following abbreviations are used in Appendix A:

adj.	adjusting
a. o.	and others
cert.	certificates
coll.	collateral
cons.	consolidated
constr.	construction
conv.	convertible
cum.	cumulative
dev.	development
div.	divisional
ext.	extension
gen.	general
impr.	improvement
incm.	income

m.	mortgage
non-cum.	noncumulative
prefs.	preferred shares
prior.	priority
ref.	refunding
subs.	subsidiary

See Appendix D for a complete list of abbreviations of railroad names.

■ 1856

IC {1855} Alstorphius & Van Hemert/Teixeira de Mattos?
7% constr. bonds $12,885,000   86
IC {1855} Alstorphius & Van Hemert/Teixeira de Mattos?
6% freeland bonds $3,000,000   100

■ 1857

MC {?} ?
8% 1st m. $2,000,000   ?
IC Alstorphius & Van Hemert/Teixeira de Mattos
commons/cert.   [$7,000,000]   ?
NOJ&GN {?} B. H. Schroeder & Co.
8% 1st m. $2,000,000   ?
GH&H {1857} G. A. van der Voort
8% 1st m.   [$1,000,000+]   95

■ 1860

IC {1860} Alstorphius & Van Hemert
8% 1st m. $1,500,000   *

■ 1864

AGW {?} G. H. Levita, Antwerp?
7% 1st m. Ohio div. $4,000,000 [$3,000,000]   ?
AGW {1863} ?
7% 2nd m. Ohio div. $4,000,000   66
AGW {1864} Gebr. Boissevain/Teixeira de Mattos
8% debentures   £2,800,000   90
StP&P {1862} Kerkhoven
7% 1st section $1,200,000 [$625,000]   66

■ 1865

AGW {1865} Gebr. Boissevain? Teixeira de Mattos?
7% cons. m.   £6,000,000   80

StP&P   {1865} Kerkhoven/H. C. Voorhoeve
    7% cons. m. $2,800,000 [$760,000]   70
IC   {1865} Teixeira de Mattos
    6% redemption bonds   ?   *

■ 1866

StP&P   {1866} Kerkhoven/H. C. Voorhoeve
    7% 2nd section $3,000,000 [$907,000]   ?

■ 1867

W&M   {1867?} Gebr. Boissevain
    6% 1st m. $1,000,000   not listed

■ 1868

Erie   Wertheim & Gompertz
    commons/cert.   ?   50?
WW   {1868} Hertz
    7% 1st m.   £200,000 [£75,000]   69
C&NW   Broes & Gosman
    commons/cert.   ?   74
C&NW   Broes & Gosman
    7% prefs./cert.   [majority]   ?
CRI&P   Broes & Gosman
    commons/cert.   ?   83

■ 1869

MC   Wertheim & Gompertz
    commons/cert.   ?   ?
PFW&C   {1869} Wertheim & Gompertz
    7% guaranteed commons   ?   107
A&C   {1869} Commandiet Kas
    8% prior. m. $3,000,000   85.50
RRI&StL   {1869} S. de Vita
    7% 1st m. $9,000,000   72.75
SPM   {1868} J. Cahen
    6% 1st m. $1,000,000   66.50
UP,SB   {1869} Becker & Fuld/Wertheim & Gompertz
    6% 1st m. $4,250,000   70.50
StP&P   {1869} Kerkhoven/H. C. Voorhoeve
    7% 1st m. $6,000,000 [$3,520,000]   70
CalP   {1869} S. de Vita
    7% ext. bonds $3,500,000   73

■ 1870

B&O Wertheim & Gompertz		
commons/cert.	?	110
FWM&I {1869} Commandiet Kas		
7% 1st m.	$1,800,000	78.50
CCC&I Gebr. Boissevain/Kerkhoven		
commons/cert.	?	74.50
CMV&D {1870} Wertheim & Gompertz		
7% cons. m.	$1,500,000 [$741,000]	80
L&N {1868} Elix & Broekman		
7% 1st m.	$1,000,000	not listed
StL&SE {1869} Hertz		
7% 1st m.	$3,500,000 [$1,644,000]	74
PR {1869} Commandiet Kas		
7% 1st m. conv.	?	72.60
JP&M {1870} Holjé & Boissevain/Milders		
8% State of Florida	$4,000,000 [$3,000,000]	85
C&NW {1870} Broes & Gosman/Piek		
7% Iowa Midland	[$1,350,000]	82.50
WW {1868} Hertz		
7% 1st m.	£200,000 [£75,000]	71
C&SW {1869} Holjé & Boissevain/Rotterdamsche Bank		
7% 1st m.	$5,000,000	82
DMV {1868} Franco Mendes/Matthes		
8% 1st m.	$2,690,000 [$774,000]	85
NM {1865} Elix & Broekman		
7% 1st m.	$6,000,000	75.75
PRly {1869} Commandiet Kas		
7% 1st m.	$1,800,000 [$1,414,000]	70
UP {1869} H. Oyens & Sons		
6% 1st m.	$27,000,000 [$4,498,000]	78.50
(already circulating since 1869)		
KP {1869} S. de Vita		
7% Denver ext.	$6,395,000 [$454,000+]	70
DP {1869} Holjé & Boissevain/Milders		
7% 1st m.	$2,500,000 [$1,413,000]	?
D&BV {1870} Wertheim & Gompertz		
7% 1st m.	[$550,000; all]	75
CP {1865–67} Elix & Broekman		
6% 1st m.	$25,885,000	71.75
(already circulating in 1865)		
O&C {1870} Ter Meulen & Boeken		
7% 1st m.	$5,000,000 [$113,500+]	72

■ 1871

StP&P   {1871} Kerkhoven a. o. for Lippmann, Rosenthal
7% St. Vincent ext. $15,000,000 [$11,400,000]   70
TC/GR&I   {1869?} F. W. Oewel
7% 1st m.   ?   ?
AM&O   {1871} Holjé & Boissevain/Milders
7% cons. m. $9,500,000 [$2,000,000+]   79.50
FR   {1869} Hertz
7% 1st m. $2,500,000 [$520,000]   74
E&P   {?} F. W. Oewel
8% 1st m.   [$3,000,000]   79.50
C&NW   {1871} Broes & Gosman/Piek
7% Madison ext.   [$3,150,000]   82.25
C&NW   {1871} Broes & Gosman/Piek
7% Menomenee ext.   [$2,700,000]   85
K&MB   {1871} Rotterdamsche Bank/Associatie Cassa
8% 1st m.   [$600,000; all?]   82.75
PRly   {1870} Ter Meulen & Boeken
7% 1st m. $2,000,000 [$700,000]   70
MKT   {1871} Leembruggen a. o. for Becker & Fuld/Wertheim
7% 1st m. $16,000,000 [majority]   80.6
UP   Broes & Gosman?
commons   ?   24
Ca&Or   {1869} Teixeira de Mattos
6% 1st m. A $2,000,000   81
DRG   {1870} Van Vloten & De Gijselaar, for Wertheim
7% 1st m.   [$6,382,500]   70

■ 1872

GC&S   {1870} Elix & Broekman
7% 1st m. $2,000,000   83.50
W&StP   {1871} Broes & Gosman
7% 1st m.   [$4,375,000]   86.50
BH&E   Wertheim & Gompertz/Teixeira de Mattos a. o.
commons $1,000,000   8–13
M&P   {1865?} Berlin & Hymans
7% 1st m. $1,500,000 [$901,000]   ?
CMV&D   {1872} Wertheim & Gompertz
7% 1st m. ext. $1,000,000 [$368,000]   90
M&E   {1871} Amsterdamsche Bank
7% 1st m. $1,250,000   89.75
C&O   {1871} Cahen/Teixeira de Mattos
6% 1st m.   ?   82

P&M   {1872} Wertheim & Gompertz
   7% 1st m.   [$2,000,000]   82.50

C&StL   {1871} Wertheim & Gompertz
   7% 1st m.   [$2,500,000]   81

C&NW   {1872} Broes & Gosman/Piek
   7% North Western Union   [$3,500,000]   87

C&SW   {1871} Gebr. Boissevain/Rotterdamsche Bank
   7% Atchison Branch $1,000,000 [$407,000]   85

CM&StP   {1869} Holjé & Boissevain/Rotterdamsche Bank
   7% Iowa div. $1,000,000 [$900,000]   83

CM&StP   {1872} Elix & Broekman
   7% River div.   £800,000 [£200,000]   90.50

CM&StP   Gebr. Boissevain/Kerkhoven
   commons/cert.   ?   ?
   7% prefs./cert.   ?   ?

M&StL   {1871} Jos. Hess
   7% 1st m. $1,100,000   82.50

TP&Wa   {1870} Elix & Broekman
   7% cons. m.   [$500,000]   72

CM&C   {1872} Hertz
   7% 1st m. $2,775,000   77

AC   {1871} Hertz
   8% 1st m. $700,000 [$400,000]   76.25

ATSF   {1869} Gebr. Boissevain/Rotterdamsche Bank
   7% 1st m. $2,700,000 [$700,000]   81.50

CP   {1870} Teixeira de Mattos
   6% San Joaquin $6,080,000   86

O&C   {1870} Hertz
   7% 1st m. $3,800,000   75.60

■ 1873

C&NW   {1872} Broes & Gosman
   7% cons. m. $12,343,000 [$5,000,000]   83

StP&P   {1873} Kerkhoven/H. C. Voorhoeve a. o.
   10% receiver's cert.   ?   85

Ca&Or   {1872} Teixeira de Mattos
   6% 1st m. B $2,000,000   ?

■ 1874

MKT   Becker & Fuld/Wertheim & Gompertz
   prefs.   ?   20

CalP   {1874?} Elix & Broekman
   6% 2nd m. $2,000,000   *
   (part refunding, part new)

■ 1875

UP   Broes & Gosman
    commons/cert.   ?   75
    (already circulating since 1871)

■ 1876

DM&FD   {1875} Broes & Gosman
    6% 1st m.   [majority]   43*
    6% income bonds   [$1,200,000]   not listed
    commons   ?   *
    prefs.   ?   *
MKT   {?} Becker & Fuld/Wertheim & Gompertz
    6% 2nd m. incm. $6,000,000 [$5,591,000]   ?

■ 1877

MP&N   {1877} Wertheim & Gompertz
    7% 1st m.   [$2,000,000]   *
RR&M   Kerkhoven/H. C. Voorhoeve a. o.
    commons   [$200,000]   ?

■ 1878

IC   {1878} Elix & Broekman
    6% Springfield div. $2,000,000   100*
C&NW   {various} Broes & Gosman
    7% subs. lines   [$900,000]   92

■ 1879

CS   Broes & Gosman
    commons/cert.   ?   62.25
CS   {1878} Elix & Broekman
    3–5% 1st m.   limited number   not listed
P&E   {1879} Wertheim & Gompertz
    8% 1st m.   [$300,000]   ?
P&E   {1879} Wertheim & Gompertz
    7% 2nd m.   [$400,000]   *
    7% prefs.   [$500,000]   *
    commons   [$500,000]   *
StPM&M   {1879} Lippmann, Rosenthal
    7% 1st m.   [$6,000,000]   *
KP   {1879} Kerkhoven
    6% cons. m.   [$247,000+]   *
O&C   {1879} O&C Committee/Amsterdamsche Bank
    6% 1st m. $1,700,000   85

O&C   ?
   commons   ?   *
   prefs.   ?   *
PR&A   {1878} ?
   6% 1st m.   ?   *

■ 1880

NYP&O   {1880} Broes & Gosman
   6% prior lien $5,500,000   92
LS&MS   Hubrecht
   commons/cert.   ?   ?
PRR   Wertheim & Gompertz
   commons/cert.   ?   ?
NYO&W   Gebr. Boissevain/Teixeira de Mattos
   commons/cert.   [$2,000,000+]   33
C&O   {1878} Broekman & Honders
   6% 1st m.   [$1,800,000]   72
NC&StL   {?} ?
   6% 1st m.   ?   100*
CM&StP   {1879} Broekman & Honders
   6% Western Union div. $4,000,000   101.50
CB&Q   Hubrecht
   commons/cert.   ?   102
TP&We   {1879} Stadnitski & Van Heukelom
   7% 2nd m. inc. bonds   [$480,000]   ?
   commons/cert.   ?   ?
WStL&P   {?} Hubrecht
   7% prefs./cert.   ?   70
M&W   {1879} L. Calisch for Alsberg, Goldberg
   6% 1st m. $1,100,000   94
StLW&W   {1879} Alsberg, Goldberg
   6% 1st m. $2,000,000   98.50
StL&SF   Hubrecht
   7% 1st prefs./cert.   ?   80
MKT   Wertheim & Gompertz a. o.
   commons/cert.   [$9,617,000]   50
StPM&M   {1879} Lippmann, Rosenthal
   6% 2nd m.   ?   *
StPM&M   Stadnitski & Van Heukelom
   commons/cert.   ?   80
UP   {1879} Ad. Boissevain/Ten Have & Van Essen
   6% coll. trust $4,800,000 [$3,194,000]   105.50
ATSF   Hubrecht
   commons/cert.   [$4,959,400]   ?

CP   Teixeira de Mattos/Dutch CP Shareholders Co.
    commons/cert.   [$2,350,000]   84.50
SP   {1880} Teixeira de Mattos
    6% 1st m. $10,000,000   95.75
DRG   {1879} Broekman & Honders
    7% cons. m. $5,000,000 [$1,165,000]   95
DRG   Hubrecht
    commons/cert.   ?   ?

■ 1881

NYLE&W   Broes & Gosman
    6% prefs./cert.   ?   74
C&A   {1880} Broes & Gosman
    6% 1st m.   [$5,961,000]   ?
BP&W/BNY&P   Hubrecht
    commons/cert.   ?   ?
N&W   {1881} Kerkhoven
    6% gen. m.   ?   *
L&N   {1881} Wertheim & Gompertz
    6% 1st m. St. Louis $3,500,000   *
    (part refunding, part new)
L&N   {1881} Wertheim & Gompertz
    6% 1st m. St. Louis $3,500,000   74
L&N   {1880} Broekman & Honders
    3% 2nd m. St. Louis $3,000,000   55*
    (part refunding, part new)
L&N   {1880} Broekman & Honders
    6% sinking fund m. $2,000,000 [$550,000]   103.75
L&N   Wertheim & Gompertz
    commons/cert.   [several millions]   ?
FT   {1881} Hubrecht
    6% 1st m./cert.   [$500,000+]   *
CStL&NO   Broes & Gosman
    commons/cert.   [$3,000,000]   73
StL&C   {1881} Wertheim & Gompertz
    5% 1st m. income   [$2,600,000]   *
StL&C   Wertheim & Gompertz
    commons/cert.   [$3,800,000]   ?
DM&FD   {1880} Broes & Gosman
    6% ext. bonds $5,000,000 [$600,000]   101
CM&StP   {1881} Everts & Schmidt
    5% Pacific Western div. $24,400,000   95
CM&StP   {1881} Oyens & Sons
    5% Lake Superior div. $1,360,000 [$1,000,000+]   92

C&GT   {1880} Wertheim & Gompertz
 7% 2nd m. inc. $4,000,000   *
A&P   {1880} Alsberg, Goldberg
 6% 1st m. $16,000,000   102
StL&SF   Hubrecht
 commons/cert.   ?   40
 2nd prefs./cert.   ?   65
StPM&M   {1880} Lippmann, Rosenthal/Gebr. Boissevain
 6% Dakota ext. $6,000,000   106

■ 1882

BNY&P   {1881} Alsberg, Goldberg
 6% cons. m. $7,000,000   104.50
FC&W   Hubrecht
 5% 1st m.   ?   *
 commons/cert.   ?   *
IC   Broes & Gosman
 4% leased lines stock   [$3,000,000]   *
CO&SW   {1881} Wertheim & Gompertz
 5–6% 1st m.   [$3,500,000]   ?
C&GT   {1882} Wertheim & Gompertz
 5% 2nd m. $6,000,000   *
StL&SF   {1881} Alsberg, Goldberg
 6% gen. m. $4,000,000   97.50

■ 1883

BNY&P   Hubrecht
 6% prefs./cert.   ?   60
MP   Broes & Gosman
 commons/cert.   ?   98
UP   {1882} Ad. Boissevain/Ten Have & Van Essen
 5% coll. trust $4,500,000 [$4,202,000]   93
DRG   {1883} Hubrecht
 5% gen. m. $2,500,000 [$656,000]   ?

■ 1884

CS   {1883} Broes & Gosman
 5% 2nd m. $2,000,000   86.50
L&N   {1884} Wertheim & Gompertz
 6% 10–40 adjustment $1,700,000 [$750,000]   ?
MKT   {1880} W. F. Piek
 5–6% gen. cons. m. $45,000,000 [$7,762,000]   ?
C&NW   {1883} Edersheim
 5% sinking fund debentures $10,000,000   92

■ 1886

CA&C   Wertheim & Gompertz
   commons/cert. $4,000,000 [$3,999,300]   *
CA&C   {1886} Wertheim & Gompertz
   6/5% 1st m.   [$1,000,000]   96*
StL&C   {1886} Wertheim & Gompertz
   4% 1st m.   [$4,000,000; $1,300,000 new]   ?
StLA&T {1886} W. F. Piek
   6% 1st m.   [$750,000+]   par
StLS&A {1886} Alsberg, Goldberg
   5% 1st m.   ?   99
StPM&M {1883} Tutein Nolthenius & De Haan
   6% cons. m. $13,000,000   102
StPM&M {1883} Jan Kol
   4.5% cons. m. $5,100,000   98.50
T&NO   {1882} Broekman & Honders
   6% 1st m. $1,200,000   103.50
DRG   {1886} Hubrecht
   4% cons. m. $42,000,000   *
   5% prefs./cert.   ?   *

■ 1887

WNY&P   {1887} no broker
   3–4% 2nd m. $7,000,000 [$433,000+]   *
WNY&P   {1887} H. Oyens & Sons
   5% 1st m. $10,000,000   96.50
MSSM&A {1886} Broekman & Honders
   5% 1st m. $900,000 [$250,000+]   92.25
CStP&KC {1886} Hope & Co.
   5% 1st m. $2,000,000   92.50
A&P   {1887} Alsberg, Goldberg
   4% 1st m.   [$4,364,000+]   *
StPM&M {1887} Tutein Nolthenius & De Haan
   4% Montana ext. $8,000,000   96.50
O&C   {1887} ?
   5% 1st m.   ?   *
CA&C   {1887} Wertheim & Gompertz
   5% 1st m. $1,800,000   96*
   (part refunding, part new)

■ 1888

CO&SW   {1881} Jos. Thors
   6% 2nd m.   ?   ?

ETV&G   {?} Hijmans & Sons
  5% 1st m.   [$1,700,000]   ?
  (second part of same loan sold by Jos. Thors, 1890)
IC   {1888} Gebr. Boissevain/Teixeira de Mattos
  4% coll. loan $15,000,000   99.50
KCFS&M   {1886} Dutch StL&SF Assoc.
  4% prefs./cert.   ?   ?
  4% ref. m. $60,000,000   90
EM   {1888} Ad. Boissevain
  5% 1st m. $5,000,000 [$1,500,000]   96.50
UP   {1888} Ad. Boissevain/Kerkhoven
  5% equipment notes $800,000 [$387,000]   ?
U&N   {1886} Ad. Boissevain
  5% cons. m. $1,800,000 [$1,193,000]   97
U&N   {1888} Kerkhoven
  5% equipment notes   [$975,000]   97
ATSF   {1881} Labouchère, Oyens & Co.
  6% 1st m. $15,000,000 [$900,000]   105.50
O&C   {1887} Ed. Dentz
  5% 1st m.   ?   92.25
DRG   {1888} Hubrecht
  5% impr. m. $8,335,500   82
L&N   {1888} Wertheim & Gompertz
  5% coll. trust $2,500,000   94.50

■ 1889

C&O   {1889} Broekman & Honders/Teixeira de Mattos
  5% cons. 1st m. $30,000,000   ?
FC&P   Hubrecht
  commons/cert.   ?   *
FC&P   {1888} Hubrecht
  5% 1st m.   ?   *
Wabash   Hubrecht
  prefs./cert.   ?   *
  6% debentures/cert. {1889}   ?   *
MoC   {1887} Ad. Boissevain
  6% 1st m. $6,000,000 [$1,100,000+]   108.60
GN   Tutein Nolthenius & De Haan
  5% prefs./cert.   ?   *
StPM&M   {1889} Van Loon for Hope & Co.
  4% Pacific ext.   £2,000,000   82
UP   {1889} Ad. Boissevain/Kerkhoven
  5% equipment notes $1,890,000 [$576,000]   97.25

UPL&C   {1888} Ad. Boissevain
    5% 1st m. $4,400,000 [$1,863,000]   97.25
OSL&UN   {1889} Broekman & Honders
    5% cons. m. $12,000,000   94.25
CP   {1889} Teixeira de Mattos
    5% 1st m. $2,500,000   .100.25

■ 1890

C&E   Dutch C&A Committee
    4–5% 1st m.   [$7,068,000+]   85*
    (part refunding, part new)
C&E   Dutch C&A Committee
    5% income bonds   [$1,500,000]   35*
    (part refunding, part new)
CA&C   {1890} Wertheim & Gompertz
    6% 2nd m.   [$600,000]   ?
KU   {1888} Oyens & Sons
    5% 1st m.   [$1,600,000]   95.50
FC&W   {1890} Broekman & Honders
    5% 1st m.   £500,000   94.50
MKT   {1890} Dutch MKT Association
    4% 1st m. $40,000,000 [$14,720,000]   80
    4% 2nd m. $20,000,000 [$7,071,500+]   ?
    4% prefs./cert. $13,000,000 [$882,000]   ?
    commons/cert. $47,000,000 [$15,558,000]   10
    (part refunding, part new)
MKT   {1890} Amsterdamsche Bank
    5% 1st m. D&W $1,340,000 [$600,000]   87
OSL&UN   {1889} Ad. Boissevain
    5% coll. trust $5,500,000   93.75
ATSF   {1889} Hubrecht
    4% gen. m. $150,000,000 [$30,100,000]   *
    5% incm. bonds/cert. $80,000,000   *

■ 1891

StLSW   {1889} W. F. Piek
    4% 1st m.   ?   *
MoC   {1887} Amsterdamsche Bank
    5% 1st m. $2,000,000   96.50
SF&NP   {1889} Alsberg, Goldberg
    5% 1st m. $4,000,000 [$400,000]   94.50

■ 1892

PCC&StL   {1890} Teixeira de Mattos
    4.5% cons. m. A $10,000,000   100.75
IC   {1890} Gebr. Boissevain/Teixeira de Mattos
    4% Cairo Bridge $3,000,000   96
StL&SF   {1890} Alsberg, Goldberg
    4% cons. m. $11,000,000 [$2,968,000]   *
ATSF   {1892} Hope & Co.
    2.5–4% 2nd m. A $80,000,000 [$8,530,500]   *
    4% 2nd m. B $5,000,000 [$602,000]   66.75

■ 1893

C&O   {1892} Teixeira de Mattos
    4.5% gen. m. $47,000,000 [limited number]   75
FC&W   {1893} Broekman & Honders
    cons. 1st m. $7,800,000   ?
ETV&G   {1893?} ?
    gen. m.   [$996,000]   *
IC   {1893} Gebr. Boissevain/Teixeira de Mattos
    4% coll. loan $4,000,000   93
CGW   {1893} Hope & Co.
    4% debentures/cert.   ?   *
    5% prefs./cert.   ?   *
UT   {1893} Tutein Nolthenius & De Haan
    5% 1st m. $2,000,000 [$1,550,000]   87.50
ATSF   {1883} Hope & Co.
    6% 5-year guarantee fund notes ?   ?
T&NO   {1886} Teixeira de Mattos
    6% 1st m.   [$500,000]   104.50

■ 1894

Erie   {?} Broes & Gosman ?
    4% 2nd prefs.   ?   16
NC&StL   {1888} Wertheim & Gompertz
    5% 1st cons. m.   [$500,000]   99.25
SR   {1894} Dutch SR Shareholders Assoc. (Wertheim)
    5% non-cum. prefs.   ?   ?
    (part exchange of earlier ETV&G, part new)
KCP&G   {1893} Tutein Nolthenius & De Haan
    5% 1st m. $23,000,000 [$7,277,100]   60

■ 1895

L&JB {1895} Broes & Gosman
    4% 1st m.   [$2,700,000]   94
N&W   Dutch N&W Shareholders Assoc.
    4% non-cum. prefs./cert.   ?   44
L&N {1895} Wertheim & Gompertz
    4.5% 1st m. M&M div. $4,500,000   100
L&E {1895} Oyens & Sons
    5% gen. m.   [$1,500,000]   50*
M&StL {1894} Teixeira de Mattos
    5% cons. m. $5,000,000   98.50
KCP&G   Tutein Nolthenius & De Haan
    commons/cert.   [$12,660,000]   15
KCSB   {?} Tutein Nolthenius & De Haan
    6% 1st m.   ?   ?
    commons/cert.   [$1,792,000+]   25
ATSF   Hubrecht
    commons/cert.   ?   *
ATSF   Dutch ATSF Shareholders Assoc.
    5% prefs./cert.   ?   *
ATSF {1895} Hope & Co.
    4% gen. m.   ?   *
    4% adj. bonds   ?   *
SR {1894} Wertheim & Gompertz
    5% 1st cons. coll. trust $120,000,000 [$250,000+]   ?
WNY&P {1895} Amsterdamsche Bank
    2–4% gen. m. $10,000,000   30*
WNY&P {1895} Amsterdamsche Bank
    5% incm. bonds   ?   10*

■ 1896

N&W   {?} Broes & Gosman
    commons/cert.   ?   4
    4% cons. m. {1896} $62,500,000   75
NP   {1896} Teixeira de Mattos/Wertheim & Gompertz
    4% prior lien $96,000,000   85

■ 1897

StL&SF {1896} Dutch StL&SF Assoc.
    commons/cert.   ?   4*
    4% 1st prefs./cert.   ?   ?*
    4% 2nd non-cum. prefs./cert.   ?   10*
    4% cons. m.   ?   90*

UP {1897} Broes & Gosman
    4% 1st m. $75,000,000 [$3,422,000]   102*
UP {1897} Broes & Gosman
    4% non-cum. prefs./cert.   [$2,500,000+]   *
    commons/cert.   [$1,702,500]   *
OSL {1897} Dutch OSL Assoc.
    5% cons. m.   ?   *
    5% incm. bonds A   ?   *
    5% incm. bonds B   [$11,000,000]   *

■ 1898

B&O Wertheim & Gompertz
    4% prefs./cert.   ?   71–81
IC {1898} Amsterdamsche Bank/Banque de Paris
    3.5% St. Louis div. $5,000,000   94.50
IC {1898} Amsterdamsche Bank/Banque de Paris
    3.5% Louisville div. $20,000,000   94.50
SP {1897} Teixeira de Mattos
    5% 1st cons. m. $10,000,000   101.25
DRG {1898} Teixeira de Mattos
    4.5% cons. m. $13,282,500   *

■ 1899

CP {1899} Teixeira de Mattos
    4% ref. m. $100,000,000   *
    3.5% ref. m. $20,000,0000   *
SP {1899} Teixeira de Mattos
    4% coll. bonds $29,000,000   ?
SP Gebr. Boissevain/Teixeira de Mattos
    commons/cert.   [$3,000,000]   ?

■ 1900

Erie {1896} Jos. Thors
    3/4% general lien   [$600,000+]   83
CA&C {1900} Dutch CA&C Assoc.
    4% cons. m.   ?   90
C&O Algemeene Trust Mij.
    commons/cert.   ?   40
SR Broes & Gosman a. o.
    commons/cert.   [$900,000+]   ?
M&O {1900} Wertheim & Gompertz
    4% coll. trust   [$1,000,000]   *

KCS   {1900} Dutch KCP&G/KCS Assoc.

3% 1st m.	[$5,000,000]	?*
4% non-cum. prefs./cert.	?	30*
commons/cert.	?	?*

NP   Wertheim & Gompertz

commons/cert.	?	?

SP   {1900} Teixeira de Mattos

4.5% 2–5 year notes	$10,000,000	97.75

■ 1901

P&R   Algemeene Trust Mij./Vermeer

commons/cert.	?	56
1st prefs./cert.	?	74
2nd prefs./cert.	?	46.50

GTW   {1900} Wertheim & Gompertz?

4% 1st m.	?	*
4% 2nd m. inc. bonds	[$1,500,000]	*

StL&SF   {1901} Alsberg, Goldberg

4% ref. m.	$12,000,000	96.75
(part refunding, part new)		

KCFS&M   {1901} Dutch StL&SF Assoc.

4% 1st m. ref.	$60,000,000	90
4% prefs./cert.	?	?

KCS&GT   {?} no broker

4% 1st m.	[$100,000]	56–65

NP   {1896} Ten Have & Van Essen

4% St. Paul & Duluth div.	$20,000,000	?

UP   {1901} Broes & Gosman

4% 1st lien conv.	$100,000,000	par

■ 1902

CRI&P   ?

4/6% prefs.	?	*

CRI&P   {1902} Teixeira de Mattos

4% coll. trust	$75,000,000 [$8,500,000]	95

C&S   {1898} Alsberg, Goldberg

commons/cert.	?	17
4% 1st prefs./cert.	?	67
4% 2nd prefs./cert.	?	33.50

OSL   {1901} Broes & Gosman

4% partial loan	$36,000,000	90

NOR   Broes & Gosman

commons/cert.	?	16
prefs./cert.	?	56

■ 1903

MKT   {1903} S. F. van Oss
   5% 1st m. Texas & Okla. $2,347,000   ?
ATSF   {1903} Van Loon, for Hope & Co.
   4% Eastern Oklahoma $10,000,000   94
DRG   {1886} Hope & Co.
   4% cons. m.   ?   90.25
RGW   {1899} Van Loon, for Hope & Co.
   4% 1st cons. & coll. m.   ?   90.25

■ 1904

CB&Q   {1899} Ad. Boissevain
   3.5% Illinois div. $12,000,000 [$400,000]   95
L&A   {1902} Van der Werff & Hubrecht a.o.
   5% 1st m. $2,724,000   101
OSL   {1904} Broes & Gosman
   4% coll. loan $100,000,000   *
   (part refunding, part new)
ATSF   {1895} Hope & Co.
   4% gen. m. $10,000,000   par
CP   {1904} Teixeira de Mattos
   4% Lucin Cut-off $8,300,000 [$1,400,000+]   98
SP   Gebr. Boissevain/Teixeira de Mattos
   7% prefs./cert.   ?   ?
SA&AP   {1893} Labouchère, Oyens, for Rotterdamsche Bank
   4% 1st m. $17,500,000 [$200,000+]   89.25
KCR&L   {1903} F. Glasbergen, for Ad. Boissevain
   5% 1st lien & ref. m. $25,000,000   98.50
DUR   {1902} H. Oyens & Sons
   4.5% 1st conv. m. $8,200,000   94.50
CR   {1903?} De Clercq & Van Essen
   4.5% 1st & ref. m. $12,500,000   97.60

■ 1905

PRR   {1905} Ad. Boissevain
   3.5% convertibles $100,000,000   101
N&W   {1904} Gebr. Boissevain
   4% 1st m. div.   ?   97
DM&FD   {1905} Glasbergen, for Alsberg, Goldberg/Labouchère
   4% 1st m. $3,072,000   96.50
   (in part redemption, rest new)
MC&FD   {1905} Ad. Boissevain
   4% 1st m. $1,000,000   91.75

WM&P {1900} Van der Werff & Hubrecht
  4% 1st m. $5,524,000   91.40
MP   {1905} Banque de Paris et des Pays-Bas
  4% first m. $50,000,000 [$6,376,000+]   94.50
T&P   Broes & Gosman
  commons/cert.   ?   38.50
MKT   {1904} Jos. Hess, for Oyens & Sons
  4% 1st ref. m. $40,000,000   87.25
ATSF   {1905} Hope & Co./Dutch ATSF Shareholders Assoc.
  4% conv. bonds $50,000,000   ?
SP   {1905} Teixeira de Mattos
  4% gen. m. $75,000,000   97
HL&R   {1905} Wiegman's Bank
  5% 1st m. $850,000 [$49,000+]   91.50
C&ME   {1902} Van der Werff & Hubrecht, J. Eck, Oppenheim
  5% 1st m. $4,600,000 [$1,642,000+]   99.25
KCS&GT   {1897} no broker
  4% 1st m.   [$500,000]   65–67

■ 1906

NYC&HR   {1897?} Ad. Boissevain
  3.5% ref. m.   limited number   93.25
CRI&P   {1904} Teixeira de Mattos
  4% 1st ref. m. $11,000,000   95.40
Wabash   Van der Waag
  commons   ?   ?
Wabash   {1906} Ad. Boissevain
  4% equipment notes   ?   not listed
WPT   {1904} Everts & Schmidt
  4% 2nd m.   [$1,400,000]   46.75
StLSW   Buitenl. Bankvereeniging/Ten Have & Van Essen
  commons   ?   27
KCS   {1906} Tutein Nolthenius & De Haan
  5% 6-year coll. notes   ?   95
OC   {1905} Van der Werff & Hubrecht/S. F. van Oss
  5% 1st m.   [$852,000]   93.40
IM   {1906} Gerritsen & Selle
  4.5% coll. trust   ?   82
  prefs./cert.   ?   25.60
BT   {1905} De Clercq & Van Essen
  5% cons. m.   [$1,000,000]   96
KCOB&E   {?} Westendorp
  4% 1st m.   [limited sum]   #

▪ 1907

C&S {1905} Möller & Kijzer
    4.5% ref. m. $10,000,000   78
UP {1907} Broes & Gosman
    4% conv. m. $75,000,000   90
ATSF {1907} Hope & Co.
    5% conv. bonds $30,000,000   ?
MS {1907} Westendorp/Oppenheim & Van Till
    5% 1st m.   ?   92.50

▪ 1908

N&W {1906} Gebr. & Ad. Boissevain/Rotterdamsche Bank
    4% conv. loan $34,000,000   97.50
Wabash {1906} Van der Waag
    4% 50-year ref. & ext.   ?   60
MKT {1906} Jos. Hess
    4.5% gen. m. $20,000,000   90
StPM&M {1883/1908} Lippmann, Rosenthal
    4% cons. m. $8,000,000   *
HC {1908} Ad. Boissevain
    6% 2.5-year conv. notes $15,000,000   98.50
KCM&O {1900} Westendorp/Ten Have & Van Essen
    4% 1st m. $4,000,000   71#
    4% non-cum. prefs. $2,000,000   31.50#
    commons $2,000,000   19#
MStP&SSM Westendorp
    commons   ?   123#

▪ 1909

SR {1906} Lutomirski
    4% dev. & gen. m. $75,000,000   ?
StL&SF {1907} Teixeira de Mattos
    5% gen. lien $17,000,000 [$1,750,000]   89
MP {1909} Amsterdamsche Bank/Hope & Co.
    5% 1st ref. conv. m. $30,000,000 [$900,000+]   95.75
KCS {1909} Tutein Nolthenius & De Haan/Ad. Boissevain
    5% ref. & improvement $15,000,000   95
SP {1909} Gebr. Boissevain/Teixeira de Mattos
    4% conv. loan $82,000,000   96
DRG {1905} Ad. Boissevain
    5% 1st & ref. m. $28,000,000   92.25
WP {1903} Ad. Boissevain/Broes & Gosman
    5% 1st m./cert. $50,000,000 [$3,200,000]   97

■ 1910

CH&D   {1909} Van Loon, for Hope & Co./Teixeira de Mattos
    4% 1st and ref. m.   [Dfl 500,000]   92
RIA&L   {1904/1910} Teixeira de Mattos
    4.5% 1st m. $11,000,000   96.25
TStL&W   {1907} Alsberg, Goldberg
    4% coll. trust $20,000,000   86.25
CGW   {1909} Hope & Co.
    commons/cert.   ?   30*
StL&SF   {1910} Teixeira de Mattos
    5% 3-year notes $8,000,000   97.75
SP   {1910} Van Loon, for Hope & Co.
    4% San Francisco Terminal $25,000,000   92.50

■ 1911

WSS   {1910} Gebr. Boissevain
    4% 1st m. $5,000,000   96
SAL   {1909} Gebr. Boissevain
    4% ref. m. $19,000,000   83.25
MP   {1911} Teixeira de Mattos
    5% 3-year notes $20,000,000   98.60
HE   {?} Teixeira de Mattos
    5% 1st cons. m.   ?   97.25
NOT   {1903} Ad. Boissevain
    4% 1st m. $4,000,000   88.25#

■ 1912

N&W   {1906/1912} Gebr. & Ad. Boissevain/Rotterdamsche Bank
    4% conv. loan $13,000,000   110
SAL   {1909} Gerritsen & Selle
    5% 2nd m. adj. $25,000,000 [300,000+]   ?
CRI&P   {1912} Teixeira de Mattos
    5% 20-year debentures $20,000,000   97.25
CM&StP   {1912} Broes & Gosman
    4.5% conv. bonds   ?   par
StL&SF   {1912} Alsberg, Goldberg
    6% 2-year notes   [$419,000]   99
WPT&W   Gebr. Boissevain
    6% prefs./cert. $6,500,000   79

■ 1913

M&O   {1913} Banque de Paris et des Pays-Bas
    5% 1st m. St. Louis div.   ?   *

SEL&T   {?} Gebr. Boissevain/Teixeira de Mattos
    6% 1st m.   [$800,000]   98

∎ 1914

CGW   {1909} Van Loon/Ad. Boissevain
    4% 1st m.   ?   73
SP   {1914} Gebr. Boissevain/Teixeira de Mattos
    5% conv. loan $55,000,000   ?

Appendix B

Alphabetical Survey of Dutch Investment in Individual American Railroads

Investments are listed alphabetically, railroad by railroad. Railroads merged into larger companies are generally listed under the new larger company, with a reference under the original name. Numbers given are consecutive issues of securities by one company or group of companies in chronological order as introduced in Amsterdam. Unless otherwise noted, prices are given as a percentage of par.

The following abbreviations are used in Appendix B.

A.	Amsterdam
AASE	Archives of the Amsterdam Stock Exchange
AE	*Amsterdamsch Effectenblad*
a. o.	and others
auth.	authorized
cert.	certificates
coll.	collateral
comm.	committee
cons.	consolidated
constr.	construction
conv.	convertible
cum.	cumulative
curr.	currency
def.	default(ed)
div.	divisional
ext.	extension
gen.	general
impr.	improvement
inc.	incorporated
incm.	income
int.	interest
intr.	introduced

m.	mortgage
NAE	*Nieuw Algemeen Effectenblad*
non-cum.	noncumulative
pref.	preferred
pr. comm.	protective committee
R.	Rotterdam
rec.	receiver(ship)
ref.	refunding
reinc.	reincorporated
>	converted into
<	converted from

See Appendix D for a complete list of abbreviations of railroad names.

▪ Alabama & Chattanooga

See under Southern Railway.

▪ Arkansas Central

Inc. 1871, 3′6″ gauge, 1873/74 rec., 1877 reorg. as Arkansas Midland, 1901 part of St. Louis, Iron Mountain & Southern.[1]

#1: 8% 1st m. loan of 1871 per 1891, total $1,200,000.

Intr. 1872 L. Hertz at 76.25, giving an actual interest of 10.50%.[2] First portion of $575,000 chiefly sold in A., next portion of $400,000 chiefly in London.[3] Def. 1873 or 1874; last quoted in A. in 1874 at 63; Dutch holdings disappeared without trace after notices about reorganization of the road appeared in the Dutch press.[4]

---

1. Hilton, *American Narrow Gauge*, pp. 313–14.
2. Notice in *NAE* 7 May 1872; see also Dinger, *Overzicht* 1873, pp. 785–86.
3. Notice in *NAE* 16 May 1874.
4. Notice in *NAE* 8 September 1876.

▪ Atchison, Topeka & Santa Fe

Inc. 1860 as Atchison & Topeka, 1863 reorg. as Atchison, Topeka & Santa Fe Railroad, rec. 1893, reorg. 1896 as Atchison, Topeka & Santa Fe Railway.[1]

#1: 7% 1st m. loan of 1869 per 1899.

Intr. 1872 Rotterdamsche Bank–Gebr. Boissevain at 81.50; $2,700,000 available in A.; $700,000 sold on first day; proposal to convert unpaid coupons of 1874–75 into 2nd m. bonds rejected by Dutch and paid in gold instead.[2]

Quotations in A. around 50 in 1874, later rallied to par in 1878 and 119 in 1881; in 1884 most Dutch-held bonds reported sold to U.S. because of high prices.[3] 1889 > #4 and #5.

#2: common shares, $100 each, intr. 1880 Hubrecht in cert. of 1, 5, or 10 shares; first dividend in 1879, 6% in the early 1880s; in 1895 48,594 shares (out of 1 million) deposited with Dutch pr. comm.[4] In 1895 $100 of #2 > $100 of #11 after payment of $10 in cash.

#3: 6% loan of 1881 per 1911, total $15,000,000.

Intr. 1888 Labouchère, Oyens at 105.50; $900,000 available in A.; not much trade but listed.[5] In 1889 > #4 and #5.

#4: 4% gen. m. loan of 1889 per 1989, total $150,000,000.

Intr. 1890 Hubrecht.[6] In 1895 $30,100,000 (out of $118,000,000) deposited with pr. comm. In 1895 $1,000 of #4 > $750 of #9 + $400 of #10.

#5: 5% income bonds of 1889, total $80,000,000. Cert. issued by Hubrecht 1890; in 1892 > #6.

#6: 2.5% (4% after 1896) Class A 2nd m. loan of 1892, total $80,000,000, used to replace #5 at par; in 1895 $8,530,500 deposited with pr. comm. In 1895 $1,000 of #6 > $1,130 of #12 after payment of 4% in cash.

#7: 4% class B 2nd m. loan of 1892, not more than $5,000,000 to be issued annually; in 1895 $602,000 (out of $9,000,000) deposited with pr. comm. In 1895 $1,000 of #7 > $1,180 of #12 after payment of 4% in cash.

Intr. 1892 Hope & Co. at 66.75.[7]

#8: 6% guarantee fund notes of 1888, which had matured 1891 and had been renewed for 5 years in 1893, total $9,000,000.

Intr. 1893 Hope & Co., Ketwich & Voombergh, Wed. W. Borski; cert. issued by Administratie Kantoor of Guépin, Boissevain and Van Marken; sales brisk.[8]

ATSF in rec. 1893, Dutch pr. comm. formed; Dr. Joh. Luden (Hope & Co.) member of international reorganization committee; Stephen Little reported on the company's books on behalf of the committee.[9] "King" plan for reorganization published 1895.[10] Dutch bondholders accepted plan, after strong resistance of some, among whom J. C. Loman was the most persistent.[11]

New securities issued were:

#9: 4% gen. m. loan of 1895 per 1995, total $98,000,000; in price lists at A. 1896; in 1904 Hope & Co. offered $10,000,000 more of same; quoted around par.[12]

#10: 4% adjustment bonds (income bonds, cum. after 1900) of 1895 per 1995, total $51,728,310. First int. of 3% paid in 1897 and quoted at 79, 4% from 1899 and quoted around par.

#11: common shares, total $102,000,000. Cert. issued by Hubrecht; quoted 4–8 initially, just below par in 1902, and at 125 in 1909.[13] Still in price lists at A. in 1993.

#12: 5% non-cum. pref. shares, total $11,485,951. Cert. of 5 or 10 prefs. issued by Dutch Assoc. of Preferred Shareholders.

#13: 4% 1st m. Eastern Oklahoma loan of 1903 per 1928, total $10,000,000, most sold in U.S., remainder in Holland.

Intr. 1903 Van Loon for Hope & Co. at 94, "limited sum"; soon quoted around par.[14]

#14: 4% conv. loan of 1905 per 1955, total $50,000,000, conv. at par into common stock between 1906 and 1918.

Intr. 1905–6 Hope & Co.–Dutch ATSF Shareholders Assoc.; more of same sold in 1910; most converted before 1911, but bonds still listed in 1939.[15]

#15: 5% conv. loan of 1907 per 1917, total $30,000,000, conv. into common stock before 1913.

Intr. 1907 Hope & Co.; quoted at 122 in 1910, down to par in 1914.[16]

▪ Oklahoma Central

Inc. 1904 as Canadian Valley & Western, 1905 name changed to Oklahoma Central, rec. 1908, 1914 reorg. as Oklahoma Central Railroad and leased to ATSF, bought by ATSF 1917.[17]

#16: 5% 1st m. loan of 1905 per 1945, total $2,640,000.

Intr. 1906 Van der 'Werff & Hubrecht–S. F. van Oss & Co. at 93.40; quoted in A. at 40 in 1910; down to 0.2% of par in 1914; def. 1908 and $852,000 in Dutch-held bonds deposited with pr. comm.; new securities created at 1914 reorganization never listed in A., but $25 paid out for every $1,000 bond in 1917.[18]

---

1. Waters, *Steel Trails*; Bryant, *History*.

2. Notice in *NAE* 14 June 1872; Dinger, *Overzicht* 1873, p. 788; on the int. problems Loman, *Supplement*, p. 289; *NAE* 30 December 1873.

3. Pik, *Amerikaansche spoorwegwaarden*, pp. 10–14; Santilhano, *Amerikaansche spoorwegen*, p. 11.

4. Weeveringh, *Noord-Amerikaansche spoorwegfondsen*, pp. 11–18; undated circular (1880) by Hubrecht in AASE file 111, no. 10B.

5. Request for listing of the 6% bonds by Labouchère, Oyens, 11 April 1888, in AASE file 111, no. 13. All 1895 figures given here are taken from a list by Hope, 13 June 1895, and numbered 5 among papers in a separate envelope in AASE file 111; in AASE file 111, no. 98, is another list, with generally the same figures for Dutch holdings. However, the class B's (#7) are given there as $642,000 instead of $602,000.

6. Details of the conversion in Van Oss, *American Railroads*, pp. 568–69; Waters, *Steel Rails*, pp. 197–98; request for listing of the fours and the income bonds, 1 February 1890, in AASE file 111, no. 26A.

7. Details in Bryant, *History*, p. 160; Waters, *Steel Trails*, pp. 204–5; circular of Hope, 31 May 1892, in AASE file 111, no. 32B.

8. Request by Hope for inclusion of the 6% notes, 15 November 1893, in AASE file 111, no. 40; request by the Administratie Kantoor for listing of the cert., 20 November 1893, in no. 45; see also Waters, *Steel Trails*, pp. 195, 203; details of the guarantee fund notes in Daggett, *Railroad Reorganization*, p. 203.

9. The minute-book of the Dutch committee has been found in AASE, but without any inventory number; for the Dutch side of the Atchison reorganization this has been used; other papers of the comm. are in AASE file 111A. Bryant, *History*, pp. 164–68; Waters, *Steel Trails*, pp. 205–19; and Daggett, *Railroad Reorganization*, pp. 210–16, give details of the reorganization. A copy of Little's printed report in AASE file 111, no. 57; in no. 61 is a copy of the printed report of Robert Moore, consulting engineer of St. Louis, on the condition of the physical plant of the railroad.

10. Printed plan of reorganization (in Dutch) with covering letter by Hope & Co., 10 April 1895, in AASE file 111A, no. 3; the details of the conversion have been taken from this plan, also given by Bryant, *History*, pp. 167–68.

11. Printed circular of the committee, 10 April 1895, in AASE file 111, no. 114; Loman's printed circular, 17 April 1895, in AASE file 111A, no. 4.

12. Hope & Co. to Stock Exchange, 20 April 1896, in AASE file 111, no. 121; the 1904 sale in Hope & Co. to same, 13 February 1904, in AASE file 111, no. 142; also *Van Oss' Effectenboek* 1903 and later editions.

13. Hubrecht to Stock Exchange, 8 April 1897, in AASE file 111, no. 130.

14. *Van Oss' Effectenboek* 1904, pp. 642 and 1093; request for listing by Hope & Co., 4 June 1903, in AASE file 111, no. 140.

15. *Van Oss' Effectenboek* 1909, p. 1190; 1912, p. 1241. Requests for inclusion in the price

lists by Hope & Co., 17 October 1905; 13 September and 8 December 1910, in AASE file 111, nos. 145, 155, and 157.

16. Request for listing of the 5% bonds, 24 September 1907, in AASE file 111, no. 149.

17. For a history of the OCR see Veenendaal, "The Oklahoma Central Railroad" and "Railroads, Oil and Dutchmen."

18. Van der Werff & Hubrecht to Stock Exchange, 5 June 1908, in AASE file 836 (no numbers); minutes of the 14 September 1908 meeting and account of bonds deposited in same file; details of the reorganization in *Van Oss' Effectenboek* 1915–16, and in file 836.

■ Atlantic & Pacific

See under St. Louis & San Francisco.

■ Atlantic & Great Western

See under New York, Lake Erie & Western.

■ Atlantic, Mississippi & Ohio

See under Norfolk & Western.

■ Baltimore & Ohio

Inc. 1828, 1896 in rec., reinc. 1898.[1]

#1: Common shares, $100 each.

Intr. 1870 Wertheim & Gompertz at 110 in cert. of 1 or 5 shares; trade in A. dull; last quoted 1878 just below par. Old cert. > 1898 new cert. of 10 commons issued by Wertheim & G.; quoted at 73 in 1899.

#2: 4% preferred shares.

Intr. 1898 Wertheim & G. at 80, in cert. of 10 prefs.; trade in A. lively; cert. cancelled 1972, with 222 cert. of 10 commons and 89 of 10 prefs. still outstanding.[2]

■ Cincinnati, Hamilton & Dayton

Inc. 1846, in rec. 1873 and again 1906–7, 1909 controlled by B&O, new reorganization 1916 and taken over by B&O.[3]

#3: 4% 1st & ref. m. loan of 1909 per 1959, total $7,500,000, chiefly sold in London. Intr. 1910 Van Loon for Hope & Co. and Teixeira de Mattos at 92; Dfl 500,000 sold one month after intr.; quoted at 76 in 1914. In 1920 > 4% B&O bonds or redeemed at 70%; new B&O bonds not listed in A.[4]

---

1. For a history of the B&O see Dilts, *The Great Road*; Hungerford, *Story of the Baltimore & Ohio*; Stover, *History of the Baltimore & Ohio*.

2. Dinger, *Overzicht* 1873, pp. 759–60; Pik, *Amerikaansche spoorwegwaarden*, pp. 26–29. Loman, *Supplement* 1880, p. 266, is the last to mention the B&O commons; Weeveringh, *Noord-Amerikaansche spoorwegfondsen*, omits them altogether; the 1972 figures in AASE file 272.

3. For a history of the CH&D see Condit, *Railroad and the City*, pp. 16–20; Stover, *History*, pp. 210, 227.

4. AASE file 967, where the Dutch prospectus is to be found. Teixeira de M. to Stock Exchange Board, 13 April 1910. Also, *Van Oss' Effectenboek* 1912, p. 1266.

■ Boston, Hartford & Erie

Inc. 1864, bankrupt 1870, reinc. 1875 as New York & New England, rec. 1893, taken over by New York, New Haven & Hartford.[1]
#1: Common shares BH&E.
Intr. 1872 Wertheim & Gompertz/Teixeira de Mattos and Lion Hertz(?) at 8–13, with BH&E already in rec.; about 10,000 shares sold; dropped from A. price lists 1873.[2]

---

1. Harlow, *Steelways*, pp. 196–205; and Baker, *Formation*, pp. 45–70.
2. AASE file 23, nos. 12–13 and 16 contain papers concerning the BH&E; file 23 is that of the Erie itself, so the archivist of the Stock Exchange did mix up things a bit. The suit against Hertz in Den Tex, *Amerikaansche spoorwegen*, p. 18. Reports of meetings called by Beurscomité in *NAE* of 5 April and 14 May 1872; Dinger, *Overzicht* 1873, p. 797, also warns against the BH&E shares.

■ Buffalo, New York & Philadelphia

See under Pennsylvania Railroad.

■ Cairo & St. Louis

See under Mobile & Ohio.

■ California & Oregon

See under Southern Pacific.

■ California Pacific

See under Southern Pacific.

■ Canada, Michigan & Chicago

Inc. 1871, but never built.[1]
#1: 7% 1st m. gold loan of 1872 per 1902, total $2,750,000, sold in London by Sutton, Miller & Comp. at £157 per $1,000 bond.
Intr. 1872 L. Hertz at 77; only one quotation found in A. at 35 in 1874.[2]

---

1. Meints, *Michigan Railroads*, p. 45.
2. Announcement by Lion Hertz in *NAE* 3 September 1872; Dinger, *Overzicht* 1873, p. 789; D. R. Adler, *British Investment*, p. 206, gives a first price in London of £157; Dinger mentions £166.

■ Canada Southern

See under New York Central.

■ Central Pacific

See under Southern Pacific.

■ Central Railroad of New Jersey

Inc. 1850.[1]

7% 1st m. loan never listed in A., but from 1858 Hope & Co. of A. held $24,000 in their investment fund.[2]

---

1. E. Anderson, *The Central Railroad.*
2. AE 9 February 1858; Bogen, *Anthracite Railroads*, p. 64. See Chapter 15 for details of Hope's investment fund.

■ Chesapeake & Ohio

Inc. 1868 as Chesapeake & Ohio Railroad from earlier Virginia Central and Covington & Ohio, in rec. 1873, reinc. as Chesapeake & Ohio Railway 1876, leased 1886–87 to Newport News & Mississippi Valley, rec. 1887, reinc. 1888.[1]

#1: 6% 1st m. loan of 1869, total $15,000,000.

Intr. 1872 Jos. Cahen/Teixeira de Mattos at 82; def. November 1873.[2] After reorganization > 6% 1st m. (#2).

#2: 6% 1st m. loan per 1908, < #1; old $1,000 bond > $900 of #2 + $100 in new 6% 2nd m. income bonds + $310 in new 1st prefs. (#4). Int. to be paid half in gold, half in scrip until 1881.[3] The 2nd m. income bonds (per 1918) were never listed in A.

Intr. 1880 (firsts only) Broekman & Honders at 72, rising to par by 1884; after def. $1,200,000 of Dutch owners assented to refunding proposals of J. P. Morgan, $600,000 did not; 1888 > 5% 1st cons. m. loan (#6).[4]

#3: Common shares.

#4: First preferred shares.

#5: Second preferred shares.

Intr. 1880 by Broekman & Honders, but little trade; dropped from price lists in A. 1884.[5] Dutch not involved in the conv. of ##3, 4, and 5 into new shares in 1888.

#6: 5% 1st cons. m. loan per 1939, total $30,000,000; < #2.

Each old $1,000 bond > $666 of #6 + $333 in new 1st prefs. Bonds quoted over par, 119 in 1902; redeemed 1939 at par.[6]

#7: 4.5% gen. m. loan of 1892 per 1992, total $70,000,000, of which $47,000,000 actually issued by 1911.

Intr. 1893 Teixeira de Mattos at 75, "limited number."[7] Soon quoted over par; in 1939 at 99; dropped from price lists in 1982 after merger of C&O and B&O into CSX Corporation.

#8: Common shares of new C&O, $100 each.

Intr. 1899 Algemeene Trust Maatschappij in cert. of 10 shares at 40; dividends 2% since 1899; 4.25% in 1910, and quoted at par. In 1939 Algemeene Trust Maatschappij still held 118,500 commons; dropped from price lists in A. 1982.[8]

---

1. Turner, *Chessie's Road*; Nelson, *Chesapeake & Ohio Railway.*
2. Turner, *Chessie's Road*, pp. 68–89; NAE of 30 January and 2 February 1872; Dinger, *Overzicht* 1873, pp. 783–84; NAE of 25 November 1873; Pik, *Amerikaansche spoorwegwaarden*, pp. 44–45.

3. Details of conversion in Turner, *Chessie's Road*, p. 100; Loman, *Supplement*, pp. 286–87; printed circular by Broekman & Honders, 1880, in AASE file 91, no. 2.

4. Broekman & H. to Stock Exchange, 24 September 1887, and minutes of meeting of 29 September, in AASE file 91, nos. 22 and 24; the number of bonds in Dutch hands in no. 28.

5. Santilhano, *Amerikaansche spoorwegen*, p. 95; request for listing of sixes and stock in AASE file 91, nos. 8 and 13.

6. See circular by Drexel, Morgan & Co., in Dutch and English, 9 February 1889, in AASE file 91, no. 31, for details of conversion.

7. Prospectus of Teixeira de M., 28 November 1893, in AASE file 91, no. 45.

8. *Van Oss' Effectenboek* 1903 and later editions; press cutting from the *Telegraaf*, 18 April 1940.

■ Chesapeake, Ohio & Southwestern

See under Illinois Central.

■ Chicago & Atlantic

See under New York, Lake Erie & Western.

■ Chicago & Erie

See under New York, Lake Erie & Western.

■ Chicago & North Western

Inc. 1864.[1] One later subsidiary of C&NW was traded in Amsterdam before the C&NW itself; this was:

■ West Wisconsin

Inc. 1867, rec. 1875, reorg. 1878 as Chicago, St. Paul & Minneapolis, acquired 1883 by C&NW.

#1: 1st m. sterling loan of 1868, total £800,000 ($4,000,000), in 4 series of £200,000 each.

Intr. 1868 Lion Hertz, £75,000 of 1st series at 69.[2] Same sum of 2nd series sold at 71 by same 1870; def. 1875.[3] No Dutch pr. comm., but Broekman & H. and Wertheim & G. active in reorganization with English comm.; outcome not recorded, but according to Wertheim there had been hundreds of Dutch bondholders.[4]

■ Chicago & North Western

#2: Common shares, intr. 1868 Broes & Gosman in cert. of 1, 5, or 10 shares; dividend 10% in 1871, but none in 1874–77.

#3: 7% pref. shares, intr. 1868 by same; majority soon in Dutch hands, much trade in A.; dividends at 7% except for 1875–77; quoted in A. at par in 1879; all-time high of 265 in 1902; two Dutch directors on the board after 1869.[5] One of them, J. L. ten Have, called Jay Gould, who was on the C&NW board 1877–84, "dishonest and objectionable in every way."[6] Both commons and prefs. dropped from price lists in A. in 1952.

#4: 8% 1st m. loan of 1870 per 1900, total $1,350,000, of Iowa Midland Railroad, controlled by C&NW.

Intr. 1870 Broes & Gosman/Piek at 82.50, redeemed 1894 by C&NW.[7]

#5: 7% 1st m. Madison ext. loan of 1871 per 1911, total $3,150,000, only sold in A.; sinking fund of $23,000 annually. Intr. 1871 Broes & G./Piek at 82.25; brisk trade in A.; quoted at par after 1879, 125 in 1900.

#6: 7% 1st m. Menominee ext. loan of 1871 per 1911, total $2,700,000, only sold in A.; sinking fund $20,000 annually.

Intr. 1871 by same as #5 at 85; much trade, same quotations as #5. Both redeemed 1911.[8]

#7: 7% 1st m. North Western Union loan of 1872 per 1917, total $3,500,00, sold only in A.

Intr. 1872 Broes & G. at 87; redeemed 1917.[9]

#8: 7% 1st m. loan of Winona & St. Peter Railroad of 1871 per 1916, guaranteed by C&NW, total $4,375,000, sold only in A.; sinking fund provided.

Intr. 1872 Broes & G. at 86.5; quoted over par after 1879; redeemed 1916.[10]

#9: 7% cons. m. loan of 1872 per 1902, auth. $48,000,000. Intr. 1873 Broes & G. at 83, $5,000,000 sold in A.; quoted at par from 1879 until redemption in 1902.[11]

For the pseudo investment fund set up by Broes & Gosman in 1878 under the name of "First Mortgage Railway Bonds," see Chapter 15.

#10: 5% sinking fund debentures of 1883 per 1933, total $10,000,000 intended for purchase of stock in Chicago, St. Paul, Minneapolis & Omaha Railroad; sinking fund of $200,000 annually from 1888.

Intr. 1884 S. E. Edersheim at 92; "limited sum," but regular quotations around par in A. until redemption in 1933.[12]

---

1. For the history of the C&NW see *Yesterday and Today*; Casey and Douglas, *Pioneer Railroad.*

2. AE 7 August 1868; Dinger, *Overzicht* 1873, pp. 729–30.

3. Notices in *NAE* 13 May 1873 and 6 April 1875.

4. AASE file 45, no. 1 contains correspondence between Broekman & H. and the Stock Exchange, 11 and 17 April 1878. Correspondence between Bruff, engineer sent out by English comm., and Wertheim & G., 25, 28, and 31 May and 3 June 1878, in nos. 3–6; printed copies of a reorganization proposal of 24 April 1877 and of a letter from the English Bondholders' Committee, 15 May 1877, in nos. 1F and 1G.

5. Grodinsky, *The Iowa Pool*, pp. 14, 27–28; Pik, *Amerikaansche spoorwegwaarden*, p. 58; Loman, *Supplement*, pp. 222–25; Weeveringh, *Noord-Amerikaansche spoorwegfondsen*, pp. 59–65.

6. Grodinsky, *The Iowa Pool*, p. 76.

7. Pik, *Amerikaansche spoorwegwaarden*, p. 58.

8. Dinger, *Overzicht* 1873, pp. 716–19; AASE file 48, no. 6 contains the Dutch prospectus of the Menominee ext. loan; that of the Madison ext. has not been found. It is remarkable how small file 48 is, considering the enormous amount of money involved in the several C&NW loans.

9. Dinger, *Overzicht* 1873, pp. 721–23; AASE file 48, no. 11 contains the Dutch prospectus; Pik, *Amerikaansche spoorwegwaarden*, p. 54.

10. Dinger, *Overzicht* 1873, pp. 719–21; *Van Oss' Effectenboek* 1903, p. 476. AASE file 48, nos. 1 and 4 contain Ten Have to Stock Exchange, 24 August 1872, about the guarantee by the

C&NW, and Dutch prospectus of the W&StP loan, January 1872. The land grant was forfeited when the road was not finished on 3 March 1873.

11. AASE file 48, no. 15 contains the Dutch prospectus of the consolidated loan, 12–13 September 1873; Pik, *Amerikaansche spoorwegwaarden*, pp. 48–49.

12. AASE file 48, no. 37 contains the prospectus of Edersheim, 16 January 1884; Weeveringh, *Noord-Amerikaansche spoorwegfondsen*, p. 62.

■ Chicago & Southwestern

See under Chicago, Rock Island & Pacific.

■ Chicago, Burlington & Quincy

Inc. 1856.[1]

#1: Common shares, said to be held in Holland before 1880. Intr. 1880 Hubrecht over par in cert., prices soon at 120–30; Dutch translations of annual reports since 1880.[2] Hill-Morgan started buying commons at $200 and by 1901 almost 97 percent was in their hands; quotations in A. ended. After breakup of Northern Securities Company, trade in A. resumed, first quoted in 1912 at 190; last two Dutch cert. canceled in 1958.

#2: 3.5% 1st m. Illinois div. loan of 1899 per 1949, used to retire older bonds.

Intr. Ad. Boissevain just below par; by 1904 $400,000 sold in A.; still quoted in 1939 at 59–61.[3]

■ Rockford, Rock Island & St. Louis

Inc. 1868, rec. 1871, reorg. as St. Louis, Rock Island & Chicago 1876, sold to CB&Q 1878.

#3: 7% 1st m. gold loan of 1869, total $9,000,000, sold chiefly in Germany.

Intr. 1869 S. de Vita at 72.50.[4] Def. 1871, German pr. comm.; half of each bond > $500 in prefs., int. on other half continued from 1873, unpaid coupons > 4% cert.; 1874 all payment of int. ended.[5] Dutch owners sold their holdings at around 5 cents on the dollar to German parties; CB&Q paid $1,570,000 for RRI&StL; bondholders got around 13.5% of their holdings and had to pay 765 reichsmarks for every $1,000 bond, but few Dutchmen participated.[6]

■ Colorado & Southern

Inc. 1898 from earlier lines, from 1908 controlled by CB&Q.[7]

#4: Common shares, total $31,000,000.

#5: 4% 1st preferred shares, total $8,500,000.

#6: 4% 2nd preferred shares, total $8,500,000.

##4, 5, and 6 intr. 1902 Alsberg, Goldberg at 17, 67, and 33.50 respectively.[8] Few dividends, little trade in A., but in 1939 three cert. of #4 and one each of #5 and #6 still outstanding, dropped from price lists only in 1960.

#7: 4.5% ref. & ext. gold loan of 1905 per 1935, $100,000,000 auth.

Intr. 1907 Möller & Kijzer at 78, $10,000,000 available.[9] Prices soon just under par until 1914; redeemed 1935.

1. Overton, *Burlington Route*.

2. AASE file 117 contains circular by Hubrecht about the exchange of original shares for cert., December 1880; annual reports in Dutch for 1880 and 1881 also in this file. Also Weeveringh, *Noord-Amerikaansche spoorwegfondsen*, pp. 46–47; and Santilhano, *Amerikaansche spoorwegen*, pp. 113, 557.

3. AASE file 117, no. 12B contains Boissevain to Stock Exchange, 7 September 1904; also *Van Oss' Effectenboek* 1905, p. 767, and later editions.

4. Announcement in *NAE* 13 April 1869.

5. Notices in *NAE* 19 December 1871; 2 and 30 July 1872; 3 February 1874; Dinger, *Overzicht* 1873, p. 732.

6. Notices in *NAE* 18 July 1876 and 23 October 1877; Loman, *Supplement*, p. 233. The purchase price of $1,570,000 is given in *NAE* 6 October 1876; Overton, *Burlington Route*, pp. 149–51, has $2,000,000.

7. Overton, *Gulf to the Rockies*.

8. *Van Oss' Effectenboek* 1903, p. 485; AASE file 665, no. 1; in no. 37 is Alsberg, Goldberg to Stock Exchange, 29 March 1939, which gives figures for 1939.

9. AASE file 665, nos. 3 and 3A, contains Möller & Kijzer to Stock Exchange, 13 January 1908, and Dutch prospectus, 30 December 1907.

■ Chicago Great Western

Inc. 1893 out of Chicago, St. Paul & Kansas City of 1886, rec. 1907, reorg. 1909.[1]

#1: 5% 1st m. loan of 1886 per 1936 of CStP&KC, total $2,000,000, mostly taken up in England.

Intr. 1887 Hope & Co. at 92.50.[2] Int. 1889 not paid, int. 1890–92 > 5% priority sterling loan, not listed in A.

Coupons of a 5% Minnesota & Northwestern loan also > sterling loan. This M&N loan apparently held in Holland, but never listed.[3] English pr. comm. 1892, with J. G. Sillem of Hope & Co. as Dutch member. Old $1,000 CStP&KC 5% bond > $500 of 4% (income) debentures (#2) + $600 of 5% pref. shares (#3).[4]

#2: 4% (income) debentures of new Chicago Great Western Railway; Hope & Co. issued cert. for these; trade slow in A. and quotations down from 90 in 1900 to 36 in 1908; int. paid regularly; in 1909 > new prefs. (#5).

#3: 5% pref. shares of CGW, intr. in A. in cert. of Hope & Co.; quoted at 85 in 1904, down to 18 in 1908.[5] Def. 1907, reorg. as CGW Railroad 1909; #3 > #4.

#4: common shares < 5% pref. shares (#3) at 120%; Hope & Co. intr. cert. in 1910; no dividend ever; first price in A. 30 below par, down to 12 in 1914; in 1939 quoted at $1 per $1,000 cert. In 1934 $129,000 (par value) of commons still held in Holland.

#5: pref. shares of CGW < debentures (#2) at 110%, intr. 1910 by Hope & Co. in cert.; quoted at $3 per $1,000 cert. in 1939.[6]

#6: 4% 1st m. loan of 1909 per 1959.

Intr. 1914 Van Loon & Co./Ad. Boissevain at 73; most bonds held in Holland < Wisconsin, Minnesota & Pacific (#8); still quoted in 1939 at 13.[7]

■ Mason City & Fort Dodge

Inc. 1881, 1901 bought by CGW, 1910 dissolved.

#7: 4% 1st m. loan of 1905 per 1955, total $12,000,000.

Intr. 1905 Ad. Boissevain at 91.75, $1,000,000 available in A.[8] At corporate dissolution of MC&FD in 1910 this loan continued by CGW, and partly > CGW bonds and shares; last quoted in A. in 1928 at 49.

■ Wisconsin, Minnesota & Pacific

Inc. 1883 from earlier lines, 1899 leased to CGW, 1901 bought by same, 1910 dissolved.

#8: 4% 1st m. loan of 1900 per 1950, total $5,524,000.

Intr. 1905 Van der Werff & Hubrecht at 91.40, limited number.[9] This loan not disturbed at 1910 reorganization, but CGW stopped payment of int. in 1912; British pr. comm. In 1913 $1,000 WM&P bond #8 > $500 4% CGW bonds (#6) + $500 prefs. (#5) + $123.74 cash for unpaid coupons; dropped from price lists in A. 1914.[10]

---

1. For a history of the CGW, see Grant, *Corn Belt*.

2. AASE file 223, no. 1C contains a Dutch prospectus of this loan, issued by Hope & Co.

3. Details of conversion of AASE file 223, nos. 6A and B. Hope & Co. to Stock Exchange, 30 January 1890, in AASE file 223, no. 9.

4. Grant, *Corn Belt*, pp. 32–34; printed circular by Hope & Co. in AASE file 223, 13C.

5. AASE file 944, no. 3C; on the formation of the CGW, the Amsterdam Stock Exchange closed its old file 223 and opened a new one, 944. Van Oss, *American Railroads*, p. 533.

6. Press cutting 12 June 1909, in AASE file 944, no. 10, gives Hope's announcement of the conversion; details also in Grant, *Corn Belt*, pp. 74–75.

7. Boissevain and others to Stock Exchange, February 1914, with request for listing of the 4% loan, in AASE file 944, no. 16.

8. Grant, *Corn Belt*, pp. 60–63. AASE file 775, no. 1 contains the request for listing by Boissevain.

9. Grant, *Corn Belt*, pp. 50–51, 59. AASE file 778, no. 1 contains the request by Van der Werff for listing of the WM&P bonds.

10. Press cutting (translated from the London *Times*), undated [1912], about English committee and the depositing of bonds, in AASE file 778, no. 36; details of conversion in a circular of English committee and announcement by Ad. Boissevain, 29 October 1912, in nos. 37 and 38.

■ Chicago, Milwaukee & St. Paul

Inc. 1873 from earlier lines, of which Milwaukee & St. Paul was the most important.[1]

#1: 7% 1st m. curr. Iowa-Dakota div. loan of 1869 per 1899 of Milwaukee & St. Paul, total $1,000,000, of which $900,000 sold in Holland.

Intr. 1872 Holjé & Boissevain/Rotterdamsche Bank at 83; quoted soon at 110.[2]

#2: 7% 1st m. River div. gold loan of 1872 per 1902, total $4,000,000 or £800,000. Marketed in London by Morton, Rose & Co.

Intr. 1872 Elix & Broekman at 90.5; £200,000 available in A.[3] Both #1 and #2 conv. into pref. shares; by 1892 about half of both converted.[4]

#3: Common shares.

#4: Preferred shares.

Both intr. 1872 Administratie Kantoor of Gebr. Boissevain/Kerkhoven in cert. of $500 or $1,000; prices of commons at 80 in later 1870's, over par in 1880, when first dividend was declared; infrequent trade.[5] In 1879 cert. transferred to Broes & Gosman. First annual report in Dutch 1883, Dutch director F. A. Müller 1872–76.

#5: 6% 1st m. Western Union div. loan of 1879 per 1909, total $4,000,000.

Intr. 1880 Broekman & Honders at 101.50.[6] Not listed in A.

#6: 5% 1st m. Pacific Western div. (North Dakota lines) loan of 1881 per 1921, total $24,400,000, but not all issued in same year.

Intr. 1881 Everts & Schmidt at 95; in 1883 Speyer Bros., London, offered $1,500,000 more in A. at 97.[7] Quotations frequent and high, around 120 in 1900.

#7: 5% 1st m. Chicago & Lake Superior div. gold loan of 1881 per 1921, total $1,360,000; sold by Borthwick, Wark & Co. in London, but only small sums; remainder in Holland.

Intr. 1882 H. Oyens & Sons at 92, at the request of Borthwick; dull trade in early years, later more frequent, and quoted around 108.[8]

#8: 4% 25-year gold bonds of 1909 were offered in A. by unknown party, but never listed.[9] Intended for construction of the Pacific Division (line to Seattle).

#9: 4.5% conv. gold bonds of 1912 per 1932, with preferential rights for stockholders; conv. into commons.

Intr. 1912 Broes & Gosman, results unknown, and possibly immediately converted into shares and never listed as bonds.[10]

---

1. Derleth, *Milwaukee Road*.

2. *NAE* 2 February 1872, announcement by Holjé & Boissevain/Rotterdamsche Bank; Weeveringh, *Noord-Amerikaansche spoorwegfondsen*, pp. 51–56; Pik, *Amerikaansche spoorwegwaarden*, pp. 114–18.

3. Greenberg, *Financiers and Railroads*, pp. 57–58; AASE file 73, no. 2, and *NAE* 26 March 1872.

4. D. R. Adler, *British Investment*, p. 206; AASE file 95, no. 1 contains Elix & Broekman to Stock Exchange, 30 May 1873.

5. *NAE* 8 March 1872, announcement by Gebr. Boissevain, Kerkhoven, and Rotterdamsche Bank about opening of Administratie Kantoor for CM&StP shares; Weeveringh, *Noord-Amerikaansche spoorwegfondsen*, p. 54.

6. Announcement by Broekman & Honders in *NAE* 6 February 1880; Loman, *Supplement*, p. 230.

7. Weeveringh, *Noord-Amerikaansche spoorwegfondsen*, p. 54; AASE file 95, no. 11 contains a prospectus by Everts & Schmidt; in no. 12 is the prospectus in English, 1883.

8. Weeveringh, *Noord-Amerikaansche spoorwegfondsen*, p. 54; *Van Oss' Effectenboek* 1903, p. 479; AASE file 95, no. 19 contains H. Oyens & Sons to Stock Exchange, 23 June 1882; Van Oss, *American Railroads*, p. 473.

9. AASE file 95, no. 22 gives an outline of the issue of $28,000,000 in 4% 25-year bonds.

10. AASE file 95, nos. 26 and 28.

▪ Chicago, Rock Island & Pacific

Inc. 1866 from earlier roads as Chicago, Rock Island & Pacific Railroad, reorg. 1880 as CRI&P Railway 1880.[1]

#1: Common shares, creation of 1866, total $4,900,000.

Intr. 1868 Broes & Gosman at 83, in cert. of 1, 5, or 10 shares; dividends of 8–10%, quotations over par in 1870.[2] Stock dividends of 100% in 1880: one share of rail*road* > two of new rail*way*.[3] Circulating in large numbers in Holland. In 1902, when quoted at 200, > ##10, 11, and 12.

■ Chicago & Southwestern

Inc. 1869, rec. 1872, reorg. as Iowa Southern & Missouri Northern, subsidiary of CRI&P.[4]

#2: 7% 1st m. loan of 1869 per 1899, total $5,000,000, int. guaranteed by CRI&P. Sold in Germany and Holland.

Intr. 1870 Holjé & Boissevain/Rotterdamsche Bank at 82; def. 1872, but coupons paid (in currency, not in gold) by CRI&P; quotations up to 125 in the 1880s; continued at 1876 reorganization.

#3: 7% Atchison Branch loan of 1871 per 1901, total $1,000,000, supposedly also guaranteed by CRI&P.

Intr. 1872 Gebr. Boissevain/Rotterdamsche Bank at 85; intended for German market, but because of Franco-Prussian War sold in A. only.[5] Def. 1872, and CRI&P refused to pay int.; Rotterdamsche Bank started lawsuit to obtain guarantee, but in 1875 the court finally decided that CRI&P was under no obligation to pay coupons. By 1873 $407,000 of Dutch Atchison Branch bonds deposited, 1878 declared worthless.[6]

■ Kansas & Missouri Bridge

Inc. 1869.[7]

#4: 8% 1st m. curr. loan 1871, total $600,000, sold only in Holland by Rotterdamsche Bank/Associatie Cassa at 82.75; int. guaranteed by C&SW.[8] Def. 1872, unpaid coupons bought by Rotterdamsche Bank; 1874 bonds deposited; 1876 bridge sold at foreclosure to P. C. A. M. van Weel, representative of Dutch bondholders.[9] Leavenworth Bridge Company then formed, and securities exchanged; outcome uncertain: in 1879 the bridge was controlled by the CRI&P.[10]

■ Des Moines Valley

Inc. 1865, rec. 1871, 1873 northern half of line reorg. as Des Moines & Fort Dodge, 1888 leased to CRI&P, 1905 leased to Minneapolis & St. Louis.

#5: 8% 1st m. loan of 1868 per 1898, total $4,690,000.

Intr. 1870 H. Franco Mendes/J. A. Matthes & Co. at 85; initially $400,000 sold.[11] Def. 1871, road sold in two sections, northern one reinc. as DM&FD.[12] Dutch pr. comm. 1873. In 1874 $2,000 of DMV bonds > $1,000 of 6% DM&FD bonds (#6) + $1,000 in 6% income bonds (#7) + $840 in new prefs. + $1,000 in new commons; for expenses each owner had to pay Dfl 159 for every $2,000 in old bonds; in A. 774 cert. of DMV bonds participated; nonassenting owners paid off in cash at 16%.[13] No dividends paid.

■ Des Moines & Fort Dodge

#6: 6% 1st m. loan per 1905, total $1,200,000, almost all held in Holland < #5; cert. issued by Broes & Gosman; int. reduced to 4% in 1887, but guaranteed by CRI&P as lessor; Broes & G. had asked for 5%, but CRI&P refused. Regular quotations in A., high of 101 in 1881.[14] Redeemed 1905 with #9.

#7: 6% income bonds per 1905, total $1,200,000, resulted from conversion of #5; 6% paid in 1881 only; almost all held in Holland, but not listed in A.; int. reduced to 2.5% in 1887, but from then on guaranteed by CRI&P.

#8: 6% ext. bonds of 1881 per 1905, total auth. $5,000,000, but only $672,000 issued, mostly sold in Holland.

Intr. 1881 Broes & G. at 101.[15] 1885–88 int. reduced to 3%. Redeemed 1905 with #9.

#9: 4% 1st m. loan of 1905 per 1935, guaranteed by new lessor Minneapolis & St. Louis, total $3,072,000. Used to redeem #6 and #8 in cash at 97%; bonds of #6 and #8 also > #9 at par + $30 cash bonus, and many Dutch opted for this. Also sold 1881 by F. Glasbergen for Alsberg, Goldberg and Labouchère, Oyens & Co. at 96.50; much trade, quoted just below par until 1910.[16] In 1933 at 0.25% of par, 1940 at 1, with M&StL in rec.

▪ Chicago, Rock Island & Pacific

In 1902 new management set up two holdings, the Rock Island Company of New Jersey, and the Chicago, Rock Island & Pacific Railroad of Iowa.

New stock was issued:

#10: common shares of RIC of New Jersey.

#11: 4–6% pref. shares of RIC of New Jersey; 114,000 Dutch owners of ##10 and 11 in 1914 represented in reorganization scheme and lost everything.[17]

#12: 4% coll. trust gold loan (per 2002), total $75,000,000, of CRI&P Railroad of Iowa; collateral was same sum in commons of CRI&P Railway. One old (#1) share ($100) > $100 of #10 + $70 of #11 + $100 of #12. Most Dutch converted, as quotations of #1 stop in 1902.[18] Of 4% coll. trust loan $8,500,000 held in Holland at reorganization of 1917.[19]

#13: 5% 10-year loan of 1903, to finance purchase of St. Louis & San Francisco; never officially listed in A. but known to have been held in Holland.[20]

#14: 4% 1st and ref. m. loan of CRI&P Railway, auth. $163,000,000, underwritten by Speyer & Co., New York.

Intr. 1906 Gebr. Teixeira de Mattos, part of $11,000,000 at 95.40.[21]

#15: 5% 20-year debentures of CRI&P Railway of 1912, total $20,000,000.

Intr. 1912 Gebr. Teixeira de M. at 97.25.[22] In 1917 > new 6% pref. shares.

Railroad def. 1914, Dutch pr. comm. formed.[23]

▪ Rock Island, Arkansas & Louisiana

Inc. 1904, subsidiary of CRI&P.[24]

#16: 4.5% 1st m. gold loan of 1904 per 1934, total $30,000,000, coupons payable in dollars, sterling, Reichsmark, francs, and guilders, guaranteed by CRI&P. A later portion of $11,000,000 underwritten by Speyer Bros., London, and Gebr. Teixeira de M. in 1910.

Intr. 1910 Teixeira de M. at 96.25.[25] Not disturbed by default of CRI&P in 1914; continued after 1934, and finally redeemed by CRI&P in 1952.

1. Hayes, *Iron Road*.
2. Dinger, *Overzicht* 1873, pp. 709–10; Pik, *Amerikaansche spoorwegwaarden*, pp. 58–63.
3. Weeveringh, *Noord-Amerikaansche spoorwegfondsen*, pp. 65–66; Hayes, *Iron Road*, pp. 99–100; *NAE* 11 June 1880.
4. Hayes, *Iron Road*, pp. 73–74; Glaab, *Kansas City*, pp. 48–49.
5. Dinger, *Overzicht* 1873, pp. 711–713. In AASE file 48, Chicago & *North* Western, papers pertaining to the Chicago & *South* Western have been included by mistake; nos. 6 and 7 contain correspondence between Boissevain/Rotterdamsche Bank and the Stock Exchange about the main line and the Atchison branch loans.
6. Loman, *Supplement*, pp. 221–22. Notices in *NAE* 3 December 1872, 17 January 1873, and 7 September 1875. Gebr. Boissevain to Stock Exchange, 1 October 1873, in AASE file 48, no. 10. Loman, *Supplement*, p. 222; Pik, *Amerikaansche spoorwegwaarden*, p. 63; notices in *NAE* 26 January 1877 and 8 February 1878.
7. Glaab, *Kansas City*, pp. 1–9; Hayes, *Iron Road*, p. 77–80.
8. *NAE* 4 July 1871. The only details of this loan on the Dutch market have been found in the financial press of the time; investors' guides make no mention of this loan. AASE file 111, which contains the papers of the Atchison, Topeka & Santa Fe, has material on the Kansas & Missouri Bridge, although the Atchison had nothing to do with it.
9. *NAE* 5 December 1873; 27 October, 6 November 1874; 22 August 1876.
10. *NAE* 25 December 1877, and 21 June 1881; *Poor's Manual* 1879, p. 821.
11. Dinger, *Overzicht* 1873, pp. 761–62; *NAE* 29 March 1870, 16 May 1871.
12. Notices in *NAE* 15 January, 22 March, and 4 November 1873.
13. Loman, *Supplement*, pp. 267–68; details in *NAE* 3 March, and 31 December 1874; Pik, *Amerikaansche spoorwegwaarden*, pp. 79–84.
14. Details in Santilhano, *Amerikaansche spoorwegen*, p. 217; notices in *NAE* 24 July and 25 August 1885; printed circular, July 1885, in AASE file 135, no. 6B.
15. AASE file 135, no. 1 contains the request by Broes & Gosman for listing of the extension bonds; Dutch prospectus in no. 4. File 135 contains no papers of earlier Des Moines & Fort Dodge loans.
16. *Van Oss' Effectenboek* 1905, p. 1316; AASE file 135, no. 9.
17. *Van Oss' Effectenboek* 1918–19.
18. Details of conversion in *Van Oss' Effectenboek* 1903, p. 482; 1904, p. 657; and 1905, p. 773.
19. Van Pellecom, *Kapitaalexport*, pp. 123–24.
20. Details of this loan in *Van Oss' Effectenboek* 1904, p. 658.
21. AASE file 687, no. 6 contains a request for inclusion of 4% loan in the Amsterdam price lists, 21 March 1906.
22. AASE file 687, no. 19; *Van Oss' Effectenboek* 1912, p. 1265.
23. Minutes of the meeting of the committee, 12 May 1914, in AASE file 687, no. 24; other papers relative to the reorganization also in same file. Van Pellecom, *Kapitaalexport*, pp. 123–24.
24. Hayes, *Iron Road*, pp. 173–74.
25. AASE file 974, no. 1 contains the Dutch prospectus of this loan, and request for listing, 25 April 1910.

■ Chicago, St. Louis & New Orleans

See under Illinois Central.

■ Chicago, St. Paul & Kansas City

See under Chicago Great Western.

■ Cincinnati, Hamilton & Dayton

See under Baltimore & Ohio.

■ Cleveland, Akron & Columbus

See under Pennsylvania Railroad.

■ Cleveland, Cincinnati, Chicago & St. Louis

See under New York Central.

■ Cleveland, Mount Vernon & Delaware

See under Pennsylvania Railroad.

■ Colorado & Southern

See under Chicago, Burlington & Quincy.

■ Dallas & Waco

See under Missouri, Kansas & Texas.

■ Denver & Boulder Valley

See under Union Pacific.

■ Denver & Rio Grande

Inc. 1870, 3′ gauge, 1878–80 leased to Atchison, Topeka & Santa Fe, 1884 rec., 1886 reorg. as Denver & Rio Grande Rail*road*.[1]

#1: 7% 1st m. gold loan of 1870 per 1900, total $2,225,000.

Intr. 1871 Van Vloten & De Gijselaar for Wertheim & Gompertz at 70; $1,230,000 sold in A.[2] Int. in 1877 paid in 7% notes instead of cash.[3] Quotations in A. up from 19 in 1877 to par in 1878; other parts of this same loan sold in A. later; undisturbed at the 1886 reorganization; total of $6,382,000 deposited with Dutch pr. comm. 1885; exchanged 1898 for #9.

#2: 7% cons. m. ext. loan of 1879 per 1909, total $5,000,000, with coupons in $ and £.

Intr. 1880 Broekman & Honders at 95, "limited number," but brisk trade and regular quotations with a high of 118 in 1881.[4] In 1886 > 4% firsts (#5) at par + $700 in new preferred shares (#7); total of $1,165,500 deposited with Dutch pr. comm.

#3: common shares, $100 each.

Intr. 1880 Hubrecht in cert. of 5 or 10 shares; first quoted over par, down to 6 in 1884. At least $656,000 deposited with pr. comm.; in 1886 > new commons after payment of $6 per share, for which $12 in new prefs (#7) was given.[5]

#4: 5% gen. m. loan of 1883 per 1913, auth. $30,000,000, but only $2,500,000 sold; shareholders had preferential rights.

Intr. 1883 Hubrecht at 75 (for shareholders); in price lists at A. and quoted at 53 at the end of 1883, at 17 in 1884; separate pr. comm. 1885; 1886 > prefs.: $1,000 of #4 > $700 in prefs. (#7).[6]

Railroad def. 1884, two Dutch pr. comm., Dutch representative (T. H. A. Tromp) with British counterparts to Colorado.[7]

New securities created 1886:

#5: 4% cons. m. loan of 1886 per 1936, auth. $42,000,000, issued $28,650,000 initially; see also #9 and #10.

Listed in A. from 1886, and widely held in Holland; quoted at par 1899–1907, down to 77 in 1914.

#6: common shares, in new cert. issued by Hubrecht; no dividends ever; quotations low, down to 5 in 1914.

#7: 5% non-cum. pref. shares; 5% reached 1901, nil after 1912; quoted at par 1901, down to 10 in 1914.

#8: 5% improvement m. gold loan of 1888 per 1928, total $8,335,500, used for widening to standard gauge.

Intr. 1888 Hubrecht at 82; brisk trade; quoted over par until 1911.[8]

#9: 4.5% cons. m. loan, unissued portion of #5, total now issued $13,282,250 underwritten by Kuhn, Loeb & Co. and Speyer & Co., used to withdraw old sevens of 1870 (#1).

Intr. 1898 Teixeira de Mattos; quoted well over par, down to 90 in 1913.[9]

#10: 4% cons. m. loan, another portion of #5.

Intr. 1903 Hope & Co. at 90.25, "limited number" available in A.; current market price then 96–98.[10]

#11: 5% 1st and ref. m. gold loan of 1905 per 1955, auth. $150,000,000, but not more than $28,000,000 actually issued, underwritten by Blair & Co., William Salomon & Co., and Wm. A. Reed & Co.; used for buying 2nd m. bonds of Western Pacific.

Intr. 1909 Ad. Boissevain at 92.25; down to 44 in 1914.[11]

■ Rio Grande Western

Inc. 1882 as Denver & Rio Grande Western, reorg. 1889 as Rio Grande Western, 1901 part of Denver & Rio Grande.

#12: 4% 1st cons. and coll. m. loan of 1899 per 1949, underwritten by Kuhn, Loeb & Co.

Intr. 1903 Van Loon for Hope & Co. at 90.25, "limited sum" available in A.; quoted at 75 in 1912; few quotations after that year, but still in price lists in 1939.[12]

---

1. For a history of the Denver & Rio Grande see Athearn, *Rebel of the Rockies*, and Hilton, *American Narrow Gauge*, pp. 344–52.

2. *NAE* 28 February 1871; Dinger, *Overzicht* 1873, pp. 776–77; *NAE* 17 November 1871; O. M. Wilson, *Denver and Rio Grande Project*, p. 12.

3. James W. Barclay, chairman of English bondholders pr. comm., to Stock Exchange, Amsterdam, 23 July 1877, in AASE file 35, no. 17; in no. 13 announcement by Stock Exchange that English bondholders had agreed to payment of interest in 7% notes, 15 September 1877; letter from William Palmer to Wertheim & G. with same information, Colorado Springs, 3 July 1877, in no. 17; also notice in *NAE* 7 September 1877, by Wertheim & G.

4. Loman, *Supplement*, pp. 279–80; notice in *NAE* 9 March 1880; request for inclusion in the price lists by Broekman & H., 28 August 1880, in AASE file 35, no. 35.

5. Notice in *NAE* 31 December 1880; Weeveringh, *Noord-Amerikaansche spoorwegfondsen*, p. 75; request for listing of the common stock by Hubrecht, 3 October 1881, and permission, 12 November 1881, in AASE file 35, no. 43. For the separate committee of junior bondholders and shareholders see announcement by Piek in *NAE* 11 December 1885; minutes of meeting of the 5% gen. m. bondholders in same of 22 December 1885.

6. Notice by Hubrecht in *NAE* 26 October 1883; Santilhano, *Amerikaansche spoorwegen*, pp. 208–9.

7. Notices about the formation of a Dutch committee in *NAE* 1 August and 12 December 1884; minutes of meetings of committee, 2 July 1884, in AASE file 35, no. 75; Tromp's report has not been found in the archives of the Amsterdam Exchange, although a copy of it must have been deposited there. Details of the conversion in Van Oss, *American Railroads*, p. 678; also notices of Dutch committee in *NAE* 11 December 1885, and of 23 April 1886, and 28 February 1887, in AASE file 35, nos. 111 and 112.

8. *Van Oss' Effectenboek* 1903, p. 487, and later editions; the request for listing, September 1888, in AASE file 35, no. 121.

9. Request for inclusion in the price lists by Teixeira de Mattos, 22 August 1898, in AASE file 35, no. 127.

10. Request for inclusion in the price lists by Hope & Co., 29 January 1903, in AASE file 35, no. 132A.

11. *Van Oss' Effectenboek* 1909, p. 1227; Boissevain's request for listing, February 1909, in AASE file 35, no. 135B.

12. *Van Oss' Effectenboek* 1904, pp. 664 and 1020, and later editions.

▪ Denver & Rio Grande Western

See under Denver & Rio Grande.

▪ Denver Pacific

See under Union Pacific.

▪ Des Moines & Fort Dodge

See under Chicago, Rock Island & Pacific.

▪ Des Moines Valley

See under Chicago, Rock Island & Pacific.

▪ East Tennessee, Virginia & Georgia

See under Southern Railway.

▪ Eastern Railway of Minnesota

See under Great Northern.

▪ Elizabethtown & Paducah

See under Illinois Central.

■ Erie Railroad
See under New York, Lake Erie & Western.

■ Florida Railroad
See under Seaboard Air Line.

■ Florida Central & Peninsular
See under Seaboard Air Line.

■ Fort Wayne, Muncie & Cincinnati
See under New York Central.

■ Galveston, Houston & Henderson
Inc. 1853.[1]
> #1: 8% 1st m. loan of 1857, total $2,625,000, chiefly sold in Paris.
> Intr. 1857 G. A. van der Voort at 95.[2] Def. 1860, Dutch pr. comm.[3] More bonds sold in A. to redeem earlier loans, total of Dutch-held bonds estimated at $1,000,000 par value, wiped out 1871.[4]

---

1. For a history of the GH&H see Reed, *History of the Texas Railroads*, pp. 75–79 and 352–56; about the land grant see Van Zant, *Early Economic Policies*, pp. 25 and 45; J. S. Adams, *Contemporary Metropolitan America*, vol. 4, p. 143.
2. AE 10 July 1857.
3. Minutes of meeting of 18 May in *AE* 12 June 1860.
4. See detailed discussion in Chapter 11.

■ Gilman, Clinton & Springfield
See under Illinois Central.

■ Grand Trunk of Canada
Only the American subsidiaries of this Canadian company will be covered here.[1]

■ Peninsular Railway
Inc. 1865, rec. 1872, reorg. 1873, merged into Chicago & Lake Huron 1878.[2] Sold at foreclosure 1879, and 1880 merged into new Chicago & Grand Trunk Railway, controlled from the start by Grand Trunk of Canada; rec. 1890, 1900 reinc. as Grand Trunk Western, still under Grand Trunk of Canada control.
> #1: 7% 1st m. Michigan Section loan of 1869 per 1899, total $1,700,000, sold in London, Frankfurt, and A.
> Intr. 1870 Commandietkas at 70, giving an effective rate of 10%.[3] At least $1,414,000 sold in A.; in 1880 > #3.
> #2: 7% 1st m. Indiana Section loan of 1870 per 1900, total $2,000,000, but only $700,000 issued, all sold in A.

Intr. 1871 Ter Meulen & Boeken at 70.[4] In 1880 > #3. Both #1 and #2 def. 1872; Wertheim & Gompertz issued cert. in exchange for deposited bonds.[5] Peninsular sold 1879 to H. W. Smithers for Dutch bondholders for $500,000.[6]

#3: 7% 2nd m. incm. loan of Chicago & Grand Trunk of 1880 per 1930, total issued $4,000,000. In 1880 < #1; $1,000 old Michigan Section > $1,000 C&GT #3; $1,000 Indiana Section > $500 C&GT #3.[7] New securities included in A. price lists from 1881, quoted between 66 and 91; interest rarely paid. In 1882 > #4.

#4: 5% 2nd m. (fixed interest) loan of 1882 per 1922, total $6,000,000, guaranteed by Grand Trunk.

$1,000 of #3 + $500 cash > $1,500 of #4; 80% of Dutch bondholders agreed.[8] New loan in A. price lists; def. 1890, Dutch pr. comm.; at least $830,000 in Dutch hands; in 1899 > #5.

#5: 4% 2nd m. incm. loan of 1900 per 1950 of Grand Trunk Western < #4: $4,000 of #4 > $1,000 of #5.

Intr. 1901, altogether $1,500,000 in Dutch hands; 1% paid between 1902 and 1904, 4% only in 1906, and quoted around 70; redeemed at 85 below par 1910.[9]

#6: 4% 1st m. loan of Grand Trunk Western of 1900 per 1950, intr. A. in 1901; still quoted in 1939 at 66.

---

1. See for the early history of the Grand Trunk, G. R. Stevens, *History*, pp. 34–137; Currie, *Grand Trunk*, pp. 3–245.
2. Meints, *Michigan Railroads*, p. 124.
3. *NAE* 22 February and 4 March 1870.
4. Dinger, *Overzicht* 1873, pp. 751–54.
5. *NAE* 28 March 1872 contains an anonymous article on failure of the company; also *NAE*, 10 December 1872; Loman, *Supplement* (1880), pp. 254–58. The cert. were included in the Amsterdam price lists together with the original bonds at the request of several Amsterdam brokers. AASE file 75 (Port Huron), nos. 1 and 2, contains letters from stockbrokers to Stock Exchange, July and November 1872. AASE file 98 (Peninsular Railway), no. 1, contains Honders & Sons to Stock Exchange, 19 December 1878. Number of bonds deposited in Wertheim & Gompertz to Stock Exchange, January 1879, in AASE file 98, no. 2.
6. Notice in *NAE* 7 November 1879, with details of the conversion, as given by Wertheim & G.
7. AASE file 114 (Chicago Grand Trunk), no. 2, contains a circular issued by Wertheim & G., 12 November 1879; Currie, *Grand Trunk*, p. 228, notes that the GT paid 12.5% of the par value of the Port Huron & Lake Michigan/Peninsular bonds, but it is probable that he means the stock of the Port Huron, not the bonds. Wertheim & G. to Stock Exchange, 5 November 1881, in AASE file 114, no. 5. At that time 73% of all bondholders had already agreed to the conversion plan; Currie, *Grand Trunk*, p. 381, gives a slightly different story of the conversion.
8. Circular, 11 October 1881, by Wertheim & G. in AASE 114.
9. AASE 114, nos. 15, 18, contains a list of those present or represented at bondholders' meeting of 31 October 1899. Details of the conversions in *Van Oss' Effectenboek* 1903, p. 495; 1912, p. 1285.

■ Great Northern

Inc. 1857 as Minnesota & Pacific, reinc. 1862 as St. Paul & Pacific, rec. 1873, reorg. 1879 as St. Paul, Minneapolis & Manitoba, 1889 leased to Great Northern Railway, which was inc. in that year.[1]

▪ St. Paul & Pacific

#1: 7% 2nd/3rd m. First Section loan of 1862 per 1892, total $1,200,000, marketed through Robert Benson & Co. in London, but chiefly taken up in Holland.
Intr. 1864 Kerkhoven at 66.[2] At least $625,000 sold in A.

#2: 7% cons. m. loan of 1865 per 1896, total $2,800,000, mostly used to retire earlier loans, but $780,000 sold on the European market.
Intr. 1866 Kerkhoven/Voorhoeve at 70.[3] At least $760,000 sold in A. and R.

#3: 7% 2nd m. Second Section loan of 1866 per 1899, total $3,000,000.
Intr. 1866 Kerkhoven/Voorhoeve.[4] At least $907,000 sold in A. and R.

#4: 7% 1st m. loan of 1869 per 1899, total $6,000,000.
Intr. 1869 Kerkhoven/Voorhoeve at 70; $1,200,000 retained by brokers and invested in U.S. government bonds to guarantee int. for 3 years.[5] At least $3,520,000 sold in A. and R.

#5: 7% 1st m. St. Vincent Ext. loan of 1871 per 1901, total $15,000,000.
Intr. 1871 Lippmann, Rosenthal/Kerkhoven/Van Rinsum/Leembruggen/Voorhoeve at 70; 20% of issue set apart in U.S. government bonds to guarantee int. for 3 years.[6] At least $11,400,000 sold in A. and R.

In 1873 all in def. (#5 in 1874); Dutch pr. comm. 1874.[7]

#6: 10% 5-year rec. cert. of 1873, total $5,000,000; redeemed at par in 1879.[8]

In 1879 majority of all Dutch-held bonds sold to the J. J. Hill consortium: #1 at 75%; #2 at 28; #3 at 30; #4 at 35; #5 at 13.75, mostly paid in new 7% St. Paul, Minnesota & Manitoba bonds (#8).[9]

▪ Red River & Manitoba

Inc. 1877 by J. J. Hill to build a connecting line between StP&P St. Vincent Ext. and main line.

#7: common shares of $40, intr. by Dutch pr. comm. 1879 at Dfl 94.50; $200,000 sold; 1879 bought in at Dfl 95.38.[10]

▪ St. Paul, Minneapolis & Manitoba

#8: 7% 1st m. land grant sinking fund gold loan of 1879 per 1909, total $8,000,000.
Intr. 1879 Lippmann, Rosenthal, and mostly held in Holland as a result of sale of StP&P securities; regular quotations in A. over par; redeemed 1909 at par.[11]

#9: 6% 2nd m. gold loan of 1879 per 1909, total $8,000,000.
Intr. 1880 Lippmann, Rosenthal; regular quotations in A.; 1908 > 4% StPM&M bonds (#16), rest redeemed at par 1909.

#10: common shares ($100) created 1879.
Intr. 1880 Stadnitski & Van Heukelom at 80 in cert. of 1, 5, or 10 shares; dividends high, after 1890 6% guaranteed by Great Northern; partly > #20, but in 1902 still 4,536 StPM&M commons held in Holland; 1907 last $10,000 bought by GN at 175.[12]

#11: 6% 1st m. Dakota ext. loan of 1880 per 1910, total $6,000,000.
Intr. 1881 Gebr. Boissevain/Lippmann, Rosenthal at 106; in 1908 partly > 4% StPM&M loan (#16), rest redeemed at par 1909.[13]

#12: 6% cons. m. loan of 1883 per 1933, auth. $50,000,000, of which just over $13,000,000 issued; preferential rights for shareholders; underwritten by syndicate of Kuhn, Loeb & Co. See also #13 and #16.

Intr. 1883 Stadnitski/Tutein Nolthenius & De Haan at 102, shareholders at 90; regular quotations in A., at 141 in 1899, well over 120 after that year.[14]

#13: 4.5% cons. m. loan of 1887 per 1933, part of #12, total $18,000,000.

Intr. 1887 Jan Kol at 98.50; $5,100,000 available in A., but actual sales not known; in 1908 partly > 4% GN loan (#22), but most redeemed at par in 1933.[15]

#14: 4% 1st m. Montana Ext. loan of 1887 per 1937, auth. $25,000,000, issued $8,000,000.

Intr. 1887 Stadnitski & van H./Tutein Nolthenius & De H. at 96.50; brisk sales, regular quotations around par.[16]

#15: 4% 1st m. Pacific Ext. loan of 1890 per 1940, auth. £6,000,000, of which £2,000,000 issued, and mostly sold through Barings of London.

Intr. 1890 Van Loon for Hope & Co. at 82; trade sluggish, few quotations found in A., but in price lists until 1940.[17] After collapse of Barings remainder of this issue deposited with Great Northern as coll. for #22.

#16: 4% cons. m. loan of 1908, part of #12, total now $8,000,000, mostly used for redemption of #9 and #11.

Intr. 1908 Lippmann, Rosenthal for bondholders of #9 and #11; regular quotations of new fours in A.[18]

■ Montana Central

Inc. 1887, controlled by Great Northern.

#17: 6% 1st m. gold loan of 1887 per 1937, total $6,000,000, guaranteed by StPM&M.

Intr. 1889 Ad. Boissevain at 108.60; at least $1,100,000 sold in A.; regular quotations around 125.[19]

#18: 5% 1st m. gold loan of 1887 per 1937 (part of #17), total now $2,000,000, guaranteed by StPM&M.

Intr. 1891 Amsterdamsche Bank at 96.50; regular quotations around 115.[20]

■ Eastern Railway of Minnesota

Inc. 1887, controlled by Great Northern.

#19: 5% 1st m. gold loan of 1888 per 1908, total $5,000,000, marketed by Lee, Higginson & Co., guaranteed by StPM&M.

Intr. 1888 Ad. Boissevain at 96.50; quota for A. of $1,500,000 sold easily.[21]

■ Great Northern

Inc. 1890, leased StPM&M for 999 years.

#20: 6% pref. shares, $25,000,000 total, partly < #10: $100 StPM&M commons + $50 cash > $100 GN 6% prefs.

Intr. 1890 Tutein Nolthenius & De H., which organized conversion for Dutch shareholders; new GN shares in price lists and regularly quoted; 1898 > #21.

#21: common shares, 1898 < #20; high dividends of 7% or over, quoted in A. in 1906 at a high of 348.[22] Most Dutch owners declined the exchange for Northern Securities Company stock in 1901. In 1928 $308,000 still in Dutch hands.

#22: 4% coll. trust bonds of 1892 per 1902, total $15,000,000; coll. was unsold part of #15.

Intr. 1892 Tutein Nolthenius & De H. for existing shareholders at 72; most declined and sold the claim for Dfl 300 for every $1,000 in shares; bonds never included in price lists.[23]

#23: 4.25% 1st and ref. m. loan of 1914, total auth. $15,000,000, offered but never listed in A.[24]

---

1. For a history of the Great Northern see Hidy, Hidy, and Scott, *Great Northern*; also Saby, "Railroad Legislation."

2. Notice in *AE* 22 January 1864; Dinger, *Overzicht* 1873, pp. 686–87.

3. Notice in *AE* 6 March 1866.

4. Dinger, *Overzicht* 1873, p. 688; Santilhano, *Amerikaansche spoorwegen*, pp. 356–57.

5. Dinger, *Overzicht* 1873, pp. 690–91.

6. Ibid., pp. 691–93; notice in *NAE* 11 July 1871.

7. Notices in *NAE* 13 May and 17 and 24 June 1873; notice about the election of pr. comm. in AASE file 36, no. 9.

8. Notices in *NAE* 22 August, 2 and 26 September, and 11 November 1873; also Dinger, *Overzicht* 1873, pp. 695–96; Swain, *Economic Aspects*, pp. 90, 116. The redemption in *NAE* 4 March 1879; Loman, *Supplement*, pp. 206–7.

9. Details of the sale in *NAE* 12 February 1878; Pik, *Amerikaansche spoorwegwaarden*, pp. 143–44; A. Martin, *James J. Hill*, pp. 150–51; Pyle, *Life*, vol. 2, Appendix 6. Pik, p. 152, neatly computes the total price.

10. Notices in *NAE* 17 and 24 July, 7 August, and 7 September 1877; A. Martin, *James J. Hill*, pp. 161–63; Loman, *Supplement*, p. 212.

11. *NAE* 3 October 1879; press cutting (from *Algemeen Handelsblad?*) 6 October 1879, in AASE file 36, no. 24. AASE file 1068, no. 2A contains the request of Lippmann & Rosenthal for inclusion in the price lists of the 6% loan, 24 May 1880; also Weeveringh, *Noord-Amerikaansche spoorwegfondsen*, pp. 139–40.

12. Weeveringh, *Noord-Amerikaansche spoorwegfondsen*, p. 139; *Van Oss' Effectenboek* 1903, p. 533, and later editions; Hidy, Hidy, and Scott, *Great Northern*, pp. 52–53, 70. Request by Stadnitski for inclusion of the certificates in the price lists, 28 December 1880, in AASE file 1068, no. 8.

13. Weeveringh, *Noord-Amerikaansche spoorwegfondsen*, p. 140; *Van Oss' Effectenboek* 1903, p. 534, and later editions.

14. Notice by Stadnitski & Van Heukelom in *NAE* 26 October 1883; AASE file 1068, no. 20, contains an announcement by Tutein Nolthenius & De Haan, 12 April 1883.

15. Weeveringh, *Noord-Amerikaansche spoorwegfondsen*, p. 140; AASE file 1068, no. 28, contains a cutting from a German newspaper, 1886, about this loan.

16. Request for inclusion in the price lists, November 1887, of the Montana Ext. bonds in AASE file 1068, no. 30; Weeveringh, *Noord-Amerikaansche spoorwegfondsen*, p. 140.

17. Van Loon's request for listing of the sterling bonds in AASE file 1068, nos. 41, 41B and 41C; the 1914 prospectus in AASE file 1070, no. 13. Also Hidy, Hidy, and Scott, *Great Northern*, pp. 78–79, and *Van Oss' Effectenboek* 1903, p. 535.

18. *Van Oss' Effectenboek* 1912, p. 1356; press cutting 15 December 1908, with Lippmann, Rosenthal's announcement in AASE file 1070, no. 7.

19. Boissevain's request for listing of the 6% Montana Central bonds, 24 January 1889, in AASE file 1069, no. 1; also *Van Oss' Effectenboek* 1903, p. 534.

20. Request for listing in AASE file 1069, no. 2; also *Van Oss' Effectenboek* 1909, p. 1269.

21. Prospectus of Eastern of Minnesota (in Dutch) and request by Boissevain for listing, April 1888, in AASE file 217, nos. 2, 3, and 6; also *Van Oss' Effectenboek* 1909, p. 1239.

22. Hidy, Hidy, and Scott, *Great Northern*, pp. 72–73; reports about the exchange of shares in AASE file 1068, no. 39, and request for listing of the GN shares in AASE file 1070, no. 2; the files 1068 (St. Paul, Minneapolis & Manitoba) and 1070 (Great Northern) run parallel for some time. Printed circular by Algemeen Kantoor van Administratie (i.e., Tutein Nolthenius & De Haan), 2 November 1907, with an undated marginal note that $10,000 in certificates was still outstanding, in AASE file 1068, no. 42.

23. Hidy, Hidy, and Scott, *Great Northern*, p. 78; prospectus of Tutein Nolthenius in AASE file 1070, no. 4.

24. American prospectus of this loan, 20 January 1914, in AASE file 1070, no. 14.

■ Illinois Central

Inc. 1852.[1]

#1: 7% construction bonds, total $12,885,000 per 1870. Traded and listed in A. from 1856. Redeemed at 120% in currency 1864 (first 3,000), and 1868 (next 1,000); remainder redeemed 1873 in gold at par, or > 7% cons. gold bonds of NOJ&GN (not held in A.), and 1881 at 110% in gold.[2]

#2: 7% freeland bonds, total $3,000,000 per 1860. Traded and listed in A. from 1856.[3] Redeemed 1860 by #4.

#3: Common shares, creation of 1857, marketed by Robert Benson in London.

Intr. 1857 Alstorphius & Van Hemert/Gebr. Teixeira de Mattos, quoted at 137 over par; in 1863 Gebr. Boissevain/Gebr. Teixeira de M. issued cert. of $100, $500, or $1,000 for IC commons, and these were listed along with original shares.[4] Fully paid up between 1857 and 1864; dividends between 4% and 8% until 1873.[5] In 1869 the Dutch held circa 26% of total commons, English 54%.[6] In 1963 187 Dutch cert. still outstanding.

#4: 8% bonds of 1860, total $1,500,000 per 1865, used for redemption of #2; organized by Alstorphius & Van H. for Dutch owners.[7] Redeemed at par 1865.

#5: 6% Springfield div. curr. bonds per 1898, $1,600,000; < 1877 GC&S bonds (#11). Listed in A. from 1878.

#6: 4% coll. gold loan 1888 per 1953, $15,000,000, sold by Speyer & Co., New York, and Speyer Elissen, Frankfurt.

Intr. 1888 Gebr. Boissevain/Teixeira de M. at 99.50, $5,000,000 available, brisk trade, quotations around par.[8]

#7: 4% Cairo Bridge loan 1890 per 1950, $3,000,000, secured by same amount of Chicago, St. Louis & New Orleans bonds in IC treasury.

Intr. 1892 Gebr. Boissevain/Teixeira de M. at 96. Little trade in A., quoted around par.[9]

#8: 4% coll. gold loan 1893 per 1953, auth. $25,000,000, for purchase of C. P. Huntington's Louisville, New Orleans & Texas Railroad; underwritten by Speyer Bros., London, and Vermilye & Co., New York, and marketed on many European bourses.

Intr. 1893 Gebr. Boissevain/Teixeira de M. at 93, brisk trade, regular quotations around par.[10]

#9: 3.5% St. Louis Div. & Terminal gold loan 1898 per 1953, auth. $10,000,000, of which half issued; underwritten by Kuhn, Loeb & Co. and Vermilye & Co., and sold throughout Europe.

Intr. 1898 Amsterdamsche Bank/Banque de Paris et des Pays-Bas at 94.50; sales sluggish, few quotations.

#10: 3.5% Louisville Div. & Terminal gold loan of 1898 per 1853, auth. $20,000,000; underwritten by same as #9.

Intr. 1898 by same as #9 at 94.50. Sales sluggish, few quotations.[11]

▪ Gilman, Clinton & Springfield

Inc. 1867, rec. 1874, reorg. 1876 and leased to IC; 1877 bought by IC.

#11: 7% 1st m. gold loan of 1870 per 1900, $2,000,000, sold by Morton, Rose & Co. in London at 90; bonds $1,000 or £200.

Intr. 1872 Elix & Broekman at 83.50. Def. 1874; American–British–Dutch reorg. comm.; road sold to bondholders 1876. In 1877 GC&S $1,000 bonds > $800 in 6% IC curr. bonds (#5), after payment of $200 (£40) in cash.[12]

▪ Chicago, St. Louis & New Orleans

Inc. 1877 as New Orleans, St. Louis & Chicago from New Orleans, Jackson & Great Northern and Mississippi Central; bought by IC 1882 and reorg. as Chicago, St. Louis & New Orleans.

In 1857 8% bonds of NOJ&GN were sold in A. by B. H. Schroeder & Co., but no trace found after 1859.[13] In 1872 Amsterdamsche Bank was said to participate in international consortium to market bonds of both NOJ&GN and MC, but no trace of these found in Holland.[14]

#12: Common shares CStL&NO, $10,000,000 total; two-thirds held by IC, rest in Holland.

Intr. 1881 Broes & Gosman at 73, cert. issued by Broes & G. 1882, of 1 ($100), 5, or 10 commons. In 1882 > "leased lines stock certificates," with 4% guaranteed by IC, all held in Holland. In 1915 Broes & G. still held Dfl 9,989,700 of these cert.[15]

▪ Elizabethtown & Paducah

Inc. 1867, rec. 1874, reorg. 1877 as Paducah & Elizabethtown, 1881 part of Chesapeake, Ohio & Southwestern.[16]

#13: 8% 1st m. curr. loan, total $3,000,000.

Intr. 1872 F. W. Oewel at 79.50, almost all sold in A.;[17] def. 1874, cert. issued by Wertheim & G./Oewel; 1879 old E&P $1,000 > $400 P&E 7% 2nd m. income bonds (#15) + $500 in prefs. + $500 in commons. Bondholders had to pay Dfl 105.56 in cash for every bond, and got $45.50 scrip for new P&E 8% 1st m. bonds (#14) in return.[18]

▪ Paducah & Elizabethtown

#14: 8% 1st m. loan, held in Holland as a result of assessments on #13; 1881 redeemed at par.

#15: 7% 2nd m. loan < E&P 8% 1st m. (#13); 1881 > 5–6% 1st m. loan of CO&SW at par (#17).

■ Paducah & Memphis

Inc. 1872, rec. 1874, sold to bondholders 1877, reorg. 1878 as Memphis, Paducah & Northern, 1881 part of Chesapeake, Ohio & Southwestern.
#16: 7% 1st m. loan of 1872 per 1902, total $2,805,000.
Intr. 1872 Wertheim & G./Oewel at 82.50; almost $2,000,000 sold in A.[19] Def. 1874; 1877 > 7% 1st m. loan of MP&N at par;[20] new def. 1880; 1881 paid off with Dfl 2,165.20 per $1,000.[21]

■ Chesapeake, Ohio & Southwestern

Inc. 1881, leased to Newport News & Mississippi Valley 1889–91, rec. 1894, bought by Illinois Central 1897.
#17: 5% (6% from 1887) 1st m. loan per 1911 < #15, brisk trade in A., quoted around 80.[22]
#18: 6% 2nd m. loan of 1881 per 1911, total $4,000,000.
Intr. 1888 Jos. Thors.[23]
What happened to the estimated $3,500,000–4,000,000 of both issues in Dutch hands is not clear; probably bought by IC at takeover of CO&SW in 1897.[24]

1. Corliss, *Main Line*; Stover, *History of the Illinois Central*. For the early history of roads and canals in Illinois see Corliss, *Trails to Rails*.
2. *AE* 20 April 1860; also Dinger, *Overzicht* 1873, pp. 659, 662–63; *AE* 23 February, 18 and 19 October 1864; *NAE* 18 July and 1 August 1873, 23 March 1875.
3. *AE* 29 February 1856. Quotations of the construction bonds have been found in later issues of the same journal. Dinger, *Overzicht* 1873, pp. 656–66; Stover, *History of the Illinois Central*, pp. 111–12.
4. *AE* 17 February, 17 April, and 1 May 1857. Dinger, *Overzicht* 1873, pp. 659–61; a list of all assessments on p. 657.
5. A list of dividends in Stover, *History of the Illinois Central*, app. viii; Pik, *Amerikaansche spoorwegwaarden*, pp. 95–99.
6. William Osborn to George Peabody, 30 September 1869, in Cochran, *Railroad Leaders*, p. 425; Stover, *Railroads of the South*, pp. 184–85.
7. *AE* 20 April 1860; also Dinger, *Overzicht* 1873, p. 659.
8. Request for inclusion in the price lists, 1888, in AASE file 67, no. 13H; also *Van Oss' Effectenboek* 1903, p. 497.
9. Request for listing, 1892, in AASE file 67, no. 20.
10. Sale of the LNO&T in Corliss, *Main Line*, pp. 242–43. Request for listing, 1893, in AASE file 67, no. 25; printed Dutch circular in no. 33.
11. Corliss, *Main Line*, pp. 284–85. Request for listing of the St. Louis bonds, 1898, in AASE file 67, no. 44; request for the Louisville bonds in no. 46. Also *Van Oss' Effectenboek* 1903, p. 499, and later editions.
12. D. R. Adler, *British Investment*, p. 205. Notice in *NAE* 17 December 1873, where it is said that the road was to be operated by the Pennsylvania. Dinger, *Overzicht* 1873, pp. 778–79. On the legal wranglings between IC and PRR over control of GC&S, see Greenberg, *Financiers and Railroads*, pp. 116–30. *NAE* 17 March and 7 August 1874, 1 June and 7 August 1877, 22 February 1878; Pik, *Amerikaansche spoorwegwaarden*, p. 96.
13. Corliss, *Main Line*, p. 189; Stover, *Iron Road*, p. 85; Stover, *History of the Illinois Central*,

p. 151. Notices by B. H. Schroeder & Co. in *AE* 18 December 1858 and 21 June 1859; also D. R. Adler, *British Investment*, p. 67, where no mention is made of the Dutch connection.

14. Brouwer, *Amsterdamsche Bank*, p. 23.

15. Notice by Broes & Gosman in *NAE* 11 March 1881; request for listing of the CStL&NO shares, 11 May 1881, in AASE file 121, no. 1. Notice by Broes & G. in *NAE* 10 March 1882; Weeveringh, *Noord-Amerikaansche spoorwegfondsen*, p. 85; call by Broes & G. for exchange of certificates, 22 July 1882, in AASE file 121, no. 2.

16. Corliss, *Main Line*, pp. 267–70; Klein, *History*, p. 104.

17. *NAE* 27 May and 30 July 1871; Dinger, *Overzicht* 1873, pp. 765–66.

18. Notice in *NAE* 19 September 1876, 19 June 1877; also Pik, *Amerikaansche spoorweg-waarden*, pp. 134–36. Details of the reorganization in *NAE* 30 September 1879; Loman, *Supplement*, pp. 269–71.

19. Dinger, *Overzicht* 1873, pp. 766–67; notice by Oewel in *NAE* 26 April 1872.

20. Notice in *NAE* 16 May 1876.

21. Pik, *Amerikaansche spoorwegwaarden*, pp. 137–39; Loman, *Supplement*, pp. 271–73; notices in *NAE* 15 and 18 March, 10 June 1881, 10 April 1882.

22. Request for inclusion in price lists of the CO&SW fives, 7 April 1882, in AASE file 354, no. 1; Weeveringh, *Noord-Amerikaansche spoorwegfondsen*, p. 40.

23. Request for listing of the seconds by Jos. Thors, 26 October 1888, in AASE file 354, no. 5.

24. Printed circular by Wertheim & G., 8 February 1894, in AASE file 354, no. 16; letter from Dutch CO&SW committee to Stock Exchange, 22 August 1894, in no. 21.

■ Iowa Midland

See under Chicago & North Western.

■ Jacksonville, Pensacola & Mobile

See under Seaboard Air Line.

■ Kansas & Missouri Bridge

See under Chicago, Rock Island & Pacific.

■ Kansas City, Fort Scott & Memphis

See under St. Louis & San Francisco.

■ Kansas City, Mexico & Orient

Inc. 1900, rec. 1912.[1]

#1: 4% 1st m. loan of 1900 per 1950.

Intr. 1908 Westendorp & Co./Ten Have & Van Essen at 71; total available in A. $4,000,000.

#2: common shares, intr. by same at 19; $2,000,000 available.

#3: 4% non-cum. pref. shares, intr. by same at 31.50; $2,000,000 available in A.[2] No listing was ever obtained for the three securities, as Arthur Stilwell's somewhat fantastic KCM&O project could not meet the stricter standards of financial responsibility imposed by the Amsterdam Stock Exchange Association after the 1907 crisis. How much Westendorp actually managed to sell is not known, but it cannot have been much.

1. Kerr and Donovan, *Destination Topolobampo*; Bryant, *Arthur E. Stilwell*, pp. 169–223; Pletcher, *Rails, Mines, and Progress*, pp. 260–95.

2. AASE file 959-28 contains only Westendorp's application for listing; the Dutch translation of the very optimistic English KCM&O prospectus is printed in *Van Oss' Effectenboek* 1908, pp. 1708–10, without further comment.

▪ Kansas City Outer Belt & Electric Railroad

Inc. 1900 to serve as terminal company for the Kansas City, Mexico & Orient.

#1: 4% 1st m. 50-year loan.

Intr. 1906 Westendorp & Co.; no application for listing found and probably very little sold.[1]

---

1. For the KCOB&E see *Van Oss' Effectenboek* 1907, p. 1497; for the related Mexico & Orient Townsite Company, offered by Westendorp in 1908, ibid., 1909, pp. 1244, 1602; later editions of the *Effectenboek* make no mention of these securities. No file found in AASE.

▪ Kansas City, Pittsburg & Gulf

See under Kansas City Southern.

▪ Kansas City Southern

Inc. 1893 as Kansas City, Pittsburg & Gulf, rec. 1899, reorg. 1900 as Kansas City Southern.[1]

#1: 5% 1st m. gold loan of 1893 per 1923, total $23,000,000.

Intr. 1895 Tutein Nolthenius & De Haan at 60; other brokers also sold these bonds in A.; quoted at 70 in 1897; def. 1899, Dutch pr. comm. and association formed 1899 and cert. issued; total of $7,277,100 deposited in 1900.[2] In 1900 $1,000 of #1 > $750 of #6 + $500 of #8.

#2: common shares, intr. by Dutch Assoc. of those interested in the KCP&G in 1895; $1,000 cert. issued by Tutein Nolthenius & De Haan; by 1897, 885 of these had been sold; quoted at 15; in 1900, $12,660,000 deposited with pr. comm.[3] In 1900 each share > one of #7 after payment of $10.

▪ Kansas City Suburban Belt

Inc. 1886, rec. 1899.

#3: 6% 1st m. loan, sold in A. by Tutein Nolthenius & De H., but with little success; never listed in A. In 1900, $1,000 of #3 > $1,330 of #6 + $250 of #8.

#4: common shares, intr. 1895 by Tutein Nolthenius & De H.; 5,000 ($100 each) sold in A. at 25; cert. issued by Hubrecht also in price lists. Def. 1899, Dutch assoc. and pr. comm. formed 1899; $1,792,000 in shares held in Holland.[4] Probably > #7 and #8 in 1900, but details are lacking.

▪ Union Terminal

Inc. 1893, rec. 1899.

#5: 5% 1st m. loan of 1893 per 1923, total $2,000,000.

Intr. 1893 Tutein Nolthenius & De H./J. de Goeijen at 87.50; Rutgers & De Beaufort sold same bonds; total sold in A. at least $1,550,000.[5] In 1900, $1,000 of #5 > $1,000 of #6 + $250 of #8.

■ Kansas City Southern

New securities were created in 1900:[6]

#6: 3% 1st m. loan of 1900 per 1950; at least $5,000,000 of these in Dutch hands as a result of conversion; never quoted higher than 75; at 46.50–55.50 in 1939.

#7: common shares ($100), held in Holland in original shares and cert. issued by Tutein Nolthenius & De H.; quoted regularly with a high of 49 in 1910; no dividends; in 1934, 2,705 commons in cert. still held in Holland, plus unknown number of original shares; quoted at $4.50–$7.90 in 1939.

#8: 4% non-cum. pref. shares, held as originals and as cert. issued by same as #7; first dividend in 1907, quoted around 30, at 72 in 1908.[7] In 1934, 44,286 prefs. in cert. held in Holland, plus unknown number of original shares; quoted at $10.25–$17.65 in 1939.

#9: 5% 6-year coll. trust notes of 1906, intr. in A. at 95, soon at par; in 1909 > #10.

#10: 5% ref. and improvement loan of 1909 per 1950, total auth. $21,000,000; $10,000,000 issued initially.

Intr. 1909 Tutein Nolthenius & De Haan at 95 for shareholders; in 1911 Ad. Boissevain offered $5,000,000 more of the same at 101.[8] Quoted at 44.75–56 in 1939.

---

1. For a history of the KCP&G see Veenendaal, "The Kansas City Southern."

2. AASE file 454, no. 37, contains minutes of the first meeting of 25 September 1899; no. 42 gives details of the certificates which were actually issued by Ad. Boissevain. The 1900 figures in Bosch, *Nederlandsche beleggingen*, p. 673; they differ somewhat from others found in the AASE: a copybook of the Dutch KCP&G committee, not included in the regular KCP&G file and not numbered, has been found through the help of Mr. Herbert W. Günst, archivist of the Stock Exchange; it gives a total of $26,000,000 (par value) of KCP&G securities, both shares and bonds, held in Holland.

3. AASE file 454, no. 5, contains a prospectus of the Dutch Association. Figures are conflicting, but a statement in AASE file 454, no. 15, gives a sum of $3,472,500 in KCP&G bonds and shares held by the association as of 31 July 1896; the number of 885 cert. is in no. 16.

4. AASE file 370, no. 1, contains the Dutch prospectus of the Belt Railway; the figures of the pr. comm. in minutes of meeting of 5 October 1899 and list of securities present, AASE file 370A, no. 1.

5. AASE file 344, no. 1, contains a request for inclusion in the price lists by Rutgers & De Beaufort of $285,000 of these bonds, 4 January 1894; Dutch prospectus issued by Tutein Nolthenius & De Goeijen in no. 5; totals sold by Rutgers in no. 15.

6. Details of the conversion in *Van Oss' Effectenboek* 1903, pp. 499–506.

7. *Van Oss' Effectenboek* 1903, p. 505; AASE file 578, no. 1, contains a request for listing of both common and preferred shares.

8. *Van Oss' Effectenboek* 1912, pp. 1296, 1603.

■ Kansas City Suburban Belt

See under Kansas City Southern.

■ **Kansas Pacific**

See under Union Pacific.

■ **Kentucky Union**

See under Louisville & Nashville.

■ **Lake Shore & Michigan Southern**

See under New York Central.

■ **Lexington & Eastern**

See under Louisville & Nashville.

■ **Louisiana & Arkansas**

Inc. 1898, reorg. 1902.[1]

#1: 5% 1st m. gold loan of 1902 per 1927, total $7,000,000.
Intr. 1904 Van der Werff & Hubrecht/Joh. Eck & Sons/Oppenheim & Van Till at 101.50, limited sum available in A.; regular quotations around par until redemption in 1927.[2]

---

1. A history of the L&A in A. E. Brown, "The Louisiana & Arkansas Railway."
2. AASE file 739, nos. 1A and 1F, contain the Dutch prospectus of the loan and request for listing by Van der Werff & Hubrecht, 22 October 1904; *Van Oss' Effectenboek* 1905, p. 1286; also Oppenheim, *Reminiscences and Impressions*, pp. 41–46.

■ **Louisville & Jeffersonville Bridge**

See under New York Central.

■ **Louisville & Nashville**

Inc. 1854, controlled by Atlantic Coast Line from 1902.[1]

#1: 7% 1st m. loan of 1868 per 1898, total $8,000,000, marketed by Drexel, Harjes, of Paris, and Drexel & Co. of Philadelphia.
Intr. 1870 Elix & Broekman at 79.50; $1,000,000 available; only partly sold, and not listed in A.[2]
#2: 6% 1st m. St. Louis Div. loan of 1881 per 1921, total $3,500,000. Mostly < old 7% St. Louis Southeastern bonds (#9): each old $1,000 bond > $1,000 new L&N 6% bond + $300 in new 3% L&N bonds (#3) after payment of Dfl 103.25 per bond toward expenses of conversion; handled by Wertheim & Gompertz.
Also intr. 1882 as new by Wertheim at 74; quoted at par 1882, at 127 in 1899, and at 108 in 1914, shortly before redemption.[3]
#3: 3% 2nd m. St. Louis Div. of 1880 per 1980, total $3,000,000. Partly < #9.
Intr. 1881 Broekman & Honders at 55; quoted at 36 in 1884, at 72 soon after; in 1939 still quoted at 54–66.[4]

#4: 6% sinking fund gold notes per 1910, $2,000,000 total, of which $1,450,000 sold in London.

Intr. 1881 Broekman & Honders $550,000 at 103.75; quoted around 105 until redemption at par in 1910.[5]

#5: Common shares, $100 each.

Intr. 1881 Wertheim & Gompertz in cert. of 1, 5, or 10 shares; prices low, much bought.[6] After the L&N crisis of 1884, new common stock was issued, $5,000,000 at 25 below par; Wertheim sold part of this new stock in A. at 26 to shareholders. Several millions of dollars (par value) in L&N commons circulating in Holland by that time.[7] Later additions to capital in 1890 and 1912 also sold in A.[8] Quotations at par in 1901, 163 in 1912; still quoted at $28–$50 in 1939, and lively trade continuing until well after World War II.

#6: 6% 10–40 year bonds, total $1,700,000, underwritten by Kuhn, Loeb & Co. at 57.50.

Intr. 1885 Wertheim & G., $750,000 sold. In 1896 all bonds outstanding were called in.[9]

#7: 5% coll. trust 1st m. loan of 1888 per 1931, total $7,000,000, marketed by Raphael & Sons of London.

Intr. 1888 Wertheim & G. at 94.50; little sold, and quotations rare, but generally at par; listed until redemption in 1931.[10]

#8: 4.5% 1st m. Mobile & Montgomery Div. loan of 1895 per 1945, total $4,500,000. Intr. 1895 Wertheim & G. at par; eagerly taken up and much trade reported; prices soon over par; still quoted at 76 in 1939.[11]

■ St. Louis & Southeastern

Inc. 1869, 1873 in rec., sold to Nashville, Chattanooga & St. Louis 1879, NC&StL bought by L&N 1880.[12]

#9: 7% 1st m. loan of 1869 per 1894, total $3,250,000, sold by George Opdyke & Co. of New York, also in Frankfurt by F. E. Fuld and in Berlin by Robert Thode.

Intr. 1870 Lion Hertz at 74, next portion 1871 also at 74.[13] At least $1,644,000 sold in A.; def. Nov. 1873; 1876 > 6% 1st m. bonds of NC&StL at par, unpaid coupons paid with $1,000,000 of 3% 2nd m. NC&StL bonds.[14] After takeover of NC&StL by L&N this loan was continued.

■ Nashville, Chattanooga & St. Louis

Inc. 1873, taken over by L&N 1880, but corporate identity retained until 1897.

#10: 1st m. loan, 1876 < #9. Quotations in A. over par from 1880 until redemption 1894.

#11: 5% 1st cons. m. loan of 1888 per 1928, auth. $20,000,000, total issued by 1902 $7,500,000.

Intr. 1894 Wertheim & G., $500,000 sold at 99.25; little trade; quoted in A. over par until redemption.[15]

▪ Kentucky Union

Inc. 1854, 1891 rec., 1894 reinc. as Lexington & Eastern, taken over by L&N 1913.[16]
#12: 5% 1st m. gold loan 1888 per 1928, marketed in New York by J. Kennedy
Todd & Co.
Intr. 1890 Oyens & Sons, $1,600,000 at 95.50.[17] Def. 1893, > 5% Lexington &
Eastern gen. m. bonds; $1,000 KU > $500 L&E + $200 in commons; no int. paid
until 1900; $1,500,000 in cert. issued by Oyens.[18] New reorg. 1901, int. reduced to
2%, 3% 1906–11; L&N started buying at 85 in 1910; dropped from price lists in A.
1913.[19]

---

1. Klein, *History*; Herr, *Louisville & Nashville*.
2. Notice by Elix & Broekman in *NAE* 29 March 1870; Dinger, *Overzicht* 1873, pp. 764–65;
Santilhano, *Amerikaansche spoorwegen*, p. 287.
3. Weeveringh, *Noord-Amerikaansche spoorwegfondsen*, pp. 89–90; *NAE* 22 March 1881.
Printed notice by Wertheim & G./Oewel on this exchange, 18 March 1881, in AASE file 74, no.
6E. *Van Oss' Effectenboek* 1903, p. 508.
4. Weeveringh, *Noord-Amerikaansche spoorwegfondsen*, p. 90.
5. *NAE* 9 August 1881; *Van Oss' Effectenboek* 1903, p. 508; 1912, p. 1303.
6. Announcement of the opening of a department for L&N commons in AASE file 74,
no. 9A.
7. Dutch prospectus for commons and 10–40 year bonds, 8 October 1884, in AASE file 74,
no. 17B; announcement by Wertheim & G. in *NAE* 9 October 1884.
8. Wertheim & G. in *Algemeen Handelsblad* 7 February 1890, in AASE file 74, no. 33; press
cutting, 27 November 1912, in no. 47.
9. Wertheim & G. to Stock Exchange, 7 March 1885, in AASE file 74, no. 20.
10. *Van Oss' Effectenboek* 1903, p. 509.
11. Request for listing of M&M bonds, 7 October 1895, in AASE file 74, no. 35.
12. Herr, *Louisville & Nashville*, pp. 63–64.
13. Dinger, *Overzicht* 1873, pp. 756–57; Dutch prospectus of this loan in AASE file 74, no. 1.
14. Pik, *Amerikaansche spoorwegwaarden*, pp. 106–10; announcement in *NAE* 10 April 1874,
28 July, 14 August 1874; official deposition by J. C. G. Pollones, 14 February 1876, in AASE file
74, no. 7B: of the first 1869 loan 1,196 bonds had been deposited; of the 1871 loan 498, making a
total 1,694 bonds of $1,000 each. *NAE* 8 October 1875, and 28 November 1879; Loman,
Supplement, pp. 259–63.
15. *Van Oss' Effectenboek* 1903, p. 521; Dutch prospectus, 8 December 1894, in AASE file
366, nos. 1 and 4.
16. Klein, *History*, p. 401.
17. Dutch prospectus and official request by Oyens & Sons for listing, 16 June 1890, in AASE
file 296, nos. 1A and B.
18. Printed circular in Dutch, 4 April 1894, in AASE file 296, no. 10; in no. 8 is a request for
listing and details of reorganization.
19. *Van Oss' Effectenboek* 1903, p. 506; 1904, p. 679.

▪ Marietta & Pittsburg

See under Pennsylvania Railroad.

▪ Mason City & Fort Dodge

See under Chicago Great Western.

■ Michigan Central

See under New York Central.

■ Milwaukee & St. Paul

See under Chicago, Milwaukee & St. Paul.

■ Minneapolis & St. Louis

Inc. 1870, leased to Lake Superior & Mississippi 1871–74, 1888 rec., reorg. 1894.[1]

> #1: 7% 1st m. loan of 1871 per 1911, guaranteed by LS&M and in turn by the Northern Pacific, which had leased the LS&M.
> Intr. 1872 Josias Hess at 82.50; $1,200,000 available in A.[2] After collapse of NP in 1873, guarantee and leases cancelled, but M&StL did not default; Dutch holdings last quoted in 1875 at 16, and not mentioned after.
> #2: 5% cons. m. loan of 1894 per 1934, total $10,000,000.
> Intr. 1895 Gebr. Teixeira de Mattos at 98.50; brisk trade, quotations soon around par.[3]

> For the Des Moines & Fort Dodge loans of 1905, guaranteed by the M&StL, see under Chicago, Rock Island & Pacific.

-----

1. Donovan, *Mileposts.*
2. Dinger, *Overzicht* 1873, p. 787; Bosch, *Nederlandse beleggingen*, p. 161; NAE 28 May 1872.
3. AASE file 382, nos. 1 and 2, contains prospectus in Dutch of Teixeira de M. and request for listing of the 5% bonds; also *Van Oss' Effectenboek* 1903, p. 518.

■ Minneapolis, St. Paul & Sault Sainte Marie

Inc. 1888 out of Minneapolis, Sault Sainte Marie & Atlantic of 1884, controlled by Canadian Pacific.[1]

> #1: 5% 1st m. gold loan of MSSM&A of 1886 per 1926, total $8,200,000; chiefly marketed by Morton, Rose & Co. in London.
> Intr. 1887 Broekman & Honders at 92.50; $900,000 available in A.; $250,000 sold in a few weeks.[2] Reorganization of 1888 did not disturb this loan, interest then guaranteed by CP, but at 4% until redemption in 1926.
> #2: Common shares, intr. 1908 Westendorp & Co. at 123.
> Listing officially "postponed until more information will have been released to the public," according to a handwritten marginal note on Westendorp's request.[3]

-----

1. Hammer, "Genesis of a Miller's Road," pp. 23–28; Innis, *A History*, pp. 137–39.
2. AASE file 213, Broekman & H. to Stock Exchange Board, November 1887; Dutch translation of English prospectus by Morton, Rose & Co. also in this file.
3. AASE file 959-27.

■ Minnesota & Northwestern

See under Chicago Great Western.

- ## Missouri & Western
See under St. Louis & San Francisco.

- ## Missouri, Kansas & Texas
Inc. 1865 as Union Pacific Railway Southern Branch, renamed Missouri, Kansas & Texas Railway 1869, rec. 1874 but reorg., new rec. 1888, reorg. 1890, new rec. 1915, reorg. 1920 as Missouri-Kansas-Texas.[1]

#1: 6% 1st m. UP,SB loan of 1869 per 1899, total $4,250,000, chiefly marketed in Germany, France, and Holland.

Intr. 1869 Becker & Fuld/Wertheim & Gompertz at 70.50; regular quotations in A. from 1869, but only listed officially 1871.[2] Coupons of 1874 and 1875 not paid but funded, partly in new prefs., partly in new income bonds; in 1890 paid off at par.

#2: 7% 1st m. MKT loan of 1871, total $3,855,000, underwritten by Becker & F./Wertheim & G.; more of same sold by them and also in other European bourses in 1872.

Intr. 1871 Leembruggen, Guépin & Muysken/C. van Rinsum Jr. for underwriters at 80.60.[3] At least $5,942,000 held in Holland in 1875; 1874–75 coupons not paid, but funded in new 2nd m. income bonds; Dutch pr. comm.[4] Interest payments on #1 and #2 resumed 1879; in 1890 paid off at par.

#3: pref. shares, resulting from funding of unpaid coupons of #1 and #2; listed only 1874–76, replaced by #4.

#4: 6% 2nd m. income bonds of 1878, in price lists from 1880; at least $6,000,000 held in Holland, replaced 1884 by #5.

#5: 5% cons. m. loan of 1880 per 1920, auth. $45,000,000, underwritten by Mercantile Trust Co. of New York.

Intr. 1884 W. F. Piek, partly to withdraw #4; unpaid coupons of #4 also > #5: $600 in coupons of #4 > $1,000 of #5. In 1886 Van Vloten & De Gijselaar intr. more of same, but at 6%; no quotations of these found, but held in Holland.[5] In 1890 $1,000 of fives > $550 of #7 + $500 of #8 + $200 of #10; $1,000 of sixes > $640 of #7 + $550 of #8 + $275 of #10.

#6: common shares, intr. 1880 by several brokers; no dividend ever; quoted at 54 in 1881, at 9–23 in 1884.[6] In 1890 > #9 after payment of $10, for which $10 of #8 was given.

Dutch pr. comm. for shareholders and 5–6% consols formed 1887, and formal Dutch Assoc. 1888; road in rec. 1888. Second pr. comm. formed 1888 for sixes #1 and sevens #2.[7] Dutch holdings in 1890 given as: $4,416,000 of 5% consols (#5), and $3,346,000 in 6% consols; in common shares $9,020,000.[8]

New securities were issued in 1890:[9]

#7: 4% 1st m. loan of 1890 per 1990, total $40,000,000; in price lists at A. 1890 at the request of Dutch MKT Assoc.; quoted around 80, with a high of 102 in 1906, and down to 82 in 1914.

#8: 4% 2nd m. loan of 1890 per 1990, total $20,000,000; in price lists at A. 1890; quoted lower than the firsts, with a high of 91 in 1906.

#9: common shares, $100 each, auth. $47,000,000, but not all issued; in Holland held in cert. of 5 or 10 shares issed by Dutch MKT Assoc.; in 1900, 102,210 shares reported in hands of Assoc., in 1905, 155,580, declining to around 100,000 after 1910.

$10: 4% pref. shares, total $13,000,000, in cert. issued by Dutch MKT Assoc.; number in Dutch hands generally around 2,000, grown to 5,136 in 1912.[10]

#11: 5% 1st m. Dallas & Waco loan of 1890 per 1940, total $1,340,000, guaranteed by MKT from 1891.

Intr. 1892 Amsterdamsche Bank at 87; $600,000 sold in A.; quoted at 111 in 1905, down to par in 1914.[11] Last quoted in A. in 1937 at 64–70.25.

#12: Missouri, Kansas & Eastern (Boonville–St. Louis line) bonds, reported to be introduced circa 1892, but apparently never sold in A.[12]

#13: 4.5% gen. m. sinking fund loan of 1906 per 1936, total $20,000,000.

Intr. 1908 Jos. Hess at 90; limited sales; quotations later mostly around 80.[13]

#14: 4% 1st m. ref. loan of 1904 per 2004, auth. $40,000,000.

Intr. 1904 Jos. Hess for H. Oyens & Sons at 87.25; little sold and never in price lists at A.[14]

#15: 5% 1st m. Texas & Oklahoma loan of 1903 per 1943, total $2,347,000.

Intr. 1903 S. F. van Oss & Co.; never listed in A.[15]

New def. 1915, Dutch pr. comm. formed; in 1918 total Dutch holdings as deposited with pr. comm. are given as: $14,720,000 in firsts (#7); $7,071,500 in seconds (#8), with more suspected of being held; $15,711,000 in commons (#9); $882,000 in prefs. (#10); $454,000 in Dallas & Waco (#11).[16]

---

1. For a general history of the Missouri, Kansas & Texas see Masterson, *The Katy Railroad*; for its early days see Morrison, "The Union Pacific Southern Branch," pp. 173–88.

2. Announcement by Becker & Fuld and Wertheim & Gompertz in *AE* 15 June 1869; their prospectus of June 1869 in AASE file 8, no. 1; also Dinger, *Overzicht* 1873, pp. 734–36; request by Wertheim & G. for listing of the Southern Branch sixes, 6 March 1871, in no. 5.

3. *NAE* 16 May 1871 and 4 November 1873; Dinger, *Overzicht* 1873, pp. 736–38; request for inclusion in the price lists of the MKT sevens by Wertheim & G., 4 January 1872, in AASE file 8, no. 5A.

4. Request for a committee in a letter from Mesdag & Sons, brokers in Groningen, to Stock Exchange, 14 March 1874, in AASE file 8, no. 15; the 1875 figure of Dutch holdings in report from the *Nederlandsche Financier-Dagelijksche Beurscourant* of 12 February 1875 in no. 45; also *NAE* 12 February 1875.

5. Request for listing of the fives by Piek, 5 January 1884, in AASE file 8, no. 74; Van Vloten & De Gijselaar's request for the sixes, 17 November 1886, in no. 96; notice by Piek about conversion of income bonds in *NAE* 6 November 1883.

6. Request for inclusion in price lists of MKT commons, 13 January 1880, in AASE file 8, no. 68.

7. AASE file 8, nos. 105, 106, and 208 give particulars of the formation of the Nederlandsche Vereeniging in March 1888. The minutes of the board of the Vereeniging are also in the AASE in an unmarked file. Also Masterson, *The Katy Railroad*, p. 240; Klein, *Life and Legend*, pp. 412, 428–29; press cutting from *Nederlandsche Financier-Dagelijksche Beurscourant* 8 June 1888 in AASE file 8, no. 208. The figures for consols held in Holland in papers concerning the joint action by shareholders and 5% and 6% bondholders, September 1888, in AASE file 8, nos. 209, 220; the figures given were noted during a meeting on 5 September 1888. Minutes of meeting of

the comm. for the sixes and sevens on 17 October 1888 in no. 225, and other papers of this comm. in nos. 230–31.

8. Press cutting of 5 March 1890 in an unmarked box containing papers of the MKT reorganization, in AASE, no number.

9. *Proposed Plan of Reorganization*, November 1889, and Dutch translation, 27 November 1889, in AASE file 8A; also printed circular by the Nederlandsche Vereeniging, 15 February 1890, giving details of the plans.

10. Correspondence of the Nederlandsche MKT Vereeniging is in AASE file 8A; the figures for 1905 in a letter, 27 November 1905, in no. 117, while later figures have been taken from "List of Dutch and German Stockholders" in no. 128A.

11. Dutch prospectus, issued by the Nederlandsche Vereeniging of Dallas & Waco bonds in AASE file 8A, no. 7.

12. Undated draft about a Dutch syndicate of several bankers and brokers who were to take up $400,000 in Missouri, Kansas & Eastern bonds, in AASE file 8A, no. 10.

13. Request for inclusion in the price lists of the 4.5% bonds, 13 January 1908, in AASE file 8A, no. 265.

14. *Van Oss' Effectenboek* 1905, pp. 821, 1331.

15. *Van Oss' Effectenboek* 1905, p. 1287, prints the prospectus of this loan.

16. Figures taken from AASE file 8A, nos. 271 and 272, which give lists of the securities deposited with the two committees in 1915. The 1918 figures in Van Pellecom, *Kapitaalexport*, pp. 122, 128.

∎ Missouri Pacific

Inc. 1876 from earlier roads.[1]

#1: Common shares, $100 each.

Intr. 1883 Broes & Gosman at 98, in cert. of 5 or 10 shares; trade brisk but few quotations, generally over par; dividends 7% until 1888, lower thereafter, and nil from 1909 until rec. of 1915; by that time few in Dutch hands.[2]

#2: 4% 1st m. loan of 1905 per 1945, auth. $50,000,000, to be used partly for support of Western Pacific and other Gould roads.

Intr. 1905 Banque de Paris et des Pays-Bas, Amsterdam Branch, at 94.50; brisk trade and $6,376,000 sold before arrival of actual bonds; in 1908 other brokers requested inclusion of more bonds in price lists of A.[3]

#3: 5% 1st ref. conv. m. gold loan of 1909 per 1959, auth. $175,000,000; conv. into commons at par between 1912 and 1932.

Intr. 1910 Amsterdamsche Bank/Hope & Co. at 95.75; after rec. of 1915, $900,000 of these deposited with Dutch pr. comm.[4]

#4: 5% 3-year secured gold notes of 1911, total $20,000,000.

Intr. 1911 Teixeira de Mattos at 98.60; other series of same of 1912 also sold in A.; not redeemed in 1913–14 but continued at 6% until 1916.[5]

---

1. The early history of the Missouri Pacific in J. L. Kerr, *A Western Pioneer*; the corporate link with the Southwest branch in Miner, *St. Louis-San Francisco*.

2. Request for inclusion in price lists, 19 December 1883, and Dutch prospectus in AASE file 1302, no. 1; also Santilhano, *Amerikaansche spoorwegen*, p. 341.

3. Dutch prospectus of the loan and request for listing, 3 April 1905, in AASE file 1302, no. 11; request of several other brokers of 1908 in no. 19.

4. Request for inclusion in price lists, 29 January 1910, in AASE file 1302, no. 27; also *Van Oss' Effectenboek* 1912, p. 1315; Van Pellecom, *Kapitaalexport*, p. 125.

5. Request for inclusion of these notes, 27 May 1911, in AASE file 1302, nos. 29 and 30; also *Van Oss' Effectenboek* 1912, p. 1315, and later editions; request for listing of the 6% notes, 4 June 1914, in AASE file 1302, no. 32.

■ Mobile & Ohio

Inc. 1848, controlled by Southern Railway from 1901.[1]

■ Cairo & St. Louis

Inc. late 1860s, rec. 1877, reorg. 1881 as St. Louis & Cairo, 1885 leased for 45 years to Mobile & Ohio.[2]

#1: 7% 1st m. gold loan of 1871 per 1901, total $2,500,000.

Intr. 1872 Wertheim & G./Oewel at 81; late in 1872 remainder offered at 80 by same; almost all sold in A.[3] Def. 1874, rec. 1877, Dutch pr. comm. 1878.[4] 1882 > 5% 1st m. bonds of StL&C (#3).

#2: Common shares; in 1880, 15,000 out of total of 50,000 in Dutch hands.[5]

■ Saint Louis & Cairo

#3: 5% 1st m. income bonds, total $2,600,0000 per 1921, < #1 at par; all in Dutch hands.[6] Int. paid: 5% in 1882, 3% in 1883, 2% in 1884, none in other years. In 1886 > #5.

#4: Common shares, total $6,500,000; unpaid coupons of old C&StL bonds (#1) > $500 in new commons for every bond. $3,800,000 held in Holland in cert. issued by Wertheim & G.[7] No dividends ever, quotations low; in 1900 > #6.

#5: 4% 1st m. loan of 1886 per 1931, total $4,000,000. Old StL&C 5% $1,000 income bonds (#3) + $400 cash > $1,500 new 4% bonds. Of 2,600 income bonds in Dutch hands, 2,527 assented to conversion.[8] Brisk trade, quoted around par, redeemed 1931 by M&O.

■ Mobile & Ohio

#6: 4% coll. trust loan of 1900 per 1930, meant to withdraw StL&C shares (#4); $3,000 in commons > $1,000 in new M&O 4% bonds, shares to be held by M&O as collateral. In 1904 all but $8,000 of old "Dutch" shares exchanged.[9] Bonds quoted at 80–94. In 1913 > #7.

#7: 5% St. Louis Div. loan per 1927, < #6 at par in 1913. Conversion executed by Banque de Paris et des Pays-Bas, Amsterdam Branch.[10] Bonds quoted around par until redemption in 1927.

---

1. Lemly, *Gulf, Mobile & Ohio*, pp. 308–14.

2. Hilton, *American Narrow Gauge*, pp. 383–86.

3. D. R. Adler, *British Investment*, makes no mention of the Cairo & St. Louis. Notices by F. W. Oewel in *NAE* 23 February and 3 September 1872; also Dinger, *Overzicht* 1873, pp. 784–85.

4. AASE file 85, no. 1, contains the official announcement of Wertheim & G./Oewel to Stock Exchange of the formation of a protective committee, 29 May 1878; also Wertheim & G./Oewel to Stock Exchange, 3 December 1878, in no. 3.

5. Copy of shareholders list in AASE file 85, no. 6.

6. Notices in *NAE* 23 and 31 May 1882. If all certificates, 2,495 (assenting) + 1,163 (not found) + 1 (refusing) = 3,659 were to be counted as full $1,000 bonds, the gross total would be more than the $2,500,000 of the original 7% loan, so it is probable that Wertheim & G. also issued cert. for half bonds, as was often done.

7. Santilhano, *Amerikaansche spoorwegen*, pp. 437–38; *NAE* 31 May 1882.

8. Wertheim & G. to Stock Exchange, undated [1886], and 15 June 1886, in AASE file 85, nos. 10D and 11; also notice in *NAE* 4 December 1885 and 15 January 1886; *Van Oss' Effectenboek* 1903, p. 510.

9. *Van Oss' Effectenboek* 1903, p. 521; 1905, p. 823.

10. *Van Oss' Effectenboek* 1915–16, vol. 2, p. 677.

▪ Montana Central

See under Great Northern.

▪ Morris & Essex

Inc. 1835, leased to Atlantic & Great Western 1865, controlled by Delaware, Lackawanna & Western from 1865.[1]

#1: 7% 2nd m. loan of 1871 per 1901, total $1,250,000, guaranteed by DL&W, underwritten by Bank für Handel und Industrie, Darmstadt, and the Frankfurter Bankverein.

Intr. 1872 Amsterdamsche Bank, probably soon sold to Germany, never listed in A.[2]

---

1. Bogen, *Anthracite Railroads*, pp. 91–94; Casey and Douglas, *Lackawanna Story*, pp. 69–86; for the Morris Canal and Banking Company see Drago, *Canal Days in America*, pp. 111–25.

2. *NAE* 5 and 19 January 1872; Bosch, *Nederlandse beleggingen*, p. 161; Dinger, *Overzicht* 1873, pp. 781–82.

▪ Nashville, Chattanooga & St. Louis

See under Louisville & Nashville.

▪ New Orleans Terminal Railroad

Inc. 1903, controlled by Southern Railway.

#1: 4% 1st m. gold loan of 1903 per 1953, total $14,000,000, underwritten by Lee, Higginson & Co. of Boston and Higginson & Co. of London.

Intr. 1911 Ad. Boissevain at 88.25; $4,000,000 available in A.; application for listing by Boissevain 7 March 1811, but withdrawn for undisclosed reasons 11 March 1911.[1]

---

1. AASE file 959-44 holds only Boissevain's official request with a marginal note: "Withdrawn."

▪ New York Central

Inc. 1914 as New York Central Lines. Of predecessor roads the following involved the Amsterdam capital market:

■ Michigan Central

Inc. 1847, controlled by New York Central & Hudson River Railroad from 1877.[1]

#1: 8% 1st m. conv. 25-year bonds, total $2,000,000.

Traded in A. from 1857; Hope & Co. bought $94,000 of these in 1858; never listed in A.; probably soon > common shares.[2]

#2: Common shares, $100 each.

Hope & Co. acquired $107,000 in commons in 1858; in 1869 Wertheim & Gompertz intr. cert. of 1, 5, or 10 commons; Hope & Co. held $130,000 in 1880. Bought back by Vanderbilt interests, 1898; offer > 3.5% NYC&HR bonds at 115%; new offer 1922 at 345% in cash; after 1922 only one cert. of 1869 still outstanding, finally dropped from price lists 1937.[3]

■ Lake Shore & Michigan Southern

Inc. 1844, 1869 name of LS&MS adopted, controlled by Vanderbilt interests from 1869.[4]

#3: Common shares, mostly held by Vanderbilt.

Intr. 1880 Hubrecht in cert., little trade, never listed in A.[5]

■ New York Central & Hudson River

Consolidated from earlier lines 1869.[6]

#4: Common shares, chiefly sold in London from 1869, small numbers also sold in Holland.

In 1922 new cert. intr. in exchange for earlier ones; in 1966 636 cert. ($1,000 each) still outstanding in A.[7]

#5: 3.5% ref. m. loan per 1997.

Intr. 1906 Ad. Boissevain at 93.25; "limited number" sold, still listed in 1939.[8]

■ Canada Southern

Inc. 1869, bankrupt 1876, taken over by Vanderbilt interests and finished, leased to MC 1882.[9]

#6: Common shares, $100 each.

Intr. 1879 Broes & Gosman in cert. of 1, 5, or 10 shares, at 62.25; dividends disappointing, and prices down to 50; after 1886 MC and later NYC guaranteed 2.5% (later 3%) dividend. Dropped from price lists in A. in 1980.[10]

#7: 3% (5% after 1880) 1st m. loan of 1878 per 1908, guaranteed by NYC&HR, extended by MC 1908 at 6%, redeemed at par 1913.

Intr. 1879 Elix & Broekman at 80, "limited number," never listed but still held in Holland in 1913.[11]

#8: 5% 2nd m. curr. loan of 1883 per 1913, guaranteed by MC, redeemed 1913 at par, or > 5% loan of 1912; the latter never held in Holland.

Intr. 1884 Broes & Gosman, $2,000,000 at 86.50, quoted over par since 1895.[12]

▪ Fort Wayne, Muncie & Cincinnati

Inc. 1869 as Fort Wayne, Muncie & Cincinnati, 1881 reorg. as Fort Wayne, Cincinnati & Louisville, 1890 merged into Lake Erie & Western, which was bought by Vanderbilt in 1882 and operated as part of Lake Shore/NYC system; sold to New York, Chicago & St. Louis (Nickel Plate) 1922.[13]

#9: 7% 1st m. loan of Fort Wayne, Muncie & Cincinnati of 1869, total $1,800,000; sold in Berlin and Breslau.

Intr. 1870 Commandietkas at 78.5, listed only in that year. In 1874 it was reported that $1,000,000 of this loan was held in Boston, with rest in Germany and Holland. No further data found.[14]

▪ Cleveland, Cincinnati, Chicago & St. Louis

Inc. 1838 as Cleveland, Columbus & Cincinnati, 1868 reinc. as Cleveland, Columbus, Cincinnati & Indianapolis, 1889 merged into Cleveland, Cincinnati, Chicago & St. Louis (Big Four), controlled by NYC&HR from 1899.[15]

#10: Common shares of CCC&I, $100 each.

Intr. 1870 Gebr. Boissevain/Kerkhoven in cert. of 5 or 10 shares, at 74.50; dividends and prices high until 1873, then both down; popular in A. and 1880 Broes & Gosman intr. more of same. In 1889 > cert. of commons of CCC&StL by Broes & G., in price lists until 1931.[16]

#11: 4% gen. m. loan of CCC&StL, to be intr. in 1911 in A., but never listed.[17]

▪ Louisville & Jeffersonville Bridge

Inc. 1887, 1890 taken over jointly by CCC&StL (75%) and Chesapeake & Ohio (25%).[18]

#12: 4% 1st m. loan of 1895 per 1945, guaranteed by CCC&StL and C&O, total $4,500,000.

Intr. 1895 Broes & Gosman at 94; $2,700,000 sold in A. initially, remainder in 1909; quoted at 78 in 1939.[19]

1. Stevens, *Beginnings*; Harlow, *The Road*, pp. 213–32.
2. First mention of MC 8% bonds in *AE* of 27 October 1857, and 9 February 1858; purchase by Hope in *AE* of 21 February 1860.
3. Bosch, *Nederlandse Beleggingen*, p. 155; Loman, *Supplement*, p. 187; Dinger, *Overzicht* 1873, pp. 732–34. Oewel requested inclusion of MC cert. in price lists in July 1871, after a sufficient number had been sold: AASE file 110. Loman, *Supplement*, pp. 234–35; Pik, *Amerikaansche spoorwegwaarden*, pp. 110–14; *Van Oss' Effectenboek* 1903, p. 517, and later editions.
4. Harlow, *The Road*, pp. 250–91.
5. Santilhano, *Amerikaansche spoorwegen*, p. 267.
6. Harlow, *The Road*, pp. 196–97.
7. NAE of 22 February 1881; Pierce, *Railroads of New York*, pp. 6–8. AASE file 119, no. 74.
8. AASE file 119, no. 4A; *Van Oss' Effectenboek* 1909, p. 1281.
9. Tennant, *Canada Southern Country*.
10. AASE file 84, no. 1; Weeveringh, *Noord-Amerikaansche spoorwegfondsen*, p. 24.
11. Santilhano, *Amerikaansche spoorwegen*, p. 52; *Van Oss' Effectenboek* 1912, p. 1392. Pik, *Amerikaansche spoorwegwaarden*, pp. 171–74, had little praise for these bonds.

12. *NAE* 28 March 1884. AASE file 84, nos. 7, 17; *Van Oss' Effectenboek* 1903, p. 554.

13. Hampton, *Nickel Plate*; Rehor, *Nickel Plate Story*.

14. The Commandietkas offered $1,800,000 of Fort Wayne, Muncie & Indianapolis (sic) bonds in *NAE* 29 March 1870; also unsigned article in *NAE* of 11 December 1874; the Fort Wayne, Muncie & Indianapolis is not found in Edson, *Railroad Names*, and Fort Wayne, Muncie & Cincinnati must have been meant.

15. Harlow, *The Road*, pp. 344–89.

16. AASE file 33. For some reason unknown the file of the CCC&I/CCC&StL has been combined with that of the Marietta & Pittsburg, although there is no connection between the two; CCC&I documents start at no. 216. Also Weeveringh, *Noord-Amerikaansche spoorwegfondsen* 1887, pp. 70–72; Loman, *Supplement*, p. 278.

17. AASE file 33, no. 217.

18. Harlow, *The Road*, p. 395; Condit, *Railroad and the City*, p. 98.

19. AASE file 394, nos. 1, 8, and 13.

▪ New York, Lake Erie & Western

Inc. 1832 as Erie Railway, in rec. 1859, reorg. 1860, in rec. 1875, reorg. as New York, Lake Erie & Western Railroad 1878, in rec. 1893, reinc. as Erie Railroad 1896.[1]

#1: common shares, $100 each.

Intr. 1868 Wertheim & Gompertz in cert. of 1, 5, or 10 shares. Highest quotation at 59 in 1873, down to 7 in 1876. In 1878 > cert. of commons of NYLE&W, original shares of same also traded in A; quotations between 1879 and 1884 down from 50 to 12. In 1896 > Erie Railroad commons (#3).[2]

#2: 6% pref. shares of NYLE&W, created 1878.

Intr. 1881 Broes & Gosman as cert.; original prefs. already traded in A. since 1878, but only New York prices given until 1883, when quoted in A. between 74 and 82, down to 23 in 1884. In 1896 > 4% prefs. of Erie (#4).[3]

▪ Erie Railroad

#3: common shares Erie Railroad created 1896: old NYLE&W commons > new Erie commons at par, after payment of $12 per share.

Listed in A. from 1896, starting at 11, rising to 52 in 1905, down to 32 in 1914; no dividends; in 1938 quoted at $1–$2.60.

#4: 4% pref. shares Erie created 1896: old prefs. > new prefs. on payment of $8 per share.

Listed in A. from 1896 at 28, 80 in 1905, down to 32 in 1914. Some dividends paid between 1901 and 1907.[4] Quoted in 1938 at $2.40–$7.20.

#5: 4% 2nd pref. shares Erie created 1896.

Listed in A. since 1896 at 16, up to 75 in 1905, 31 in 1914; some dividends paid in 1905 and 1906; regular quotations of both prefs. and commons in A. and trade reported as lively. Last quoted in 1937 at $7–$21.

#6: 3% (4% from 1898) general lien loan of 1896 per 1996, total $140,000,000.

Intr. 1900 Jos. Thors at 83; after 1908 several coupons could not be paid, but were bought up by Morgan & Co.[5] Quoted at 10–19 below par in 1939, with Erie again in receivership.

■ Atlantic & Great Western Railway

Inc. 1860 from earlier lines, reorganized 1865, in rec. 1867, reinc. 1871, in rec. 1874, reinc. 1880 as New York, Pennsylvania & Ohio Railroad, leased to NYLE&W 1883, merged into Erie 1896.[6]

#7: 7% 1st m. loan Ohio Division, total $4,000,000 per 1876.

Intr. G. H. Levita, Antwerp 1864.[7] Regular quotations since 1864. Later reports state that at least $3,000,000 of this loan was held in Holland.[8] Continued through receivership and finally redeemed 1879 at $1,152, or > #11.[9]

#8: 7% 2nd m. loan Ohio Division of 1863 per 1888, total $4,000,000, sold chiefly in London.

Intr. 1864 by ? at 66.[10] Regular quotations from 1864.

#9: 8% debentures, total £2,800,000 per 1867.

Intr. 1864 Gebr. Boissevain/Teixeira de Mattos at 90.[11] Regular quotations since 1864.

#10: 7% cons. m. loan of 1865 per 1890, total £2,771,600.

Intr. 1865 by Gebr. Boissevain/Teixeira de M. at 80, regular quotations.[12]

■ New York, Pennsylvania & Ohio

#11: 6% prior lien NYP&O loan of 1880 per 1895, total $8,000,000, int. only to be paid when earned, but cum.; renewed 1895 at 4.5% by Erie until 1935.

Intr. 1879 ($5,500,000) Broes & Gosman at 92; partly < #7; lively trade, quoted at 110 since 1896; around par after 1914 until redemption in 1935.[13]

■ Chicago & Atlantic

Inc. 1880, controlled by NYLE&W, rec. 1884, 1890 reinc. as Chicago & Erie Railroad.

#12: 6% 1st m. loan of 1880 per 1920, total $6,500,000, guaranteed by NYLE&W.

Intr. 1881 Broes & Gosman;[14] Dutch pr. comm. had $5,961,000 of these bonds in 1890. In 1890 > 4–5% C&E 1st m. (#13).

■ Chicago & Erie

#13: 4–5% 1st m. loan C&E per 1982, total $12,000,000.

Listed in A. from 1890; between $7,000,000 and $10,000,000 was in Dutch hands.[15] Quoted 1939 at 59–61.

#14: 5% 2nd m. income bonds C&E, total $10,000,000.

Listed in A. from 1890; at least $1,500,000 held in Holland. In 1895 > Erie shares.

---

1. Mott, *Between the Ocean*; Hungerford, *Men of Erie*; Condit, *Port of New York*, vol. 1, pp. 53–64; Flint, *Railroads of the United States*, pp. 172–89.

2. Dinger, *Overzicht* 1873, pp. 707–9; Pik, *Amerikaansche spoorwegwaarden*, pp. 84–89; the conversion into NYLE&W shares in Weeveringh, *Noord-Amerikaansche spoorwegfondsen*, pp. 105–8.

3. *NAE* 15 November 1881; Weeveringh, *Noord-Amerikaansche spoorwegfondsen*, p. 107.

4. Correspondence on reorganization between J. S. Morgan and Amsterdam Stock Exchange, August–September 1895, in AASE file 23, nos. 100–107; details also in Daggett, *Railroad Reorganization*, pp. 66–72.

5. Jos. Thors to Stock Exchange, 21 March 1900, in AASE file 23, no. 126. *Van Oss' Effecten-boek* 1909, p. 1235; 1912, p. 1284. Edward Harriman personally advanced $5,500,000 to the Erie in 1908 to avoid a receivership. Klein, *Union Pacific*, vol. 2, p. 178.

6. Hungerford, *Men of Erie*, pp. 180–99; Flint, *Railroads*, pp. 191–203. For McHenry see R. D. Adler, *British Investment*, pp. 100–101.

7. Levita's announcement in *AE* 30 March 1864.

8. Pik, *Amerikaansche spoorwegwaarden*, pp. 14–15; Oewel in *NAE* 23 September 1870.

9. Details in Loman, *Supplement*, pp. 200–204; also notices in *NAE* 2 December 1879 and 27 April 1880.

10. Anonymous notice in *AE* 19 October 1864.

11. Advertisement by Gebr. Boissevain/Teixeira de M. in *AE* 29 November 1864.

12. *AE* 29 May and 15 December 1865; also Dinger, *Overzicht* 1873, pp. 668–72.

13. Van Oss, *American Railroads*, p. 414. Announcement by Broes & Gosman in *NAE* 2 December 1879; Weeveringh, *Noord-Amerikaansche spoorwegfondsen*, pp. 111–13. Request for listing by Ten Have & Van Essen, 15 June 1880, in AASE file 97, no. 5.

14. *NAE* 3 July 1881 and 6 July 1882; also Weeveringh, *Noord-Amerikaansche spoorweg-fondsen*, pp. 41–43. The request for listing of C&A sixes by Broes & G., 31 August 1881, in AASE file 127, no. 1.

15. On 5 November 1890 the Dutch committee requested listing of $7,068,000 of C&E firsts, plus $894,000 of income bonds; in a letter by several stockbrokers to Stock Exchange, 11 November 1890, it was stated that at least $1,500,000 of the income bonds had been distributed in Amsterdam: AASE file 127, nos. 32 and 33. On 16 March 1891 the Amsterdamsche Bank requested inclusion of 500 more of firsts: AASE file 127, 40. AASE file 23 (Erie), nos. 101 and 103, gives details of C&E income bonds at the 1895 Erie reorganization.

■ New York, Ontario & Western

Inc. 1866 as New York & Oswego Midland Railroad, in rec. 1873, reinc. 1879 as New York, Ontario & Western Railway, 1886 reorganized. Controlled by NYNH&H 1904–12.[1]

#1: Common shares, created 1879, each $100; no voting rights.

Intr. 1880 Wertheim & Gompertz at 33 in cert. of 10 shares; original shares also traded. No dividends until 1904, quoted at 7 in 1884.[2] English and Dutch pr. comm. formed 1884, voting rights regained by common shareholders. Amsterdamsch Trustee Kantoor opened new department for common shares 1905, but success was limited, as trade was in original shares chiefly.[3] The Dutch Administratie Kantoor in 1932 held $1,474,000 in commons, plus an unknown number of original shares in private hands; quoted at $0.37 per share in 1939. Company folded in 1957.

1. Pierce, *Railroads of New York*, pp. 33–35, 84–85; Helmer, *O. & W.*; Condit, *Port of New York*, vol. 1, pp. 72–73.

2. AASE file 116 contains a printed circular by Wertheim & Gompertz in no. 1; notice on dividends in *NAE* 11 February 1881.

3. Notice by Amsterdamsch Trustee Kantoor in AASE file 116, no. 39; *Van Oss' Effectenboek* 1909, p. 1283.

■ Norfolk & Western

Inc. 1881 from several lines, of which most important was:

■ Atlantic, Mississippi & Ohio

Inc. 1870 from Norfolk & Petersburg Railroad, Southside Railroad, and Virginia & Tennessee, under presidency of William Mahone, the "Railroad Bismarck" of his time.[1]

#1: 7% cons. m. loan of 1871, total $15,000,000, of which $9,500,000 was to be marketed in London by John Collinson. Part of this English loan also offered in A. Intr. 1871 Holjé & Boissevain/A. J. & M. Milders at 79.50.[2] Def. 1875; joint English-Dutch pr. comm. formed, dissolved 1877. In 1881 cons. m. bonds at 95% > new 6% N&W bonds (#2), or cash. Most Dutch opted for cash: Dfl 3,230.63 for every $1,000 bond plus interest since 1875. Kerkhoven executed exchange, and claimed to have paid off 2,190 old bonds, so Dutch holdings in AM&O consols had exceeded $2,000,000.[3]

■ Norfolk & Western

Inc. 1881, rec. 1895, reinc. as Norfolk & Western Railway in 1896.

#2: 6% gen. m. loan of 1881 per 1931, total $11,000,000. Partly < from #1; held in Holland, but not listed in A. 1896 > 4% 1st cons. m. of N&W (#6).

#3: 5% equipment notes, $1,000,000 sold in 1888 by Blake, Boissevain of London and Gebr. Boissevain at 85.[4] In 1896 > 4% consols (#6) at par + 48% in new prefs. (#4).[5]

#4: Pref. shares, issued in 1891, taken up by Ad. Boissevain, among others, but not listed in A. until 1896.[6] Cert. of 5 or 10 shares issued by Nederlandsche Vereeniging of Norfolk & Western Shareholders and old prefs. exchanged for new 4% non-cum. prefs. of N&W Railway after payment of $12.30 per share. Prices started at 44, 1899 at 90. In 1933 $180,900 held by the Administratie Kantoor.[7]

#5: Common shares, created 1896, total $66,000,000.

Intr. 1896 Broes & Gosman in cert. of 5 or 10 shares; first dividend 1901; quotations started at 4 in 1896, 59 in 1901, around par from 1909; at $164 per share in 1939.[8]

#6: 4% 1st cons. m. loan of 1896 per 1996, total $62,500,000. Partly < #2: old $1,000 bond > $625 in 4% bonds + $750 in new prefs. (#4). Widely held in Holland and listed in A. since 1896, starting at 75 and rising to slightly over par by 1905. Quoted at 83–95 in 1939.[9]

#7: 4% 1st div. and gen. m. loan of 1904 per 1944.

Intr. 1905 Gebr. Boissevain at 97; last quoted 1933 at 54–98.

#8: 4% conv. loan of 1906, total $34,000,000, underwritten at 97.50 by consortium with Gebr. Boissevain, Ad. Boissevain, and Rotterdamsche Bank among the members. Conv. into common stock before 1917. Little sold, consortium dissolved 1908, but bonds listed in A. from 1908, soon over par. Second portion of same loan, now $13,000,000, issued 1912 and sold by same. Soon rose to 110; most conv. into common stock; last quoted at 95 in 1933.[10]

---

1. Lambie, *From Mine to Market*; Blake, *William Mahone of Virginia*, gives an overly flattering portrait of this controversial figure.

2. Notice in *NAE* 3 October 1871; Dinger, *Overzicht* 1873, pp. 779–81; Collinson's English prospectus in AASE file 14, no. 1.

3. *NAE* 20 April and 3 June 1881. Accounts of the Dutch committee, dated 14 August 1883, in AASE file 14, no number.

4. Frederick Kimball to A. J. Dull, 6 April 1888, quoted in Cochran, *Railroad Leaders*, p. 375.

5. *Van Oss' Effectenboek* 1903, p. 529, and later editions.

6. Lambie, *From Mine to Market*, pp. 129–30.

7. *Van Oss' Effectenboek* 1903, p. 528, and later editions.

8. Lambie, *From Mine to Market*, p. 187. No file on the Norfolk & Western has been found in the archives of the Amsterdam Stock Exchange.

9. *Van Oss' Effectenboek* 1903, p. 529, and later editions.

10. *Van Oss' Effectenboek* 1909, p. 1287.

▪ North Missouri

See under Wabash Railroad.

▪ Northern Pacific

Inc. 1870, rec. 1873, reorg. 1874, rec. 1893, reorg. 1896.[1]

#1: 4% prior lien gold loan of 1896 per 1996, auth. $130,000,000, sold in London, Frankfurt, and New York in several portions.

Intr. 1896 Teixeira de Mattos at 85; lively trade, regular quotations in A.; dropped from price lists 1965; $20,000,000 more of same offered in 1901 by Ten Have & Van Essen, dropped from price lists 1971.[2]

#2: Common shares.

Intr. 1900 Wertheim & Gompertz in cert.; most bought up by Northern Securities Company 1902, but cert. still listed in A. in 1939.[3]

---

1. For the history of the NP see Smalley, *Northern Pacific*, and Rentz, *Northern Pacific*.

2. AASE file 425; request by Teixeira de M., 8 June 1896, in no. 1; Dutch prospectus in no. 2; the 1901 prospectus of Ten Have & Van Essen and application for listing in no. 14; see also Rentz, *Northern Pacific*, p. 200.

3. AASE file 425, no. 12, gives the Dutch prospectus; *Van Oss' Effectenboek* 1903, p. 529.

▪ Northwestern Pacific

See under Southern Pacific.

▪ Oklahoma Central

See under Atchison, Topeka & Santa Fe.

▪ Oregon & California

See under Southern Pacific.

▪ Oregon Short Line

See under Union Pacific.

▪ Oregon Short Line & Utah Northern

See under Union Pacific.

■ Paducah & Elizabethtown

See under Illinois Central.

■ Paducah & Memphis

See under Illinois Central.

■ Pennsylvania Railroad

Inc. 1846 as Pennsylvania Railroad Company.[1]
#1: Common shares, $50 each.
Intr. 1880 Wertheim & Gompertz in cert. of 2, 10, or 20 shares; listed in A. until
replaced by new cert. at merger of PRR with NYC into Penn Central; dropped 1979.
In 1881, 29.3% of common stock of PRR held in England, 47.4% in 1895; in same
years 0.5% in other countries (including Holland), 1.5% in 1895.[2]
#2: 3.5% conv. 10-year bonds of 1905 per 1915, total $100,000,000; $150 in bonds >
$100 in commons.
Intr. 1905 Ad. Boissevain at 101; unconverted portion redeemed at par 1915.[3]

■ Pittsburgh, Fort Wayne & Chicago

Inc. 1856 as PFW&C Rail*road*, 1862 reinc. as PFW&C Rail*way*, leased to PRR 1869.[4]
#3: Common shares, $100 each, created 1869, total just over $10,000,000 and
guaranteed by PRR at 7%.
Intr. 1869 Wertheim & Gompertz at 107, in cert. of 1, 5, or 10 shares; prices dropped
to 80, and Pik deemed them unsafe, as the guarantee was transferred to the Pennsylvania Company, a holding company for all lines leased or operated by PRR west of
Pittsburgh. Dividends were paid, however, and quotations rose to 175 in 1900; 140
in 1939; last 27 cert. canceled 1956.[5]

■ Traverse City

Inc. 1871, merged into Grand Rapids & Indiana 1883; GR&I leased to PFW&C 1869,
same year transferred to PRR.
#4: 7% 1st m. loan.
Intr. 1871 F. W. Oewel, listed until 1873; probably same as 7% 1st m. loan of GR&I
per 1889, mostly sold in Germany, but mentioned in A. in 1873.[6]

■ Marietta & Pittsburg

Inc. 1870, rec. 1873, reinc. 1874 as Marietta, Pittsburg & Cleveland, 1880 reinc. as
Cleveland & Marietta, 1895 bought by PRR.
#5: 7% 1st m. loan per 1895 of $1,500,000 marketed by Winslow, Lanier & Comp.
Intr. 1872 Berlin & Hymans; def. 1873, loan not disturbed at reorganization of 1874,
but later in 1874 > 7% cons. m.; 901 Dutch and 457 English bondholders assented;
new bonds listed at 40, dropped to 7 in 1875; Dutch holdings probably sold to
England by 1881 and dropped from lists in A.[7]

■ Cleveland, Mount Vernon & Delaware

Inc. 1869, controlled by PRR through FWP&C, in rec., reorg. 1881 as Cleveland, Akron & Columbus Rail*road*, 1886 reorg. as CA&C Rail*way*.[8]

#6: 7% cons. m. loan of 1870 per 1900, total $1,500,000.

Intr. 1870 Oewel/Wertheim & Gompertz at 80; $200,000 redeemed in 1872 from part of #7.

#7: 7% Columbus Ext. loan of 1872 per 1902, total $1,000,000.

Intr. 1872 by Oewel/Wertheim & G. at 90.[9] Int. on coupons 1875 through 1877 of both #6 and #7 paid half in gold, half in cert. of deferred debt, 1877 stopped altogether.[10] After new default 1886 > common shares of new CA&C Railway: one old $1,000 bond > 10 common shares (#8).

■ Cleveland, Akron & Columbus

#8: Common shares created 1886, total $4,000,000; all but 7 shares held in cert. of Wertheim & G.[11] Quotations started at around 50, dropped to 15 in 1887; cert. exchanged 1895 for new cert. issued by Dutch Association of Shareholders of American Railroads, quoted at 40–65; Dutch-held shares gradually bought by PRR; remainder bought by PRR 1911: a first offer of 85 below par was refused; PRR then raised its bid to 92 and Dutch owners sold out.[12]

#9: 6% 1st m. loan of 1886, total $600,000, all in Dutch hands.

Intr. 1886 Wertheim & G. for existing shareholders; 1887 > 5% loan (#10).

#10: 5% 1st m. loan of 1887 per 1927, total $1,800,000, partly < #9, most in Dutch hands.

Intr. 1887 Wertheim & G. at 90; quoted well over par, redeemed by PRR 1927.[13]

#11: 6% equipment trust notes of 1890.

Intr. 1890 Wertheim & G.; $600,000 sold in A., not listed.[14]

#12: 4% cons. m. loan of 1899 per 1939.

Intr. 1899 Cleveland, Akron & Columbus Vereeniging in cert. of $400 at 90; last quoted in 1937 at 70.[15]

■ Buffalo, New York & Philadelphia

Inc. 1883 from several smaller lines, one of them the Buffalo, Pittsburg & Western Railroad, 1885 in rec., reinc. 1887 as Western New York & Pennsylvania Rail*road*, 1895 reinc. as WNY&P Rail*way*.[16]

#13: Common shares of BP&W, $100 each.

Intr. 1881 Hubrecht, in cert. at 47.5; in 1883 > cert. of shares of BNY&P, no dividends; quoted at 5.5 in 1884.[17] In 1886–87 > new WNY&P RR commons after payment of $6 per share. In 1895 $200 in commons > $150 in new WNY&P Rly commons + $25 in 5% income bonds (#18) after payment of $7 per $200.

#14: 6% pref. shares BNY&P, $100 each.

Intr. 1883 Hubrecht, in cert. (also one-half share at $50) at 60; quoted at 9 in 1884. In 1886–87 > new WNY&P RR commons after payment of $4 per share.

#15: 6% cons. m. loan of 1881 per 1921, total $11,000,000, underwritten by J. &

W. Seligman of New York, and marketed by Seligman Bros. in London, Seligman &
Stettheimer of Frankfurt, and the Banque de Bruxelles in Belgium.

Intr. 1882 Alsberg, Goldberg at 104.50.[18] In 1886–87 > 3–4% 2nd m. of WNY&P
(#16). No separate Dutch pr. comm., but close collaboration with Germans. Dutch
shareholders got 4 representatives on the WNY&P board of 13, same as 2nd m.
holders.[19]

#16: 3–4% 2nd m. loan of 1886–87, total $20,000,000; listed in A. from 1887; def.
1893; Dutch pr. comm. formed. In 1895 > 2–4% gen. m. loan (#19) at 50% + 25%
in 5% 25-year income bonds (#20) + 25% in other (worthless) securities.

#17: 5% 1st m. loan of 1887 per 1937, total $10,000,000.

Intr. 1887 H. Oyens at 96.5; not disturbed at 1895 reorganization and redeemed at
par in 1937 by PRR.[20]

#18: Common shares WNY&P Rly, in 5-year voting-trust cert., listed in A. from
1895; PRR bought commons in 1905 at $9 per $50 share. Not all Dutch sold out,
and in 1925 PRR bought most of remainder at 30 below par; a few cert. continued to
be held until Hubrecht canceled them and > original shares in 1928.[21]

#19: 2–4% gen. m. loan of $10,000,000, listed in A. from 1895, at 30 in 1896, rising
to 82 in 1914; still listed in 1939, at 76.

#20: 5% 25-year income bonds, listed in A. from 1895, no int. ever paid; quoted at
10 in 1896, at 20 in 1904, just before being bought up by PRR in 1905 at 30 and
dropped from the lists in A.

■ Pittsburgh, Cincinnati, Chicago & St. Louis

Inc. 1890 by PRR.[22]

#21: 4.5% cons. m. loan Series A of 1890 per 1940, guaranteed by PRR, underwrit-
ten by Kuhn, Loeb of New York, and Speyer Bros. of London.

Intr. 1892 Teixeira de Mattos at 100.75; quoted around par until redemption.[23]

1. Burgess and Kennedy, *Centennial History*; Ward, *J. Edgar Thomson*.
2. AASE file 112, no. 1, contains a notice by Wertheim & Gompertz about opening of
department for PRR commons. Lists of stock ownership in Burgess and Kennedy, *Centennial
History*, Appendix E.
3. AASE file 112, no. 7, contains a request for listing of 3.5% bonds by Ad. Boissevain & Co., 1
December 1905. There was uneasiness among Dutch shareholders about this addition to the
capital stock and they feared lower dividends. James McCrea, PRR president, soothed their
feelings in a letter to the chairman of the Amsterdam Stock Exchange, 13 December 1909, in
AASE file 112, no. 8.
4. Burgess and Kennedy, *Centennial History*, pp. 176–219; Dinger, *Overzicht* 1873, pp. 728–
29; Weeveringh, *Noord-Amerikaansche spoorwegfondsen*, pp. 122–25.
5. Request for listing by Wertheim & G., 24 February 1869, in AASE file 994, no. 1; the
announcement in *NAE* of 15 January 1869. Pik, *Amerikaansche spoorwegwaarden*, pp. 152–55;
Bonbright and Gardiner, *Holding Company*, p. 71.
6. Notice by Oewel in *NAE* 30 July 1872. Dinger, *Overzicht* 1873, p. 790; Burgess and
Kennedy, *Centennial History*, pp. 200–202.
7. AASE file 33 also holds papers of the Cleveland, Cincinnati, Chicago & St. Louis. Berlin & Hymans's request for listing of the M&P sevens, 19 July 1872, in no. 8A. Dinger, *Overzicht*
1873, p. 783; Bosch, *Nederlandse Beleggingen*, p. 161; *NAE* 3 February 1874; Swain, *Economic*

Aspects, p. 85. On the number of bonds exchanged by Berlin & H. in 1874 see letters to Stock Exchange, 23 April, 27 August, 18 September, 7 and 21 December 1874, in AASE file 33, nos. 13, 14, 15A, 16A; in no. 204 see Hymans & Sons to Stock Exchange, 17 May 1881. Pik, 1879, and Weeveringh, 1887, do not mention the M&P's loan anymore.

8. Burgess and Kennedy, *Centennial History*, pp. 185–86; 229–30.

9. Oewel in *NAE* 5 May 1871. Dinger, *Overzicht* 1873, pp. 773–74.

10. *NAE* 7 July 1874; notice on deferred interest payment in *NAE* 5 February 1875; also Pik, *Amerikaansche spoorwegwaarden*, pp. 66–69.

11. Weeveringh, *Noord-Amerikaansche spoorwegfondsen*, pp. 68–70; Swain, *Economic Aspects*, p. 102; *NAE* 18 April 1882. Printed circular of Wertheim & G. and F. W. Oewel, February 1882, in AASE file 115, no. 3B; printed circular of Wertheim & G., 28 November 1885, with details of financial arrangements, in no. 3D. A. C. Wertheim to Stock Exchange, 1 April 1886, in no. 5A.

12. Circular of Ad. Boissevain & Co., 17 March 1911, and results of meeting of 20 March, in AASE file 115, no. 30; press cutting, 25 April 1911, in no. 31. Also *Van Oss' Effectenboek* 1912, p. 1267.

13. Dutch prospectus of the 5% loan in AASE file 115, no. 8F.

14. Dutch prospectus of the 6% notes in AASE file 115, nos. 9A–D.

15. *Van Oss' Effectenboek* 1903, p. 483.

16. Burgess and Kennedy, *Centennial History*, pp. 483–85.

17. Notice in *NAE* 3 January 1881; also Santilhano, *Amerikaansche spoorwegen*, p. 34; Weeveringh, *Noord-Amerikaansche spoorwegfondsen*, pp. 21–24.

18. Notice in *NAE* 18 April 1882; Weeveringh, *Noord-Amerikaansche spoorwegfondsen*, p. 23. The Dutch prospectus of the 6% loan in AASE file 139, no. 3.

19. The default in *NAE* 6 January and 10 April 1885; printed circular on terms of conversion by Hubrecht, 17 March 1886, in AASE file 139, no. 15; circular of 16 June 1886 in no. 16.

20. Correspondence between several brokers and Stock Exchange on the reorganization, May 1893, and report of meeting of 10 May 1893, in AASE file 139, nos. 31–33. Details of conversion in printed circulars by Hubrecht, September 1893–94, in nos. 39–44.

21. Burgess and Kennedy, *Centennial History*, p. 485; *Van Oss' Effectenboek* 1903, p. 549, and later editions. Notice in *Algemeen Handelsblad*, 5 September 1928, in AASE file 139, no. 70.

22. Burgess and Kennedy, *Centennial History*, p. 192.

23. Dutch prospectus and request for listing, 3 July 1892, in AASE file 988, nos. 1A and B; *Van Oss' Effectenboek* 1903, p. 536, and later editions.

■ Pere Marquette

Inc. 1900 from several smaller roads, 1905–7 controlled by Cincinnati, Hamilton & Dayton; rec. 1912.

#1: 4% ref. m. loan of 1905 per 1955, total $60,000,000, guaranteed by CH&D.
Intr. 1905 Van der Werff & Hubrecht/Van Oss & Co. at 92.40; in A. $6,000,000 available.[1] Def. 1912, no Dutch pr. comm.; in 1917 > common shares, one $1,000 bond > $1,104 in commons; nonparticipating owners got $117.01 in cash for every bond; new shares never listed in A.

1. *Van Oss' Effectenboek* 1909, p. 1298.

■ Philadelphia & Reading

Inc. 1833 as Philadelphia & Reading Railroad, several times in rec. and reorg.; seen as highly speculative by European investors.[1]

#1: Common shares, $100 each.

Intr. 1901 Algemeene Trust Maatschappij/Vermeer at 56, in cert. of 10 shares; first dividend paid in 1904; shares quoted at 80 in 1904, 173 in 1910, when dividend hit 6%.

#2: 4% 1st pref. shares.

Intr. 1901 by same at 74; rising when 4% dividend was reached in 1903.

#3: 4% 2nd pref. shares.

Intr. 1901 by same at 46,50; 4% paid since 1904. All cert. of ##1, 2, and 3 canceled in 1912 and dropped from price lists in A.; most bought up by PRR.[2]

---

1. For a history of the Reading see Hare, *History of the Reading*; Bogen, *Anthracite Railroads*, pp. 19–75. For its financial performance, see Singer, *Die Amerikanische Bahnen*, pp. 179–81; and Van Oss, *American Railroads*, pp. 307–44. For the Reading Company, formed in 1897 as a holding company for the railroad and its mining interests, see Bonbright and Means, *Holding Company*, pp. 247–49.

2. Application by Vermeer & Co. for listing of P&R stock in AASE file 598, no. 1. Also *Van Oss' Effectenboek* 1903, p. 538.

■ Pittsburgh, Cincinnati, Chicago & St. Louis

See under Pennsylvania Railroad.

■ Pittsburgh, Fort Wayne & Chicago

See under Pennsylvania Railroad.

■ Port Royal

Inc. 1871, reinc. 1878 as Port Royal & Augusta, 1897 part of Atlantic Coast Line.[1]

#1: 7% conv. loan of 1869 per 1889, $2,500,000, coupons payable in New York, London, Frankfurt, and Amsterdam.

Intr. 1870 Commandietkas at 72.60.[2] Quotations low, despite an optimistic letter where exchange of St. Paul & Pacific bonds for Port Royal bonds was recommended.[3] Def. Nov. 1873; last quotations in A. in 1875 at 12 under par.[4] 1876 $1,000 PR > $600 new 6% PR&A 2nd m. bonds + $300 in commons. Little trade in these new sixes in A.; last quoted 1884 at 17; commons never listed.[5]

---

1. Prince, *Atlantic Coast Line Railroad*, pp. 85–86; Stover, *Railroads of the South*, pp. 267–70.

2. Dinger, *Overzicht* 1873, p. 772; D. R. Adler, *British Investment*, makes no mention of this loan. Notice in *NAE* 5 April 1870.

3. Notice by "Iemand die goed ingelicht is" (well-informed person) in *NAE* 25 October 1872.

4. *NAE* 3 March 1874, 3 August 1875.

5. Pik, *Amerikaansche spoorwegwaarden*, pp. 160–63; also Loman, *Supplement*, pp. 274–75.

■ Red River & Manitoba

See under Great Northern.

■ Rio Grande Western

See under Denver & Rio Grande.

■ Rock Island, Arkansas & Louisiana

See under Chicago, Rock Island & Pacific.

■ Rockford, Rock Island & St. Louis

See under Chicago, Burlington & Quincy.

■ St. Louis & Cairo

See under Mobile & Ohio.

■ St. Louis & San Francisco

Inc. 1876 out of South Pacific, Atlantic & Pacific and others, controlled by Atchison, Topeka & Santa Fe 1890–96, rec. 1893, reorg. 1896, controlled by Chicago, Rock Island & Pacific 1908–9.[1]

■ South Pacific

Inc. 1868, merged with Atlantic & Pacific 1870.
#1: 6% 1st m. loan of 1868 per 1888, total $7,250,000.
Intr. 1869 Joseph Cahen at 66.5, total available in A. $1,000,000.[2] Regular quotations in A., high of 103 in 1880. Loan not disturbed at 1876 merger; redeemed at par 1888.

■ Atlantic & Pacific

Inc. 1866, merged with South Pacific but both companies continued under old names because of legal problems.[3] Rec. 1875, and Missouri lines reorg. as St. Louis & San Francisco, while lines in Indian Territory continued under old name; new rec. 1893, Western Div. sold to Atchison, Topeka & Santa Fe, remainder to StL&SF.[4]
#2: 6% 1st m. Western Division (Albuquerque–Needles, Calif.) loan of 1880 per 1910, int. guaranteed by ATSF and StL&SF jointly, total $16,000,000.
Intr. 1881 Alsberg, Goldberg at 102.[5] In 1886 int. reduced to 4%.[6] At ATSF receivership in 1893 A&P def.; Dutch pr. comm. and $4,364,000 exchanged for cert. in A; more than $5,000,000 in Germany.[7] In 1897 > 4% ATSF bonds and prefs.: $1,000 of #2 > $446.95 in 4% gen. m. ATSF bonds + $489.51 in ATSF pref. shares.[8]
#3: 6% 1st m. Central Div. (Seneca–Sapulpa, Indian Territory) loan, total held in Holland $2,794,000; sold to StL&SF in 1898 for $300,000 in gold + $1,500,000 in new StL&SF 5% bonds.[9]

■ St. Louis & San Francisco

#4: 6% 1st m. Missouri & Western gold loan of 1879 per 1919, total $1,100,000, underwritten at 94 by Seligman & Stetheimer of Frankfurt and Alsberg, Goldberg of A.; sinking fund provided.

Intr. 1879 by L. Calisch & Son for Alsberg, Goldberg; not disturbed by consecutive reorganizations of StL&SF; in 1904 $135,000 still outstanding; last quoted in A. in 1909 at 120.[10] After 1901 > #16: $1,000 of #4 > $1,282.05 of #16 or $1,250 cash.

#5: 6% 1st m. St. Louis, Wichita & Western loan of 1879 per 1919, total $2,000,000, underwritten by same as #4; sinking fund; not disturbed by reorganizations.

Intr. 1879 Alsberg, Goldberg at 98.50; limited sum available in A.; trade dull; last quoted in A. in 1910 at 103.[11] After 1901 > #15: $1,000 of #5 > $1,179.49 of #16 or $1,150 cash.

#6: 7% 1st pref. shares, total $4,500,000.

Intr. 1880 Hubrecht at 80; first dividend 1881, quotations in A. over par, brisk trade; also cert. of 5 and 10 prefs. issued by Hubrecht. In 1890 > at par in StL&SF 4% consols per 1990, guaranteed by ATSF (#11); $11,000,000 of these held in Holland.[12]

#7: second pref. shares; 1890 > ATSF commons: 8 StL&SF 2nd prefs. > 11 ATSF commons.

#8: common shares; both #7 and #8 intr. Alsberg, Goldberg at the request of Seligman & Co. of New York; cert. issued by Hubrecht, commons at 40, 2nd prefs. at 65; no dividends.[13] In 1890 > ATSF commons: 4 StL&SF commons > 3 ATSF commons.

#9: 6% gen. m. St. Louis Ext. loan of 1881 per 1931.

Intr. 1882 Alsberg, Goldberg at 97.50; $4,000,000 available in A.; parts also sold at 5% int.; regular trade and quotations at 110 in A., mostly of sixes; not disturbed by 1896 and 1915 reorganizations; redeemed 1931.[14] After 1901 partly > #16: $1,000 of #9 > $1,369.23 of #16 or $1,335 cash.

#10: 5% 1st m. St. Louis, Salem & Arkansas gold loan per 1931, total $1,000,000.

Intr. Alsberg, Goldberg at 99, but little trade and never listed in A.[15]

#11: 4% cons. m. of 1890, < #6. StL&SF in rec. 1893, Dutch pr. comm. and formal association of bondholders formed.[16] All earlier StL&SF loans undisturbed at 1896 reorganization, but 4% consols > new #12 and #14. Total of 2,968 of Dutch-held cert. of old 4% consols was converted in 1897.

#12: common shares of new StL&SF Railroad. In 1908 > for Rock Island securities, but after def. of this road again regularly quoted in A.; no dividend ever.

#13: 4% non-cum. 1st pref. shares of same; 4% paid from 1898–1912.

#14: 4% non-cum. 2nd pref. shares of same; 4% paid 1902–6; quoted at 80 in A. 1902, at 3 in 1914.

#15: 4% cons. m. loan of 1896 per 1996, auth. $50,000,000; widely held in Holland and generally quoted between 90 and par; mostly > into #16 after 1909.

##12–15 initially marketed together in blocks of $3,020 each; 2,901 blocks sold in A.; Dutch-held shares made out in name of Dutch Association of StL&SF shareholders, which issued cert. in return; all four securities listed in A.[17] After 1901 partly > #16: $1,000 of #15 > $1,025.64 of #15 or $1,000 cash.

#16: 4% ref. loan of 1901, auth. $30,000,000; mostly used to redeem earlier loans; underwritten by Seligman & Co. of New York, Seligman Bros. of London, Seligman & Stettheimer of Frankfurt, Seligman Frères et Cie. of Paris, Berliner Handels-Gesellschaft, Schweizerische Bankverein, and Alsberg, Goldberg of A.

Intr. 1901 Alsberg, Goldberg at 96.75.[18] Quoted around 90 in A., at 68 in 1914; Dutch pr. comm. formed in 1914.

#17: 5% general lien loan of 1907 per 1927, underwritten by international consortium headed by Speyer Bros. of New York, with Teixeira de Mattos as Dutch member; $10,000,000 sold in France, $6,000,000 in Germany, and $17,000,000 available in A. but not all sold.

Intr. 1909 Teixeira de M. at 89; sales brisk, at least $1,750,000 sold in A.[19] Def. 1913; Dutch pr. comm. formed.

#18: 5% 3-year notes of 1910, total $8,000,000.

Intr. 1910 Teixeira de M. at 97.75, "limited sum."[20] Redeemed at par in 1912 and replaced by #19.

#19: 6% 2-year notes of 1912.

Intr. 1912 Alsberg, Goldberg at 99, "limited sum."[21] More than $400,000 sold in A.[22]

■ Kansas City, Fort Scott & Memphis

Inc. 1888 out of earlier roads, 1901 reorg. and taken over by StL&SF.

#20: 4% pref. shares of KCFS&M, guaranteed by parent StL&SF.

Intr. 1901 Dutch StL&SF Shareholders Assoc. in cert. issued by Amsterdamsch Administratie Kantoor voor Buitenlandsche Waarden; 4% paid regularly, quotations in A. around 80.[23] In 1916 > new StL&SF securities.

#21: 4% ref. gold loan of 1901 per 1936, total $60,000,000; guaranteed by StL&SF.

Intr. 1901 Dutch StL&SF Shareholders Assoc. at 90; loan not disturbed by 1916 reorganization of parent StL&SF, continued after 1936, last quoted in A. in 1939 at 20 below par.

---

1. For the early corporate history of the St. Louis & San Francisco see Miner, *St. Louis-San Francisco.*

2. Notice in *AE* 26 August 1869; Dinger, *Overzicht* 1873, p. 747.

3. Miner, *St. Louis-San Francisco*, p. 72; notice of the merger in *NAE* 26 May 1871.

4. Miner, *St. Louis-San Francisco*, pp. 85–94; notice of the merger and the incorporation of the new StL&SF company in *NAE* 19 September 1876. For a history of the Atlantic & Pacific see Myrick, *Railroads of Nevada*, vol. 2, pp. 762–76.

5. Weeveringh, *Noord-Amerikaansche spoorwegfondsen*, pp. 19–20; notice in *NAE* 8 April 1881; AASE file 120, no. 5, contains the request for inclusion in the price lists, 28 April 1881; no. 7 is the prospectus in Dutch.

6. Printed circulars by Alsberg, G. about the conversion in AASE file 120, nos. 9 and 11; request for inclusion of the fours, 5 February 1887, in no. 12A.

7. Minutes of meeting of 22 January 1894 in AASE file 120, no. 18; figures of deposited bonds in Veltman (chairman of pr. comm.) to Stock Exchange, 17 November 1894, in no. 27; printed circular of comm. with call for depositing of bonds, May 1894, in no. 22.

8. Printed circular, 5 January 1897, of Dutch comm. and letter from Veltman to Stock Exchange, 1 March 1897, giving details, in AASE file 120, nos. 30, 32.

9. Letter from Veltman to Stock Exchange, 17 March 1898, giving details, in AASE file 120, no. 34. The actual sale of the bonds had taken place on 18 December 1897.

10. Loman, *Supplement*, pp. 247–48; notice in *NAE* 5 September 1879; AASE file 58, no. 2, contains the request by Alsberg, G. for inclusion in price lists, 18 July 1879; Dutch prospectus in no. 3; *Van Oss' Effectenboek* 1903, p. 513, and later editions.

11. Weeveringh, *Noord-Amerikaansche spoorwegfondsen*, p. 135; *Van Oss' Effectenboek* 1903, p. 514. Request for inclusion in price lists, 16 June 1880, in AASE file 58, no. 7; Dutch prospectus in no. 19.

12. Weeveringh, *Noord-Amerikaansche spoorwegfondsen*, p. 135; Waters, *Steel Trails*, pp. 200–201; Van Oss, *American Railroads*, p. 582.

13. Seligman & Co. to Alsberg, G., New York, 27 January 1881, in AASE file 58, no. 24; requests for inclusion in price lists, 8 February 1881, in no. 25; Weeveringh, *Noord-Amerikaansche spoorwegfondsen*, p. 135; Santilhano, *Amerikaansche spoorwegen*, pp. 445–47.

14. Notice in *NAE* 18 July 1882; Dutch prospectus issued by Alsberg, G., in AASE file 58, no. 37; *Van Oss' Effectenboek* 1903, p. 513, and later editions.

15. Prospectus in AASE file 58, no. 47.

16. Request for inclusion in price lists of the StL&SF 4% consols, 12 February 1892, in AASE file 58, no. 49A; appointment of comm., 29 January 1894, in nos. 57 and 59; minutes of meeting, undated (early 1894) in nos. 58, 60.

17. Articles of incorporation of the Dutch association, 6 March 1894, in AASE file 58, no. 69; circular letter to bondholders in no. 70; nos. 81 and 85 give details of reorganization; request for inclusion of all new securities by the Dutch Assoc., 4 November 1896, in no. 93; details of the blocks in nos. 86 and 92; the number of Dutch-held cert. in J. de Gijselaar to Stock Exchange, 26 November 1896, in no. 99.

18. Request for inclusion in price lists, 10 September 1901, in AASE file 58, no. 113; also *Van Oss' Effectenboek* 1903, p. 514. The conversion of the earlier loans into #16 in printed circular in Dutch, 16 and 28 May 1901, by Alsberg, G. in no. 111.

19. Request for inclusion in price lists, 4 February 1909, and Dutch prospectus in AASE file 58, no. 126; also *Van Oss' Effectenboek* 1912, p. 1361; total sold in Teixeira de M. to Stock Exchange, 19 June and 16 July 1913, in file 58A, no. 6.

20. Request for inclusion in price lists, 15 March 1910, and Dutch prospectus in AASE file 58, no. 131; also *Van Oss' Effectenboek* 1912, p. 1361.

21. Request for inclusion of these notes in price lists, 27 September 1912, and Dutch prospectus in AASE file 58A, no. 3.

22. Press cutting, 23 July 1913, and Alsberg, G. to Stock Exchange, 11 November 1913, in AASE file 58A, nos. 10 and 12.

23. Request for inclusion in price lists by the Dutch StL&SF Assoc. of both the preferred shares and the 4% refunding mortgage bonds, 27 November 1901, in AASE file 661, no. 1; no. 6 gives the Dutch and the American prospectus.

■ St. Louis & Southeastern

See under Louisville & Nashville.

■ St. Louis, Arkansas & Texas

See under St. Louis Southwestern.

■ St. Louis, Kansas City & Northern

See under Wabash Railroad.

■ St. Louis, Salem & Arkansas

See under St. Louis & San Francisco.

■ St. Louis South Western

Inc. 1891 from earlier St. Louis, Arkansas & Texas of 1886, which consisted of 3′ gauge Tyler Tap Railroad and Texas & St. Louis Railway among others.[1] Bought by Southern Pacific 1932.

> #1: 6% 1st m. loan of StLA&T of 1886 per 1936, total $10,000,000; bonds deposited with Central Trust Co. of New York, which issued cert. in return; these cert. traded. Intr. 1887 W. F. Piek at par, but already listed in A. since 1886; $750,000 sold.[2] Def. 1889; cert. > #2.
>
> #2: 4% 1st m. loan of StLSW of 1889 per 1989. Each $1,000 6% cert. of StLA&T > $1,030 of #2 + $250 in 4% 2nd m. bonds + $200 in pref. shares; conversion executed by Piek; 4% firsts listed in A. from 1892 and only dropped in 1962. New StLSW 4% seconds never listed in A., although prospectus for this loan has been found.[3]
>
> #3: common shares StLSW. Intr. 1906 Buitenlandsche Bankvereeniging/Ten Have & Van Essen at 27; quotations regular but never higher than 39, no dividends ever, last quoted 1925; Dutch holdings sold by 1931.[4]
>
> #4: 5% 1st Terminal and unifying m. loan of 1912 per 1952. Never listed in A., but coupons made out in dollars and guilders, and during later receivership it was learned that some of these bonds were in fact held in Holland.[5]

1. For the history of the narrow-gauge Texas & St. Louis see Hilton, *American Narrow Gauge*, pp. 316–19; J. E. Anderson, *Brief History*.

2. AASE file 204, no. 2A contains details of Piek's sales; also Weeveringh, *Noord-Amerikaansche spoorwegfondsen*, p. 130.

3. Details of the conversion in *Van Oss' Effectenboek* 1903, p. 509; prospectus of the 4% second m. loan in AASE file 204, no. 7; Piek's request for inclusion of the 4% first m. bonds in no. 11.

4. Official request for inclusion of the commons in price lists, May 1906, in AASE file 204, no. 12. Boissevain and Teixeira de Mattos to Stock Exchange Board, 28 October 1931, in AASE file 204, no. 17; they ask why the commons are still being listed when there are none in Dutch hands anymore.

5. Correspondence about this loan in unmarked folder in AASE file 204.

■ St. Louis, Wichita & Western

See under St. Louis & San Francisco.

■ St. Paul & Pacific

See under Great Northern.

■ St. Paul, Minneapolis & Manitoba

See under Great Northern.

■ San Antonio & Aransas Pass

See under Southern Pacific.

- ## Seaboard Air Line

Inc. 1900 from many earlier roads, of which the following were known in Amsterdam.

- ### Florida Railroad

Inc. 1856, def. 1873, reinc. as Florida Transit 1881, reorg. 1883 as Florida Transit & Peninsular, 1884 merged with Florida Central & Western into Florida Railway & Navigation, rec. 1886, reorg. 1889 as Florida Central & Peninsular Railway, 1900 part of Seaboard Air Line.[1]

> #1: 7% 1st m. loan of 1869, total $2,500,000, sold by Drake Bros. of New York.
> Intr. 1871 L. Hertz $520,000 at 74; def. 1873; Dutch-American pr. comm. 1879; 1881 > 6% 1st m. Florida Transit bonds: $3,000 FR bonds > $1,000 FT bonds; cert. issued by Hubrecht.[2] FT bonds not disturbed by 1884 merger into FR&N. Def. 1885; Dutch pr. comm. In 1889 > FC&P 5% bonds at par (#4).

- ### Jacksonville, Pensacola & Mobile

Inc. 1869, 1881 part of Florida Central & Western.

> #2: 8% Florida State loan of 1870 per 1900, total $4,000,000, in support of JP&M.
> Intr. 1870 Holjé & Boissevain/Milders at 85; def. 1873; at least $1,384,000 sold in A.[3] 1882 > JP&M 5% bonds: $3,000 state bonds > $1,000 5% JP&M bonds + $500 in commons + $300 income scrip; Hubrecht issued cert. for JP&M commons; no dividend, quotations in A. around 26, bonds around 75.[4] Dutch holdings in JP&M further increased after judgment of U.S. Supreme Court 1879.[5] JP&M bonds continued at 1881 merger; def. 1885; Dutch pr. comm. In 1889 > 5% FC&P bonds at par (#4).

- ### Florida Central & Peninsular

> #3: Common shares < old JP&M commons, in cert. of Hubrecht; listed in A. until 1902.
> #4: 5% 1st m. gold loan of 1888 per 1918, < old FT and JP&M bonds at par; Dutch holdings large; quotations over par in A.[6]
> #5: 5% sterling loan of 1890 per 1930, total £500,000.
> Intr. 1890 Broekman & Honders at 94.50; quoted at 110, but little trade in A.; redeemed 1930.
> #6: 5% cons. m. loan of 1893 per 1943, total $7,800,000.
> Intr. 1893 Broekman & Honders; soon quoted over par, in 1939 at 26.50.[7]

- ### Seaboard Air Line

> #7: 4% ref. gold loan of 1909 per 1959, auth. $125,000,000, underwritten by Blair & Co., Ladenburg, Thalmann, New York; Middendorf, Williams & Co., Baltimore; Robert Fleming, London; Ad. and Gebr. Boissevain, Amsterdam.
> Intr. 1911 by Ad. and Gebr. Boissevain at 83.25; sales considerable; quoted at 75–80; dropped from price lists in A. 1952.[8]

#8: 5% adjustment m. gold loan of 1909 per 1949, total $25,000,000; interest paid only when earned, but cum.

Intr. 1912 Gerritsen & Selle at 82.75; at least $300,000 in A.; last quoted at 52 in 1930; wiped out 1940.[9]

---

1. Prince, *Seaboard Air Line Railway.*
2. Dinger, *Overzicht* 1873, p. 771; announcement by Hertz in *NAE* 18 July 1871; *NAE* 3 October 1873; Pik, *Amerikaansche spoorwegwaarden*, pp. 90–94; Loman, *Supplement*, p. 274; *NAE* 8 April 1879.
3. Stover, *Railroads of the South*, pp. 94–95; Dinger, *Overzicht* 1873, pp. 650–51; McGrane, *Foreign Bondholders*, pp. 298–304; minutes of meetings of Dutch Florida bondholders in *NAE* 13 and 20 April 1877.
4. Details of agreement in *NAE* 2 September 1882.
5. See Chapter 10.
6. *Van Oss' Effectenboek* 1903, p. 492, and later editions.
7. Ibid., p. 493, and later editions.
8. Dutch prospectus of this loan and request by Ad. Boissevain for listing, April 1911, and 1 April 1912, in AASE file 1037, nos. 1 and 4; also *Van Oss' Effectenboek* 1912, p. 1355.
9. *Van Oss' Effectenboek* 1912, p. 1355, and later editions. Request for inclusion in price lists by Gerritsen & Selle, January 1912, in AASE file 1037, nos. 3 and 3A.

■ South Pacific

See under St. Louis & San Francisco.

■ Southern Pacific

The corporate and financial history of the present-day Southern Pacific Lines system is complex.[1] Only those securities of the Southern Pacific and its predecessor and constituent companies that found their way to the Dutch capital market will be listed here.

■ Central Pacific

Inc. CP Rail*road* 1861, leased Southern Pacific 1884; reinc. as CP Rail*way* 1899.[2]

#1: 6% 1st m. loan of 1867 per 1897.
Intr. 1870 Elix & Broekman at 71.75; after 1877 prices over par until redemption.[3]
#2: 6% San Joaquin Valley of 1870 per 1900, total $6,080,000.
Intr. 1872 Teixeira de Mattos at 86; after 1879 prices over par until redemption.[4]
#3: common shares, intr. 1880 Teixeira de M. at 84.5, dropped to 31 in 1884; 1899 > common shares of SP (#20). In 1898, of a total of $68,000,000 of CP common stock, $52,000,000 was held in Europe, most in England and the remainder in Holland and Germany.[5]
#4: 5% 1st (?) m. loan of 1889, total $11,000,000, of which $2,500,000 was held in Germany, and some in Holland.
Intr. 1889 Teixeira de M. at 101; in 1899 > half in 4% bonds (#5) + 70–90% in 3.5% bonds (#6).[6]
#5: 4% 1st ref. m. loan of 1899 per 1949, total $100,000,000, guaranteed by SP.
Listed in A. from 1899, mostly around par; 1939 at 48–58, redeemed 1949.
#6: 3.5% gold bonds of 1899 per 1929, total $20,000,000, guaranteed by SP.

Listed in A. from 1899, usually just below par; widely held; $11,000,000 redeemed by 1911, remainder in 1929.

#7: 4% Through Short Line (Lucin Cut-off) 1st m. loan of 1904 per 1954, total $8,300,000, guaranteed by SP, underwritten by Speyer & Co.

Intr. 1904 Teixeira de Mattos at 98; more than $1,400,000 sold; quoted at par until 1929, redeemed 1954.[7]

■ California Pacific

Inc. 1865, controlled by CP 1871.[8]

#8: 7% 1st m. loan of 1869 per 1889, total $2,250,000.

Held in A. but never listed.[9]

#9: 7% 1st m. loan (Extension Co.) of 1869 per 1889, total $3,500,000, mostly held in Germany; 1874 > half in 6% CalP bonds (#10) + Reichsmark 144 in cash.

Intr. 1869 S. de Vita at 73; quoted at 92 in 1872, 28 in 1875.

#10: 6% 2nd m. loan per 1891, total $2,000,000, guaranteed by CP, 1891 continued by CP at 4.5%, redeemed 1893–94.

Listed in A. from 1875, and more sold by Elix & Broekman later.[10]

■ California & Oregon

Inc. 1869, since 1870 controlled by CP.

#11: 6% 1st m. loan per 1888, total $2,000,000, guaranteed by CP.

Intr. 1871 Teixeira de M. at 81; rose to par 1879, 110 in 1881.[11]

#12: 6% 1st m. loan per 1892, total $5,800,000, of which $2,000,000 was offered in London in 1873 through Speyer Bros. at 79.5, but mostly sold in A. by Teixeira de M. and known as Series B; renewed in 1892 at 5%; in 1899 > CP 4% (#5).[12]

■ Oregon & California

Inc. 1865 as Oregon Central, reinc. 1869 as Oregon & California, def. 1873, reorg. 1879, def. 1885, reorg. 1887.[13]

#13: 7% 1st m. loan of 1870 per 1890, total $5,000,000, sold chiefly in Germany and Switzerland through Bischoffsheim of Frankfurt am Main; second portion of same loan of $3,800,000 sold 1872 in Germany; 1873 German pr. comm. with one Dutch member. In 1879 > common and pref. shares of reorganized O&C (#14).[14] New 6% "committee" loan issued 1879 to remove original incorporator Ben Holladay, total $2,500,000 (#15).

Intr. 1870 Ter Meulen & Boeken at 72; second portion 1872 by Lion Hertz at 75.60.

#14: commons and prefs. < old 7% loan (#13); included in the A. price lists. In 1887 O&C prefs. > CP commons at 50%; O&C commons > CP commons at 25%.[15]

#15: 6% "committee" loan, intr. 1879 by Amsterdamsche Bank at 85; in 1881 > 6% 1st m. bonds of O&C itself; 1885 > #16.[16]

#16: 5% 1st m. loan of 1887 per 1927, guaranteed by SP; listed in A. from 1887; Ed. Dentz sold more of same in 1888 at 93.25; continued 1899; redeemed by SP 1927.[17]

▪ Southern Pacific

Inc. 1865 as SP Railroad, reinc. 1870 as SP Railroad of California, leased to CP until 1885, when CP was leased to SP; holding company SP Company of Kentucky inc. 1884, which leased both SP and CP.

#17: 6% 1st m. loan of 1875 and following years, per 1910 and later, total (Series E and F) $10,000,000; marketed by Speyer Bros. of London, L. Speyer Elissen of Frankfurt, and E. J. Meyer of Berlin; sinking fund provided from 1882.
Intr. 1880 Teixeira de M. at 95.75; rose to 114 in 1904; redeemed between 1905 and 1912.[18]

#18: 5% 1st cons. m. loan of 1897 per 1937, total $21,500,000, of which $10,000,000 marketed by Speyer consortium 1898.
Intr. 1898 Teixeira de M. at 101.25; redeemed 1905 at 107.50.[19]

#19: 4% coll. gold bonds of 1899 per 1949 (coll. was CP common stock), total $29,000,000; marketed by Speyer consortium.
Intr. 1899 Teixeira de M. at just under par; prices stable; in 1939 between 31 and 45; redeemed 1949.[20]

#20: SP (of Calif.) common shares, < CP commons (#3) in 1899.
Listed in A. from 1899 at 31; rose to 138 in 1909, and around par afterwards. Gebr. Boissevain and Gebr. Teixeira de M. issued $1,000 cert. of 10 commons 1904; $377,000 in these reported sold in 1904, but original shares also circulating.[21] In 1900, out of a total of 2,000,000 shares, B. W. Blijdenstein & Co., C. W. Blijdenstein & Co. (Twentsche Bank) had 1,900 shares, Ad. Boissevain 50, E. Enthoven 28,100, and a few other Dutchmen some hundreds more. Van Deventer and Van der Veer, of New York, held 3,950 and 9,100 respectively, probably proxies for European (Dutch?) owners.[22]

#21: 7% pref. shares created 1904, total $40,000,000; issued at par to existing stockholders; $1,000 in commons could buy $200 in prefs.; in 1907 new offer of $300 in prefs. for $2,000 in commons.
Intr. 1904 Boissevain/Teixeira de M.; last quoted in 1909 at 119.[23]

#22: 4.5% 2- and 5-year gold notes of 1900, total $10,000,000; marketed by Speyer and partners; redeemed at par 1905, or > 4% 2- and 5-year notes + $42.50 cash.
Intr. 1900 Teixeira de M. at 97.25; at par until redemption; new 4% notes of 1905 never listed in A.[24]

#23: 4% ref. m. loan of 1905 per 1955, total $160,000,000; marketed by Speyer.
First part of this loan ($75,000,000) intr. 1905 Teixeira de M. at 97; prices between 95 and par, dropped to 47–54 in 1939.[25]

#24: 4% conv. gold loan of 1909 per 1929, total $82,000,000, with preferential rights for shareholders. Conv. until 1919: $130 in bonds > $100 in commons.
Intr. 1909 Gebr. Boissevain/Teixeira de M. at 96; many owners did convert, but bonds listed in A. until redemption 1929.[26]

#25: 4% 1st m. San Francisco Terminal loan of 1910 per 1950, total $50,000,000, with coupons in dollars and guilders.
Intr. 1910 Van Loon for Hope & Co. at 92.50; 1914 quoted at 82–92, 1939 at 57–70.[27]

#26: 5% conv. gold loan of 1914 per 1934, total $55,000,000, with preferential rights for shareholders; conv. before 1924.

Intr. 1914 Gebr. Boissevain/Teixeira de M. just under par; quoted at 44–57 in 1933; redeemed 1934 at par.[28]

■ Texas & New Orleans

Inc. 1860, 1885 taken over by SP, together with Morgan's Louisiana & Texas Railroad & Steamship Co., but continued operating as T&NO.[29]

#27: 6% 1st m. Sabine Division loan of 1882 per 1912, total $2,000,000.

Intr. ($1,200,000) 1886 Broekman & Honders at 103.75; $500,000 more in 1893 by Teixeira de M. at 104.50; quoted at 115 in 1899, redeemed at par 1912 by SP.[30]

■ San Antonio & Aransas Pass

Inc. 1884, 1892 under SP control, 1903 independent, 1925 again under SP control.[31]

#28: 4% 1st m. loan of 1893 per 1943, total $25,000,000, guaranteed by SP, of which only $17,500,000 actually issued.

Intr. 1904 Labouchère, Oyens for Rotterdamsche Bank at 89.25; at least Dfl 500,000 sold before bonds were listed, despite some uncertainty about SP guaranteed after new independence of SA&AP; quoted around 90, 1939 at 42–46.[32]

■ Northwestern Pacific

Inc. 1907 by ATSF and SP jointly out of earlier roads, among which the narrow-gauge North Pacific Coast and the standard-gauge San Francisco & North Pacific Railway of 1889.[33]

#29: SF&NP 5% 1st m. sinking fund loan of 1889 per 1919, total $4,000,000, underwritten by Ladenburg, Thalmann & Co. of New York, sold in Germany by Gebr. Bethmann and Von Erlanger und Söhne, Frankfurt am Main; int. payable in New York, Frankfurt, and Amsterdam.

Intr. ($400,000) 1891 Alsberg, Goldberg at 94.50; on inc. of Northwestern Pacific these bonds not disturbed and continued until redemption at par in 1919; highest quotation at 114 in 1900.[34]

---

1. Daggett, *Chapters*; Hofsommer, *Southern Pacific*; on Collis P. Huntington see Lavender, *The Great Persuader*.

2. Daggett, *Chapters*, pp. 1–61.

3. Dinger, *Overzicht* 1873, pp. 740–42; Pik, *Amerikaansche spoorwegwaarden*, pp. 31–37.

4. Dinger, *Overzicht* 1873, p. 744; Teixeira de M. had an unusually large full-page advertisement for these bonds in *NAE* 13 January 1872.

5. Weeveringh, *Noord-Amerikaansche spoorwegfondsen*, pp. 31–34; Daggett, *Chapters*, p. 148; AASE file 81.

6. Prospectus of Teixeira de M. in AASE file 81, no. 62; in Germany these bonds had been offered at 99.50 below par. Teixeira de M. to Stock Exchange, 3 November 1897, in nos. 73–74: a total of $8,004,000 of these bonds was reported deposited in New York, almost all from Germany. *Van Oss' Effectenboek* 1903, p. 540, and later editions.

7. Hofsommer, *Southern Pacific*, pp. 14–17; *Van Oss' Effectenboek* 1905, p. 1315, and later editions. Request for listing by Teixeira de M., 20 January 1905, in AASE file 81, no. 102.

8. Daggett, *Chapters*, pp. 107–10. J. de Frémery, Dutch consul in San Francisco, had his doubts about the financial stability of the CalP. See his *Californië*, vol. 1, p. 50.

9. Dinger, *Overzicht* 1873, pp. 738–39.

10. Notices in *NAE* 4 August 1874, 24 September 1875, and 26 November 1878; also Pik, *Amerikaansche spoorwegwaarden*, pp. 37–40; Loman, *Supplement*, pp. 241–43; request by Broekman for listing of $92,000 in new 6% bonds, 20 December 1877, in AASE file 65, no. 2; on the extension by the CP see Teixeira de M. to Stock Exchange, 7 January 1891, in nos. 4 and 5A.

11. Notice in *NAE* 16 May 1871; Dinger, *Overzicht* 1873, pp. 743–44. Request for listing of C&O bonds, 15 November 1872, in AASE file 63, no. 1A; the rest of file 63 holds papers relating to the Oregon & California, a different railroad altogether.

12. Notice about the renewal of these bonds at 5% in AASE file 63, nos. 29A and 30; Teixeira de M. requested listing of $4,358,000 of the fives, but not all of this was held in Holland.

13. Lewty, *Columbia Gateway*, pp. 28–29; Ganoe, "Oregon & California Railroad"; about Holladay, incorporator of O&C, see Lucia, *Saga of Ben Holladay*.

14. Dinger, *Overzicht* 1873, pp. 758–59; Pik, *Amerikaansche spoorwegwaarden*, p. 130. Regarding the German committee see *NAE* 1 April 1873; F. S. van Nierop to Stock Exchange, 6 November 1873, in AASE file 63, no. 1; notices in *NAE* 11 November 1873, 20 January 1874; minutes of meeting of committee, 8 October 1874, in AASE file 63, no. 3.

15. Details of conversion in Weeveringh, *Noord-Amerikaansche spoorwegfondsen*, pp. 114–15, and AASE file 63, nos. 23, 25.

16. Loman, *Supplement*, pp. 264–65; Pik, *Amerikaansche spoorwegwaarden*, pp. 131–33; notices in *NAE* 4, 21 March 1879.

17. Details of conversion in Weeveringh, *Noord-Amerikaansche spoorwegfondsen*, pp. 114–15; *Van Oss' Effectenboek*, 1903, p. 531.

18. Loman, *Supplement*, pp. 291–92; Dutch prospectus in AASE file 55, no. 4; *Van Oss' Effectenboek* 1903, p. 541.

19. *Van Oss' Effectenboek* 1904, p. 723, and later editions; Dutch prospectus in AASE file 55, no. 11.

20. *Van Oss' Effectenboek* 1903, p. 540, and later editions.

21. *Van Oss' Effectenboek* 1905, p. 853. AASE file 55, nos. 38 and 39 hold correspondence about the issue of certificates.

22. Huntington Library, San Marino, Calif., Henry E. Huntington Papers HEH 9946, contains Southern Pacific Co., Stockholders of record on March 15th, 1900.

23. *Van Oss' Effectenboek* 1905, p. 853; AASE file 55, nos. 38, 44.

24. *Van Oss' Effectenboek* 1903, p. 539, and later editions.

25. *Van Oss' Effectenboek* 1909, p. 1322, and later editions.

26. *Van Oss' Effectenboek* 1912, p. 1369; request for listing in AASE file 55, no. 50.

27. On the San Francisco extensions and electrification see Hofsommer, *Southern Pacific*, pp. 60–61; *Van Oss' Effectenboek* 1912, p. 1369. No request for listing has been found in AASE file 55, although correspondence of Hope & Co. in no. 51 indicates strong Dutch interest.

28. *Van Oss' Effectenboek* 1915–16, vol. 1, appendix 126, and vol. 2, p. 742. Request for listing by Boissevain/Teixeira de M. in AASE file 55, no. 63.

29. Hofsommer, *Southern Pacific*, pp. 158–76; Baughman, *Charles Morgan*.

30. Weeveringh, *Noord-Amerikaansche spoorwegfondsen*, pp. 140–42; request for listing by Teixeira de M. in AASE file 191, no. 1; correspondence between Teixeira and Stock Exchange, 1893, in no. 5.

31. Hofsommer, *Southern Pacific*, pp. 163–64.

32. Request for listing, 25 October 1904, in AASE file 738, no. 1A. *Van Oss' Effectenboek* 1905, p. 1293, gives Labouchère, Oyens, as the Dutch underwriter, with Möller & Kijzer acting for them; material in no. 1A clearly names the Rotterdamsche Bank as underwriter.

33. Hilton, *American Narrow Gauge*, pp. 329–30; Stindt and Dunscomb, *Northwestern Pacific*, pp. 13, 22–26; Hofsommer, *Southern Pacific*, pp. 45, 57, 135.

34. Dutch prospectus, 31 October 1891, in AASE file 316, no. 1B; request for listing in no. 1A. *Van Oss' Effectenboek* 1903, p. 843.

■ Southern Railway

Inc. 1894 from Richmond Terminal, East Tennessee, Virginia & Georgia, and others.[1]

■ Alabama & Chattanooga

Inc. 1868, def. 1871, 1877 reinc. as Alabama Great Southern, from 1896 part of Southern Railway.

#1: 8% priority m. gold loan, total $3,000,000, sold by J. Henry Schroeder in London and the Erlanger firms in Frankfurt and Paris.

Intr. 1869 Commandietkas at 85.5, def. 1871.[2] German pr. comm.; last quoted in A. in 1874 at 15; 1878 > 2–4% Alabama State bonds; the latter never listed in A.[3]

■ East Tennessee, Virginia & Georgia

Inc. 1869, rec. 1885, controlled by Richmond Terminal 1886, 1892 rec., part of Southern Railway 1894.[4]

#2: 5% 1st m. extension loan.

Intr. 1888 Hijmans & Sons; 1890 Jos. Thors.[5] Some $1,000,000 sold in A., rec. 1892; Dutch pr. comm.[6] In 1894, $1,000 ETV&G > $250 5% bonds (#3) + $800 prefs. (#4).[7]

■ Southern Railway

#3: 5% 1st cons. m. and coll. trust loan per 1994, < #2. At least $250,000 held in Holland, but not much trade; last quoted in A. in 1937 at 77.

#4: 5% non-cum. pref. shares, some $800,000 held in Holland in name of Nederlandsche Vereeniging ter behartiging van de belangen van preferente aandeelen der Southern Railway Company (Neth. Assoc. of preferred shareholders) founded 1894; also sold by Broes & Gosman in cert. and blocks of 10 original shares; dividends from 1897; 5% in 1902; quoted at $14–$26.50 in 1939; dropped from price lists in A. 1953.[8]

#5: Common shares in blocks of 10, sold from 1900 by Kalker & Polack (claimed to have sold 9,000 shares), A. H. Keyser & Sons, Twentsche Bank, Mendes Gans & Co., Incasso Bank; $1,000 cert. issued by Broes & Gosman.[9] Quoted at $9.60–$17.25 in 1939; dropped from lists in A. 1983.

#6: 4% development and gen. m. loan of 1906 per 1956, auth. $200,000,000, $75,000,000 issued by 1911.

Intr. 1909 D. Lutomirski at 79.40; limited sum, sales strong; quoted around 70, in 1939 35–48.[10]

---

1. Klein, *Richmond Terminal*; B. Davis, *The Southern Railway*; and Harrison, *Legal Development of the Southern Railway*.

2. D. R. Adler, *British Investment*, pp. 125–29; announcement in *AE* 19 August 1869; *NAE* 21 February, 27 June 1871.

3. D. R. Adler, *British Investment*, p. 128; notices in *NAE* 27 June and 25 July 1876; announcement in *NAE* 26 November 1878.

4. Klein, *Richmond Terminal*, pp. 6–9, 62–65.

5. AASE file 247, no. 1A, contains the request for listing by Hijmans, 15 October 1888; in nos. 4/4A Dutch prospectus of the loan and Thors's request for listing, 2 May 1890. File 247 is marked East Tennessee, Virginia & Georgia, but also holds the later Southern Rly. papers; usually a new file was opened when a company reorganized under a different name.

6. Minutes of meeting of 26 January 1893, in AASE file 247, no. 8; Hijmans to Stock Exchange, 23 January 1893, and circular letter of pr. comm., 24 June 1893, in nos. 9 and 14.

7. There is some uncertainty about the terms of the conversion: Dutch-held extension bonds were rumored to have been converted into ETV&G consols first; in that case they should have been exchanged dollar for dollar for new Southern 5% bonds in the Morgan plan, according to the table given by Klein, *Richmond Terminal*, pp. 274–75. As the later Dutch sources clearly show that each $1,000 worth of the Dutch ETV&G bonds was converted into $250 worth of new bonds and $800 worth of preferred shares, the conversion into ETV&G consols must have been annulled or may never have taken place at all. Circular letters of the pr. comm. 24 June and 2 August 1893, in AASE file 247, nos. 13 and 14.

8. AASE file 247, no. 17, contains the request of the Dutch committee for listing of the 5% consols and the prefs., 10 January 1895.

9. AASE file 247, no. 20, contains the request by the brokers mentioned, 12 December 1900; Broes & Gosman's request for listing of its certificates, of the same day, in no. 21.

10. Lutomirski's request, 22 February 1909, in AASE file 247, no. 25.

■ Texas & New Orleans

See under Southern Pacific.

■ Texas & Oklahoma

See under Missouri, Kansas & Texas.

■ Texas & Pacific

Inc. 1872 from earlier roads such as Frémont's Memphis, El Paso & Pacific; rec. 1884, reorg. 1887 and closely connected with Missouri Pacific.[1]

#1: Common shares, intr. 1905 Broes & Gosman in original shares and cert. of 5 or 10; no dividend ever; quotations in A. dropping from 38.50 in 1905 to 11 in 1914; last Dutch-held share sold in 1955.[2]

1. Van Zant, *Early Economic Policies*, p. 29; J. L. Kerr, *A Western Pioneer*, pp. 25–27; Mercer, *Railroads and Land Grant Policy*, pp. 43–47; Watson and Brown, *Texas & Pacific Railway*.

2. *Van Oss' Effectenboek* 1909, p. 1326; Dutch prospectus, 5 September 1905, in AASE file 776, no. 1.

■ Toledo, Peoria & Western

Inc. 1864 as Toledo, Peoria & Warsaw, rec. 1873, reorg. 1880 as Toledo, Peoria & Western and leased to Wabash, St. Louis & Pacific, def. 1884, reorg. 1885 and independent again.

#1: 7% cons. m. loan of TP&Wa of 1870 per 1910, total $6,200,000, used chiefly for redemption of earlier loans.

Intr. 1871 Elix & Broekman at 72; $500,000 available in A.[1] Def. 1873, Dutch pr. comm. 1877.[2] In 1879 > #2.

#2: 7% 2nd m. pref. income bonds of TP&We, guaranteed by Wabash at 4%; conv. into Wabash prefs. at owners' wish; unpaid coupons from 1873 paid with $352 in TP&We commons, which were in turn conv. into Wabash commons.[3] Cert. for income bonds and shares of TP&We issued by Stadnitski & Van Heukelom; def. 1884; $480,000 still not converted.[4] New Dutch pr. comm. 1885, but $464,000 of Dutch-held inc. bonds wiped out in reorg. of TP&W of 1885.[5]

#3: Common shares of TP&We, see under #2.

1. Dinger, *Overzicht* 1873, pp. 777–78.
2. Pik, *Amerikaansche spoorwegwaarden*, pp. 163–66; *NAE* 8 May 1875; notices by Elix & Broekman in *NAE* 25 July 1876, and 16 February 1877.
3. Loman, *Supplement*, pp. 280–82; *NAE* 16 December 1879, and 27 February 1880; details of the arrangement in *NAE* 13 April and 21 December 1880; AASE file 46, no. 16A, contains details of conversion.
4. *NAE* 4 July and 12 August 1884.
5. AASE file 46, nos. 18 and 20, contains details of the results achieved by the committee; no. 21B gives totals of Dutch-held income bonds.

■ Toledo, St. Louis & Western

Inc. 1900 out of Toledo, St. Louis & Kansas City, which was originally a 3'-gauge road and part of the projected Narrow Gauge Trunk.[1]

#1: 4% 10-year coll. trust loan of 1907, Series A and B, total $12,000,000, used for the purchase of a controlling interest in the Chicago & Alton.

Intr. 1910 Alsberg, Goldberg at 86.25; only Series A available in A.; def. 1914; no Dutch pr. comm.[2]

1. For the Narrow Gauge Trunk see Hilton, *American Narrow Gauge*, pp. 101–17; for a history of the TStL&W, or Clover Leaf, see Rehor, *Nickel Plate Story*, pp. 119–67.
2. *Van Oss' Effectenboek* 1912, p. 1376.

■ Traverse City

See under Pennsylvania Railroad.

■ Union Pacific

Inc. 1864, rec. 1893, reorg. as Union Pacific Railroad 1897.[1]

Securities of the UP itself were only traded in A. from about 1869, but several of its later subsidiaries were known there much earlier.

■ Kansas Pacific

Inc. 1863 as Union Pacific Eastern Division, renamed Kansas Pacific 1869, rec. 1876, 1880 part of Union Pacific.[2]

#1: 7% 1st/3rd m. Denver Ext. loan of 1869 per 1899, total $6,395,000, chiefly sold in Germany.

Intr. 1870 S. de Vita at 70; def. 1873; no Dutch pr. comm.[3] In 1879 partly > #2, but remainder continued and int. paid by UP after 1880; in 1896 at least $454,000 still in Dutch hands and > #21 at par.

#2: 6% cons. m. loan of 1879 per 1919, partly < #1; in 1896 $247,000 of consols in Dutch hands.[4] In 1897 > #21 and #23: $1,000 of #2 > $500 of #21 + $1,100 of #23.

■ Denver Pacific

Inc. 1869, controlled by Kansas Pacific, rec. 1878, part of Union Pacific 1880.[5]

#3: 7% 1st m. loan of 1869 per 1899, total $2,500,000.

Intr. 1870 Holjé & Boissevain/Milders; much trade and some $1,500,000 sold in A. and R.; quoted at 61–80 in 1870.[6] Def. 1878; Dutch pr. comm.

#4: 7% 1st m. Denver & Boulder Valley loan of 1870 per 1900, total $550,000.

Intr. 1870 Wertheim & Gompertz at 75; whole issue sold in A.[7] Def. 1878; Dutch pr. comm.

DP placed in hands of Dutch bondholders 1879; 1,413 DP bonds sold to Jay Gould in 1879 at 74 percent of par, 358 D&BV bonds at 57.[8]

■ Utah & Northern

Inc. 1871 as 3'-gauge Utah Northern, 1878 reorg. as Utah & Northern, 1889 merged with Oregon Short Line (UP).[9]

#5: 5% cons. 1st m. loan of 1886 per 1926, total $1,800,000, sold by Lee, Higginson & Co; int. guaranteed by UP.

Intr. 1888 Ad. Boissevain at 97; in 1896, $1,193,000 of these in Dutch hands.[10] Continued at 1896 reorganization and redeemed 1926 at par.

#6: 5% equipment bonds, guaranteed by UP.

Intr. 1888 Kerkhoven; $971,000 sold in A. in 1888–89.[11] Paid off in cash at par 1896.

■ Oregon Short Line & Utah Northern

Inc. 1889, 1897 reorg. as Oregon Short Line, controlled by Union Pacific.

#7: 5% coll. trust loan of 1889 per 1909, secured by shares of Oregon Railway & Navigation; int. guaranteed by UP.

Intr. 1890 Ad. Boissevain at 93.75; lively trade in A.; in 1897 > at par for new 5% inc. bonds B (#9).[12]

#8: 5% cons. m. loan per 1946, total $12,000,000, guaranteed by UP.

Intr. 1889 Broekman & Honders at 94.25; brisk trade.[13] In 1897 > new bonds: $1,000 of #8 > $500 in new OSL 5% cons. m. bonds (#10) + $500 in new 5% income bonds A (never listed in A.) + $1,000 in new commons (#11).

#9: 5% income bonds Series B of 1897, total $14,841,000, of which $11,000,000 was held in Holland in cert. issued by Dutch Oregon Short Line Assoc. In 1899 > UP 4% prefs. (#23).

#10: 5% cons. m. loan of 1897, < #8, and listed in A., but few quotations found.

#11: common shares of new OSL, < #8, and held in Holland in cert. issued by Oregon Short Line Assoc. In 1899 > UP common stock at par and dropped from price lists in A.

#12: 4% participating gold loan of 1901 per 1925, auth. $82,500,000, issued $36,000,000; collateral was UP's holding of Northern Securities Co. stock; underwritten by Kuhn, Loeb & Co.

Intr. 1902 Broes & Gosman at 90, with preferential rights for stockholders; soon quoted at par; in 1904 > #13.

#13: 4% ref. m. loan of 1904 per 1929, auth. total $100,000,000.

Intr. 1904 Broes & Gosman, but little trade and never listed in A.[14]

■ Union Pacific

#14: 6% 1st m. loan of 1866–69 per 1896–99, in several series, totalling $27,000,000. Intr. 1870 H. Oyens & Sons at 78.50, but already regularly quoted in A. in 1869.[15] In 1896, $3,996,000 in Dutch hands; other figures give $4,498,000; in 1896 > #21 at par + 50% in new prefs. #23.

#15: common shares, first quoted (at 24) in A. in 1871, when Broes & G. announced that it took care of interests of Dutch shareholders.

Intr. 1875 Broes & G. in cert. of 1, 5, or 10 shares; quoted at 128 in 1881, when dividends were between 6% and 8%; in price lists officially 1877.[16] In 1896 > #22 for $15 in cash.

#16: 6% coll. trust bonds of 1878 per 1908, total $4,800,000; coll. was stock of branch line companies.

Intr. 1880 Ad. Boissevain/Ten Have & Van Essen at 105.50.[17] In 1896, $3,194,000 in Dutch hands.

#17: 5% coll. trust bonds of 1882 per 1907, total $4,500,000.

Intr. 1883 by same at 93.[18] In 1896, $4,200,000 in Dutch hands.

#18: 5% equipment bonds of 1888, total $795,929, taken up by Barings and Blake, Boissevain of London.

Intr. 1888 Ad. Boissevain/Kerkhoven; $387,000 sold in A.[19]

#19: 5% equipment m. bonds of 1889, total $1,890,000.

Intr. 1889 Kerkhoven at 97.50; Dfl 1,440,000 ($576,000) sold in A.[20]

#20: 5% 1st m. loan of Union Pacific, Lincoln & Colorado of 1888 per 1918, total $4,400,000.

Intr. 1888 Ad. Boissevain at 97.25; never listed in A. but in 1896, $1,917,000 of these bonds in Holland.[21]

UP def. 1893, reorg. 1896; all existing first mortgage bonds were converted into new 4% bonds (#21) plus common (#22) and 4% preferred stock (#23).[22] Dutch pr. comm. and formal association founded 1894, which issued cert. in return for bonds.[23] Separate Oregon Short Line Assoc. founded 1894; Dutch member (A. A. H. Boissevain) of international reorganization committees of UP and OSL.

#21: 4% 1st m. loan of 1897 per 1947, total $100,000,000 (reduced to $75,000,000). Listed in A. from 1897, at least $3,422,000 in Dutch hands; quoted at 102 in 1897 and around par later.[24] In 1939 still quoted at 79–88.

#22: common shares, in cert. of 5 or 10 shares issued by Broes & G.; $1,702,000 held in Holland as result of the conversion; in 1933, $5,230,000 held by Broes & G. against cert.; in 1939 quoted at $65–$82 per share of $100.

#23: 4% non-cum. pref. shares, < #9 and #20; cert. issued by Broes & G. and also sold new in A.[25] In 1933, $2,890,000 held by Broes & G. against cert.; in 1939 quoted at $58–$70.

#24: 4% 1st lien conv. loan of 1901 per 1911, total $100,000,000, to be used for buying of Southern Pacific and other stock; conv. into commons before 1906. Intr. 1901 Broes & Gosman; brisk trade; quoted at 103–124 in 1901; most conv. before 1906, but $550,000 redeemed at par in 1911.[26]

#25: 4% conv. loan of 1907 per 1927, total $75,000,000, to be used for betterments, equipment, and purchase of stock of other roads; conv. into commons before 1917. Intr. 1907 Broes & G. at 90; soon quoted over par, with a high of 123 in 1909.[27]

#26: 4% 1st lien and ref. m. loan of 1908 per 2008, total $50,000,000, underwritten by Kuhn, Loeb & Co., Baring Bros., and Glyn, Mills, Currie & Co.; coupons in dollars and pounds. Prospectus printed and published in Holland, but bonds never listed in A. and probably few sold.[28]

---

1. For a history of the Union Pacific see Klein, *Union Pacific*, vols. 1 and 2; a financial history in Trottman, *History*; Athearn, *Union Pacific Country*, is an excellent social history of the UP and of the area traversed by its lines.

2. A history of the Kansas Pacific in G. L. Anderson, *Kansas West*.

3. Dinger, *Overzicht* 1873, pp. 748–49; notice in German about cessation of interest payment in *NAE* 28 October 1873.

4. Details of conversion in Trottman, *History*, pp. 149–55; also Loman, *Supplement*, pp. 248–51. Trottman (p. 153, 160) errs where he states that no KP firsts, but only junior securities, were actually converted into consols; Weeveringh, *Noord-Amerikaansche spoorwegfondsen*, p. 147, is correct in stating that the old firsts, among them the Denver Extensions, still existed. In AASE a file marked "Union Pacific Copie Boek," without any number, has been found. The 1896 figures given here are taken from a letter of G. Vissering to A. A. H. Boissevain, 29 December 1896, in this file.

5. Jessen, *Railroads*, pp. 11– 24.

6. *NAE* 1 March 1870; Dinger, *Overzicht* 1873, pp. 749–50; prospectus of this loan in AASE file 31, no. 1.

7. *NAE* 16 June 1871 and 25 October 1872; also Dinger, *Overzicht* 1873, pp. 750–51.

8. Minutes of meeting of 12 March 1877 in AASE file 31, no. 5; no. 7 is a statement of Dutch holdings: a little less than $2,000,000 of DP bonds is in Dutch hands; report of meeting also in *NAE* 16 March 1877; in no. 17 draft of the final report drawn up by the Dutch committee, 23 April 1880; the story of the Dutch interest in the Denver Pacific has been taken from this report; a notice in *NAE*, 12 August 1879, also gives details of the transaction with Gould.

9. A history of the Utah & Northern in Hilton, *American Narrow Gauge*, pp. 533–36; Klein, *Union Pacific*, vol. 1., pp. 356–58.

10. Request for inclusion in the price lists, 24 September 1888, by Ad. Boissevain, in AASE file 218, no. 8A; no. 8B is the Dutch prospectus.

11. Request for inclusion in the price lists by Kerkhoven, 6 February 1888, and printed circular, 31 December 1887, in AASE file 218, nos. 1 and 2; request for inclusion of more of the same, 12 March 1888, in no. 5.

12. Request for inclusion in the price lists by Ad. Boissevain, 9 July 1890, and Dutch prospectus in AASE file 218, nos. 11C and D. For the 1897 reorganization see Trottman, *History*, pp. 261/277–78; "Plan and Agreement for the Reorganization of the Oregon Short Line & Utah Northern Railway Company," Boston, 20 February 1896, in Huntington Library, San Marino, Calif., catalog no. 230557. For the conversion see printed circular by Oregon Short Line Vereeniging, 15 July 1897, in AASE file 218, no. 31.

13. Broekman & Honders to Stock Exchange, 17 July 1890, in AASE file 218, no. 13A: Broekman had inspected the OSL&UN himself; also *Van Oss' Effectenboek* 1903, p. 532; Dutch prospectus, April 1890, in no. 14D.

14. Request for inclusion in the price lists by Broes & Gosman, 7 August 1902, in AASE file 218, no. 41; in no. 42 is a Dutch and an American prospectus of the same loan; also *Van Oss' Effectenboek* 1903, p. 532, and 1909, p. 1204.

15. Dinger, *Overzicht* pp. 745–46; request for inclusion in the price lists by Oyens & Sons, 10 July 1871, in AASE file 62, no. 1A.

16. *NAE* of 21 November 1871 for the announcement of Broes & G., and same of 2 December 1873 for an anonymous warning against UP shares: "Union shares are wastepaper; mind your purses; qui vivra verra." Request for inclusion of the commons in the price lists by Jarman & Sons, 30 August 1877, in AASE file 62, no. 1; no. 2 holds a letter from several brokers to the Stock Exchange, 4 September 1877, in which they argue in favor of inclusion of both original shares and certificates in the price lists.

17. Weeveringh, *Noord-Amerikaansche spoorwegfondsen*, p. 146; AASE file 62, no. 4, contains a request for inclusion of the sixes in the price lists by Ten Have & Van E., 3 May 1880; Dutch prospectus, 25 March 1880, in no. 7.

18. Weeveringh, *Noord-Amerikaansche spoorwegfondsen*, p. 147; AASE file 62, no. 13: request for listing of the fives, 12 May 1883.

19. Request for inclusion of the 5% equipment bonds in the price lists by Ad. Boissevain/Kerkhoven, 24 July 1888, in AASE file 62, no. 23.

20. Dutch prospectus by Kerkhoven, January 1889, in AASE file 62, no. 31B.

21. Although always called the Lincoln & Colorado in Holland, the official name of the road was Union Pacific, Lincoln & Colorado. Ad. Boissevain to Stock Exchange, 17 November 1888, in AASE file 62, no. 25; Dutch prospectus of this loan, 26 October 1888, in no. 26.

22. For the several reorganization schemes that did not come to fruition see Trottman, *History*, pp. 252–61; Daggett, *Railroad Reorganization*, pp. 244–50. For the condition of the UP and its possibilities see S. F. van Oss, "The Union Pacific," in *Supplement to the Stock Exchange*, 21 October 1893, copy in AASE file 62, no. 38. Details of the conversion in Daggett, *Railroad Reorganization*, pp. 250–53; Trottman, *History*, pp. 262–72.

23. AASE file 62, nos. 44, 50, and 51.

24. Union Pacific Vereeniging to Kas Vereeniging, 24 February 1898, in Union Pacific Copie Boek, AASE. The fours were included in the price lists at the request of the Amsterdamsche Bank, 18 February 1898, in AASE file 62, no. 62.

25. Request for inclusion of commons and prefs. in price lists by Broes & G., 19 February 1898, in AASE file 62, no. 64.

26. Klein, *Union Pacific*, vol. 2, pp. 89–90, 165–66; request for inclusion in the price lists by Broes & G., 1901, in AASE file 62, no. 64; *Van Oss' Effectenboek* 1903, p. 547.

27. Request for listing by Broes & G., 23 October 1907, in AASE file 62, no. 67; also *Van Oss' Effectenboek* 1909, p. 1335.

28. *Van Oss' Effectenboek* 1909, p. 1664.

■ Union Pacific Eastern Branch

See under Union Pacific.

■ Union Pacific, Lincoln & Colorado

See under Union Pacific.

■ Union Pacific Southern Branch

See under Missouri, Kansas & Texas.

▪ Union Terminal
See under Kansas City Southern.

▪ Utah & Northern
See under Union Pacific.

▪ Wabash Railroad
Inc. 1889 from earlier Wabash, St. Louis & Pacific of 1879 and other lines.[1] Rec. 1912 and reorg. as Wabash Railway 1915. Of constituent roads the first to enter the Amsterdam market was:

▪ North Missouri
Inc. 1855, def. 1871, reorg. as St. Louis, Kansas City & Northern, which was consolidated with other roads into the Wabash, St. Louis & Pacific in 1879.

#1: 7% 1st m. loan of 1865 per 1895, total $6,000,000.

Intr. 1870 Elix & Broekman for F. W. Oewel at 75.75; very popular and seen as good investment.[2] Not disturbed at 1871 reorganization and still widely held in A.; not disturbed by 1879 consolidation and continued under original name, but slowly sold off by Dutch; last quotation found in 1882, but listed until redemption in 1895; some uncertainty about this redemption.[3]

▪ Wabash, St. Louis & Pacific
#2: 7% non-cum. preferred shares.

Intr. 1880 Hubrecht at 70, in cert. of 5 or 10 shares; 6% dividend paid in 1881, not out of earnings but out of capital; no dividends after 1881.[4] Quotations in A. down from par in 1881 to 10 in 1884; after inc. of Wabash Railroad in 1889 > prefs. of new Wabash, after payment of $8 per $100 share; for these cash payments 6% debentures Series B were given (#4).[5] Quoted in A. at a high of 62 in 1909, down to 2 in 1914; in 1933, $485,000 in prefs. of then Wabash Railway still held in Holland.

#3: common shares; lively trade in A. but not listed until 1906.

Intr. 1906 J. C. van der Waag; no dividends ever; quoted at 27 in 1909, at 1 percent of par in 1914.[6] In 1933, $3,299,300 in commons still held in Holland; quoted just above zero.

#4: 6% debentures Series B of 1889 resulting from assessments on #2.

Intr. 1889 Hubrecht in $1,000 cert.; annual interest of 1%, 2%, 4%, and 3% paid between 1908 and 1911, nothing afterwards; no A. quotations found after 1911.

#5: 4% equipment notes of 1906, running 1–10 years, total $6,200,000.

Intr. 1906 Ad. Boissevain, and seen as extremely safe; not listed because of short duration.[7]

#6: 4% 1st ref. and ext. loan of 1906, intended to withdraw debentures (#4).

Intr. 1908 Van der Waag at 60, "sizable number" sold before being listed in A.[8] Dr. Joh. Luden, of Hope & Co., was member of international reorg. comm. All Dutch holdings of shares and bonds converted into new Wabash Railway prefs. A and B, in

cert. of Administratie Kantoor van Aandeelen der Wabash Railway Co.; B's largely >
A's and commons after 1915.

1. For a short history of the Wabash see Swartz, "Wabash Railroad."
2. Dinger, *Overzicht* 1873, pp. 754–56; Loman, *Supplement*, pp. 258–59; positive article by
"Americanus" in *NAE* 25 March 1870; Pik, *Amerikaansche spoorwegwaarden*, pp. 126–28.
3. Godzen & Van Eele, Amsterdam stockbrokers, to Stock Exchange Board, 16 July 1895, in
AASE file 1246, no. 14.
4. Van Oss, *American Railroads*, pp. 504–6; AASE file 1246, no. 1, contains the first Wabash
annual report (1881) in Dutch.
5. Details of conversion in AASE file 1246, nos. 6–11.
6. Request for listing by Van der Waag, 25 April 1906, in AASE file 1246, no. 17.
7. *Van Oss' Effectenboek* 1907, p. 1549.
8. Van der Waag to Stock Exchange, 23 November 1908, in AASE file 1246, no. 18.

■ Wabash Pittsburgh Terminal

Inc. 1904 to provide last link in transcontinental railroad assembled by George Gould;
rec. 1908; 1917 reorg. as Pittsburgh & West Virginia.
#1: 4% 2nd m. loan of 1904 per 1954, total $20,000,000.
Intr. 1906 Everts & Schmidt, "limited sum," but at least $1,400,000 sold in A.[1]
Def. 1908; A. A. H. Boissevain acted as representative of Dutch bondholders, with
John W. Castles of New York for the Americans; at reorganization of 1917 these
bonds wiped out.[2]

1. AASE file 745, nos. 1 and 1H, contains the request by Everts & Schmidt and Dutch
prospectus of the loan; they mention $1,150,000 as sold in Holland.
2. AASE file 745, no. 7F, contains Boissevain to Stock Exchange, 5 September 1908.

■ West Wisconsin

See under Chicago & North Western.

■ Western Pacific

Inc. 1903, rec. 1914, reorg. 1916.[1]
#1: 5% 1st m. gold loan of 1903 per 1933, total $50,000,000, guaranteed by Den-
ver & Rio Grande.
Intr. 1909 Ad. Boissevain at 97; also in cert. of $100, $200, and $400 by Broes,
Gosman, "to accommodate small savers."[2]
Def. 1914, Dutch pr. comm.; one Dutch member of international reorganization
comm.; in 1915, $3,200,000 of Dutch-held bonds (6.5% of total) deposited.[3]

1. For a history of the WP see DeNevi, *The Western Pacific*, and Myrick, *Railroads of Nevada*,
vol. 1, pp. 316–33.
2. AASE file 1435, nos. 1 and 2, contains request for inclusion of the bonds in the price lists,
May 1909, and announcement by Broes, Gosman of opening of a department for these bonds;
also *Van Oss' Effectenboek* 1909, p. 1226.
3. Details of reorganization in *Van Oss' Effectenboek* 1918–19 and later editions; the 1915
figures in Van Pellecom, *Kapitaalexport*, pp. 122–23.

■ Wilmington & Manchester

Inc. 1852, 1870 reinc. as Wilmington, Columbia & Augusta, 1885 part of Atlantic Coast Line.[1]

> #1: 6% £200,000 ($1,000,000) loan of 1866, sold by Robert Benson.
>
> Intr. 1867 Gebr. Boissevain, Confederate cotton loan 7% bonds taken in payment; results of sale unknown but W&M bonds never listed in A.[2]

1. Dozier, *Atlantic Coast Line*, pp. 75–76; 127–30.
2. Announcement in *AE* 3 October 1867; D. R. Adler, *British Investment*, does not mention this loan of the W&M; Dinger, *Overzicht* 1873, pp. 600–601.

■ Winona & St. Peter

See under Chicago & North Western.

■ Winston Salem Southbound

Inc. 1910 jointly by Norfolk & Western and Atlantic Coast Line.

> #1: 4% 1st m. gold loan of 1910 per 1960, $5,000,000, sold by Brown Bros. & Co. and W. Salomonson of New York; interest guaranteed by N&W and ACL.
>
> Intr. 1911 Gebr. Boissevain at 96; still quoted in A. in 1939 at 79.75.[1]

1. *Van Oss' Effectenboek* 1912, pp. 1389, 1601; AASE file 1030, no. 1, contains the request for listing by Gebr. Boissevain, 7 February 1911.

■ Wisconsin, Minnesota & Pacific

See under Chicago Great Western.

Streetcars, Interurbans, and Miscellaneous

■ Bush Terminal Company (Brooklyn)

> #1: 5% cons. m. loan of 1905 per 1955.
>
> Intr. 1906 De Clercq & Van Essen at 96; $1,000,000 sold in A.; in rec. 1933, reorg. 1937, but bonded debt undisturbed; still listed in A. in 1939 and quoted at 24.[1]

1. Condit, *Port of New York*, vol. 2, 107–8; AASE file 759, and *Van Oss' Effectenboek* 1940.

■ Chicago & Milwaukee Electric Railroad

> #1: 5% 1st m. loan per 1922, total $4,600,000.
>
> Intr. 1905 Van der Werff & Hubrecht/Joh. Eck & Sons/Oppenheim & Van Till at 99.25; in first week $600,000 sold; 1908 rec.; Dutch pr. comm. formed; cert. issued; redeemed in cash at 62.50% in 1911; total of Dutch holdings exchanged $1,642,000. Road reorganized as Chicago, North Shore & Milwaukee in 1917.[1]

1. AASE file 750, no. 1, contains a Dutch prospectus of the C&ME and official request for listing by Van der Werff & Hubrecht, 20 January 1905. The number of Dutch bonds in Van der Werff & H. to Stock Exchange, 2 July and 11 September 1908, in nos. 4 and 5; also *Van Oss' Effectenboek* 1909 and 1911. A file, unnumbered and undated, pertaining to the C&ME has been found in the AASE.

■ Connecticut Railway & Lighting Company

#1: 4.5% 1st and ref. m. sinking fund loan of 1904, total $12,500,000.

Intr. 1904 De Clercq & Van Essen at 97.6; company controlled by New York, New Haven & Hartford from 1906, but this loan was continued and quoted around par in A.[1]

1. AASE file 749 contains no papers from the period before 1914; material relevant to the Connecticut Railway loan has been taken from *Van Oss' Effectenboek* 1905, 1296; also Mason, *Street Railway in Massachusetts*, 62–69; these bonds remained in the Amsterdam price lists until 1940, but by then most bonds had been bought back by the company.

■ Detroit United Railways

#1: 4.5% 1st cons. m. loan of 1902 per 1932, total $8,200,000.

Intr. 1904 H. Oyens & Sons at 94.50; quoted around 95 until dropped from price lists in A. in 1931.[1]

1. AASE file 756; also O'Geran, *A History*.

■ Havana (Cuba) Electric Railway

A New York company.

#1: 5% 1st cons. m. loan per 1952.

Intr. 1911 Gebr. Teixeira de Mattos at 97.25; "limited sum" available in A.; undisturbed at the 1912 merger into the Havana Electric Railway, Light & Power Co. and still listed in A. in 1939.[1]

1. *Van Oss' Effectenboek* for 1918–19, 1934, and 1940.

■ Helena Light & Railway Company

#1; 5% 1st m. sinking fund loan of 1905 per 1925, total $850,000.

Intr. 1905 Wiegman's Bank at 91.50; company managed by the well-known firm of White & Co., which had recently built an electric interurban between Haarlem and Amsterdam; little success with the sale of bonds of the Helena, Montana, line; only 49 cert. of $1,000 each were outstanding in 1927, when the HL&R defaulted.[1]

1. In AASE file 788, no. 7D, Amsterdamsche Bank to Stock Exchange, 7 July 1930, gives the number of 49 cert.; in 1927 the company was reorganized as the Helena Gas & Electric Company; $1,000 in old bonds could be exchanged for $600 in new bonds plus $400 cash, but the new securities were listed in A. only until 1932. See also Oppenheim, *Reminiscences*, 85–88; he considered the HL&R bonds safe as houses.

■ Hudson Companies (New York)

Construction company set up to build the Hudson & Manhattan Tunnels.

#1: 6% 2.5-year conv. gold notes, underwritten by Harvey Fisk & Sons, total $15,000,000.

Intr. 1908 Ad. Boissevain at 98.5, "limited sum" available in A.; bonds > 4.5% 1st m. bonds of parent Hudson & Manhattan Railroad, but the latter never listed in A.[1]

1. Walker, *Fifty Years of Rapid Transit*, pp. 284–91; *Van Oss' Effectenboek* 1909, p. 1635.

■ Interborough Rapid Transit (New York)

#1: 4.5% coll. trust loan of 1906 per 1956.

Intr. 1906 at 82; dropped from price lists in A. 1925.

#2: pref. shares, intr. 1909 Gerritsen & Selle at 25.60 in cert. issued by Nederlandsch Administratie en Trustkantoor of A.; exchanged for new cert. of 6% prefs. of reorganized Interborough Consolidated Company in 1915; new cert. never listed.[1]

1. Walker, *Fifty Years of Rapid Transit*, pp. 182–99; *Van Oss' Effectenboek* 1912, p. 1467; ibid. 1915–16, vol. 2, p. 798.

■ Kansas City Railway & Light Company

#1: 5% 1st lien ref. loan of 1903 per 1913, total $25,000,000.

Intr. 1904 by F. Glasbergen for Ad. Boissevain at 98.50; in rec. but coupons paid until redemption and quoted around 90 in A.[1]

1. *Van Oss' Effectenboek* 1905, pp. 643, 1303, and later editions; with the 1915 reorganization $1,000 in old bonds could be exchanged for $700 in 5% 1st m. bonds of the new Kansas City Railways plus $300 in bonds of the Kansas City Light & Power; these two never listed in A.

■ Manila Suburban Railways

A Connecticut company.

#1: 5% 1st m. sinking fund loan of 1907 per 1947, underwritten by Rosen, Stillman & Co.

Intr. 1907 Westendorp & Co./Oppenheim & Van Till at 92.50; still listed in A. in 1934, but most > bonds of Associated Gas & Electric Co.[1]

1. *Van Oss' Effectenboek* for 1918–19, 1934, and 1940.

■ New Orleans Railways

#1: common shares, intr. 1902 Broes & Gosman in cert. of $1,000 at 16; no dividends; quoted in A. at 3 in 1905, at 37 thereafter.

#2: pref. shares, intr. by same but sold at 56; quoted at 80 in 1907; dividend 4%, and 5% or 6% after 1905.

NOR reorganized 1905 as New Orleans Railways & Light Company, taken over 1911 by American Cities Company. Old commons got 35% in new ACC 6% prefs. +

25% in ACC commons; $1,113,200 exchanged by Broes & Gosman. Old prefs. got 83.30% in ACC prefs. + 16.60% in ACC commons; $283,000 exchanged by Broes & G.[1]

---

1. AASE file 773; also Blain, *A Near Century*, pp. 67–71; *Van Oss' Effectenboek* 1903 and later editions. American figures in *United States Census Office, Bulletin 3, Street and Electric Railways*. For the activities of brokers Oppenheim & Van Till in New Orleans, see Oppenheim, *Reminiscences*, p. 49; the 1911 conversion in Broes & G. to Stock Exchange, 19 June 1911, in AASE file 773, no. 22.

▪ Santiago (Cuba) Electric Light & Traction Company

Controlled by Electric Bond & Share Co. of New York.

#1: 6% 1st m. loan per 1958.

Intr. 1913 Gebr. Boissevain/Gebr. Teixeira de Mattos at 98; $800,000 sold in A.; redeemed 1927 and dropped from price lists.[1]

---

1. *Van Oss' Effectenboek* for 1918–19, 1934, and 1940.

▪ West Penn Traction & Water Power Company

#1: 6% pref. shares, intr. 1912 Gebr. Boissevain at 79 in cert. of $500 or $1,000; total offered in A. $6,500,000; dividends regular and quotations in A. high.[1]

---

1. Hilton and Due, *Interurban Railways*, pp. 202, 299–300; AASE file 1111; at the reorganization of the company in 1926, the old cert. were exchanged for 7% prefs. of the West Penn Electric Co.; the latter still listed in A. in 1939.

Dutch Protective Committees and International Committees with Dutch Members

In most cases, the first named was the chairman of the committee and the last named the secretary. Sources for this appendix are De Iongh, *Gedenkboek 1876–1926*, Bijlage II; and material from the Archives of the Amsterdam Stock Exchange.

■ 1860

Galveston, Houston & Henderson

L. H. Weetjen; G. A. van der Voort; M. S. Boon Hartsinck.

■ 1871

Des Moines Valley

The firms of: H. Franco Mendes; J. A. Matthes & Co.; H. Oyens & Sons; Burdet & Druijvesteyn.

■ 1873

St. Paul & Pacific

The firms of: Chemet & Weetjen; Kerkhoven & Co.; Lippmann, Rosenthal & Co.; Tutein Nolthenius & De Haan; Wurfbain & Co.; Voorhoeve & Co. (Rotterdam); J. Carp (Utrecht).

Oregon & California

German committee, with F. S. van Nierop as sole Dutch member.

■ 1875

Missouri, Kansas & Texas

F. S. van Nierop; G. A. Croockewit; E. Fuld; P. A. L. van Ogtrop; H. J. de Marez Oyens; A. C. Wertheim; J. H. Wijsman.

- 1876

Atlantic, Mississippi & Ohio

P. A. van Oosterwijk Bruyn; J. Carp; H. P. Goedkoop; H. J. de Marez Oyens; J. C. de Marez Oyens; W. F. Piek; James C. Parrish (Philadelphia). A short-lived joint British-Dutch committee had H. J. de Marez Oyens and W. F. Piek as Dutch members.

Toledo, Peoria & Warsaw

P. A. van Oosterwijk Bruyn; J. H. Broekman, Jr.; H. J. de Marez Oyens; and a secretary.

Gilman, Clinton & Springfield

Joint American-British-Dutch committee: George Bliss; Charles S. Seyton; H. J. de Marez Oyens.

- 1877

Denver Pacific

J. L. ten Have; A. R. Jolles; A. C. Wertheim; W. F. Piek.

State of Florida

Jac. Wertheim; C. D. Willard (Washington).

- 1884

Chicago & Atlantic

H. J. de Marez Oyens; J. L. ten Have; W. F. Piek; R. van Rees.

Denver & Rio Grande

H. J. de Marez Oyens; P. C. A. M. van Weel; T. H. A. Tromp; and others.

Denver & Rio Grande (5% bonds and shares)

W. F. Piek; J. L. ten Have.

New York, Ontario & Western

P. A. L. van Ogtrop; A. C. Wertheim; M. Westendorp; P. J. Loman; R. van Rees (secretary); H. W. Smithers (Louisville).

- 1885

Florida Central & Western

T. Cool; H. F. R. Hubrecht; J. M. Rodenberg.

Florida Transit

J. H. Broekman, Jr.; J. C. Loman; A. Roelvink.

Toledo, Peoria & Western

J. H. Broekman, Jr.; P. A. van Oosterwijk Bruyn; and others.

- 1887

Missouri, Kansas & Texas

F. S. van Nierop; P. A. L. van Ogtrop; L. C. van Heukelom; H. J. de Marez Oyens; R. van Rees; A. L. Wurfbain.

▪ 1888

Missouri, Kansas & Texas (7% bonds and Southern Branch 6% bonds)

M. C. van Hall; A. C. Wertheim; A. D. de Marez Oyens; H. P. Berlage; J. C. Loman.

▪ 1891

Chicago, St. Paul & Kansas City

British committee, with J. G. Sillem as sole Dutch member.

▪ 1892

East Tennessee, Virginia & Georgia

A. C. Wertheim; H. J. de Marez Oyens; A. Hijmans; A. Palache; R. van Rees; J. L. Gunning.

▪ 1893

Western New York & Pennsylvania

F. S. van Nierop; P. A. van Oosterwijk Bruyn; W. F. Piek; G. M. Titsingh; J. H. Wijsman; and a secretary.

Union Pacific

P. A. L. van Ogtrop; M. C. van Hall; H. P. Berlage; A. A. H. Boissevain; P. A. Dijkshoorn (Rotterdam); A. A. H. Boon Hartsinck (Arnhem); J. H. Nachenius; H. J. de Marez Oyens; A. C. Wertheim; G. Vissering.

St. Louis & San Francisco

J. L. N. de Gijselaar; T. Cool; S. Alsberg; H. J. Heemskerk; H. J. Waller; A. H. Wertheim.

Atlantic & Pacific

H. C. Veltman, Jr.; P. A. van Oosterwijk Bruyn; G. C. B. Dunlop; L. Goldberg; J. C. F. Knapp, Jr.; H. Bensman.

Oregon Short Line & Utah Northern

P. A. L. van Ogtrop; H. P. Berlage; J. H. Broekman, Jr.; A. A. H. Boon Hartsinck (Arnhem); D. Rahusen; R. van Rees; A. Roelvink; J. L. Gunning.

Chesapeake Ohio & Southwestern

A. C. Wertheim; J. C. Loman; J. Luden; H. Teixeira de Mattos; A. C. van Heemskerck Veeckens; E. J. Everwijn Lange, Jr.

▪ 1895

Atchison, Topeka & Santa Fe

P. A. L. van Ogtrop; M. C. van Hall; A. J. A. Gillissen; J. H. Nachenius; A. D. de Marez Oyens; J. C. Sweijs; J. L. Gunning; R. Bloembergen.

Atchison, Topeka & Santa Fe (second mortgage bonds)

A. C. Wertheim; D. A. Fock; S. Piek; J. G. Steneker; J. H. Wijsman; E. J. Everwijn Lange, Jr.

Norfolk & Western

F. S. van Nierop; M. C. van Hall; H. P. Berlage; J. H. van Eeghen; H. F. R. Hubrecht; H. M. Huydecoper; J. L. Pierson; G. Vissering.

■ 1897

Central Pacific

H. C. Veltman, Jr.; J. C. Loman; H. P. Berlage; G. C. B. Dunlop; J. H. Wijsman; A. F. van Hall.

■ 1899

Kansas City, Pittsburg & Gulf

H. J. de Marez Oyens; H. P. Berlage; R. Bloembergen; E. van Essen; J. de Goeijen, Jr.; A. C. Laane; J. H. Wijsman; A. F. van Hall.

Kansas City Suburban Belt

J. L. N. de Gijselaar; R. Bloembergen; E. van Essen; J. de Goeijen, Jr.; T. Gilissen; H. van Kempen; A. F. van Hall.

Chicago & Grand Trunk

P. A. L. van Ogtrop; J. L. N. de Gijselaar; J. C. Loman; J. Luden; S. Piek.

■ 1908

Oklahoma Central

Aug. Kalff; J. Kalker; G. A. W. van Lanschot; S. F. van Oss (The Hague); P. J. J. Jonas van 's Heer Arendskerke; J. A. van Sonsbeeck.

Chicago & Milwaukee Electric

A. F. van Hall; J. F. van Essen; J. G. Gleichman; P. G. Hubrecht; A. Oppenheim (The Hague); H. Portheine; J. C. Stoop; J. A. van Sonsbeeck.

■ 1915

Western Pacific

A. de Bijll Nachenius; P. J. J. Jonas van 's Heer Arendskerke; C. E. J. de Bordes; W. M. J. van Lutterveld; F. P. Muysken; A. Offers; P. Sanders; J. D. Santilhano.

Missouri Pacific (4% bonds)

H. M. Roelofsz; C. van Oldenborgh; L. H. J. F. van Bevervoorden tot Oldemeule; D. Lutomirski; M. Milders; D. H. W. Patijn; J. D. Schoon; G. Hijmans.

Missouri Pacific (5% bonds)

W. M. J. van Lutterveld; G. W. A. van Laer; L. R. Gratama; N. Levenkamp; F. P. Muysken; IJ. A. Schuller tot Peursum; J. J. Vierhout; J. D. Santilhano.

Missouri, Kansas & Texas (4% first mortgage bonds)

B. W. van Vloten; A. de Bijll Nachenius; C. E. J. de Bordes; L. H. J. F. van Bevervoorden tot Oldemeule; A. F. van Hall; J. van der Kooy; A. C. van Heemskerck Veeckens; A. S. van Nierop.

Missouri, Kansas & Texas (4% second mortgage bonds)

J. H. Wijsman; J. Stroeve; J. Kerkhoven; W. Marcelis; W. W. van der Meulen; C. W. Lunsingh Scheurleer; H. K. Westendorp; J. A. van Sonsbeeck.

Abbreviations of Railroad Names

AC	Arkansas Central
ACL	Atlantic Coast Line
A&C	Alabama & Chattanooga
AGW	Atlantic Great Western
AM&O	Atlantic, Mississippi & Ohio
A&P	Atlantic & Pacific
ATSF	Atchison, Topeka & Santa Fe
BH&E	Boston, Hartford & Erie
BNY&P	Buffalo, New York & Philadelphia
B&O	Baltimore & Ohio
BP&W	Buffalo, Pittsburg & Western
BT	Bush Terminal
C&A	Chicago & Atlantic
CA&C	Cleveland, Akron & Columbus
Ca&Or	California & Oregon
CalP	California Pacific
CB&Q	Chicago, Burlington & Quincy
CCC&I	Cleveland, Columbus, Cincinnati & Indianapolis
CCC&StL	Cleveland, Cincinnati, Chicago & St. Louis
C&E	Chicago & Erie
C&GT	Chicago & Grand Trunk
CGW	Chicago Great Western
CH&D	Cincinnati, Hamilton & Dayton
CM&C	Canada, Michigan & Chicago
C&ME	Chicago & Milwaukee Electric
CM&StP	Chicago, Milwaukee & St. Paul
CMV&D	Cleveland, Mount Vernon & Delaware
C&NW	Chicago & North Western

C&O	Chesapeake & Ohio
CO&SW	Chesapeake, Ohio & Southwestern
CP	Central Pacific
CR	Connecticut Railways
CRI&P	Chicago, Rock Island & Pacific
CS	Canada Southern
C&S	Colorado & Southern
C&StL	Cairo & St. Louis
CStL&NO	Chicago, St. Louis & New Orleans
CStP&KC	Chicago, St. Paul & Kansas City
C&SW	Chicago & Southwestern
D&BV	Denver & Boulder Valley
DL&W	Delaware, Lackawanna & Western
DM&FD	Des Moines & Fort Dodge
DMV	Des Moines Valley
DP	Denver Pacific
DRG	Denver & Rio Grande
DUR	Detroit United Railways
D&W	Dallas & Waco
EM	Eastern of Minnesota
EO	Eastern Oklahoma
E&P	Elizabethtown & Paducah
Erie	Erie Railway
ETV&G	East Tennessee, Virginia & Georgia
FC&P	Florida Central & Peninsular
FC&W	Florida Central & Western
FR	Florida Railroad
FR&N	Florida Railroad & Navigation
FT	Florida Transit
FT&P	Florida Transit & Peninsular
FWM&C	Fort Wayne, Muncie & Cincinnati
FWM&I	Fort Wayne, Muncie & Indianapolis
GC&S	Gilman, Clinton & Springfield
GH&H	Galveston, Houston & Henderson
GN	Great Northern
GR&I	Grand Rapids & Indiana
GTW	Grand Trunk Western
HC	Hudson Companies
HE	Havana Electric
HL&R	Helena Light & Railway
IC	Illinois Central
IM	Interborough Metropolitan
JP&M	Jacksonville, Pensacola & Mobile
KCFS&M	Kansas City, Fort Scott & Memphis

KCM&O	Kansas City, Mexico & Orient
KCOB&E	Kansas City Outer Belt & Electric
KCP&G	Kansas City, Pittsburg & Gulf
KCR&L	Kansas City Railways & Light
KCS	Kansas City Southern
KCSB	Kansas City Suburban Belt
KCS&GT	Kansas City, Shreveport & Gulf Terminal
K&MB	Kansas & Missouri Bridge
KP	Kansas Pacific
KU	Kentucky Union
L&A	Louisiana & Arkansas
L&E	Lexington & Eastern
L&JB	Louisville & Jeffersonville Bridge
L&N	Louisville & Nashville
LNO&T	Louisville, New Orleans & Texas
LS&M	Lake Superior & Mississippi
LS&MS	Lake Shore & Michigan Southern
MC	Michigan Central
MC&FD	Mason City & Fort Dodge
M&E	Morris & Essex
MKT	Missouri, Kansas & Texas
M&N	Minnesota & Northwestern
M&O	Mobile & Ohio
MoC	Montana Central
M&P	Marietta & Pittsburg
MP	Missouri Pacific
MP&C	Marietta, Pittsburg & Cleveland
MP&N	Memphis, Paducah & Northern
MS	Manila Suburban
MSSM&A	Minneapolis, Sault Sainte Marie & Atlantic
M&StL	Minneapolis & St. Louis
MStP&SSM	Minneapolis, St. Paul & Sault Sainte Marie
M&W	Missouri & Western
NC&StL	Nashville, Chattanooga & St. Louis
NM	North Missouri
NOJ&GN	New Orleans, Jackson & Great Northern
NOR	New Orleans Railways
NOT	New Orleans Terminal
NP	Northern Pacific
N&W	Norfolk & Western
NYC	New York Central
NYC&HR	New York Central & Hudson River
NYLE&W	New York, Lake Erie & Western
NYNH&H	New York, New Haven & Hartford

NYO&W	New York, Ontario & Western
NYP&O	New York, Pennsylvania & Ohio
OC	Oklahoma Central
O&C	Oregon & California
OSL	Oregon Short Line
OSL&UN	Oregon Short Line & Utah Northern
PCC&StL	Pittsburgh, Cincinnati, Chicago & St. Louis
P&E	Paducah & Elizabethtown
PFW&C	Pittsburgh, Fort Wayne & Chicago
PH&LM	Port Huron & Lake Michigan
P&M	Paducah & Memphis
PM	Pere Marquette
P&R	Philadelphia & Reading
PR	Port Royal
PR&A	Port Royal & Augusta
PRly	Peninsular Railway
PRR	Pennsylvania Railroad
RGW	Rio Grande Western
RIA&L	Rock Island, Arkansas & Louisiana
RIC	Rock Island Company of New Jersey
RRI&StL	Rockford, Rock Island & St. Louis
RR&M	Red River & Manitoba
SA&AP	San Antonio & Aransas Pass
SAL	Seaboard Air Line
SEL&T	Santiago Electric Light & Traction
SF&NP	San Francisco & North Pacific
SP	Southern Pacific
SPM	South Pacific Railroad of Missouri
SR	Southern Railway
StLA&T	St. Louis, Arkansas & Texas
StL&C	St. Louis & Cairo
StLS&A	St. Louis, Salem & Arkansas
StL&SE	St. Louis & South Eastern
StL&SF	St. Louis & San Francisco
StLSW	St. Louis South Western
StLW&W	St. Louis, Wichita & Western
StPM&M	St. Paul, Minneapolis & Manitoba
StP&P	St. Paul & Pacific
TC	Traverse City
T&NO	Texas & New Orleans
T&P	Texas & Pacific
TP&Wa	Toledo, Peoria & Warsaw
TP&We	Toledo, Peoria & Western
TStL&W	Toledo, St. Louis & Western

U&N	Utah & Northern
UP	Union Pacific
UPL&C	Union Pacific, Lincoln & Colorado
UP,SB	Union Pacific, Southern Branch (MKT)
UT	Union Terminal (Kansas City)
Wabash	Wabash Railroad
W&M	Wilmington & Manchester
WM&P	Wisconsin, Minnesota & Pacific
WNY&P	Western New York & Pennsylvania
WP	Western Pacific
WPT	Wabash Pittsburgh Terminal
WPT&W	West Penn Traction & Water
WStL&P	Wabash, St. Louis & Pacific
W&StP	Winona & St. Peter
WSS	Winston-Salem Southbound
WW	West Wisconsin

Reference Matter

Notes

The following abbreviations are used in the Notes:

AASE   Archives of the Amsterdam Stock Exchange
AE   *Amsterdamsch Effectenblad*
NAE   *Nieuw Algemeen Effectenblad*

See the sections on Manuscript Collections and Periodicals at the beginning of the Bibliography, pp. 317–18. See Appendix D for a complete list of abbreviations for the various railroads.

Please note that authors' names containing particles (Van Winter, De Vries) are listed in the Bibliography under the family name rather than the particle. For example, a citation in these notes such as

Van Winter, *Het aandeel*, . . .

will be found in the Bibliography under

Winter, P. J. van, *Het aandeel*, . . .

■ *Chapter One*

1. Today the area of the country is somewhat greater because of large-scale drainage projects. Population at present is over 15 million.

2. For the general history of the Dutch Republic a good, succinct survey is C. Wilson, *The Dutch Republic*. For its financial history, see Veenendaal, "Fiscal Crises." For economic history see Israel, *Dutch Primacy*.

3. The best survey of Dutch colonial history in English is Boxer, *The Dutch Seaborne Empire*; newer and more complete, but in Dutch, is Van Goor, *De Nederlandse Koloniën*.

4. A good survey of the later history of both the Netherlands and Belgium is Kossmann, *The Low Countries*.

5. De Jong, *Geschiedenis*, vol. 1; Buist, "Geld"; De Jonge, "Economisch Leven."

6. Ridder, *Conjunctuur-analyse*, p. 59; also Bos, "Vermogensbezitters," pp. 554–57.

7. De Jonge, "Economisch Leven," p. 55.

8. Ridder, *Conjunctuur-analyse*, pp. 64, 86; Van Tijn, *Twintig jaren*, p. 38.

9. Van Tijn, *Twintig jaren*, p. 211.

10. Van Tijn, *Amsterdam en diamant*, pp. 23–24, 42–56; Van Tijn, *Twintig jaren*, p. 234.

11. Ridder, *Conjunctuur-analyse*, pp. 66–67; Van Tijn, *Twintig jaren*, pp. 45, 51–60.

12. [Van Oosterwijk Bruyn], *Finantieele beschouwingen 1868*, pp. 6–9. For new thoughts on the availability or lack of capital for domestic enterprise see Jonker, "Lachspiegel van de vooruitgang."

13. Neal, *Financial Capitalism*, p. 179.

14. Bosch, *Nederlandse beleggingen*, p. 28.

15. Platt, *Foreign Finance*, pp. 8–10, 21–22.

16. [Van Oosterwijk Bruyn], *Nieuwe finantieele beschouwingen 1869*, pp. 13–14; Platt, *Foreign Investment*, pp. 112–14, 129.

17. Knapen, *De lange weg*; Platt, *Foreign Investment*, pp. 40–47, 67–73; [Van Oosterwijk Bruyn], *Nieuwe finantieele beschouwingen 1869*, pp. 7–9; Van Horn, "Russische schulden."

18. Platt, *Foreign Finance*, pp. 89–95; [Van Oosterwijk Bruyn], *Nieuwe finantieele beschouwingen 1869*, pp. 9–13.

19. [Van Oosterwijk Bruyn], *Nieuwe finantieele beschouwingen 1869*, p. 15.

20. Van Weede, *Indische reisherinneringen*, pp. 519–20.

21. [Van Oosterwijk Bruyn], *Nieuwe finantieele beschouwingen 1869*, p. 16. About New Granada see Herring, *History of Latin America*, pp. 501–2.

22. De Klerck, *De verarming van Nederland*, p. 54; Berghuis, *Ontstaan*, p. 84.

23. Regarding Dutch help for the United States in general see Van Winter, *Het aandeel*; also Riley, *International Government Finance*, pp. 186–90. Regarding foreign investment in America see Wilkins's invaluable *History of Foreign Investment in the United States*, especially pp. 29–37.

24. The price agreed on was $15 million, but only $11,250,000 was required to be paid in bonds; the rest consisted of claims of American citizens against the French government regarding confiscated shipping, which the U.S. government agreed to take over. Van Winter, *Het aandeel*, vol. 2, pp. 378–85.

25. Van Winter, *Het aandeel*, vol. 2, pp. 386–88; Buist, *At Spes non Fracta*, pp. 57–62, 188–90; Bosch, *Nederlandse Beleggingen*, pp. 35–36.

26. Platt, *Foreign Finance*, p. 145; Wilkins, *Foreign Investment*, pp. 53–55.

27. Dinger, *Overzicht 1851*, p. 229.

28. Ridder, *Conjunctuur-analyse*, p. 198.

29. Regarding the Holland Land Company see Evans, *The Holland Land Company*; and Van Winter, *Het aandeel*, vol. 2, pp. 223–334.

30. Van Winter, *Het aandeel*, vol. 2, pp. 192–96.

31. In financial parlance *per* means "reaching maturity in," the year of mandatory redemption of a loan.

32. Dinger, *Overzicht 1851*, pp. 214–21; Wilkins, *History of Foreign Investment*, pp. 61–72.

33. Dinger, *Overzicht 1851*, pp. 222–24; Bosch, *Beleggingen*, pp. 49–50.

34. Van Winter, *Het aandeel*, vol. 2, pp. 204–22.

35. Ibid., pp. 302, 412.

36. Ibid., pp. 415–16; Dinger, *Overzicht 1851*, p. 228; Bosch, *Nederlandse beleggingen*, p. 48.

37. Van Winter, *Het aandeel*, vol. 2, p. 412; Bosch, *Nederlandse beleggingen*, p. 51.

38. Bosch, *Nederlandse beleggingen*, p. 51; Dinger, *Overzicht 1873*, p. 608.

39. John Gamble came from Virginia to Florida and became a landowner and banker there. Schweikart, *Banking*, pp. 52, 198.

40. McGrane, *Foreign Bondholders*, pp. 223–44, 265; Winkler, *Foreign Bonds*, pp. 270–76; Dinger, *Overzicht 1851*, p. 229.

41. Van Winter, *Het aandeel*, vol. 2, p. 307.

42. Bosch, *Nederlandse beleggingen*, p. 50; Dinger, *Overzicht 1851*, pp. 229–30.

43. Van Winter, *Het aandeel*, vol. 2, pp. 413–14; McGrane, *Foreign Bondholders*, pp. 170–85, gives slightly different figures. Schweikart, *Banking*, p. 139, gives only $3 million as Hope's share.

44. Dinger, *Overzicht* 1851, pp. 225–26.

45. Pierson, "Handel en het bankwezen," pp. 182–86.

46. Dinger, *Overzicht* 1873, pp. 640–49; Bosch, *Nederlandse Beleggingen*, p. 126. In 1902 Louisiana passed a law restricting foreign participation in its banks. Wilkins, *History of Foreign Investment*, p. 458.

47. Van Winter, *Het aandeel*, vol. 2, pp. 418–19; Wilkins, *Foreign Investment*, also mentions several American banks and canal companies in which there was Dutch interest, but little or no trace of these investments has been found in Amsterdam.

48. Platt, *Foreign Finance*, pp. 146–47.

49. Wilkins, *History of Foreign Investment*, pp. 102–4. Platt, *Foreign Finance*, pp. 150–51, seems to be too low in his estimates of Dutch holdings of Union loans. He explains this as a result of the large sums locked up in Louisiana, but these did not amount to much during the period under discussion; moreover, the Louisiana Citizens Bank was paying interest regularly again.

50. Wilkins, *History of Foreign Investment*, pp. 104; Dinger, *Overzicht* 1873, pp. 592–98.

51. Bosch, *Nederlandse beleggingen*, p. 135; for the foreign share in the U.S. loans during these years see Wilkins, *History of Foreign Investment*, pp. 102–13.

52. Dinger, *Overzicht* 1873, pp. 600–602; Bosch, *Nederlandse beleggingen*, pp. 132–34.

53. McGrane, *Foreign Bondholders*, pp. 319–20; Dinger, *Overzicht* 1873, pp. 637–39.

54. Dinger, *Overzicht* 1873, p. 654; Bosch, *Nederlandse beleggingen*, p. 136.

55. Dinger, *Overzicht* 1873, pp. 652–54.

■ *Chapter Two*

1. Van Tijn, *Twintig jaren*, pp. 38–39, 209–12. For a recent survey of the development of banking in the Netherlands, see J. de Vries, "Nederlandse financiële imperium," and Wijtvliet, *Expansie en dynamiek*.

2. Rijxman, A. C. *Wertheim*, pp. 23–24, 147.

3. The brothers Isaäc Eduard (1832–85) and Abraham Louis (1839–1908) Teixeira de Mattos, members of the Netherlands nobility (*jonkheer*), operated the family firm during the 1860's and 1870's. Later Abraham Louis's son Henri Teixeira de Mattos (1867–1924) became a partner as well. *Nederland's Adelsboek* 45 (1952): pp. 314–17.

4. Brouwer, *Amsterdamsche Bank*, pp. 16–17; Wilkins, *The History*, p. 112.

5. *NAE*, 14 January 1876.

6. For the early history of Hope and Company see Buist, *At Spes non Fracta*, pp. 3–69; for the history of the Labouchère family see *Nederland's Patriciaat* 49 (1963): pp. 210–29; for that of Van Loon and Company see J. de Vries, ed., *Herinneringen en dagboek*, vol. 1, p. 151.

7. For the history of the (De Marez) Oyens family see *Nederland's Patriciaat* 72 (1988): pp. 370–80.

8. For the history of the Boissevain family see *Nederland's Patriciaat* 72 (1988): pp. 48–123; for that of Blake, Boissevain and Company see Wilkins, *The History*, p. 477.

9. For the history of the Kerkhoven family see *Nederland's Patriciaat* 35 (1949): pp. 131–41; for that of the Van Oosterwijk Bruyn family see *Nederland's Patriciaat* 4 (1913): pp. 80–81.

10. For the history of the Piek family see *Nederland's Patriciaat* 10 (1919): p. 351; for that of the Van Ogtrop family see *Nederland's Patriciaat* 37 (1951): p. 264.

11. For the history of the Hubrecht family see *Nederland's Patriciaat* 66 (1982): p. 175. Paul

François Hubrecht (1829–92), lawyer and businessman, was director of the Rotterdamsche Bank from 1863 to 1869.

12. For the history of the Bischoffsheim family see *La Grande Encyclopédie* vol. 6 (Paris, s.a.): p. 928; *Dictionnaire de Biographie Française* vol. 6 (Paris, 1954).

13. Van Tijn, *Twintig jaren*, p. 39; J. de Vries, "Nederlandse financiële imperium," p. 25. On the development of modern banking in the Netherlands, see Harthoorn, *Hoofdlijnen moderne bankwezen*; Hirschfeld, *Ontstaan moderne bankwezen*, p. 15; M. de Vries, *Tien jaren geschiedenis*; Wijtvliet, *Expansie en dynamiek*; and Kymmel, *Geschiedenis algemene banken*. For the history of the Rothschilds see R. Davis, *The English Rothschilds*.

14. Brugmans, *Begin van twee banken*, p. 55; Wijtvliet, *De overgang*.

15. Brandes de Roos, *Industrie*, vol. 1, p. 98.

16. M. de Vries, *Tien jaren geschiedenis*, pp. 22–25; Brugmans, *Begin van twee banken*, p. 56.

17. Brugmans, *Begin van twee banken*, pp. 77–106; J. de Vries, "Nederlandse Financiële Imperium," p. 28.

18. J. de Vries, "Nederlandse financiële imperium," p. 27.

19. Van Tijn, *Twintig jaren*, p. 215; M. de Vries, *Tien jaren geschiedenis*, pp. 29–33.

20. Brouwer, *Amsterdamsche Bank*; M. de Vries, *Tien jaren geschiedenis*, pp. 44–53. Frederik Salomon van Nierop was married to Emilie Regina Gompertz and thus was a relative of Wertheim, again illustrating the closely knit Amsterdam financial community.

21. Brouwer, *Amsterdamsche Bank*, p. 23.

22. C. Adler, *Jacob H. Schiff*, vol. 1, pp. 194–95.

23. Riemens, *Financiële ontwikkeling*, pp. 63–65; Santilhano, *Amerikaansche spoorwegen*, pp. ix–x.

24. *AE*, 17 June 1864.

25. *AE*, 29 January 1867.

26. Rijxman, *A. C. Wertheim*, pp. 147–49; *NAE*, 11 December 1883.

27. *NAE*, 14 January 1881.

28. *NAE*, 31 December 1880 and 25 March 1884.

29. Daggett, *Chapters*, p. 148; AASE file 81, nos. 19–28, contains correspondence between several stockbrokers and the Stock Exchange Committee on this subject; see also a printed brochure, dated 1881, on this matter in no. 28.

30. Huntington Library, Henry E. Huntington Papers HEH 1489, proxies to be sent to San Francisco, March 25, 1893; a similar list from 1895 (HEH 1490) gives substantially lower figures for Van Deventer (26,130) and Van der Veer (29,029), while Bretherton has about the same number of proxies.

31. Correspondence between the English Association and the Stock Exchange Committee, mostly dating from 1887, in AASE file 81, nos. 43–48; the figure of $23,000,000 is given in a letter of 16 March 1887, in no. 48.

32. AASE file 81 (no detailed numbering) contains articles of incorporation of the Maatschappij and correspondence with the London Company, mostly from 1897; see also minutes of the Amsterdam meeting of 2 July 1897, also in file 81, without further number.

■ Chapter Three

1. For a history of the Stock Exchange see De Iongh, *Gedenkboek 1876–1926*; J. de Vries, *Een eeuw vol effecten*; and Günst, *Trommelpapier*.

2. J. de Vries, *Een eeuw vol effecten*, pp. 45–47.

3. Regarding the provincial *Bond* see Van der Werf, *De bond*.

4. J. de Vries, *Een eeuw vol effecten*, p. 104.

5. For the hectic days of 1914 see ibid., pp. 130–40.

6. About the buildings see Weismann, *De beurs te Amsterdam*; De Iongh, *Gedenkboek*, pp. 78–79.

7. Spanjaard, *Nederlandsche diplomatieke*, pp. 174, 224–32.

8. Spanjaard, *Nederlandsche diplomatieke*, pp. 207–9, 356. This may be the case mentioned by Schweikart, *Banking in the South*, p. 304, regarding $800,000 in silver placed in the safety of the Dutch consulate in 1862 and seized by Union troops.

9. Minister of Foreign Affairs to Amsterdam Stock Exchange Committee, The Hague, 13 March 1867, in AASE file 26 (Atlantic & Great Western), no. 18.

10. N. G. Pierson to his wife, 19 July 1870, in Van Maarseveen, ed., *Briefwisseling van N. G. Pierson*, vol. 1, p. 450.

11. Croockewit, "Amerikaansche schetsen," p. 91; the list of Dutch consulates has been taken from the annual *Staats Almanak*.

12. NAE, 5 November 1878; De Fremery, *Californië*, vol. 1, pp. 48–50. James de Fremery (1826–99) founded the merchant firm of Gildemeester, De Fremery and Company in San Francisco in 1849 (which operated after 1855 under the name De Fremery and Company). After his return to the Netherlands in 1891 he acquired a reputation as editor of medieval records of the county of Holland. *Nieuw Nederlandsch Biografisch Woordenboek*, vol. 3, p. 419. Leiden: A. W. Sijthoff, 1914.

13. Van Minnen, *Yankees onder de zeespiegel*, p. 97.

14. Ibid., pp. 102–3.

15. For a history of the Netherlands South African Railway and Dutch influence in the Transvaal see Van Winter, *Onder Krugers Hollanders*. Regarding entrepreneurial imperialism see Davis and Huttenback, *Mammon and the Pursuit of Empire*; and Davis and Wilburn, eds., *Railway Imperialism*.

16. Riemens, *Financiële ontwikkeling*, p. 67; De Jong, *Geschiedenis*, vol. 1, pp. 336–48.

17. William A. Osborn to the president of the Amsterdam Stock Exchange, 22 September 1864, in AASE file 67, no. 2.

18. Dinger, *Overzicht 1873*, pp. 662–63; *AE*, 23 February, 18 and 19 October 1864.

19. Bosch, *De Nederlandse beleggingen*, pp. 20–21.

20. Kymmel, *Geschiedenis algemene banken*, p. 27.

21. Bosch, *De Nederlandse beleggingen*, pp. 8–10. Regarding capitalization of Dutch domestic railways see Van den Broeke, *Financiën en financiers*; Jonker, "Lachspiegel van de vooruitgang."

22. For the history of the investment funds in Holland see Chapter 15 and Berghuis, *Ontstaan en ontwikkeling*.

23. Bosch, *Nederlandse beleggingen*, pp. 14–15.

24. Kymmel, *Geschiedenis algemene banken*, pp. 51, 71, 86–87, 189; Jongman, *Nederlandse geldmarkt*, pp. 149–60.

25. Jongman, *Nederlandse geldmarkt*, p. 153.

26. Ibid., pp. 158–62.

27. Capefigue, *Histoire*, vol. 3, pp. 75–76.

28. Brayer, *William Blackmore*, vol. 2, p. 335; Lewis, *America's Stake*, pp. 457–60. For the Scots see W. G. Kerr, *Scottish Capital*.

29. Joh. de Vries, *Een eeuw vol effecten*, p. 103. For the affair in Barneveld see Ramshorst and Crebolder, *Sporen door de Gelderse Vallei*, p. 30.

30. De Valk and Van Faassen, eds., *Dagboeken*, p. 227.

31. Kymmel, *Geschiedenis algemene banken*, pp. 30, 189.

32. Wilkins, *History of Foreign Investment*, pp. 216–18.

33. Henry B. Ledyard, president of the Michigan Central, to Charles F. Cox, vice president of the Canada Southern, 12 June 1888, quoted in Cochran, *Railroad Leaders*, p. 403.

■ *Chapter Four*

1. Dinger, *Overzicht* 1851.

2. Van Oosterwijk Bruyn, *Amerikaansche fondsen als geldbelegging*. His *Finantieele beschouwingen* was published anonymously in Amsterdam in 1868. His *Nieuwe finantieele beschouwingen* was published in 1869 under the initials W. v. O. B. Willem van Oosterwijk Bruyn (1829–1903) and his younger brother Pieter Adolf (1837–1900) were partners of Kerkhoven and Company, just as their father, Jacob van Oosterwijk Bruyn (1794–1876), more famous as a poet and writer, had been before them. See *Nederland's Patriciaat* 4 (1913), pp. 80–81.

3. Platt, *Foreign Finance*, pp. 92–96.

4. Weeveringh, *Noord-Amerikaansche spoorwegfondsen*, Amsterdam, 1870; the second edition under the same title was published in Haarlem in 1887.

5. Den Tex, *Amerikaansche spoorwegen*; published in 1873.

6. Pik, *Amerikaansche spoorwegwaarden*; published in Groningen in 1879.

7. Santilhano, *Amerikaansche spoorwegen*; published in 1884. Van Oss, *American Railroads as Investments*, 1893; this title was published jointly by American, British, and Dutch publishers. See also Van Oss, *Amerikaansche spoorwegwaarden*, 1903.

8. On the economic and/or financial press in England and the Netherlands see Vissink, *Economic and Financial Reporting*, pp. 122–32.

9. *NAE*, 27 June 1873.

10. Gevers Deynoot, *Aanteekeningen*, pp. 137–38; he had visited the Dutch East Indies on an an earlier trip in 1862 and published an account of that journey in his *Herinneringen* of 1864.

11. Bancroft, *Geschiedenis der Vereenigde Staten van Noord-Amerika*, of which the first and only volume came out in Holland in 1868.

12. Rae, *Westward by Rail*; Blackmore, *Colorado*. Both books were favorably reviewed by Dozy in *De Gids* 35 (1871).

13. See, for example, Dozy's review of G. J. Chester's *Transatlantic Sketches in the West Indies, South America, Canada and the United States* in *De Gids* 34 (1870).

14. Verschuur, *Door Amerika*; published in 1877.

15. Cohen Stuart, *Zes maanden*, p. 76.

16. Ibid., pp. 186–88.

17. Ralph Waldo Emerson, "The Young American," quoted in Marshall, "Steel Wheels," p. 39; see also Ward, *Railroads and the Character*, pp. 38–40.

18. Marshall, "Steel Wheels," p. 39; Cohen Stuart, *Zes maanden*, p. 276.

19. Marshall, "Steel Wheels," p. 41; Cohen Stuart, *Zes maanden*, p. 290. For Thoreau's less favorable opinions on railroads see Ward, *Railroads and the Character*, pp. 31–32. N. J. den Tex, already mentioned above, reviewed Cohen Stuart's book in *De Gids* 38 (1875): pp. 367–73; he is full of praise for its optimistic but honest description of America and considered the work a good antidote against all negative reports by those "disappointed persons, who had lost their fortune in reckless speculation in American rails."

20. Van 't Lindenhout, *Zes weken tusschen de wielen*, p. 234.

21. Wijnaendts Francken, *Door Amerika*, pp. 87, 191–99.

22. Tutein Nolthenius, *Nieuwe wereld,* was first published in Haarlem in 1900; the second edition, with an epilogue, came out in 1902.

23. Van Reigersberg Versluys, *Amerika,* pp. 38–39.

24. Boissevain, *Van 't Noorden,* vol. 1, pp. 116–20.

25. [Van Oosterwijk Bruyn], *Finantieele beschouwingen, 1868,* pp. 4–6; Bosch, *Nederlandse beleggingen,* p. 141.

26. Boissevain, *Van 't Noorden,* vol. 2, p. 325.

27. Van Hinte, *Netherlanders in America,* pp. 322–28.

28. Ibid., p. 539.

29. Croockewit, "Amerikaansche schetsen." For a history of the Dutch emigration to the United States in general see Van Hinte, *Netherlanders in America.* For the movement toward Michigan in the 1840's see Stokvis, *De Nederlandse Trek.* Adriaan Eliza Croockewit (1839–1917) was an Amsterdam lawyer and judge and was related to Gustaaf Adolf Croockewit (1833–1910), director of several Amsterdam shipping companies. See *Nederland's Patriciaat* 72 (1988): p. 190.

30. De Veer, "Ons Hollanders in Michigan."

31. *Van Oss' Effectenboek* 1909, p. 1298.

32. *AE,* 11 December 1866.

33. J. H. Kloos, *Minnesota*; published in 1867.

34. Van Schevichaven, *Minnesota*; published in 1872.

35. Knuppe, *Land en dollars*; published in 1883.

36. Martin, *James J. Hill,* p. 139.

37. For the Dutch involvement in the Maxwell Land Grand Company see Veenendaal, "'Dutch' Towns."

38. Van Schevichaven, *Minnesota,* p. 73. Mickelson, *Northern Pacific,* does not mention Itman, although he does note some promotional activities on the part of Jay Cooke in Holland.

39. Den Tex, "Naar Amerika," p. 422.

40. Gerstäcker, *Naar Amerika*; Den Tex, "Naar Amerika," p. 422.

41. Van Hinte, *Netherlanders in America,* p. 704.

42. N. G. Pierson to his father, 17 August 1864, in Van Maarseveen, *Briefwisseling,* vol. 1, p. 190.

43. On the financial history of the Dutch railways see Van den Broeke, *Financiën en financiers.*

44. I am indebted for this information to Dr. Maureen A. Jung of Sacramento, California, who is preparing a book about the early mining companies in California.

45. Trollope, *North America,* vol. 1, p. 220.

46. Ibid., pp. 195–96.

47. Trollope, *The Way We Live Now,* p. 59; Albert Grant (1830–99) was the Irish-born son of W. Gottheimer, partner in a foreign "fancy" business (importer of luxury goods) in London. Grant actively promoted many railroad schemes in England and abroad and proved to be very adept at inducing small investors such as clergymen, widows, and spinsters to sink their money in his dubious schemes. He became an Italian baron in 1868 and died in poverty. *Dictionary of National Biography,* Supplement vol. 2 (London, 1901), p. 338.

48. Pike, *Zuid-Carolina*; translated by B. Scholten and published in the Netherlands in 1875. The original title is *The Prostrate State: South Carolina under Negro Government.*

49. For the history of the Port Royal railroad see Prince, *Atlantic Coast Line Railroad,* pp. 85–86; Stover, *Railroads of the South,* pp. 267–70.

50. H., "Het Maatschappelijk Kansspel," pp. 267–82.

51. "Een Makelaar in Effekten," in *De groote bankgoochelaar Langrand Dumonceau*, pp. 23–24; published in 1870.

52. Huizenga, *Amerikaansche spoorwegtoestanden*; published between 1873 and 1875, with an afterword, *Nog iets over de "sporen,"* published in 1875. Huizenga became editor of *De Nieuwe Financier* in 1875.

53. De Klerck, *De verarming*.

54. De Klerck, *De verarming*, pp. 30–31, 51, 56–57.

■ *Chapter Five*

1. This chapter is largely based on Ripley, *Railroads*; Sakolski, *American Railroad Economics*; Bonbright, *Railroad Capitalization*; Cleveland and Powell, *Railroad Promotion*; Chandler, *Patterns*; D. R. Adler, *British Investment*; and Wilkins, *History of Foreign Investment*, pp. 190–228.

2. Ward, *J. Edgar Thomson*, pp. 74–75.

3. Ripley, *Railroads*, p. 10.

4. Ulmer, *Capital in Transportation*, p. 169.

5. Cleveland and Powell, *Railroad Promotion*, pp. 286–87.

6. Mercer, *Railroads*, p. 3. For state aid to railroads see Goodrich, *Government Promotion*; Pierce, *Railroads of New York*.

7. Ripley, *Railroads*, pp. 143–45.

8. Ibid., p. 142.

9. Ulmer, *Capital in Transportation*, pp. 155–57.

10. For the Boston influence in general see Johnson and Supple, *Boston Capitalists*. For John Murray Forbes see J. L. Larson, *Bonds of Enterprise*.

11. Quoted from Johnson and Supple, *Boston Capitalists*, p. 101.

12. Chandler, *Patterns*, pp. 248–61.

13. Wilkins, *History of Foreign Investment*, p. 76.

14. Ibid., p. 198, quoting figures given by Leland Jenks.

15. See also Platt, *Foreign Finance*, pp. 155–61.

16. Wilkins, *History of Foreign Investment*, pp. 223–28.

17. Swain, *Economic Aspects*; Ripley, *Railroads*, pp. 371–87.

18. Klein, *Life and Legend*, pp. 329–30, 348–50.

■ *Chapter Six*

1. Dilts, *The Great Road*, pp. 238–39.

2. See Chapter 1.

3. For the history of the Illinois Central see Corliss, *Main Line of Mid-America*; Stover, *History of the Illinois Central*. For the promoters behind the IC see Corliss, *Trails to Rails*. About David Neal see Johnson and Supple, *Boston Capitalists*, pp. 136–40.

4. It is not quite clear which Labouchère Neal saw. Samuel Pierre Labouchère (1778–1867) was a partner in Hope and Company, as was his son Henri Matthieu (1807–69). *Nederland's Patriciaat* 49 (1963): pp. 210–11.

5. Brownson, *History*, p. 60. Charles Devaux, in partnership with M. Uziëlli, also of London, had taken up 14,000 shares (£20 each) of the Dutch Rhenish Railway in 1845, and was also one of the concessionaires of that company. Van den Broeke, *Financiën en financiers*, pp. 63–64, 256–57.

6. For the Schuyler fraud see Harlow, *Steelways*, pp. 186–88.

7. *AE*, 29 February 1856. In later issues regular quotations of these bonds have been found.

8. *AE*, 17 February, 17 April, and 1 May 1857; Dinger, *Overzicht* 1873, pp. 659–61.

9. Brownson, *History*, pp. 41–42; *AE*, 17 July 1857, 16 March and 22 June 1858.

10. William Osborn to George Peabody, 30 September 1869, in Cochran, *Railroad Leaders*, p. 425; also Stover, *Railroads of the South*, pp. 184–85. About Dulman's appointment see Mercer, *E. H. Harriman*, p. 28.

11. Gevers Deynoot, *Aanteekeningen*, pp. 137–38.

12. Notices by B. H. Schroeder and Company in *AE*, 18 December 1858 and 21 June 1859; also D. R. Adler, *British Investment*, p. 67, where no mention is made of the Dutch connection. The house of Bernhard Hinrich Schroeder in Amsterdam was closely related to the much more important house of J. Henry Schröder of London, and they often acted together. Roberts, *Schroders*, pp. 61–62, and Appendix I(ii).

13. Harlow, *The Road*, pp. 213–32; Gates, *Illinois Central*, p. 70. For the Michigan Central locomotive "Foreigner" see Moshein and Rothfus, "Rogers Locomotives," p. 13.

14. *AE*, 27 October 1857 and 9 February 1858. For Hope and Company's investment fund, see Chapter 15.

15. Dinger, *Overzicht* 1873, pp. 732–34; AASE file 110. Oewel requested inclusion of the MC certificates in the price lists only in July 1871, after a sufficient number had been sold.

16. Loman, *Supplement*, pp. 234–35; Pik, *Amerikaansche spoorwegwaarden*, pp. 110–14.

17. *Van Oss' Effectenboek* 1903, p. 517, and editions of 1924, 1934, and 1940.

18. Burgess and Kennedy, *Centennial History*, pp. 64–68; Thompson is not mentioned by D. R. Adler, *British Investment*, during these years. For more on Thomson see Ward, *J. Edgar Thomson*, p. 11.

19. Hungerford, *Men of Erie*, p. 143; Mott, *Between the Ocean*, pp. 115–18. Charles Moran (1811–95) was later (1884) the sole owner of the narrow-gauge Nevada, California & Oregon railroad; see Myrick, *Railroads of Nevada*, vol. 1, pp. 350–51.

20. Mott, *Between the Ocean*, pp. 128–29.

21. About the Atlantic & Great Western see Hungerford, *Men of Erie*, pp. 180–99; Flint, *Railroads of the United States*, pp. 191–203. For McHenry see D. R. Adler, *British Investment*, pp. 100–103. About Peto's role see Joby, *Railway Builders*, p. 113; Jenks, *Migration of British Capital*, pp. 255–58. About the early A&GW bonds on the Dutch market see *AE*, 22 January 1864; for Levita's announcement see *AE*, 30 March 1864. The quote about McHenry from the *New York Herald* is in Hungerford, p. 190.

22. Oberholtzer, *Jay Cooke*, vol. 2, p. 150.

23. Chandler, *The Visible Hand*, p. 155.

24. About Palmer see Anderson, *William Jackson Palmer*. For a history of the Denver & Rio Grande see Athearn, *Rebel of the Rockies*; Hilton, *American Narrow Gauge Railroads*, pp. 344–52.

25. About William Bell see Athearn, *Westward the Briton*; and *Rebel of the Rockies*, pp. 19–20.

26. Bell, *New Tracks*; Athearn, *Rebel of the Rockies*, pp. 28–29. D. R. Adler, *British Investment*, makes no mention of any bond issue of the Denver & Rio Grande being introduced in London in these years.

27. Fisher, *A Builder of the West*, p. 156.

28. Brayer, *William Blackmore*, vol. 2, pp. 44–50; Fisher, *A Builder of the West*, p. 195; *NAE*, 28 February 1871; and Dinger, *Overzicht* 1873, pp. 776–77. Oewel's commission is in Brayer, vol. 2, pp. 100–101.

29. *NAE*, 17 November 1871; O. M. Wilson, *Denver and Rio Grande Project*, p. 12.

30. Brayer, *William Blackmore*, vol. 2, p. 66. Brayer's (or Blackmore's) arithmetic seems to be wrong: the net total comes to only 55.5 percent.

31. Edward M. McCook to Samuel M. L. Barlow, Denver, 27 July 1871, in Huntington Library, Barlow Papers, box 76, 11.

32. Dinger, *Overzicht* 1873, pp. 792–95; see also Veenendaal, "'Dutch' Towns," pp. 315–22.

33. Athearn, *Rebel of the Rockies*, p. 37; O. M. Wilson, *Denver and Rio Grande Project*, p. 26; Brayer, *William Blackmore*, vol. 2, pp. 173–74; and Fisher, *A Builder of the West*, p. 246.

34. Beadle, *The Undeveloped West*, p. 443; also Athearn, *Rebel of the Rockies*, p. 34. Ten Kate, *Reizen en onderzoekingen*, p. 310.

35. Parsons to Weetjen, chairman of the Amsterdam Stock Exchange, telegram dated Paris 21 July 1873, and note of 4 August 1873, in AASE file 8, no. 5A.

36. A report of Warren's visit to Amsterdam is in *NAE*, 21 April 1874; see also Loman, *Supplement*, pp. 284–85.

37. *NAE* of 28 July and 14 August 1874.

38. G. M. Boissevain to Mahone, 2 January 1875, draft in AASE file 14, no. 23.

39. For a history of the Kansas City, Pittsburg & Gulf see Veenendaal, "The Kansas City Southern"; for a biography of Stilwell, see Bryant, *Arthur E. Stilwell*.

40. About S. F. van Oss see Veenendaal, "The Dutch Connection."

■ Chapter Seven

1. F. W. Stevens, *Beginnings*, pp. 205–7.

2. Van Winter, *Het aandeel*, vol. 2, p. 412.

3. Van Winter, *Het aandeel*, vol. 2, p. 227; Pierce, *Railroads of New York*, p. 15.

4. Pierce, *Railroads of New York*, p. 206.

5. Shaw, "Profitability," p. 61.

6. Shaw, "Profitability," p. 65.

7. Gunnarsson, *The Story*; Burgess and Kennedy, *Centennial History*, pp. 129–34; Alexander, *On the Main Line*; Stover, *Iron Roads*, p. 54.

8. Frederik Willem Oewel (1826–83), son of Johann Andreas Georg Oewel (died 1855), was probably of German origin, to judge by the name of his father, and started his career as a grocer in Amsterdam before he went into the stockbroking business. In 1860 Frederik Willem married Clara Catharina Schaap (1843–1902), and they had one son, Frederik Willem, Jr. (1867–1925). Frederik Willem Oewel, Sr., had an older brother—Johan Andreas George, who settled in Wytheville, Virginia, in 1872—on the Atlantic, Mississippi & Ohio Railroad. F. W. Oewel is mentioned as a partner of Wertheim and Gompertz until 1881–82. Rijxman, *A. C. Wertheim*, p. 147, and data from the Centraal Bureau voor Genealogie, The Hague.

9. Notice by Oewel in *NAE* of 30 July 1872.

10. Advertisement for the A&GW 8% debentures by Gebr. Boissevain and Gebr. Teixeira de Mattos in *AE* of 29 November 1864.

11. Benjamin Moran (relation of Charles Moran of the Erie?) to Thomas H. Dudley, London, 4 December 1865, in Huntington Library, Dudley Papers DU 3081.

12. *AE* of 29 May and 15 December 1864; also Dinger, *Overzicht* 1873, pp. 668–72.

13. Report of meeting of Bond, Debentures, and Shareholders, London, 22 October 1867, in AASE file 26, no. 54. Pik, *Amerikaansche spoorwegwaarden*, pp. 14–15; Oewel in *NAE*, 23 September 1870.

14. Jenks, *Migration of British Capital*, p. 260.

15. D. R. Adler, *British Investment*, pp. 106–9; notices in *AE*, 10 and 29 January, 5 February, 15 March, and 17 April 1867. Papers of the Dutch A&GW committee in AASE file 26, nos. 1–16.

16. *AE*, 23 July and 8 October 1867. Oewel's report, dated April 1867, in AASE file 26, no. 29. McHenry was described there as sanguine and extravagant, needing a quiet and solid person next to him. A copy of the report of the Committee of Investigation, 1867, is also in AASE file 26.

17. Minister of Foreign Affairs to Stock Exchange Committee, 13 March 1867, in AASE file 26, no. 18.

18. Correspondence about McClellan's appointment is in Huntington Library, Barlow Papers; see McClellan to Barlow, Vichy (France), 3 June 1867, in BW 63, vol. 1.

19. James McHenry to S. L. M. Barlow, London, 5 March 1870, in Huntington Library, Barlow Papers BW 72, no. 22. D. R. Adler, *British Investment*, pp. 112–14. See Oewel's plan in Dinger, *Overzicht* 1873, pp. 680–81; the English plan is on pp. 681–82, and in *NAE*, 24 and 28 May 1870.

20. Notices in *NAE*, 21 June and 23 September 1870; Dinger, *Overzicht* 1873, pp. 682–83.

21. Bunge, Burlage and Company to Barlow, New York, 22 July 1869, in Huntington Library, Barlow Papers BW 69. The letter was signed by Jacob F. de Neufville.

22. Correspondence between Bischoffsheim and Goldschmidt, A&GW Rly Official Scheme of Reorganization, London, and McClellan, Thurman and Butler, trustees, about the Oewel certificates, 22 January, 12, 21, and 26 February, and 14 March 1872, in Huntington Library, Barlow Papers, BW 78.

23. Announcement by a "well informed firm" in *NAE*, 22 March 1872.

24. Details in Loman, *Supplement*, pp. 200–204; also notices in *NAE*, 2 December 1879 and 27 April 1880.

25. *NAE*, 27 May and 30 July 1871; Dinger, *Overzicht* 1873, pp. 765–66.

26. Corliss, *Main Line*, p. 268. Notice in *NAE*, 19 September 1876; also Pik, *Amerikaansche spoorwegwaarden*, pp. 134–36. Details of the reorganization also in *NAE*, 30 September 1879.

27. Corliss, *Main Line*, pp. 261–66; Dinger, *Overzicht* 1873, pp. 766–67. Notice about the introduction of the bonds by Oewel in *NAE*, 26 April 1872; notice in *NAE*, 16 May 1876, on the reorganization.

28. Annual report of the Administratie Kantoor van Amerikaansche Spoorwegwaarden of Wertheim and Gompertz and partners, in *NAE*, 5 November 1878.

29. Brayer, *William Blackmore*, vol. 2, p. 151.

30. Van Motz, *Colorado*, was published in 1874. For Van Motz himself see Brayer, *William Blackmore*, vol. 2, p. 229.

31. *NAE*, 28 February 1871; Dinger, *Overzicht* 1873, pp. 776–77.

32. Brayer, *William Blackmore*, vol. 1.

33. *NAE*, 21 January 1871; Brayer, *William Blackmore*, vol. 1, pp. 86, 91–92.

34. See Talbot and Hobart, *Biographical Dictionary* 1885, p. 214.

35. Brayer, *William Blackmore*, vol. 1, pp. 96–97.

36. For Oewel's commission see Brayer, *William Blackmore*, vol. 2, pp. 100–101.

37. Nicolaas Jacob den Tex (1836–99), attorney in Amsterdam and later director of a large shipping firm there. He had married Hester Boissevain (1842–1914), of the famous banking family, and his elder brother Cornelis Jacob Arnold den Tex was burgomaster of Amsterdam from 1868 to 1879. *Nieuw Nederlandsch Biografisch Woordenboek* 4 (Leiden, 1918), p. 1304.

38. Mickelson, *Northern Pacific*, p. 11.

39. Oberholtzer, *Jay Cooke*, vol. 2, pp. 217–20.

40. Den Tex's "Naar Amerika" came out in *De Gids* in 1874; one year earlier he had published his guide for investors, *Amerikaansche spoorwegen*.

41. Hidy, "Dutch Investor in Minnesota," p. 154.

42. Notices in *NAE* of 29 June and 30 July 1875 and 14 January 1876. Agreement, dated 1 March 1876, in AASE file 8, no. 55. Also notice in *NAE* of 5 May 1876.

43. Printed report (in Dutch) by G. D. l'Huilier, a French engineer sent out by Meyer, dated January 1874, in AASE file 8, no. 14. Croockewit's opinion in *NAE* of 15 and 22 December 1874. Gustaaf Adolf Croockewit (1833–1910) came from a family of sugar refiners and himself was a director of a large Amsterdam steamship company. His cousin was Adriaan Eliza Croockewit, whom we have encountered as a writer on the United States. *Nederland's Patriciaat* 72 (1988), pp. 180 and 190.

44. *NAE*, 5 May 1876.

45. *Proposed Plan of Reorganization*, dated November 1889, and Dutch translation of same, dated 27 November 1889, in AASE file 8, nos. 230 and 231.

46. *NAE*, 19 January 1877, gives the minutes of the Amsterdam meeting.

47. Galton had inspected the American railroads already in 1857 and published his findings in his *Report to the Lords*.

48. Short notice about Galton's and De Marez Oyens's findings in *NAE*, 12 May 1877.

49. William K. Ackerman, then president of IC, to H. J. de Marez Oyens, 8 May 1878, about the ridiculously low rates charged by other roads for hauling grain to the East. Cochran, *Railroad Leaders*, p. 239.

50. William H. Osborn, then president of the Chicago, St. Louis & New Orleans, to William K. Ackerman, 30 December 1880. Cochran, *Railroad Leaders*, p. 426.

51. Notices in *NAE* of 4 September 1885 and 15 January 1886.

52. Jacobus Wertheim (1827–86), an Amsterdam lawyer since 1851 and substitute judge there since 1867. *Nederland's Patriciaat* 72 (1988), p. 495.

53. English report to MP&C bondholders, dated 9 August 1877, in AASE file 33, no. 20. Notice in *NAE* of 16 January 1877, and correspondence of Francis Pavy with the Amsterdam Stock Exchange in the summer of 1877 in file 33. Also Berlin and Hymans to Stock Exchange, 29 August 1877, in file 33, no. 59.

54. Loman, *Supplement*, p. 285; *NAE* of 9 March 1880. Wertheim's report in AASE file 33, no. 130.

55. Hymans and Sons to Stock Exchange, 17 May 1881, in AASE file 33, no. 204. Pik (1879) and Weeveringh (1887) do not mention the Marietta & Pittsburg loan.

56. Klein, *Union Pacific*, vol. 1, pp. 651–52.

57. For the several reorganization schemes that did not come to fruition see Trottman, *History*, pp. 252–61; Daggett, *Railroad Reorganization*, pp. 244–50. About the condition of the UP and its prospects see S. F. van Oss, "The Union Pacific," in *Supplement to the Stock Exchange*, 21 October 1893, copy in AASE file 62, no. 38.

58. Klein, *Union Pacific*, vol. 2, pp. 20–22; Athearn, *Union Pacific Country*, p. 371.

59. Report of meetings of this association for 1894 in AASE file 62, nos. 44, 50, and 51. Correspondence between A. A. H. Boissevain and other members of association in "Union Pacific Copie Boek," found in AASE, but without any further number.

60. A. A. H. Boissevain to Stock Exchange Board, 5 September 1908, in AASE file 745, no. 7F.

61. In financial circles the Atchison, Topeka & Santa Fe Railroad was always known as the Atchison, while to railroad enthusiasts the company is best known as the Santa Fe.

62. Circular of Hope and Company dated 31 May 1892, in AASE file 111, no. 32B.

63. Request by Hope and Company for inclusion of the 6% notes, dated 15 November 1893,

in AASE file 111, no. 40. See also Waters, *Steel Trails*, pp. 195, 203. Details about the guarantee fund notes in Daggett, *Railroad Reorganization*, p. 203.

64. For details of the reorganization see Bryant, *History*, pp. 164–68; Waters, *Steel Trails*, pp. 205–19; and Daggett, *Railroad Reorganization*, pp. 210–16. A copy of Little's printed report, in AASE file 111, no. 57. In no. 61 is a copy of the printed report of Robert Moore, consulting engineer of St. Louis, on the condition of the physical plant of the Santa Fe and its subsidiaries.

65. Printed plan of reorganization (in Dutch) with covering letter by Hope and Company dated 10 April 1895, in AASE file 111A, no. 3. The details of the conversion have been taken from this plan; they are also given by Bryant, *History*, pp. 167–68.

66. The figures of the conversion given by Hope are taken from a list dated 13 June 1895, and numbered 5 among papers in a separate envelope in AASE file 111. In no. 98 is another list with generally the same figures for the Dutch holdings.

67. *Biografisch Woordenboek van Nederland*, vol. 2 (Amsterdam, 1985), pp. 413–14.

68. Veenendaal, "The Dutch Connection," pp. 254–58.

69. *Biografisch Woordenboek van Nederland*, vol. 1 (The Hague, 1980), pp. 389–90; also Veenendaal, "Gerrit Middelberg."

70. Veenendaal, "Railroads, Oil, and Dutchmen."

71. Veenendaal, "Guilders for Gold."

72. Jonkheer Louis den Beer Poortugael (born 1865), nobleman-banker and partner of Oppenheim and Van Till; his sister Catharina Louisa was married to Cornelis E., Baron van Till, one of the other partners of the firm.

■ *Chapter Eight*

1. Undated and unsigned article from *The Times*, probably before 1878, quoted from Brayer, *William Blackmore*, vol. 2, p. 283.

2. Wilkins, *History of Foreign Investment*, p. 97; D. R. Adler, *British Investment*, pp. 172–75.

3. A partial list is given by De Iongh, *Gedenkboek 1876–1926*, pp. 113–23, where 30 such Dutch committees for American railroads are mentioned before 1915. A complete list is given here in Appendix C.

4. D. R. Adler, *British Investment*, pp. 178–79.

5. Jean Charles Gérard Pollones (d. 1909) was one of the best known notaries public in Amsterdam, specializing in deals involving the sale of securities.

6. Request for an MKT committee in a letter from Mesdag and Sons, brokers in Groningen, to Stock Exchange Committee, 14 March 1874, in AASE file 8, no. 15; Pollones to Stock Exchange Committee, 24 November 1874, in no. 36.

7. Notices in *NAE* of 28 October 1873, and 13 February, 29 March, and 6 April 1877.

8. Notice about the German committee in *NAE,* 1 April 1873.

9. *NAE*, 20 February, 6 July, and 18 December 1877, and 1 March 1878; press cuttings from the Amsterdam *Algemeen Handelsblad*, July 1877, in AASE file 14, no numbers.

10. Accounts of the Dutch AM&O committee, 14 August 1883, in AASE file 14, no number.

11. Greenberg, *Financiers and Railroads*, pp. 116–30; Dinger, *Overzicht* 1873, pp. 778–79; notice in *NAE* of 17 December 1873.

12. Cohen Stuart, *Zes maanden in Amerika*, p. 267.

13. Loman, *Supplement*, pp. 267–68; *NAE*, 3 March 1874. See also Appendix B for details.

14. Notices in *NAE* of 24 July and 25 August 1885, and printed circular, July 1885, in AASE file 135, no. 6B.

15. Dinger, *Overzicht* 1873, pp. 777–78.

16. Loman, *Supplement*, pp. 280–82; *NAE*, 16 December 1879, and 27 February, 13 April, and 21 December 1880. AASE file 46, no. 16A, also gives details of the conversion.

17. *NAE*, 4 July and 12 August 1884.

18. AASE file 46, nos. 18, 20, and 21B, give details of the results achieved by the committee.

19. Joseph Price to Stock Exchange Committee, 16 January 1884, in AASE file 116, no. 13.

20. Winslow to Price, 24 January 1884, in AASE file 116, no. 17.

21. Wertheim and Gompertz to Stock Exchange Committeee, 8 February 1884, and report of subsequent meeting, in AASE file 116, no. 19.

22. Notice in *NAE*, 5 August 1884, and printed report of Dutch committee, Amsterdam, 29 July 1884, in AASE file 116.

23. Dutch committee to Stock Exchange Committee, February 1885, in AASE file 116, no. 35.

24. Athearn, *Rebel of the Rockies*, p. 149. Notices about the formation of a committee in *NAE* of 1 August and 12 September 1884; minutes of meeting of committee, 2 July 1884, in AASE file 35, no. 75.

25. Tromp's report has not been found in the archives of the Amsterdam Stock Exchange, although a copy must have been deposited there. See also Athearn, *Rebel of the Rockies*, pp. 150–51.

26. Notices of Dutch committee 23 April 1886 and 28 February 1887 in AASE file 35, nos. 111 and 112. For details of the conversion of the several securities see Appendix B.

27. Announcement by Piek in *NAE*, 11 December 1885; minutes of the meeting of the 5-percent general mortgage holders in *NAE*, 22 December 1885.

28. A brochure entitled "Mededeelingen van het comité tot waarneming der belangen van de houders van 6pct eerste hypotheek-obligatiën ten laste der Chicago & Atlantic Spoorweg-Mij" (Report of the 6% C&A Rly. Bondholders Committee) in AASE file 127, no. 0, gives details of the procedures of the committee. The certificates were included in the price lists as of 22 November 1884.

29. Details of the purchase of the second mortgage bonds by Oyens in a printed circular, dated 21 October 1890, in AASE file 127, no. 30; a printed circular, dated 1 May 1890, with details of the fund in no. 28B.

30. Details of the activities of the committee in a letter to the Stock Exchange, dated 23 March 1891, in AASE file 127, no. 43.

31. *NAE*, 4 September 1885.

32. *NAE*, 15 January 1886.

33. AASE file 114, nos. 15 and 18, contains a list of those present or represented at the meeting of 31 October 1899.

34. AASE file 223, no. 1C, holds the Dutch prospectus of this loan. For a history of the Chicago Great Western, see Grant, *Corn Belt*.

35. Details of the conversion in AASE file 223, nos. 6A and B. Hope and Company to Stock Exchange Board, 30 January 1890, in no. 9.

36. Printed circular of Hope and Company in AASE file 223, no. 13C; also Grant, *Corn Belt*, pp. 32–34.

37. D. R. Adler, *British Investment*, p. 176; Klein, *Great Richmond Terminal*, pp. 135–42.

38. AASE file 247, no. 1A, is the request for inclusion in the price lists by Hijmans, dated 15 October 1888; nos. 4 and 4A hold the Dutch prospectus of the loan and Thors's request for inclusion, 2 May 1890. File 247 is marked East Tennessee, Virginia & Georgia, but also holds the later Southern Railway papers. Usually a new file would be opened when a company reorganized under a different name.

39. Minutes of meeting of 26 January 1893, in AASE file 247, no. 8.

40. Hijmans to Stock Exchange Committee, 23 January 1893, and circular letter of protective committee, 24 June 1893, in AASE file 247, nos. 9 and 14.

41. There is some confusion about the terms of the conversion: if the Dutch-held Extension bonds were indeed converted into ETV&G consols, they should have been exchanged dollar for dollar for new Southern Railway 5-percent bonds under the Morgan plan, according to the table given by Klein, *Great Richmond Terminal*, pp. 274–75. As the later Dutch sources clearly show that the Dutch ETV&G bonds were converted 25 percent into bonds and 80 percent into preferred shares, the conversion into ETV&G consols must have been annulled or may never have taken place at all.

42. Circular letters of the protective committee, 24 June and 2 August 1893, in AASE file 247, nos. 13 and 14.

43. Correspondence among several Amsterdam brokers and Stock Exchange Board, May 1893, in AASE file 139, nos. 31–32; report of meeting on 10 May 1893 in no. 33.

44. Details of the conversion in printed circulars of Hubrecht, September 1893, September 1894, in AASE file 139, nos. 39–44.

45. Burgess and Kennedy, *Centennial History*, p. 485; *Van Oss' Effectenboek* 1903, p. 549, and later editions.

46. Minutes of meeting of 22 January 1894, in AASE file 120, no. 18; figures of deposited bonds in Veltman to Stock Exchange Board, 17 November 1894, AASE file 120, no. 27. Printed circular of committee with call for depositing of the bonds, dated May 1894, in no. 22.

47. Printed circular, 5 January 1897, of the Dutch committee, and letter from Veltman to Stock Exchange Committee, 1 March 1897, giving all details, in AASE file 120, nos. 30, 32.

48. Letter from Veltman to Stock Exchange Board, 17 March 1898, giving all details, in AASE file 120, no. 34. The actual sale of the bonds took place on 18 December 1897.

49. Appointment of committee, 29 January 1894, in AASE file 58, nos. 57 and 59.

50. Minutes of meeting, undated (early 1894), in AASE file 58, no. 60.

51. Articles of incorporation of the Nederlandsche Vereeniging, etc., dated 6 March 1894, in AASE file 58, no. 69; circular letter to bondholders in no. 70.

52. Daggett, *Railroad Reorganization*, p. 216.

53. AASE file 58, nos. 81 and 85, gives details of the reorganization.

54. Request for inclusion of all new securities by the Nederlandsche Vereeniging, dated 4 November 1896, in AASE file 58, no. 93; details about the blocks in nos. 86 and 92.

55. Jules de Gijselaar to Stock Exchange Board, Amsterdam, 26 November 1896, in AASE file, 58, no. 99.

56. Printed circular of Wertheim and partners, 8 February 1894, in AASE file 354, no. 16.

57. Letter from Dutch CO&SW committee (i.e., Wertheim) to Stock Exchange Board, 22 August 1894, in AASE file 354, no. 21.

58. Gerard Vissering (1865–1937), son of a Dutch Minister of Finance, was a lawyer who had chosen banking as his profession. He was director of the Amsterdamsche Bank from 1900 to 1906 and president of the Nederlandsche Bank, the Dutch Central Bank, from 1912 to 1931. *Biografisch Woordenboek van Nederland*, 3 (The Hague, 1989), pp. 628–30.

59. *Van Oss' Effectenboek* 1903, p. 528, and later editions.

60. There is an unnumbered file in AASE pertaining to the Chicago, Milwaukee Electric, from which most details have been taken. See also Hilton and Due, *Interurban Railways*, pp. 335–36.

61. Van Pellecom, *Kapitaalexport*, pp. 123–24.

62. *Van Oss' Effectenboek* 1912, p. 1315; Van Pellecom, *Kapitaalexport*, p. 125.

63. Athearn, *Rebel of the Rockies*, pp. 228–30; Van Pellecom, *Kapitaalexport*, pp. 122–23; and *Van Oss' Effectenboek* 1918–19.

64. Broekman and Honders to Stock Exchange Board, 24 September 1887, and minutes of meeting of 29 September, in AASE file 91, nos. 22 and 24.

65. AASE file 91, no. 28.

66. Circular of Drexel, Morgan and Company, in Dutch and English, 9 February 1889, gives details of the conversion. AASE file 81, no. 31.

67. Correspondence between J. P. Morgan and the Amsterdam Stock Exchange Board, August-September 1895, in AASE file 23, nos. 100–107.

68. Request for listing of the WM&P bonds by Van der Werff and Hubrecht in AASE file 778, no. 1.

69. Press cutting (translated from the London *Times*), undated, on the English committee and the depositing of the bonds, in AASE file 778, no. 36; details of the conversion in circular of the English committee and notice by Gebr. Boissevain, 29 October 1912, in nos. 37 and 38.

■ Chapter Nine

1. Joseph Price, representative of the British shareholders, to the Amsterdam Stock Exchange Committee, 16 January 1884, in AASE file 116, no. 13. Also General E. F. Winslow, president of the NYO&W, to Price, 24 January 1884, in no. 17; report of the meeting held in Amsterdam, 14 February 1884, in no. 19. Report by Van Rees sent to America to assist H. W. Smithers, representative of the Dutch shareholders, 29 July 1884, in AASE file 116, no number; also notice in *NAE*, 5 August 1884. Regarding the lack of support by individual Dutch shareholders see Van Ogtrop, chairman of Dutch committee, to Stock Exchange Committee, February 1886, in AASE file 116, no. 35.

2. Klein, *History*, pp. 214–20; Herr, *Louisville and Nashville*, p. 73.

3. For a history of the Denver Pacific see Klein, *Union Pacific*, vol. 1, pp. 344–53; Jessen, *Railroads of Northern Colorado*, pp. 11–23.

4. *NAE*, 1 March 1870; Dinger, *Overzicht* 1873, pp. 749–50; the prospectus of this loan is in AASE file 31, no. 1.

5. *NAE*, 16 June 1871 and 25 October 1872; also Dinger, *Overzicht* 1873, pp. 750–51.

6. Minutes of meeting of 12 March 1877 in AASE file 31, no. 5; no. 7 is a statement of the Dutch holdings, which indicates that just under $2 million worth of DP bonds were in Dutch hands. A report of this meeting is also in *NAE*, 16 March 1877.

7. Notices in *NAE*, 4 and 10 April 1877.

8. *NAE*, 21 May 1878.

9. In AASE file 31, no. 17, is a draft of the final report drawn up by the Dutch committee intended for the Stock Exchange Committee and dated 23 April 1880; the story of the Dutch interest in the Denver Pacific has been taken from this report, and the quotation has been translated. A notice in *NAE* of 12 August 1879 also gives details of the transaction with Gould.

10. *NAE*, 13 December 1878.

11. Klein, *Union Pacific*, vol. 1, p. 408, says that Gould bought the Denver "Extension" bonds in Amsterdam, but he seems to confuse these extension bonds, which were part of the Kansas Pacific issues, with the real Denver Pacific bonds.

12. Klein, *Life and Legend*, p. 237.

13. Final account of the Committee in AASE file 31, no. 16. Details of payments in press cutting, 16 September 1879, in no. 12; also *NAE*, 19 September 1879 and 27 April 1880.

14. F. Stoop of Dordrecht to Stock Exchange Committee, undated, in AASE file 31, no. 13.

15. Hilton, *American Narrow Gauge*, pp. 101–17. For a capsule history of the Cairo & St. Louis, see ibid., pp. 383–86.

16. D. R. Adler, *British Investment*, makes no mention of the Cairo & St. Louis.

17. Notices by F. W. Oewel in *NAE*, 23 February and 3 September 1872; see also Dinger, *Overzicht* 1873, pp. 784–85.

18. Notice by Oewel in *NAE*, 31 March 1874.

19. Pik, *Amerikaansche spoorwegwaarden*, pp. 29–31.

20. AASE file 85, no. 1, contains the official announcement of Wertheim and Gompertz and F. W. Oewel to the Stock Exchange Committee of the formation of a protective committee, 29 May 1878.

21. Copy of shareholders list in AASE file 85, no. 6.

22. Notice in *NAE*, 8 February 1881.

23. Notices in *NAE*, 23 and 31 May 1882. If all certificates (2,495 + 1,163 + 1 = 3,659) were counted as full $1,000 bonds, the total would be more than the $2.5 million of the original 7-percent loan, so it is probable that Wertheim and Gompertz also issued certificates for half bonds, as was often done.

24. Santilhano, *Amerikaansche spoorwegen*, pp. 437–38; *NAE*, 31 May 1882.

25. Wertheim and Gompertz to Stock Exchange Board, undated [1886] and 15 June 1886, in AASE file 85, nos. 10D and 11; also notice in *NAE*, 15 January 1886. Also notice by Wertheim and Gompertz in *NAE*, 4 December 1885, and *Van Oss' Effectenboek* 1903, p. 510.

26. Regarding the two loans on the Amsterdam market see *NAE*, 22 February and 4 March 1870; also Dinger, *Overzicht* 1873, pp. 751–54.

27. *NAE*, 28 March 1872, contains an anonymous article about the failure of the company.

28. The certificates were included in the Amsterdam price lists in addition to the original bonds at the request of several Amsterdam brokers. AASE file 75 (Port Huron), nos. 1 and 2, contains letters from stockbrokers to Stock Exchange Committee, July and November 1872.

29. Honders and Sons to Stock Exchange Committee, 19 December 1879, in AASE file 98 (Peninsular Railway), no. 1. Wertheim and Gompertz to Stock Exchange Committee, January 1879, in AASE file 98, no. 2.

30. Notice in *NAE*, 7 November 1879, with details about the conversion as given by Wertheim and Gompertz.

31. Circular issued by Wertheim and Gompertz, 12 November 1879, in AASE file 114 (Chicago Grand Trunk), no. 2. Currie, *Grand Trunk*, p. 228, notes that the GT paid 12.5 percent of the par value of the Port Huron/Peninsular bonds, but it is probable that he means the stock of the Port Huron, not the bonds.

32. Wertheim and Gompertz to Stock Exchange Committee, 5 November 1881, in AASE file 114, no. 5. At that time 73 percent of all bondholders had already assented to the conversion plan; Currie, *Grand Trunk*, p. 381, gives a slightly different story of the conversion.

33. Glaab, *Kansas City*, pp. 1–9; Hayes, *Iron Road*, pp. 77–80.

34. *NAE*, 4 July 1871. The only details of this loan on the Dutch market have been found in the financial press of the time. The usual investors' guides make no mention of it. AASE file 111, which contains the papers of the Atchison, Topeka & Santa Fe, also gives some information about the Kansas & Missouri Bridge Company, although the Atchison had nothing to do with the bridge.

35. *NAE*, 5 December 1873.

36. *NAE*, 27 October, 6 November 1874.

37. *NAE*, 22 August 1876. Pieter C. A. M. van Weel (1839–1920) was a lawyer and notary public in Dirksland (South Holland). His elder brother was David van Weel (1838–1911), also a lawyer and a director of the Rotterdamsche Bank. *Nederland's Patriciaat* 51 (1965), p. 314.

38. *NAE*, 25 December 1877 and 21 June 1881.

39. *Poor's Manual* 1879, p. 821.

40. Burgess and Kennedy, *Centennial History*, pp. 185–86; 229–30.

41. Dinger, *Overzicht* 1873, pp. 773–74; Oewel in *NAE*, 5 May 1871.

42. *NAE*, 7 July 1874.

43. Notice in *NAE*, 5 February 1875; see also Pik, *Amerikaansche spoorwegwaarden*, pp. 66–69.

44. Pik, *Amerikaansche spoorwegwaarden*, p. 69.

45. Notice in *NAE*, 20 January 1880.

46. Pollones to Wertheim and Gompertz, 18 December 1880, in AASE file 115, no. 1.

47. Weeveringh, *Noord-Amerikaansche spoorwegfondsen*, pp. 68–70; Swain, *Economic Aspects*, p. 102; *NAE*, 18 April 1882. Printed circular by Wertheim and Gompertz and F. W. Oewel, dated February 1882, in AASE file 115, no. 3B.

48. Printed circular by Wertheim and Gompertz with the details of the financial arrangements, dated 28 November 1885, in AASE file 115, no. 3D.

49. Wertheim to Stock Exchange Board, 1 April 1886, in AASE file 115, no. 5A.

50. Ernest Louis Smithers (1867–1940) was born in England and ended his career as director of the Louisville & Nashville Railroad. *Who Was Who in America*, 1, 1151.

51. Dutch prospectus of the 5-percent loan in AASE file 115, no. 8F.

52. Nederlandsche Vereeniging to Stock Exchange Board, 19 August 1895, in AASE file 115.

53. Nederlandsche Vereeniging to Stock Exchange Board, 30 May 1900, in AASE file 115.

54. *Van Oss' Effectenboek* 1903, p. 483.

55. Circular of Ad. Boissevain and Company, dated 17 March 1911, and results of meeting of 20 March, in AASE file 115, no. 30.

56. *Van Oss' Effectenboek* 1912, p. 1267; press cutting dated 25 April 1911, with details, in AASE file 115, no. 31.

■ *Chapter Ten*

1. The first successful transatlantic cable was laid in 1866 between Valentia Harbour in Ireland and Heart's Content Bay, Newfoundland, after an unlucky attempt the year before. Isambard Kingdom Brunel's giant steamship *Great Eastern* was used for the purpose. Rolt, *Victorian Engineering*, p. 215.

2. Clews, *Fifty Years*, p. 242.

3. Joseph Seligman to Seligman Brothers of London, 25 July 1872, quoted in Miner, *St. Louis–San Francisco*, p. 89.

4. Quoted in Harlow, *The Road*, p. 292.

5. Baker, *Formation*, pp. 45–70; Harlow, *Steelways*, pp. 196–205.

6. Papers concerning the Boston, Hartford & Erie may be found in AASE file 23, nos. 12, 13, and 16. File 23 is that of the Erie Railroad itself, so the archivist of the Amsterdam Stock Exchange did mix up things a bit. For the lawsuit against Hertz see Den Tex, *Amerikaansche spoorwegen*, p. 18.

7. *NAE*, 5 April and 14 May 1872. Dinger, *Overzicht* 1873, p. 797, also warns against the BH&E shares.

8. On railroad construction companies see Chandler, *The Railroads*, pp. 54–57; E. P. Ripley, *Railroads: Finance and Organization*, pp. 10–31.

9. Clews, *Fifty Years*, pp. 243–45.

10. Trottman, *History*; Fogel, *The Union Pacific*.

11. For the history of the Arkansas Central/Arkansas Midland see Hilton, *American Narrow Gauge*, pp. 313–14. There were very few other American railroads built to this gauge of 3.5 feet or 1,067 mm. In the British colonies it was quite common, however, and it was also used on a large scale in the Dutch East Indies.

12. McGrane, *Foreign Bondholders*, pp. 292–93.

13. Notices in *NAE*, 7 May 1872 and 16 May 1874; see also Dinger, *Overzicht* 1873, pp. 785–86.

14. Notice in *NAE*, 8 September 1876.

15. King, *Southern States*, p. 284.

16. The state bonds would have netted $1,446,250 at the 65 below par mentioned by D. R. Adler, *British Investment*, p. 205, while the $750,000 worth of Arkansas Central bonds sold in Europe at 75 below par would have netted $562,500, making a grand total of $2,008,750. This total does not include any bonds sold in the United States, for which no figures are available. The second mortgage bonds worth $700,000 have also been left out, as it is not certain that they were actually sold. *Poor's Manual* for 1876–77 gives $15,000 per mile in state aid, totaling $720,000, plus $500,000 in levee bonds, plus some $750,000 in subscriptions from counties and towns, plus 200,000 acres of land. It is doubtful whether any of these county subscriptions were ever paid in full, but they certainly were not by the counties and towns that were never actually reached by the railroad. For the cost of narrow-gauge construction see Hilton, *American Narrow Gauge*, p. 51.

17. D. R. Adler, *British Investment*, p. 205.

18. Notice in *NAE*, 17 December 1873, where it is also said that the road was to be operated by the Pennsylvania. Dinger, *Overzicht* 1873, pp. 778–79. About the legal wranglings between the Illinois Central and Pennsylvania groups over control of the GC&S, see Greenberg, *Financiers and Railroads*, pp. 116–30.

19. *NAE*, 17 March and 7 August 1874.

20. For the KCP&G business see Chapter 14 and Veenendaal, "The Kansas City Southern."

21. See Veenendaal, "Railroads, Oil and Dutchmen."

22. For the early history of the St. Louis & San Francisco see Miner, *St. Louis-San Francisco*, pp. 40–68 and appendix.

23. Trollope, *North America*, vol. 2, pp. 138–42.

24. Miner, *St. Louis–San Francisco*, p. 72; Mark Twain and Charles Dudley Warner, *The Gilded Age: A Tale of Today*.

25. Beadle, *Undeveloped West*, p. 352.

26. Notice in *AE*, 26 August 1869; Dinger, *Overzicht* 1873, p. 747.

27. Stover, *Railroads of the South*, pp. 94–95.

28. Dinger, *Overzicht* 1873, pp. 650–51.

29. McGrane, *Foreign Bondholders*, pp. 298–304; minutes of meeting of Dutch Florida bondholders in *NAE*, 13 and 20 April 1877.

30. Jacobus Wertheim, an Amsterdam attorney, was a cousin of Abraham Carel Wertheim of Wertheim and Gompertz.

31. Details of the conversion in *NAE*, 2 September 1882; see also Appendix B.

32. McGrane, *Foreign Bondholders*, pp. 303–4.

33. Prince, *Seaboard Air Line Railway*, pp. 74–75.

34. Dinger, *Overzicht* 1873, p. 771; announcement in *NAE*, 18 July 1871.

35. *NAE*, 3 October 1873.

36. Pik, *Amerikaansche spoorwegwaarden*, pp. 90–94.

37. Loman, *Supplement*, p. 274; *NAE*, 8 April 1879.

38. Stover, *Railroads of the South*, pp. 88–90. For the state aid in Alabama see Doster, *Railroads in Alabama Politics*, pp. 4–6.

39. D. R. Adler, *British Investment*, pp. 125–29.

40. Announcement in *AE*, 19 August 1869.

41. *NAE*, 21 February and 27 June 1871.

42. Loumans and Company, stockbrokers of Amsterdam, to Stock Exchange Committee, 16 December 1871, in AASE file 105, no. 1.

43. D. R. Adler, *British Investment*, p. 128; notices in *NAE*, 27 June and 25 July 1876.

44. Announcement in *NAE*, 26 November 1878.

45. Announcement in *NAE*, 13 April 1869.

46. Donovan, *Mileposts*, p. 79; Casey and Douglas, *The Lackawanna Story*, p. 129. Truesdale was later president of the Minneapolis & St. Louis and the Delaware, Lackawanna & Western.

47. Dinger, *Overzicht* 1873, pp. 731–32.

48. Notice in *NAE*, 18 July 1876 and 23 October 1877; Loman, *Supplement*, p. 233. The purchase price of $1,570,000 is given in *NAE*, 6 October 1876; Overton, *Burlington Route*, pp. 149–51, gives a price of $2 million.

49. For a history of the Erie Railway see Mott, *Between the Ocean*; Hungerford, *Men of Erie*; Condit, *Port of New York*, vol. 1, pp. 53–64; Flint, *Railroads of the United States*, pp. 172–89.

50. Mott, *Between the Ocean*, p. 138.

51. For the "Erie Wars" see Klein, *Life and Legend*, pp. 80–91; Mott, *Between the Ocean*, pp. 155–64; and C. F. Adams, *A Chapter of Erie*, reprinted in Hicks, *High Finance in the Sixties*, pp. 20–119.

52. Dinger, *Overzicht* 1873, pp. 707–9; Pik, *Amerikaansche spoorwegwaarden*, pp. 84–89.

53. A. Martin, *Railroads Triumphant*, p. 373; Grant, "Life and Death."

54. Notice about the cooperation between Bischoffsheim and Goldschmidt, Satterthwaite, and Wertheim and Gompertz, in *NAE*, 4 January 1870. Report by the English committee of H. L. Raphael, H. L. Bischoffsheim, R. A. Heath, and E. F. Satterthwaite, in AASE file 23, nos. 1–2.

55. McHenry asked Dutch shareholders for support by depositing their shares with Bischoffsheim and Goldschmidt. *NAE*, 19 December 1871.

56. Samuel F. Butterworth to S. L. M. Barlow, Paris, 27 March 1872, in Huntington Library, Barlow Papers BW 79, part 2. More congratulations for Barlow, from U.S. Senator Thomas F. Bayard, Washington, D.C., 13 March 1873, are in Barlow Papers BW 78, part 2.

57. The recommended exchange of Austro-Hungarian railway stock for Erie is in *NAE*, 1 March 1872.

58. Mott, *Between the Ocean*, pp. 234–35; the quote from an English newspaper is on p. 234. Sir Henry Whatley Tyler (1827–1908), Captain, Royal Engineers, and inspector of railways for the British Board of Trade until 1877; from that year until 1895 he was president of the Grand Trunk of Canada.

59. Correspondence, circulars, and reorganization proposals originating with the English committees over the years 1872–78 are found in AASE file 23, nos. 20–69. The Dutch seem to have left the management of their affairs entirely to the British.

60. For Holladay see Lucia, *Saga of Ben Holladay*, pp. 266–86. For the early history of the Oregon & California see Ganoe, "Oregon & California Railroad."

61. Dinger, *Overzicht* 1873, pp. 758–59.

62. Lucia, *Saga of Ben Holladay*, pp. 318–19; Dinger, *Overzicht* 1873, p. 759.

63. F. S. van Nierop to Stock Exchange Committee, 6 November 1873, in AASE file 63, no. 1; notice in *NAE*, 11 November 1873.

64. Minutes of the meeting of 8 October 1874, in AASE file 63, no. 3.

65. Loman, *Supplement*, pp. 264–65; notice in *NAE*, 4 and 21 March 1879.

66. Pik, *Amerikaansche spoorwegwaarden*, pp. 130–33.

67. Notices in *NAE*, 28 March and 10 December 1872.

68. About the reorganization of the ATSF see Bryant, *History*, pp. 164–68; Waters, *Steel Trails*, pp. 205–19; and Daggett, *Railroad Reorganization*, pp. 210–16. A copy of Little's printed report is in AASE file 111, no. 57. A copy of the printed report of Robert Moore, consulting engineer of St. Louis, on the physical plant of the road is in AASE file 111, no. 61.

69. G. M. Boissevain to Stock Exchange Committee, 17 March 1873, in AASE file 21. In that year Cimarron numbered 75 American and European inhabitants plus some 150 Spanish-Mexicans. Veenendaal, "'Dutch' Towns," pp. 316–17.

70. Berghuis, *Ontstaan*, p. 148; see also Chapter 15.

■ *Chapter Eleven*

1. For a history of the Galveston, Houston & Henderson see S. G. Reed, *History of the Texas Railroads*, pp. 75–79 and 352–56.

2. About the land grant see Van Zant, *Early Economic Policies*, pp. 25 and 45.

3. J. S. Adams, *Contemporary Metropolitan America*, vol. 4, p. 143.

4. King, *Southern States*, p. 131.

5. I used the second edition of Considérant, *Au Texas*, reprinted in 1975 with an introduction in English.

6. Clews, *Fifty Years*, pp. 59–67.

7. V. H. Taylor, *The Franco-Texan Land Company*.

8. *AE*, 10 July 1857. G. A. van der Voort was one of the better known Amsterdam brokers and held a position of trust as secretary of the commission charged with the keeping of the assets of the dissolved Amsterdam Brokers Guild in 1853–54. Van Malsen, *Geschiedenis*, p. 133.

9. *AE*, 7 April 1858.

10. Edouard, comte d'Alton Shée de Lignères (1810–74), of Irish-French ancestry, a renowned French radical politican and railway director. During the Second Empire he lived in political retirement and devoted himself to his many business ventures. *Dictionnaire de Biographie Française*, vol. 2 (Paris, 1934), pp. 343–46.

11. Notices (in French) by the Comité Européen in *AE*, 24 June, 12 August, and 20 December 1859.

12. Notice in *AE*, 13 March 1860.

13. Notice in *AE*, 11 April 1860.

14. Minutes of meeting of 18 May in *AE*, 12 June 1860.

15. Dinger, *Overzicht* 1873, pp. 696–702.

16. Notice in *AE*, 26 February 1861.

17. AASE file 1554, no. 2**.

18. AASE file 1554, no. 14, contains a survey by the French committee of the financial history of the GH&H, dated 12 July 1861.

19. In AASE file 1554, no. 52, is a succinct survey compiled by Weetjen of the GH&H affairs up to 27 September 1867. Most of the information presented here has been taken from that survey.

20. Heydecker's letter in AASE file 1554, no. 47A. E. Kauffman, probably a partner in the same firm as Heydecker, was Dutch consul in Galveston from 1845; it is not recorded why he did not act himself. In 1871 Kauffman was succeeded as consul by Th. Wagner.

21. Copy of a letter from Tucker and Leane, Galveston, 22 March 1867, in AASE file 1554, no. 47C.

22. Notice in *AE*, 10 October 1867.

23. Notice in *AE*, 15 May 1868.

24. Letters from Kuyper van Harpen, merchant of Rotterdam, to Weetjen, dated Rotterdam, 13 September and 23 December 1869, in AASE file 1554, nos. 56 and 57.

25. Dinger, *Overzicht* 1873, p. 700; notices in *NAE*, 28 January and 8 February 1870.

26. Copy of Heydecker's letter to Van Zuylen van Nijevelt, Galveston, 9 June 1870, in AASE file 1554, no. 60.

27. Dinger, *Overzicht* 1873, pp. 701–2; S. G. Reed, *History of the Texas Railroads*, pp. 352–53.

28. Notice in *NAE*, 20 April 1877; Loman, *Supplement*, p. 215.

29. B. de Vries, *Electoraat en elite*, pp. 99–100. Luns was particularly unlucky in his investments; besides the GH&H bonds he also owned many acres of the Poyasian Land Grant, of the imaginary state of Poyas, and 444 certificates of the Bank of the United States of Philadelphia, then defunct.

30. These computations are based on an incomplete resumé (in French), dated 7 May 1860, in AASE file 1554, no. 2*.

31. Beadle, *The Undeveloped West*, p. 797.

■ *Chapter Twelve*

1. For a history of the Great Northern Railway and its predecessors, including the Minnesota & Pacific, see Hidy, Hidy, and Scott, *Great Northern*.

2. Saby, "Railroad Legislation."

3. Hidy, Hidy, and Scott, *Great Northern*, pp. 5–6.

4. Saby, "Railroad Legislation," p. 55.

5. A. Martin, *James J. Hill*, pp. 117–20.

6. Notice in *AE*, 22 January 1864; Dinger, *Overzicht* 1873, pp. 687–88.

7. Hidy, Hidy, and Scott, *Great Northern*, p. 8, mentions Lippmann and Rosenthal.

8. Notices in *AE*, 6 March 1866; Dinger, *Overzicht* 1873, p. 687. Saby, "Railroad Legislation," p. 58, gives the lower figure, plus some unspecified acreage of swampland.

9. Notice in *AE*, 19 May 1868.

10. Dinger, *Overzicht* 1873, p. 688; Santilhano, *Amerikaansche spoorwegen*, pp. 356–57.

11. Hidy, "Dutch Investor in Minnesota," p. 154.

12. Dinger, *Overzicht* 1873, pp. 690–91.

13. Lamb, *History*, p. 56; Pyle, *Life*, vol. 1, p. 161. Regarding the missing $8 million see Holbrook, *James Hill*, p. 43.

14. Dinger, *Overzicht* 1873, pp. 691–93; notice in *NAE*, 11 July 1871.

15. Notice by Lippmann and Rosenthal in *NAE*, 29 November 1872.

16. Pyle, *Life*, vol. 1, p. 177.

17. Notices in *NAE*, 13 May, 17 and 24 June 1873; notice about the election of a protective committee also in AASE file 36, no. 9.

18. Cohen Stuart, *Zes maanden in Amerika*, pp. 289–90.

19. Pyle, *Life*, vol. 1, p. 177; Russell, *Stories*, pp. 17–19.

20. Notices in *NAE*, 22 August, 2 and 26 September, and 11 November 1873; Dinger, *Overzicht* 1873, pp. 695–96; and Swain, *Economic Aspects*, pp. 90, 116.

21. Notices in *NAE*, 30 December 1873, 13 March 1874.

22. Minutes of bondholders' meetings in *NAE*, 28 September, 12 and 29 October, 12 November 1875, 14 July, 22 August 1876. Pyle, *Life*, vol. 1, pp. 193–97.

23. Defense of Lippmann in *NAE*, 22 October 1875.

24. Cutting from the *St. Paul Daily Press*, 18 September 1874, in AASE file 36, no. 17; also Holbrook, *James Hill*, p. 55; A. Martin, *James J. Hill*, pp. 127–28.

25. Saby, "Railroad Legislation," p. 137.

26. Notices in *NAE*, 12 and 29 May 1877.

27. A. Martin, *James J. Hill*, p. 128; Pyle, *Life*, vol. 1, p. 157.

28. For the connection between Stephen and Morton, Rose and Company see Greenberg, "Capital Alliances," pp. 26–27.

29. Pyle, *Life*, vol. 1, pp. 212–17, and vol. 2, Appendix 2.

30. Pyle, *Life*, vol. 1, pp. 218–19, and vol. 2, Appendix 3.

31. Details in *NAE*, 2 and 16 October 1877. Unidentified press cutting of 29 September 1877, in AASE file 36, no number.

32. Pik, *Amerikaansche spoorwegwaarden*, pp. 142–43; Pyle, *Life*, vol. 1, p. 224; and A. Martin, *James J. Hill*, pp. 144–48.

33. Details of the sale in *NAE*, 12 February 1878; Pik, *Amerikaansche spoorwegwaarden*, pp. 143–44. See also A. Martin, *James J. Hill*, pp. 150–51; Pyle, *Life*, vol. 1, p. 226, and vol. 2, Appendix 6.

34. Pik, *Amerikaansche spoorwegwaarden*, p. 152, neatly figured the exact price.

35. *NAE*, 1 March and 30 July 1878.

36. A. Martin, *James J. Hill*, pp. 154–57.

37. Figures in Loman, *Supplement*, pp. 211–12; those given in *NAE*, 18 July and 22 August 1879, differ slightly.

38. *NAE*, 17 and 24 July, 7 August, and 7 September 1877. See also A. Martin, *James J. Hill*, pp. 161–63; Loman, *Supplement*, p. 212.

39. *NAE*, 4 March 1879; Loman, *Supplement*, pp. 206–7.

40. Notices by the Committee in *NAE*, 29 July and 8 August 1879.

41. Notice by 't Hooft in *NAE*, 4 and 18 November 1879. Two printed circulars by 't Hooft, 1 and 28 August 1879, in AASE file 36, nos. 20 and 23. See also A. Martin, *James J. Hill*, pp. 356–60.

42. Van Oss, *American Railroads*, p. 655; 't Hooft gives his figures in *NAE* of 15 April 1881, and although he claims that they are much higher than those offered in 1879, the real difference is minimal; for the extension bonds no new price is given.

43. Holbrook, *James Hill*, p. 65.

44. Lamb, *History*, p. 63.

45. Engelbourg, "John S. Kennedy."

46. Van Schevichaven, *De Noord-Amerikaansche*, p. 67. In the archives of the Amsterdam Exchange an unmarked file on Kerkhoven, Minnesota, has been found, which gives some particulars of the Kerkhoven firm and of the history of the town. The locomotive Kerkhoven is listed in Keyes and Middleton, "Great Northern," p. 42.

■ *Chapter Thirteen*

1. For a general history of the Missouri, Kansas & Texas see Masterson, *The Katy Railroad*; for its early days see Morrison, "The Union Pacific," pp. 173–88.

2. King, *Southern States*, p. 187.

3. Announcement by Becker and Fuld and Wertheim and Gompertz in *AE*, 15 June 1869; their prospectus of June 1869 in AASE file 8, no. 1. See also Dinger, *Overzicht* 1873, pp. 734–36.

4. Anonymous articles in *NAE*, 15 March 1870 and 17 March 1871; a favorable report by Ernest Frignet, apparently a Frenchman, and titled general European agent of the MKT, dated 10

January 1871, in AASE file 8, no. 3. Frignet writes that traffic is increasing and that the sales of land are good. Requests by Wertheim and Gompertz for inclusion of the Southern Branch sixes in the price lists, dated 6 March 1871, in AASE file 8, no. 5.

5.   *NAE*, 16 May 1871, and 4 November 1873; Dinger, *Overzicht* 1873, pp. 736–38. Request for inclusion in the price lists of the MKT sevens by Wertheim and Gompertz, dated 4 January 1872, in AASE file 8, no. 5A.

6.   Telegram from Parsons to Weetjen, chairman of the Stock Exchange Committee, Paris, 21 July 1873; and note 4 August 1873, in AASE file 8, nos. 7 and 10.

7.   Hafen and Rister, *Western America*, pp. 447–48; King, *Southern States*, pp. 196–200; Holbrook, *Story*, pp. 217–18; and Beadle, *The Undeveloped West*, p. 785.

8.   They closed on 8 September 1873, Jay Cooke ten days later. Lewty, *Columbia Gateway*, p. 12. Parsons's announcement in *NAE*, 30 January 1874.

9.   Details of the arrangement in *NAE*, 12 and 30 June 1874.

10.   L'Huilier's printed report (in Dutch), dated January 1874, is in AASE file 8, no. 14. About Croockewit's findings see *NAE*, 15 and 22 December 1874. Gustaaf Adolf Croockewit (1833–1910) came from a family of sugar refiners and was a director of a large Amsterdam steamship company. A cousin of his was Adriaan Eliza Croockewit, whom we have met as a writer on the United States. *Nederland's Patriciaat* 72 (1988), pp. 180 and 190.

11.   Request for a committee in a letter from Mesdag and Sons, brokers in Groningen, to Stock Exchange Committee, 14 March 1874, in AASE file 8, no. 15; Pollones to Stock Exchange Committee, 24 November 1874, in no. 36. Report from the *Nederlandsche Financier-Dagelijksche Beurscourant* of 12 February 1875 in AASE file 8, no. 45. See also *NAE*, 12 February 1875.

12.   Notices in *NAE*, 29 June and 30 July 1875, and 14 January 1876. Agreement, dated 1 March 1876, in AASE file 8, no. 55. About the French see *NAE*, 5 May 1876.

13.   T. Haskins Du Puy was a railroad engineer in the service of the Pennsylvania for a time. See Ward, *J. Edgar Thomson*, p. 105.

14.   Pik, *Amerikaansche spoorwegwaarden*, pp. 119–23; Loman, *Supplement*, pp. 237–38; Overton, *Burlington Route*, p. 170; and Klein, *Life and Legend*, p. 250.

15.   Request for inclusion of the fives by Piek, dated 5 January 1884, in AASE file 8, no. 74. Van Vloten and De Gijselaar's request for the sixes, dated 17 November 1886, in no. 96. Notice by Piek about conversion of income bonds in *NAE*, 6 November 1883.

16.   Request for inclusion in price lists of MKT common shares, dated 13 January 1880, in AASE file 8, no. 68.

17.   Notices in *NAE*, 6 and 30 January, 6 and 13 February 1885. Piek to Stock Exchange Committee, 29 October 1887, in AASE file 8, p. 101. Traffic figures in Klein, *Life and Legend*, p. 405.

18.   AASE file 8, nos. 105, 106, and 208 give particulars of the formation of the Nederlandsche Vereeniging in March 1888. The minutes of the board of the Vereeniging are also in AASE, but in a file without any number or further description, and were only found accidentally. The story about the activities of the Vereeniging is chiefly built on these minutes, unless stated otherwise.

19.   Masterson, *Katy Railroad*, p. 240; Klein, *Life and Legend*, pp. 412, 428–29. See also press cutting from *Nederlandsche Financier-Dagelijksche Beurscourant*, 8 June 1888, in AASE file 8, no. 208.

20.   *Report of the Committee Appointed by the Executive Committee of the Board of the M, K & T Rly*, August 1888, by G. Clinton Gardner, Thos. Bedford Atkins, and Wm. P. Robinson, in AASE file 8.

21.   Papers concerning the joint action by shareholders and 5- and 6-percent bondholders,

September 1888, in AASE file 8, nos. 209 and 220. The figures given were noted during a meeting on 5 September 1888.

22. Minutes of meeting of 17 October 1888 in AASE file 8, no. 225; other papers of this committee in nos. 230–31.

23. *Proposed Plan of Reorganization*, dated November 1889, and a Dutch translation, dated 27 November 1889, in AASE file 8; also printed circular by the Nederlandsche Vereeniging, dated 15 February 1890, giving details of the plans. *De grieven tegen het 7 pct. Missouri, Kansas-Comite* by Van der Schooren, also in AASE file 8, elaborates on the lack of persuasion on the part of the Van Hall committee. A letter of that committee to the Stock Exchange Committee, dated April 1890, explaining the reasons for going along with the Olcott plan, in AASE file 8, no. 241.

24. Press cutting of 5 March 1890 in an unmarked box, containing papers of the MKT reorganization, in AASE, no number; also in this box are minutes of the Nederlandsche Vereeniging, dated 16 January 1892.

25. These figures have been taken from a list, dated 1900, in minutes of the Nederlandsche Vereeniging in AASE, unnumbered box.

26. A regular correspondence between Rouse and Van Nierop of the Nederlandsche Vereeniging is in AASE file 8A; the figures for 1905 in a letter, dated 27 November 1905, in no. 117, while the 1909 figures have been taken from a "List of Dutch and German Stockholders" of that year in no. 128A.

27. Figures taken from AASE file 8A, nos. 271 and 272, which give lists of the securities deposited with the two committees in 1915. An undated note in AASE file 8C gives the figure for the second mortgage bonds in 1922. Van Pellecom, *Kapitaalexport*, pp. 122 and 128, gives the 1918 figures. All later figures are from *Van Oss' Effectenboek* over the years until 1940.

■ *Chapter Fourteen*

1. Glaab, *Kansas City*, p. 32.

2. For a history of the KCP&G see Veenendaal, "The Kansas City Southern," pp. 291–310; for a biography of Stilwell see Bryant, *Arthur E. Stilwell*.

3. AASE file 454, no. 2; the prospectus of the Vereeniging N.V. in no. 5.

4. Figures are conflicting, but a statement in AASE file 454, no. 15, gives the latter figure for 31 July 1896.

5. AASE file 454, 16.

6. Tutein Nolthenius, *Nieuwe wereld*; this work went through two editions.

7. Daniel Gideon Boissevain (1867–1940) was first sent to the London office of Blake, Boissevain and Company before setting up the Boissevain office in New York.

8. AASE file 370, no. 1, contains the Dutch prospectus of the Belt Railway.

9. AASE file 344, no. 1, holds the request for inclusion in the price lists by Rutgers and De Beaufort of $285,000 worth of these bonds, dated 4 January 1894. The Dutch prospectus issued by Tutein Nolthenius and De Goeijen is in no. 5; totals sold by Rutgers are in no. 15.

10. Lamping, *De Kansas City's*, vols. 1 and 2; Van Oss, *Amerikaansche spoorwegwaarden*, pp. 33–34, 81.

11. Minutes of meeting of 5 October 1899 and list of securities present or represented are in AASE file 370A, no. 1.

12. AASE file 454, no. 37, contains the minutes of the first meeting of 25 September 1899; no. 42 gives details of the certificates, which were actually issued by Ad. Boissevain.

13. Bosch, *Nederlandse beleggingen*, p. 673, gives these figures. They differ somewhat from others found in the archives of the stock exchange.

14. Details of the conversion in *Van Oss' Effectenboek* 1903, pp. 499–506.

15. De Goeijen to Jules N. L. de Gijselaar, 16 July 1900, in AASE file 370A, no number.

16. This copybook is not included in the regular KCP&G file and is not numbered. It was found accidentally through the help of Mr. Herbert W. Günst, archivist of the stock exchange.

17. *Van Oss' Effectenboek* 1903, p. 505; AASE file 578, no. 1, contains the request for inclusion in the price lists of both common and preferred shares.

18. Details in Appendixes A and B.

19. Details of the syndicates may be found in *Van Oss' Effectenboek* 1904, pp. 531–36; AASE file 359 contains the Arkansas Construction Company Syndicate papers, and file 402 holds those of the Kansas City Terminal Construction Company Syndicate.

20. *Van Oss' Effectenboek* 1906, pp. 851 and 1296.

▪ *Chapter Fifteen*

1. For the early history of the first Dutch investment funds see Berghuis, *Ontstaan*, pp. 46–73.

2. Dinger, *Overzicht* 1851, pp. 215–21.

3. Dinger, *Overzicht* 1873, pp. 618–19, gives a complete list of all securities thus acquired.

4. Berghuis, *Ontstaan*, pp. 91–94.

5. Dinger, *Overzicht* 1873, pp. 625–26; Loman, *Supplement*, pp. 186–87.

6. The figures have been taken from Dinger, *Overzicht* 1873, pp. 797–801, and Berghuis, *Ontstaan*, pp. 118–26.

7. Berghuis, *Ontstaan*, p. 130.

8. The figures have been taken from *Van Oss' Effectenboek* 1915–16, vol. 1, pp. 1008–10.

9. Berghuis, *Ontstaan*, p. 178.

10. The figures have been taken from Dinger, *Overzicht* 1873, pp. 802–3.

11. Huizenga, *Amerikaansche spoorwegtoestanden*, vol. 7, p. 44.

12. Berghuis, *Ontstaan*, p. 148.

13. Figures taken from Loman, *Supplement*, pp. 299–300.

14. Figures taken from *Van Oss' Effectenboek* 1915–16, pp. 1012–13.

15. Berghuis, *Ontstaan*, pp. 158–60.

16. Ibid., pp. 165–68.

17. Figures taken from *Van Oss' Effectenboek* 1915–16, p. 1011.

18. Berghuis, *Ontstaan*, pp. 167–68.

19. Announcement by Broes and Gosman in *NAE* of 15 October 1878; also Weeveringh, *Noord-Amerikaansche spoorwegfondsen*, p. 65; *Van Oss' Effectenboek* 1909, p. 1209; Pik, *Amerikaansche spoorwegwaarden*, p. 58.

20. Berghuis, *Ontstaan*, pp. 180–88.

21. Ibid., pp. 196–99.

▪ *Conclusion*

1. The figures in Bosch, *Nederlandse beleggingen*, p. 136, are not quite complete.

2. See Wilkins, *The History*, p. 121, for some comparisons.

3. Berghuis, *Ontstaan*, pp. 77, 99, 101.

4. Kiliani, *Grossbanken-Entwicklung*, pp. 11, 29, 56.

5. Figures based on Lewis, in Wilkins, *History of Foreign Investment*, p. 194. Lewis may be too high in her figure of $300 million for German-owned American railroad securities in 1914. German figures are even more contradictory than the Dutch. Kabisch, in his recent *Deutsches Kapital*, pp. 116–18, gives only $74 million of German-held American railroad securities before 1914.

His figures are based on a U.S. government report of 1918 and are much too low because many securities had already been sold through neutral countries by then to avoid sequestration. Other estimates suggest that some $425 million in U.S. railroad paper was held in Germany in 1913, after a high of $1,000 million in 1906, an almost unbelievably high figure. Kabisch, *Deutsches Kapital*, p. 124.

6. Van Pellecom, *Kapitaalexport*, p. 45.

7. Meijers, "Buitenlandsche beleggingen," pp. 273–75.

8. Wilkins, *The History*, Table 5.5 on p. 156; Staley, *War and the Private Investor*, pp. 523–24.

Bibliography

Please note that authors' names containing particles (Van Winter, De Vries) are listed in the Bibliography under the family name rather than the particle. For example, a listing in the Bibliography under

Winter, P. J. van, *Het aandeel*, . . .

will be cited in the Notes as

Van Winter, *Het aandeel*, . . .

■ Manuscript Collections

The most important single source of documents for this study was the Archives of the Amsterdam Stock Exchange, hereafter AASE. These archives, preserved in the basement of the building of the Vereeniging voor de Effectenhandel (Stock Exchange Association) represent its activities over more than a century.

By far the most useful documents for this study have been the files of the securities listed in Amsterdam over the years. After the formation of the *Vereeniging* (then spelled with two e's) in 1876, every government, company, or public institution that listed its securities in Amsterdam was allotted a number—in chronological sequence—by the secretary of the *Vereeniging*. For companies that had already obtained their listing before 1876, a number was given more or less at random; for instance, the Missouri, Kansas & Texas got the number 8, while the Illinois Central, actually the first American railroad traded in Amsterdam, got 67, and the Galveston, Houston & Henderson, the second in Amsterdam, got 1554. Apparently this last number was assigned during a much later reorganization of the archives. Once allotted, the number was retained throughout the company's corporate life as long as its securities were listed in Amsterdam. The Union Pacific file number 62 is still open and growing every year.

Whenever companies merged their old files were generally closed and a new one opened with a higher number. The old files were shelved and have in most cases never been opened since. When a company continuing operations had its securities withdrawn from the Amsterdam price lists for reasons of default, redemption, or just plain lack of interest and trade, its file was also closed and shelved.

Some files hold only a few scraps of paper; others may run into several meters of bundles, including sometimes long-running series of annual reports, balance sheets, and such. A few of the railroads with similar names have been mixed up at some time in the past. For example, the Chicago & North Western and the Chicago South Western share a common file though they have no corporate links. The Norfolk & Western file has not been found, although it must have existed. The file of its predecessor road, the Atlantic, Mississippi & Ohio, has been found.

A few files have had an A added to the original number to designate a separate file for the reorganization or protective committee of that particular railroad. In other cases, papers of protective committees have been found without a separate file, dispersed among the documents in the regular file. And a few protective committees have had their papers kept together, but without any number or name given. Some of these have been found accidentally; others may well be somewhere in the cellars of the Stock Exchange, unknown to anyone. It was impossible to institute a systematic search among the vast masses of paper, especially because as a result of the installation of an advanced computerized system for listings and sales in the Stock Exchange hall proper, all the cellars underneath were covered with a thick layer of white chalk dust on top of the layer of black dust that had accumulated over the last hundred years.

Another source of important documents has been the Huntington Library in San Marino, California. Among its vast holdings are the Barlow Papers, catalogued in chronological sequence and containing the correspondence between Samuel Barlow, American lawyer and financier, and hundreds of his correspondents all over the world, among them a few Dutchmen. Other documents, correspondence, stockholders' lists, and such have been found elsewhere among the Huntington Library's holdings and are cited at the appropriate places.

American railroad archives as such have not been used. One compelling reason for not using them was the physical impossibility of traveling to all the many railroad companies involved. Another reason was the state of the stockbooks of most railroad companies, which generally give little information about the actual owners of the stock. Many times shares were still in the names of earlier owners or in those of clerks and servants of American railroad tycoons, who thus continued to exercise the voting rights, while the actual owner might live thousands of miles across the Atlantic.

■ Periodicals

Of the many financial periodicals in the Netherlands, the *Amsterdamsch Effectenblad* (AE) has been used for the years between 1855 and 1870, and thereafter the *Nieuw Algemeen Effectenblad* (NAE). The library of the Stock Exchange has a complete set of the *Prijscourant* from 1795, replaced by the *Amsterdamsch Effectenblad* and after 1870 by the *Nieuw Algemeen Effectenblad*. For reasons of convenience and accessibility, this series in the Stock Exchange building has been used. Other periodicals have been used occasionally when necessary.

■ Books and Articles

Adams, Charles F., Jr. *A Chapter of Erie*. Boston: Fields, Osgood, 1869.

Adams, John S., ed. *Contemporary Metropolitan America*. 4 vols. Cambridge, Mass.: Ballinger, 1976.

Adler, Cyrus. *Jacob H. Schiff: His Life and Letters*. 2 vols. Garden City, N.Y.: Doubleday, Doran, 1928.

Adler, Dorothy R. *British Investment in American Railways 1834–1898*. Charlottesville: University Press of Virginia, 1970.

Alexander, Edwin P. *On the Main Line: The Pennsylvania Railroad in the Nineteenth Century*. New York: Bramhall House, 1971.

Ames, Charles E. *Pioneering the Union Pacific: A Reappraisal of the Builders of the Railroad.* New York: Appleton-Century-Crofts, 1969.

Anderson, Elaine. *The Central Railroad of New Jersey's First 100 Years.* Easton, Pa.: Center for Canal History and Technology, 1984.

Anderson, George L. *General William J. Palmer: A Decade of Railroad Building 1870–1880.* Colorado Springs: The Colorado College, 1936.

——. *Kansas West.* San Marino, Calif.: Golden West Books, 1963.

Anderson, Jacob E. *A Brief History of the St. Louis Southwestern Railway Lines.* [St. Louis: St. Louis Southwestern Railway, 1947].

Athearn, Robert G. *Rebel of the Rockies: A History of the Denver and Rio Grande Railroad.* New Haven, Conn.: Yale University Press, 1962.

——. *Union Pacific Country.* Lincoln: University of Nebraska Press, 1976.

——. *Westward the Briton.* New York: Scribners, 1953.

Baker, George P. *The Formation of the New England Railroad Systems.* Cambridge, Mass.: Harvard University Press, 1937.

Bancroft, George. *Geschiedenis der Vereenigde Staten van Noord Amerika.* Vol. 1. Groningen: Wolters, 1868.

Bankwezen: een geschiedenis en bronnenoverzicht. Historische Bedrijfsarchieven 1. Amsterdam: NEHA, 1992.

Barnes, Irston R. *The Economics of Public Utility Regulation.* New York: F. S. Crofts, 1947.

Baughman, James P. *Charles Morgan and the Development of Southern Transportation.* Nashville, Tenn.: Vanderbilt University Press, 1968.

Beadle, J. H. *The Undeveloped West: or Five Years in the Territories.* 1873. Reprint New York: Arno Press, 1973.

Beebe, Lucius. *The Central Pacific and the Southern Pacific Railroads.* Berkeley, Calif.: Howell-North, 1963.

Bell, William A. *New Tracks in North America: A Journal of Travel and Adventure Whilst Engaged in the Survey for a Southern Railroad to the Pacific Ocean During 1867–1868.* London: Chapman & Hall, 1870. Reprint Albuquerque, N.Mex.: Horn & Wallace, 1965.

Berghuis, W. H. *Ontstaan en ontwikkeling van de Nederlandse beleggingsfondsen tot 1914.* Assen: Van Gorcum, 1967.

Blackmore, William. *Colorado: Its Resources, Parks, and Prospects as a New Field for Emigration: With an Account of the Trenchera and Costilla Estates, in the San Luis Park.* London: S. Low, 1869.

Blain, Hugh M. *A Near Century of Public Service in New Orleans.* New Orleans, La.: New Orleans Public Service, 1927.

Blake, Nelson M. *William Mahone of Virginia: Soldier and Political Insurgent.* Richmond, Va.: Garrett & Massie, 1935.

Bogen, Jules I. *The Anthracite Railroads: A Study in American Railroad Enterprise.* New York: Ronald Press, 1927.

Boissevain, Charles. *Van 't Noorden naar 't Zuiden; Schetsen en indrukken van de Vereenigde Staten van Noord-Amerika.* 2 vols. Haarlem: H. D. Tjeenk Willink, 1881–1882.

Bonbright, James C. *Railroad Capitalization: A Study of the Principles of Regulation of Railroad Securities.* New York: Columbia University Press, 1920.

Bonbright, James C., and Gardiner C. Means. *The Holding Company: Its Public Significance and Its Regulation.* New York: McGraw-Hill, 1932.

Bos, N. J. P. M. "Vermogensbezitters en bevoorrechte belastingbetalers in de negentiende eeuw." *Bijdragen voor de Geschiedenis der Nederlanden* 105, no. 4 (1990): 553–77.

Bosch, K. D. *De Nederlandse beleggingen in de Verenigde Staten.* Amsterdam: Elsevier, 1948.

Boxer, Charles R. *The Dutch Seaborne Empire 1600–1800.* London: Hutchinson, 1965.

Brandeis, Louis D. *Other People's Money and How the Bankers Use It.* New York: Frederick A. Stokes, 1914.

Brandes de Roos, R. *Industrie, Kapitalmarkt und Industrielle Effekten in den Niederlanden: Ein Beitrag zur Kenntnis der Niederländischen Industrie und der Faktoren, welche die Beschaffung ihrer Anlage-Kapitalien beeinflussen.* 2 vols. The Hague: M. Nijhoff, 1928.

Brayer, Herbert O. *William Blackmore.* 2 vols. Denver, Colo.: Bradford-Robinson, 1949.

Broeke, W. van den. *Financiën en financiers van de Nederlandse spoorwegen 1837–1890.* Zwolle: Waanders, 1985.

Brooks, John G. *As Others See Us: A Study of Progress in the United States.* New York: MacMillan, 1908.

Brouwer, S. *De Amsterdamsche Bank 1871–1946.* Amsterdam: De Amsterdamsche Bank, 1946.

Brown, A. E. "The Louisiana & Arkansas Railway: Structure and Operation in the Age of Steam." *Railroad History* 144 (Spring 1981): 51–59.

Brown, A. Theodore, and Lyle W. Dorsett. *K. C.: A History of Kansas City, Missouri.* Boulder, Colo.: Pruett, 1979.

Brown, Cecil K. *A State Movement in Railroad Development: The Story of North Carolina's First Effort to Establish an East and West Trunk-Line Railroad.* Chapel Hill: University of North Carolina Press, 1928.

Brownson, Howard G. *History of the Illinois Central Railroad to 1870.* Ph.D. diss., University of Illinois, 1909.

Brugmans, I. J. *Begin van twee banken.* Rotterdam, 1963.

———. *De economische conjunctuur in Nederland in de 19e eeuw.* Amsterdam: Noord-Hollandsche, 1936.

Bryant, Keith L., Jr. *Arthur E. Stilwell: Promoter with a Hunch.* Nashville, Tenn.: Vanderbilt University Press, 1971.

———. *History of the Atchison, Topeka and Santa Fe Railway.* Lincoln: University of Nebraska Press, 1974.

———. *Railroads in the Age of Regulation, 1900–1980.* New York: Facts on File, 1988.

Buckley, Peter, and Brian Roberts. *European Direct Investment in the USA Before World War I.* New York: St. Martin's Press, 1982.

Buist, Marten G. *At Spes non Fracta: Hope & Co. 1770–1815.* The Hague: M. Nijhoff, 1974.

———. "Geld, bankwezen en handel in de Noordelijke Nederlanden, 1795–1844." In *Algemene Geschiedenis der Nederlanden* vol. 10, pp. 289–322. Haarlem: Fibula-Van Dishoeck, 1981.

Burgess, George H., and Miles C. Kennedy. *Centennial History of the Pennsylvania Railroad Company, 1846–1946.* Philadelphia, Pa.: The Pennsylvania Railroad Comp., 1949.

Busbey, T. A., ed. *The Biographical Directory of the Railway Officials of America.* Chicago, 1893.

Buss, Dietrich G. *Henry Villard: A Study of Transatlantic Investments and Interests, 1870–1895.* New York: Arno Press, 1978.

Cairncross, A. K. *Home and Foreign Investment 1870–1913: Studies in Capital Accumulation.* Cambridge, Eng.: Cambridge University Press, 1953.

Cameron, Rondo. *Banking in the Early Stages of Industrialization.* New York: Oxford University Press, 1967.

Camijn, A. J. W. *Samen effectief: Opkomst, bloei en ondergang van de Vereeniging van Effectenhandelaren te Rotterdam.* Rotterdam: Historische Publikaties Roterodamum, 1987.

Campbell, E. G. *The Reorganization of the American Railroad System, 1893–1900.* New York: Columbia University Press, 1938.

Capefigue, J. B. H. R. *Histoire des Grandes Opérations Financières.* 4 vols. Paris: 1855–60.

Carey, John W. *The Organization and History of the Chicago, Milwaukee & St. Paul Railway Company.* N.p., [1892].

Carosso, Vincent P. *Investment Banking in America: A History.* Cambridge, Mass.: Harvard University Press, 1970.

———. *More Than a Century of Investment Banking: The Kidder, Peabody & Co. Story.* New York: McGraw-Hill, 1979.

———. *The Morgans: Private International Bankers 1854–1913.* Cambridge, Mass.: Harvard University Press, 1987.

Casey, Robert J. *Pioneer Railroad: The Story of the Chicago and North Western System.* New York: McGraw-Hill, 1948.

Casey, Robert J., and W. A. S. Douglas. *The Lackawanna Story: The First Hundred Years of the Delaware, Lackawanna and Western Railroad.* New York: McGraw-Hill, 1951.

Caudle, Robert E. *History of the Missouri Pacific Lines.* Houston, Tex., 1949.

Chandler, Alfred D., Jr. *Patterns of American Railroad Finance, 1830–1850.* Cambridge, Mass.: MIT Press, 1955.

———. *The Railroads: The Nation's First Big Business.* New York: Harcourt, Brace & World, 1965.

———. *The Visible Hand: The Managerial Revolution in American Business.* Cambridge, Mass.: Harvard University Press, 1977.

Chazanof, William. *Joseph Ellicott and the Holland Land Company: The Opening of Western New York.* Syracuse, N.Y.: Syracuse University Press, 1970.

Chernow, Ron. *The House of Morgan: An American Banking Dynasty and the Rise of Modern Finance.* New York: Simon & Schuster, 1990.

Clark, Ira G. *Then Came the Railroads: The Century from Steam to Diesel in the Southwest.* Norman: University of Oklahoma Press, 1958.

Clark, Thomas D. *A Pioneer Southern Railroad from New Orleans to Cairo.* Chapel Hill: University of North Carolina Press, 1936.

Cleveland, Frederick A., and Fred W. Powell. *Railroad Promotion and Capitalization in the United States.* New York: Longmans, Green, 1909.

Clew, Henry. *Fifty Years in Wall Street.* New York: Irving, 1908.

Clifford, Howard. *Rails North: The Railroads of Alaska and the Yukon.* Seattle, Wash.: Superior, 1981.

Cochran, Thomas C. *Railroad Leaders 1845–1890: The Business Mind in Action.* Cambridge, Mass.: Harvard University Press, 1953.

Cohen, Norm. *Long Steel Rail: The Railroad in American Folk Song.* Urbana: University of Illinois Press, 1981.

Cohen Stuart, Martinus. *Zes maanden in Amerika.* 2nd ed. Haarlem: Tjeenk Willink, 1879.

Commager, Henry S. *America in Perspective: The United States through Foreign Eyes.* New York: Random House, 1947.

Condit, Carl W. *The Port of New York.* 2 vols. Chicago: University of Chicago Press, 1980–81.

———. *The Railroad and the City: A Technological and Urbanistic History of Cincinnati.* Columbus: Ohio State University Press, 1977.

Considérant, Victor. *Au Texas.* 2nd ed. Brussels and Paris, 1855. Repr. R. V. Davidson, ed. Philadelphia: Porcupine Press, 1975.

Corliss, Carlton J. *Main Line of Mid-America: The Story of the Illinois Central.* New York: Creative Age Press, 1950.

———. *Trails to Rails: A Story of Transportation Progress in Illinois.* Chicago: Illinois Central System, 1934.

Cronau, Rudolf. *Im Wilden Westen: Eine Künstlerfahrt durch die Prairien und Felsengebirge der Union.* Braunschweig: Oskar Löbbecke, 1890.

Croockewit, A. E. "Amerikaansche schetsen." In *De Gids* 34 (1870): pp. 66–98, 117–36.

Crump, Spencer. *Henry Huntington and the Pacific Electric.* Corona del Mar, Calif.: Trans-Anglo Books, 1978.

Currie, A. W. *The Grand Trunk Railway of Canada.* Toronto: University of Toronto Press, 1957.

Daggett, Stuart. *Chapters on the History of the Southern Pacific.* 1922. Repr. New York: Augustus M. Kelley, 1966.

———. *Railroad Reorganization.* 1908. Repr. New York: Augustus M. Kelley, 1967.

Daniels, Winthrop. *American Railroads: Four Phases of Their History.* Princeton, N.J.: Princeton University Press, 1932.

Davis, Burke. *The Southern Railway: Road of the Innovators.* Chapel Hill: University of North Carolina Press, 1985.

Davis, Clarence B., and Kenneth E. Wilburn, eds. *Railway Imperialism.* New York: Greenwood Press, 1991.

Davis, L. E., and R. A. Huttenback. *Mammon and the Pursuit of Empire: The Political Economy of British Imperialism 1860–1912.* Cambridge, Eng.: Cambridge University Press, 1986.

Davis, Richard. *The English Rothschilds.* London: Collins, 1983.

DeNevi, Don. *The Western Pacific.* Seattle, Wash.: Superior, 1978.

Derleth, August. *The Milwaukee Road: Its First Hundred Years.* New York: Creative Age Press, 1948.

Dilts, James D. *The Great Road: The Building of the Baltimore & Ohio, the Nation's First Railroad, 1828–1853.* Stanford, Calif.: Stanford University Press, 1993.

Dinger, J. *Overzicht van alle ter beurse van Amsterdam verhandeld wordende binnen—en buitenlandse effecten.* Amsterdam: Erve H. van Vucht, 1851.

———. *Overzicht van alle ter beurze van Amsterdam verhandeld wordende binnen—en buitenlandse effecten.* 5th ed., 2 vols. Amsterdam: J. M. E. & G. H. Meijer, 1873.

Dodge, Grenville M. *How We Built the Union Pacific.* N.p., n.d.

Donovan, Frank P., Jr. *Mileposts on the Prairie: The Story of the Minneapolis & St. Louis Railway.* New York: Simmons-Boardman, 1950.

Doster, James F. *Railroads in Alabama Politics, 1875–1914.* University of Alabama Studies, no. 12. Birmingham: University of Alabama Press, 1957.

Dozier, Howard D. *A History of the Atlantic Coast Line Railroad.* Boston: Houghton Mifflin, 1920.

Dozy, R. P. A. "Lectuur over Noord-Amerika." In *De Gids* 34 (1870): pp. 385–410.

———. "Studiën over de Vereenigde Staten." In *De Gids* 35 (1871): vol. 1, pp. 193–219 and 425–54; vol. 2, pp. 101–31.

Drago, Harry S. *Canal Days in America: The History and Romance of Old Towpaths and Waterways.* New York: Clarkson N. Potter, 1972.

Ducker, James H. *Men of the Steel Rail: Workers on the Atchison, Topeka & Santa Fe Railroad, 1869–1900.* Lincoln: University of Nebraska Press, 1983.

Edelstein, Michael. *Overseas Investment in the Age of High Imperialism: The United Kingdom, 1850–1914.* New York: Columbia University Press, 1982.

Edson, William D. *Railroad Names: A Directory of Common Carrier Railroads Operating in the United States 1826–1982.* Potomac, Md.: William D. Edson, 1984.

125 Jaar Commissiehandel in Effecten: 1 Januari 1812–1937, Kerkhoven & Co. Amsterdam, 1937.

80 Years of Transportation Progress: A History of the St. Louis South Western Rly. Tyler, Tex.: St. Louis South Western Railway, n. d.

Emeis, M. G. *Honderdzestig jaar kassierderij.* Amsterdam: Kas Associatie, 1966.

Engelbourg, Saul. "John S. Kennedy, 1830–1909." In Robert L. Frey, ed., *Railroads in the Nineteenth Century,* pp. 216–19. New York: Facts on File, 1988.

Evans, Paul D. *The Holland Land Company.* Buffalo, N.Y.: Buffalo Historical Publications, 1924.

Fahey, John. *The Inland Empire: Unfolding Years, 1879–1929.* Seattle: University of Washington Press, 1986.

Fisher, John S. *A Builder of the West: The Life of General William Jackson Palmer.* Caldwell, Idaho: Caxton, 1939.

Fitch, Edwin M. *The Alaska Railroad.* New York: Praeger, 1967.

Flint, Henry M. *Railroads of the United States, Their History and Statistics.* Philadelphia, 1868.

Fogel, Robert W. *Railroads and American Economic Growth.* Baltimore, Md.: Johns Hopkins University Press, 1964.

———. *The Union Pacific.* Baltimore, Md.: Johns Hopkins University Press, 1960.

Forbes, John D. *J. P. Morgan, Jr., 1867–1943.* Charlottesville: University of Virginia Press, 1984.

Frederick, J. V. *Ben Holladay, the Stagecoach King: A Chapter in the Development of Transcontinental Transportation.* Glendale, Calif.: Arthur H. Clark, 1940.

Fremery, J. de. *Californië: Uittreksels uit consulaire jaarverslagen.* Vol. 1. Leiden: E. J. Brill, 1876. Vol. 2, 1876–1890. The Hague: W. P. van Stockum, 1891.

Frey, Robert L., ed. *Railroads in the Nineteenth Century.* New York: Facts on File, 1988.

Friedricks, William B. *Henry E. Huntington and the Creation of Southern California.* Columbus: Ohio State University Press, 1992.

Galton, Douglas. *Report to the Lords of the Committee of the Privy Council for Trade and Foreign Plantations, on the Railways of the United States.* London: Eyre & Spottiswoode, 1857–58.

Ganoe, John T. "The History of the Oregon & California Railroad." *Quarterly of the Oregon Historical Society* 25, no. 3 (1924): 236–83; no. 4: 330–52.

Gates, Paul W. *The Illinois Central Railroad and Its Colonization Work.* Cambridge, Mass.: Harvard University Press, 1934.

Gerstäcker, Friedrich. *Naar Amerika. Een verhaal.* Amsterdam: Van Kampen & Zn., 1873.

Gevers Deynoot, W. *Aanteekeningen op eene reis door de Vereenigde Staten van Noord-Amerika en Canada in 1859.* The Hague: M. Nijhoff, 1860.

———. *Herinneringen eener reis naar Nederlandsch-Indië in 1862.* The Hague: M. Nijhoff, 1864.

Girault, René. *Emprunts russes et investissements français en Russe 1887–1914.* Paris: Armand Colin, 1973.

Glaab, Charles N. *Kansas City and the Railroads: Community Policy in the Growth of a Regional Metropolis.* Madison: State Historical Society of Wisconsin, 1962.

Glaab, Charles N., and A. Theodore Brown. *A History of Urban America.* New York: Macmillan, 1967.

Glasgow, George. *The Scottish Investment Trust Companies.* London: Eyre & Spottiswoode, 1932.

Gömmel, Rainer. "Enstehung und Entwicklung der Effektenbörse im 19. Jahrhundert bis 1914." In Hans Pohl, ed., *Deutsche Börsengeschichte,* pp. 133–210. Frankfurt am Main: Fritz Knapp, 1992.

Goodrich, Carter. *Government Promotion of American Canals and Railroads, 1800–1890.* New York: Columbia University Press, 1960.

Goor, Jurjen van. *De Nederlandse Koloniën: geschiedenis van de Nederlandse expansie.* The Hague: SDU, 1994.

Gordon, John S. *The Scarlet Woman of Wall Street: Jay Gould, Jim Fisk, Cornelius Vanderbilt, the Erie Railway Wars, and the Birth of Wall Street.* New York: Weidenfeld & Nicolson, 1988.

Grant, H. Roger. *The Corn Belt Route: A History of the Chicago Great Western Railroad Company.* De Kalb: Northern Illinois University Press, 1984.

——. "Life and Death of Erie Lackawanna." *Trains* 52, no. 2 (Feb. 1992): 32–39.

Greenberg, Dolores. *Financiers and Railroads, 1869–1889: A Study of Morton, Bliss & Company.* Newark: University of Delaware Press, 1980.

——. "A Study of Capital Alliances: The St. Paul & Pacific." *Canadian Historical Review* 57 (1976): 25–29.

Grodinsky, Julius. *The Iowa Pool: A Study in Railroad Competition, 1870–1884.* Chicago: University of Chicago Press, 1950.

——. *Jay Gould: His Business Career, 1867–1892.* Philadelphia: University of Pennsylvania Press, 1957.

De groote bankgoochelaar Langrand Dumonceau en de Amerikaansche spoorweg-aktiën aan de Amsterdamsche Beurs. Amsterdam: Frijlink, 1870.

Gunnarson, Robert L. *The Story of the Northern Central Railway.* Sykesville, Md.: Greenberg, 1991.

Günst, Herbert W. *Trommelpapier; 115 Jaar Vereniging voor de Effectenhandel.* Amsterdam: Beursdata, 1991.

H. "Het Maatschappelijk Kansspel." *Onze Tijd,* New Series, no. 3 (1868), vol. 2, pp. 267–82.

Hafen, LeRoy R., and Carl C. Rister. *Western America: The Exploration, Settlement, and Development of the Region Beyond the Mississippi.* 2nd ed. Englewood Cliffs, N.J.: Prentice-Hall, 1950.

Hammer, Kenneth M. "Genesis of a Miller's Road: The Minneapolis, St. Paul & Saulte Ste. Marie." *Railroad History* 146 (Spring 1982): 23–28.

Hampton, Taylor. *The Nickel Plate Road: The History of a Great Railroad.* Cleveland, Ohio: World, [1947].

Hare, Jay V. *History of the Reading.* Philadelphia: J. H. Strock, 1966.

Harlow, Alvin F. *The Road of the Century: The Story of the New York Central.* New York: Creative Age Press, 1947.

——. *Steelways of New England.* New York: Creative Age Press, 1946.

Harrison, Fairfax. *A History of the Legal Development of the Railway System of the Southern Railway Co.* Washington, D.C., 1901.

Harthoorn, P. C. *Hoofdlijnen uit de ontwikkeling van het moderne bankwezen in Nederland vóór de concentratie.* Rotterdam: Strömberg, 1928.

Hayes, William E. *Iron Road to Empire: The History of 100 Years of the Progress and Achievements of the Rock Island Lines.* New York: Simmons-Boardman, 1953.

Hedges, James B. *Henry Villard and the Railways of the Northwest.* New Haven, Conn.: Yale University Press, 1930.

Heimburger, Donald J. *Wabash.* River Forest, Ill.: Heimburger House, 1984.

Helmer, William F. *O. & W.: The Long Life and Slow Death of the New York, Ontario & Western Railway.* Berkeley, Calif.: Howell-North, 1959.

Helps, Sir Arthur. *Life and Labours of Mr. Brassey.* Repr. London: Augustus M. Kelley, 1969.

Herr, Kincaid. *The Louisville and Nashville Railroad 1850–1913.* Rev. ed. Louisville, Ky.: Louisville & Nashville Railroad, 1964.

Herring, Hubert. *A History of Latin America.* New York: Alfred A. Knopf, 1955.

Hicks, Frederick C. *High Finance in the Sixties: Chapters from the Early History of the Erie Railway.* New Haven, Conn.: Yale University Press, 1929.

Hidy, Muriel E. "A Dutch Investor in Minnesota, 1866: The Diary of Claude August Crommelin." *Minnesota History* (December 1960): 152–60.

———. *George Peabody: Merchant and Financier, 1829–1854*. New York: Arno Press, 1978.

Hidy, Ralph W. *The House of Baring in American Trade and Finance: English Merchant Bankers at Work*. Cambridge, Mass.: Harvard University Press, 1949.

Hidy, Ralph W., Muriel E. Hidy, and Roy V. Scott. *The Great Northern Railway: A History*. Boston: Harvard Business School Press, 1989.

Hilton, George W. *American Narrow Gauge Railroads*. Stanford, Calif.: Stanford University Press, 1990.

———. *The Cable Car in America*. Berkeley, Calif.: Howell-North, 1971.

Hilton, George W., and John F. Due. *The Electric Interurban Railways in America*. 2nd ed. Stanford, Calif.: Stanford University Press, 1964.

Hinte, Jacob van. *Netherlanders in America: A Study of Emigration and Settlement in the Nineteenth and Twentieth Centuries in the United States*. Ed. by Robert P. Swierenga and Adriaan de Wit. Grand Rapids, Mich.: Baker Book House, 1985.

Hirschfeld, H. M. *Het ontstaan van het moderne bankwezen in Nederland*. Rotterdam: Nijgh & Van Ditmar, 1922.

Hofsommer, Donovan L. *Katy Northwest: The Story of a Branch Line Railroad*. Boulder, Colo.: Pruett, 1976.

———. *The Southern Pacific: A History, 1901–1985*. College Station: Texas A & M University Press, 1986.

Holbrook, Stewart H. *James Hill: A Great Life in Brief*. New York: Alfred A. Knopf, 1955.

———. *The Story of the American Railroads*. New York: Bonanza Books, 1947.

Holton, James L. *The Reading Railroad: History of a Coal Age Empire*. 2 vols. Laury's Station, Pa.: Garrigues House, 1989–92.

Horn, N. A. van. "Russische schulden aan Nederland na de revolutie." *Bijdragen en Mededelingen betreffende de Geschiedenis der Nederlanden* 108, no. 3 (1993): 431–44.

Huizenga, T. A. *Amerikaansche spoorwegtoestanden*. 12 vols. Groningen: Gebr. Hoitsema, 1873–75.

Hull, Clifton E. *Shortline Railroads of Arkansas*. Norman: University of Oklahoma Press, 1969.

Hungerford, Edward. *Men of Erie: A Story of Human Effort*. New York: Random House, 1946.

———. *The Story of the Baltimore & Ohio Railroad 1827–1927*. New York: Putnam, 1928.

Innis, Harold A. *A History of the Canadian Pacific Railway*. Repr. Toronto: University of Toronto Press, 1971.

Iongh, A. W. de. *Gedenkboek 1876–1926 Vereeniging voor den Effectenhandel*. Amsterdam: Vereeniging voor den Effectenhandel, 1926.

Israel, Jonathan I. *Dutch Primacy in World Trade 1585–1740*. Oxford: Oxford University Press, 1989.

Jackson, W. Turrentine. *The Enterprising Scot: Investors in the American West after 1873*. Edinburgh: Edinburgh University Press, 1968.

Jenks, Leland H. *The Migration of British Capital to 1875*. New York: Alfred A. Knopf, 1927.

Jessen, Kenneth. *Railroads of Northern Colorado*. Boulder, Colo.: Pruett, 1982.

Joby, R. S. *The Railway Builders: Lives and Works of the Victorian Railway Contractors*. Newton Abbot, Eng.: David & Charles, 1983.

Johnson, Arthur M., and Barry M. Supple. *Boston Capitalists and Western Railroads: A Study in the Nineteenth-Century Railroad Investment Process*. Cambridge, Mass.: Harvard University Press, 1967.

Johnson, Walter A. "Brief History of the Missouri-Kansas-Texas Railroad Lines." *The Chronicles of Oklahoma* 24, no. 3 (1946): 340–58.

Jong, A. M. de. *Geschiedenis van de Nederlandsche Bank.* 4 vols. Haarlem: J. Enschedé, 1930–1967.

Jonge, J. A. de. "Het Economisch Leven in Nederland 1844–1873." In *Algemene Geschiedenis der Nederlanden* vol. 12, pp. 53–76. Haarlem: Fibula-Van Dishoeck, 1977.

———. *De industrialisatie in Nederland tussen 1850 en 1914.* Amsterdam: Scheltema & Holkema, 1968.

Jongh, B. H. de. *Beschouwingen over eenige effecten—en credietvormen in hun beteekenis voor de financiering van de onderneming.* The Hague: M. Nijhoff, 1922.

Jongman, C. D. *De Nederlandse geldmarkt.* Leiden: Stenfert Kroese, 1959.

Jonker, J. "In het middelpunt en toch aan de rand: Joodse bankiers en effectenhandelaren, 1815–1940." In H. Berg, T. Wijsenbeek, and E. J. Fischer, eds., *Venter, fabriqueur, fabrikant: Joodse ondernemers en ondernemingen in Nederland, 1796–1940*, pp. 92–113. Amsterdam: NEHA, 1994.

———. "Lachspiegel van de vooruitgang: het historiografische beeld van de Nederlandse industrie-financiering in de negentiende eeuw." *NEHA-Bulletin* 5 (1991): 5–23.

Josephson, Matthew. *The Robber Barons.* 1932. Repr. New York: Harcourt, Brace & World, 1962.

Kabisch, Thomas R. *Deutsches Kapital in den USA: von der Reichsgründung bis zur Sequestrierung und der Freigabe.* Stuttgart: Klett-Cotta, 1982.

Kahn, Otto H. *Reflections of a Financier: A Study of Economic and Other Problems.* London: Hodder & Stoughton, 1921.

Kate, H. F. C. ten. *Reizen en onderzoekingen in Noord-Amerika.* Leiden: E. J. Brill, 1885.

Kennan, George. *E. H. Harriman: A Biography.* 2 vols. Boston: Houghton Mifflin, 1922.

Kerr, Duncan J. *The Story of the Great Northern Railway and James J. Hill.* Princeton, N.J.: Princeton University Press, 1939.

Kerr, John L. *The Story of a Western Pioneer: The Missouri Pacific, an Outline History.* New York: Railway Research Society, 1928.

Kerr, John L., and Frank Donovan. *Destination Topolobampo: The Kansas City, Mexico and Orient Railway.* San Marino, Calif.: Golden West Books, 1968.

Kerr, Joseph G. *Historical Development of the Louisville and Nashville Railroad System.* Louisville, Ky.: Louisville & Nashville Railroad, 1926.

Kerr, W. G. *Scottish Capital on the American Credit Frontier.* Austin: Texas State Historical Association, 1976.

Keyes, Norman C., Jr., and Kenneth R. Middleton. "The Great Northern Railway Company: All-Time Locomotive Roster, 1861–1970." *Railroad History* 143 (Autumn 1980): 20–162.

Kiliani, Richard. *Die Grossbanken-Entwicklung in Holland und die Mitteleuropäische Wirtschaft.* Leipzig: Felix Meiner, 1923.

King, Edward. *The Southern States of North America.* London: Blackie, 1875.

Klein, Maury. *The Great Richmond Terminal: A Study in Businessmen and Business Strategy.* Charlottesville: University of Virginia Press, 1970.

———. *History of the Louisville & Nashville Railroad.* New York: Macmillan, 1972.

———. "In Search of Jay Gould." *Business History Review* 52, no. 2 (Summer 1978): 166–99.

———. *The Life and Legend of Jay Gould.* Baltimore: Johns Hopkins University Press, 1986.

———. *Union Pacific.* 2 vols. New York: Doubleday, 1987–89.

Klerck, A. W. de. *De verarming van Nederland met betrekking tot den aanvoer van Amerikaansche spoorwegaandeelen.* Amsterdam: J. Clausen, 1886.

Kloos, G. J. *De handelspolitieke betrekkingen tusschen Nederland en de Vereenigde Staten van Amerika 1814–1914.* Amsterdam: H. J. Paris, n. d.

Kloos, J. H. *Minnesota in zijne hulpbronnen, vruchtbaarheid en ontwikkeling geschetst voor land-verhuizers en kapitalisten.* 2nd ed. Amsterdam: H. de Hoogh, 1867.

——. *Report Relative to the Resources, Population and Products of the Country along the Brainerd and St. Vincent Extensions of the St. Paul and Pacific Railroad.* St. Paul, Minn.: Pioneer Printing, 1871.

Knapen, B. *De lange weg naar Moskou: Nederlandse relaties tot de Sovjet-Unie, 1917–1942.* Amsterdam: Elsevier, 1985.

Knuppe, J. *Land en dollars in Minnesota en Dakota: Inlichtingen voor landverhuizers.* Rotterdam: Van Hengel & Eeltjes, 1883.

Kossmann, Ernst H. *The Low Countries 1780–1940.* Oxford: Oxford University Press, 1978.

Krooss, Herman E., and Martin A. Blyn. *A History of Financial Intermediaries.* New York: Random House, 1971.

Krooss, Herman E., and Charles Gilbert. *American Business History.* Englewood Cliffs, N.J.: Prentice-Hall, 1972.

Kuznets, Simon. *Capital in the American Economy: Its Formation and Financing.* Princeton, N.J.: Princeton University Press, 1961.

Kymmel, J. *Geschiedenis van de algemene banken in Nederland 1860–1914.* Amsterdam: NIBE, 1992.

Lamb, W. Kaye. *History of the Canadian Pacific Railway.* New York: Macmillan, 1977.

Lambie, Joseph T. *From Mine to Market: The History of Coal Transportation on the Norfolk and Western Railway.* New York: New York University Press, 1954.

Lammers, A. "'Een landschap der Vereenigde Staten, allerbedrijvigst gestoffeerd'; De Gids over Amerika 1837–1877." *Americana 'Tijdschrift voor de Studie van Noord-Amerika* 3, no. 1 (1989): 38–52.

Lamping, I. A. *De De Goeijen's: Toelichting en Kritiek.* 2 vols. The Hague: Van Stockum, 1896.

——. *De Kansas City's.* 2 vols. The Hague: Van Stockum, 1899.

Larson, Henrietta M. *Jay Cooke, Private Banker.* Cambridge, Mass.: Harvard University Press, 1936.

Larson, John L. *Bonds of Enterprise: John Murray Forbes and Western Development in America's Railway Age.* Boston: Graduate School of Business Administration, Harvard University, 1984.

Lavender, David. *The Great Persuader.* Garden City, N.Y.: Doubleday, 1970.

Lemly, James H. *The Gulf, Mobile and Ohio: A Railroad That Had to Expand or Expire.* Homewood, Ill.: Richard D. Irwin, 1953.

Lennep, F. J. E. van. *Een weduwe aan de Amsterdamse beurs; Borski saga 1765–1960.* Haarlem: H. D. Tjeenk Willink, 1973.

Lewis, Cleona. *America's Stake in International Investments.* Washington, D.C.: Brookings Institution, 1938.

Lewis, Oscar. *The Big Four: The Story of Huntington, Stanford, Hopkins and Crocker, and of the Building of the Central Pacific.* New York: Alfred A. Knopf, 1938.

Lewty, Peter J. *To the Columbia Gateway: The Oregon Railway and the Northern Pacific, 1879–1884.* Pullman: Washington State University Press, 1987.

Licht, Walter. *Working for the Railroad: The Organization of Work in the Nineteenth Century.* Princeton, N.J.: Princeton University Press, 1983.

Lindenhout, J. van 't. *Zes weken tusschen de wielen, of de Hollanders in Amerika.* Nijmegen: P. J. Milborn, 1887.

Loman, J. C. *Supplement op den vijfden druk van J. Dinger's overzicht van alle ter beurze van Amsterdam verhandeld wordende binnen—en buitenlandse effecten.* Amsterdam: J. M. E. & G. H. Meijer, 1880.

Lucas, Henry S. *Dutch Immigrant Memoirs and Related Writings.* 2 vols. Assen: Van Gorcum, 1955.

Lucia, Ellis. *The Saga of Ben Holladay, Giant of the Old West.* New York: Hastings House, 1959.

Lustig, Hugo. *Nordamerikanische Eisenbahnwerte: Handbuch für Bankiers und Kapitalisten.* Berlin: Minenverlag, 1909.

Lyle, Katie L. *Scalded to Death by the Steam: Authentic Stories of Railroad Disasters and the Ballads That Were Written About Them.* Chapel Hill, N.C.: Algonquin Books, 1988.

Lynch, Terry, and W. D. Caileff, Jr. *Kansas City Southern: Route of the Southern Belle.* Boulder, Colo.: Pruett, 1987.

Maarseveen, J. G. S. J. van, ed. *Briefwisseling van Nicolaas Gerard Pierson 1839–1909.* Vol. 1, *1851–1884.* Amsterdam: De Nederlandsche Bank, 1990.

McCarter, Steve. *Guide to the Milwaukee Road in Montana.* Helena: Montana Historical Society Press, 1992.

McGrane, Reginald C. *Foreign Bondholders and American State Debts.* New York: Macmillan, 1935.

McKay, John P. *Tramways and Trolleys: The Rise of Urban Mass Transport in Europe.* Princeton, N.J.: Princeton University Press, 1976.

"Makelaar in Effekten, Een." *De groote bankgoochelaar Langrand Dumonceau en de Amerikaansche spoorweg-aktiën aan de Amsterdamsche beurs, of de zeden van onzen tijd.* Amsterdam: A. Frijlink, 1870.

Malsen, H. van. *Geschiedenis van het makelaarsgild te Amsterdam 1578–1933.* Amsterdam: W. ten Have, 1933.

Marshall, Ian. "Steel Wheels on Paper: The Railroad in American Literature." *Railroad History* 165 (Autumn 1991).

Martin, Albro. *Enterprise Denied: Origins of the Decline of American Railroads, 1897–1917.* New York: Columbia University Press, 1971.

———. *James J. Hill and the Opening of the Northwest.* New York: Oxford University Press, 1976.

———. *Railroads Triumphant: The Growth, Rejection, and Rebirth of a Vital American Force.* New York: Oxford University Press, 1992.

Martin, William E. *Internal Improvement in Alabama.* Baltimore, Md.: Johns Hopkins University Press, 1902.

Mason, Edward S. *The Street Railway in Massachusetts: The Rise and Decline of an Industry.* Cambridge, Mass.: Harvard University Press, 1932.

Masterson, V. V. *The Katy Railroad and the Last Frontier.* Norman: University of Oklahoma Press, 1952.

Meijers, E. M. "Buitenlandsche beleggingen van kapitaal." *Vragen des Tijds* 1917, 2:271–96.

Meints, Graydon M. *Michigan Railroads and Railroad Companies.* East Lansing: Michigan State University Press, 1992.

Mendes da Costa, J. *Het A. B. C. van den Amsterdamschen effectenhandel met bijzonderheden der voornaamste buitenlandse effectenbeurzen.* 4th ed. Amsterdam: J. H. de Bussy, 1931.

Mercer, Lloyd J. *E. H. Harriman: Master Railroader.* Boston: Twayne, 1985.

———. *Railroads and Land Grant Policy: A Study in Government Intervention.* New York: Academic Press, 1982.

Merrill, Horace S. *Bourbon Democracy of the Middle West, 1865–1896.* Baton Rouge: Louisiana State University Press, 1953.

Meyer, Balthasar H. *History of Transportation in the United States before 1860.* Repr. New York: Peter Smith, 1948.

Michie, R. C. *The London and New York Stock Exchanges 1850–1914*. London: Allen & Unwin, 1987.

Mickelson, Sig. *The Northern Pacific Railroad and the Selling of the West*. Sioux Falls, S. Dak.: Center for Western Studies, 1993.

Middleton, William D. *The Interurban Era*. Milwaukee, Wis.: Kalmbach, 1961.

Miller, John A. *Fares Please! A Popular History of Trolleys, Horse-Cars, Street-Cars, Buses, Elevateds, and Subways*. New York: Dover, 1960.

Miner, H. Craig. *The St. Louis-San Francisco Transcontinental Railroad: The Thirty-fifth Parallel Project, 1853–1890*. Lawrence: University of Kansas Press, 1972.

Minnen, C. A. van. "Percepties van een Amerikaans gezant; Harmanus Bleecker in Nederland (1839–1842)." *Americana* 1, no. 1 (1987): 15–33.

——. *Yankees onder de zeespiegel: De Amerikaanse diplomaten in de lage landen en hun berichtgeving 1815–1850*. Amsterdam: Bataafsche Leeuw, 1991.

Moody, John. *The Railroad Builders: A Chronicle of the Welding of the States*. New Haven, Conn.: Yale University Press, 1920.

Morrison, James D. "The Union Pacific, Southern Branch." *Chronicles of Oklahoma* 14 (1936): 173–88.

Moshein, Peter, and Robert R. Rothfus. "Rogers Locomotives: A Brief History and Construction List." *Railroad History* 167 (Autumn 1992): 13–147.

Mott, Edward H. *Between the Ocean and the Lakes: The Story of Erie*. 2nd ed. New York: Collins, 1901.

Motz, Albert J. G. W. van. *Colorado uit een geographisch en huishoudkundig oogpunt beschouwd*. Deventer: W. F. P. Enklaar, 1874.

Mourik Broekman, M. C. van. *De Yankee in denken en doen: karakterteekening van het Amerikaansche leven*. Haarlem: H. D. Tjeenk Willink, 1914.

Myers, Gustavus. *History of the Great American Fortunes*. 3 vols. Chicago: Charles H. Kerr, 1910.

Myrick, David F. *New Mexico's Railroads*. Rev. ed. Albuquerque: University of New Mexico Press, 1990.

——. *Railroads of Nevada and Eastern California*. 2 vols. Berkeley, Calif.: Howell-North, 1962–63.

Neal, Larry. "The Disintegration and Re-integration of International Capital Markets in the Nineteenth Century." *Business and Economic History*, 2nd. series, 21 (1992): 84–96.

——. *The Rise of Financial Capitalism: International Capital Markets in the Age of Reason*. Cambridge, Eng.: Cambridge University Press, 1990.

Nederland's Patriciaat. The Hague: Centraal Bureau voor Genealogie, annual publication since 1910.

Nelson, James P. *The Chesapeake and Ohio Railway*. Richmond, Va., 1927.

Neu, Irene D. *Erastus Corning: Merchant and Financier 1794–1872*. Ithaca: Cornell University Press, 1960.

Nordhoff, Charles. *California for Health, Pleasure and Residence: A Book for Travellers and Settlers*. New York: Harper Brothers, 1873.

Noyes, Alexander D. *Forty Years of American Finance: A Short Financial History of the Government and People of the United States Since the Civil War, 1865–1907*. New York: Putnam, 1909.

Oberholtzer, E. P. *Jay Cooke: Financier of the Civil War*. 2 vols. Philadelphia: George W. Jacobs, 1907.

O'Connor, Richard. *Iron Wheels and Broken Men: The Railroad Barons and the Plunder of the West.* New York: Putnam, 1973.

O'Geran, Graeme. *A History of the Detroit Street Railways.* Detroit, Mich.: Conover Press, 1931.

Oosterwijk Bruyn, W. van. *Amerikaansche fondsen als geldbelegging.* Amsterdam: H. de Hoogh, 1866.

[———.] *Finantieele beschouwingen bij den aanvang van het jaar 1868.* Amsterdam: H. de Hoogh, 1868.

[———.] *Nieuwe finantieele beschouwingen: een handleiding bij geldbelegging in fondsen bij den aanvang van het jaar 1869.* Amsterdam: H. de Hoogh, 1869.

Oppenheim, A. *Reminiscences and Impressions.* New York: Caulon Press, 1906.

Ormes, Robert M. *Railroads and the Rockies: A Record of Lines in and near Colorado.* Denver, Colo.: Sage Books, 1963.

Oss, S. F. van. *American Railroads as Investments: A Handbook for Investors in American Railroad Securities.* New York: Putnam/Amsterdam: Gebr. Binger, 1893.

———. *Amerikaansche spoorwegwaarden.* Groningen, 1903.

"An Outline History of the Erie." *Railroad History* 131 (1974): 5–11.

Overton, Richard C. *Burlington Route: A History of the Burlington Lines.* Lincoln: University of Nebraska Press, 1965.

———. *Burlington West: A Colonization History of the Burlington Railroad.* New York: Russell & Russell, 1967.

———. *Gulf to the Rockies: The Heritage of the Fort Worth and Denver, Colorado and Southern Railways, 1861–1898.* Austin: University of Texas Press, 1953.

Pas, J. J. *Benton county in den staat Minnesota, als geschikte plaats voor eene kolonie van Nederlandsche landbouwers.* Amsterdam: C. van Helden, 1868.

Pellecom, A. C. van. *De Nederlandse kapitaalexport.* Unpublished manuscript, 1919, in Economische Historische Bibliotheek, Amsterdam.

Pierce, Harry H. "Anglo-American Investors and Investment in the New York Central Railroad." In Joseph R. Frese and Jacob Judd, eds., *An Emerging Independent American Economy 1815– 1875*, pp. 127–60. Tarrytown, N.Y.: Sleepy Hollow Press, 1980.

———. *Railroads of New York: A Study of Government Aid 1826–1875.* Cambridge, Mass.: Harvard University Press, 1953.

Pierson, N. G. "De handel en het bankwezen van den staat Louisiana." *Tijdschrift voor Staathuishoudkunde en Statistiek* 18 (1859): 177–93.

Pik, J. *De Amerikaansche spoorwegwaarden: bijdrage tot de kennis der te Amsterdam verhandelde fondsen.* Groningen: Erven B. van der Kamp, 1879.

Pike, James S. *The Prostrate State: South Carolina under Negro Government.* New York: Appleton, 1874.

———. *Zuid-Carolina onder negerbestuur: een bijdrage tot de kennis van Amerika.* Doesburg: R. van Hinloopen Labberton, 1875.

Platt, D. C. M. *Britain's Investment Overseas on the Eve of the First World War: The Use and Abuse of Numbers.* New York: St. Martin's, 1986.

———. *Foreign Finance in Continental Europe and the United States, 1815–1870.* London: Allen & Unwin, 1984.

Pletcher, David M. *Rails, Mines, and Progress: Seven American Promoters in Mexico, 1867–1911.* Ithaca, N.Y.: Cornell University Press, 1958.

Poor's Manual of the Railroads of the United States. New York, 1870/71–1914.

Prince, Richard E. *Atlantic Coast Line Railroad: Steam Locomotives, Ships and History.* Green River, Wyo.: R. E. Prince, 1966.

———. *Seaboard Air Line Railway: Steamboats, Locomotives and History*. Green River, Wyo.: R. E. Prince, 1969.

Pyle, Joseph G. *The Life of James J. Hill*. 2 vols. Garden City, N.Y.: Doubleday, 1917.

Quiett, Glenn C. *They Built the West: An Epic of Rails and Cities*. 1934. Repr. New York: Cooper Square, 1965.

Rae, William F. *Westward by Rail: The New Route to the East*. New York: Appleton, 1871.

Ramshorst, A. van, and G. Crebolder. *Sporen door de Gelderse Vallei*. Barneveld: BDU, 1980.

Reed, M. E. *New Orleans and the Railroads 1830–1860*. Baton Rouge: Louisiana State University Press, 1961.

Reed, Robert C. *Train Wrecks: A Pictorial History of Accidents on the Main Line*. Seattle, Wash.: Superior, 1958.

Reed, S. G. *A History of the Texas Railroads and of Transportation Conditions under Spain and Mexico, and the Republic and the State*. Houston, Tex.: St. Clair, 1941.

Rehor, John A. *The Nickel Plate Story*. Milwaukee, Wis.: Kalmbach, 1965.

Reibnitz, Kurt von. *Amerika's internationale Kapitalwanderungen*. Sozialwissenschaftliche Forschungen, Abt. 4, Heft 3. Berlin, 1926.

Reigersberg Versluys, J. C. van. *Amerika: indrukken, aanteekeningen, opmerkingen*. The Hague: M. Nijhoff, 1917.

Renooy, D. C. *De Nederlandsche emissiemarkt 1904–1939*. Amsterdam: J. H. de Bussy, 1951.

Renz, Louis T. *The History of the Northern Pacific*. Fairfield, Wash.: Ye Galleon Press, 1980.

Ridder, J. *Een conjunctuur-analyse van Nederland 1848–1860*. Amsterdam: H. J. Paris, 1935.

Riegel, Robert E. *The Story of the Western Railroads: From 1852 through the Reign of the Giants*. 1926. Repr. Lincoln: University of Nebraska Press, 1964.

Riemens, H. *De financiële ontwikkeling van Nederland*. Amsterdam: Noord-Hollandsche, 1949.

Rijxman, A. S. A. C. *Wertheim 1832–1897: een bijdrage tot zijn levensgeschiedenis*. Amsterdam: Keesing, 1961.

Riley, James C. *International Goverment Finance and the Amsterdam Capital Market 1740–1815*. Cambridge, Eng.: Cambridge University Press, 1980.

Ripley, E. P. *Railroads: Finance and Organization*. New York: Longmans, Green, 1915.

Ripley, William Z. *Railroads, Rates and Regulation*. New York: Longmans, Green, 1913.

Roberts, Richard. *Schroders: Merchants & Bankers*. London: Macmillan, 1992.

Rolt, L. T. C. *Victorian Engineering*. Harmondsworth, Eng.: Penguin Books, 1974.

Roos, F. de. *De algemene banken in Nederland*. Utrecht: A. Oosthoek, 1949.

Russell, Charles E. *Stories of the Great Railroads*. Chicago: Charles H. Kerr, 1914.

Saby, Rasmus S. "Railroad Legislation in Minnesota 1849 to 1875." *Collections of the Minnesota Historical Society* 15 (1915): 1–188.

Sakolski, A. M. *American Railroad Economics: A Text-book for Investors and Students*. New York: Macmillan, 1913.

Santilhano, J. D. *Amerikaansche spoorwegen: overzicht van de in Nederland verhandeld wordende Amerikaansche spoorwegfondsen*. Rotterdam: Nijgh & Van Ditmar, 1884.

Schevichaven, S. R. J. van. *De Noord-Amerikaansche staat Minnesota*. Amsterdam: C. F. Stemler, 1872.

Schlagintweit, R. von. *Die Santa Fe—und Südpacificbahn in Nordamerika*. Köln, 1884.

Schukking, W. H. C. *Beurswetgeving: wettelijke regeling van effectenhandel, beurs—en emissiewezen*. Groningen: J. B. Wolters, 1947.

Schweikart, Larry. *Banking in the American South, from the Age of Jackson to Reconstruction*. Baton Rouge: Louisiana State University Press, 1987.

Shaughnessy, Jim. *Delaware and Hudson*. Berkeley, Calif.: Howell-North, 1967.

Shaw, Robert B. "The Profitability of Early American Railroads." *Railroad History* 132 (Spring 1975): 56–69.

Simon, Matthew. "The Pattern of New British Portfolio Foreign Investment 1865–1914." In John H. Adler, ed., *Capital Movements and Economic Development*, pp. 33–70. London: Macmillan, 1967.

Singer, J. *Die Amerikanischen Bahnen und Ihre Bedeutung für die Weltwirtschaft.* Berlin: Franz Siemenroth, 1909.

Slotkin, Richard. *The Fatal Environment: The Myth of the Frontier in the Age of Industrialization 1800–1890.* New York: Atheneum, 1985.

Smalley, Eugene V. *History of the Northern Pacific Railroad.* New York: Putnam, 1883.

Smiley, Gene. "The Expansion of the New York Securities Market at the Turn of the Century." *Business History Review* 55, no. 1 (Spring 1981): 75–84.

Smith, M. F. J. *Tijd-affaires aan de Amsterdamsche beurs.* The Hague: M. Nijhoff, 1919.

Smith, W. Prescott. *The Book of the Great Railway Celebrations of 1857.* New York: Appleton, 1858.

Snell, Joseph, and Don Wilson. "The Birth of the Atchison, Topeka and Santa Fe Railroad." *The Kansas Historical Quarterly* 34, no. 3 (Summer 1968): 113–42, and no. 4 (Fall 1968): 325–64.

Soest, Jan J. van. *Een bijdrage tot de kennis van de beteekenis der Nederlandsche beleggingen in buitenlandsche fondsen voor de volkswelvaart.* Utrecht: Kemink, 1938.

Spanjaard, L. *Nederlandse diplomatieke en andere bescherming in den vreemde 1795–1914.* The Hague: M. Nijhoff, 1923.

Spence, Clark C. *British Investments and the American Mining Frontier 1860–1901.* Ithaca, N.Y.: Cornell University Press, 1958.

Spooner, Frank C. *Risks at Sea: Amsterdam Insurance and Maritime Europe.* Cambridge, Eng.: Cambridge University Press, 1983.

Staley, Eugene W. *War and the Private Investor.* Garden City, N.Y.: Doubleday, 1935.

Stevens, Frank W. *The Beginnings of the New York Central Railroad: A History.* New York: Putnam, 1926.

Stevens, G. R. *History of the Canadian National Railways.* New York: Macmillan, 1973.

Stilgoe, John R. *Metropolitan Corridor: Railroads and the American Scene.* New Haven, Conn.: Yale University Press, 1983.

Stilwell, Arthur E. *Cannibals of Finance: Fifteen Years' Contest with the Money Trust.* Chicago: Farnum, 1912.

Stindt, Fred A., and Guy L. Dunscomb. *The Northwestern Pacific Railroad.* Redwood City and Modesto, Calif.: Stindt and Dunscomb, 1964.

Stokvis, Pieter R. D. *De Nederlandse trek naar Amerika 1846–1847.* Leiden: Universitaire Pers, 1977.

Stover, John F. *American Railroads.* Chicago: University of Chicago Press, 1961.

———. *History of the Baltimore & Ohio Railroad.* West Lafayette, Ind.: Purdue University Press, 1987.

———. *History of the Illinois Central Railroad.* New York: Macmillan, 1975.

———. *Iron Road to the West: American Railroads in the 1850s.* New York: Columbia University Press, 1978.

———. *The Life and Decline of the American Railroad.* New York: Oxford University Press, 1970.

———. *The Railroads of the South, 1865–1900: A Study in Finance and Control.* Chapel Hill: University of North Carolina Press, 1955.

Studenski, Paul, and Herman E. Krooss. *Financial History of the United States.* 2nd ed. New York: McGraw-Hill, 1963.

Swain, Henry H. *Economic Aspects of Railroad Receiverships.* New York: American Economic Association, 1898.

Swartz, William. "The Wabash Railroad." *Railroad History* 133 (Fall 1975): 5–35.

Talbot, E. H., and H. R. Hobart, eds. *The Biographical Directory of the Railway Officials of America.* Chicago and New York: Railway Age, 1885.

Taylor, George R., and Irene Neu. *The American Railroad Network 1861–1900.* Cambridge, Mass.: Harvard University Press, 1956.

Taylor, Virginia H. *The Franco-Texan Land Company.* Austin: University of Texas Press, 1969.

Tennant, Robert D., Jr. *Canada Southern Country.* Erin, Ont.: The Boston Mills Press, 1991.

Tex, N. J. den. *Amerikaansche spoorwegen op de Amsterdamsche beurs.* Amsterdam: P. N. van Kampen, 1873.

———. "Naar Amerika." *De Gids* 38 (December 1874): 417–57.

Thomas, Brinley. "The Historical Record of International Capital Movements to 1913." In John H. Adler, ed., *Capital Movements and Economic Development,* pp. 3–32. London: Macmillan, 1967.

Tiffany, N. M., and F. Tiffany. *Harm Jan Huidekoper.* Cambridge, Mass.: Riverside Press, 1904.

Tijn, Th. van. *Amsterdam en diamant.* Amsterdam: A. van Moppes, 1976.

———. *Twintig jaren Amsterdam: de maatschappelijke ontwikkeling van de hoofdstad, van de jaren '50 der vorige eeuw tot 1876.* Amsterdam: Scheltema & Holkema, 1965.

Trelease, Allen W. *The North Carolina Railroad, 1849–1871, and the Modernization of North Carolina.* Chapel Hill: University of North Carolina Press, 1991.

Trescott, Paul B. *Financing American Enterprise: The Story of Commercial Banking.* New York: Harper & Row, 1963.

Trollope, Anthony. *North America.* 2 vols. 1862. Repr. Gloucester, Eng.: Alan Sutton, 1987.

———. *The Way We Live Now.* London: Chatto & Windus, 1876.

Trottman, Nelson. *History of the Union Pacific: A Financial and Economic Survey.* 1923. Repr. New York: Augustus M. Kelley, 1966.

Turner, Charles W. *Chessie's Road.* 2nd ed. Alderson, Va.: The Chesapeake & Ohio Historical Society, 1986.

Tutein Nolthenius, R. P. J. *Nieuwe wereld: indrukken en aanteekeningen tijdens eene reis door de Vereenigde Staten van Noord-Amerika.* 2nd ed. Haarlem: H. D. Tjeenk Willink, 1902.

Twain, Mark (Samuel L. Clemens), and Charles D. Warner. *The Gilded Age: A Tale of Today.* 1873. Reprint Indianapolis: Bobbs-Merrill, 1972.

Ulmer, Melville J. *Capital in Transportation, Communications, and Public Utilities: Its Formation and Financing.* Princeton, N.J.: Princeton University Press, 1960.

———. *Trends and Cycles in Capital Formation by United States Railroads, 1870–1950.* New York: National Bureau of Economic Research, 1954.

United States Census Office, Bulletin 3. *Street and Electric Railways.* Washington, D.C.: Government Printing Office, 1903.

Valk, J. P. de, and M. van Faassen, eds. *Dagboeken en aantekeningen van Willem Hendrik de Beaufort 1874–1918.* 2 vols. The Hague: Instituut voor Nederlandse Geschiedenis, 1993.

Van Oss' Effectenboek. Groningen: Noordhoff, annual publication since 1903.

Van Zant, Lee. *Early Economic Policies of the Government of Texas.* El Paso: The University of Texas, 1966.

Veenendaal, Augustus J., Jr. "The Dutch Connection: Salomon Frederik van Oss and Dutch Investment in Oklahoma." In *The Chronicles of Oklahoma* 65, no. 3 (Fall 1987): 252–67.

———. "'Dutch' Towns in the United States." In Robert S. Kirsner, ed., *The Low Countries and*

Beyond, pp. 309–22. Publications of the American Association for Netherlandic Studies, no. 5. Lanham, Md.: University Press of America, 1993.

———. "An Example of 'Other People's Money': Dutch Capital in American Railroads." *Business and Economic History*, 2nd series, 21 (1992): 147–58.

———. "Fiscal Crises and Constitutional Freedom in the Netherlands, 1450–1795." In Philip T. Hoffman and Kathryn Norberg, eds., *Fiscal Crises, Liberty, and Representative Government, 1450–1789*, pp. 96–139. Stanford, Calif.: Stanford University Press, 1994.

———. "Gerrit Middelberg: een veelzijdig spoorwegingenieur uit de negentiende eeuw." *Jaarboek voor de Geschiedenis van Bedrijf en Techniek* no. 1 (1984): 231–55.

———. "Guilders for Gold: Dutch Interest in the Alaska Central Railway Company." *Alaska History* 2, no. 2 (Fall 1987): 19–32.

———. "The Kansas City Southern Railway and the Dutch Connection." *Business History Review* 61, no. 2 (Summer 1987): 291–316.

———. "Nederlands kapitaal plaveit de weg van Kansas City naar de Golf van Mexico." *Jaarboek voor de Geschiedenis van Bedrijf en Techniek* 6 (1989): 119–38.

———. "The Oklahoma Central Railroad: A 'Dutch' Railroad in the United States." *Railroad History* 166 (Spring 1992): 80–102.

———. "Railroads, Oil and Dutchmen: Investing in the Oklahoma Frontier." *The Chronicles of Oklahoma* 63, no. 1 (Spring 1985): 4–27.

Veer, Theo de. "Ons Hollanders in Michigan." *Eigen Haard* 1907, pp. 628–34 and 804–8; 1908, pp. 43–48 and 552–55.

Verschuur, G. *Door Amerika: reisherinneringen.* Amsterdam: Gebr. Binger, 1877.

Vissering, G. *Het oude en het moderne giroverkeer.* Amsterdam: J. H. de Bussy, 1908.

Vissink, H. G. A. *Economic and Financial Reporting in England and the Netherlands: A Comparative Study over the Period 1850 to 1914.* Assen: Van Gorcum, 1985.

Vries, Boudien de. *Electoraat en elite: sociale structuur en sociale mobiliteit in Amsterdam 1850–1895.* Amsterdam: Bataafsche Leeuw, 1986.

Vries, Joh. de. *Een eeuw vol effecten: historische schets van de Vereniging voor de Effectenhandel en de Amsterdamse effectenbeurs 1876–1976.* Amsterdam: Vereniging voor de Effectenhandel, 1976.

———. *Geschiedenis van de Nederlandsche Bank.* Vol. 5, *1914–1948.* Amsterdam: De Nederlandsche Bank, 1989.

———. "Het Nederlandse financiële imperium: schets van de geschiedenis van het Nederlandse bankwezen." In *Bankwezen: geschiedenis en bronnenoverzicht*, pp. 13–58. Amsterdam: NEHA, 1992.

———, ed. *Herinneringen en dagboek van Ernst Heldring 1871–1954.* 3 vols. Groningen: Wolters-Noordhoff, 1970.

Vries, M. de. *Tien jaren geschiedenis van het Nederlandsche bankwezen en de Nederlandsche conjunctuur, 1866–1876.* The Hague: M. Nijhoff, 1921.

Walker, James B. *Fifty Years of Rapid Transit 1864–1917.* 1918. Repr. New York: Arno Press, 1970.

Ward, James A. "Early Railroad Empire Builders." *Railroad History* 160 (Spring 1989): 5–21.

———. *J. Edgar Thomson: Master of the Pennsylvania.* Westport, Conn.: Greenwood Press, 1980.

———. *Railroads and the Character of America 1820–1887.* Knoxville: University of Tennessee Press, 1986.

Ware, Louise. *George Foster Peabody: Banker, Philanthropist, Publicist.* Athens: University of Georgia Press, 1951.

Waters, L. L. *Steel Trails to Santa Fe*. Lawrence: University of Kansas Press, 1950.

Watson, Don, and Steve Brown. *Texas & Pacific Railway*. Cheltenham, Ont.: The Boston Mills Press, 1978.

Webb, William. *The Southern Railway System: An Illustrated History*. Erin, Ont.: The Boston Mills Press, 1986.

Weede, H. M. van. *Indische reisherinneringen*. Haarlem: H. D. Tjeenk Willink, 1908.

Weeveringh, J. J. *Handleiding tot de geschiedenis der staatsschulden, ten dienste van allen die belang hebben bij effecten en effectenhandel*. 2 vols. Haarlem: A. C. Kruseman, 1852–55.

———. *De Noord-Amerikaansche spoorwegfondsen aan de Amsterdamsche beurs*. 2nd. ed. Haarlem: Erven F. Bohn, 1887.

Weismann, A. W. *De beurs te Amsterdam 1835–1903*. Amsterdam: B. Wolf Jzn., 1904.

Werf, D. C. J. van der. *De bond, de banken en de beurzen: de geschiedenis van de Bond voor den Geld—en Effectenhandel in de Provincie (1903–1974)*. Amsterdam: NIBE, 1988.

Wertheim, Alexander H. *Het Emissie-Syndicaat*. Amsterdam: Gebr. Binger, 1891.

Westermann, J. C. *The Netherlands and the United States: Their Relations in the Beginning of the Nineteenth Century*. The Hague: M. Nijhoff, 1935.

White, John H., Jr. *American Locomotives: An Engineering History, 1830–1880*. Baltimore, Md.: Johns Hopkins University Press, 1968.

———. *The American Railroad Passenger Car*. 2 vols. Baltimore, Md.: Johns Hopkins University Press, 1978.

Wijk, F. W. van. *De Republiek en Amerika 1776 tot 1782*. Leiden: E. J. Brill, 1921.

Wijk, G. O. van. *Brieven uit Amerika*. Amsterdam: Gebr. Binger, 1895.

Wijnaendts Francken, C. J. *Door Amerika: reisschetsen, indrukken en studiën*. Haarlem: H. D. Tjeenk Willink, 1892.

Wijtvliet, C. A. M. *Expansie en dynamiek: de ontwikkeling van het Nederlandse handelsbankwezen 1860–1914*. Amsterdam: NIBE, 1993.

———. *De overgang van commanditaire naar naamloze vennootschap bij de Twentsche Bankvereeniging: in de ban van B. W. Blijdenstein 1861–1917*. Amsterdam: NIBE, 1988.

Wilkins, Mira. *The Emergence of Multinational Enterprise: American Business Abroad from the Colonial Era to 1914*. Cambridge, Mass.: Harvard University Press, 1970.

———. *Foreign Enterprise in Florida: The Impact of Non-U.S. Direct Investment*. Gainesville: University Presses of Florida, 1979.

———. *The History of Foreign Investment in the United States to 1914*. Cambridge, Mass.: Harvard University Press, 1989.

Wilson, Charles. *The Dutch Republic and the Civilisation of the Seventeenth Century*. New York: McGraw-Hill, 1977.

Wilson, Neill, and Frank Taylor. *Southern Pacific: The Roaring Story of a Fighting Railroad*. New York: McGraw-Hill, 1952.

Wilson, O. Meredith. *The Denver and Rio Grande Project 1870–1901*. Salt Lake City, Utah: Howe Brothers, 1982.

Wilson, William H. *Railroad in the Clouds: The Alaska Railroad in the Age of Steam, 1914–1945*. Boulder, Colo.: Pruett, 1977.

Winkler, Max. *Foreign Bonds: An Autopsy. A Study of Defaults and Repudiations of Government Obligations*. Philadelphia: Roland Swain, 1933.

Winter, P. J. van. *Het aandeel van den Amsterdamschen handel aan den opbouw van het Amerikaansche gemeenebest*. 2 vols. The Hague: M. Nijhoff, 1927–33.

———. *Onder Krugers Hollanders: geschiedenis van de Nederlandsche Zuid-Afrikaansche Spoorweg-Maatschappij*. 2 vols. Amsterdam: J. de Bussy, 1937–38.

Wood, Charles R. *Northern Pacific: Main Street of the Northwest.* Seattle, Wash.: Superior, 1968.

Yesterday and Today: A History of the Chicago and North Western Railway System. 3rd. ed. Chicago, 1910.

Young, Harold H. *Forty Years of Public Utility Finance.* Charlottesville: University Press of Virginia, 1965.

Zanden, J. L. van. *De industrialisatie in Amsterdam 1825–1914.* Bergen, N.H.: Octavo, 1987.

Index

In this index "f" after a number indicates a separate reference on the next page, and "ff" indicates separate references on the next two pages. A continuous discussion over two or more pages is indicated by a span of numbers. *Passim* is used for a cluster of references in close but not consecutive sequence.

Library of Congress Cataloging-in-Publication Data

Veenendaal, A. J.
    Slow train to paradise : how Dutch investment helped
build American railroads / Augustus J. Veenendaal, Jr.
        p.   cm.
Includes bibliographical references and index.
ISBN 0-8047-2517-9 (alk. paper)
1. Railroads—United States—Finance—History.
2. Investments, Dutch—United States—History.   I. Title
HE2751.V43   1996
385′.1—dc20
95-11959   CIP   Rev.
⊛ This book is printed on acid-free recycled paper.

Original printing 1996

Last figure below indicates year of this printing

06 05 04 03 02 01 99 98 97 96